Peak Bouldering

Alan James

Text, topos and crag photography
by Adrian Berry and Alan James
Action photography as credited
Edited by Alan James
Printed in Europe on behalf of Latitude Press Ltd.
Distributed by Cordee (www.cordee.co.uk)

All maps by ROCKFAX
Some maps based on original source data
from openstreetmap.org

Published by ROCKFAX in May 2014
© ROCKFAX 2014
www.rockfax.com

We only use paper made from wood fibre
from sustainable forests and produced according
to ISO 14001 environmental standard

ISBN 978 1 873341 72 8

Cover: Naomi Buys on *Not to Be Taken Away* (V5 6C) -
page 137 - at the Plantation, Stanage. Photo: Mike Hutton

Northern Peak

Sheffield Craas

Stanage Area

Burbage Valley

Derwent Edges

The Limestone

Central Grit

Staffordshire

South Peak

In a back street in Liverpool a small wall was created in 1998 by a passion to prove to the world that climbing wa
can be fun and inspiring places to climb and train. Awesome Walls Climbing Centres aim to provide frequent well s
routes and boulder problems in a clean and friendly atmosphere!

Introduction. **4**
    Acknowledgments and Advertisers 10
Logistics **12**
    Tourist Information, When to Go 14
    Accommodation, Pubs and Shops 16
    Climbing Walls 18
Climbing Information **20**
    Access 22
    Safety 24
    Topos, Maps and Symbols 28
    Bouldering Grades 30
    Circuits 32
    Destination Planner 34

Northern Peak. **38**
    Wimberry 40
    Tintwistle Knarr. 51
    Black Tor. 56
    Hobson Moor Quarry 62
    New Mills Tor 65
    The Woolpacks 68
    Derwent 80
Sheffield Crags **88**
    Wharncliffe 90
    Rivelin. 96
    Bell Hagg 102
Stanage Area. **108**
    Bamford 110
    Stanage High Neb 114
    Stanage Plantation 126
    Stanage Popular End 160
    Stanage Far Right. 164
Burbage Valley **178**
    Higgar Tor 180
    Burbage West 192
    Burbage North 200
    Burbage South Edge 218
    Burbage South Valley 234
    Millstone Area 252
    Houndkirk Moor 268
Derwent Edges **272**
    Froggatt. 274
    Curbar. 290
    Baslow 310
    Gardom's 322
    Birchen Edge 338
The Limestone **346**
    Stoney. 348
    Rubicon. 356
    Raven Tor 360
    Blackwell Dale 365
Central Grit **272**
    Alport Area 368
    Rabbit Warren. 374
    Harland Edge 376
    Robin Hood's Stride 378
    Cratcliffe 388
    Clifftop Boulder 402
    Eagle Tor. 404
    Stanton Moor 406
    Rowtor Rocks 416
    Matlock 424
    Amber Valley. 426
    Eastwood Rocks. 434

Staffordshire **436**
    The Roaches 438
    The Skyline. 466
    The Five Clouds 474
    Ramshaw 482
    Newstones and Baldstones 490
    Gib Torr. 500
    Wolf Edge 502
South Peak **506**
    Black Rocks 508
    Harborough Rocks 512
    Shining Cliff. 516
    Churnet Valley 518

Problem Index. **532**
Crag Index. **543**
Area Map and General Index. **544**

Northern Peak

Sheffield Crags

Stanage Area

Burbage Valley

Derwent Edges

The Limestone

Central Grit

Staffordshire

South Peak

Audrey Seguy grappling with the rounded holds on *Beach Ball* (**V6** *7A*) - *page 254* - at the Secret Garden. Photo: Adrian Berry

Bouldering means different things to different people. Some find joy in seeking out intense, hard problems in hidden locations, while others spend sessions with friends, working at their limits to tick mutual goals. Others have a more relaxed approach, ticking as many problems in a circuit as possible, just for the joy of movement and being in a beautiful location.

Northern Peak

Sheffield Crags

Stanage Area

Burbage Valley

Derwent Edges

The Limestone

Central Grit

Staffordshire

South Peak

David Noddings climbing *Crescent Arete* (**V2** 5c) - *page 134* - at Stanage Plantation Area. Photo: Alan James

With a variety of crags and easy access all this is possible in the Peak area. The main attractions are the extensive gritstone crags that stretch from Wimberry in the northwest, through the eastern edges and the central grit crags, and on to Staffordshire. The range and concentration of the bouldering is immense and varied, sometimes on the edges themselves, sometimes on the blocks dotted around and beneath the crag. As an additional attraction there is some intense limestone bouldering with fingery eliminates and powerful stamina traverses.

This book brings everything together in a massive 544 pages. There are 3394 distinct problems described on 66 separate crags (compared to 1600 problems on 38 crags back in the 1998 book). We have also included over 60 bouldering circuits which are pitched at a relatively low level with 17 dedicated to problems at **V0+** 5a and under, and a further 43 circuits set at a harder level.

The book doesn't cover all of the bouldering on offer in the Peak - that would be almost impossible for a single book. Eliminates and combination problems are only included where they are popular, and sit-down starts tend to be mentioned as add-ons to most problems unless they are particularly significant. There are also plenty of small areas that there hasn't been room to include, but many of these are of only of minor interest.

This book has all you need to choose and find the best areas for you, and to get the most out of your visits. It has enough bouldering to last most people a lifetime.

Northern Peak | Sheffield Crags | Stanage Area | Burbage Valley | Derwent Edges | The Limestone | Central Grit | Staffordshire | South Peak

Northern Peak

Sheffield Crags

Stanage Area

Burbage Valley

Derwent Edges

The Limestone

Central Grit

Staffordshire

South Peak

Problem Names

When we published the first Peak Bouldering Rockfax guidebook in 1998, we took the liberty of naming certain problems to aid navigation. Since then, a number of other guidebooks have been published, more new names have been introduced, and it has become apparent that it is essential to give every problem a name to avoid confusion between different information sources. In this book we have followed the convention of using the names established in previous books. Where there is a discrepancy, we have gone with the more common name and these have now also been updated on UKC Logbooks. If a problem has been documented for the first time in this book, we have made up a name for it. These names are generally descriptive ones only.

First Ascents

Many of the problems in this book have been climbed for years and who did what first is impossible to establish. In the last twenty years more problems have been claimed by individuals and some of this information has been documented in other information sources although it is still relatively incomplete. The true record of exactly who climbed what, and when, is likely to never be achieved for bouldering since no one really knows. In this book we haven't included any first ascent information next to the problems. This information can be added to the UKC logbook record, which will become available for online 'app' versions of this book in the future.

Key Previous Guides

Bouldering in the Peak District only really started being documented on its own right back in 1994 with Allen Williams's first book. Since then several dedicated books have followed, including the Peak Bouldering Rockfax of 1998. The BMC guidebooks to the Peak area have also started to include much more bouldering information.

We are very grateful to all those who have worked on previous guidebooks. The key books are listed below.

Peak Bouldering Rockfax 1998

Bouldering in the Peak District - Allen Williams *(OTE 1994)*

Peak Plus - Bouldering in the Peak District Vol II

- Jason Myers *(OTE 1995)*

Peak Bouldering *(right)* - Allen Williams and Alan James *(Rockfax 1998)*

Peak District : Bouldering

- Rupert Davies and Jon Barton *(Vertebrate Graphics 2004)*

Peak District Bouldering - Rupert Davies, John Coefield and Jon Barton *(Vertebrate Publishing 2011)*

BMC Peak Area Guidebooks - Various authors *(BMC 2004 to 2012)*

Neil Kershaw palming his way up *Slap Bass Odyssey* (**V8** *7B*) - *page 381* - at Robin Hood's Stride. Photo: Adam Long

Northern Peak

Sheffield Crags

Stanage Area

Burbage Valley

Derwent Edges

The Limestone

Central Grit

Staffordshire

South Peak

Northern Peak

Sheffield Crags

Stanage Area

Burbage Valley

Derwent Edges

The Limestone

Central Grit

Staffordshire

South Peak

The Rockfax website rockfax.com is a mine of useful information about climbing all over Europe. You can order all of our books and download many PDF MiniGUIDES and updates, which both complement the printed books, and cover new areas. It will also be the main place to look when we develop the smartphone app version of our guidebooks.

Rockfax Route Database

The website is also the home of the Rockfax Route Database which contains a listing of every problem in this book, and most other Rockfax books as well - that's over 35,000 routes and boulder problems! Using this database you can vote on grades and star ratings, and submit feedback about the routes and problems. The data already received has been vital in the production of this guide - thanks to all those who have contributed. The current version of the Rockfax Route Database has been updated to reflect the descriptions of the routes in this edition of the book so you can start use it to keep everyone informed about any changes or your own opinions on grades, stars and the routes in general.

UKC Logbooks

An incredibly popular method of logging your climbing is to use the UKClimbing.com Logbooks system. This database lists more than 276,000 routes, over 18,000 crags and, so far, users have recorded more than 3.2 million ascents! To set up your own Logbook all you need to do is register at UKClimbing.com and click on the Logbook tab. Once set up you will be able to record every ascent you make, when you did it, what style you climbed it in, who you did it with and each entry has a place for your own notes. You can also add your vote to the grade/star system linked to the Rockfax database. The Logbook can be private, public or restricted to your own climbing partners only.

Using your Smartphone with this Book

We plan to have a fully-functioning 'app' version of this guidebook available in the future, but until then, you can still use your smartphone to aid in getting to the crags. To do this you need to use a navigation app with the blue box coordinates that are displayed with the parking locations. Just enter the coordinates into your web browser, or navigation app, to take you straight from your current location to the parking. Since these coordinates are quite difficult to enter, we have included QR Codes on the maps. Using a QR Code reader app like **Scan** (for iOS) or **Google Goggles** (for Android) you can scan the QR Code and choose to open the result direct into the **Google Maps** navigation app on your phone.

Northern Peak

Sheffield Crags

Stanage Area

Burbage Valley

Derwent Edges

The Limestone

Central Grit

Staffordshire

South Peak

Jon Fullwood high up on *Chip Shop Brawl* (**V7** *7A+*) - *page 116* - at Stanage End. Photo: Adam Long

As the biggest Rockfax ever, this book has taken quite some effort to assemble. Many days have been spent by both authors rambling over the moors, in search of 'small green rocks' to document and photograph. We are indebted to the many climbers who cheerfully moved their bags and mats out of the way for us to take uncluttered photos, and to others who pulled on (without their spotters) so we could inject a bit of action into the topos.

We are extremely grateful to everyone who has helped contribute to the documentation of bouldering in the Peak District over the years. Thanks to Allen Williams whose original books provided an excellent foundation for this one. A major source of information for us has been PeakBouldering.info which is maintained by Gareth Cokell and Robin Mueller. Special mention is needed for Robin who has diligently proofread this book, making many corrections to the harder problems in particular.

The photographs in this book have come from a number of people. Adam Long and Mike Hutton both gave us access to their huge collections and we have used many of those brilliant images. Thanks also to Jamie Moss, Simon Rogers, Duncan Skelton, Christian Fox, Stuart McNeil, Tim Glasby, Paul Phillips, David Bond, Daniel Rushforth and Rob Greenwood for their contributions.

Thanks are also due to our proofreaders. In this case a very special mention is needed for Jaimella Espley who offered her proofreading skills at an early stage and has been a real pleasure to work with. Chris Craggs has also been very diligent as usual. We are also grateful to Rebecca Ting, Andy Harris, Jon Fullwood and Tom Ripley for their help.

Thanks to Sherri Davy for advertising, Stephen Horne for technical matters and Duncan Campbell for some fun crag research trips.

Adrian - I would particularly like to thank Audrey Seguy and Jamie Veitch for, amongst numerous other things, hiking up to the Woolpacks with me when no other bugger would. Thanks too to little Raphael for the pleasure of carrying him all the way there and back.

Alan - I would like to thank Sam for accompanying me on many a research trip. I would also like to dedicate this book to my mother Liz James who passed away in February 2014.

Alan James and Adrian Berry, March 2014

We are grateful to the following advertisers for their support of this guidebook.

Equipment Manufacturers

Black Diamond - *Outside back cover*
www.blackdiamondequipment.com

Beta Climbing Designs - *Page 27*
betaclimbingdesigns.com

Mammut - *Inside front cover*
www.mammut.ch

Marmot - *Inside back cover*
www.marmot.com

Entre-prise - *Page 19*
www.entre-prises.com

Wild Country - *Page 25*
www.wildcountry.com

Climbing Walls

Awesome Walls - *Page 2*
Liverpool, Stockport, Stoke-on-Trent, Sheffield, Dublin
www.awesomewalls.co.uk

ClimbingCentres.co.uk - *Back cover flap*
Manchester, Harrogate, Reading
climbingcentres.co.uk

Shops

Alpkit - *Page 17*
alpkit.com

Cotswold Outdoor - *Page 15*
Multiple shops nationwide
cotswoldoutdoor.com

High Sports - *Page 23*
Shrewsbury
www.highsports.co.uk

Rock On - *Page 31*
London, Guildford, Birmingham
www.rockonclimbing.co.uk

Outside - *Opposite*
Hathersage
www.outside.co.uk

Guiding and Accommodation

Thornbridge Outdoors - *Page 29*
www.thornbridgeoutdoors.co.uk

Northern Peak
Sheffield Crags
Stanage Area
Burbage Valley
Derwent Edges
The Limestone
Central Grit
Staffordshire
South Peak

eat
shop
climb

Outside
outside.co.uk

Shop & Café
Main Road, Hathersage S32 1BB

© Nic Mullin: Tom Peckitt
The Joker F8A Stanage Plantation

Peak Bouldering
Logistics

Northern Peak

Sheffield Crags

Stanage Area

Burbage Valley

Derwent Edges

The Limestone

Central Grit

Staffordshire

South Peak

Claire Carter on *Joe's Arete* (**V3** *6A*) - *page 455* - Upper Tier Boulders at the Roaches. Photo: Alan James

Northern Peak

Sheffield Crags

Stanage Area

Burbage Valley

Derwent Edges

The Limestone

Central Grit

Staffordshire

South Peak

Mountain Rescue
In the event of an accident requiring the assistance of Mountain Rescue:
Dial 112 and ask for 'POLICE - MOUNTAIN RESCUE'
All mountain rescue incidents in the Peak District area fall under the responsibility of Derbyshire Constabulary. If in any doubt request Derbyshire Police Operations Room.

Mobile Phones
Many of the crags described in this section of the book have reasonable mobile phone coverage across the major networks. The exceptions are isolated and exposed places such as the moors of Kinder and Derwent where coverage can be intermittent or not available at all. In an emergency it could be a while before help arrives in these very remote locations.

Tourist Information Offices
If you are short of ideas about what to do on a wet day or need some accommodation, take a look at the Tourist Information Offices. They contain much more information than it is possible to include in these pages.
Glossop - Victoria Street. Tel: 01457 855920
Sheffield - Surrey Street. Tel: 0114 221 1900
Buxton - Pavilion Gardens. Tel: 01298 25106
Bakewell - Old Market Hall, Bridge Street. Tel: 01629 816558
Leek - Market Place. Tel: 01538 483741
Chesterfield - Rykneld Square. Tel: 01246 345777
Ashbourne - 13 Market Place. Tel: 01335 343666
More information and other travel tips are at **www.visitpeakdistrict.com**

When to Go
Peak Bouldering can offer something on most days of the year. Crisp winter conditions, while ideal for the harder problems on gritstone, can make more leisurely circuit bouldering awkward if the ground is horribly boggy underfoot and north-facing walls are green and wet. Spring can offer perfect conditions when the crags and ground dry out and it isn't too hot. Once the summer arrives, shade can usually be found on certain crags, or a trip to the higher moorland boulders is in order where there may well be a cooling breeze, although midges can be a problem. In the autumn the foliage can choke some of the grit areas but good conditions can also usually be found.

Temperature °C	Jan	Feb	Mar	Apr	May	Jun	Jul	Aug	Sep	Oct	Nov	Dec
Average Max Temp (°C)	6	6	9	10	14	17	20	19	15	12	8	5
Average Min Temp (°C)	1	1	3	3	6	9	11	11	8	6	3	1
Average Rain Days/Month	9	10	8	6	6	5	6	6	7	7	8	6

Getting Around
The easiest way to access most of the crags in this book is by car and the approach descriptions are written assuming you are using one. Certain crags are accessible using public transport, and train stations are marked on the maps. Bus coverage for the Peak District is reasonable. The best website for finding train information is **www.thetrainline.com**. The best website for finding bus information is **www.traveline.info**

COTSWOLD
outdoor

BRINGING YOU THE
MOST INNOVATIVE KIT
EVERY YEAR SINCE 1974

1977
MOUNTAIN EQUIPMENT CASCADE
JACKET, ONE OF THE FIRST EVER
GORE-TEX® JACKETS PRODUCED

2014
THE STORY CONTINUES
THE LHOTSE JACKET
ENGINEERED WITH THE NEW GORE-TEX® PRO

MOUNTAINEERING. It's you versus the elements and the Lhotse Jacket
is here to level the playing field. It's made from GORE-TEX® Pro, which is
more rugged and up to 28% more breathable than previous generations
of GORE-TEX® Pro. So let the wind howl and the rain pour; a legend is
coming through.

STORES NATIONWIDE
COTSWOLDOUTDOOR.COM

Engineered with

MOUNTAIN
EQUIPMENT

Northern Peak

Sheffield Crags

Stanage Area

Burbage Valley

Derwent Edges

The Limestone

Central Grit

Staffordshire

South Peak

Accommodation

There are many campsites scattered throughout the area, from small and basic to very plush - **www.ukcampsite.co.uk** Useful websites for different types of accommodation are:
www.peakdistrictonline.co.uk
www.ukclimbing.com/listings

Youth Hostels - There are numerous Youth Hostels in the Peak District, check out **www.yha.org.uk**

Pubs

Pubs are an integral part of the climbing experience for many. The Peak District is blessed with many fine hostelries which make great locations for an après-climb pint where you can discuss the highs and lows of your day. A few are listed below.

The King William - on the main road in Greenfield.
The Fox House - near Burbage South.
The Grouse - above the parking area for Froggatt.
Robin Hood Inn - parking area for Birchen.
The Moon - on the main road in Stoney Middleton.
The Angler's Rest - passed on the approach to Raven Tor.
The Druid - directly below Rowtor Rocks in Birchover.
The Rock - in Upper Hulme near the Roaches and the Newstones.

Climbing Shops

More shops listed at -
www.ukclimbing.com/listings

Outside - *page 11*
Main Road, Hathersage
Tel: 01433 651936
www.outside.co.uk

Cotswold Outdoor - *page 15*
Bridge Street, Bakewell
Tel: 01629 812231
cotswoldoutdoor.com

Cotswold Outdoor - *page 15*
Castle Buildings, Nottingham
Tel: 0115 9576890
cotswoldoutdoor.com

Cotswold Outdoor - *page 15*
Oxford Road, Manchester
Tel: 0161 2364123
cotswoldoutdoor.com

High Sports - *page 23*
Shrewsbury, SY1 1XJ
Tel: 01743 231649
www.highsports.co.uk

Crag X - 45 Mowbray Street, Sheffield.
Go Outdoors - Hill Street, Sheffield.
Go Outdoors - Main Road, Hathersage.
Hitch 'n' Hike - Mytham Bridge, Hope Valley.
Jo Royle - Market Place, Buxton.
The Crag Station - Kinders Lane, Greenfield.

Samuel James-Louwerse climbing *Buckstone Groove* (**V1** 5b) - *page 125* - on the Buckstone below Stanage. Photo: Alan James

ALPKIT

BOULDERMATS MADE FOR CLIMBERS BY CLIMBERS

www.alpkit.com/boulder

Ben Meakin Western Eyes, 7C+ Burbage West

Northern Peak

Sheffield Crags

Stanage Area

Burbage Valley

Derwent Edges

The Limestone

Central Grit

Staffordshire

South Peak

Awesome Walls Sheffield *Page 2*
Garter Street, Sheffield.
Tel: 0114 244 6622
Large dedicated climbing centre.

Awesome Walls Stockport *Page 2*
The Engine House, Stockport.
Tel: 0161 494 9949
Large dedicated climbing centre.

Awesome Walls Stoke *Page 2*
Sefton Road, Stoke-on-Trent.
Tel: 01782 341919
Bouldering wall with some leading lines.

www.awesomewalls.co.uk

Audley Climbing Centre
Nantwich Road, Stoke.
peakpursuits.co.uk

Alter Rock
St. James Church, Derby.
www.alter-rock.co.uk

Broughton Recreation Centre
Camp Street, Salford.
broughtonpower.wetpaint.com

Glossop Leisure Centre
High Street East, Glossop.

Kilnworx Climbing Centre
Wycliffe Street, Burslem.
kilnworx.org

Manchester Wall *Cover flap*
St Benedict's Church, Bennett Street,
Manchester. Tel: 0161 230 7006
Large dedicated climbing centre
www.manchesterclimbingcentre.com

Nottingham Climbing Centre
212 Noel St, Nottingham.
www.nottingham-climbing.co.uk

Rock Over Climbing
45 Julia Street, Manchester.
rockoverclimbing.com

Rope Race
Goyt Mill, Upper Hibbert Lane, Marple.
www.roperace.co.uk

The Climbing Unit
Mason's Place Business Park, Chaddesden.
theclimbingunit.com

The Climbing Works
Little London Road, Sheffield.
www.climbingworks.com

The Depot
4 King Edward Street, Nottingham.
theclimbingdepot.com

The Edge, Sheffield
John Street, Sheffield.
www.sheffield-climbing.co.uk

The Foundry, Sheffield
45 Mowbray Street, Sheffield.
www.foundryclimbing.com

If you are rained off in the Peak, or if you just want to top up your power
in the winter months, the climbing walls above are well worth considering.
More information and more walls are on the UKClimbing website at
www.ukclimbing.com/walls/

- Lead routes
- Bouldering

- Cafe
- Major shop

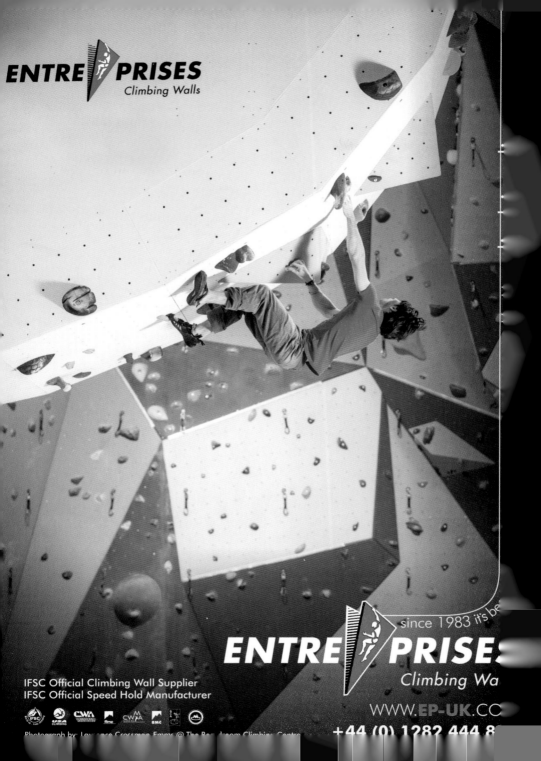

Northern Peak

Sheffield Crags

Stanage Area

Burbage Valley

Derwent Edges

The Limestone

Central Grit

Staffordshire

South Peak

Peak Bouldering
Climbing Information

Sheffield Crags

Stanage Area

Burbage Valley

Derwent Edges

The Limestone

Central Grit

Staffordshire

South Peak

Mike Haves on *Spider Crack* (**V5** *6C+*) - *page 263* - at Owler Tor. Photo: Paul Phillips

The majority of crags in this book have been climbed on for many years and we are lucky to enjoy almost unrestricted access to nearly all of the problems in the book. In a few cases there may be temporary restrictions because of nesting birds, or special approach arrangements. These details are covered in the text, or indicated by signs on the approach to the crags.

In general all that is required to maintain this access is reasonable behaviour. Try to leave a place in better shape than you found it; take only pictures and leave only footprints; and abide by the Country Code.

Access arrangements can change and we recommend that, when unsure, you use the BMC Regional Access Database to check what the up-to-date situation is.
You can check RAD here - **thebmc.co.uk/modules/RAD/** or install the BMC RAD app from your iOS or Android app store.

BMC RAD app

If you do encounter problems then contact the BMC Access and Conservation representative. They are always happy to discuss any problems and often the BMC's involvement at an early stage can defuse a situation before it escalates into a serious access dispute.

Erosion

The popularity of bouldering in recent years has caused some serious ground erosion especially under popular problems. The increased use of bouldering mats has helped slow down this erosion but there are still some areas where the last blade of grass disappeared a long time ago and all that is left is a dusty/muddy pit.
Overuse of chalk and vigorous brushing have also had an impact on the rock, especially on grit crags where the rock is soft or the surface layer has been worn away.
Are there any ways we can stop this?
Well ultimately probably not but there are ways to slow down the erosion and minimise it so that the impact is spread over time and different areas.
- Use less chalk.
- Use bouldering mats, even on low problems.
- Only brush the holds gently with plastic brushes.
- Don't stray from the popular paths.

Parking

All the crags in this book have described parking areas which have been indicated with GPS coordinates and QR codes on the maps. Please use these parking areas! If there is one thing above all others that annoys landowners, it is having their drive/field blocked by someone's car. In one or two cases parking may involve you spending some money.

British Mountaineering Council

British Mountaineering Council, 177-179 Burton Road, Manchester, M20 2BB.
Tel: 0870 010 4878 Fax: 0161 445 4500
Web: **www.thebmc.co.uk**
Email: **office@thebmc.co.uk**

Somewhere over the rainbow is a crag that I climbed on. Photo: Adrian Berry

Northern Peak

Sheffield Crags

Stanage Area

Burbage Valley

Derwent Edges

The Limestone

Central Grit

Staffordshire

South Peak

Part of the enjoyment of bouldering comes from experiencing the same pleasure of moving over rock as climbing longer routes, but without the encumbrance of gear and the dangers associated with roped climbing. That's not to say that there are no dangers. Indeed, it often seems that climbers are more likely to receive minor injuries from bouldering than any other branch of the sport. Knowing how to moderate these dangers by landing safely, using mats correctly, how to spot properly and knowing your limits are the keys to staying safe.

Landing Safely

When landing it is all about correct use of your legs. A thick bouldering mat may give five centimetres of compression to reduce the impact of landing - your legs give you ten times that, but only if you bend them. Aim to land with your legs slightly bent and squat down to absorb the force of the fall through your leg muscles.

If the idea of jumping off onto mats from a couple of metres up makes you nervous then it is a good idea to practise this by jumping off from gradually greater heights when attempting a particular problem. Being relaxed mentally will allow you to avoid tensing up physically and possibly injuring yourself when you fall.

Bouldering Mats

Bouldering mats (or pads) have gone a long way towards making falling from boulder problems safer and dramatically increasing the popularity and difficulty levels achieved in the sport. They soften the impact, can be used to level uneven landings and protect from awkward blocks and other obstacles.

Bouldering mats are not a guarantee of safety - to start with you have to actually land on one. Even the biggest of mats is unlikely to cover all the possible landing sites and, the higher you climb, the wider the potential landing area becomes.

If you are using multiple mats it is usually wiser to cover a wider area, paying attention to joining up the edges - landing on the edge of a mat is a recipe for an ankle injury. Try to keep the landing area flat and resist the temptation to put one more mat in the middle which might present a further edge. For highball problems, multiple pads 'stacked' on top of each other is commonplace but watch out again for edges and keep the landing area flat. Falling onto a stack of pads two to three deep will reduce the impact, but is a smaller target area with a dangerous big edge if you half land on your 'stack'.

Mike Langley on *Hourglass Left* (**V4** *6B*) - *page 146* - at Stanage. Because the edge of the mat is directly under the climber, the upper mat probably creates more of a hazard than it removes. Photo: Adrian Berry

Landing Zone

An uneven or sloping landing zone can make even the shortest of problems dangerous. Creating a level base to place your pad will significantly decrease the likelihood of injury. This can be done by using other smaller mats, or rucksacks or nearby small blocks. A common awkward landing is where the edge slopes away under the crag. In these cases there is little you can do apart from engage good spotters.

Snowballing - One of the best ways to level out a landing zone is to wait until there is a snow drift under a buttress. In these conditions you can carve out a level platform for your mats. This can be so effective that there are some problems that have only ever been 'snowballed' above a drift and await an ascent in more conventional conditions.

WILD COUNTRY

Naomi Buys, NTBTA '6c, Grand Hotel, Stanage Plantation. Ph: Nadir Khan

#PureClimbing

Northern Peak

Sheffield Crags

Stanage Area

Burbage Valley

Derwent Edges

The Limestone

Central Grit

Staffordshire

South Peak

Spotting

There is an art to spotting well that is usually only learned through experience. The objective of spotting is to reduce the risk of injury to the climber. However the first rule is to make sure you're not going to get hurt yourself.

There is a point above which spotting is merely an act of encouragement, and that point is probably a lot lower than many people think. You might feel the emotional need for a spot on highball problems, but if you fall from a good few metres up, your spotters won't be able to do anything (and will probably scatter - if they've got any sense). The point at which a spot is no longer effective depends on the relative size of the spotter and the climber. A general rule of thumb is that, if the climber is beyond reach, he/she is beyond spotting and it is more useful to adjust the positions of the mats than to try to spot. You may still be able to deflect them from blocks and obstacles.

In terms of technique, it is important to note that you're not trying to catch the climber. The aims are to keep them upright so they can land on their feet as much as possible, and to direct them towards a soft landing and away from hazards like rocks and tree stumps. To do this you need to be able to react rapidly to the falling climber. Having your hands almost in contact with the climber is ideal - and if they need reassurance you can tap them with your fingers so they know you're there. Take care to keep your thumbs out of the way to avoid injuring them when fielding the climber.

Where you place your hands on their body depends on the steepness of the problem. The steeper the problem the higher up the back you need to spot and on a horizontal roof problem you will want your hands level with their shoulders. On vertical or slabby problems, there's not much point in trying to grab the climber's sides - they will slide straight through. This leaves only one place to grab - the bottom.

It is a good idea to communicate whether you wish to be spotted before setting off rather than getting into a panic when high up and yelling for spotters. When you fall into the trusty arms of your spotter, do them a favour and keep your

Can you have too many spotters? Eve Lancashire being well supported on *Cleo's Edge* (**V2** 5c) - *page 212* - at Burbage North. Photo: Alan James

arms up. The instinct is to maintain balance and prepare for impact by lowering your arms and sticking our elbows out - elbowing your friend in the face is not a good way to replay them for caring for you.

In situations where you want to prevent someone from running/rolling off down a hill, consider using a spare bouldering mat as a sort of shield to stop them without causing you injury.

tenaya

world's first **9a onsight**

Alexander Megos

Topo Key

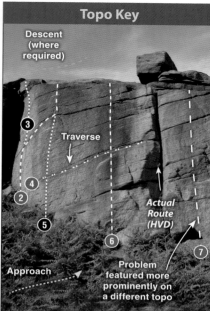

- Descent (where required)
- Traverse
- Actual Route (HVD)
- Approach
- Problem featured more prominently on a different topo

Map Key

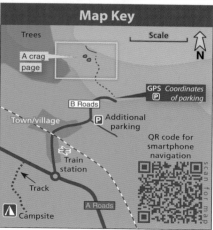

- Trees
- A crag page
- Scale
- N
- B Roads
- GPS Coordinates of parking
- Town/village
- Additional parking
- QR code for smartphone navigation
- Train station
- Track
- Campsite
- A Roads

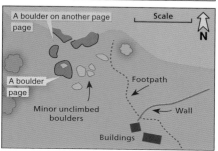

- A boulder on another page page
- Scale
- N
- A boulder page
- Footpath
- Minor unclimbed boulders
- Wall
- Buildings

Route Symbols

 1	A good problem which is well worth climbing.
2	A very good problem, one of the best on the crag.
3	A brilliant problem, one of the best in the Peak.
	Powerful climbing; roofs, steep rock, low lock-offs or long moves off small holds.
	Sustained climbing; either lots of hard moves (including on slabs) or pumpy traverses.
	Fingery climbing with significant small holds on the hard sections.
	A highball problem or one with a bad landing.
	A long reach is helpful, or even essential, for one or more of the moves.
	A dynamic move is required.
	Sit-down start required at this grade.
	Graunchy climbing. Wide cracks or thrutchy moves (not specifically for hand and fist cracks).
	Technical climbing. Not used in this book since most of the problems are technical.
	Rounded climbing. Not used in this book since most gritstone problems have rounded moves.

Crag Symbols

	Angle of the approach walk to the boulders with approximate time.
Lots of sun	Approximate time that the boulder/face is in the direct sun (when it is shining).
Sheltered	The boulder can offer an option when the weather is bad. Shelter from wind or a sun-trap.
Windy	The boulder is exposed to bad weather and will catch the wind if it is blowing.
Seepage	The boulder suffers from seepage.
Dry in the rain	The boulder may offer dry climbing in the rain.
Green	The rock can be green and dirty after prolonged rain.
	Deserted - Currently under-used and usually quiet. Less good problems or a remote area.
	Quiet - Less popular sections on major areas, or good areas with awkward approaches.
	Busy - You will seldom be alone when conditions are good. Good bouldering and easy access.
	Crowded - The most popular sections of the crags which are always busy when in condition.

Northern Peak

Sheffield Crags

Stanage Area

Burbage Valley

Derwent Edges

The Limestone

Central Grit

Staffordshire

South Peak

scan for map

thornbridge **outdoors**

Courses & Coaching

Peak Accommodation

"Leon Zablocki at Bell Hagg" Photo by Alex Ekins

MOUNTAIN TRAINING ENGLAND

AMI ASSOCIATION OF MOUNTAINEERING INSTRUCTORS

iTC IMMEDIATE TEMPORARY CARE

There are three recognised grading systems for bouldering - the **V Grade**, starting at **VB, V0-, V0, V0+, V1, V2,** to **V14**; the **Font Grade**, written *6A, 6A+, 6B, 6B+, ...* to *8C* (with a capital letter to distinguish it from the similar looking sport grade); and the **UK Technical Grade**, written *4a, 4b, 4c, 5a, 5b, 5c*. These three systems are an attempt to measure the overall difficulty of a problem and none of them takes into account the danger level of a highball problem, or one with a bad landing. This similarity means that the grades can be easily converted from one system to the other.

The **V Grade** is popular in the USA and at climbing walls in the UK and has been used in a number of previous bouldering guidebooks in the UK. The **Font** system was established in the mecca for boulderers - Fontainebleau - and is popular amongst the majority of keen boulderers but suffers from inconsistencies in the lower grades. The **UK Technical Grade** is familiar to those who go traditional climbing but has also been used historically to grade boulder problems in the Peak District, and in places like Southern Sandstone in the UK.

In this book we have taken a new approach which aims to appeal to everyone by giving two grades for every problem. You can choose which system you want to use and we have standardised the conversions, although this has left some subdivisions in the Font grade (e.g. **V4** can be *6B* or *6B+*). For lower grade problems (below **V3** *6A*) we have used the UK Technical Grade instead of the inconsistent Font Grade since most British climbers getting into the sport understand and use UK Technical Grades as part of their trad climbing.

Colour Codes

The problems are all given a colour-coded dot corresponding to a grade band. The colour represents a level that a climber should be happy at, hence boulder problems tend to be technically harder than the equivalent coloured trad routes because the length of the climbing tends to be shorter

and the climber doesn't need to worry about the protection, although obviously some highball problems can be extremely serious. See page 32 for information on the Circuit Colour-codes.

Bouldering Grades

V Grade	Font Grade	UK Technical Grade
VB	3	4a
V0-	3+	4b
V0	4	4c
V0+	4+	5a
V1	5	5b
V2	5+	5c
V3	6A / 6A+	6a
V4	6B / 6B+	
V5	6C / 6C+	6b
V6	7A	
V7	7A+	
V8	7B / 7B+	6c
V9	7C	
V10	7C+	
V11	8A	7a
V12	8A+	
V13	8B	
V14	8B+	
V15	8C	

Northern Peak | Sheffield Crags | Stanage Area | Burbage Valley | Derwent Edges | The Limestone | Central Grit | Staffordshire | South Peak

Bouldering circuits have long been popular amongst people wanting to get a lot of climbing done across an area. They are used as training, or just familiar routine circuits practised by frequent visitors. They can also be a great way to sample an area the first time you visit, and this is where the pre-defined circuits in this book come in.

We have included 60 circuits mainly in the easier grade range. These have been sub-divided into Green (up to **V0+** 5a), Orange (up to **V2** 5c) and Red (up to **V5** 6C+). There is some variation in difficulty level between individual circuits, particularly the Red zone where, for example, the two Red Circuits at the Roaches are significantly easier than the those at Froggatt or in the Churnet. Each circuit has a tick box for when you manage to complete it.

The circuits are indicated using the a 'C' symbol by the route name (see right) and are designed to be easily followed in numerical

> **8** **Wall Past Slot** . . . . ③④🕏 [   ] **V0+** 5a
> The far left-hand side of the slab.

order. They vary in length and problems can appear on two circuits (as above) since there is some overlap, especially the Orange problems.

The colour of a circuit indicates its level of difficulty, rather than reflecting the colour of problems included. All the Red Circuits contain some easier Orange problems, and all the Green Circuits contain a few Orange **V0+** 5a problems. Orange Circuits can include problems of all three colours.

No Black Circuits have been included mainly because there are very few climbers that operate at a high enough level to actually complete a Black Circuit. Of course the circuits in this book are only guidelines and you can make up your own, or combine and extend the included circuits.

Circuit	Problems	VB 4a	VO- 4b	VO 4c	VO+ 5a	V1 5b	V2 5c	V3 6A	V3 6A+	V4 6B	V4 6B+	V5 6C	V5 6C+	Page
Wimberry	25	Wimberry Green												
	23			Wimberry Orange										40
	25						Wimberry Red							
Woolpacks	15	Woolpacks Green												
	24			Woolpacks Orange										70
Stanage High Neb	22					Stanage End and High Neb Red								116
	13	Buckstone Causeway Green												
	13			Buckstone Causeway Orange										125
Stanage Plantation	26	Plantation Green												
	39		Plantation Orange											132
	30					Plantation Red								
Stanage Popular	20					Stanage Popular Red								162
Stanage Far Right	20	Stanage Far Right Green												
	24		Stanage Far Right Orange											165
	22					Stanage Far Right Red								167
Higgar Tor	20	Higgar Tor Green												
	20			Higgar Tor Orange										183
	17					Higgar Tor Red								

Northern Peak | Sheffield Crags | Stanage Area | Burbage Valley | Derwent Edges | The Limestone | Central Grit | Staffordshire | South Peak

Circuit

Circuit	Problems	VB 4a	V0- 4b	V0 4c	V0+ 5a	V1 5b	V2 5c	V3 6A	V3 6A+	V4 6B	V4 6B+	V5 6C	V5 6C+	Page
Burbage West	18		Burbage West Orange											198
Burbage North	32	Burbage North Green												202
	35		Burbage North Orange											
	29			Burbage North Red										
Burbage South Valley	30	Burbage South Valley Green												236
	30		Burbage South Valley Orange											
	20				Burbage South Valley Red									
Millstone Area	17		Mother Owler Area Orange											258
	22				Millstone Area Red									
Froggatt	20				Froggatt Red									276
	17		Pinnacle Orange											284
Curbar Edge	25	Curbar Edge Orange												303
	25				Curbar Edge Red									
Curbar Field	11	Curbar Field Green												309
	20		Curbar Field Orange											
Baslow	26				Baslow Edge Red									313
Gardom's North	13				Gardom's North Red									324
	12		Gardom's North Orange											326
Birchen	16				Birchen Red									341
	16	Birchen Three Ships Green												342
Robin Hood's Stride	15	The Stride Green												380
	19		The Stride Orange											
	20				The Stride Red									
Cratcliffe	20				Cratcliffe Red									390
	17	Cratcliffe Green												392
	16		Cratcliffe Orange											
Roaches Lower	25	Roaches Lower Green												441
	30		Roaches Lower Orange											
	30			Roaches Lower Red										
Roaches Upper	18	Roaches Upper Green												455
	24		Roaches Upper Orange											
	25			Roaches Upper Red										
The Skyline	15	The Skyline Green												468
	20		The Skyline Orange											
	29			The Skyline Red										
Ramshaw	13		Ramshaw Orange											485
	24			Ramshaw Red										
Newstones/ Baldstones	15	Newstones Green												492
	19		Newstones/Baldstones Orange											
	29			Newstones/Baldstones Red										
Harborough	19	Harborough Green												513
Churnet	31				Churnet Red									521

	Problems	Circuits	up to V0 Easy to 4c	V0+ to V2 5a to 5c/6a	V3 to V5 6A to 6C+	V6 to V13 7A to 8B+
Northern Peak						
Wimberry	92	●○●	27	28	23	14
Tintwistle Knarr	36		1	7	15	13
Black Tor	37		5	9	12	11
Hobson Moor Quarry	24		6	9	7	2
New Mills Tor	22		1	7	11	3
The Woolpacks	54	●○	12	27	15	–
Derwent	68		5	33	24	6
Sheffield Crags						
Wharncliffe	30		–	4	15	11
Rivelin	28		–	2	12	14
Bell Hagg	35		8	16	10	1
Bamford	21		3	3	13	2
Stanage Area						
Stanage High Neb	96	●○●	9	34	28	25
Stanage Plantation	225	●○●	28	60	61	76
Stanage Popular End	36	●	6	23	5	2
Stanage Far Right	118	●○●	23	44	37	14
Burbage Valley						
Higgar Tor	78	●○●	16	31	19	12
Burbage West	54	○	5	17	15	17
Burbage North	154	●○●	28	50	36	40
Burbage South Edge	112		9	29	35	39
Burbage South Valley	136	●○●	33	66	20	17
Millstone Area	110	○●	9	29	36	36
Houndkirk Moor	29		1	16	10	2
Derwent Edges						
Froggatt	94	●●	10	23	25	36
Curbar	165	●○●	23	53	45	44
Baslow	84	●	7	26	26	25
Gardom's	88	○●	2	20	35	31
Birchen	80	●●	21	28	18	13

Northern Peak | Sheffield Crags | Stanage Area | Burbage Valley | Derwent Edges | The Limestone | Central Grit | Staffordshire | South Peak

Approach	Sun	Wind	Seepage	Dry in Rain	Summary	Page	
10 - 25 min	Sun and shade	Windy			An extensive boulderfield spread across a steep hillside. Excellent for circuits, but can be exposed and cold.	40	Northern Peak
30 min	Sun and shade				A complex jumble of boulders with some interesting problems. Out of the way and unlikely to be busy.	51	
15 - 19 min	Morning	Windy			An exposed hillside with some fine isolated boulders. Quite remote and unlikely to be busy.	56	
1 min	Sun and shade	Sheltered			A roadside quarry with a famous traverse and some good vertical problems.	62	Sheffield Crags
5 min	Sun and shade	Sheltered		Dry in the rain	Some hard problems and traverses in a very sheltered urban setting with one ever-dry wall.	65	
90 min	Sun and shade	Windy			A very remote and exposed set of beautiful moorland boulders and rock formations. A long walk in and some soft rock.	68	
15 - 30 min	Afternoon	Windy			Remote and wild rock formations on the beautiful moors. A long walk in, but good when in condition.	80	Stanage Area
20 - 40 min	Sun and shade	Sheltered			A few small areas spread along the edge in a wooded setting. Mostly in the higher grades.	90	
10 - 16 min	Sun and shade	Sheltered			Some quality hard problems dotted along the main edge. Mostly in a wooded setting and good for dry winter days.	96	
10 - 11 min	Not much sun	Sheltered		Dry in the rain	A north-facing edge on the outskirts of Sheffield. Nothing of any great quality, but quick and easy access.	102	
15 - 20 min	From mid morning	Windy			A beautiful edge with limited bouldering, but a few worthwhile harder problems.	110	Burbage Valley
5 - 25 min	Afternoon	Windy			The most remote section of Stanage with a number of areas which are well spread out. A few good circuits.	114	
10 - 20 min	From mid morning	Windy			One of the most extensive areas in the book with many brilliant problems and some great long circuits. Usually busy.	126	
8 - 18 min	From mid morning	Windy			A combination of short routes and boulder problem starts on the busiest section of Stanage Edge.	160	Derwent Edges
6 - 15 min	Lots of sun	Windy			Lots of great small areas dotted along the continuation of the main edge. Some excellent circuits.	164	
5 min	Sun and shade	Windy		Dry in the rain	Some great bouldering spread around the small edge of the tor. Good for circuits. Some of the landings are bad..	180	
3 - 5 min	Morning	Windy			Good hard bouldering and a few top class problems. East facing, so it offers shade in the afternoon in the warmer months.	192	The Limestone
2 - 23 min	From mid morning	Windy		Dry in the rain	An excellent edge with plenty of bouldering on the edge itself and on the blocks below. Good circuits.	200	
12 - 20 min	Evening	Windy			Shady northwest-facing crag with some quality hard problems. Not good for circuits and some very bad landings.	218	
10 - 20 min	Lots of sun	Windy			One of the best boulderfields around with some brilliant boulders and great circuits. Always busy when conditions are good.	234	Central Grit
8 - 15 min	Lots of sun	Windy			Some good natural blocks above Millstone, and hard problems on the quarried edge itself.	252	
5 - 15 min	Sun and shade	Windy			Two minor locations - one offering a short, shady, north-facing edge and the other a lone block in the middle of the moor.	268	
1 - 20 min	Afternoon	Windy			Some good hard problems on the wooded area and main crag and easier offerings on the boulders above.	274	Staffordshire
3 - 30 min	Afternoon	Windy		Dry in the rain	Several locations spread along the edge and some brilliant and popular boulders in the field below.	291	
5 - 22 min	Afternoon	Windy			A small edge and isolated block. Quite a bit of lower grade bouldering on offer but it is mostly highball/soloing.	310	South Peak
5 - 25 min	Sun and shade	Windy			Three good concentrated areas with some isolated harder problems in between.	322	
12 - 15 min	From mid morning	Windy			Hard bouldering on the edge and an easy circuit on the blocks above.	338	

Faded symbol means that only some of the bouldering is sheltered / suffers from seepage / is dry in the rain

		Problems	Circuits	up to V0 Easy to 4c	V0+ to V2 5a to 5c/6a	V3 to V5 6A to 6C+	V6 to V13 7A to 8B+
The Limestone	Stoney	66		1	8	18	39
	Rubicon	27			6	10	11
	Raven Tor	31				7	24
	Blackwell Dale	31				6	25
	Alport Area	24			5	8	11
Central Grit	Rabbit Warren	18		4	12	2	
	Harland Edge	15		1	9	5	
	Robin Hood's Stride	78	● ○ ●	11	24	20	23
	Cratcliffe	92	● ○ ●	16	28	22	26
	Clifftop Boulder	18			4	8	6
	Stanton Moor	72			15	28	29
	Rowtor Rocks	47			6	17	24
	Matlock	15			5	9	1
	Amber Valley	52		1	10	24	17
Staffordshire	The Roaches	252	● ○ ●	52	93	70	37
	The Skyline	66	● ○ ●	17	20	23	6
	The Five Clouds	28			6	9	13
	Ramshaw	55	○ ●	4	18	19	14
	Newstones Baldstones	76	● ○ ●	11	27	27	11
	Gib Torr	16			5	6	5
	Wolf Edge	27		3	16	7	1
Southern Crags	Black Rocks	26		3	5	9	9
	Harborough Rocks	32	●	15	14		3
	Shining Cliff	10			4	2	4
	Churnet Valley	114	●	1	18	51	44

Northern Peak | Sheffield Crags | Stanage Area | Burbage Valley | Derwent Edges | The Limestone | Central Grit | Staffordshire | South Peak

Approach	Sun	Wind	Seepage	Dry in Rain	Summary	Page	Region
10 min	Sun and shade	Sheltered		Dry in the rain	Technical eliminates on polished limestone in a handful of locations on this historic crag. Not too everyone's taste.	350	Northern Peak
3 min	Lots of sun	Sheltered	Seepage	Dry in the rain	Hard problems and some difficult traverses in a sun-trap. Often inaccessible in the winter when flooded.	356	Northern Peak
Roadside	Lots of sun	Sheltered	Seepage	Dry in the rain	Some of the hardest problems and traverses in the Peak. The rock is polished and often wet in winter. A sun-trap at other times.	360	Northern Peak
1 min	Sun and shade	Sheltered	Seepage	Dry in the rain	Three roadside walls with a few hard problems. They generally suffer from some seepage, although one section dries quickly.	365	Sheffield Crags
2 min	Sun and shade	Sheltered	Seepage		Two contrasting venues - one vertical wall of highballs in a lovely location, another steep cave with some powerful problems.	368	Sheffield Crags
25 min	Lots of sun	Windy			An isolated edge with a small set of mid-grade problems. Never busy and a beautiful setting. Can be combined with Harland Edge.	374	Stanage Area
20 - 24 min	Lots of sun	Windy			An isolated edge with a small set of mid-grade problems. Never busy and a beautiful setting. Can be combined with Rabbit Warren.	376	Stanage Area
10 - 15 min	Sun and shade	Sheltered		Dry in the rain	A beautiful cluster of varied boulders scattered around this small edge with some good circuits. Plenty for a long day.	378	Stanage Area
10 - 20 min	Sun and shade	Sheltered	Seepage		A superb boulderfield with lower-grade problems and some quality hard bouldering on the edge and wooded area of the main crag.	388	Burbage Valley
10 min	Lots of sun				A small crag with a good steep prow and walls either side. A limited set of problems, but some of high quality.	402	Burbage Valley
2 - 20 min	Sun and shade	Sheltered			Several small clusters of blocks and edges around the moor. A few high-quality problems.	406	Burbage Valley
2 - 4 min	Sun and shade	Sheltered	Seepage		A great location on a small tor with some fascinating rock formations and carvings. Excellent hard bouldering.	416	Derwent Edges
2 - 4 min	Not much sun / Sheltered				Two small crags on the northern edge of the town of Matlock. A few good highball problems only.	424	Derwent Edges
4 - 10 min	Morning				Three small edges in a picturesque valley. Mostly hard problems in amongst some dense vegetation.	426	Derwent Edges
3 - 30 min	From mid morning	Windy			Superb and extensive bouldering on boulders and the edge. Six excellent circuits and quality across the grades.	438	The Limestone
25 - 40 min	From mid morning	Windy			Several beautiful and exposed locations above the Roaches with some good hard problems and circuits.	466	The Limestone
10 - 15 min	From mid morning	Windy			A few isolated locations including one brilliant boulder. Can be combined easily with the Roaches.	474	The Limestone
2 - 10 min	Morning	Windy			An east-facing edge with a few good areas in the mid and high grades.	482	Central Grit
2 - 12 min	Morning	Windy			An excellent spot with good bouldering on the two edges and quality problems across the grade range. Mostly east-facing.	490	Central Grit
1 min	Morning	Windy			A few high-quality problems on a small, east-facing crag.	500	Central Grit
10 min	Morning	Windy			Isolated bouldering on a short edge in four separate sections.	502	Staffordshire
1 - 5 min	Sun and shade	Sheltered			Three contrasting areas near the crag. One has some lower-grade slabs and the others offer very hard highball slabs and walls.	508	Staffordshire
5 min	Lots of sun				A nice limestone edge with short routes and problems. Mostly in the lower grades.	512	Staffordshire
10 - 15 min	Lots of sun	Sheltered			A small sheltered area with a limited set of decent problems.	516	South Peak
8 - 18 min	Sun and shade	Sheltered		Dry in the rain	A wooded set of small sandstone crags offering hard bouldering and traverses.	518	South Peak

Faded symbol means that only some of the bouldering is sheltered / suffers from seepage / is dry in the rain

Northern Peak

Northern Peak

Sheffield Crags

Stanage Area

Burbage Valley

Derwent Edges

The Limestone

Central Grit

Staffordshire

South Peak

Audrey Seguy on *Novel Adaptation* (**V3** *6A*) - *page 77* - at the Woolpacks. Photo: Adrian Berry

About 5km

N

Uppermill

A635

A6024

Hepworth

Greenfield

Wimberry
next page

Black Tor
p.56

A628

Tintwistle Knarr
p.51

Stalybridge

Hobson Moor Quarry
p.62

Bleaklow (633m)
△

M67

Mottram

Glossop

Derwent
p.80

A624

A57

Marple

Kinder (636m)
△

The Woolpacks
p.68

Bamford
p.110

Hayfield

New Mills

New Mills Tor
p.65

Edale

Disley

A6

Hope

Bamford

	No star	🕸	🕸	🕸
VB to V0 Easy to 4c	5	17	5	-
V0+ to V2 5a to 5c	3	22	3	-
V3 to V5 6A to 6C+	3	13	7	-
V3 to V5 7A upwards	3	3	3	5

This collection of boulders is the Chew Valley's best bouldering venue with everything needed for a good session. Although Wimberry is far from the madding crowds of Eastern Grit, it has long been a favourite of the Lancashire and Manchester set and is highly developed and popular. Unlike virtually every other crag in the Chew area, you don't need to slog up a big hill to get to the bouldering, although there is a bit of hill slogging between the boulders. The grit is solid with some very sloping holds. Most of the problems are a perfect height and generally the landings are fine. The rock is very coarse in places and can have spectacular pebbles sticking out.

Circuits

There are three excellent circuits at Wimberry.

Conditions

Although this area of the Chew Valley is notorious for its bad weather (the main crag faces north and is very exposed) the boulders are relatively sheltered and do get plenty of sun. The rock can be green, especially by the brooks, but will dry quickly.

The **Wimberry Green Circuit**
25 problems dotted across the boulders up to the Salmon Boulder. There are a few slightly high problems on the Tank but these are mostly above good landings.

The **Wimberry Orange Circuit**
A 23-problem circuit up to **V2** 5c. It includes a few highball Green problems and requires walking all the way up the hill to the Top Slab.

The **Wimberry Red Circuit**
Another longish 25 problem circuit. There is one classic **V6** 7A but it is mostly V4 and below.

Wimberry Crag

Top Slab p.50

Fish Boulder p.48

Salmon Boulder p.49

Matterhorn p.46

Stream Boulder p.43

Shell Shot p.45

The Tank p.44

Sloping Top p.43

Sugar Loaf p.42

Northern Peak

Sheffield Crags

Stanage Area

Burbage Valley

Derwent Edges

The Limestone

Central Grit

Staffordshire

South Peak

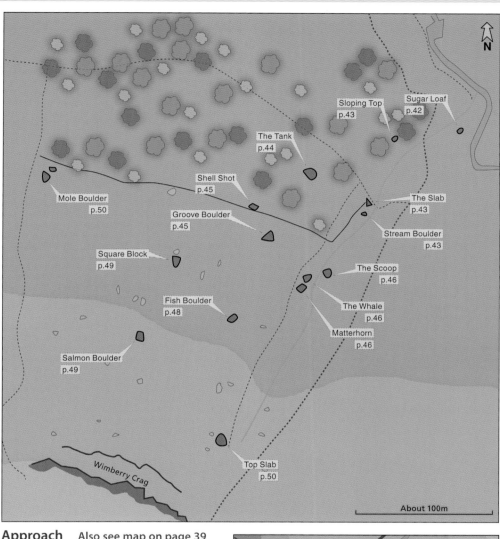

Sloping Top
p.43

Sugar Loaf
p.42

The Tank
p.44

Shell Shot
p.45

Mole Boulder
p.50

Groove Boulder
p.45

The Slab
p.43

Stream Boulder
p.43

Square Block
p.49

The Scoop
p.46

Fish Boulder
p.48

The Whale
p.46

Matterhorn
p.46

Salmon Boulder
p.49

Top Slab
p.50

Wimberry Crag

About 100m

Approach   Also see map on page 39

The area is south of the A635 Chew Valley to Greenfield road, just to the east of Greenfield. (See map on previous page for general location). Turn off the A635 at a sharp bend into Bank Lane. This leads to parking spots by the reservoir. Follow the track past the yachting club (no parking here) and below the walled plantation. Turn right onto a path just before a bridge. This leads to The Sugar Loaf.

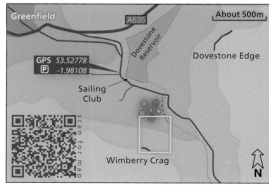

Greenfield

A635

About 500m

Dovestone Reservoir

Dovestone Edge

GPS 53.52778
P -1.98108

Sailing Club

scan for map

Wimberry Crag

N

Northern Peak

Sheffield Crags

Stanage Area

Burbage Valley

Derwent Edges

The Limestone

Central Grit

Staffordshire

South Peak

Sugar Loaf

The undercut Sugar Loaf is the first boulder you come to by the brook and a great place to start a circuit.
Approach - See map on page 41.

1 Artificial Route ... V0+ 5a
The rib and wall above. **V8** 7B from sitting.

2 Green Wall V0 4c
Follow the old chips.

3 Right Arete V2 5c
The right side of the arete.

4 Way Down V0- 4b
Also the easiest way up.

5 Angus V4 6B
The graffiti-covered face and rib. The sitting start is **V7** 7A+.

6 Angus Right V4 6B
From the starting hold on *Angus*, move out right.

7 Rib Left V1 5b
The arete climbed on its left-hand side, and slab above.

8 Rib Right V0- 4b
The same arete climbed on its right-hand side, and slab above.

9 Left Arete V2 5c
The arete. **V6** 7A from sitting.

10 Local Hero ...... V4 6B+
The centre of the wall, following chips. Avoiding all the chips is **V6** 7A. It is a fingery **V10** 7C+ from sitting.

11 Baxter's Wall .... V3 6A+
As for *Local Hero* but move right to the arete.

12 Baxter's Wall Direct .. V2 5c
A touch easier than the original. The sitting start is **Brush Electric, V9** 7C - take the lip of the mini-roof as an undercut.

13 Sugar Loaf Girdle V5 6C
A traverse of the boulder in either direction.

Northern Peak

Sheffield Crags

Stanage Area

Burbage Valley

Derwent Edges

The Limestone

Central Grit

Staffordshire

South Peak

Sloping Top
A horrific sloping top which gives some nasty mantels.
Approach - See map on page 41.

🔟4 **Left Arete** . . . . ⑥ 🕸 🔧 [　　] **V1** 5b
The left arete of the stream face.

🔟5 **Letterbox Slot** . ⑦⑦ 🕸 🔧 [　　] **V2** 5c
Undercut the slot to start. *Orange Circuit continues on page 44.*

🔟6 **Fat Slapper** . . . . . . ⑧ 🕸 🔧 [　　] **V4** 6B+
The arete. **V6** 7A from sitting and avoiding the chipped hold.
Red Circuit continues on page 44.

🔟7 **Slap Happy** . . . . 🕸 🔧 [　　] **V5** 6C+
Slap and mantel. **V8** 7B+ from a crouching start.

🔟8 **Slapstick** . . . . 🕸 🔧 [　　] **V5** 6C
The short rib to the right. The sitting start is **The Grey Road**,
V9 7C.

The Stream Boulder and The Slab
The next two boulders are up the brook, below a
steepening in the slope.
Approach - See map on page 41.

🔟9 **Shallow Water** . . . . [　　] **V3** 6A
Climb the groove above the stream.

2⃣0 **Stream Slab** . . . . ⑤ 🕸 [　　] **VB** 4a
The easy wall.

2⃣1 **Stream Arete** . . . . ⑥ 🕸 [　　] **V0** 4c
The pleasant short arete.

The chipped slab has two nice problems.

2⃣2 **Chipper** . . . . ⑦ 🕸 [　　] **VB** 4a
Grease up the chips.

2⃣3 **The Slab** . . . . ⑧ 🕸 [　　] **V0** 4c
The right arete. *Green Circuit continues on page 44.*

The Scoop p.46

The Matterhorn p.46

The Whale p.46

The Stream Boulder

The Slab

Northern Peak

Sheffield Crags

Stanage Area

Burbage Valley

Derwent Edges

The Limestone

Central Grit

Staffordshire

South Peak

The Tank

In the woods on the west (right looking uphill) of the stream is a big lump of a boulder that looks a bit like a tank although not as much as its namesake at Burbage South.

Approach - See map on page 41.

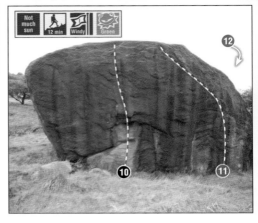

❶ **Left Slab** . . . . ⑧ ⑨ 🌣 ▢ **V0+** 5a
The slab left of the crack.

❷ **Diagonal Crack** . . . ⑩ 🌣 ♥ ▢ **V0-** 4b
The prominent diagonal crack.

❸ **Tanked Up** . . . . . . ⑪ 🌣 ♥ ▢ **V0-** 4b
The wall left of the arete.

❹ **Chipper** . . . . . ⑨ ⑫ 🌣 ♥ ▢ **V0** 4c
The left-hand side of the arete following chipped holds.

❺ **Moby Dick** . . . . ⑨ ⑩ 🌣 ♥ ▢ **V2** 5c
The right-hand side of the arete is a lot harder.

❻ **Enhancing Hero** . . . ⑩ 🌣 🔧 ▢ **V5** 6C
The wall between the arete and the crack. **V8** 7B from sitting.

❼ **Elephant's Bum** . . . . . ⑪ 🌣 ▢ **V1** 5b
The awkward crack. **V5** 6C+ from sitting.
Orange Circuit continues on page 46.

❽ **Bum-Slide** . . . . ⑪ 🌣 ▢ **V4** 6B
The slab just right.

❾ **Stateside** . . . . . . 🌣 🔧 🔧 ▢ **V8** 7B+
The poor side-pulls allow the right arete to be climbed.

❿ **Unclimbed Dyno** . . . . 🔧 ▢ **?**
An unclimbed problem, at the time of writing...

⓫ **Think Tank** . . . . . ⑫ 🌣 🔧 ▢ **V4** 6B
The line of flakes, started from the arete.

⓬ **Beginners' Slab** . . . . . ⑬ 🌣 ▢ **VB** 4a
The low-angled slab with chips.

Shell Shot

Shell Shot

Uphill from the Tank is a pyramidal boulder by a fence.
Approach - See map on page 41.

⓭ Take Cover . . . . . 🕴🏃❤️ ▭ **V7** *7A+*
The wall on thin edges with a hard finish.

⓮ Howitzer . . . . ⑬🕴 ▭ **V3** *6A*
The arete on its left-hand side.

⓯ Shell Shot . . . . ⑭🕴 ▭ **V0** *4c*
The left arete.

⓰ Shell Shock. . . . . ⑮🕴 ▭ **V0-** *4b*
The small slab to the right. *Green Circuit continues on page 46.*

⓱ The Cannon. . . . . . ⑭🕴🏃 ▭ **V3** *6A*
Up to the flakes on the right.

The Groove Boulder

This is uphill and slightly leftwards from Shell Shot.
Approach - See map on page 41.

⓲ Groove . . . . ⑮🕴 ▭ **V4** *6B*
The short groove on the east side of the boulder.
Red Circuit continues on page 46.

⓳ Groove Traverse . . . . 🏃 ▭ **V7** *7A+*
Gain the top of *Groove* by traversing the top of the boulder from
close to the right arete.

⓴ Handrail . . . . 🕴🍎 ▭ **V2** *5c*
From sitting, gain the handrail and follow it to a mantel onto
the top.

Northern Peak | Sheffield Crags | Stanage Area | Burbage Valley | Derwent Edges | The Limestone | Central Grit | Staffordshire | South Peak

The Scoop

The lowest of three boulders close to the stream with a prominent scoop in its downward face.
Approach - See map on page 41.

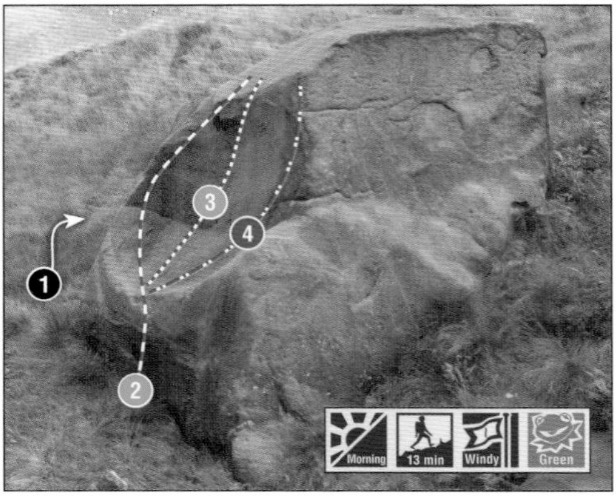

1 Steve's Wall .... 2★ ☐ **V7** *7A+*
The slab just left of the arete.

2 Scoop Left .... (12) 1★ ☐ **V2** 5c
The scoop, exiting leftwards.

3 Scoop Centre....... (13) 1★ ☐ **V2** 5c
The scoop, exiting directly.

4 The Scoop.......... (16) 2★ ☐ **VB** 4a
The scoop, exiting rightwards.

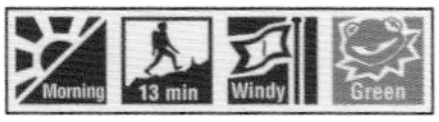

The Whale

The Whale lies below the Matterhorn, by the stream.

5 Pockets .... (16)(14) 1★ ☐ **V2** 5c
The wall via a trio of pockets.

6 Grit Style .... (17) 2★ ☐ **V4** *6B*
Just right, climb the wall without using the crack.

7 Whalebone .... ☐ **V0** 4c
Climb the crack.

8 Whale Traverse ..... 1★ ☐ **V8** *7B*
Starting at the crack of *Whalebone*, traverse left to *Pockets*.

9 The Flake .... ☐ **V0-** 4b
The flake. Eliminating the pockets is **V7** *7A+*.

Just above is the Matterhorn Boulder.

10 The Nipple .... (18) 1★ ☐ **V3** *6A*
Just right of the arete, climb the wall via a 'nipple'.

11 West's Route.. (19)(15) 2★ ☐ **V2** 5c
The centre of the face.

12 Winsome ...... 3★ ☐ **V7** *7A+*
The slab left of the arete is very thin and very classic.

13 Zmutt Ridge ..... (20)(16) 1★ ☐ **V2** 5c
The arete.

14 South Arete........ (17) 1★ ☐ **V0-** 4b
Another arete.

15 South Face Direct . (17) 1★ ☐ **V1** 5b
Follow small holds up the slab right of the arete.

16 South Face .... (18) 1★ ☐ **V0-** 4b
Follow chipped holds up the face. *Photo opposite.*

17 Eliminator....... (21)(18) 1★ ☐ **V2** 6a
An eliminate between two lines of chipped holds.
Orange and Red Circuits continue on page 48.

18 Hörnli Ridge .... (19) 1★ ☐ **VB** 4a
The easiest way up, and down. *Green continues on page 48.*

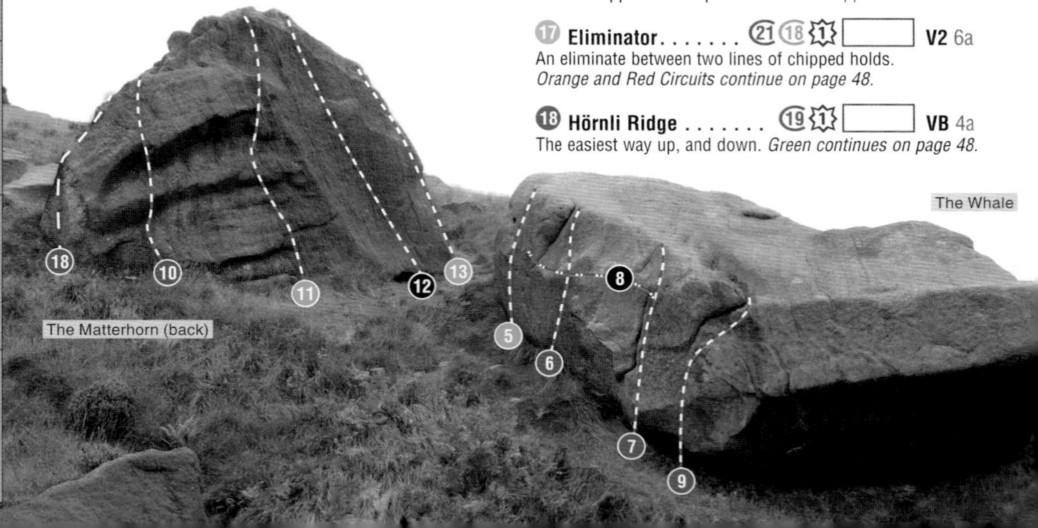

Northern Peak

Sheffield Crags

Stanage Area

Burbage Valley

Derwent Edges

The Limestone

Central Grit

Staffordshire

South Peak

The Matterhorn

Named because of its resemblance to the Matterhorn, it has a couple of excellent faces and includes one of the classic problems of the area.
Approach - See map on page 41.

Lots of sun | 13 min | Windy | Green

Adrian Berry on *South Face* (**V0-** 4b) - *opposite* - Matterhorn Boulder. Photo: Duncan Skelton

Northern Peak

Sheffield Crags

Stanage Area

Burbage Valley

Derwent Edges

The Limestone

Central Grit

Staffordshire

South Peak

The Fish Boulder

Uphill and a little to the right is this excellent block.
Approach - See map on page 41.

1 **You're Joking** . . . . . . 　　　　　 **V8** *7B*
Start hanging the crimps and go for the top.

2 **Fish Groove** . . . . . 　　　　　 **V4** *6B+*
The groove - starting low on the poor crimps is V8.

3 **Fish Arete** . . . . 　　　　 **V6** *7A*
Climb the double aretes. **V8** *7B+* from sitting.

4 **The Fish Slab** . . . . . . 　　　　 **VB** *4a*
The left side of the slab.

5 **Fish Slab Central** . . 　　　　　 **V0+** *5a*
A middle of the slab via a pair of flakes.

6 **Fish Slab Right** . . . . . 　　　　 **V1** *5b*
The right side of the slab. *Orange Circuit continues on page 50.*

7 **The Coarse Traverse**

. . . . 　　　　　 **V6** *7A*
Traverse the edge all the way to the nose.

8 **Not So Coarse** . . . . . . 　　　　 **V3** *6A*
Do half the previous problem then exit to the top.

9 **Dark Matter** . . . 　　　　　　 **V9** *7C*
From a low hold, gain the top via some slopers.

10 **Fish Dish** . . . . 　　　　 **V4** *6B*
Starting at the rib, gain the top via dishes. Starting down and left in the break is **V5** *6C+*. *Red Circuit continues on page 50.*

11 **Fish Eye** . . . . 　　　　 **V0** *4c*
Climbs past a sloping shelf.

12 **Fish Traverse** . . . . . . 　　　　 **V6** *7A*
Follow the holds below the top from right to left. Finishing up *Fish Dish*. Straight up is **V3** *6A+*.

13 **Grouper** . . . . 　　 **V4** *6B*
Mantel the lip.

Northern Peak

Sheffield Crags

Stanage Area

Burbage Valley

Derwent Edges

The Limestone

Central Grit

Staffordshire

South Peak

The Square Block

About 50m right (west) of The Fish is a low block.
Approach - See map on page 41.

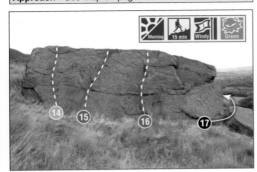

14 Square Arete . . . . VO+ 5a
The short wall just right of the arete.

15 Groove . . . . VB 4a
The groove in the centre of the face.

16 Grooves . . . . VO- 4b
The groove further right.

17 Arch Enemy V6 7A
Follow the thin holds just right of the tiny arch.

18 Scoop Mantel V2 5c
Mantel into the scoop just to the right.

On the far side of the boulder below are two short problems.

19 Cave Dweller V2 5c
Pull out of the 'cave' on slopers.

20 Cave Traverse V3 6A
Start up *Cave Dweller* and traverse slopers right to the arete.

The Salmon Boulder

Hike straight up the hill from Square Block and you reach
the Salmon Boulder.
Approach - See map on page 41.

21 Poached . . . . VO- 4b
The scoop.

22 Smoked . . . . VO 4c
The rib just right.

23 Le Petit Tank . . . . VO+ 5a
From the left, follow edges to the top. Start sitting at the left
arete for **V1** 5b, and start sitting on the right arete at **V4** 6B.
This is the last problem in the Green Circuit.

24 Raw . . . . VO+ 5a
Starting from the block, climb the arete..

25 Leap . . . . VO- 4b
Link the three pockets on the wall just right. V4 from sitting.

Northern Peak

Sheffield Crags

Stanage Area

Burbage Valley

Derwent Edges

The Limestone

Central Grit

Staffordshire

South Peak

Top Slab

The highest boulder here has some good slab climbing - but is a bit on the high side.
Approach - See map on page 41.

Mole Boulder

The Mole Boulder is at the south-west corner of the plantation, just outside the fence.
Approach - See map on page 41.

① **Peas of Mine** . . . . . ㉑ ⚡ 🖐 [ ] **V1** 5b
The left side of the slab.

② **Sip in Side** . . . . . . ㉒ ⚡ 🖐 [ ] **V0** 4c
The centre of the slab. *Photo this page.*

③ **Pool Wall** . . . . ㉓ ⚡ 🖐 [ ] **V0+** 5a
The wall above the pool. *The last problem in the Orange Circuit.*

❹ **Directissima** . . . . ⚡ 🧗 [ ] **V8** 7B+
Start by jumping into the large dimple then follow the brush marks up the thin slab.

❺ **Mr Mole** . . . . ㉔ ⚡ [ ] **V5** 6C
The right arete on its left.

❻ **Mrs Mole** . . . . ㉕ ⚡ [ ] **V1** 5b
The wall right of the arete. *The last problem in the Red Circuit.*

	No star	✧	✧✧	✧✧✧
VB to V0 Easy to 4c	-	1	-	-
V0+ to V2 5a to 5c	1	6	-	-
V3 to V5 6A to 6C+	-	10	5	-
V3 to V5 7A upwards	-	11	2	-

Tintwistle is a small venue in a beautiful location with a good set of mainly harder problems. The approach is lengthy but straightforward following the quarry track up the hill. The quarry of Tintwistle, with its famous arete climb, makes a worthy addition for those who wish to mix their routes and bouldering.

Approach   Also see map on page 39

The A628 Woodhead Pass runs between the M67 (Manchester) and the M1 (Barnsley). Tintwistle is 3 miles (4.5km) from the eastern end of the M67. From Tintwistle, head 1.3 miles (2.1km) east. Just before you reach a wooded area there is a small parking area on the left for four cars (five at a push). Pass through the gate (unlocked but vehicles are not allowed). Hike up the track, ignoring a couple of tracks leading off right into the forest. Pass through a locked gate and continue up until the ground levels out and you come to the quarry on your left. The boulders are down to your right. Approach with care over the scree to reach the Top Boulders.

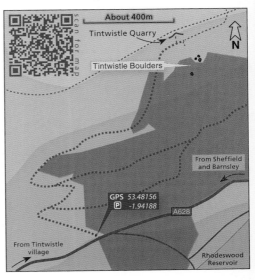

About 400m

Tintwistle Quarry

Tintwistle Boulders

N

From Sheffield and Barnsley

GPS 53.48156
ⓟ -1.94188   A628

From Tintwistle village

Rhodeswood Reservoir

Conditions

The boulders face all directions so there should be some sun and some shade available at all times. The lack of popularity means that the problems can get dirty so be prepared to brush them carefully after wet weather.

The Soul Deep Boulder. Photo: Adrian Berry

Sheffield Crags | Stanage Area | Burbage Valley | Derwent Edges | The Limestone | Central Grit | Staffordshire | South Peak

Northern Peak

Sheffield Crags

Stanage Area

Burbage Valley

Derwent Edges

The Limestone

Central Grit

Staffordshire

South Peak

Top Boulders

These are the first boulders you reach when approaching down the scree from the track.

Approach - See map on page 51.

❶ Nikita . . . . ⬚ V4 *6B+*
From sitting at an undercut and a gaston, gain the left arete and follow this to finish. Finishing on the right-hand side is **V8** *7B*.

❷ Leon . . . . ⬚ V8 *7B*
From sitting, climb the right-hand arete.

There are two problems on the other side of the Nikita Boulder.

❸ La Femme Fatale
. . . . ⬚ V8 *7B+*
The left arete of the back of the block. A bad landing.

❹ La Femme Slab . . . . ⬚ V2 *5c*
The centre of the slab.

The Soul Deep Boulder is the tall block down towards the trees.

❺ Left Side. . . . . ⬚ V2 *5c*
Climb the left-side of the rippled slab.

❻ Centre . . . . ⬚ V2 *5c*
The centre of the rippled slab.

❼ Arete on Left . . . . ⬚ V2 *5c*
The right-hand side of the rippled slab.

Lots of sun **30 min**

On the other side of this boulder.

❽ Soul Deep . . . . ⬚ V4 *6B+*
Climb the wall out of the pit. **V8** *7B* from sitting.

A little further down is a narrow pinnacle.

❾ Small Arete . . . . ⬚ V5 *6C*
From sitting, climb the pinnacle.

Around to the right is the undercut **Mr. Brightside Boulder**.

❿ Underpass . . . . ⬚ V5 *6C*
Starting under the roof on the left block, span out to the lip and mantel onto the slab.

⓫ Mr. Brightside ⬚ V6 *7A*
From sitting, traverse the edge to the lip and mantel the lip on the left.

⓬ Layaway Wall . . . ⬚ V4 *6B*
Start as for *Mr. Brightside* and climb directly up the wall.

⓭ Small Wall . . . . V0+ *5a*
The wall just right.

⓮ Fire Fly . . . . ⬚ V5 *6C+*
From sitting, climb the wall just left of the arete.

The Back Side Arete Boulder presents a nice tall slab.

⓯ Left Slab. . . . . ⬚ V3 *6A*
The left side of the slab.

⓰ Back Side Arete . . ⬚ V5 *6C+*
The arete on its right-hand side from sitting.

Nikita

Soul Deep

Northern Peak

Sheffield Crags

Stanage Area

Burbage Valley

Derwent Edges

The Limestone

Central Grit

Staffordshire

South Peak

Mr. Brightside

Northern Peak

Sheffield Crags

Stanage Area

Burbage Valley

Derwent Edges

The Limestone

Central Grit

Staffordshire

South Peak

Mr. Brightside
p.53

Back Side Arete
p.53

The Big Boulder

The largest boulder here is just down and right (looking uphill) of the previous boulders.
Approach - See map on page 51.

1 Mad as a Badger . . . . ☼ 🎒   **V3** *6A*
The left arete of the wall.

2 The Thief . . . . ☼ 🔲   **V5** *6C*
Climb the wall just right of the arete.

3 Seam Wall . . . . ☼ 🔲   **V5** *6C+*
The centre of the rippled wall.

4 Two Pocket Wall . . . . ☼   **V4** *6B*
The wall left of the arete, via a couple of pockets.

5 Right Arete . . . . ☼   **V1** *5b*
The arete on its left-hand side.

6 Debstar . . . . ☼ 🔲   **V6** *7A*
Traverse the west face to finish as for *Mad as a Badger*.

7 Big Slab . . . . ☼ 🔲   **V0** *4c*
The south side of the slab.

Northern Peak · Sheffield Crags · Stanage Area · Burbage Valley · Derwent Edges · The Limestone · Central Grit · Staffordshire · South Peak

The east face of the boulder provides some harder problems.

8 Whispa Loudly. . . **V6** *7A*
The left arete of the east face of the boulder.

9 The Ramp. **V6** *7A*
From sitting at a shelf, move up to the arete and pull around onto the slab.

10 The Dark Side . . . **V6** *7A*
From sitting, climb the left side of the face to the good hold on the arete.

11 Midnight Monster **V6** *7A*
Start up *The Dark Side* and carry on up the wall, eliminating the arete.

12 Broken Moon. **V6** *7A*
Follow the holds up the middle of the face.

13 Acapella **V11** *8A*
From sitting on the arete, follow poor holds up the arete.

14 Hard Moon . . **V9** *7C*
Finishing out left from *Acapella.*

The Tree Boulder
Head 50m down into the trees, roughly in the direction of where you parked and you will come across the Tree Boulder. Unfortunately this block is currently severely obstructed by a large fallen tree and most of the problems on its north side are inaccessible.
Approach - See map on page 51.

15 Pocket Slab. **V4** *6B*
The slab left of the arete via a small pocket.

16 Forestation **V1** *5b*
The left-hand side of the arete.

17 Deforestation **V6** *7A*
The arete on its right-hand side, eliminating the better holds further left. **V8** *7B* from sitting.

18 The Porthole . . . . **V5** *6C+*
The right side of the south face of the block via a big pocket.

19 The Enigma. **V11** *8A*
Start *The Porthole* from sitting with left hand on the arete.

20 The Rib **V4** *6B*
Climb the fingery rib.

Problems further right are, at time of writing (Spring 2014), obscured by a large fallen tree. The problems are:
Easy Wall, V0+ *5a.* **Pocket Wall, V0+** *5a* climbs to the shot-hole. **The Hanging Arete, V2** *5c from sitting.* **Overhanging Arete, V4** *6B* follows the edge of the north-west corner of the block right then continues up the arete. **Straight No Chaser, V9** *7C* the arete from sitting. **Dream Chaser, V8** *7B+* hand traverse left to the arete then rock onto the slab. **The Groove, V0-** *4b.* **Thin Slab, V6** *7A* and then we're onto *Pocket Slab.*

	No star	☆1	☆2	☆3
VB to V0 easy to 4c	1	4	-	-
V0+ to V2 5a to 5c	2	4	3	-
V3 to V5 6A to 6C+	3	7	1	1
V3 to V5 7A upwards	2	5	2	2

Northern Peak

Sheffield Crags

Stanage Area

Burbage Valley

Derwent Edges

The Limestone

Central Grit

Staffordshire

South Peak

Black Tor is a beautiful, quiet spot with plenty to go at, though mostly in the higher grades. The problems are dotted around on various blocks below the indistinct edge on the west side of the valley that leads up to the crag of Laddow. It is very different to the more popular edges, and getting from problem to problem isn't on well-formed paths. Much of the ground is covered with pristine vegetation, so care needs to be taken not to disturb it.

Approach   Also see map on page 39

Black Tor is a short walk from the Crowden Youth Hostel on the A628 Woodhead Pass Road linking Sheffield to Manchester. There is a large car park just off the road near the Youth Hostel. If this is full there are usually a few parking places before you get to the narrow road that leads to the campsite. From the car park, walk up the road towards the campsite. Opposite the campsite entrance is a track signed to the Youth Hostel. Head up here until you reach a bridge leading to the hostel, now turn right and follow a path for about 250m. Pass through a gate and over the stepped weir, and continue up to join The Pennine Way, following this briefly until a path leads off to the left towards Black Tor.

Conditions

The problems are mostly east-facing, so get here in the morning if you are after sun, and in the afternoon if you're looking for shade. Give the area a few days to dry out after rain, especially in the winter and be prepared to brush the problems which are likely to be dirty.

High Edge Boulders
p.59

The Looking Glass Slab
p.59

Atari Boulder
p.58

The Weasel Boulders

p.58

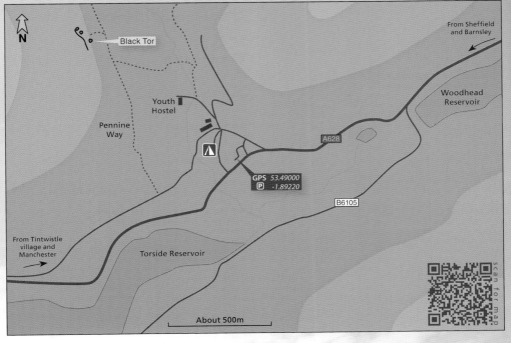

N

Black Tor

From Sheffield
and Barnsley

Woodhead
Reservoir

Youth
Hostel

Pennine
Way

A628

GPS 53.49000
P -1.89220

B6105

From Tintwistle
village and
Manchester

Torside Reservoir

About 500m

scan for map

Seldom Seen Kid
p.61

Wolverine Boulder
p.60

Northern Peak
Sheffield Crags
Stanage Area
Burbage Valley
Derwent Edges
The Limestone
Central Grit
Staffordshire
South Peak

Northern Peak

Sheffield Crags

Stanage Area

Burbage Valley

Derwent Edges

The Limestone

Central Grit

Staffordshire

South Peak

The Weasel Boulders

These are the first boulders you reach on the approach. They offer a mixture of good warm-ups and fingery desperates without much in between. There are some more problems squeezed onto the back side of the blocks which are not described here.
Approach - See map on page 57.

1 Playing with Fire . . . . 🌣 V11 *8A*
An incredibly fingery pull from a dire edge to a better one.

2 One Move . . . . 🌣 V2 5c
Another fingery problem, but rather more amenable than the previous one.

3 Middle Block Slab . . . . . . 🌣 V0 4c
The slab on the left side of the middle block.

4 Angry Love . . 🌣 V5 *6C+*
From sitting at a layaway, move up and climb the arete.

5 Technical Love 🌣 V8 *7B*
Start as for *Angry Love* then head out right, ignoring all the good holds.

6 Slab Arete Left . . . . 🌣 V0- 4b
The left arete of the smooth slab.

7 The Left Slab . . . . 🌣 V2 5c
Climb the wall left of centre.

8 The Right Slab . . . . 🌣 V0- 4b
Climb the wall right of centre.

9 Right Arete . . . . 🌣 V0 4c
The right arete.

Just above the Weasel Boulders is a solitary problem.

10 Atari . . . . 🌣 V7 *7A+*
From sitting, climb the two aretes until you can swing left to finish in the heather.

High Edge Boulders and The Looking Glass Slab

Atari Boulder

The Looking Glass Slab

*The first couple of problems are on **The Looking Glass Slab** which is an isolated boulder down below the High Edge Boulders - see overview photo on page 56.*

⓫ **The Looking Glass** . . . V7 *7A+*
The middle of the slab is a brilliant problem.

⓬ **The Looking Glass Arete** . . V5 *6C*
The arete.

High Edge Boulders
Well above the Weasel Boulders is a mini-edge offering a good concentration of mostly hard problems.
Approach (also see overview and map on page 57) - There's no major path up here so it's a matter of finding the least destructive way you can. The most logical route is to head around the left side of the Weasel Boulders and head towards the grassy col that brings you to the right-hand side of the blocks. This can take you via The Looking Glass block if you so wish.

⓭ **The Mantel** V5 *6C*
From sitting at slopers move up to a mantel to finish.

⓮ **The Traverse** . . . . V4 *6B+*
Starting as for *The Mantel*, hand traverse right to finish as for the following problem.

⓯ **Escape From Monday**
. . . . V6 *7A*
The arete on its left-hand side from sitting.

⓰ **Twins** . . . . V4 *6B+*
Climb the twin aretes.

⓱ **Crack** . . . . VB *4a*
Climb the crack.

⓲ **Layaway Wall** V3 *6A*
The wall just right of the crack.

⓳ **The Ill Defined**. . . V7 *7A+*
The vague arete, climbed on its right-hand side.

A few metres to the right is another block with more to go at:

⓴ **Sit Start Wall** . . . V4 *6B*
From sitting, follow edges up the wall.

㉑ **The Fin**. V5 *6C*
Climb the right-side of the crack from sitting.

㉒ **The Wall**. . . . . V3 *6A+*
The middle of the wall from sitting.

㉓ **Right Arete** . . . . V4 *6B+*
The right arete, from sitting.

Northern Peak

Sheffield Crags

Stanage Area

Burbage Valley

Derwent Edges

The Limestone

Central Grit

Staffordshire

South Peak

Northern Peak

Sheffield Crags

Stanage Area

Burbage Valley

Derwent Edges

The Limestone

Central Grit

Staffordshire

South Peak

Technician's Day Out

Wolverine Boulder

Wolverine Boulder Area

A good collection of blocks at the north end of Black Tor.
Approach (also see overview and map on page 57)
- Although it is possible to contour around from the High
Edge Boulders, it is easier to approach more directly
from below. There is no obvious path, so choose your
approach line with care.

*The first four problems are on a miniature outcrop just above
the Wolverine Boulder -* **Technician's Day Out.**

❶ Slap Problem . . . . 〔icon〕 [ ] **V4** *6B*
The left-hand block, starting low.

❷ Technician's Day Out
. . . . 〔icons〕 [ ] **V8** *7B*
The right side of the arete - chockstones in the crack are out.

❸ Means to an End . . . . . . 〔icon〕 [ ] **V6** *7A*
Starting on some undercuts, move up and left to finish.

❹ The Crack . . . . [ ] **V2** *5c*
Starting as for *Means to and End*, climb the crack.

The main area of interest here is the Wolverine Boulder.

❺ Mollie Sugden . . . . 〔icon〕 [ ] **V2** *5c*
The left arete of the block.

❻ Baby Wolverine . . . . 〔icon〕 [ ] **V2** *5c*
The face, following the easiest line.

❼ PK's Hammer . . . . 〔icon〕 [ ] **V2** *5c*
The vague rib. From sitting it is **Crowden Girls, V7** *7A+.*

❽ The Arete . . . . 〔icon〕 [ ] **V2** *5c*
Climb the arete on its left-hand side.

❾ Flaky Bake . . . . 〔icon〕 [ ] **V2** *5c*
The arete on its right-hand side. **V6** *7A* from sitting.

❿ The Groove . . . . 〔icons〕 [ ] **V6** *7A*
The groove right of the arete, eliminating both the arete and the
flake just right.

⓫ One Arm . . . . [ ] **V1** *5b*
Follow the flake. **V5** *6C+* from sitting.

Above and left of the Wolverine Boulder is the angular, undercut
Thug's Day Out Boulder.

⓬ Thug's Day Out . . . . 〔icon〕 [ ] **V8** *7B*
At the left side of the boulder, starting on undercuts, gain and
follow edges up the wall, and exit out left.

*Heading further around to the right, you soon come across
a sizeable buttress. Below this buttress is a pit containing a
problem called* **Phantom Lights, V8** *7B+, which follows a series
of poor edges up a boulder in the pit, finishing at a tree.*

Thug's Day Out

Wolverine Boulder

Seldom Seen Kid

Keep heading right for another 50m (see overview on page 56) and you reach **Seldom Seen Kid**.

13 Seldom Seen Kid. ⚡🎯🧗 ▭ **V10** *7C+*
The left arete.

14 Pennine Way Variation
. . . . ⚡🎯🧗 ▭ **V5** *6C*
The centre of the slab.

Northern Peak

Sheffield Crags

Stanage Area

Burbage Valley

Derwent Edges

The Limestone

Central Grit

Staffordshire

South Peak

Northern Peak

Sheffield Crags

Stanage Area

Burbage Valley

Derwent Edges

The Limestone

Central Grit

Staffordshire

South Peak

	No star	⚝	⚝	⚝
VB to V0 Easy to 4c	5	1	-	-
V0+ to V2 5a to 5c	4	5	-	-
V3 to V5 6A to 6C+	1	2	3	1
V3 to V5 7A upwards	-	2	-	-

A good roadside venue with a variety of problems across the grades. There are a few good traverses, most notably the long pumpy traverse of the Back Wall, plus plenty of decent straight-up problems too, including some at relatively friendly grades.

Approach   Also
see map on page 39
The crag is only seconds from roadside parking and is a good place for a quick fix. The minor road to the cliff is accessed by turning east off the A6018 at the top of the Mottram cutting (a tight right turn when coming from the Glossop direction) almost opposite the Waggon and Horses

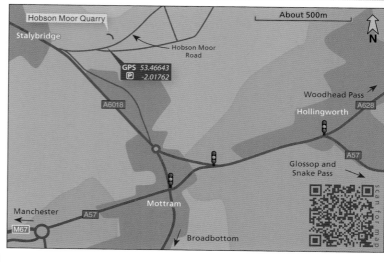

pub. Take the left-hand branch where it forks and the quarry soon appears on the left. There is parking for 10 or so cars on the right. Leave nothing valuable in the car.

Conditions

The quarry is quite sheltered from the wind, does not tend to seep, and dries quickly after rain. The walls face south and southwest and it is often possible to chase some sun or shade. 'Hobby Moor' the perfect spot for an evening workout.

❶ Back Wall Traverse . . 🎯🖌️⬜ **V4** *6B*
Traverse the long wall from either end but usually from the left. Finish on the ledges on the arete, before the corner. Well pumpy and unfeasibly long.

❷ Sunshine Traverse 🎯🖐️🖌️⬜ **V3** *6A+*
Traverse the small flat slab left of the main corner using the thin breaks.

❸ Basic Traverse. . . . . . 🎯🖌️⬜ **V3** *6A+*
A low traverse from the corner to the arete.

❹ Basic Training Start . . 🎯🧗⬜ **V8** *7B+*
Climb the wall with powerful moves on undercuts. The thin crack is out of bounds at this grade.

❺ Steve Ring Home Start . . . . . . ⬜ **V4** *6B*
The wall between the corner and the arete, when you're standing on the starting hand-holds, you're done.

❻ Pillar Face . . . . 🎯🗡️⬜ **V6** *7A*
Link the two slots on the small separate pillar.

❼ Pillar Arete . . . . 🎯⬜ **V1** *5b*
From the same slot reach the sharp arete which forms the right edge of the block.

❽ Dragon's Slab . . . . 🧗⬜ **V1** *5b*
Mantel the slab.

Northern Peak

Sheffield Crags

Stanage Area

Burbage Valley

Derwent Edges

The Limestone

Central Grit

Staffordshire

South Peak

⑨ Percy 97 . . . . ▨ ▨ ☐ **V3** 6A+
Crimp up the edges above the graffiti to the ledge. There is a much harder eliminate version where you start with your left hand on the right-hand crimp at **V10** 7C+.

⑩ Percy Left-hand . . . . . ▨ ▨ ☐ **V2** 5c
The wall on small edges.

⑪ Percy Right-hand . . . . ▨ ▨ ☐ **V0+** 5a
This one uses side-pulls and low edges.

⑫ Triangle Left . . . . ▨ ▨ ☐ **V3** 6A+
Follow crimps left of the triangular hold.

⑬ Triangle . . . . ▨ ▮ ▨ ☐ **V4** 6B
Up the blank wall and rib above the large triangular hole.

⑭ Triangle Arete . . . . ▨ ☐ **V2** 5c
The arete on its left-hand side.

⑮ Easy Crack . . . . ☐ **VB** 4a
The left-hand of the twin cracks.

⑯ Slippery Groove . . . . ☐ **V0-** 4b
The easy groove.

⑰ Edgy Slab . . . . ☐ **VB** 4a
Follow holds up the slab.

The next two problems are on the level above.

⑱ High Wall . . . . ▨ ☐ **V0** 4c
The wall just left of the arete.

⑲ High Arete . . . . ▨ ☐ **V2** 5c
The arete on its left-hand side.

The final five problems are on a separate northwest-facing wall which faces into the quarry.

⑳ Green Wall . . . . ▨ ▨ ☐ **VB** 4a
Climb the edges on the left-hand side.

㉑ Green Ramp . . . . ☐ **V0** 4c
The ramp and slots to the right.

㉒ Rib . . . . ▨ ▨ ☐ **V1** 5b
Climb the vague rib on the left of the flat wall, right of the shattered grooves and corners.

㉓ The Seam . . . . ☐ **V1** 5b
Delicately up to the thin seam to the right.

㉔ Flakes . . . . ☐ **V1** 5b
Climb the in-cut flakes right again.

	No star	☼	☼☼	☼☼☼
VB to V0 Easy to 4c	1	-	-	-
V0+ to V2 5a to 5c	2	5	-	-
V3 to V5 6A to 6C+	-	4	6	1
V3 to V5 7A upwards	-	2	1	-

Far below the streets of New Mills is a spectacular gorge which is well worth a visit. Below the viaduct is a steep set of walls with a number of routes and an excellent selection of boulder problems and traverses, many of which will stay dry in heavy rain.

Approach   Also see map on page 39

There is limited (paid) parking on the small loop road behind the bus turning-circle in the centre of New Mills. If this is full, or you fancy climbing for longer than a hour or two, there are various quiet side streets nearby where parking is possible. From behind the bus turning circle a steep path leads down to the left-hand end of the cliff.

Conditions

The crag is steep enough to stay dry in light rain and the tree canopy in summer adds to this shelter. The steepest part of the cliff is right under the viaduct, and this stays dry even in monsoon conditions. The walls do face south, so can catch the sun, but they are also shaded by the tree cover and bridge pillars.

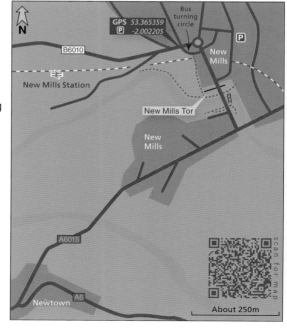

Northern Peak

Sheffield Crags

Stanage Area

Burbage Valley

Derwent Edges

The Limestone

Central Grit

Staffordshire

South Peak

Northern Peak

Sheffield Crags

Stanage Area

Burbage Valley

Derwent Edges

The Limestone

Central Grit

Staffordshire

South Peak

Alcove Area

The first wall you encounter on the approach is the Alcove Area. A little further right is the Grim Reaper Wall.

1 Alcove Traverse V2 5c
A left-to-right traverse of the back wall, past the corner, and across the side wall as far as the *The Steeple*.

2 Alcove Wall V9 7C
Use an undercut to gain edges then pop for a good hold. Big holds on the right are out of bounds.

3 Porky's Wall V3 6A
The left-hand line up the wall.

4 Porky's Wall Right-hand . . V2 5c
The wall, keeping left of the crack.

5 Piggy's Crack . . . . . . V0+ 5a
The crack.

6 The Steeple V1 5b
The arete.

Sun and shade | 5 min | Sheltered

Grim Reaper Wall

Sun and shade | 5 min | Sheltered

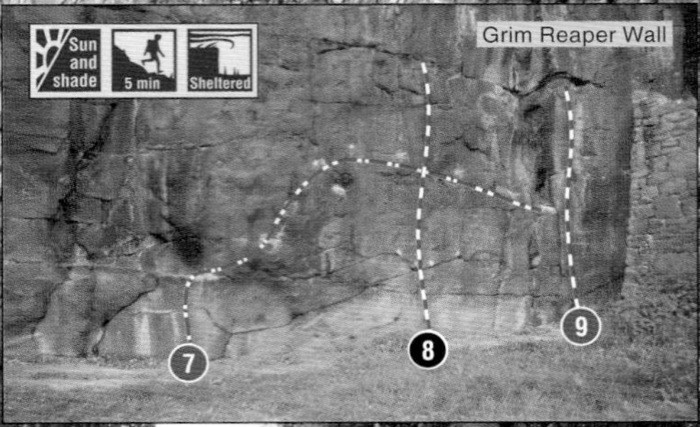

To the right of a tall arete is the **Grim Reaper Wall**.

7 Grim Reaper Traverse V3 6A+
The fingery left-to-right traverse of the wall starting on the low break and finishing just before *Sandy Arete*.

8 Grim Reaper Direct
. . . . V7 7A+
The hard direct start to an E5 route.

9 Sandy Arete . . . . V3 6A+
The arete just left of the brick wall.

Descent

Grim Reaper Wall - 8m

Viaduct Wall

Viaduct Wall and Bionics Wall

Under the viaduct at the right-hand end of the face is a good clean wall with plenty of good problems. Descend by jumping ... if you can't reverse back down.

⑩ Viaduct Wall Traverse. **V1** 5b
The traverse of the wall, in either direction, or both for a pumpier workout.

⑪ Viaduct Crack . . . . **V0+** 5a
Follow thin cracks.

⑫ Viaduct Eliminate **V5** 6C
The wall just right using the pinch with your right hand, continuing to the ledge. The dyno finish is **V7** 7A+.

⑬ Viaduct Wall . . . . **V3** 6A+
The wall to the good ledge.

⑭ Honcho Left. **V5** 6C
A left-hand start to finish as for *Honcho*.

⑮ Honcho. . . . . **V4** 6B+
From the jug, continue direct past the overlap to finish at a jug.

⑯ Honcho Right-hand . . **V5** 6C
A right-hand start to *Honcho* starting just left of the arete.

⑰ Deception **V0** 4c
The cracks.

The continuation of the wall to the right is **Bionics Wall**.

⑱ Bionics Wall Low Left. **V5** 6C+
From the low flake, take the triangular hold as a side-pull with your right hand and move back left to finish.

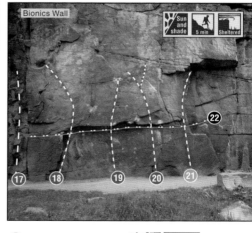

Bionics Wall

⑲ Bionics Wall Direct . . **V3** 6A+
Starting on a pair of side-pulls, pop for the ledge.

⑳ Bionics Wall Right . . . **V4** 6B+
Start with your left hand on an undercut and your right hand on a side-pull. Pull up to the sloper then up left to finish at the jugs. Finishing directly to the right-most jugs is worth **V6** 7A.

㉑ Hallelujah Start . . . . **V0+** 5a
The flakes to the break.

㉒ Bionics Traverse . **V7** 7A+
The low traverse of the wall. Start on jugs just right of *Hallelujah Start* and continue left to the crack of *Deception*.

Northern Peak

Sheffield Crags

Stanage Area

Burbage Valley

Derwent Edges

The Limestone

Central Grit

Staffordshire

South Peak

	No star	☗	☗	☗
VB to V0 Easy to 4c	1	11	-	-
V0+ to V2 5a to 5c	3	15	9	-
V3 to V5 6A to 6C+	7	6	2	-
V3 to V5 7A upwards	-	-	-	-

For those really wishing to get away from it all, there is
The Woolpacks. This large boulderfield on Kinder is at first
glance a bouldering paradise that makes you wonder why
you haven't heard more about it. Unfortunately most of
the boulders are just a bit too small, and the rock typically
has a dusty surface which can spit you off at any moment
no matter what the conditions. Don't be put off - it's still well worth a visit and there is more
than enough good bouldering to justify the long approach, especially in the mid to lower
grades.

The area has not been documented previously, and names have been made up to make
clear reference possible. The authors do not claim any first ascents. It should also be noted
that there are many more problems available than the ones mentioned here however the
rock quality may not be as good so please take care if you explore.

Circuits

We have described two circuits which cover most of the easier problems.

Approach   Also see map on page 39

The Woolpacks are approached from the Edale Valley which is also the start of the Pennine
Way. Drive up the valley, past Edale (train station) to Barber Booth where the road veers
left. Turn right here and drive along a minor road and park near a railway bridge. Continue
on foot. After a kilometre the track turns sharp right. Continue along the track and onto the
Pennine Way heading west. Continue up the steep climb (known as Jacob's Ladder) and
stick to paths leading off to the right, following the rim of the plateau. The path will take you
right into the heart of the boulderfield. The walk is about 6km in total and takes around 90
minutes if you're reasonably fit. It is also possible to approach, or descend, via Crowden
Clough, but this is steeper.

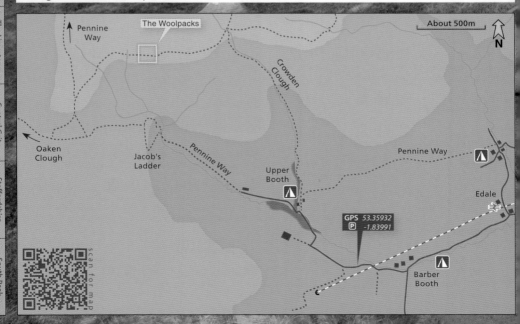

Conditions

This is very much a summer venue and should be reserved for days when it's warm and dry - any bad weather will feel much worse up here. Since it is such a remote venue, getting an ankle injured up here is likely to be a very unpleasant experience especially as you probably won't get a mobile phone signal. It goes without saying that this isn't a suitable location to come on your own.

Rock Quality

There is a lot of soft rock on the Woolpacks. The problems covered here are on the solid rock sections only but please still be careful with the holds you use and don't over brush them.

Audrey Seguy on *The Tortoise* (**V5** *6C+*) - *page 78* - in the Galapagos Boulders. Photo: Adrian Berry

Northern Peak

Sheffield Crags

Stanage Area

Burbage Valley

Derwent Edges

The Limestone

Central Grit

Staffordshire

South Peak

Northern Peak

Sheffield Crags

Stanage Area

Burbage Valley

Derwent Edges

The Limestone

Central Grit

Staffordshire

South Peak

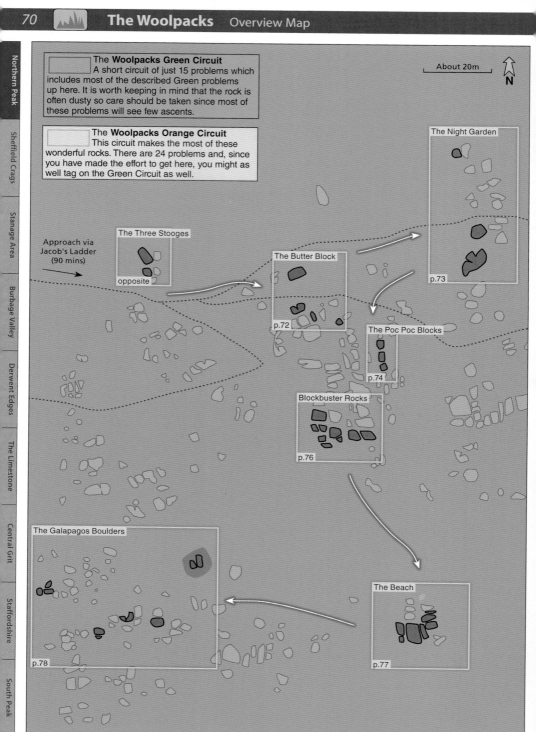

The **Woolpacks Green Circuit**
A short circuit of just 15 problems which includes most of the described Green problems up here. It is worth keeping in mind that the rock is often dusty so care should be taken since most of these problems will see few ascents.

The **Woolpacks Orange Circuit**
This circuit makes the most of these wonderful rocks. There are 24 problems and, since you have made the effort to get here, you might as well tag on the Green Circuit as well.

About 20m

N

The Night Garden

p.73

The Three Stooges

opposite

The Butter Block

p.72

Approach via Jacob's Ladder (90 mins)

The Poc Poc Blocks

p.74

Blockbuster Rocks

p.76

The Galapagos Boulders

p.78

The Beach

p.77

Northern Peak
Sheffield Crags
Stanage Area
Burbage Valley
Derwent Edges
The Limestone
Central Grit
Staffordshire
South Peak

The Three Stooges

This is the first documented area encountered on the approach via Jacob's Ladder, just left of the main approach path.

1 Larry's Launch. **V2** 5c
Jump to a the sloper then pop to the top. Not quite as hard as it looks.

2 Vaudeville Crack **V2** 5c
The off-width crack yields to a variety of techniques.

3 Slap Stick. **V3** 6A
Jump and take the arete with your left hand and the sloper out right with your right and continue to the top.

4 Short 'n' Curly . . . . . . **V4** 6B+
The arete is climbed via a powerful mantel on a sloper.

5 Curly's Crack. **V1** 5b
The proper off-width crack just right.

6 Moe's Meander **V0-** 4b
The left arete of the third block.

7 Knee-bar Crack . . . **V2** 5c
The hanging off-width crack.
Orange Circuit continues on page 72.

8 Nertsery Crack. **V0-** 4b
Just around to the right. *Green Circuit continues on page 72.*

The Night Garden
p.73

The Poc Poc Blocks
p.74

Blockbuster Rocks
p.76

The Three Stooges

Northern Peak

Sheffield Crags

Stanage Area

Burbage Valley

Derwent Edges

The Limestone

Central Grit

Staffordshire

South Peak

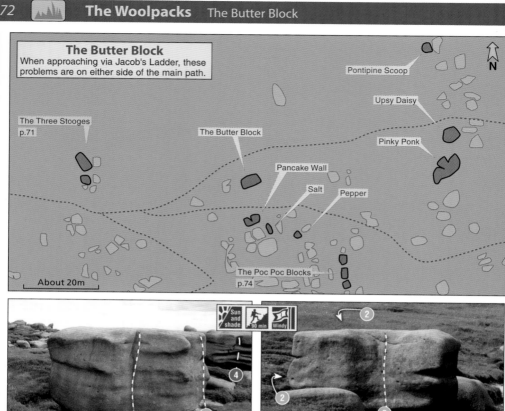

The Butter Block
When approaching via Jacob's Ladder, these problems are on either side of the main path.

Pontipine Scoop

Upsy Daisy

The Three Stooges
p.71

The Butter Block

Pinky Ponk

Pancake Wall

Salt

Pepper

The Poc Poc Blocks
p.74

About 20m

N

Sun and shade / 90 min / Windy

The Butter Block

❶ **Green Runnel** **V3** *6A*
The runnel.

❷ **Butter Knife** **V2** 5c
The pocketed arete.

❸ **Butter Scoop** . . . . **V0+** 5a
Pockets up the scoop.

Pancake Wall

Sun and shade / 90 min / Windy

The final two problems are directly opposite the Butter Block.

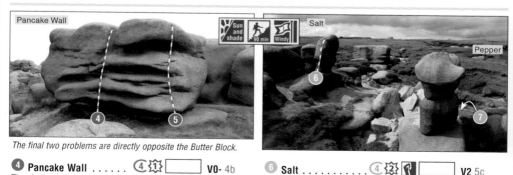

Salt

Pepper

❹ **Pancake Wall** **V0-** 4b
The sloping ledges to a scoop.

❺ **Pancake Edge** **V0-** 4b
The arete via rounded ledges.

❻ **Salt** **V2** 5c
The crimpy arete.

❼ **Pepper** **V1** 5b
Clamp up the back of the boulder. *See photo opposite.*

Pontipine Scoop

The Night Garden
Some good boulders at the east end of the boulderfield.

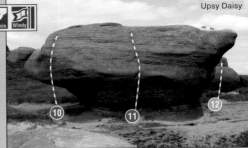

Upsy Daisy

8 Pontipine Scoop .... 6 ☼ [ ] **V2** 5c
The left scoop.

9 Wottinger Scoop .... 7 ☼ [ ] **V2** 5c
The scooped arete.

10 Makka Pakka's Press .... 🔲 [ ] **V3** 6A
Mantel off the sloper.

11 Tombliboo Trouble ... ☼ 🔲 [ ] **V3** 6A
Another powerful mantel.

12 Upsy Daisy .... 8 ☼ [ ] **V1** 5b
Jump into the scoop.

Pinky Ponk

13 Iggle .... ☼ 🔲 [ ] **V4** 6B
Starting low at the pocket, gain the lip then mantel.

14 Piggle .... 🔲 [ ] **V5** 6C
A powerful mantel.

15 Haahoo .... 9 6 ☼ [ ] **V0** 4c
Into the bowl at the back of the boulder.

16 Pinky Ponk ...... 10 ☼ 🔳 [ ] **V2** 5c
Link a couple of finger-rails to the top.

17 Ninky Nonk .... 11 ☼ [ ] **V2** 5c
Start with your left foot in the pocket.
Orange Circuit continues on page 75.

18 Og-Pog .... 7 ☼ [ ] **V0-** 4b
The easy scoop. *Green Circuit continues on page 76.*

Adrian Berry on *Pepper* (**V1** 5b) - *opposite.*

Northern Peak

Sheffield Crags

Stanage Area

Burbage Valley

Derwent Edges

The Limestone

Central Grit

Staffordshire

South Peak

Jamie Veitch on *Poc Poc* (**V2** 5c) - *opposite* -
The Poc Poc Blocks. Photo: Adrian Berry

The Night Garden
p.73

The Night Garden p.73

The Poc Poc Blocks

Some distinctive slender, free-standing blocks situated just beyond the **Butter Blocks**.
Approach - See map on pages 70.

1 Poc Poc **V2** 5c
The face via some pockets. *Photo opposite.*

2 Bop . . . . **V5** 6C+
Jump to sloper then mantel.

3 Neep . . . . **V3** 6A+
A mantel.

4 Gully Crack **V2** 5c
The crack in the gully below and left of the previous problems.
Orange Circuit continues on page 76.

Northern Peak

Sheffield Crags

Stanage Area

Burbage Valley

Derwent Edges

The Limestone

Central Grit

Staffordshire

South Peak

Northern Peak

Sheffield Crags

Stanage Area

Burbage Valley

Derwent Edges

The Limestone

Central Grit

Staffordshire

South Peak

Blockbuster Rocks

A collection of decent problems right in the middle of The Woolpacks, just beyond the Poc Poc Blocks.
Approach - See map on pages 70.

1 **The Runnel** . . . . VO- 4b
The lovely runnel.

2 **Jaws** . . . . VO- 4b
The notched arete.

3 **Holds Actually** V2 5c
The arete which has some holds.

4 **Pocket Money** V2 5c
Start at the big pocket at the back of the boulder and clamp your way up. Finish out right.

5 **High School Musical** VO+ 5a
A good high problem up the arete. Finish out left (easier) or out right (wilder). *Photo this page.*

Audrey Seguy on *High School Musical* (**VO+** 5a) - *this page* - on the Blockbuster Rocks. Photo: Adrian Berry

Northern Peak

Sheffield Crags

Stanage Area

The rest of the problems on Blockbuster Rocks are on the south side, facing The Beach.

6 **The Edge of Love** . . . . ⑩ ⌂ [____] **V0-** 4b
The short left arete.

7 **The Edge of Reason** . . ⑰ ⌂ [____] **V1** 5b
The right-hand arete.

8 **Wide Eyes Shut** . . ⌂ 🏃 [____] **V4** *6B*
The wide crack is harder than it looks.

9 **Pressed** . . . . 🏃 [____] **V3** *6A*
Sloper and mantel.

The Beach
An isolated collection of boulders with its own beach. The rocks are at the south-eastern edge of the boulderfield.
Approach - See map on pages 70.

Burbage Valley

11 **Shark Attack** . . . . [____] **V1** 5b
The short arete with a mantel to finish.

12 **Maya** . . . . [____] **V0-** 4b
The corner.

13 **Novel Adaptation** . . . . . . ⌂ [____] **V3** *6A*
The overlaps right of the corner. *Photo on page 38.*

10 **Parallel Universe** . . . . [____] **V3** *6A*
Link the stacked blocks via a good slot.

Derwent Edges

The Limestone

Central Grit

Staffordshire

14 **Phi Phi** . . . . ⑪ ⌂ [____] **V0+** 5a
The short arete and corner above.

15 **Hidden Paradise** . . ⑱ ⑫ ⌂ [____] **V0+** 5a
The nobbly wall.
Orange and Green Circuits continue on page 78.

South Peak

Northern Peak
Sheffield Crags
Stanage Area
Burbage Valley
Derwent Edges
The Limestone
Central Grit
Staffordshire
South Peak

The Galapagos Boulders

From the Three Stooges head down to the right - the most obvious block is Solly's Island, an isolated pinnacle which, unless it has been very dry, typically has a moat surrounding it.

The Tortoise

Baltra Flake

1 Solly's Island V2 5c
The most prominent line following the inviting features.
Photo this page.

There are a few other lines on this block - notably the distinctive wall just right, which may be awaiting an ascent.

2 The Tortoise . . . . V5 6C+
Through the bulge and up the 'tortoise-shell'. *Photo page 69.*

Around to the right are a couple of good, short cracks.

3 Baltra Flake . . . . . VO+ 5a
Monkey up the good flake.

4 Darwin's Crack . . . V2 5c
The right crack. Having the correct sized knee is useful.

Solly's Island

Audrey Seguy being well-spotted on *Solly's Island* (**V2** 5c) - *this page*. Photo: Adrian Berry

Northern Peak

Sheffield Crags

Stanage Area

Burbage Valley

Derwent Edges

The Limestone

Central Grit

Staffordshire

South Peak

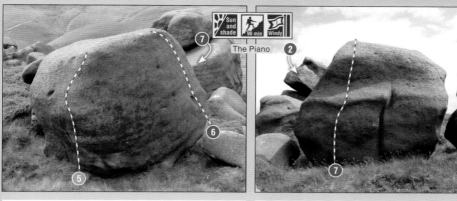

The Piano

Just west of The Tortoise is The Piano block.

5 Genovesa 22 **V2** 5c
The slab starting from a good hold for the left hand.

6 Isabela Slab 14 **V0-** 4b
Step onto the green slab at the sloping pocket.

7 The Piano . . . . **V4** 6B+
Start with your left hand on the arete, and your right hand on the rounded side-pull and somehow get stood on the sloping ledge.

Blockbuster Rocks
p.76

The Three
Stooges

The Beach

Solly's Island

Volcan Wolf

The Tortoise

About 20m

N

Baltra Flake

The Piano

Volcan Wolf

The next two problems are a little further west and on the other side of a vague col.

8 Volcan Wolf 23 **V1** 5b
Link the big pockets.

9 Grapsus 24 15 **V0** 4c
Pass the recessed feature. *This is the last problem on both the Orange and the Green Circuit.*

	No star	✿	✿	✿
VB to V0 Easy to 4c	2	3	-	-
V0+ to V2 5a to 5c	9	13	9	2
V3 to V5 6A to 6C+	5	13	5	1
V3 to V5 7A upwards	1	2	3	-

The edges above the reservoirs of Ladybower and Derwent are wonderful wild bits of gritstone with some superb and spectacular rock formations, situated in an area of dramatic moorland. The bouldering is well spread out and the long walk in and exposed aspect mean that it is never likely to become popular. The three spots covered offer some decent problems but some can get quite high and this isn't a good place to boulder alone since it could be a while before anyone finds you if you were to hurt yourself in a fall.

Approach   Also see map on page 39

The best approach for all three areas documented is from the Cutthroat Bridge lay-by on the A57 Sheffield to Glossop road. It is a large lay-by, separated from the road by trees, and usually home to a tea wagon. The bridge from where the paths start is further down the hill. To get onto the moor, follow one of two well-marked paths onto the ridge from where the main bouldering spots can be clearly seen. It is also possible to walk in from parking on the bend beyond the Strines Inn which is on a side road off the A57.

scan for map

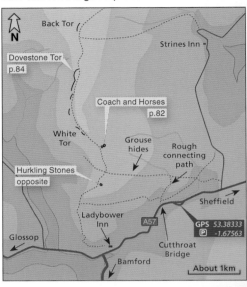

Conditions

The crags up here are very exposed and it is not a good idea to be anywhere near the place when the weather is bad. Good cool conditions are uncommon but exploring on a warm days can be more fun than pushing the limits of friction.

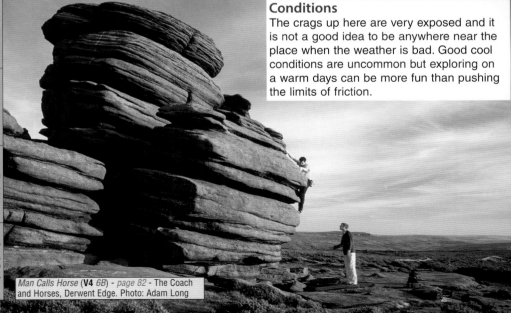

*Man Calls Horse (**V4** 6B) - page 82 - The Coach and Horses, Derwent Edge. Photo: Adam Long*

Northern Peak | Sheffield Crags | Stanage Area | Burbage Valley | Derwent Edges | The Limestone | Central Grit | Staffordshire | South Peak

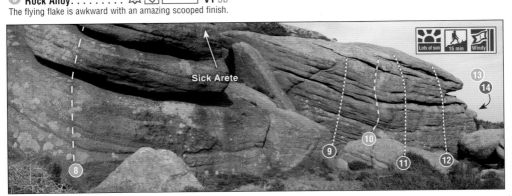

Hurkling Stones

The problems here are surprisingly good considering their unimpressive appearance on the approach trudge. There are a few nice slabs and walls as well as one or two interesting rock features to struggle with.

1 Baby Bulge **V0** 4c
The short problem on the left.

2 Arete and Seam . . . . **V0+** 5a
The left-hand arete of the slab.

3 Hurkling Towards Earth . . . **V3** 6A+
The wall just right of the arete using the thin seam on the left.

4 Pothole Slab . . . . **V4** 6B+
A delightful rock-up move on the thin slab finishing at a bowl.

5 The Gurgling Green Streak **V5** 6C
Holdless friction and pebble climbing up the green streak.

6 Little Arete . . . . **V0+** 5a
The arete to the left of the wide crack.

7 Other Arete **V3** 6A
The arete on the other side of the crack.

8 Rock Ahoy **V1** 5b
The flying flake is awkward with an amazing scooped finish.

To the right is an impressive arete - Sick Arete, E6 6c.

9 Wall Past Flake . . . . **V3** 6A+
The little wall has a hard mantel finish.

10 All Sloping Arete **V2** 5c
The arete on its left.

11 Captain Ahab . . . . **V5** 6C+
Powerful undercutting just right of the arete.

12 Wall Above Flake . . . . **V3** 6A+
The wall further right has a horrible 'flop or drop' finish.

Around the corner is a short wall.

13 Flake Bulge . . . . **V0+** 5a
The wall above a ledge.

14 The Arete . . . . **V3** 6A+
Climb the arete.

Northern Peak | Sheffield Crags | Stanage Area | Burbage Valley | Derwent Edges | The Limestone | Central Grit | Staffordshire | South Peak

Northern Peak

Sheffield Crags

Stanage Area

Burbage Valley

Derwent Edges

The Limestone

Central Grit

Staffordshire

South Peak

Jupiter Collision

❶ Shelf Wall V3 *6A*
The wall past sloping breaks. Gnarlier than it looks.

❷ Low Coach . . . . V3 *6A+*
Start low and climb the arete.

❸ Jupiter Collision . . . . V7 *7A+*
From a low start, follow poor slopers to a hard finish.

❹ Man Calls Horse V4 *6B*
The left-hand side of the arete from sitting. *Photo on page 80.*

❺ Arete on Right . . . . . . V4 *6B+*
The right-hand side of the arete from sitting. No side-pull.

❻ Side-pull Wall V1 *5b*
The left side of the wall from the big side-pull.

❼ Side-pull Stretch . . . . V0+ *5a*
The middle of the wall.

❽ The Scoop V2 *5c*
From a sitting start, pull into the scoop.

❾ Roof Left . . . . V3 *6A+*
The left side of the roof.

❿ Roof Right V1 *5b*
The right side of the roof.

⓫ Steep Nose V1 *5b*
Another rounded roof.

⓬ Summit Bid . . . . V0+ *5a*
The easiest way to the summit is easier if you find the chip.

The Scoop

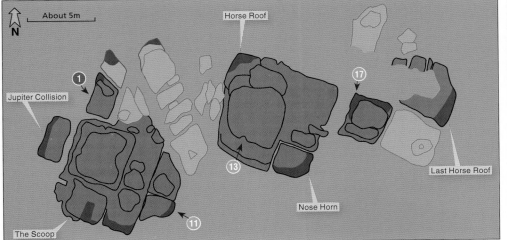

Jupiter Collision

Horse Roof

Last Horse Roof

Nose Horn

The Scoop

The Coach and Horses

The 'coach' is the big one, and the 'horses' are the little ones. The quality problems are well spread around.
Approach (see map on page 80) - The rocks lie further north along the track from the Hurkling Stones and are also best approached from the Cutthroat Bridge lay-by.

⑬ The Runnel . . . . 🔲 **V0+** 5a
An exposed problem up the nice runnel.

⑭ Nose Horn . . . . . . 🔲 **V2** 5c
Starting low, move up and pull through the rounded horn.

Nose Horn

⑮ Horn Arete . . . . 🔲 **V2** 5c
The arete to the right.

Last Horse Roof

⑯ Last Horse Roof . . . . 🔲 **V2** 6a
The furthest horse has a long roof.

The rest of the problems are around the back of the horses.

⑰ Green Roof . . . . 🔲 **V2** 6a
A very green bulging roof.

⑱ Dark Green Traverse . . . . . 🔲 **V1** 5b
Traverse the vertical wall.

Horse Roof

⑲ Horse Roof Direct 🔲 **V5** 6C
Yawn out through the roof using a good flake. Pull up right of the nose.

⑳ Horse Roof . . 🔲 **V5** 6C
Hand traverse the lip of the roof from right to left and finish by pulling over.

Northern Peak | Sheffield Crags | Stanage Area | Burbage Valley | Derwent Edges | The Limestone | Central Grit | Staffordshire | South Peak

Northern Peak

Sheffield Crags

Stanage Area

Burbage Valley

Derwent Edges

The Limestone

Central Grit

Staffordshire

South Peak

Dovestone Tor

The vast and beautiful moorland around Dovestone Tor provides an amazing backdrop to some excellent esoteric bouldering. You won't find too much chalk on the problems here and there is plenty of grass beneath them and always will be. This is obviously not a place to come in anything approaching bad weather. It is really exposed and can often be very windy. As is usually the case with exposed crags, they dry quickly, aren't too green and don't suffer from too much seepage.

Approach (see map on page 80) - Walk up past the Coach and Horses and keep going until you reach a surprising flag-stone path. Follow this, over the top of the Tor, to reach the bouldering area on the far side.

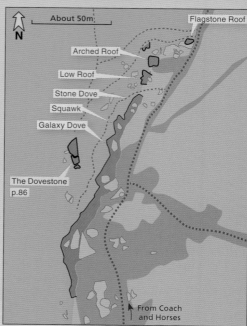

Flagstone Roof

The first problems are on a low roof next to the flagstone path.

① Flagstone Roof Left . . . . . ☷ [ ] **V1** 5b
Start low and reach a good hold on the lip. Pull over to finish.

② Flagstone Roof Right . ☷ 🧗 [ ] **V3** 6A+
The roof further right has a thin edge on the lip - use this.

Standing alone in front of the main tor is a weird shaped block.

③ Odd Block . . . . ☷ [ ] **V1** 5b
The far arete is the most enjoyable line of ascent of the block.

④ Arched Roof . . . . ☷ [ ] **V0** 4c
Back on the main edge is a small arched roof.

⑤ Arch Right . . . . ☷ [ ] **V0** 4c
The wall just to the right of the arch.

⑥ Chicken Head . . . . . . ☷☷ 🌱 [ ] **V1** 5b
Virtually a route. Climb over the roof right of a groove passing a high chicken head.

⑦ Roof Route . . . . ☷☷ 🌱 [ ] **V5** 6C
Climb the big roof via a flaky lower wall. The top-out is not too hard but quite high.

8 Low Roof Left . . . . . . 🕯️🔲 **V2** 5c
On the impressive low roof, start low on a square hold and climb out of the side on friable flakes.

9 Low Roof Middle . . . . 🕯️🔲 **V3** 6A+
The middle line through the roof finishing at the notch.

10 Low Roof Right . . 🕯️🔲 **V2** 5c
Climb the widest part of the roof, above an occasional puddle.
V1 5b if finished slightly right.

Further right is another undercut buttress.

11 Stone Dove Sidewall . . . . 🔲 **V0** 4c
The left-hand side of the steep wall.

12 Stone Dove Left . . . . . 🕯️🔲 **V1** 5b
The right-hand side of the roof starting low.

13 Stone Dove Right . . . . 🕯️🔲 **V1** 5b
Same start as the previous problem but move up and right onto the arete.

14 Stone Dove Crack . . . . 🕯️🔲 **V0+** 5a
The crack in the wall.

15 Chicken Head Rockover . . 🕯️🔲 **V1** 5b
Rock-over on a tiny chicken head on the wall right of the crack.

16 Squawk Traverse Direct 🕯️🔲 **V7** 7A+
The direct start to *Squawk Traverse*.

17 Squawk Traverse . . . . 🕯️🔲 **V5** 6C
Start as for *Squawk* and traverses left to the jammed block.

18 Squawk . . . . 🕯️🔲 **V4** 6B
The arete from a low start.

The next buttress right has a fine arete.

19 Stingray Arete . . . . 🕯️🔲 **V2** 5c
The arete taken on its right-hand side.

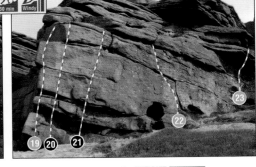

20 Galaxy Dove . . . . 🕯️🔲 **V6** 7A
Gain the thin edge right of the arete and dyno for the top. The sit start is **V7** 7A+.

21 Interstellar Pigeon . 🕯️🔲 **V7** 7A+
Start low on a left-hand lay-away. Reach the edge then dyno for sloper and pocket.

22 The Cavendish . . . . 🔲 **V0+** 5a
Climb the crack then pull upwards.

23 Jug of Justice . . . . 🔲 **V1** 5b
The roof using a jug on the lip.

Northern Peak

Sheffield Crags

Stanage Area

Burbage Valley

Derwent Edges

The Limestone

Central Grit

Staffordshire

South Peak

The Dovestone

The huge boulder below the crag is unique in the Peak District and worth the approach on its own. The main face has a series of sculpted pockets, also known 'huecos', which provide some interesting and varied problems.

Approach (see map on page 80) - The best approach is to continue over the top of the crag and drop down under the other bouldering spots. It can also be reached from the southern end of the crag.

1 **Perfect Porthole Problem** **V2** 5c
The left-hand side of the wall has an amazing porthole.

2 **Huway-cold** **V2** 5c
A sloper is all you have to get the next huecos.

3 **Huway-day** **V1** 5b
The huecos near the arete give another wonderful problem. The top one may be full of water.

4 **Half a World Huway** **V6** 7A
The arete on it left-hand side to the hueco.

5 **Hip Hip Huway** . . . . **V5** 6C+
The arete on its right-hand side is nasty. No huecos here.

6 **Play Huway** **V1** 5b
Another one hold problem.

7 **Up Up and Huway** . . . **V0** 4c
The crack is okay.

Adrian Berry on *Curving Arete* (**V4** 6B) - *this page* - on The Dovestone. Photo: Tim Glasby

Northern Peak

Sheffield Crags

Stanage Area

Burbage Valley

Derwent Edges

The Limestone

Central Grit

Staffordshire

South Peak

Afternoon | 30 min | Windy

8 **Curving Arete** **V4** 6B
The fine arete on its left-hand side. *Photo this page.*

9 **The Dove from Above** .   **V8** 7B+
The sit start is worth an entry on its own. Start at a dink on the arete and slap up into the stand up version.

10 **Small Roof Left** . . . . .   **V3** 6A+
From a sitting start heave over the small roof.

11 **Small Roof Right** **V4** 6B
Further right the roof requires a cunning foot jam.

Northern Peak

Sheffield Crags

Stanage Area

Burbage Valley

Derwent Edges

The Limestone

Central Grit

Staffordshire

South Peak

Paul Phillips pulling along *Mini Beak* (**V6** *7A*) - *page 99* - above the quarry at Rivelin. Photo: Alan James

Stocksbridge

Wharncliffe
p.90

Wharncliffe
Side

Chapeltown

Outibridge

Bell Hagg
p.102

Rivelin
p.96

Sheffield

Northern Peak

Sheffield Crags

Stanage Area

Burbage Valley

Derwent Edges

The Limestone

Central Grit

Staffordshire

South Peak

Sheffield Crags

	No star	☆	☆☆	☆☆☆
VB to V0 Easy to 4c	-	-	-	-
V0+ to V2 5a to 5c	2	2	-	-
V3 to V5 6A to 6C+	6	7	2	-
V3 to V5 7A upwards	-	9	2	-

Wharncliffe offers some very esoteric bouldering for the connoisseur with the main interest being a few excellent problems in the mid-to-hard grades. The bouldering spots are situated away from the main edge in the woods to the south. The tree cover offers sheltered climbing but also make much of the rock very green. Although easier problems have been climbed here, they are mostly poor and not worth seeking out. Striking rock paintings by local artists/vandals add to the ambience.

Circuits

No prescribed circuits are included since the place doesn't really lend itself to a circuit approach. Ticking off all the starred red problems would make for a testing day's work.

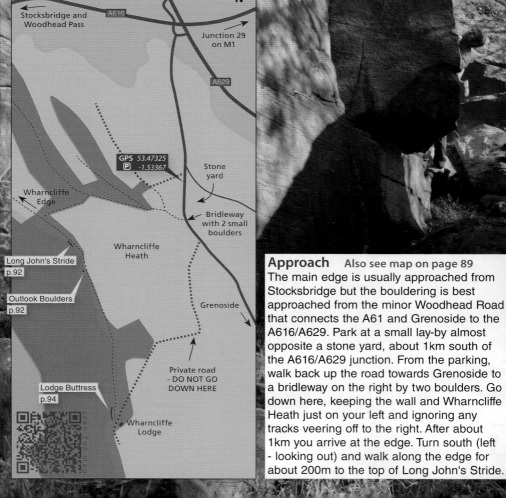

About 500m

← Stocksbridge and Woodhead Pass

A616

Junction 29 on M1

A629

GPS 53.47325
P -1.53367

Stone yard

Wharncliffe Edge

Bridleway with 2 small boulders

Wharncliffe Heath

Long John's Stride p.92

Outlook Boulders p.92

Grenoside

Private road - DO NOT GO DOWN HERE

Lodge Buttress p.94

Wharncliffe Lodge

Approach   Also see map on page 89

The main edge is usually approached from Stocksbridge but the bouldering is best approached from the minor Woodhead Road that connects the A61 and Grenoside to the A616/A629. Park at a small lay-by almost opposite a stone yard, about 1km south of the A616/A629 junction. From the parking, walk back up the road towards Grenoside to a bridleway on the right by two boulders. Go down here, keeping the wall and Wharncliffe Heath just on your left and ignoring any tracks veering off to the right. After about 1km you arrive at the edge. Turn south (left - looking out) and walk along the edge for about 200m to the top of Long John's Stride.

Northern Peak · Sheffield Crags · Stanage Area · Burbage Valley · Derwent Edges · The Limestone · Central Grit · Staffordshire · South Peak

Northern Peak

Sheffield Crags

Stanage Area

Burbage Valley

Derwent Edges

The Limestone

Central Grit

Staffordshire

South Peak

Conditions

The rock tends to get very green, especially after rain. Some of the problems can seem horribly dirty if you are the first to arrive but the more popular ones do clean up in dry spells. The crag gets afternoon sun although this is often filtered through the trees. It is sheltered from the wind.

Alan James having a look at *Long John's Arete* (**V4** *6B*) - *next page* - at Long John's Arete, while the 'Erganweasel' looks on. Photo: Alan James

Long John's Stride

This is the last section of quality routes on the edge when coming from the north and also the beginning of the bouldering. Although there are only a few problems here, they are pretty good. As with everything at Wharncliffe, they are usually green. The 'Erganweasel' graffiti is not to be encouraged but it does give the place a curious other-worldly feel.

Approach (see map on page 90) - Walk south (left - looking out) along the cliff-top path from the point you arrive at the edge. Long John's Stride is the first significant section of rock you come to.

Outlook Boulders

Although this is only a minor venue, it does have a couple of good problems and is worth looking in as you walk past. It is very green and dirty for much of the time.

Approach (see map on page 90) - From the top of Long John's Stride, walk along the crag-top path for about 4 minutes, until you pass a prominent buttress on the left of the track. This is Chase Buttress. Continue for about 200m to two boulders slightly hidden on the right of the track.

The first problems are on the short walls down and right as you approach between the two boulders.

❶ Impish **V5** *6C*
The undercut arete gets quite high.

❷ Imp Wall. . . . . **V3** *6A+*
Climb the wall using some slopers.

❸ Long John's Arete . . . **V4** *6B*
The sharp arete above a poor landing. *Photo on previous page.*

❹ Erganweasel **V3** *6A*
Start low on the right-hand side of the graffiti block and traverse across left and up to the top left-hand edge.

❺ Slab and the Beanstalk . . . . . . **V3** *6A+*
An eliminate up the wall left of the corner.

❻ Sneaky Little Fingers . **V6** *7A*
The side-wall requires a big span.

❼ Pixie's Arete . . . . **V0+** *5a*
Climb the sharp arete. High but with holds.

❽ Lembas Arete **V3** *6A*
Climb the bold arete.

❾ Lembas . . . . **V5** *6C+*
The front face is even bolder.

Down below is another boulder with three V3 problems and one V7. It is almost always covered in dirty green slime. See peakbouldering.info *Wharncliffe > Lower Wall for details.*

⑩ Kim Span **V6** *7A*
Start on a low hold below the roof and then make a huge span to crinkles on the lip. Pull over to the top.

⑪ Dirty Roof **V4** *6B*
The lower right-hand side of the roof is dirty.

⑫ Link Up . . . . **V3** *6A+*
Traverse the rounded lip all the way to *Outlook Roof*.

⑬ Hard Mantel **V4** *6B*
Manteling direct over the roof is hard!

⑭ Outlook Roof **V3** *6A*
Climb the roof on positive holds then pull round. The best problem on this section.

⑮ Pete's Route **V1** *5b*
Around to the right, climb the right-hand side of the roof.

Northern Peak

Sheffield Crags

Stanage Area

Burbage Valley

Derwent Edges

The Limestone

Central Grit

Staffordshire

South Peak

Lodge Buttress

Probably the best bouldering at Wharncliffe is found on the distant area by Wharncliffe Lodge. It is also remarkably difficult to find if you don't know the area but the Dragon's Den area is worth seeking out if you are up to the grades.

Approach (also see map on page 90) - Follow this carefully since this area is hard to find. From Long John's Stride, follow the crag-top path for 18 minutes, passing Outlook Boulders. Avoid any paths breaking off to the right. Continue until you join a much larger track by some buildings (Wharncliffe Lodge). You have now passed Lodge Buttress so backtrack 50m to where the edge comes near to the path. Go down a gully a little further right (looking out) to get to the base of Lodge Buttress. Alternatively, if you are carrying a pad, it is easier to go along the big track for about 50m, until just past a woods on the right. Then cut right into the woods here and double back under the edge.

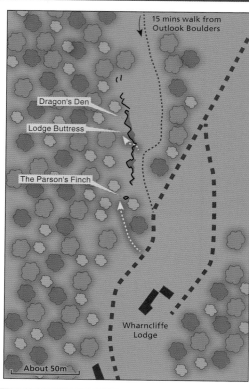

To the left of the Dragon's Den are some very esoteric problems. See peakbouldering.info for details.

❶ Dragon Slayer . . . . . . **V7** *7A+*
Climb the prow to its end, then up the arete. No right wall.

❷ The Dragon's Den . . . . . . **V3** *6A+*
Span to the lip from undercuts, then pull up the wall.

❸ Big Flake **V1** 5b
The big flake itself requires a big heave.

❹ Sweet Move **V8** *7B*
From the start of *Jorge Easy*, span left into the flake and finish up *The Dragon's Den*.

Dragon's Den

Lodge Buttress

Northern Peak
Sheffield Crags
Stanage Area
Burbage Valley
Derwent Edges
The Limestone
Central Grit
Staffordshire
South Peak

⑤ Jorge **V8** *7B*
Climb the arete avoiding all decent holds out right.

⑥ Jorge Easy **V4** *6B*
Jorge using a big flat hold out right. Quite hard.

⑦ Jorge Jr **V6** *7A*
Jorge using the sloping pocket rather than the big flat hold.

⑧ Crouching Tiger . . . **V7** *7A+*
Dyno from a nothing break to the seam.

⑨ Blunted **V6** *7A*
From a very low start on an edge, pull up the rib. Avoiding the footblock is **V7** *7A+*.

⑩ Sweet Release **V10** *7C+*
A powerful link-up. Start up *Blunted*, then traverse the thin break leftwards to a hard span to the flake. Finish up *The Dragon's Den*.

Up and right of the Dragon's Den is the main Lodge Buttress.

⑪ Ogilvie's Direct . . . . . **V4** *6B+*
The finger crack is sustained. Traverse the pockets left to get off.

⑫ Curvaceous . . . . **V7** *7A+*
The blunted arete to a sloper. Good but technical.

⑬ Ogilvie's Slab **V2** *5c*
Step off a boulder and teeter up to the sloping hold. Jump off.

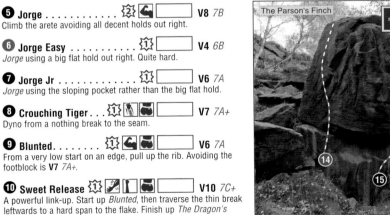

The Parson's Finch

Not much sun

There are a few more problems in the sprawl of edge and boulders stretching rightwards. The best of this is the perched Parson's Finch block passed on the lower approach.

⑭ Crazy Legs Crane **V4** *6B*
Climb up and left.

⑮ The Parson's Finch **V8** *7B*
The line of sloping holds up the front of the block. Start with your feet at the back.

	No star	✦	✦✦	✦✦✦
VB to V0 Easy to 4c	-	-	-	-
V0+ to V2 5a to 5c	-	1	1	-
V3 to V5 6A to 6C+	1	4	6	1
V3 to V5 7A upwards	1	7	4	2

Northern Peak

Sheffield Crags

Stanage Area

Burbage Valley

Derwent Edges

The Limestone

Central Grit

Staffordshire

South Peak

Paul Phillips climbing *Cool Running Left-hand* (**V4** *6B*) - *page 99* - on the left-hand end of Rivelin Edge. Photo: Alan James

Rivelin doesn't have a history of bouldering, but the development of some hard problems, and the re-categorisation of some of the shorter routes, has meant that there is now enough to justify a visit albeit only for those operating in the harder grades. There is very little in the Orange and Green band although Rivelin is excellent for routes at this level. Some of the best problems do see frequent ascents but many will need to be cleaned, especially after prolonged periods of bad weather.

Approach   Also see map on page 89

The crag lies just off the A57, just west of Sheffield. Turn off the A57 over the dam below Rivelin Reservoirs and park in a small car park. Walk back over the dam and cross the road. A path leads up through the woods. Follow this bearing first right, then turning left at a junction up towards the edge.

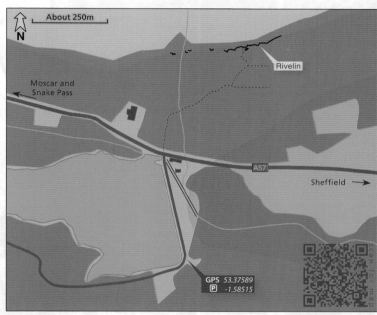

About 250m

N

Moscar and Snake Pass

Rivelin

A57

Sheffield →

GPS 53.37589
P -1.58515

Conditions

Rivelin is south-facing and very sheltered and is often a place that you can get some climbing done when the rest of the Peak is grim. The tree cover keeps the sun off in the summer but also makes some of the problems very green.

Northern Peak

Sheffield Crags

Stanage Area

Burbage Valley

Derwent Edges

The Limestone

Central Grit

Staffordshire

South Peak

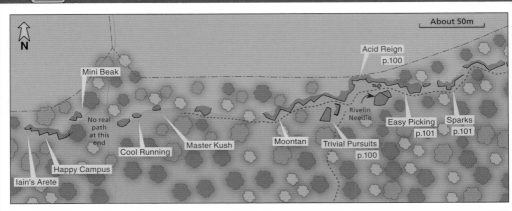

The Quarry and Edge - Left

The far left end of the crag and right end of the quarry give very esoteric bouldering with a number of hard destination problems only. The tree cover offers some shade in warmer weather but means that the place is green in the winter and slow to dry.

Approach - From the edge by the Needle, walk left below the crag. *Moontan* is the first problem reached. The next boulders are further left into the trees and a clear path is often hard to find. For the quarry, continue past the last routes buttress to a stream. Scramble a little way up this to the top and then walk left to *Mini Beak*. The other walls are down below this.

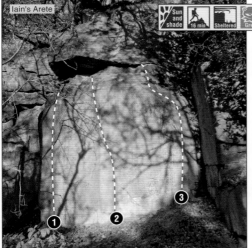

The next block along is undercut, and has three hard problems.

❹ Happy Campus . . . . . 〔1〕 ⬛ V8 *7B*
The undercut arete. Starting from the back is **No Class, V8** *7B+*. Approaching from the left is **Cheeses of Nazareth, V4** *6B+*.

❺ Cheeks 'n' Beaks . . . . 〔1〕 ⬛ V8 *7B+*
The wall via some small holds.

❶ Iain's Arete . . . . . . 〔1〕 ⬛⬛ V8 *7B*
The sharp arete, climbed on its right with a dynamic approach.

❷ Nik's Wall . . . . 〔2〕 ⬛ V11 *8A*
The wall via some tiny holds.

❸ Non Rib . . . . 〔1〕 V7 *7A+*
The right arete.

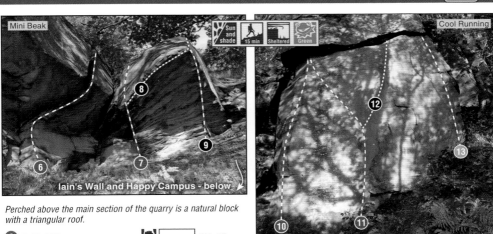

Perched above the main section of the quarry is a natural block with a triangular roof.

6 Boffwidth . . . . 🏋️ ⬜ **V4** *6B*
The wide, steep crack - no bridging! Can be jammed all the way at around **V6** *7A*.

7 Mini Beak Rib . . . . 🔁 ⬜ **V4** *6B+*
Starting low, climb through the roof and finish up the left arete.

8 Mini Beak . . . . 🔁 ⬜ **V6** *7A*
Starting as for *Mini Beak Rib*, follow the lip rightwards then finish up the right arete on its right-hand side.
Photo on page 88.

9 Beak No Weevil . . 🔁 ⬜ **V7** *7A+*
From a sitting start with feet above the break, gain the jug on the arete, then the top.

Just right of the tall Birch Buttress is a short wall.

10 Cool Running Left-hand 🔁 ⬜ **V4** *6B*
The left side of the wall. *Photo on page 96.*

11 Cool Running . . . . . . 🔁 ⬜ **V4** *6B+*
The centre of the wall, trending left to finish.

12 Faze Action . . . . 🔁 ⬜ **V8** *7B+*
The direct finish to *Cool Running* is very thin.

13 Hot Dog . . . . ⬜ **V1** *5b*
Climb the arete on its left-hand side. **V0** *4c* on its right.

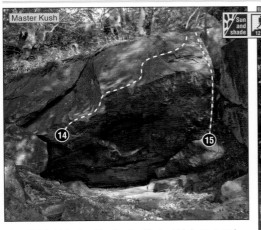

At a slightly higher level is a leaning block which forms a roof.

14 Purple Haze . . . . 🔁 ⬜ **V7** *7A+*
From a jug, traverse right using the lip and crimps above, finishing on top. Sticking to the lip holds is a bit harder at **V8** *7B*.

15 Master Kush . . . . 🔁 ⬜ **V10** *7C+*
The right arete, starting low is desperate.

The main continuous section of the edge has a thin wall just left of the route *Kremlin Krack*.

16 Moontan . . . . 🔁 ⬜ **V7** *7A+*
The fingery wall to the break. The upper wall has a move of similar difficulty although you will need a rope for that one - **E5**.

Northern Peak · Sheffield Crags · Stanage Area · Burbage Valley · Derwent Edges · The Limestone · Central Grit · Staffordshire · South Peak

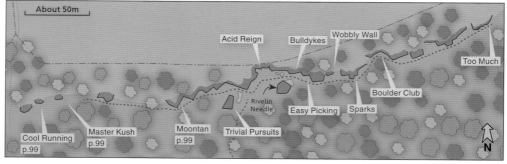

Cool Running p.99 — Master Kush p.99 — Moontan p.99 — Trivial Pursuits — Acid Reign — Bulldykes — Wobbly Wall — Too Much — Boulder Club — Rivelin Needle — Easy Picking — Sparks

About 50m

N

Rivelin Edge

The edge continues the theme of a small number of good quality hard problems. The aspect is more open than further left which means that some of the problems are cleaner. The crag is sunny and generally sheltered from the wind, though it can be too hot in summer.
Approach - The main approach deposits you roughly in the location of *Acid Reign*, which is just behind the prominent pinnacle of Rivelin Needle.

Behind the Rivelin Needle is a short blank wall and arete.

❸ **Acid Reign** . . . . 🔲 **V5** *6C*
The square arete to a tough last move.

Just a few metres along the edge the next two problems can be found on an isolated block just below the path that skirts the base of the edge.

❶ **Trivial Pursuits 1** . . . . 🔲 **V3** *6A+*
The cracks on the left.

❷ **Trivial Pursuits 2** . . . . 🔲 **V3** *6A*
The cracks on the right.

The walls behind the Rivelin Needle are a bit high but there is one decent problem.

❹ **Where Bulldykes Daren't** . . 🔲 **V4** *6B+*
The faint rib.

The next problem is in a little bay before the prominent arete of the route The Brush Off.

⑤ Easy Picking . . . . 〔2〕 ☐ **V4** *6B*
Climb the start of the route to a flake then slink off leftwards.

Around to the right of The Brush Off buttress.

⑥ Fumf . . . . 〔1〕 ☐ **V1** *5b*
The arete is good.

⑦ Wobbly Wall . . . . 〔2〕 ☐ **V1** *5b*
The middle of the wall is even better.

⑧ Europe After Rain. . . . 〔1〕 ☐ **V6** *7A*
Another excellent highball, the last move is a heart-stopper.

Further along you soon reach the prominent crack and arete of the route Auto da Fe, the lower left arete of this buttress is the home of the next problem.

⑨ Sparks . . . . 〔2〕 ☐ **V8** *7B*
Climb the arete on some small edges and a poor sloper. Stay left, and step off left when you reach the break. There is a slightly easier variation moving right to finish.

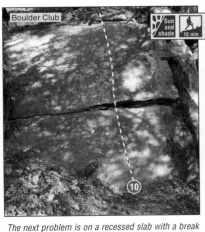

The next problem is on a recessed slab with a break

⑩ Boulder Club . . . . 〔1〕 ☐ **V5** *6C+*
The fingery slab via a tough rock-over using a thin slot. No arete. The original version was further left but has shed a hold.

⑪ Chimp A . . . . ☐ **V7** *7A+*
The undercut arete.

At the far end of the crag, past the Altar Crack Buttress, are two highball wall climbs that are just about boulder problems.

⑫ Too Much . . . . 〔2〕 ☐ **V3** *6A+*
Climb the thin cracks. Probably too high for most but the landing isn't bad, and the hard bit is at half-height.

⑬ Altered . . . . 〔1〕 ☐ **V3** *6A+*
The wall to the right is shorter but has a sloping landing.

Northern Peak | Sheffield Crags | Stanage Area | Burbage Valley | Derwent Edges | The Limestone | Central Grit | Staffordshire | South Peak

	No star	✪	✪✪	✪✪✪
VB to V0 Easy to 4c	4	4	-	-
V0+ to V2 5a to 5c	4	11	1	-
V3 to V5 6A to 6C+	2	4	4	-
V3 to V5 7A upwards	-	1	-	-

Bell Hagg is a well used crag on the outskirts of Sheffield consisting of a series of buttresses of varying heights. Although there are many recorded routes, most people come here for the bouldering. The proximity to Sheffield has led to the place being intensely used over the years hence there are at least five eliminates for every problem listed. The three buttresses covered are steep and undercut. Most problems do top out but some can get quite high, especially on Lurcher Buttress, so it is important to work out your retreat before setting off.

Approach   Also see map on page 89

The edge is situated on the north-facing slope below Hallamshire Golf Course. The best approach is from the A57 Snake Pass road. As you enter/leave Sheffield look out for a side road called Coldwell Lane. Turn up here then take the first right. Drive to the end and park on a dirt section. Walk along a level path for 50m then take the steps that lead up on the left. Follow the path through the woods for 350m to the corner of the golf course. After 10m you reach two stone posts of uneven height, head off right along a narrow trail for 50m to reach Burglar Buttress. The other buttresses described here can be reached by walking along the base from Burglar Buttress.

You can also approach by bus, or drive, up Sandygate Road from Crosspool. When you arrive at the golf course, walk across the course on the well-marked path next to the club house. This will bring you out in the trees above Burglar Buttress.

Conditions

The crag faces north and is partially hidden by trees, which mean it is very green and damp during the winter but it is a fine place to climb during a dry spring, summer or autumn. Some of it is steep enough to stay dry in light rain. The rock is a soft grit and can be friable and loose especially on Burglar Buttress.

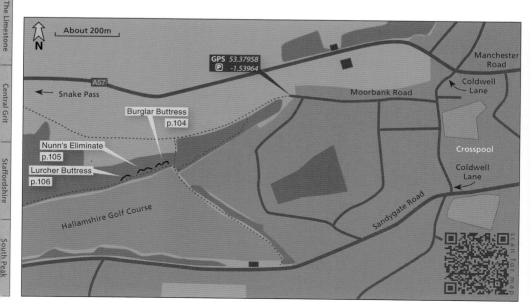

Side tabs: Northern Peak · Sheffield Crags · Stanage Area · Burbage Valley · Derwent Edges · The Limestone · Central Grit · Staffordshire · South Peak

Northern Peak

Sheffield Crags

Stanage Area

Burbage Valley

Derwent Edges

The Limestone

Central Grit

Staffordshire

South Peak

Johnny Camateras on *Getaway* (**V2** 5c) - *next page* - on Burglar Buttress. Photo: Adrian Berry

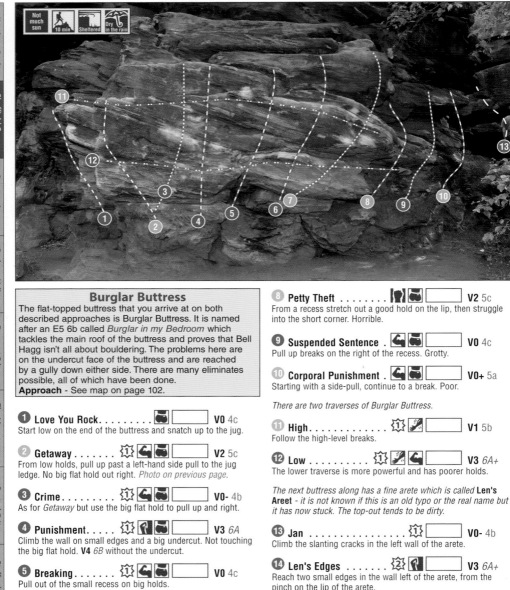

Burglar Buttress

The flat-topped buttress that you arrive at on both described approaches is Burglar Buttress. It is named after an E5 6b called *Burglar in my Bedroom* which tackles the main roof of the buttress and proves that Bell Hagg isn't all about bouldering. The problems here are on the undercut face of the buttress and are reached by a gully down either side. There are many eliminates possible, all of which have been done.
Approach - See map on page 102.

❶ Love You Rock **V0** 4c
Start low on the end of the buttress and snatch up to the jug.

❷ Getaway **V2** 5c
From low holds, pull up past a left-hand side pull to the jug ledge. No big flat hold out right. *Photo on previous page.*

❸ Crime **V0-** 4b
As for *Getaway* but use the big flat hold to pull up and right.

❹ Punishment **V3** 6A
Climb the wall on small edges and a big undercut. Not touching the big flat hold. **V4** 6B without the undercut.

❺ Breaking **V0** 4c
Pull out of the small recess on big holds.

❻ Entering **V0** 4c
Start on a flat triangular hold and pull up past the breaks.

❼ Grand Larceny . . . **V0+** 5a
From the flat triangular hold pull up rightwards via big breaks and a final heave using the short arete.

❽ Petty Theft **V2** 5c
From a recess stretch out a good hold on the lip, then struggle into the short corner. Horrible.

❾ Suspended Sentence . **V0** 4c
Pull up breaks on the right of the recess. Grotty.

❿ Corporal Punishment . **V0+** 5a
Starting with a side-pull, continue to a break. Poor.

There are two traverses of Burglar Buttress.

⓫ High **V1** 5b
Follow the high-level breaks.

⓬ Low . . . . **V3** 6A+
The lower traverse is more powerful and has poorer holds.

*The next buttress along has a fine arete which is called **Len's Areet** - it is not known if this is an old typo or the real name but it has now stuck. The top-out tends to be dirty.*

⓭ Jan **V0-** 4b
Climb the slanting cracks in the left wall of the arete.

⓮ Len's Edges . . . . **V3** 6A+
Reach two small edges in the wall left of the arete, from the pinch on the lip of the arete.

⓯ Len's Areet **V2** 5c
Climb the arete anyway you can. **V3** 6A from siting.
Photo on page 107.

⓰ Alleluia . . . . **V0+** 5a
The wall right of the arete is a ramble on good breaks.

⓱ Alleluia Right . . . . **V0+** 5a
Reachy moves up the dirty right-hand side of the wall.

Len's Areet

Nunn's Eliminate

50m along the path lurks *Nunn's Eliminate* and other gems. The nature of these problems means that good spotting is advised due to the potential for pinging off backwards from the lip.

Approach - See map on page 102.

18 Monk's Other Bulge **V0** 4c
A grotty pull over the left-hand side of the roof. Descend this way from the other problems to avoid grovelling over the top.

19 Monk's Bulge **V1** 5b
Use two edges over the roof and then stretch up left.

20 Nunn's Eliminate . . . . **V3** *6A+*
Get the side-pulls in the middle of the wall and somehow use them to gain much better holds above.

21 Nunn's Right . . . . **V3** *6A+*
The roofs and wall to the right of the central weakness.

22 The Spike Problem. . . **V1** 5b
Attain the spike above the overlaps and escape left.

23 Nunn's Traverse. **V2** 5c
Traverse from left to right.

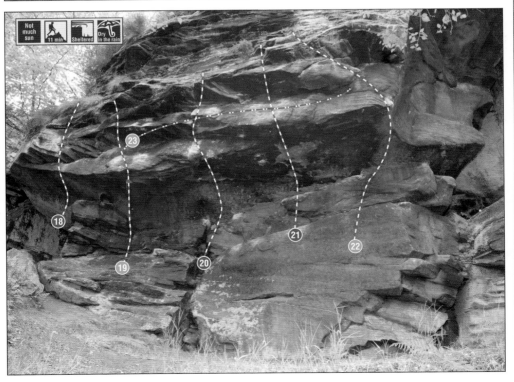

Northern Peak

Sheffield Crags

Stanage Area

Burbage Valley

Derwent Edges

The Limestone

Central Grit

Staffordshire

South Peak

Northern Peak

Sheffield Crags

Stanage Area

Burbage Valley

Derwent Edges

The Limestone

Central Grit

Staffordshire

South Peak

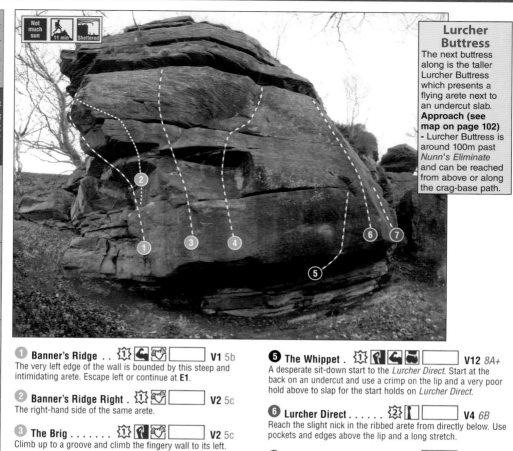

Not much sun | 11 min | Sheltered

Lurcher Buttress

The next buttress along is the taller Lurcher Buttress which presents a flying arete next to an undercut slab. **Approach (see map on page 102)** - Lurcher Buttress is around 100m past *Nunn's Eliminate* and can be reached from above or along the crag-base path.

1 Banner's Ridge . . **V1** 5b
The very left edge of the wall is bounded by this steep and intimidating arete. Escape left or continue at **E1**.

2 Banner's Ridge Right . **V2** 5c
The right-hand side of the same arete.

3 The Brig **V2** 5c
Climb up to a groove and climb the fingery wall to its left.

4 Brown's Unmentionable **V0+** 5a
The fine groove is scary.

5 The Whippet . **V12** 8A+
A desperate sit-down start to the *Lurcher Direct*. Start at the back on an undercut and use a crimp on the lip and a very poor hold above to slap for the start holds on *Lurcher Direct*.

6 Lurcher Direct **V4** 6B
Reach the slight nick in the ribbed arete from directly below. Use pockets and edges above the lip and a long stretch.

7 The Lurcher **V0** 4c
Pull easily onto the slab and follow it to the first break.

The next problems are on the two smaller blocks further right.

8 Lurcher's Nose **V1** 5b
The left arete on its left-hand side. **V4** *6B* from sitting.

9 Lurcher's Nose Front . **V3** 6A
Start low and use the left arete and holds on the slab to pull up.

10 Nose Arete Right **V4** 6B
Pull up the right arete.

11 Sitdown Groove **V4** 6B
From a low start, climb through the bulge on sloping edges, gymnastically desperate.

12 Solly's Arete **V5** 6C
From the same low start, pull up rightwards on thin edges.

Not much sun | 11 min | Sheltered

Northern Peak

Sheffield Crags

Stanage Area

Burbage Valley

Derwent Edges

The Limestone

Central Grit

Staffordshire

South Peak

Rob Jackson pulling through the crux of *Len's Areet* (**V2** 5c) - *page 104*. Photo: Adrian Berry

Northern Peak

Sheffield Crags

Stanage Area

Burbage Valley

Derwent Edges

The Limestone

Central Grit

Staffordshire

South Peak

About 1km

N

A57

Moscar

Stanage High Neb
p.114

Stanage Plantation
p.126

Bamford
p.110

Dennis Knoll

Stanage Popular
p.160

Bamford

Plantation

Stanage Far Right
p.164

North Lees
Campsite

Popular End

Burbage West
p.192

Stanage Area

Northern Peak

Sheffield Crags

Stanage Area

Burbage Valley

Derwent Edges

The Limestone

Central Grit

Staffordshire

South Peak

Sam Townsend latching the hold on *Big Air* (**V5** *6C*) - *page 135* - in the Crescent Arete area of Stanage Plantation. Photo: Mike Hutton

	No star	☆	☆☆	☆☆☆
VB to V0 Easy to 4c	-	3	-	-
V0+ to V2 5a to 5c	1	2	-	-
V3 to V5 6A to 6C+	-	8	4	1
V3 to V5 7A upwards	-	-	1	1

Perched high above Ladybower Reservoir, and opposite Win Hill, is Bamford, one of the most beautiful little edges in the Peak. It has some superb routes for roped climbing but less to offer the boulderer. Included here are three small sections that offer some quality problems mostly in the mid-grades. Confident climbers may be able to extend the set of problems by including a few of the routes in solo mode.

Access

Please use the described approach only to get to the crag. Absolutely no dogs are allowed at this crag, even dogs on leads.

Circuits

There isn't really enough here for a circuit although ticking the Red Spot problems would be a great day out.

Approach   Also see map on page 108

The edge is situated above Bamford village, and in front of the higher edge of Stanage End set back on the moor behind it. It is best approached from a minor road that connects the main Stanage High Neb parking with the A6013 road through Bamford village. There is ample parking on the roadside by a gate. Do not park anywhere else on the minor road. Follow a path, branching left almost immediately, and heading up towards the edge.

Conditions

The edge faces southwest getting plenty of sun. It is fast drying and seldom green but offers little shelter from wind or rain.

About 500m

N

Yorkshire Bridge Pub

Salmon Boulders
p.112

K Buttress
p.113

Gun Buttress
p.113

A6013

GPS 53.35204
℗ -1.67825

Bamford

From Stanage High Neb

Northern Peak · Sheffield Crags · Stanage Area · Burbage Valley · Derwent Edges · The Limestone · Central Grit · Staffordshire · South Peak

Duncan Campbell on the beautifully photogenic *Snap* (**V0-** 4b)
- *next page* - on the Salmon Boulders at Bamford. Photo: Alan James

Northern Peak

Sheffield Crags

Stanage Area

Burbage Valley

Derwent Edges

The Limestone

Central Grit

Staffordshire

South Peak

Salmon Boulders

Some isolated blocks at the very far end of the crag offer a few excellent problems in one of the most photogenic locations in the Peak.

Approach (see map on page 110) - To go direct to this area, follow the crag-top path all the way until you pass the prominent arete (Gargoyle Buttress). Continue a little further and then scramble down to the boulders.

Something Silly

*The furthest boulder is less popular than the stuff to its right but has the impressive arete of **Something Silly**.*

1 Something Silly **V5** *6C*
The left arete gets quite high.

2 Something Else **V0** *4c*
Start up the right side of the wall, then traverse the break to finish at the left arete.

The main Salmon Boulder sits proudly on the hillside and has a smaller wall to its left.

3 Win Hill . . . . **V0+** *5a*
The ramp up the wall left of the crack.

4 Lose Hill . . . . **V3** *6A+*
Fridge-hugging up the pillar on the right.

5 Ping Pong Pocket Rib . **V7** *7A+*
The left arete is excellent.

6 Flaky Fluster **V4** *6B*
Follow poor flakes up the wall too a hard finish.

7 Wriggly Crack **V0** *4c*
The crack, finished up and left.

8 Snap **V0-** *4b*
The wall on the right of the block past an undercut.
Photo on previous page.

In the centre of the edge is a shorter section around K Buttress which offers some good hard problems and highballs.

9 K Kole Arete . . . . **V4** *6B+*
The arete is climbed from the big hole.

10 KO'd **V4** *6B*
Follow the break from the back to finish up the last moves of *K Kole Arete*. **V2** *5c* if you use the foot-ledge on the wall behind.

11 The Bookend **V4** *6B*
The end of the narrow block, using both edges.

12 Bookend Right . . . . . . **V5** *6C+*
The right arete on its right-hand side.

13 The Plumber has Landed
. . . . **V4** *6B*
The thin seam between the chimney and the arete.

Something Silly

K Buttress

The middle section of the edge has some extended problems in the mid-grades.

Approach (see map on page 110) - To go direct to this area, follow the crag-top path until above the third major section of edge. Go past this and double back left under the problems.

14 Down to Earth . . . . . . **V3** *6A+*
The superb highball arete.

15 Deb . . . . **V0+** *5a*
The arete. Also known as *Crunchy Nuts*.

16 Bamboozer **V5** *6C*
Swing out right from the crack and follow edges up the wall.

17 Spike **V8** *7B*
Starting at the niche, pull through the roof and move up and left then finish direct.

Gun Buttress

The first section of edge on the crag is midway between highball problems and short routes. Included here are the safer problems but the main Gun Buttress also has plenty to offer albeit quite high.

Approach (see map on page 110) - Follow the main approach and take the path leftwards towards the first major section of the edge.

18 Long John **V3** *6A*
The arete and left side of the overhang.

19 Three Real Men Dancing . **V4** *6B+*
Climb through the roof starting from the flat jug.

20 Green Parrot **V1** *5b*
Grab the jug on the arete and pull up.

21 A Minah Variation . . . **V3** *6A*
Traverse the lip from right to left, then finish up the arete.

Northern Peak
Sheffield Crags
Stanage Area
Burbage Valley
Derwent Edges
The Limestone
Central Grit
Staffordshire
South Peak

	No star	✧	✧	✧
VB to V0 Easy to 4c	1	8	-	-
V0+ to V2 5a to 5c	5	23	4	2
V3 to V5 6A to 6C+	4	8	14	2
V3 to V5 7A upwards	3	11	7	4

Northern Peak

Sheffield Crags

Stanage Area

Burbage Valley

Derwent Edges

The Limestone

Central Grit

Staffordshire

South Peak

The northern end of Stanage offers much for the boulderer who likes solitude and who is prepared to walk a bit since the decent bouldering tends to be in isolated pockets. This can mean that you spend a fair amount of time lugging your pad around but there are some great problems and also plenty of potential for further exploration.

The better problems are mostly in the mid and hard grades with some top-notch Black Spot problems and a decent Red Circuit. For the lower grades the only sections worth considering are the Causeway and the Buckstone but these are definitely worthwhile.

Circuits

Three circuits have been included - a Red Circuit that starts at the furthest flung end of Stanage and works back towards the Causeway; and Green and Orange Circuits on the Buckstone and Causeway crags.

Conditions

This end of Stanage is as exposed as the rest, catching any wind that is going and with no shelter in the rain. However, this means that it dries very quickly and can give great conditions all year round if the weather is kind. The sun is slower to arrive at this end of Stanage and some of the most distant buttresses can be dirty and green after bad weather. The paths are often boggy making navigating between the boulders tricky.

Mike Hutton tackling the delightful *Microbe* (**V2** 5c) - *page 117* - at Stanage End. A boulder problem which is not as small as its name suggests. Photo: Mike Hutton

Stanage End
p.116

From Moscar
and the A57

About 500m

scan for map

N

Old Salt
p.117

Marble Wall
p.118

Twin Buttress
p.119

Anniversary Arete
p.121

High Neb

Blockhead Buttress
p.120

Broken Buttress
p.121

The Causeway
p.122

GPS 53.35548
-1.66018

The Buckstone
p.124

Dennis Knoll

P

Northern Peak

Sheffield Crags

Stanage Area

Burbage Valley

Derwent Edges

The Limestone

Central Grit

Staffordshire

South Peak

Approach   Also see map on page 108

The sections of Stanage to the north and south of High Neb Buttress are best approached from the Dennis Knoll parking. From here two main paths lead up to High Neb Buttress and the Causeway. All the sections can be reached from here using the paths above or below the edge. Stanage End can also be approached from Moscar on the A57 which is a slightly shorter walk.

Chip Shop Brawl

Stanage End

The remotest part of Stanage offers the prospect of solitude to those prepared to walk. The main attractions are a few top-notch hard problems.

Approach (see map on page 115) - Stanage End is reached in 20-25 minutes from Moscar parking, or around 30 minutes from High Neb Parking.

The big end slab has the undercut arete of **Chip Shop Brawl**.

1 Low Rider . . . . . . **V10** *7C+*
Start on the arete below the roof, traverse the lip and finish at a jug.

2 Incursion Direct **V3** *6A*
Starting where *Low Rider* traverses the lip, pass the roof and either finish direct (**E1**) as shown or traverse off left.

3 R.I.P.O.D.B. **V9** *7C*
Pull through the lip on slopers.

4 Chip Shop Buddy **V11** *8A*
Start up *Low Rider*. Finish as for the *Chip Shop Brawl*.

5 Chip Shop Brawl . . **V7** *7A+*
The prominent hanging arete, finishing slightly left. The arete can be climbed on its right at the same grade. *Photo on page 9.*

6 Opposition **V9** *7C*
Start up the scoop right of *Chip Shop Brawl*, then traverse the break left to the arete. The continuation awaits an ascent.

The Stanage End and High Neb Red Circuit
This Red Circuit enables you to pick out the best of this end of Stanage. It involves a lot of walking especially in the second half where there are some isolated problems.

Chip Shop Brawl

Wilbur's Wall

Northern Peak

Sheffield Crags

Stanage Area

Burbage Valley

Derwent Edges

The Limestone

Central Grit

Staffordshire

South Peak

Northern Peak

Sheffield Crags

Stanage Area

Burbage Valley

Derwent Edges

The Limestone

Central Grit

Staffordshire

South Peak

Wilbur's Wall

Afternoon | **25 min** | **Windy**

⑫ Skimmington Ride . ④ 🏃 📷 ⬜ **V4** *6B*
The *Old Salt* arete on its right hand side as far as the break.

⑬ Little Oedipus . . . . 📷 ⬜ **V7** *7A+*
Climb the initial crack of *Valediction* then traverse out right along the thin break to finish as for *Monad*.

⑭ Monad . . . . . . ⑤ 🏃 📷 🔲 ⬜ **V5** *6C+*
Jump to the hold, and continue direct. It is also possible to start by bridging in the corner to the right, which is slightly easier. Add a grade if you use the arete to avoid the jump at the start.

⑮ Quiver . . . . . . ⑥ 🏃 ▯ 📷 ⬜ **V2** *5c*
The left crack to a tricky finish.

⑯ Arrow Crack . . . . . ⑦ 🏃 📷 ⬜ **V1** *5b*
The next crack.

⑰ Blinkers . . . . ⑧ 🏃 📷 ⬜ **V1** *5b*
The wall just right.

⑱ Thin Problem Crack ⑨ 🏃 📷 ⬜ **V1** *5b*
The thin crack has a hard start.

⑲ Microbe Left . . ⑩ 🏃 🧗 📷 ⬜ **V4** *6B*
The crimpy wall.

⑳ Microbe . . . . ⑪ 🏃 📷 ⬜ **V2** *5c*
Follows a thin crack from the right-hand side of the overlap.
Photo on page 114.

㉑ Germ . . . . ⑫ 🏃 📷 ⬜ **V4** *6B*
Another great highball wall problem.

㉒ Problem Corner . . . . . 🏃 📷 ⬜ **V0+** *5a*
The prominent corner.

㉓ Flags of the World . ⑬ 🏃 📷 ⬜ **V3** *6A+*
Just right of the corner, follow crimps up the wall.

㉔ Love Handles . . . . 📷 ⬜ **V3** *6A*
Follow the flake.

㉕ Mr M'Quod and the Anti-rock Squad
. . . . ⑭ 🏃 📷 ⬜ **V2** *5c*
The arete. *Red Circuit continues on page 118.*

Wilbur's Wall *presents some cracks and aretes.*

⑦ Wilbur's Rib . . . . 📷 ⬜ **V1** *5b*
The prominent hanging arete, finishing slightly left.

⑧ Wilbur's Corner . . . . . . ① 🏃 ⬜ **V1** *5b*
The corner just right.

⑨ Wilbur's Wall . . . . ② 🏃 ⬜ **V2** *5c*
The wall just right, starting from the low break.

⑩ New York, New York ③ 🏃 📷 ⬜ **V4** *6B*
The clean arete. **V5**, *6C+* from sitting.

⑪ These Vagabond Shoes 🏃 🥾 ⬜ **V5** *6C+*
The wall from a sitting start.

Old Salt

This quarried section of Stanage boasts a great collection of micro-climbs that are best enjoyed as highball boulder problems.
Approach (see map on page 115 - It can be approached from Moscar (20 mins) or from High Neb Parking (30 mins).

Afternoon | **20 min** | **Windy**

Northern Peak

Sheffield Crags

Stanage Area

Burbage Valley

Derwent Edges

The Limestone

Central Grit

Staffordshire

South Peak

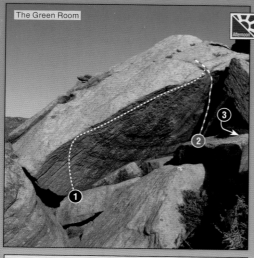

The Green Room

Hideous Hidare

Marble Wall

This quarried section of Stanage boasts a great collection of micro-climbs that are best enjoyed as highball boulder problems.
Approach (see map on page 115) - Approach from Moscar (20 mins) or Dennis Knoll (30 mins).

There are two problems in The Green Room, which is a cave made from a cluster of boulders to the left of Marble Wall area. The first problem is at the entrance to the cave.

❶ Soft Top Traverse . . . . 　　　　 **V6** *7A*
From sitting, traverse the lip to finish as for the next problem.

❷ Soft Top Beetle 　　　　 **V5** *6C*
The rib from sitting.

❸ Green Room Slap 　　　　 **V7** *7A+*
In the back of the cave, dyno from slopers to the lip. The sitting start is **V9** *7C*.

There is another problem on the other side of Marble Wall.

❹ Hideous Hidare . . . 　　　　 **V5** *6C*
The rib and slab via a sloping ledge.

*The next three problems are on the **Lone Boulder**.*

❺ Lone Boulder Arete Left . . 　　 **V0+** *5a*
The arete on its left-hand side.

❻ Lone Boulder Arete . . 　　　 **V1** *5b*
The arete on its right-hand side.

❼ Lone Boulder Slab . . . . 　　 **V0+** *5a*
The slab to the right.

Marble Wall

Hideous Hidare

The Green Room

Loan Boulder

30m to
Beauty slab →

Twin Buttress

An isolated buttress with some reasonable problems including a delightful slab.

Approach (see map on page 115) - It can be approached from Moscar or from Dennis Knoll.

8 Cutunder Crack V1 5b
The short jamming crack.

9 Bottomless Crack Direct No.1
. . . . V1 5b
From a positive hold, move left to flakes and onto the break.

10 Bottomless Crack Direct No.2
. . . . V2 5c
The wall to the right, finishing at the break.

11 Seranata Start V2 5c
From the break, gain the finishing jug dynamically.

30m to the right (looking in) is a jumble of blocks in front of the main edge with the fine **Beauty Slab**.

12 Beauty . . . . ⟨17⟩ V5 6C
The blank slab is a superb combination of pebbles and smearing. Using the right arete makes it a decent **V2** 5c.
Red Circuit continues a long way right on page 122.

13 The Beast . . . . V8 7B+
A tough mantel - no aretes are allowed.

14 Dowager's Hump V5 6C
Another mantel but this time more manageable.

100m to the right is an isolated problem under **Birthday Buttress**. *The buttress has an undercut arete on its right-hand side below a ledge and a curved roof at the top.*

15 21 Today Start . . . V6 7A
Make hard moves to get over the undercut onto the arete.
Starting from standing is **V2** 5c.

Beauty Slab

Northern Peak · Sheffield Crags · Stanage Area · Burbage Valley · Derwent Edges · The Limestone · Central Grit · Staffordshire · South Peak

Northern Peak

Sheffield Crags

Stanage Area

Burbage Valley

Derwent Edges

The Limestone

Central Grit

Staffordshire

South Peak

High Neb to the Causeway

The disjointed section of Stanage between High Neb and the Causeway has a small selection of esoteric problems for those after some solitude.

Approach (see map on page 115) - This area is best approached from Dennis Knoll parking. The main track leads up to the Causeway area at one end and there is a well-trodden path up to High Neb at the other.

Jamie's Other Roof

High Neb

Jeepers Creepers (HVS)

The first problem is at **High Neb**, *under the route Jeepers Creepers on the right-hand (looking in) side of the crag.*

1 **Fallen Archangel** . . . . ⟨☆⟩ 🔒⬜ **V5** *6C*
From sitting, pull up leftwards along the fallen arete and finally heave up onto the top slab.

About 100m right of High Neb Buttress is the first of two undercut blocks - **Jamie's Other Roof**.

2 **Jamie's Other Roof** . . ⟨☆⟩🔒⬜ **V6** *7A*
Pass the lip and continue up the face.

3 **Jamie's Other Roof Right** . 🔒⬜ **V5** *6C*
Use the right arete.

Jamie's Roof

About 100m further along is **Jamie's Roof**.

4 **Jamie's Roof** . . . . ⟨☆⟩🔒⬜ **V6** *7A*
The roof and face above.

Blockhead Buttress

The next substantial section of edge is **Blockhead Buttress.**

5 Sinew Stretch ...... [icons] ▢ **V2** 5c
The arete is hard to start and high above.

6 Headbanger .... [icons] ▢ **V2** 5c
This clean arete is also tricky to start and has a potential fall of twice the height of the problem!

7 Solomon's Seal .. [icons] ▢ **V10** 7C+
The centre of the wall via a poor flake. The sit-down from down and left is **Solomon Grundy V11** 8A.

8 The Jester ...... [icons] ▢ **V8** 7B
A slightly easier way up the wall, grab the edges and go for the top. A low start crouching on the right arete is a grade harder.

9 Slabenger .... [icons] ▢ **V6** 7A
The thin slab, avoiding the cracks.

Anniversary Arete

Anniversary
Arete (E1)

About 100m further on is **Anniversary Arete** *which has one problem at its base.*

10 Youngster's Wall .... [icons] ▢ **V6** 7A
The wall via a thin seam.

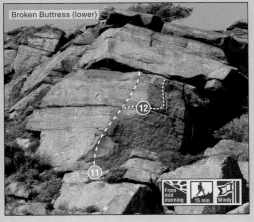

Broken Buttress (lower)

Another 200m further along and above the Causeway is a very jumbled section of blocks called collectively **Broken Buttress.**

11 Blow Out .... [icons] ▢ **V2** 5c
The blunt arete to the break.

12 Blow Peter .... [icons] ▢ **V5** 6C+
Start up *Blow Out* then move out right along the break to finish up the short crack.

Broken Buttress (upper)

High up on the right-hand side of the jumble is a flying arete (the route Prowler). The next two problems are on the south-facing side-wall of this prow.

13 Wu Tang Span .... [icons] ▢ **V6** 7A
Make a dyno from an edge and a side-pull to a flatty. Easier but more dangerous if you pull on the crispy flakes!

14 Crimp Shrimp ...... [icons] ▢ **V8** 7B
The wall to the right, from a low start.

Cock 'O The Rock
p.122

Jamie's Roof
Blockhead Buttress
Youngster's Wall
Broken Buttress

Northern Peak | Sheffield Crags | Stanage Area | Burbage Valley | Derwent Edges | The Limestone | Central Grit | Staffordshire | South Peak

Northern Peak

Sheffield Crags

Stanage Area

Burbage Valley

Derwent Edges

The Limestone

Central Grit

Staffordshire

South Peak

The Causeway

Above the section of Causeway that cuts diagonally through the edge is a set of small buttresses and slabs with a decent selection of problems including a couple of classics and a decent lower-grade section.

Approach (see map on page 115) - From Dennis Knoll parking, follow the main track up towards the edge. *Cock 'O The Rock* is left of where the stream and drystone wall run down from the crag. An alternative approach is across the field, past the Buckstone.

Cock 'O The Rock

Above and left of a small stream and drystone wall running down the hillside. Above this is a square block.

1 Cock Crack . . . . 　　　 **V2** 5c
The crack on the left.

2 Cock-a-doodle-doo . . . 　　 **V9** 7C
From a low start pull over the roof using a side-pull. Finish at the break.

3 Cock 'O The Rock . . . . 　　 **V6** 7A
Start with hands on the big sloper and climb the arete mostly on its right-hand side.

4 Rocksucker . . . . 18 **V4** 6B+
The wall just right.

5 Historical Arete 19 **V4** 6B
Follow the first break left to finish up the arete.

6 Cock Groove . . . . 　　 **V3** 6A+
The short groove on the right-side of the block.

Iain's Prow

On the opposite side of the gully with the stream is an undercut prow just left of a large hollybush.

7 Central Buttress Direct 20 **V5** 6C
The bulge is tackled with hard moves at the lip.

8 Iain's Prow 21 **V5** 6C
Jump to the lip, finish out right. The left-hand finish is **V7** 7A+.

Beaky Direct

The next problem is just above the Causeway.

9 Beaky Direct 22 **V3** 6A
Pull onto the hanging arete then mantel the ledge.
The final problem on the Red Circuit.

Cock 'O The Rock　　Iain's Prow　　Beaky Direct　　Causeway Slabs

The first of the **Causeway Slabs** *has a sloping landing.*

10 Broad Slab Left . . . . . ⑥☆ ☐ **VB** 4a
Make a high step onto the left-hand side of the slab.

11 Side-pull Slab . . . . . . ⑦☆ ☐ **V0-** 4b
The centre of the slab. Rock onto a foothold.

12 Broad Slab . . . . ⑧☆ ☐ **V0** 4c
Tackle the slab above a vertical crack.

13 Broad Rib . . . . ⑧⑨☆ ☐ **V0+** 5a
The blunt arete is easy on its left-hand side.

14 Broad Wall . . . . ⑩☆ ☐ **V0-** 4b
Climb the side-wall.

15 Rusty Left . . . . ⑨⑪☆ ☐ **V0+** 5a
The left-hand side of the next smaller slab.

16 Rusty . . . . ⑩☆ ☐ **V1** 5b
The arete is pleasant.

17 Crispy Wall . . . . ⑫☆ ☐ **V0-** 4b
The left-hand side of the hanging slab.

18 The Skid . . . . ⑪☆ ☐ **V2** 5c
The right-hand side of the hanging slab.

19 Miss Sunshine. . . . ⑫☆ 👟 ☐ **V2** 5c
Climb the nose from a low start.

20 Sunny Barger . . . . ⑬⑬☆ ☐ **V0+** 5a
The roof crack. Not as hard as roof cracks should be.
The butch finish to the Green and Orange Circuits.

21 Iraqu . . . . ☆ ☐ **V3** 6A+
The left-hand side of the undercut wall from a low start.

22 Iranu . . . . ☆ ◫ 🖐 ☐ **V6** 7A
Make a desperate rock-up the blank wall, just to the right of the vague arete.

23 Uvavu. . . . . 👟 ☐ **V1** 5b
More cunning than power.

24 Uvanu. . . . . ☆ 🖐 👟 ☐ **V8** 7B
Connect the start of *Uvavu* to *Iranu* using the thin break and your thin fingers.

Causeway Slabs

Northern Peak · Sheffield Crags · Stanage Area · Burbage Valley · Derwent Edges · The Limestone · Central Grit · Staffordshire · South Peak

Northern Peak

Sheffield Crags

Stanage Area

Burbage Valley

Derwent Edges

The Limestone

Central Grit

Staffordshire

South Peak

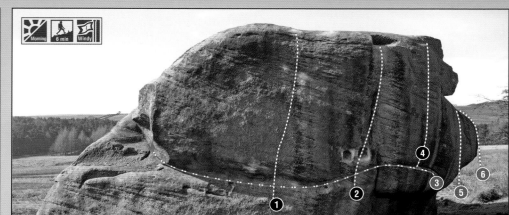

The Buckstone

The Buckstone is famous for its one dyno problem. However there is a good spread of bulging mantels and delicate slabs here which can be used in combination with the Causeway Slabs.

The block is exposed to all weather but dries quickly and gets the sun for much of the day.

Approach (see map on page 115) - Continue on the road under Stanage past the Plantation car park. You can see the Buckstone in the field on the right of the road. Park either at the little lay-by before the bend or off the road somewhere. A path leads from a gate by the road straight to the Buckstone.

❶ Spring Voyage **V9** *7C*
Use the undercut to reach the crimps, and continue to the top.

❷ The Buckstone Dyno . . **V8** *7B*
A classic dyno from the big rafter-holding chips to the flatty. Easy to get close but a different ball game to latch it.

❸ Buckstone Traverse . . **V4** *6B*
Traverse the low break leftwards under the next problem, using the chips.

❹ Ron's Wall **V9** *7C*
The bulging wall starting from the low break.

❺ Buckstone Bulge **V4** *6B*
The bulge just to the right.

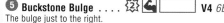

The Buckstone

The Buckette

The **Buckstone Causeway Green Circuit**
There isn't much for the lower-grade boulderer at this end of Stanage but this short circuit, combining the Buckstone and the Causeway, makes the most of what's available. It is mostly slabby problems although the landings above the Causeway are sloping. It is listed from right to left in the book.

The **Buckstone Causeway Orange Circuit**
This short circuit basically boosts the Green Circuit with a few excellent extra problems. It is listed from right to left in the book.

6 Buckaroo V5 *6C*
A hideous mantel onto the nose.

7 The Buckshelf V3 *6A*
The wall left of the rib. Use the sloping shelf for all its worth.

8 Buckrib V1 5b
Climb the blunt rib just left of the groove.

9 Buckstone Groove V1 5b
The attractive groove is excellent. If it feels too hard then you are doing it wrong. *Photo on page 16.*

10 Pass the Buck . . . . V0+ 5a
Mantel the sloping ledge to gain the slot-pocket.
Green Circuit continues on page 123.

11 Buxom . . . . VB 4a
The arete on its left-hand side is a good beginners' test in friction climbing.

12 Buxless . . . . VB 4a
The arete on its right-hand side. Avoid the big chip.

13 Buckaroo V0 4c
Connect two big chips. Tricky for the short.

14 Buck Eliminate V1 5b
The slab without using any chipped buckets is good.

15 Buckstone Wall . . . . VB
Use the huge chipped holds below the chipped runnel.
Photo this page.

The Buckette

Up the hill towards the path are two more small boulders known collectively as **The Buckette**.

16 Buckette Arete . . . . . . V3 *6A+*
The bulging arete is a powerful slopey pull.

17 Sarah V2 5c
Delicate moves up the bulging slabby wall.

18 Buckette Rib V1 5b
The rib. *Orange Circuit continues on page 123.*

Northern Peak
Sheffield Crags
Stanage Area
Burbage Valley
Derwent Edges
The Limestone
Central Grit
Staffordshire
South Peak

	No star	⚝	⚝⚝	⚝⚝⚝
VB to V0 Easy to 4c	5	15	7	1
V0+ to V2 5a to 5c	10	29	15	6
V3 to V5 6A to 6C+	6	19	28	8
V3 to V5 7A upwards	9	22	20	25

Stanage Plantation is amongst the most famous bouldering locations in the country and has many superb and high profile problems. A quick list of the iconic problems in this area illustrates the quality that can be found here: *Crescent Arete, Not To Be Taken Away, The Green Traverse, Deliverance, Careless Torque, Brad Pit, The Joker* and *The Ace*. For many climbers these iconic problems will be too difficult but there is plenty of easier stuff too.

Erosion

The Plantation has become a victim of its own popularity with some of the problems and surrounding grassy bases showing signs of wear and tear. The erosion has been especially bad in the area around The Pebble. In recent times the increasing use of bouldering pads has helped save the ground from repeated impacts and this is to be encouraged. Use your pad to protect both the ground and yourself!

Circuits

The Plantation is a great spot for circuits and this is often the best way to sample the whole area. Three have been included in this chapter.

Approach   Also see map on page 108

Park in the Plantation parking (paid) and follow the distinct path up to the crag. For the Pebble Area, head rightwards after exiting the first sections of trees. For the Crescent Arete and Far Left Areas, continue on the path and you will walk under the eponymous route.

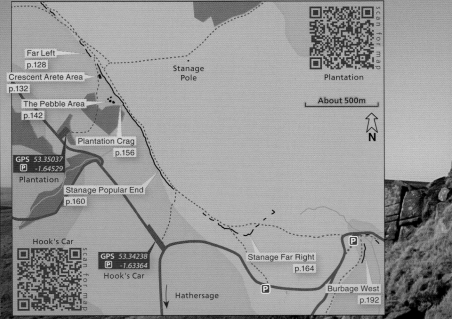

Far Left p.128
Crescent Arete Area p.132
The Pebble Area p.142
Plantation Crag p.156
GPS 53.35037 Ⓟ -1.64529 Plantation
Stanage Popular End p.160
Hook's Car
GPS 53.34238 Ⓟ -1.63364 Hook's Car
Hathersage
Stanage Pole
Plantation
About 500m
N
Stanage Far Right p.164
Burbage West p.192

Northern Peak

Sheffield Crags

Stanage Area

Burbage Valley

Derwent Edges

The Limestone

Central Grit

Staffordshire

South Peak

Jon Stewart high up on the bold *Daydreamer* (**V3** *6A+*) - *next page* - on the Far Left Area of Stanage Plantation. Photo: Jamie Moss

Conditions

The Plantation is generally southwest-facing, catching plenty of afternoon and evening sun. The exposed position means that it will catch the wind although sometimes it can whistle over the top of the edge and leave the base and the slopes below relatively sheltered. The crag and boulders dry very quickly and aren't green. On still days after June the place can be impossibly midge-ridden.

Conundrum Slabs

Nightmare Slab

Count's Buttress

Far Left

The furthest left (north) section of the Plantation area is usually completely deserted. The bouldering here is of reasonable quality but only worth seeking out for the few excellent highball smearing slabs including the classic *Daydreamer*, *Shirley's Shining Temple* and *D.I.Y.*
Approach (see map on page 127) - From the Plantation parking, continue past the Crescent Arete Area. When you have almost reached the top of the crag, break off left and follow a vague path down under the edge.

1 BGM's Mantel . . . . 🗒 ▢ **V0** 4c
Mantel through the scoop at the left side of the wall. Manteling direct without the extra ledge is **V1** 5b.

2 BGM's Crack . . . . ▢ **V0-** 4b
The layback crack.

3 Fierce Wall . . . . 🗒 ▢ **V2** 6a
Gain the pocket and move up and right past the break.

4 Arete . . . . ▢ **V1** 5b
The arete.

5 Slab . . . . ▢ **V2** 5c
The slab just to the right.

Up on the main edge, just left of the large Count's Buttress is a clean slab.

6 Little Eden Arete . . . . 🗒 ▢ **VB** 4a
The short arete is easy but don't fall off.

7 Eden Arete . . . . 🗒🗒 ▢ **VB** 4a
The higher arete just to the right. Again, don't fall.

The slab itself has five highballs with an extra drop from the ledge if you should bounce.

8 Nightmare Slab . . . . . 🗒🗒 ▢ **V3** 6A+
Finish either direct, or out right.

9 Dream Boat . . . . 🗒🗒 ▢ **V4** 6B
The slab just right.

10 Daydreamer . . . . 🗒🗒 ▢ **V3** 6A+
Start at a small flake and continue direct.
Photo on previous page.

11 Nightrider . . . . 🗒🗒 ▢ **V4** 6B
Follow the green streak.

12 Sleepwalker . . . . 🗒🗒 ▢ **V3** 6A+
A pale streak a couple of metres left of the corner.

Nightmare Slab   Shirley's Shining Temple   The Upper Tier

Conundrum Slabs

The DT's

D.I.Y. Area p.130   The Hippo p.130   Poundland p.130

From Plantation Bridleway

Northern Peak
Sheffield Crags
Stanage Area
Burbage Valley
Derwent Edges
The Limestone
Central Grit
Staffordshire
South Peak

Count's Buttress

The DT's

Below Count's Buttress is a tilted block which is difficult to see from above.

13 The DT's **V9** *7C*
Traverse the sloping lip from right to left. A real skin tester.

Shirley's Shining Temple

Back up on the main edge.

14 Shirley's Shining Temple
. . . . **V9** *7C*
An old route (E5) which is now usually done above mats as a classic highball slab.

15 Shock Horror Slab **V5** *6C*
An easier way up the slab, but still thin and high. It is **V7** *7A+* if you gain the flakes direct (without the pockets and side-pulls out right).

*Further right, and up on an **Upper Tier**, are a couple of short walls which have the following problems.*

16 Bell End **V1** 5b
The left arete is highball without a spotter to stop you rolling down the hill.

17 The Bell **V5** *6C*
The technical scoop.

At the same level, further right are a few more problems. These problems are directly above the D.I.Y. Area and best reached round to the left (looking in).

18 Scoop de Grass **V1** 5b
The scoop on the left side of the wall.

19 Breakout **V1** 5b
The wall past a break.

20 The Hank Rack **V0-** 4b
The crack.

21 Huffer Puffer . . . . **VB** 4a
Layback up the wide crack.

22 Sweep . . . . **V0+** 5a
The arete just right.

The Upper Tier

D.I.Y. Area
p.130

Northern Peak · Sheffield Crags · Stanage Area · Burbage Valley · Derwent Edges · The Limestone · Central Grit · Staffordshire · South Peak

Northern Peak

Sheffield Crags

Stanage Area

Burbage Valley

Derwent Edges

The Limestone

Central Grit

Staffordshire

South Peak

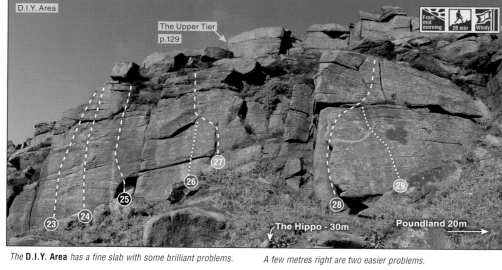

The **D.I.Y. Area** *has a fine slab with some brilliant problems.*

㉓ Black and Decker . . . . 🌟 ⬜ **V5** *6C+*
The left-hand line of the slab, finishing up the arete.

㉔ D.I.Y. . . . . 🌟🌟🌟 ⬜ **V4** *6B*
The central line of the slab is excellent.

㉕ Torture Garden . . . . . 🌟🌟  ⬜ **V6** *7A*
From the niche, follow the slab. The grade assumes you don't
bounce past the first move - **V5** *6C* if you do.

㉖ Sithee Direct . . . . 🌟🌟 ⬜ **V5** *6C*
The thin wall past the right-hand end of the overlap.

㉗ Sithee . . . . 🌟 ⬜ **V1** *5b*
A much easier start comes in from the right.

A few metres right are two easier problems.

㉘ Toxic . . . . 🌟 ⬜ **VB** *4a*
The flake moving right along the break before finishing.

㉙ Cixot . . . . 🌟 ⬜ **V0+** *5a*
The slab just right.

Beneath D.I.Y. Area is a leaning block called **The Hippo.**

㉚ The Hippo . . . . . . 🌟 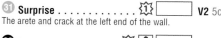 ⬜ **V7** *7A+*
The small block is out of bounds. Left is **Peahound, V8** *7B.*

20m right of the D.I.Y. Area is a short bulge - **Poundland.**

㉛ Surprise . . . . 🌟 ⬜ **V2** *5c*
The arete and crack at the left end of the wall.

㉜ Poundland . . . . 🌟🌟  ⬜ **V9** *7C*
From a poor pocket, follow slopers out left, to just short of a
crack.

㉝ Surprise Direct . . . . 🌟🌟 ⬜ **V4** *6B+*
A hard mantel on positive holds.

The Hippo

Poundland

Northern Peak

Sheffield Crags

Stanage Area

Burbage Valley

Derwent Edges

The Limestone

Central Grit

Staffordshire

South Peak

Chris Taylor 'snowballing' *Silk* (**V7** *7A+*) - *page 133* - on the Wall End Slab Area of the Plantation. Photo: Adrian Berry

Northern Peak

Sheffield Crags

Stanage Area

Burbage Valley

Derwent Edges

The Limestone

Central Grit

Staffordshire

South Peak

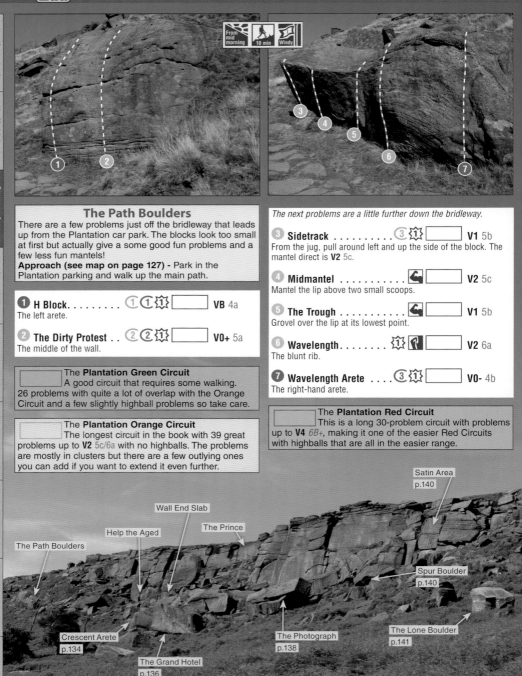

From mid morning | 10 min | Windy

The Path Boulders

There are a few problems just off the bridleway that leads up from the Plantation car park. The blocks look too small at first but actually give a some good fun problems and a few less fun mantels!

Approach (see map on page 127) - Park in the Plantation parking and walk up the main path.

❶ H Block. . . . . ①①🔄 ☐ **VB** 4a
The left arete.

❷ The Dirty Protest . . ②②🔄 ☐ **V0+** 5a
The middle of the wall.

☐ The **Plantation Green Circuit**
A good circuit that requires some walking. 26 problems with quite a lot of overlap with the Orange Circuit and a few slightly highball problems so take care.

☐ The **Plantation Orange Circuit**
The longest circuit in the book with 39 great problems up to **V2** 5c/6a with no highballs. The problems are mostly in clusters but there are a few outlying ones you can add if you want to extend it even further.

The next problems are a little further down the bridleway.

❸ Sidetrack . . . . ③🔄 ☐ **V1** 5b
From the jug, pull around left and up the side of the block. The mantel direct is **V2** 5c.

❹ Midmantel . . . . 💪 ☐ **V2** 5c
Mantel the lip above two small scoops.

❺ The Trough . . . . 💪 ☐ **V1** 5b
Grovel over the lip at its lowest point.

❻ Wavelength. . . . . 🔄 🧗 ☐ **V2** 6a
The blunt rib.

❼ Wavelength Arete . . . . ③🔄 ☐ **V0-** 4b
The right-hand arete.

☐ The **Plantation Red Circuit**
This is a long 30-problem circuit with problems up to **V4** 6B+, making it one of the easier Red Circuits with highballs that are all in the easier range.

Satin Area
p.140

Wall End Slab

Help the Aged

The Prince

The Path Boulders

Spur Boulder
p.140

The Lone Boulder
p.141

Crescent Arete
p.134

The Photograph
p.138

The Grand Hotel
p.136

Wall End Slab Area

A good collection of problems mostly on the main edge around the popular route *Wall End Slab*. Some are the starts of routes and require care to get back down.

8 Dijon Dip **V5** *6C*
The arete and capping roof. The arete start is a good **V1** 5b.

9 Silk Start .... **V7** *7A+*
The start to the E6 route *Silk*. When the snow drifts are deep, you can carry on all the way. **V9** *7C* from sitting.
Photo on page 131.

10 Fern Crack Start... **V0+** 5a
A fine piece of laybacking/jamming.

11 Polished Bump ..... **V7** *7A+*
The bulge just right of the crack.

12 Help the Aged ...... **V7** *7A+*
Hang the sloper and somehow use it to gain the break above.

13 Help Right-hand **V8** *7B*
An harder and thinner right-hand variation to *Help the Aged*.

Across to the right is the popular **Wall End Slab**.

14 Virginia Arete **V2** 5c
The left arete on its left-hand side.

15 Wall End Start .... **V0+** 5a
The slab on its left-hand side, with or without the arete. Most slip off at least once.

16 Super Duper Direct Start
.... **V0+** 5a
Centre of the slab. About **V2** 5c if you ignore all the pockets.

17 Wall End Slab Direct Start
.... **V0** 4c
Right-hand side of the slab.
Green Circuit continues on page 135.

Up and right of the main slab is a short, blunt arete.

18 Wall End Grab **V3** *6A*
A little gem up two rounded holds.

On the main edge above the last problem is a wall with a beautiful open groove on its right.

19 The Prince **V6** *7A*
The left-hand line.

20 Bunny Wailer **V5** *6C*
The wall via two small pockets.

21 Mo Tucker **V1** 5b
Just right of the groove.
Red and Orange Circuits continue on page 134.

Wall End Slab

The Prince

Northern Peak · Sheffield Crags · Stanage Area · Burbage Valley · Derwent Edges · The Limestone · Central Grit · Staffordshire · South Peak

Northern Peak

Sheffield Crags

Stanage Area

Burbage Valley

Derwent Edges

The Limestone

Central Grit

Staffordshire

South Peak

Crescent Arete

The main area of interest here is the jumble of large boulders below the prominent route *Goliath's Groove*. This is a long-standing bouldering area with many problems which have become classic test pieces over the years. The boulders face generally west-ish and get the afternoon sun. They dry quickly, are seldom green but give little shelter when the weather is bad.

Approach (see map on page 126 and overview on page 132) - Park in the Plantation parking and walk up the main path.

❶ The Storm...... **V8** *7B+*
Rock over from the rail to the top. Easy when you've done it.

❷ Deadline.......... **V7** *7A+*
Continue out right from the start of *The Storm* to finish up the arete. Originally given **V8** *7B+* but a new method has been found however it is very bold - one for snowballing!

❸ Beneath the Breadline **V8** *7B*
The finish of *Breadline* from the ground. Linked into *The Storm* via the prominent pocket is **Baseline, V9** *7C*.

❹ Breadline **V5** *6C*
From the adjacent boulder, lean across to sloping edges and continue up the arete. Safer than it looks. **Highline, V10** *7C*, keeps finger traversing along the edge into the finish of *Big Air*.

The next problem is down by the path on the famous Crescent Arete Boulder.

❺ Ron's Slab .... **V8** *7B+*
The slab left of *Crescent Arete*. It is a bit of a mystery where it actually goes since most repeats end up back on the arete. The direct start is as yet unclimbed.

❻ Crescent Arete.... **V2** *5c*
One of the finest problems around. It always feels precarious no matter how many times you have climbed it. *Photo on page 4.*

❼ Crescent Arete Right-hand
.... **V4** *6B+*
The arete on its right-hand side.

❽ Crescent Slab **V6** *7A*
Wall just right of arete, finishing up the arete.

❾ Mono Slab .... **V7** *7A+*
The superb thin pebbly slab, with a mono.

❿ Crescent Groovelet. **V2** *5c*
An excellent little groove which is harder than it looks. It is easier but not as good to the right.
Red Circuit continues on page 136.

⓫ The Snapper **V4** *6B*
Steep side-wall from a lowish start. No block out left allowed.

⓬ Snapper Arete .... **V5** *6C+*
The desperate rounded arete from a low start.

⓭ Pocket Wall. **V4** *6B*
The short wall using some rounded pockets. Nasty!

⓮ Ramp Thing **V2** *5c*
Use the sloping ledge to gain the top.

From mid morning | 10 min | Windy

Careless Torque

15 Nameless Block Mantel . . . . . [ ] **V0+** *5a*
Mantel onto the block.

16 Issue 53 . . . . ⑨ 🏠 ▯ [ ] **V1** *5b*
The steep left-hand side of the arete. Easy to skid off.

17 Back Cover . . . . ⑧ 🏠 [ ] **VB** *4a*
The right-hand side of the arete is easy.

18 Shady Slab . . . . . . ⑩ ⑨ 🏠 [ ] **V0-** *4b*
The middle of the slab stepping off the block. Harder off the
inner block, and about **V4** *6B* off the grass.

19 Shady Slab Right Arete . . . ⑩ [ ] **VB** *4a*
The right-hand arete of the short wall.

20 Big Air . . . . . . 🏠 🧗 💚 🖐 [ ] **V5** *6C*
Jump to the pocket, then make a tricky move up. Lots of pads
needed to make this a boulder problem. *Photo on page 109.*

21 Coming Up For Air . 🏠 🖐 💚 [ ] **V11** *8A*
The direct start to *Big Air*.

22 Scoops Groove . . . ⑪ ⑪ 🏠 [ ] **V0+** *5a*
The slim groove, keep traversing right at this grade.

23 Scoops Slab . . . . . ⑫ ⑫ 🏠 [ ] **V0+** *5a*
Start from the grass and use only the pocket. **V5** *6C* from sitting.

24 Scoops Arete . . . . . ⑬ ⑬ 🏠 [ ] **V0** *4c*
The arete has a tricky start. *Green Circuit continues on page 138.*

25 Grooved Arete . . . . . . ⑭ 🏠 [ ] **V1** *5b*
Groove and arete in the gully side-wall. Mantel the ledge.
The Orange Circuit continues on page 141.

Northern Peak · Sheffield Crags · Stanage Area · Burbage Valley · Derwent Edges · The Limestone · Central Grit · Staffordshire · South Peak

The Grand Hotel

The next problems are on the front of the main block which overlooks the bridleway, formerly known as the 'Grand Hotel' because of the bivvy site underneath it. This is really still part of the Crescent Arete area but it gets its own page because of the quality of the problems. **Approach (see map on page 126 and overview on page 132)** - Park in the Plantation parking and walk up the main path.

1 Careless Youth . . 2 **V10** *7C+*
The wall left of *Careless Torque* was a long-standing project. A very poor landing.

From mid morning | 10 min | Windy

2 Careless Torque. . 3 **V11** *8A*
The biggest arete of the block has a near impossible start, coming in from the right. *Photo opposite.*

3 Not to be Taken Away
. . . . 7 3 **V5** *6C*
A classic line with a hard start, especially for shorties, and a quick finish. *Photo on cover and page 25.*

4 To Be or Not to Be . . . 2 **V7** *7A+*
A direct finish/leap to *Not to be Taken Away*. Dyno to the top of the block from two little crimps!

5 Broken . . . . 8 2 **V4** *6B+*
A fine little problem up the thin flakes on the right-hand side.
Red Circuit continues on page 140.

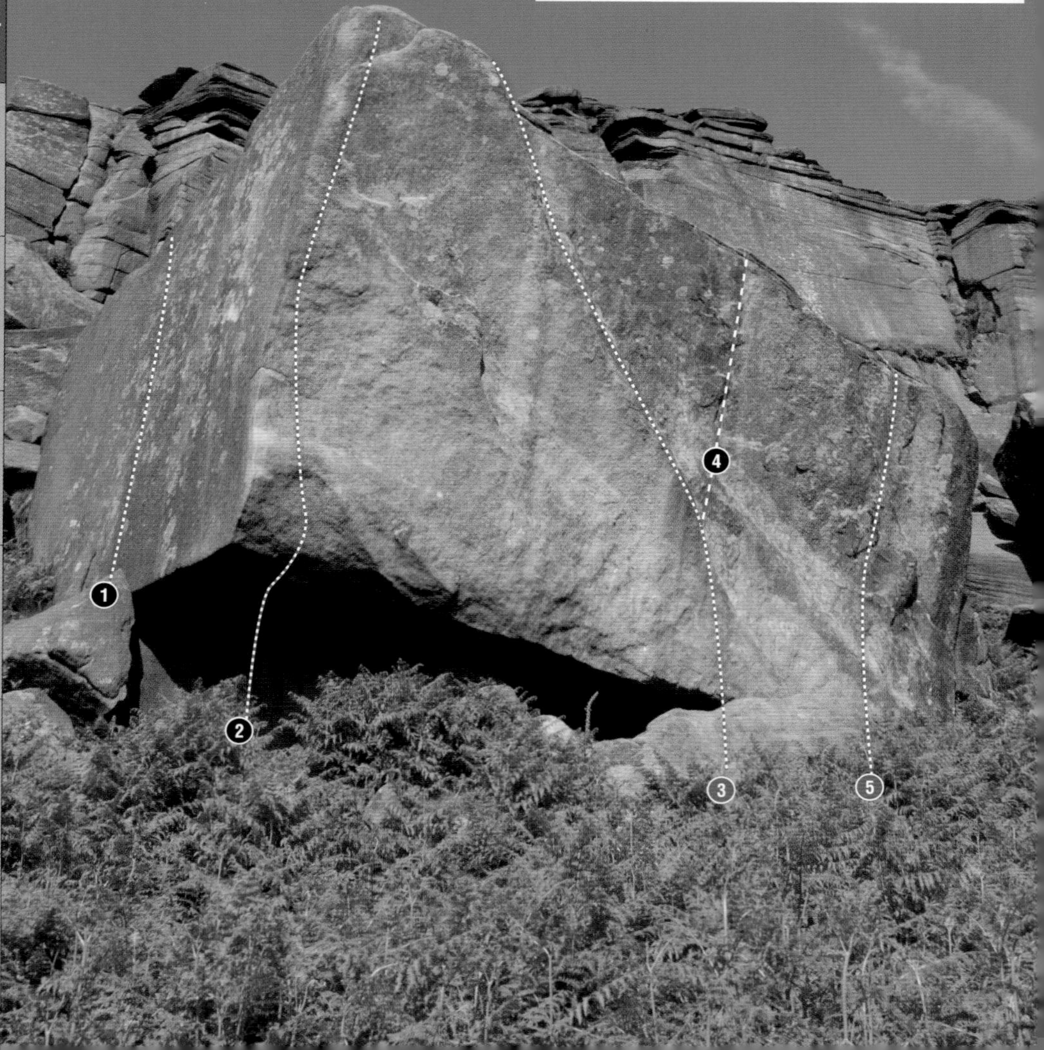

Northern Peak

Sheffield Crags

Stanage Area

Burbage Valley

Derwent Edges

The Limestone

Central Grit

Staffordshire

South Peak

Ryan Pasquill committed to *Careless Torque* (**V11** *8A*) - *opposite* -
on the Grand Hotel Boulder at the Plantation. Photo: Adam Long.

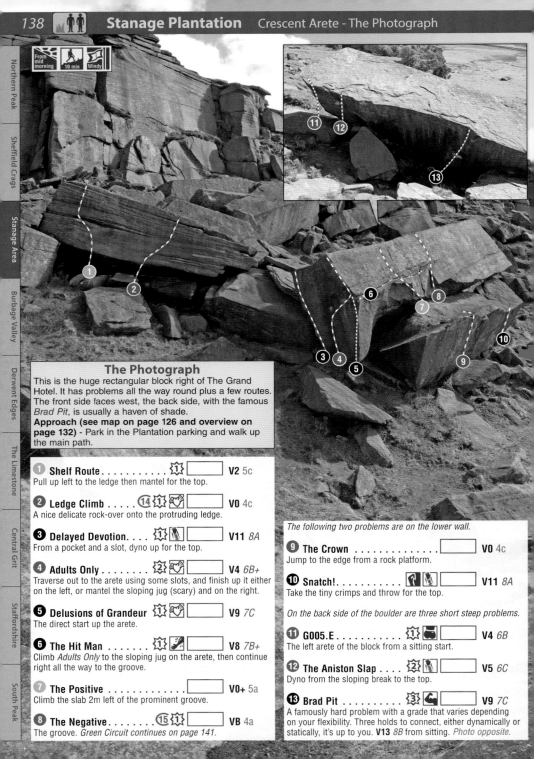

Northern Peak

Sheffield Crags

Stanage Area

Burbage Valley

Derwent Edges

The Limestone

Central Grit

Staffordshire

South Peak

The Photograph

This is the huge rectangular block right of The Grand Hotel. It has problems all the way round plus a few routes. The front side faces west, the back side, with the famous *Brad Pit*, is usually a haven of shade.

Approach (see map on page 126 and overview on page 132) - Park in the Plantation parking and walk up the main path.

❶ Shelf Route **V2** *5c*
Pull up left to the ledge then mantel for the top.

❷ Ledge Climb . . . . . **VO** *4c*
A nice delicate rock-over onto the protruding ledge.

❸ Delayed Devotion **V11** *8A*
From a pocket and a slot, dyno up for the top.

❹ Adults Only . . . . **V4** *6B+*
Traverse out to the arete using some slots, and finish up it either on the left, or mantel the sloping jug (scary) and on the right.

❺ Delusions of Grandeur **V9** *7C*
The direct start up the arete.

❻ The Hit Man . . . . **V8** *7B+*
Climb *Adults Only* to the sloping jug on the arete, then continue right all the way to the groove.

❼ The Positive . . . . **VO+** *5a*
Climb the slab 2m left of the prominent groove.

❽ The Negative . . . . **VB** *4a*
The groove. *Green Circuit continues on page 141.*

The following two problems are on the lower wall.

❾ The Crown . . . . **VO** *4c*
Jump to the edge from a rock platform.

❿ Snatch! **V11** *8A*
Take the tiny crimps and throw for the top.

On the back side of the boulder are three short steep problems.

⓫ G005.E **V4** *6B*
The left arete of the block from a sitting start.

⓬ The Aniston Slap **V5** *6C*
Dyno from the sloping break to the top.

⓭ Brad Pit **V9** *7C*
A famously hard problem with a grade that varies depending on your flexibility. Three holds to connect, either dynamically or statically, it's up to you. **V13** *8B* from sitting. *Photo opposite.*

Adam Lincoln making an evening attempt on *Brad Pit* (**V9** *7C*) - *opposite* - on the back of the Photograph Boulder at the Plantation. Photo: Adam Long

Northern Peak

Sheffield Crags

Stanage Area

Burbage Valley

Derwent Edges

The Limestone

Central Grit

Staffordshire

South Peak

Northern Peak

Sheffield Crags

Stanage Area

Burbage Valley

Derwent Edges

The Limestone

Central Grit

Staffordshire

South Peak

Satin Area

Up on the crag are a few areas worth seeking out. The Spur Boulder offers powerful problems turning the lip of a sharply undercut boulder. Further right are some ultra-thin slabs, then right again are some short aretes and walls.

Approach (see map on page 126 and overview on page 132) - Park in the Plantation parking and walk up the main path.

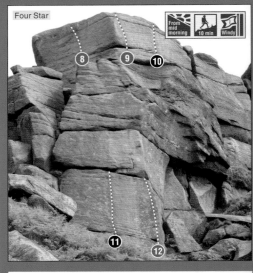

Four Star

1 Spur Traverse . . . V5 *6C+*
Traverse the roof from left to right and finish up a rib just before the gully.

2 Left Spur. V6 *7A*
The left-hand side of the roof sees few ascents.

3 Right Spur . . . . . V5 *6C+*
The centre of the roof via a square-cut edge.

4 Pressure Drop . . . . . . V7 *7A+*
The ultra-thin slab. Traverse off along the break.

5 Satin Start V6 *7A*
The thin elegant slab, traverse off along the break.

On the next wall are two more problems.

6 Pullover V1 *5b*
Unobvious move over a low roof and up the rib. Even more unobvious and awkward if you start too far right.

7 Woolly Pully . . . . V3 *6A+*
Another awkward problem just right.

There are three highball problems on a wall at the top of the edge, approached from the left.

8 A Day Without Pay . . . V5 *6C+*
Needs plenty of pads to make this micro-route a problem.

9 Louis the Loon. . . . . . V3 *6A+*
The arete on its right-hand side.

10 Sky Bouldering V6 *7A*
The faint rib just right. Sturdy spotters essential.

Back down at the base of the crag is the arete of **Four Star***.*

11 Force Tart . . . . V7 *7A+*
The very thin slab left of *Four Star*.

12 Four Star V5 *6C*
A direct start to the route *Fina*. Traverse off left at the break.

Satin

Spur Boulder

13 The Lone Arete . . . . . . 15 3 [____] **V2** 5c
The arete. Only **V0** 4c on the left but not as good.

14 The Lone Slab . . . . 11 16 2 [____] **V2** 6a
The slab over the bulge. **VB** with a run up!

15 Lone Scoop . . . . . . 12 17 3 [____] **V2** 5c
The faint groove on the right-hand side of the slab is a little easier than *The Lone Slab*. No arete.

16 Scoop Arete . . . . 18 1 [____] **V1** 5b
The arete on its left.

17 Steep Side . . . 19 16 1 📖 [____] **V0+** 5a
The ledgy wall with a jump/reach and mantel to finish.
Orange Circuit continues on page 144.

18 The Lone Ranger . . . . 13 1 [____] **V3** 6A+
Incredibly awkward little groove.
Red Circuit continues on page 144.

19 Tonto . . . . [____] **V0+** 5a
Tricky mantel over the nose. **V3** *6A+* from sitting.

20 Lone Boulder . . . . 17 1 [____] **V0** 4c
The centre of the wall. *Green Circuit continues on page 144.*

The Lone Boulder

Way below in the bracken is a beautiful lonely boulder with a fine slab which is well worth seeking out. A great place to practice your no-holds gritstone friction moves.

Sidebar tabs: Northern Peak · Sheffield Crags · Stanage Area · Burbage Valley · Derwent Edges · The Limestone · Central Grit · Staffordshire · South Peak

Adam Long on *Pebbledash Arete* (**V5** *6C+*) - *page 153* - on
the Pebble Boulder in the Plantation. Photo: Adam Long

Northern Peak

Sheffield Crags

Stanage Area

Burbage Valley

Derwent Edges

The Limestone

Central Grit

Staffordshire

South Peak

The Pebble Area
Probably the most popular area in the book with three
very important boulders - the Green Block, with its
testing traverse; the Pebble, with its many superb
problems; and The Business Boulder, for the real hard
core. The problems stay clean because of their popularity
and they receive plenty of sunshine. The Green Block is
under a big tree, hence its name, but the rest are open
and dry quickly after rain. There is little shelter here.

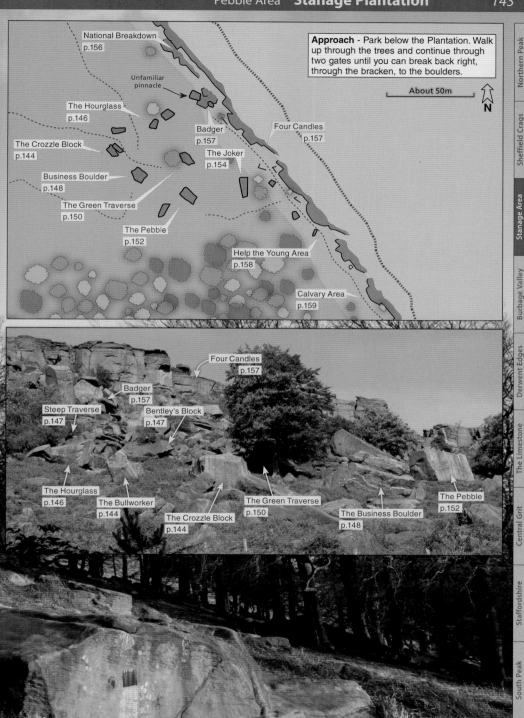

National Breakdown
p.156

Unfamiliar pinnacle

The Hourglass
p.146

Badger
p.157

Four Candles
p.157

The Crozzle Block
p.144

The Joker
p.154

Business Boulder
p.148

The Green Traverse
p.150

The Pebble
p.152

Help the Young Area
p.158

Calvary Area
p.159

Approach - Park below the Plantation. Walk up through the trees and continue through two gates until you can break back right, through the bracken, to the boulders.

About 50m

N

Four Candles
p.157

Badger
p.157

Bentley's Block
p.147

Steep Traverse
p.147

The Hourglass
p.146

The Bullworker
p.144

The Crozzle Block
p.144

The Green Traverse
p.150

The Business Boulder
p.148

The Pebble
p.152

Northern Peak | Sheffield Crags | Stanage Area | Burbage Valley | Derwent Edges | The Limestone | Central Grit | Staffordshire | South Peak

The Hourglass
p.146

Crozzle Block

Bullworker

Bullworker and the Crozzle Block

These two small boulders are the first reached on the approach. They both have good landings.

Approach - See map and overview on page 143.

1 Bull Flakes . . . . 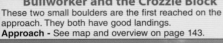 **V4** 6B
Start on some small flakes and make a stiff pull up onto a slab.

2 Bullworker . . . . . .  **V4** 6B
The blunt end of the arete using a side-pull.

3 Bullworker Slab . . . . .  **VB** 4a
Climb the left-hand side of the slab from its lowest point to the very top. Avoid grabbing the top edge too early. With no hands it is a daft but fun **No Bull, V3** 6B.

4 Bullworker Slab Traverse

. . . .  **V0+** 5a
Traverse the slab either way, without using the top.

5 Crozzle Wall . . . . 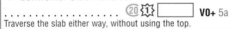 **V3** 6A+
The crozzly wall just right of the groove.

6 Crozzle Arete . . . . . 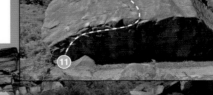 **V4** 6B
The left-hand side of the arete, jump for a sloper. Static is **V6** 7A.

7 Crozzle Arete Right-hand

. . . . **V3** 6A
The right-hand side of the arete is a touch easier.

Crozzle Block

8 **Bristol Stool** **V6** *7A*
The centre of the square face to a tricky top-out.

9 **Crozzle Slab** **V1** 5b
The weathered slab is pleasant. *Photo this page.*
Orange Circuit continues on page 146.

10 **Arete** **V0-** 4b
The juggy arete requires a balancy start.
Green Circuit continues on page 148.

The next problem is on the back of the adjacent boulder.

11 **Low Lip Traverse** . . **V2** 5c
Traverse the low face from left to right and pull over at the end.
Red Circuit continues on page 146.

Northern Peak

Sheffield Crags

Stanage Area

Burbage Valley

Derwent Edges

The Limestone

Central Grit

Staffordshire

South Peak

Claire Aspinall on *Crozzle Slab* (**V1** 5b) - *this page*. Photo: Mike Hutton

Northern Peak

Sheffield Crags

Stanage Area

Burbage Valley

Derwent Edges

The Limestone

Central Grit

Staffordshire

South Peak

The Hourglass

A super little block with several excellent hard problems. It's not high but the ground slopes away quite steeply so good spotting is needed on some problems.

Approach - See map and overview on page 143.

❶ Born Slappy . . . . ▣ ▨ ☐ **V6** *7A*
Crouching start.

❷ The Pendulum . . . . . . ✿ ♡ ☐ **V6** *7A*
The wall just left of the arete.

❸ Glass Hour Left-hand . ✿ ♡ ☐ **V7** *7A+*
The arete on its left-hand side.

❹ Glass Hour . . . . ✿ ♡ ☐ **V6** *7A*
The arete on its right-hand side.

❺ Born Snappy . . . . ✿ ⒈ ▤ ♡ ☐ **V9** *7C*
Straight up the tall front face on friable flakes. More of a route and originally done with an army of spotters.

❻ Hourglass Left . . . . . . ✿ ♡ ☐ **V4** *6B*
The left-hand side of the arete is harder and taller than the right. *Photo on page 24.*

❼ The Hourglass . . . . ⑲ ㉒ ✿ ☐ **V2** *5c*
The arete on its right-hand side, starting with the pocket and the arete.

❽ Slopey Pokey . . . . ⑳ ㉓ ✿ ☐ **V2** *5c*
Great little wall and pockets to the right of the arete.

Steep Traverse and Bentley's Block

The undercut boulder just above the Hourglass has a great little traverse and a few worthwhile other problems. Further right is another low boulder with a powerful mantel and its variation.

Approach - See map and overview on page 143.

9 Steep Traverse . . . . . 🎲 📷 ▭ **V5** *6C*
Start on the slanting ramp and traverse above an awkward landing to the big rounded arete. Pull up this.

10 Popp's Pop . . . . 🎲 ▭ **V4** *6B+*
Straight through the traverse from under the roof.

11 Steep Traverse Arete
. . . . 🎲 🎲 🎲 🎒 ▭ **V2** *5c*
The arete itself from below and left with a sort of sitting start. *Red and Orange Circuits continue on page 148.*

12 Seamless . . . . 🎒 ▭ **V5** *6C*
A neglected problem up the back of the block. Start low and pull past the seam in the wall. Often green.

Bentley's Block

The Steep Traverse

Back down and to the right (looking at the edge) is another undercut boulder with a couple of hard problems.

13 Bentley's Going to Sort You Out
. . . . 🎲 🧗 🎒 ▭ **V8** *7B+*
Start on the good edge, make a move right then rock left onto the slab. It's a hideous thrutch of a lip-turner!

14 Captain Hook. . . . . 🎲 🧗 🎒 ▭ **V8** *7B*
Start as for *Bentley's* then traverse the lip, using the sidepull in the roof, and finishing up the arete.

Crozzle Block
p.144

Steep Traverse

Bentley's Block

Northern Peak / Sheffield Crags / Stanage Area / Burbage Valley / Derwent Edges / The Limestone / Central Grit / Staffordshire / South Peak

Northern Peak

Sheffield Crags

Stanage Area

Burbage Valley

Derwent Edges

The Limestone

Central Grit

Staffordshire

South Peak

The Business Boulder

This block has a concentration of some of the best and hardest problems in the Peak on its steep west face. The other sides though give more amenable problems, including a trio of friendly classics on the uphill side.
Approach - See map and overview on page 143.

1 Black Arete . . ㉕㉕㉕ ▢ **V0+** 5a
The left-hand arete past a small overlap.

2 Black Wall . . . . ㉑㉕ ▢ **VB** 4a
The left line through the overlap.

3 Black Bulge. . . . . . ㉖㉒㉕ ▢ **V0** 4c
Start on the two low holds.

The next problems are around the corner by a dusty low alcove.

4 Nobody's Business . ㉗㉓㉕ ▢ **V0-** 4b
A tricky start. *Green Circuit continues on page 152.*

5 Slot Sitdown . . ㉒㉕ ▢ **V4** 6B
Start low on a jug and dyno up to the thin flake. A nice **V1** 5b if you start standing. *Red Circuit continues on page 152.*

6 Zippy's Traverse . . . . ㉕ ▢ **V8** 7B
From the good hold, traverse right to arete and finish up flakes.

7 Big Business . . . . . . ㉘㉕ ▢ **V1** 5b
Romp up the big flakes.
Orange Circuit continues on page 152.

8 Jerry's Finish . . . . ㉕ ▢ **V5** 6C
Rock over using edges (and avoiding the big jugs). The finish to *Jerry's Traverse*.

9 H - Top . . . . ㉕ ▢ **V8** 7B
Follow the crimps. The low start is **Danny's Problem, V10** 7C+.

10 Jerry's Traverse . . ㉕ ▢ **V10** 7C+
From the middle of the shelf, drop down low and traverse left, then do the big rock-over.

Crozzle Block
p.144

Easy way down, or
very easy way up

11 Rose and the Self-employed Business Man

. . . . **V7** *7A+*

Start in the middle of the shelf, as for *Jerry's Traverse*. From the left end of the shelf move up and follow holds below the top to a drop down done via an obligatory 'Rose' move. (**Rose move** - one hand on a hold above your head and reach through with your other hand turning the top of your body outwards. Named after a route at Buoux in France - *La Rose at le Vampire*).

12 A B Top **V4** *6B*

Starting at the left end of the shelf, spring to the top and finish.

13 Business Launch **V4** *6B*

From a pair of crimps on the middle of the shelf, launch to the lip and mantel. There is a hold on the way, which may or may not help.

14 Ben's Extension . . **V11** *8A*

Start in horizontal break around the right arete. Use a sloping hold to drop down around onto the shelf and continue along *Jerry's Traverse*. Doing this in reverse from the start of *Jerry's Traverse* is **Ben's Reverse V8** *7B*.

There are some awe-inspiring extensions and combinations.

15 Jason's Traverse

. . . . **V11** *8A*

Start along *Zippy's Traverse* but stay low at its end on side-pulls. Reverse *Jerry's Traverse* to the middle of the shelf. Dyno for the top as for *Business Launch* and pull over.

16 Malc's Traverse **V13** *8B*

Link *Ben's Extension*, *Jerry's Traverse* and *Danny's Problem*.

17 Close of Business . . . **V13** *8B*

Start with *Jason's Traverse* but carry on and finish with *Ben's Reverse*.

Victorian Overmantel

Between the Business Boulder and the trees is this short boulder with two demanding problems.

Victorian Overmantel

18 One More Inch . . . . **V7** *7A+*

Start low and take the roof just right of the arete.

19 Victorian Over Mantel. **V10** *7C+*

A typical Dawes problem with no prizes for guessing the manoeuvre required for success. Body shape and flexibility dependent.

Victorian Overmantel ⟶

Northern Peak | Sheffield Crags | Stanage Area | Burbage Valley | Derwent Edges | The Limestone | Central Grit | Staffordshire

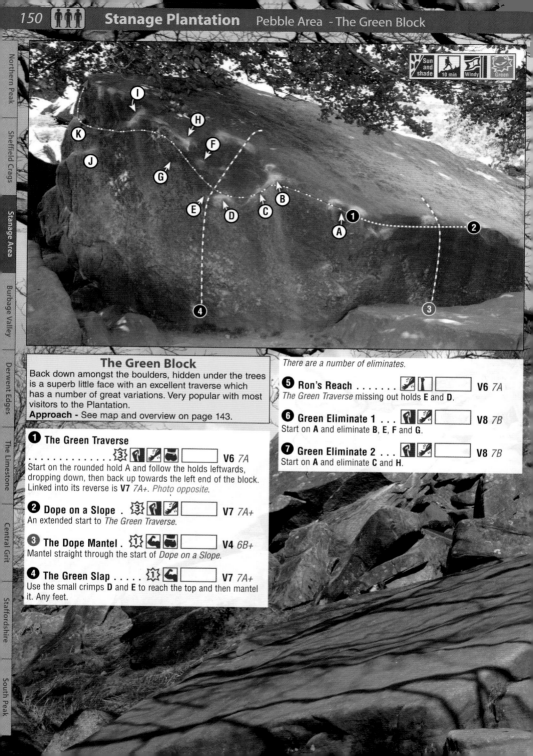

Northern Peak
Sheffield Crags
Stanage Area
Burbage Valley
Derwent Edges
The Limestone
Central Grit
Staffordshire
South Peak

The Green Block

Back down amongst the boulders, hidden under the trees is a superb little face with an excellent traverse which has a number of great variations. Very popular with most visitors to the Plantation.

Approach - See map and overview on page 143.

❶ The Green Traverse

. . . . 🔧🖐️📐🖐️⬜ **V6** 7A

Start on the rounded hold A and follow the holds leftwards, dropping down, then back up towards the left end of the block. Linked into its reverse is **V7** 7A+. *Photo opposite.*

❷ Dope on a Slope . 🔧🖐️🖐️📐⬜ **V7** 7A+

An extended start to *The Green Traverse*.

❸ The Dope Mantel . 🔧🤚🤚⬜ **V4** 6B+

Mantel straight through the start of *Dope on a Slope*.

❹ The Green Slap . . . . . 🔧🤚⬜ **V7** 7A+

Use the small crimps **D** and **E** to reach the top and then mantel it. Any feet.

There are a number of eliminates.

❺ Ron's Reach . . . . 📐🖐️⬜ **V6** 7A

The Green Traverse missing out holds **E** and **D**.

❻ Green Eliminate 1 . . . 🖐️📐⬜ **V8** 7B

Start on **A** and eliminate **B**, **E**, **F** and **G**.

❼ Green Eliminate 2 . . . 🖐️📐⬜ **V8** 7B

Start on **A** and eliminate **C** and **H**.

Northern Peak

Sheffield Crags

Stanage Area

Burbage Valley

Derwent Edges

The Limestone

Central Grit

Staffordshire

South Peak

Siomon Jacklin on *The Green Traverse* (**V6** *7A*) - *opposite* - Stanage Plantation. Photo: Alan James

The Pebble

This big rectangular block is probably the original home of bouldering in the Peak. It is rumoured that J.W.Puttrell ascended the southwest face in 18-something and visitors to Stanage have been climbing on it long before bouldering became popular. All of the faces offer problems.

Approach - See map and overview on page 143.

Southwest Face

1 **Smear Test** . . . . . . V3 *6A+*
The left-hand arete is superb and exposed.

2 **Pebble Face** . . VO *4c*
Follow the distinct line up the centre of the face and flop onto the top. Perform a handstand on the summit before descending down the far side. Can be done without hands.

3 **Pebble Face Direct.** . . V4 *6B*
The thin slab directly above the start of *Pebble Face*.

4 **Pebble Flakes** . . . . VO+ *5a*
The thin wall and flakes to join *Pebble Face*.

5 **Thin Slab** V4 *6B*
The slab just right of *Pebble Flakes*. Avoid touching the flakes.

6 **Ron's Slab II** V8 *7B*
If you keep a bit further right the slab gets very thin.

7 **Pebble Arete Left-hand**
. . . . V3 *6A+*
The fine arete starting up its left-hand side via some tricky moves.

Southeast Face

This face is home to some superb problems. You can create a number of good eliminates by trying some low starts to most of the existing problems.

8 **Pebble Arete** V2 *5c*
One of the finest problems around, up the arete, starting from the right-hand side. The sit-down start is **V6** *7A*.

9 **Andy Brown's Wall** V10 *7C+*
A harder companion to *Deliverance*.

10 **Deliverance.** . . . . V8 *7B+*
Technically ungradable and very height dependent. Start up the crack on the left (or direct) then use the side-pull in the centre of the face and very high foot smears to lunge for the top. The very tall can keep their feet lower and make a bigger but easier dyno.

11 **Delivarate** V2 *5c*
The right-hand arete of the east face gives another good problem. **V3** *6A+* from sitting.

Northeast Face

12 **Pebble Ledges Left** VO *4c*
Just right of the arete.

13 **Pebble Ledges.** . . . . VO *4c*
The easiest line on the block.
The last problem in the Green Circuit.

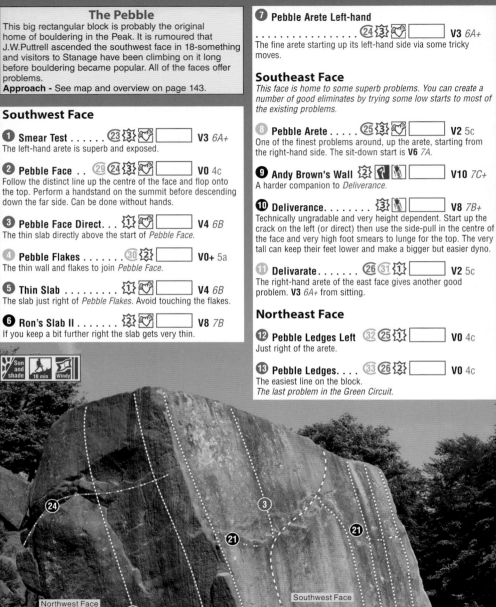

14 Bogside Flakes . . . 34 V1 5b
Central flake line of the wall. A big pull to start then it eases somewhat. Much harder if you can't reach the hold.

15 The Falls 27 V4 6B
Start up the previous problem to a side-pull then stretch up rightwards to the sloping ledge. Mantel the top.
Red Circuit continues on page 157.

16 Boston Mess . . . . V10 7C+
Excruciatingly desperate problem up the upside-down flakes. Start from a low undercut, pull on, then up left to the furthest left undercut. Grab the middle undercut then gain the ledge above. From standing it is **V5** *6C*. From the left-hand undercuts is **V7** *7A+*. Other eliminates exist.

17 Twister V8 7B
From a bum start with your hands on the right-hand side of the 'V' slot, pull up to a thin flake then leftwards to undercut some more flakes. This should bring you within reach of the ledge.

18 Bogside Arete 35 V1 5b
The arete mainly on its right-hand side finishing up a flake.
Orange Circuit continues on page 158.

Northwest Face

19 Pebbledash V4 6B
The groove with a stretch for the top. If you do this the easy way then you will get your left hand on the top first. Some do it the other way around with a scary rock-over.

20 Pebbledash Arete . . . . V5 6C+
Smear test on its left-hand side. A good problem but bad landing. *Photo on page 142.*

The Traverses

All the faces of the block can be traversed with each being a good problem in its own right and the full loop being one of the best. They are all listed here from left to right but can be done in the other direction as well.

21 Southwest Face . . . . . V7 7A+
Relatively straightforward until you need to connect the last bit to the arete.

22 Deliverance Traverse
. . . . V7 7A+
Superb balancy climbing across the *Deliverance* face. Usually very frustrating. It is harder if you are short and can't reach between the two holds.

23 Northeast Face V5 6C
The easiest face is usually climbed from right to left, starting up *Bogside Arete* and hand traverse the sloping shelf.

24 Northwest Face V6 7A
A hard (and slightly scary) last section to the arete. Another one which is often reversed or done in combination with the lower section of the arete on the right.

25 The Full Circuit V8 7B
Plenty of rests but still a testing connection. Most usually done left to right but has been done the other way as well.

Business Boulder
p.148

Business Boulder p.148

Northern Peak

Sheffield Crags

Stanage Area

Burbage Valley

Derwent Edges

The Limestone

Central Grit

Staffordshire

South Peak

Northern Peak
Sheffield Crags
Stanage Area
Burbage Valley
Derwent Edges
The Limestone
Central Grit
Staffordshire
South Peak

The Joker Block

Situated just above The Pebble, the Joker Block is the home of one of the most sought-after test pieces in the Peak. There is plenty of unclimbed rock too although not many holds.

Approach - See map and overview on page 143.

① **Caley Arete** . . . . ☆1 ▢ **V2** 5c
The arete forming the right side of the crack.

② **Honorary Caley** . . . . ☆2 ▢ **V6** 7A
The extremely thin slab without the good side-pull by the arete.

③ **The Joker** . . . . ☆ 🔒🔨🔧◣ ▢ **V11** 8A
A mega hard problem up the front face of the block. Reach the poor holds from the adjacent block and slap away for the top. *Photos on page 11 and opposite.*

④ **The Ace** . . . . . ☆ 🔒🔨🔧◣ ▢ **V13** 8B
Jerry Moffatt's classic desperate made his already hard *Joker*, even harder. Start on the hold on the edge of the cave and use the poor edges to reach the top.

⑤ **Spades** . . . . ◣ ▢ **V6** 7A
The arete from sitting.

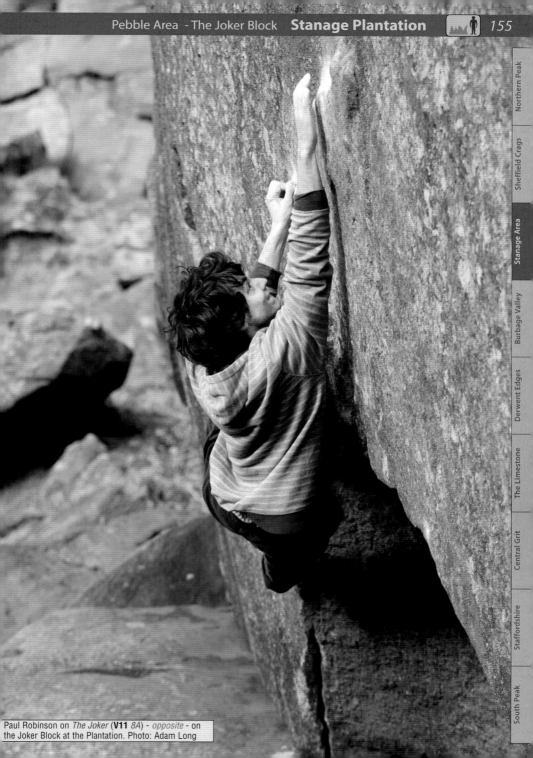

Northern Peak

Sheffield Crags

Stanage Area

Burbage Valley

Derwent Edges

The Limestone

Central Grit

Staffordshire

South Peak

Paul Robinson on *The Joker* (**V11** *8A*) - *opposite* - on the Joker Block at the Plantation. Photo: Adam Long

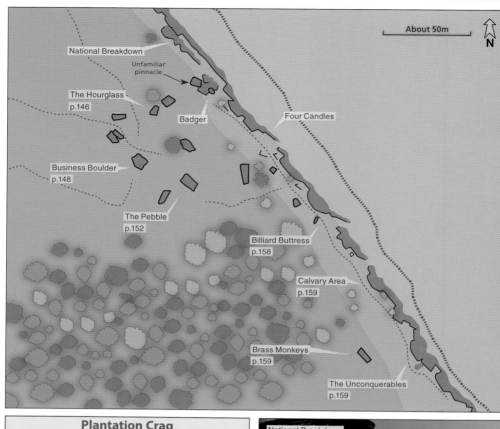

About 50m

N

National Breakdown

Unfamiliar pinnacle

The Hourglass
p.146

Badger

Four Candles

Business Boulder
p.148

The Pebble
p.152

Billiard Buttress
p.158

Calvary Area
p.159

Brass Monkeys
p.159

The Unconquerables
p.159

Plantation Crag

The section of crag above the main Plantation boulderfield has a few decent problems dotted along its length. Classic hard problems like *National Breakdown*, *Badger*, *Back in the Y.M.C.A.*, *Help the Young* and *Nightsalt* will make a visit worthwhile on its own. For those after easier grades, there are some nice Orange Circuit problems.

Approach - Walk up from the Plantation parking then turn right towards the main boulderfield. The tall pinnacle of *Unfamiliar* is visible above which gives a useful marker.

Two isolated hard problems are found high on the edge, next to the route the Hathersage Trip.

❶ **Courtesy of Jonboy...** 🎒 📷 ☐ **V8** *7B+*
The arete left of the crack.

❷ **National Breakdown ..** 🎒 📷 ☐ **V8** *7B+*
The centre of the next wall on the right.

National Breakdown

Four Candles

Help the Young Area →

There is a cluster of problems around the Unfamiliar pinnacle.

❸ Ten Shadows to Midnight
.... **V8** *7B*
In the cave above the *Unfamiliar* pinnacle, reached from its left (looking in). Climb the blunt arete from a sit start, then traverse along the lip until it is possible to top out up the slab.

❹ Savage .... **V3** *6A+*
Gain the arete with a steep pull. Good spotter required.

❺ Badger .... **V5** *6C+*
From sitting, pull up the leaning arete to a jug. Rock right from here to finish. The left-hand finish is **V6** *7A*.

High up on the edge is a short wall with a L-shaped block perched on its top. The landing is sloping.

❻ Unpredictable **V2** *5c*
A highball excursion up the centre of the wall.

❼ Zero Point .... **V0+** *5a*
Climb the juggy wall left of the arete.

❽ Four Candles Arete **V2** *6a*
An eliminate up the arete forming the right side of the crack.

❾ Four Candles **V2** *5c*
The slight rib up the wall is good.

❿ Fork 'andles **V2** *6a*
The ramp and wall above.

A few metres further right is this arete.

⓫ Rubber 'ose ..... **V3** *6A+*
Climb the arete. *This is the last problem on the Red Circuit.*

Badger

Four Candles →

Unfamiliar pinnacle

Steep Traverse Boulder
(p.147) just below

Northern Peak

Sheffield Crags

Stanage Area

Burbage Valley

Derwent Edges

The Limestone

Central Grit

Staffordshire

South Peak

Northern Peak

Sheffield Crags

Stanage Area

Burbage Valley

Derwent Edges

The Limestone

Central Grit

Staffordshire

South Peak

The popular **Billiard Buttress** has a number of problems on and around it. The first three are on a small gritty block below.

12 Through the Keyhole . 36 ☝ ☐ **V1** 5b
The face via the large keyhole pocket.

13 Loyd Left . . . . ☝ ☐ **V2** 5c
The arete on its left requires a mantel.

14 Loyd Grossman . . . . . 37 ☝ ☐ **V0+** 5a
The arete on its right, finishing on the left.

Hippocampus

Billiard Buttress (lower)

15m to the right is another leaning block.

15 Hippocampus . ☝ 🖐 🡇 🡇 ☐ **V9** 7C
The steep face from a sitting start.

16 All 14,000m Peaks. . . . . . ☝ ☐ **V4** 6B
The wall just right.

17 Oh Bubba . . . . ☝ ☐ **V0** 4c
The arete on the other side of the block.

Billiard Buttress (right)

Billiard Buttress

Hippocampus

Calvary Area

Calvary
(E4)

The Unconquerables

②④

②⑥

②⑤

The next problems are at the right-hand end of Billiard Buttress.

⑱ Back in the YMCA . . . 🕸🔺⬜ **V8** *7B+*
Poor pockets lead up the leaning wall.

⑲ Winner Stays On . . . . 🕸⬜ **V8** *7B*
The arete on its left-hand side.

⑳ Help the Young . . . . . 🕸◀⬜ **V7** *7A+*
The leaning arete gives a superb problem. Jump start at this
grade. From standing it is **V8** *7B+*. The sit down is **V10** *7C+*, and
starting sitting without the foot-block is **V11** *8A*.

*A few metres further right is a tall edge with three actual routes
that can be climbed as problems.*

㉑ Between the Two . . . . . ③⑧🕸⬜ **V1** *5b*
Start with your hand in a slot then pull up and left on edges.

㉒ Plug . . . . ⬜ **V5** *6C*
The arete. Continuing directly is a bit of an eliminate.

㉓ Pool Wall . . . . ③⑨🕸⬜ **V0** *4c*
Pull up past a sloping ledge.
The last problem on the Orange Circuit.

*Further along is the tall Calvary Buttress with a couple of
problems.*

㉔ Nightsalt . . . . 🕸🔺⬜ **V7** *7A+*
The superb hard arete.

㉕ Defying Destiny Start . 🕸🔺⬜ **V5** *6C+*
Just right of the start of the route *Calvary* is this rarely climbed
problem start to the route *Defying Destiny*.

㉖ Unconquerable Direct Start
. . . . 🕸⬜ **V3** *6A+*
The polished direct start to the route *Right Unconquerable* -
probably best to stay clear if the route is busy.

Brass Monkeys

②⑦

*The following problem lies on the large wedge-shaped boulder
below the crag, at the edge of the actual plantation.*

㉗ Brass Monkeys . . 🕸◀⬜ **V9** *7C*
Start on a block at the back of the roof. Powerful moves up the
steep northwest side of the block.

Northern Peak

Sheffield Crags

Stanage Area

Burbage Valley

Derwent Edges

The Limestone

Central Grit

Staffordshire

South Peak

Northern Peak

Sheffield Crags

Stanage Area

Burbage Valley

Derwent Edges

The Limestone

Central Grit

Staffordshire

South Peak

	No star	✪	✪✪	✪✪✪
VB to V0 Easy to 4c	-	6	-	-
V0+ to V2 5a to 5c	-	15	6	2
V3 to V5 6A to 6C+	-	-	3	2
V3 to V5 7A upwards	-	1	1	-

The well-named Popular End of Stanage has less to offer boulderers than the Plantation but there are still a few problems that are worth seeking out. Some of them comprise the starts of routes and others are just short routes in themselves. In combination with a routes guidebook (or local knowledge) there is great potential here for some exhausting circuits consisting of hard bouldering and less hard soloing of routes.

Approach   See map on page 126

Park at the main Popular End (Hook's Car) and walk up to the crag. The problems on the left-hand (northern) end can also easily be approached from the Plantation.

Conditions

As with the rest of Stanage, it is southwest-facing, catching plenty of afternoon and evening sun. The exposed position means that it will catch the wind although sometimes it can whistle over the top of the edge and leave the base relatively sheltered. The crag and boulders dry very quickly and aren't green. On still days after June the place can be impossibly midge-ridden.

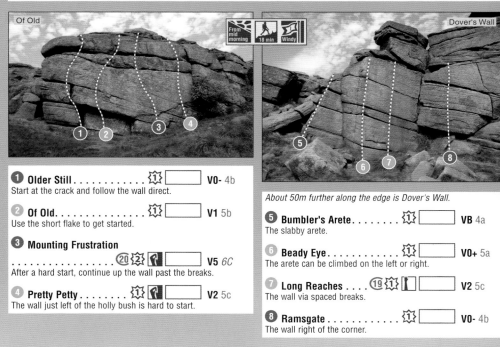

① Older Still . . . . ✪ [ ]   **V0-** 4b
Start at the crack and follow the wall direct.

② Of Old . . . . ✪ [ ]   **V1** 5b
Use the short flake to get started.

③ Mounting Frustration
. . . . 20 ✪✪ 🧗 [ ]   **V5** 6C
After a hard start, continue up the wall past the breaks.

④ Pretty Petty . . . . ✪ 🧗 [ ]   **V2** 5c
The wall just left of the holly bush is hard to start.

About 50m further along the edge is Dover's Wall.

⑤ Bumbler's Arete . . . . ✪ [ ]   **VB** 4a
The slabby arete.

⑥ Beady Eye . . . . ✪ [ ]   **V0+** 5a
The arete can be climbed on the left or right.

⑦ Long Reaches . . . . 19 ✪ [ ][ ]   **V2** 5c
The wall via spaced breaks.

⑧ Ramsgate . . . . ✪ [ ]   **V0-** 4b
The wall right of the corner.

Blue December Sky   Verandah Buttress

Of Old   Dover's Wall

Swings

Pedlar's Slab

Blue December Sky

Pedlar's Slab

About 100m further is B.A.W.'s Crawl and Pedlar's Slab area, the first three problems are just to the left.

⑨ Three Breaks . . . . ⚡ 〔　〕 **V0+** 5a
The slabby rib via three breaks.

⑩ Bouldering Matt . . . . ⚡ 〔　〕 **V0+** 5a
From a start on the right, pull around to climb the arete on its left-hand side.

⑪ Blue December Sky . . . . . ⚡ 〔　〕 **V0** 4c
Starting at the pocket, climb the wall.

⑫ The Golden Path . ⚡🐛◀ 〔　〕 **V9** 7C
The stepped arete.

⑬ Punklet . . . . ⑱⚡🐛 〔　〕 **V3** 6A+
The wall via the thin break. Traverse off at the big break.

⑭ Pedlar's Rib . . . . . ⑰⚡🐛 〔　〕 **V2** 5c
Climb the excellent arete exiting rightwards at the top.

⑮ Pedlar's Arete . . . . ⑯⚡🐛 〔　〕 **V0+** 5a
More of a scoop than an arete.

⑯ Keep Pedalling . . . . . ⚡🐛 〔　〕 **V2** 5c
An eliminate up the rib.

⑰ Pedlar's Slab . . . . . ⑮⚡🐛 〔　〕 **V2** 5c
The well-travelled slab further right.

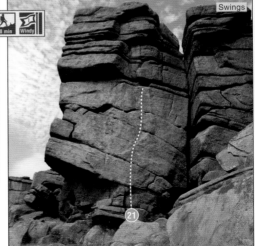

Swings

Verandah Buttress

The next buttress along is the overhang of Guillotine which is the left-hand side of the popular Verandah Buttress.

⑱ Mary Whitehouse . . ⑭⚡🐛 〔　〕 **V2** 6a
Follow the lip of the overhang rightwards then escape right.

⑲ Verandah Buttress Direct
. . . . ⚡🐛 〔　〕 **V7** 7A+
The roof direct.

⑳ Verandah Buttress . . . ⑬⚡ 〔　〕 **V1** 5b
The start of the route to the shelf is an uncomfortable struggle for most. At least **V2** 5c if you do it with style!

Further along, just before the next tall buttress (Martello Buttress) is a short wall with a decent starting problem.

㉑ Swings . . . . ⑫⚡ 〔　〕 **V2** 5c
The start to this route is a worthwhile problem on its own. Traverse off right from the break and descend the corner.
Red Circuit starts on page 162.

Desperation

Cave Arete (HVS)

22

23

The next two problems are found around Robin Hood's Cave Buttress, in the middle of the Popular End. Both are starts to routes.

22 Cave Eliminate Start

. . . . ⑪ 🧗 ⬅ ▢ **V3** *6A+*
Another start to a route that is a brilliant problem - one of the very best of its grade. Finding the hidden slot is the key.
The Red Circuit continues on page 161.

The Red Circuit continues on page 161.

23 Desperation Start . . . . ⑩ 🧗 ▢ **V3** *6A+*
The frustrating starting moves are the crux of this route, end at the break.

▢ The **Stanage Popular Red Circuit**
This relatively easy Red Circuit makes the most of the best problems on the Popular End of Stanage. There are 20 problems in all with only one **V5** *6C*. If you dropped a couple of problems from this then it would make a decent Orange Circuit. It is described from right to left since that is the way most people approach.

Rusty Wall

24 25 26 27 28

Desperation   Rusty Wall   Mantelpiece Buttress   Suzanne

Approach from Hook's Car parking

In the middle of the most popular bit of Stanage Popular is a nice compact wall with a set of face climbs that are usually done as boulder problems or solos.

24 Rugosity Wall . . . . ⑨ ☼ 🔝 [____] **V2** 5c
A hard start and a tricky pull higher up.

25 Rusty Wall . . . . . . ⑧ ☼ 🔝 [____] **V2** 6a
An excellent technical pull on poor holds, or a dead easy bounce for the tall.

26 Rusty Crack . . . . ⑦ ☼ [____] **V2** 5c
Another hard start then easier above.

27 Via Media . . . . ☼ [____] **V0** 4c
A popular VS route with a tricky start.

28 Via Dexter . . . . ⑥ ☼ 👁 [____] **V2** 5c
Direct up the wall with the difficulties getting a little high.

Much further along, at the far right-hand side of the Popular End, are three small buttresses with low roofs.

29 Mental Peace . . . . ☼ [____] **V2** 5c
The triangular roof on its left side.

30 Mantelpiece Buttress Direct
. . . . ① ☼ 🔙 [____] **V1** 5b
The roof at its widest via an inviting hanging crack.

31 Fragile Mantel . . . . . . ☼ ⬜ [____] **V0** 4c
The roof at its right-hand end via a long reach.

A few metres further right, the problems continue.

32 Square Buttress Direct
. . . . ② ☼ 🔙 [____] **V1** 5b
The front of the square buttress via a couple of small roofs.

Mantelpiece Buttress

From mid morning | 8 min | Windy

33 Ding Dong . . . . ③ ☼ 🔙 [____] **V1** 5b
The roof and left arete of the prominent low roof.

34 Suzanne . . . . ④ ☼ 🔙 [____] **V2** 6a
The centre of the roof is well worth seeking out.

35 Finale Direct . . . . . ⑤ ☼ 🔙 [____] **V3** *6A+*
The roof at its right-hand end. Red circuit ends here.

36 Finale . . . . ☼ [____] **V1** 5b
The rib just right.

From mid morning | 8 min | Windy

Suzanne

Side tabs: Northern Peak | Sheffield Crags | Stanage Area | Burbage Valley | Derwent Edges | The Limestone | Central Grit | Staffordshire | South Peak

	No star	☆1☆	☆2☆	☆3☆
VB to V0 Easy to 4c	4	17	1	1
V0+ to V2 5a to 5c	4	28	12	-
V3 to V5 6A to 6C+	-	18	19	-
V3 to V5 7A upwards	-	5	6	3

Stanage Far Right has never really grown up enough to be considered a crag. With the exception of the Cowperstone and Apparent North Buttress, there are few documented routes on the jumble of blocks and boulders dotted around under the trig point at the southern end of Stanage. However, it is the closest bit of Stanage to the road and most people drive past it on their way to the other areas.

The problems are interesting and varied with perhaps the best being in the hard fingery traverse category. *Hamper's Hang* is a classic of its type and the chalk stripe along its lip can usually be clearly seen from the road. There are also some superb low roofs and plenty to explore for the easier grade boulderer.

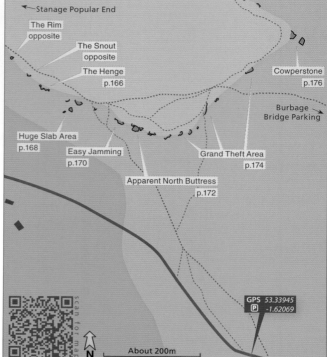

Circuits
This is another really good area for circuits. We have included three here including a very accessible Green Circuit and a very testing Red Circuit.

Approach   Also see map
on page 108
The main areas are best approached from the parking spots beside the road which drops down towards Stanage Popular End. There are usually plenty of hang-gliders and model aircraft fliers already parked there. A large path leads across the moor towards the trig point on top of Apparent North Buttress. It is also possible to approach from Burbage Bridge which is better in the ice cream van department. This is also the best approach for the Cowperstone.

Conditions
The rock at this end of Stanage has a lot in common with the stuff at Higgar Tor - finger-shredding big crystal breaks and coarse-grain slopers abound. The presence of slopers mean that you will want cool conditions for many of the problems including *Hamper's Hang*. The area is more exposed to the wind but is rarely green and dries quickly.

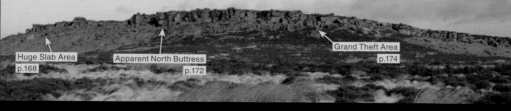

Huge Slab Area
p.168

Apparent North Buttress
p.172

Grand Theft Area
p.174

The Rim Area

The furthest blocks and boulders, heading towards the main edge from the trig point, have potential for many short problems. Some of the better ones are detailed below.

Approach - Walk up the main path to the top of the edge then continue left (looking in) until you can see the low flat roof of *The Rim*.

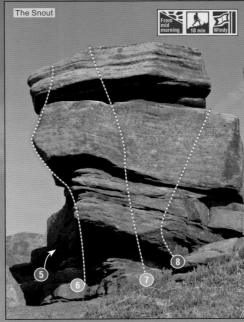

The Snout

1 Rim Flake **V2** 5c
A short problem up the left-side of the block.

2 The Rim . . . . **V3** 6A+
Follow the lip from left to right until it runs out and you can pull to the top.

3 The Rim Extension . **V4** 6B+
Extend *The Rim* by a couple of moves before dynoing for the top from a sloping edge.

4 Rimmer **V4** 6B
From a low start pull up from the hold on the extension. **Rum** is the **V0+** 5a mantel from a standing start.

20m to the right is a block with three stacked layers.

5 Snout Groove . . . . **VB** 4a
The groove is barely worth the effort.

6 The Snout **V2** 5c
The arete is good. Finish direct or scuttle off right at the break.

7 Snout Wall . . . . . . **V0+** 5a
Step up left onto the wall and continue direct.
The Green and Orange Circuits continue on page 166.

8 Eliza **V0** 4c
Start on the left and rock up before pulling back right.

The **Stanage Far Right Orange Circuit**
There is plenty to go at in this 24-problem circuit. No real highballs and mostly good landings. Combine it with the Green Circuit for an excellent 40 problem marathon.

The **Stanage Far Right Green Circuit**
A really nice Green Circuit - 20 problems, all 5a or easier, and mostly not too high.

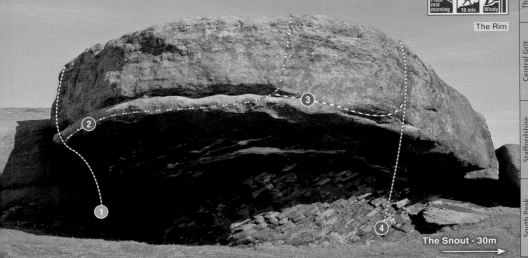

The Rim

The Snout - 30m

Northern Peak

Sheffield Crags

Stanage Area

Burbage Valley

Derwent Edges

The Limestone

Central Grit

Staffordshire

South Peak

The Henge

This section has a good concentration of low-grade boulder problems, plus some excellent harder ones.
Approach (see map on page 164) - Walk up to the edge on the main path. This short set of walls is 50m or so past the huge slab.

1 Sparky Slab. . . . . **VB** 4a
The slab left of the undercut nose.

2 Sparky **V4** 6B
The undercut nose, climbed direct in classic fridge-hugging style.

3 The Henge **V1** 5b
The highball arete via a few increasingly helpful breaks.

4 The Henge/ Hinge Connection
. . . . **V4** 6B+
Starting up *The Henge*, follow the thin break out right (no foot-ledges) to finish up *The Hinge*.

5 The Doorstep. **V5** 6C
The crimpy wall just right of the arete - not high, but has a poor landing.

6 The Hinge **V4** 6B
The middle of the wall from a low start.

7 Staircase Flake **V2** 5c
The flake, from sitting.

8 Al's Attic. **V6** 7A
Starting up *Staircase Flake*, follow the break right, past the arete and up to another break which is followed to an exit up the crack of *Quick Wall*.

9 Front Flake . . . . **V0+** 5a
Layback the crack. Add a grade for a sitting start.

10 Quick Wall . . . . **V3** 6A+
The wall just left of the corner.

11 Quick Wall Traverse . . . **V4** 6B+
Follow the break left from the corner moving up to the higher break to finish. *The Red Circuit continues on page 168.*

12 Tweedle Dee . . . . **VB** 4a
Follow breaks up the left side of the wall.

13 Steps . . . . **VB** 4a
The shallow groove in the middle of the wall.

14 Tweedle Dum . . . . . . **VB** 4a
More break pulling up the wall just right.

Slotted Wall *is to the right and set back.*

15 Hook, Line, and Sinker . . **VB** 4a
The left arete of the left-most block.

16 Right Hook **V0-** 4b
The right arete is easy but the hardest bit is the last move.

17 Slotted Arete **V0** 4c
The left arete of the next block along.
The Green Circuit continues on page 168.

18 Slotted Wall **V1** 5b
The face just right. *The Orange Circuit continues on page 168.*

See opposite

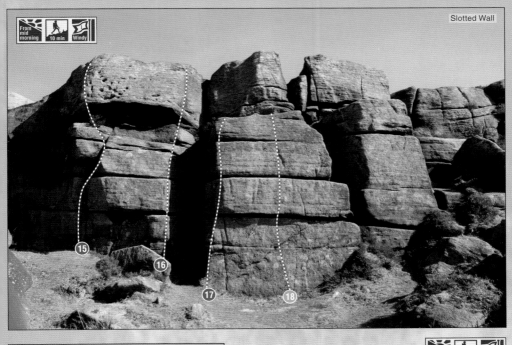

Slotted Wall

The **Stanage Far Right Red Circuit**

This is quite a hard circuit consisting of 22 problems up to **V5** *6C+* with only a few problems easier than **V3** *6A*. Combine with the Orange Circuit for a really good work out.

Slotted Wall

Northern Peak

Sheffield Crags

Stanage Area

Burbage Valley

Derwent Edges

The Limestone

Central Grit

Staffordshire

South Peak

Left of the prominent Gripple Buttress is **Pert Block**.

❶ Pert Block Arete..... ⑨ 🔅 ☐ **V0+** 5a
The left arete of the wall is best on its right-hand side.

❷ Pert Wall .... ⑩ 🔅 ☐ **VB** 4a
The centre of the wall above the mouth. It is about the same grade on either side.

❸ Pert Bloke...... ⑪ 🔅 🎒 ☐ **V0+** 5a
The right arete of the block, from sitting.

Huge Slab Area

The most conspicuous thing in this area is a huge hanging slab perched below the crag. Ths slab itself only has three problems including one hard classic, but the walls and blocks around it offer more of interest.
Approach (see map on page 164) - Head left from the main approach path to the huge slab. The first problems are on the edge behind this slab.

❹ Gripple One... ⑥ ⑫ 🔅 ☐ **V0+** 5a
The left side of the wall has a reachy start.

❺ Gripple Grapple... ④ 🔅 🔧 ☐ **V3** *6A+*
Traverse the thin rounded seams from left to right. It starts easily but has one small ankle-worrying section at the end when the moves get tricky. Only 50cm off the ground but nearly worth a heart symbol!

❻ Gripple Two........ ⑦ 🔅 ☐ **V1** 5b
Climb the wall from a good slot.

❼ Gripple Three ...... 🔅 🐾 ☐ **V1** 5b
Two good slots to start off but a poor break and a bad landing give food for thought.

❽ Gripple Graunch . 🔅 🗲 🎒 🗲 ☐ **V4** *6B*
Beef up the arete from the lowest of low starts. Hard for those over 1.5m tall.

❾ Gripple Nipple...... ⑧ 🔅 ☐ **V1** 5b
A delightful problem. Start at the crack on the left at this grade. Bouncing straight off the slot to the right is only **V0+** 5a.

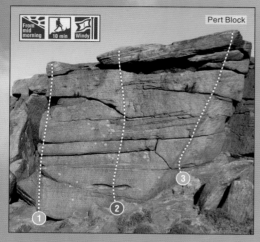

Pert Block

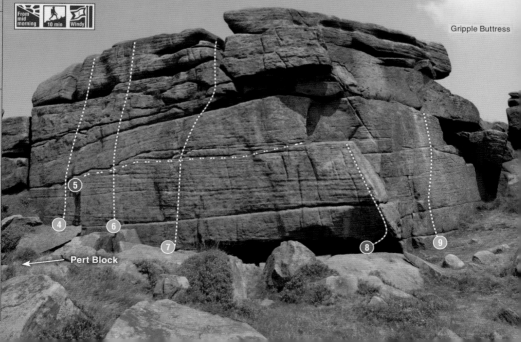

Gripple Buttress

← **Pert Block**

The next problems are on **The Cube**, *a square boulder below the huge slab and the main edge.*

10 Cube Left . . . . ☐ V1 5b
Climb the wall left of the arete. No arete.

11 Cube Arete . . . . ⑨ ✿ ☐ V1 5b
The arete on the lowest end of the block.

12 The Cube Root . . . . . . ⑩ ✿ ☐ V1 5b
The concave wall is a little trickier than its neighbour.

13 Lower Cube Traverse
. . . . ⑤ ✿ 🔒 ◀ ☐ V2 5c
The traverse of the thin break from left to right.

14 Upper Cube Traverse . ⑪ ✿ ☐ V0+ 5a
Follow the ramp-line up rightwards.

15 The Cornflake . . . . . . ✿ 🔒 ☐ V5 6C+
From the break to a shelf. The cornflake is one of the holds.

16 Slots . . . . ⑫ ✿ 📏 ☐ V1 5b
Two slots to the top. Easier for the tall.
The Orange Circuit continues on page 170.

Just above The Cube is the **Huge Slab** *that gives the area its name.*

17 The High Road . . . . . . ⑬ ✿ ☐ V0- 4b
Pull up onto the sculpted flake. Undercut to the arete then climb this to the top on its left-hand side. The direct through the notch in the flake is worth **V0**+ 5a.
Green Circuit continues on page 172.

18 A Case of Mistaken Identity
. . . . ✿ ◀ 🖐 ☐ V8 7B
From a sitting start, traverse the edge of the block and top out.

19 Huge Slab Mantel . . . . ☐ V0+ 5a
Mantel or lunge the last move of the previous problem from standing. Finish up *The High Road* or step off.

The Cube

There is an isolated problem in amongst the jumble of smaller boulders between here and the Easy Jamming Buttress.

20 The Hatchet . . . ⑥ ✿ ◀ 🔒 ☐ V5 6C
Hang the start then power up using a painful crinkle to the top of the small prow. *The Red Circuit continues on page 170.*

Gripple Buttress

Pert Block

Huge Slab

The Hatchet - 30m →

Northern Peak
Sheffield Crags
Stanage Area
Burbage Valley
Derwent Edges
The Limestone
Central Grit
Staffordshire
South Peak

Easy Jamming Buttress
Just a little further left from Apparent North is this clean block with plenty of cracks to go at.
Approach (see map on page 164) - Head left from the main approach path to the wall.

① Easy Walling V2 5c
The wall between the cracks.

② Easy Jamming . . . . . . VB 4a
The crack.

③ Trainer Failure . . . . . . V0+ 5a
The arete.

④ The Real 20 Foot Crack V0 4c
The prominent crack just right of the arete.

⑤ The Shiznit V6 7A
A dynamic problem up the wall just right of the crack.

⑥ Missile Toe . . . . V7 7A+
A one-move problem up the wall to the break.

⑦ Twin Cam V6 7A
Link the breaks with difficulty. Quite high.

⑧ Canary Traverse . . . ⑬ V1 5b
Traverse from right to left. Finish on the very far left end of the left wall. *The Orange Circuit continues on page 172.*

⑨ The Fudgie Budgie V1 5b
The arete on its right-hand side.

⑩ Minah Variation . . . ⑦ V5 6C
The wall to the right. *The Red Circuit continues on page 172.*

Easy Jamming Buttress

Apparent North Buttress
p.172

Northern Peak

Sheffield Crags

Stanage Area

Burbage Valley

Derwent Edges

The Limestone

Central Grit

Staffordshire

South Peak

Audrey Seguy on *Mating Toads* (**V2** 5c) - *page 173* - on the Apparent North Buttress at Stanage Far Right. Photo: Adrian Berry

Northern Peak

Sheffield Crags

Stanage Area

Burbage Valley

Derwent Edges

The Limestone

Central Grit

Staffordshire

South Peak

Apparent North Buttress

This beautifully sculptured buttress is by far the most impressive thing on this section of the crag. It sits below the trig point and is very obvious from the road mainly due to the *Hamper's Hang* chalk line.

Approach (see map on page 164) - The main approach leads directly to this buttress.

1 Left Leg . . . . **VB** 4a
The left side of the small face.

2 Middle Leg . . . . **VB** 4a
The centre of the face.

3 Right Leg . . . . **VB**
The right arete on its left-hand side.

4 Howdy Rowdy . . . . . . **V4** 6B+
Climb the left edge of the wall.

5 Rawhide . . . . **V7** 7A+
The little wall to the left of the arete on tiny pebbles.

6 My Crazy Head **V4** 6B
The superb little arete on the left-hand side of the gully is easier than first appearances suggest. It's **V1** 5b on the right.

7 Gully Flake **V2** 5c
From low slots, continue past a flake.

8 The Shaft **V5** 6C
From sitting at a rounded boss, climb the hanging crack to the break, then traverse the break left to finish as for *Gully Flake*.

9 Shatner's Bassoon **V6** 7A
Starting in the back of the niche, reach out to the rounded boss on *The Shaft* and cut loose. Controlling the swing is the crux. Finishing as for *The Shaft* is worth **V7** 7A+.

10 Hamper's Hang . . . . . **V7** 7A+
The classic problem at this end of the crag. A superb traverse along the juggy break and then the sloping ledge. Start at the back of the cave and connect with *North* or *Round the Horn* for the full work out.

11 Chinless Wonder **V5** 6C
The hanging arete starting from the lip.

12 Skinless Wonder . **V7** 7A+
Start up the right edge of the cave to a break - this is **V3** 6A+. Continue up the blank wall above to the top break - this is close to soloing a very hard route. Slink off right or jump onto your pile of mats.

13 Stanage Without Oxygen
. . . . **V7** 7A+
With plenty of mats this route almost becomes a boulder problem. With a snow drift it is a boulder problem.

14 Hamper's Direct. . **V6** 7A
Pull through the roof to slopers on the lip. Finish with a mantel.

15 North **V1** 5b
Follow the rising crack-line from the end of *Hamper's Hang* across to the block in the gully.

16 Round the Horn . . . **V4** 6B
The lower break is okay until you try to turn the corner. Add a bit of spice by finishing up the next problem.

From mid morning | 6 min | Windy

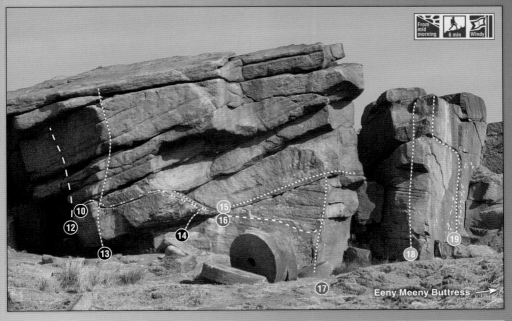

Eeny Meeny Buttress →

⓱ Magnetic North Start . ⑪ ⟨⟩ [____] **V3** *6A*
Another deceptively awkward problem up the arete. Finish right.

⓲ Mating Toads . . . . ⑫ ⑮ ⟨⟩ [____] **V2** *5c*
A typical Stanage HVS solo up the clean rib right of the gully.
Excellent but hard if you don't use the right-hand arete.
Photo on page 171.

⓳ Massacre . . . . ⑬ ⟨⟩ [____] **V2** *5c*
The quarried side-wall on its right-hand side, traversing along
the break to finish, or finish directly with less flutter at **V2** *5c*.
Photo on page 171. The Red Circuit continues on page 174.

*A little further right is a shorter **Eeny Meeny Buttress** with some
easier problems.*

⓴ Mo' . . . . [____] **V0-** *4b*
The crack has a slightly awkward finish.

㉑ Fo' . . . . ⑯ ⟨⟩ [____] **V2** *5c*
The wall just right of the crack.
The Orange Circuit continues on page 174.

㉒ Ho' . . . . ⑰ ⟨⟩ [____] **VB** *4a*
On the wall up and right, climb left of the wide crack.

㉓ Eeny . . . . ⑱ ⟨⟩ [____] **VB** *4a*
The left side of the slab right of the wide crack.

㉔ Meeny . . . . ⑲ ⟨⟩ [____] **V0-** *4b*
The middle of the slab.

㉕ Miny . . . . ⑳ ⟨⟩ [____] **V0-** *4b*
The right side of the slab has a long reach at the top which is
easier on the right. *The last problem in the Green Circuit.*

Eeny Meeny Buttress

Side tabs: Northern Peak | Sheffield Crags | Stanage Area | Burbage Valley | Derwent Edges | The Limestone | Central Grit | Staffordshire | South Peak

Grand Theft Area

The long section of edge facing southeast and dropping gently down towards the Cowperstone is a complex area of many blocks and buttresses. The selection here is probably the best since the list was drawn up by following the chalk of the many visitors who had unearthed more gems to add to the original list.

Approach (see map on page 164) - Head rightwards from the Apparent North Buttress or alternatively you can approach from Burbage Bridge.

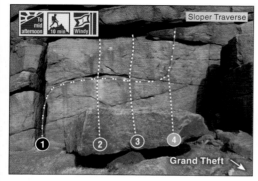

❶ Sloper Traverse . . 🔲🔲🔲 **V6** *7A*
A wicked traverse of the lower break.

❷ Slope John A. . . . . . . 🔲🔲 **V5** *6C*
Follow the big slopers to the break. Conditions vital.

❸ Slope John B. . . . . 🔲🔲🔲 **V4** *6B*
From a sitting start, climb the wall just right.

❹ Slopers Crimp Problem 🔲🔲 **V2** *5c*
Start low in the traverse break and pull up on very small edges to the main break.

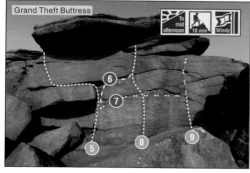

Grand Theft Buttress *has a large flat pancake block on top of it shading a similar small wall with horizontal breaks.*

❺ Petty Larceny . . . . . . 🔲🔲 **V2** *5c*
A problem which pretends to be a route. The bulge above the leaning block is surmounted by way of an unlikely finger-tip mantel. Slide off left to finish.

❻ Tea Leaf . . . . 🔲🔲 **V4** *6B*
Traverse the higher of two breaks.

❼ Almost a Hold . 🔲🔲🔲🔲 **V5** *6C+*
Another desperate thin traverse along the lower break with a stopper move. Harder from right to left.

❽ Grand Theft Start . . 🔲🔲🔲 **V2** *5c*
A route which pretends to be a problem. Climb the centre of the wall to the roof. For the heart symbol you need to pull over the roof. Cracking stuff at HVS 5c!

❾ Zorro . . . . 🔲🔲 **V1** *5b*
The breaks at the right-hand end of the wall to an exit right.

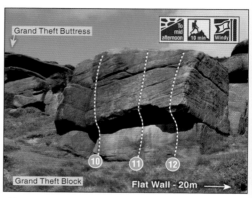

10m to the right of the Grand Theft Buttress is the **Grand Theft Block** *with these three problems.*

❿ Block Party . . . . 🔲🔲 **V1** *5b*
The left arete from sitting.

⓫ Block Wall . . . . . . 🔲🔲🔲 **V2** *5c*
Pull over the centre of the little roof and move up left. No touching the right arete. If you are small enough you can add a start traverse along the lip from the left-hand side.

⓬ Block Arete . . . . . . 🔲🔲🔲 **V2** *5c*
The right arete on its left or right-hand side.

About 20m further to the right is **Flat Wall**.

⓭ Little Left Wall . . . . . 🔲🔲 **V3** *6A+*
The left-hand side of the buttress from a good low hold via some less good ones. Bridging right is allowed at this grade.

⓮ Flat Groove . . . . . . 🔲🔲🔲 **V2** *6a*
The groove, starting as for *Little Left Wall*.

⓯ Get the Horn . . . . . 🔲🔲🔲 **V2** *5c*
Dyno from the flake to the horn.

⓰ Flat Wall Traverse . 🔲🔲🔲 **V3** *6A+*
Traverse the break from right to left, finishing up the arete.

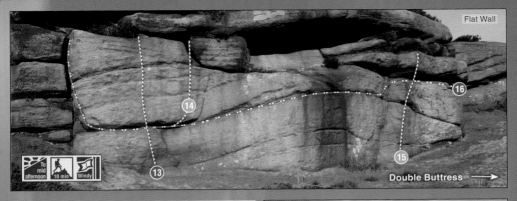

Flat Wall

⑭

⑯

⑮

⑬

Double Buttress ➝

A few metres to the right are a couple of undercut buttresses with a few problems - this is collectively **Double Buttress**.

⑰ Three Tiered Cake . . . . ㉓ ⚄ [   ] **V1** *5b*
Climb the wall past a scooped hold. Great fun.
The Orange Circuit continues on page 177.

⑱ Cave Route . . . . ⚄ 🔲 [   ] **V5** *6C*
From sitting below the roof, turn the lip then up the wall.

⑲ Crack Cave . . . . ⚄ 🔲 [   ] **V4** *6B*
The roof crack.

Another 50m further along, past the main path, is the undercut **Long Wall** *with a prominent traverse line.*

⑳ Fig Roll . . . . ⚄ 🖐 [   ] **V2** *6a*
The left-hand side of the buttress from a good low hold via some less good ones. Bridging right is allowed at this grade.

㉑ Double Flake . . . . [   ] **V0-** *4b*
The prominent flake.

Double Buttress

⑰

⑱

⑲

Long Wall - 50m ➝

㉒ Crimpy Roof . . ⑱ ⚄ 🖐 🔲 [   ] **V4** *6B*
Come direct out of the cave via some crinkly crimps on the lip.
The Red Circuit continues on page 176.

㉓ The Tea Break . . . . . . ⚄ 🖉 [   ] **V4** *6B*
Traverse the high break from right to left.

㉔ The Medicine Ball . . . . . . ⚄ [   ] **V1** *5b*
The arete at the right end of the wall.

Long Wall

⑳

㉑

㉒

㉓

㉔

Northern Peak | Sheffield Crags | Stanage Area | Burbage Valley | Derwent Edges | The Limestone | Central Grit | Staffordshire | South Peak

The Cowperstone

You can't really miss the Cowperstone, after all its been on the cover of the Stanage guide for years. Just in case you missed it though, it is the huge leaning block striated with rounded breaks which can be seen from Burbage Bridge. The climbing here lies somewhere between bouldering and route climbing. Most of the routes are in fact extended boulder problems with scary sloping top-outs but the landings are at least mostly good. There is also a famous low-level traverse which is only scary to look at.

Approach (see map on page 164) - If you only want to climb on the Cowperstone then it is best to approach it from Burbage Bridge along the big path. Otherwise you can reach it via the crag-top path from the other areas at this end of the crag.

❶ Zippattrocity . **V8** *7B+*
A rounded traverse with a capital ROUNDED. Grind your way along the lowest break from left to right and up the other side to the separate boulders. A tad pumpy. Starting at *Breakdance Start* it is **V4** *6B+*.

❷ Little Thug . . . . **V3** *6A+*
Just try to touch the gorgeous flutings on *Snug as Thug on a Jug*. Then jump off.

❸ Breakdance Start . . . . **V3** *6A+*
Start with your right hand in the lower of the two pockets and power up the arete using a very painful jam. Finish as high as you dare.

❹ Breakdance High Start . . . **V2** *5c*
Start with your right hand in the higher pocket. Also worthwhile.

❺ Leroy Slips Disc **V8** *7B*
The wall just right using an undercut and not much else.

❻ Headspin **V4** *6B*
The right-hand side of the wall. The heart flutter is for if you finish the problem over the last bulge. Slide off right to escape. Both finishes are the crux of the problem.

Chippy Buttress

Behind the Cowper Stone is **Chippy Buttress**.

7 Pudding . . . . ☐ **V2** 5c
A tiny problem up the short wall, 4m left of the arete, to a crack.

8 Salt and Vinegar . . . . ☐ **VB** 4a
The flared crack.

9 Chips . . . . ㉑ ㉔ ☐ **V2** 5c
The left-hand side of the arete.
The last problem in the Orange Circuit.

10 Peas . . . . ㉑ ☐ **V5** 6C
Mantel the ledge using everything you can get your hands on.
The full route is E4 5c and traverses in above the mantel.

11 Battered Sausage . . ㉒ ☐ **V5** 6C
Start at *Pudding* and follow the thin break up rightwards. Drop down the arete then make a long move rightwards under the bulge. Can be done the other way around.
The last problem in the Red Circuit.

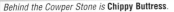

Chippy Buttress

The Back
There are a couple more problems on a bit of Stanage most people didn't know existed.
Approach (see map on page 164) - Keep walking past Chippy Buttress for about 60m or so to find a leaning slab with a roof crack. This is *Savage Me Softly*; *Fly Frisching* is a little further on.

12 Savage Me Softly . . ☐ **V5** 6C+
A typical wideboyz offering up the flared roof crack.

13 Fly Frisching . . . . ☐ **V5** 6C
Another low roof climb from a sitting start.

Northern Peak

Sheffield Crags

Stanage Area

Burbage Valley

Derwent Edges

The Limestone

Central Grit

Staffordshire

South Peak

Northern Peak

Sheffield Crags

Stanage Area

Burbage Valley

Derwent Edges

The Limestone

Central Grit

Staffordshire

South Peak

Burbage Valley

Northern Peak

Sheffield Crags

Stanage Area

Burbage Valley

Derwent Edges

The Limestone

Central Grit

Staffordshire

South Peak

Sheffield

Stanage Popular
p.160

Stanage Far Right
p.164

Burbage West
p.192

The Ox Stones
p.269

Burbage North
p.200

Hathersage

Burbage South Valley
p.234

Higgar Tor
p.180

Houndkirk Tor
p.270

Hathersage

Burbage South Edge
p.218

Owler Tor
p.262

Sheffield

Mother Cap
p.258

Millstone
p.252

Fox House

A625

A6187

Secret Garden
p.254

B6521

A625

About 1km

N

	No star	✿	✿✿	✿✿✿
VB to V0 Easy to 4c	-	14	2	-
V0+ to V2 5a to 5c	10	12	8	1
V3 to V5 6A to 6C+	4	5	10	-
V3 to V5 7A upwards	-	3	6	3

Northern Peak

Sheffield Crags

Stanage Area

Burbage Valley

Derwent Edges

The Limestone

Central Grit

Staffordshire

South Peak

Duncan Skelton on *The Big Slab* (**V0+** 5a)
- *page 184* - at Higgar Tor. Photo:Duncan Skelton

Although known mostly for its impressive leaning block and steep routes, there is plenty of bouldering on the jumble of blocks that make up the south and east faces of Higgar Tor. It can often seem very busy with walkers but usually, once you drop down from the top path, you will have peace and solitude.

Circuits

Some nice circuits can be had and three have been included - Green, Orange and Red. The landings on all these circuits aren't great so take care and do them with a spotter or two.

Conditions

The leaning block is very exposed and can be a good place to escape summer insects. The east-facing rocks are sheltered from the prevailing westerly winds and get afternoon shade. All the problems are on clean rock which dries quickly after rain.

Approach   Also see map on page 179

Park on the main Sheffield to Hathersage road which passes between Burbage and Stanage. Follow the hordes up the stepped path to the top then nip down left when you arrive at the summit area.

Stanage Far Right
p.164

Burbage West
p.192

Burbage North
p.200

Higgar Tor East

Carl Wark
p.251

Burbage South Valley
p.234

Higgar Tor South

The Sheepfold
p.251

Burbage South Edge
p.218

GPS 53.33656
P -1.61669

About 1km

Sheffield →

N

Hathersage

scan for map

Northern Peak · Sheffield Crags · Stanage Area · Burbage Valley · Derwent Edges · The Limestone · Central Grit · Staffordshire · South Peak

Leaning Block

South

A series of south-facing blocks in a sprawling mass of jumbled boulders. This area has a good grade spread including some good circuits which continue around onto Higgar East.

Approach (see map on page 180) - Walk over the top, or around the western edge of Higgar Tor.

*The first problems are at the base of the **Leaning Block**. The traverse is usually well-chalked on account of its sheltered aspect. The 'up' problems require one to know when to stop.*

❶ Block and Tackle Direct . . [   ] **V8** *7B+*
The left arete, finishing at the good holds.

❷ Leaning Block Traverse [   ] **V8** *7B+*
A pumpy traverse across the base of the block. Said by some to be easier than the route *The Rasp*!

❸ Witness the Gritness . . . . [   ] **V6** *7A*
Climb the wall right of the start of the route *The Rasp*. End at the pockety break.

Harvester

About 100m right (looking in) of the Leaning Block is the small but interesting **Harvester Wall**.

❹ The Harvester . [   ] **V4** *6B*
The striking diagonal crack, finishing through the roof.

❺ Combine Harvester . . [   ] **V5** *6C*
Traverse the break from left to right finishing up *Harvest Arete*.

❻ Pippin Dyno . . . . [   ] **V6** *7A*
Dyno or make a powerful undercut move from break to break.

❼ Harvester Dyno . . . [   ] **V4** *6B+*
Another dyno with good hands but poor feet.

❽ Harvest Arete . . . . [   ] **V2** *5c*
The blunt arete climbed on its left.

❾ Harvest Groove . . . [   ] **V0** *4c*
The crack/flake just right of the arete.

Northern Peak

Sheffield Crags

Stanage Area

Burbage Valley

Derwent Edges

The Limestone

Central Grit

Staffordshire

South Peak

Elephant's Arse

The first problem in this area is on a rounded block above the edge, which is a popular venue for weaselling for children.

⑩ Elephant's Arse . . . ④ ❄ 🔲 **V4** *6B*
The bulging wall just on slopers. It may need a firm brushing to get rid of the 'ball-bearings'. The rest of the problems are found below the edge. *Red Circuit continues on page 184.*

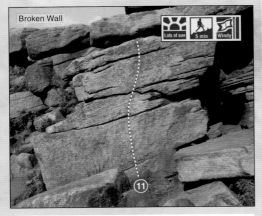

Broken Wall

The next problems are on the blocks below the edge.

⑪ Broken Wall . . . . . ② ③ ❄ 🔲 **V0** *4c*
The short wall via breaks.

Little Slab

10m to the right is **Little Slab**, *and to the right again a short wall with a few cracks.*

⑫ Little Slab . . . . ④ ③ ❄ 🔲 **V0** *4c*
The centre of the slab.
Orange and Green Circuits continue on page 184.

⑬ Pillar Eliminate . . . . 🔲 **V3** *6A+*
The pillar, eliminating all else.

⑭ Slanting Crack . . . . 🔲 **V2** *5c*
The fist-sized crack is ugly.

⑮ Straight Crack . . . . 🔲 **V1** *5b*
From a sitting start, climb the hand-sized crack.

The **Higgar Tor Green Circuit**
A decent circuit with 20 problems but some are quite highball and the landings aren't always great. It can easily be done in reverse.

The **Higgar Tor Orange Circuit**
This is a great circuit with 20 problems which can easily be done in reverse. There are a few slightly highball problems on Higgar East but most are okay.

The **Higgar Tor Red Circuit**
Although it only has 17 problems, this circuit packs a lot in. As with the other circuits, it can easily be done in reverse. There are a few highballs and some bad landings so bring your pad and your mates to spot.

Elephant's Arse

Broken Wall

Little Slab

Like Pommel p.184

Northern Peak

Sheffield Crags

Stanage Area

Burbage Valley

Derwent Edges

The Limestone

Central Grit

Staffordshire

South Peak

Northern Peak

Sheffield Crags

Stanage Area

Burbage Valley

Derwent Edges

The Limestone

Central Grit

Staffordshire

South Peak

Like Pommel

Pocket Wall

Lots of sun | 5 min | Windy

The next section has a wall with a jutting block above its right-hand end.

16 Like Pommel . . . . . ⑥ ♻ 🏴 ☐ **V4** *6B*
The nose direct using a thin ripple on the right.
Red Circuit continues on page 186.

17 Not Like Pommel . . ⑤ ⑥ ♻ ☐ **V2** 5c
The wall just right.

18 Central Wall . . ⑤ ④ ♻ 🏴 ☐ **V0+** 5a
The centre of the wall.

19 The Prow . . . . 🐑 💪 ☐ **V2** 5c
Another jutting prow with an airy finish.

About 20m further, just before a big slab is a short buttress.

20 Broken Arete . . . . ⑤ ♻ ☐ **V0-** 4b
The arete via breaks.

21 Pocket Wall. . . . . ☐ **V0+** 5a
The wall from a flake to a pocket.

The Big Slab *is a clear landmark.*

22 Big Slab Left . . . . ♻ ☐ **V1** 5b
Keeping on the left is more smeary than the middle but you can bale out to the left arete if you get scared.

23 The Big Slab . . . . . ⑦ ♻ 🐑 ☐ **V0+** 5a
Straight up the middle of the slab is superb and delicate. *Photo on page 180.*

24 Big Slab Right . . . . ⑧ ⑥ ♻ ☐ **V0+** 5a
Gain the big flake on the right-hand side.

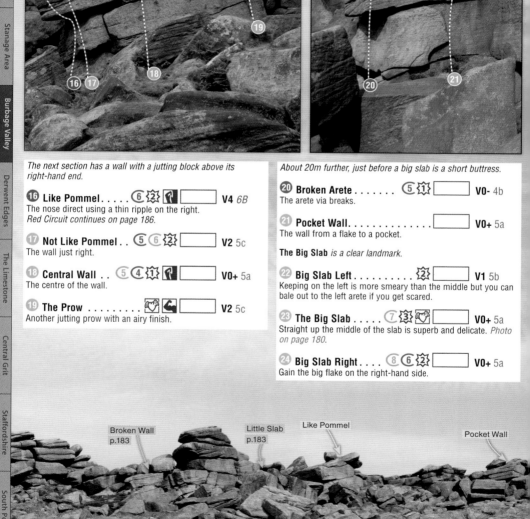

Broken Wall
p.183

Little Slab
p.183

Like Pommel

Pocket Wall

South **Higgar Tor** 185

Northern Peak · Sheffield Crags · Stanage Area · Burbage Valley · Derwent Edges · The Limestone · Central Grit · Staffordshire · South Peak

The Big Slab

25 Small Slab . . . . ⑦ V0+ 5a
The smaller slab is worthwhile.

26 Small Slab Arete . . . . ⑧ V0- 4b
The arete just right. *Green Circuit continues on page 186.*

Just to the right is a low wall which looks like it might have a good traverse - sadly it doesn't.

27 Left Arete V4 6B
The left arete from a sitting start.

28 Parquet Wall . . . . V3 6A+
The wall to the right, starting with your feet on the small shelf at the back and head past a thin seam at the lip.

Above and behind the previous wall is a distinctive jutting prow.

29 High Mantel V2 5c
Pull over and mantel the jutting prow.

The final problems worth attention on Higgar South are on a small leaning slab.

30 Rippled Slab . . . . ⑨ V2 5c
The centre of the slab requires delicate smearing.

31 Rippled Slab Arete . . . ⑩ V1 5b
The right-hand side is even more smeary but the arete for your hands makes it easier. *Orange Circuit continues on page 187.*

High Mantel

Rippled Slab

The Big Slab

High Mantel

Rippled Slab

Fingery Green Wall

Northern Peak

Sheffield Crags

Stanage Area

Burbage Valley

Derwent Edges

The Limestone

Central Grit

Staffordshire

South Peak

East

The east-facing walls on Higgar Tor give the options of climbing in the sun in the morning or avoiding it in the afternoon. The problems are good although some get a little high above bad landings. The rock can get green in the winter when it tends to stay wet after rain.

Approach (see map on page 181) - Park on the main road below Higgar and follow the popular path to the top. The Excreta Buttress is down and left and the rest of the walls are further along.

1 Seventy Degrees . . **V4** *6B*
Above the main edge is a sharp arete. Start low.

2 Fingery Green Wall **V4** *6B*
The small fingery wall. *Red Circuit continues on page 188.*

3 Bum Start Crack **V2** *5c*
The short flake left of the crack from a low start. The wider crack on its own is **V0**+ *5a*.

4 The Trunk **V2** *5c*
The arete has a precarious start and a lonely finish which makes it feel more like a solo route.

5 The Layback Crack . . . . **V0**+ *5a*
A layback crack which is better as a HVS route.

6 Precarious Rib **V0** *4c*
Start the arete on the left and finish precariously on the front.

7 The Grassy Mantel . . . **V0** *4c*
The wall past a grassy ledge. No aretes.

Fingery Green Wall

The Trunk

Green Groove

Tall Arete
p.188

Toppled Block Ar
p.188

The Trunk

Morning · 5 min · Windy

8 Small Blunt Rib . . . . . ⑩ ✩ [ ] **VB** 4a
The little blunt rib is nice.

9 Cracked Rib . . . . . ⑪ ⑪ ✩ [ ] **VO+** 5a
Trend leftwards from the rib, up the wall.
Orange Circuit continues on page 188.

10 Wide Crack . . . . ⑫ ✩ [ ] **VO-** 4b
The layback crack is easier if you jam it.

11 Green Groove . . . . . . ⑬ ✩ [ ] **VB** 4a
The green groove. *Green Circuit continues on page 188.*

Green Groove

Morning · 5 min · Windy

Toppled Block Arete
p.188

Triple Cracks
p.189

Krush Regime
p.190

The Flying Arete
p.190

Excreta Buttress
p.191

Northern Peak

Sheffield Crags

Stanage Area

Burbage Valley

Derwent Edges

The Limestone

Central Grit

Staffordshire

South Peak

Tall Arete

The next buttress has a huge tilted block on its upper half and a **Tall Arete**.

12 Sketchy Pillar . . . . V3 *6A+*
The small pillar is a bit worrying but also an excellent problem.

13 Ledge Wall . . . . . . V0+ 5a
The side-wall with a ledge. Harder if you start low - **V2** 5c.

14 Tall Arete V1 5b
The fine flying arete from some fingery holds at the start.

15 Scratchy Bun Left V5 *6C*
Use the left-hand side of the rounded arete. It is difficult to get off the ground.

16 Scratchy Bun Right. V2 5c
The arete on the block above on its right-hand side. Use the right-hand arete at this grade.

Toppled Block Arete

Across the other side of are a couple more aretes including **Toppled Block Arete**.

17 Sharp Arete . . . . ⑮ ✿ [____] **V0-** 4b
A nice little arete. Award yourself a flutter symbol if you pull on the thin flake.

18 Pillar . . . . ⑯ ✿ [____] **V0-** 4b
The narrow front face of a pillar.

Easy Slab

19 Toppled Block Arete . . . ⑮ ✿ [____] **V0+** 5a
The fine arete on a leaning tower. Use either arete at this grade.

20 Fun Crack . . . . ⑯ ✿ [____] **V0** 4c
A fun little crack in the wall.

21 Central Pillar . . . . ✿ [____] **V0+** 5a
The middle of the pillar.

The next prominent arete has a nice slab on its left and **Triple Cracks** on its right.

22 Easy Slab . . . . ⑰ ⑰ ✿ [____] **V0+** 5a
The slab isn't that easy. No arete at this grade.

23 Triple Cracks Arete . ⑫ ✿ 🔲 [____] **V3** 6A+
The arete from a sitting start. Standing it is a worthwhile **V0+** 5a.

24 Rounded Wall . . . . ⑬ ✿ 🔲 [____] **V4** 6B
The bulging wall from two side-pulls. No right arete allowed.
Red Circuit continues on page 190.

25 Triple Cracks Left . . . . ⑱ ✿ [____] **V0** 4c
The left-hand crack.

26 Triple Cracks Right . . . ⑱ ✿ [____] **V0+** 5a
The right-hand of three thin cracks.
Orange Circuit continues on page 190.

27 Front Wall . . . . ⑲ ✿ [____] **V0** 4c
The front wall of buttress via rounded ledge.
Green Circuit continues on page 190.

Triple Cracks

Northern Peak

Sheffield Crags

Stanage Area

Burbage Valley

Derwent Edges

The Limestone

Central Grit

Staffordshire

South Peak

Northern Peak

Sheffield Crags

Stanage Area

Burbage Valley

Derwent Edges

The Limestone

Central Grit

Staffordshire

South Peak

Krush Regime

The Flying Arete

Morning | 5 min | Windy

This is the first bay that you arrive at on the approach.

28 Left Arete . . . . 20 🎲 🐾 ☐ **V0** 4c
The arete is nice - high but not too worrying.
The final (or first) problem on the Green Circuit.

29 Harry's Hole . . . . . 🎲 🖐️ 🐾 ☐ **V5** 6C+
The wall right of the arete.

30 Krush Regime . 🎲 🫄 🖐️ 🐾 ☐ **V7** 7A+
Sit down in the mucky little hole, pull out on fingery holds and
continue up the wall.

31 Right Arete . . . . 🎲 🐾 ☐ **V1** 5b
The right-hand side of the tall wall is a fine little solo.

32 Bolted Pillar . . . . 19 🎲 ☐ **V1** 5b
The pillar has a tricky start. No block on the right for your feet.

33 Stretching Wall . . . . . 14 🎲 ☐ **V3** 6A+
The short wall.

34 Flying Arete Left . . 15 🎲 ✊ ☐ **V4** 6B
The arete is considerably easier on its left.

35 The Flying Arete . 🎲 ✊ 🖐️ ☐ **V7** 7A+
The much-tried arete on its right-hand side.

36 Flying Wall Left . . . . ☐ **V1** 5b
The wall above a spike block. Flop left onto the ledge.

37 Flying Wall Right . . . . ☐ **V0+** 5a
Up the cracks in the side wall.

Toppled Block Arete
p.188

Triple Cracks
p.189

Krush Regime

The Flying Arete

Excreta Buttress

38 Winnie the... 16 20 ⛄ 🖐 🔲 **V2** 6a
From a sitting start, stretch up leftwards. A dynamic approach is easier for most.
The final (or first) problem on the Orange Circuit.

39 Pooh . . . . ⛄ 🖐 🔲 **V8** 7B
Sitting start, dyno for the top (no aretes).

40 Mick's Problem . . ⛄ 🖐 🔲 **V7** 7A+
From hands in the break use a small hold to gain the top. Without using your heels it is **V9** 7C.

The next block gives the most popular and best boulder problems at Higgar in spite of the unsavoury names.

41 Quintessential Higgarisms ⛄ 🔲 **V6** 7A
The left arete.

42 Sick . . . . 17 ⛄ 🖐 🔲 **V3** 6A
Mantel or dyno the wall. The mantel is easier for the tall.
The final (or first) problem on the Red Circuit.

43 Piss . . . . ⛄ 🔲 **V8** 7B
Gain sloping holds above the roof and do something with them. Heels on the lip jugs to the left are not allowed at this grade.

44 Hemline . . . . ⛄ 🔲 **V7** 7A+
Start as for *Shit*. Span out to the lip and then traverse left along the lip to join *Sick*.

45 Shit . . . . ⛄ 🔲 **V8** 7B+
A classic. Cross the roof below *Piss* from jams in the back, and finish up *Piss*.

46 Jump to Slopers . . . . . . 🖐 🔲 **V3** 6A+
Jump from the ground to slopers.

To the right is a prominent jutting prow.

47 Dirty Higgar . . . . 🔲 **V1** 5b
Traverse the break from left to right and finish up a crack.

Excreta Buttress

Northern Peak
Sheffield Crags
Stanage Area
Burbage Valley
Derwent Edges
The Limestone
Central Grit
Staffordshire
South Peak

Northern Peak

Sheffield Crags

Stanage Area

Burbage Valley

Derwent Edges

The Limestone

Central Grit

Staffordshire

South Peak

	No star	⚜	⚜⚜	⚜⚜⚜
VB to V0 Easy to 4c	1	4	-	-
V0+ to V2 5a to 5c	2	9	6	-
V3 to V5 6A to 6C+	1	7	5	2
V3 to V5 7A upwards	1	4	5	7

Gareth Roberts on *Go West* (**V3** *6A*) - *page 196* - on Burbage West. Photo: Adrian Berry

A good area which has some famous problems and is seldom very busy. There is plenty to go at for everyone including one of the best hard problems around - *West Side Story*. There are also some excellent aretes and fingery walls to keep you busy and three mega-problems for those who think they've done everything.

Circuits
We have only included an Orange Circuit although this could easily be boosted into a Red Circuit by adding one or two of the better Red Spot problems.

Conditions
The edge faces east catching the morning sun. It is reasonably sheltered from the prevailing westerly winds but will offer nothing in the rain. There are wet streaks on a couple of the buttresses.

Approach   Also see map on page 179
The edge of Burbage West is directly opposite the first section of Burbage North. Park at large parking by the bridge, or on the roadside hereabouts, and wander across.

About 1km

GPS 53.34322
P -1.61048

Burbage Bridge
p.198

Sheffield →

Stanage Far Right
p.164

Burbage West

Burbage North
p.200

Burbage South Valley
p.234

Carl Wark
p.251

Higgar Tor
p.180

Hathersage →

The Sheepfold
p.251

Burbage South Edge
p.218

Northern Peak · Sheffield Crags · Stanage Area · Burbage Valley · Derwent Edges · The Limestone · Central Grit · Staffordshire · South Peak

West End Girls

This is the last significant section of edge as you walk away from Burbage Bridge. Although it doesn't have much, it is worth a look if you have some energy left.
Approach - See map on page 193.

1 Left Over Chips . . . . . V0+ 5a
The arete to the left. *The last problem in the Orange Circuit.*

2 Chipless V4 6B
The left-hand side of the arete without the chips. With them it is **V2** 5c.

3 Breakfast V6 7A
From a sitting start, climb the right side of the arete. **V8** 7B without the foot-block.

4 Spartacus V9 7C
The thin wall requires either a rock-over or a dyno to gain a small hold.

5 Brian . . . . V5 6C+
An easier version of *Spartacus* gaining the hold from the right.

6 West End Girls. . . . V2 5c
The central groove gets a bit high but it's okay if you keep cool.

7 Famous Grouse . . . . . V8 7B+
The bulging undercut arete. The sitting start is **V9** 7C.

8 Square Arete V2 5c
The pleasant arete.

9 Vague Nose. V4 6B
The wall past the bulge.

10 True Git V8 7B
Starting from the low break, use a layaway under the roof and plenty of technique to gain the top.

West End Girls

West End Girls | Vague Nose | West Side Story | Go West p.196 | Westworld p.197

West Side Story
The most impressive section of Burbage West is the tall walls and arete which are home to the classic *West Side Story* - one of the best wall problems in the Peak.
Approach - See map on page 193.

13 Crow Man Meets the Psychotic Pheasant
. . . . **V2** 6a
The right-hand side of the curving arete above a nasty block.

14 El Regallo del Mocho . **V7** 7A+
An eliminate up the narrow wall.

15 Crow Man Groove . . . **V0-** 4b
The groove in the centre of the right wall.

16 Crow Man Wall . . . . **V0+** 5a
A tiny eliminate up the wall right of the groove.

17 West Side Traverse . . **V4** 6B+
From the left arete, traverse the break to finish up *Rumblefish*.

18 West Side Story **V9** 7C
A brilliant micro-route up the unhelpful rib. *Photo on page 178.*

19 Ron-Side Force-It **V8** 7B
An easier variation that moves out right then back left.

20 Rumblefish **V1** 5b
A touch precarious at the top.

11 Jason's Mono Problem **V6** 7A
The wall left of the arete has a drilled mono for your left hand.

12 The Arete of Cold Gloom
. . . . **V2** 6a
The arete on its left-hand side is a gem.

Sidebar tabs: Northern Peak · Sheffield Crags · Stanage Area · Burbage Valley · Derwent Edges · The Limestone · Central Grit · Staffordshire · South Peak

Go West

The next buttress along has an undercut roof on its left and right-hand edges, separated by a wall covered with horizontal breaks.

Approach - See map on page 193.

❶ Long's Lock. . . . . **V7** *7A+*
A stiff pull through the overhang to the break. The low start from the jug is **V8** *7B+*.

❷ Western Eyes . . . **V10** *7C+*
Start at the back and climb the roof and bulging arete above.
Photo on page 17.

❸ Left Arete **V1** *5b*
The left-hand edge of the wall.
Orange Circuit continues on page 195.

❹ Middle Traverse. **V4** *6B*
Traverse the middle break from *Left Arete* to finish up *Go West*.

❺ Descent Route. **V0-** *4b*
The next line is usually used as a descent.

❻ Easy Breaks **V2** *6a*
From a low start make a long reach from some rounded breaks.

❼ Low Traverse. **V8** *7B*
Traverse the low rounded break up leftwards. Finish up *Left Arete*. Hard for the tall.

❽ Go West **V3** *6A*
The little groove is superb. Feels harder until you do it.
Photo on page 192.

❾ The Nostril . . . . **V7** *7A+*
Start on the undercut and move to the arete via a pocket.

❿ The Nose **V6** *7A*
Start low in the cave and pull out on some big rounded holds.

Westworld

This is the first buttress you come to on the approach from Burbage Bridge parking. It has a slab, a few pull-between-break style problems, plus one of the big ticks of Peak Bouldering, *Westworld*.
Approach - See map on page 193.

⑪ Scooter . . . . ☐ **V4** *6B*
The left arete.

⑫ Blazing 48s . . . . . 🌀 🔧 📄 ☐ **V11** *8A*
Scratch desperately up the pock marks.

⑬ Westworld . . . . 🌀 📄 ☐ **V11** *8A*
A desperate problem up the centre of the wall, undercutting to the poorest of holds, then slapping for the break. The sit-down is also **V11** *8A*.

⑭ Not Westworld . . . . . . 🌀 🔧 ☐ **V4** *6B+*
Climb the wall just left of the arete using an undercut. Climbed by many who then think they've done *Westworld* because of the similarity of moves and position.

⑮ West Arete . . . . 🌀 ☐ **V4** *6B*
The excellent rounded arete is best climbed on its left.

⑯ West Arete Right . . . . 🌀 ☐ **V3** *6A+*
The right side of the arete is a bit easier.

⑰ Ledgy Wall . . . . ⑨ 🌀 ☐ **V0+** *5a*
The right-hand wall past a ledge.

The first problems reached on the walk-in are on a short slab.

⑱ Chipped Slab . . . . . . ⑧ 🌀 ☐ **V0+** *5a*
Take the longest line possible on the slab using everything. It is **V1** *5b* without the chips.

⑲ Chipped Slab Right . . ⑦ 🌀 ☐ **V0** *4c*
The short right-hand side to a crack.

Northern Peak · Sheffield Crags · Stanage Area · Burbage Valley · Derwent Edges · The Limestone · Central Grit · Staffordshire · South Peak

Burbage Bridge

The tiny area below the parking by the bridge has some surprisingly worthwhile bouldering. There are only 15 problems but six of them are superb. The boulders face south and get plenty of sun.
Approach - See map on page 193.

The first problems described are on a short steep buttress, almost below the first bridge.

❶ Blocky Rib **V3** *6A*
A curious problem up the rib at the back of the small recess. Getting off the ground without using the high break is the crux. It is **V5** *6B+* from a sitting start.

❷ Rocket Man . . . . . . **V8** *7B+*
Dyno from the low break to the top of the wall.

❸ Mermaid **V6** *7A*
A desperate problem up to the twin cracks. Usually wet.

❹ Twin Crack Arete . **V5** *6C+*
The arete on its steeper left-hand side. You can pinch the arete but no holds right of the arete are allowed.

❺ Slabby Arete **V0** *4c*
The arete on its right-hand side.
Orange Circuit continues on page 197.

The next set of problems is across the stream on the **Bridge Arete Buttress** *below the pillar by the parking.*

❻ Bridge Wall **V1** *5b*
The side-wall.

❼ Bridge Arete **V2** *5c*
The arete on its left-hand side starting with hands near the arete. No foot-ledge at this grade.

❽ Little Roof . . . . . . **V4** *6B+*
Start from the low break and pull up the wall right of the arete. A touch easier if you use the arete.

❾ Bridge Traverse . . . **V2** *5c*
Traverse the break from right to left. The crux is rounding the arete.

❿ Short Arete **V0** *4c*
Climb the arete on its right. **V4** *6B* from a sitting start.

⓫ Short Arete Traverse **V1** *5b*
Traverse the break. Rounding the arete is the crux.

The **Burbage West Orange Circuit**
An 18-problem circuit with quite a difficulty range including a few green problems plus one red spot! It is listed from right to left in the book.

Bridge Arete Buttress

Directly below the pillar by the roadside parking is the **Wobble Block Buttress**.

12 Wobble Block Direct . . **V5** *6C*
The blocky left arete.

13 Wobble Block . . . . . . **V4** *6B+*
Superb! Climb direct through both roofs. The first involves pulling on slopers, which can be bypassed by reaching in from the right, dropping the grade to **V2** 5c. The wobble block itself has now gone.

14 Beached Whale Crack
. . . . **V1** 5b
Pull through the roof crack and flop at someone's feet like a....

15 Sitdown Arete **V1** 5b
The arete right of the little roof from a lowish start.

Wobble Block Buttress

Northern Peak | Sheffield Crags | Stanage Area | Burbage Valley | Derwent Edges | The Limestone | Central Grit | Staffordshire | South Peak

	No star	⛰	⛰	⛰
VB to V0 Easy to 4c	7	16	5	-
V0+ to V2 5a to 5c	5	33	9	3
V3 to V5 6A to 6C+	-	16	9	11
V3 to V5 7A upwards	3	11	16	10

Burbage North has been used for bouldering and soloing for years. It is the first place many climbers reach when driving out from Sheffield and it is ideal for a quick afternoon or evening session throughout the year. As a pure bouldering destination the problems tend to be in the higher grades and there are many destination problems such as *Banana Finger*, *Remergence*, *Blind Date*, *The Terrace* and *Voyager* - the sit-down start to the latter being one of the hardest in the country. In the right conditions, the various blocks will be busy with clusters of boulderers and heaps of mats. For those looking for lower grades the edge itself has plenty to offer. Some of the problems were originally climbed as routes and can get quite high, so may feel more like soloing. The whole length of the edge can get busy, especially the sections nearer the parking. It is also very popular with outdoor groups.

Circuits
There are three long circuits described, all of which involve quite a lot of walking. The first section of the edge is a popular solo area and some of these have been included on the circuits but they may be a bit highball for some people.

Approach   Also see map on page 179
From the parking by Burbage Bridge on the Ringinglow to Hathersage road, take the main path down the valley but almost immediately break out left along a narrower path. This leads quickly to the first walls. Other areas are best reached using the lower path and breaking up left when below them. For the most distant sections on the far southern end, stay on the crag-top path.

Conditions
The rock is superb if a little 'climbed on' It dries very quickly after rain and catches plenty of sun for those ideal winter and spring days when it is cold enough for good friction. The edge is exposed to any wind that is blowing.

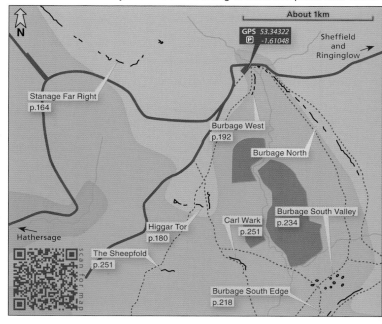

N

About 1km

GPS 53.34322
P -1.61048

Sheffield and Ringinglow

Stanage Far Right
p.164

Burbage West
p.192

Burbage North

Carl Wark
p.251

Burbage South Valley
p.234

Higgar Tor
p.180

Hathersage

The Sheepfold
p.251

scan for map

Burbage South Edge
p.218

Jo Carroll in perfect crisp winter conditions on *Banana Finger Direct* (**V5** *6C*) - *page 205*. Photo: Simon Rogers

Northern Peak

Sheffield Crags

Stanage Area

Burbage Valley

Derwent Edges

The Limestone

Central Grit

Staffordshire

South Peak

First Wall

The Chant

The bouldering at Burbage North begins on the most popular bit of the edge which is coincidentally also the closest section to the car park. These routes have been soloed for years and traditionally given route grades. Many will find them quite high but the landings are good. **Approach** - See map on page 200.

The **Burbage North Green Circuit**
A long 32 problem circuit that takes in all the edge including the very furthest section. There is quite a lot of walking and a few highballs on the initial walls.

The **Burbage North Orange Circuit**
This good long 35 problem circuit includes the whole edge including the furthest sections.

The first problem is on a little overhang left of the main crag.

1 North Roof . . . . . . ① ⚡ 🎒 [   ] **V3** *6A+*
Out from the back using the arete. This is **V5** *6C* if you move up left without the arete and the block down and left.

The climbing really gets going on **First Wall**.

2 RT Wall . . . . . ② ① ⚡ 🚪 [   ] **V2** *5c*
The wall past the carved initials is reachy.

3 Route 1 . . . . ① ⚡ [   ] **V0-** *4b*
The fine arete.

4 First Wall Traverse . . . ⚡ 📄 [   ] **V2** *5c*
The lowish traverse from left to right is entertaining.

5 Route 1.5 . . . . ③ ② ⚡ [   ] **V1** *5b*
The wall right of the arete.

6 Route 2 . . . . ② ⚡ [   ] **VB** *4a*
A good place to start.

The **Burbage North Red Circuit**
A superb circuit with some great problems up to **V4** *6B* only that makes the most of the area.

The Chant   Banana Finger   All Quiet Area   Remergence   The Tiny Slab
                        p.204   p.206   p.207   p.208

Triangle Buttress
p.204

Northern Peak
Sheffield Crags
Stanage Area
Burbage Valley
Derwent Edges
The Limestone
Central Grit
Staffordshire
South Peak

The Chant

From mid morning | 2 min | Windy

⑪ ⑫ ⑬ ⑭ ⑮ ⑯ ⑰

Northern Peak

Sheffield Crags

Stanage Area

Burbage Valley

Derwent Edges

The Limestone

Central Grit

Staffordshire

South Peak

⑦ Route 2.5 . . . . ③③⚡ ☐ **V0+** *5a*
The wall avoiding the cracks.

⑧ Route 3 . . . . ④⚡ ☐ **VB** *4a*
The easiest way up the wall.

⑨ Route 4 . . . . ☐ **V2** *5c*
Climb the wall left of the arete. There is a micro-eliminate here that is a bit harder and dubbed **Route 3.5**.

⑩ Route 5 . . . . ☐ **V0-** *4b*
The right arete of the wall.

After a short gap is another vertical wall with two prominent cracks up it.

⑪ Cranberry Wall . . . . . ⑤⚡ ☐ **VB**
Climb the narrow face.

⑫ Cranberry Crack . . . . . ⑥⚡ ☐ **VB** *4a*
The wide crack up the left side of the wall.

⑬ The Chant . . . . ④⚡ ☝ ☐ **V0+** *5a*
A superb little wall climb with a high crux. It can be started direct **V2** *5c* and finished direct at a high **V3** *6A*.

⑭ 20 Foot Crack . . . . ④⑦⚡ ☐ **V0-** *4b*
The inviting crack doesn't require jamming technique, but it does help. *Green Circuit continues on page 204.*

⑮ 20 Foot Traverse . . . . ⚡ ☝ ☐ **V1** *5b*
The low traverse.

⑯ The Curse . . . . ⑤⑤⚡ ☝ ☐ **V1** *5b*
A classic with many eliminate possibilities.
Orange and Red Circuits continue on page 204.

⑰ Lost in France . . . ⚡ ☝ ☝ ☐ **V3** *6A*
The fingery wall left of the arete. Easier on undercuts.

sh Tree Wall
p.210

The Terrace
p.211

The Sphinx
p.212

Boyager
p.214

Nicotine Stain
p.214

The End
p.216

Velvet Roof
p.215

Northern Peak

Sheffield Crags

Stanage Area

Burbage Valley

Derwent Edges

The Limestone

Central Grit

Staffordshire

South Peak

Triangle Buttress

This enclosed corner has a few fingery problems and traverses. Continue upwards or traverse off.
Approach - See map on page 200.

① Triangle Traverse . . ⑥ 🏃 **V3** *6A+*
Traverse the head-height break from left to right, past the corner.

② Low Triangle Traverse
. . . . 🏃 **V4** *6B*
The fingery low-level version to join the original is a bit harder.

③ Triangle Buttress Direct ⑥ 🏃 **V1** *5b*
An old favourite up the blunt nose to a sloping ledge. Eliminates possible.

④ Leaning Wall Start
. . . . ⑦ ⑧ 🏃 **V0+** *5a*
The wall to the break. There are a number of variations possible.

⑤ Little White Jug Start . ⑨ 🏃 **V0** *4c*
A stiff pull between thin breaks.

Banana Finger Area

A famous buttress with some excellent bouldering including one of the original classic problems of the Peak.
Approach - See map on page 200.

The first problem is found under a boulder below the main edge.

⑥ Definitive 5.12 . . . . . 🏃 **V5** *6C*
Burrow into the back of the cave and undercling your way back out again. Turning the lip gives a gut-wrenching finish. A left-hand finish is possible at **V7** *7A+*.

⑦ Easy Problem 1 . . . . ⑩ **V0-** *4b*
The left-hand line up the arete.

⑧ Easy Problem 2 . . . . ⑪ **V0-** *4b*
Climb the wall. *Green Circuit continues on page 206.*

⑨ Cinzano Roof . . . . . . 🏃 **V8** *7B*
Start from an edge and a pocket and use a flake in the roof to turn the lip. **V5** *6C* starting from the block on the right.

⑩ Monkey Crack . . . . ⑦ ⑧ 🏃 **V2** *5c*
The side-wall of Banana Finger Buttress has a little crack in it. Dynoing between the breaks is a weird **V5** *6C*.

The main event here is the undercut buttress of Banana Finger.

⑪ Banana Arete . ⑧ⓖ✿📝▢ **V2** 5c
The left-hand side of the roof, starting from a small crimp. No bridging across left allowed. Rock back right on the lip.

⑫ Banana Reverse .... ✿📝▢ **V6** 7A
Start on the good hold on the left arete and drop down onto the side-pull. Swap into the *Direct* then up to reverse *Banana Finger.*

⑬ Banana Finger Direct
. . . . ⑩✿📝▢ **V5** 6C
Brilliant pebble-pulling with a knee-bar to help.
Photo on page 201. Red Circuit continues on page 206.

⑭ Sloper Pull . . . . ✿📝▢ **V5** 6C
Gain the traverse by a nasty pull on slopers and pebbles.

⑮ Banana Finger .... ⓖ✿📝▢ **V3** 6A
One of the great Peak problems which follows the line of thin holds leftwards to an ungracious udge to get the upper break.

⑯ Banana Right-hand ⑩✿📝▢ **V2** 5c
From the start of the traverse, make a long reach to the break.

⑰ Monk On . . . . ⑪✿📝▢ **V1** 5b
The arete is easy if you slink too far rightwards, but if you tackle it on its left, it's a bit scary.

A little further along is a prominent low roof - home to three good problems.

⑱ Little Brown Thug ✿📝📦▢ **V5** 6C+
From sitting, use the arete to climb the roof on poor slopers to a rockover. Starting on the left is worth **V6** 7A.

⑲ Wednesday Climb . ⑫✿📝▢ **V1** 5b
Another route which thinks it's a boulder problem. The massive crack which cleaves the big roof is easier than it looks.
Orange Circuit continues on page 206.

⑳ Life in a Radioactive Dustbin
. . . . ✿📝📷▢ **V5** 6C
The superb roof is quite high. Controlling the swing is the key.

Northern Peak | Sheffield Crags | Stanage Area | Burbage Valley | Derwent Edges | The Limestone | Central Grit | Staffordshire | South Peak

Bracken
Crack
(HVD)

All Quiet Area

A pleasant little section which gives some nice warm-ups for the Remergence Area. It is set back from the main edge, up and left of the prominent roofs of Remergence. **Approach** - See map on page 200.

1 Hush **V1** 5b
The wall past a diagonal break.

2 Hush Arete . . . . . **V0+** 5a
The arete just to the right.

3 All Quiet on the Eastern Front

. . . . **V3** 6A+
An old classic. Finger traverse to the blunt arete from the left, then make a long pull up.

4 Captain Underpants **V8** 7B+
The wall above the start of *All Quiet*.

5 All Quiet Direct . . . . . **V7** 7A+
Climb direct using some creases and a pebble. It is slightly harder if you go very direct. The sit-down start is worth **V8** 7B.

6 The Busker . . . . . . **V0+** 5a
The face left of the crack. *Orange Circuit continues on page 208.*

7 Bracken Traverse **V2** 5c
Traverse the lowest break either way.

8 Green Slab **V0** 4c
The wall right of the crack. *Green Circuit continues on page 212.*

The next area is the taller wall of The Grogan, which is left of the main bulk of **Remergence** *Buttress.*

9 Fallen Slab Lip **V6** 7A
From a sitting start, climb the arete to slopers. Move right and up to finish. **V8** 7B if you don't use the back arete.

10 In the Flick of Time . . **V11** 8A
From a sitting start, climb the wall past a sloper.

11 Mr Sheen . . . . **V8** 7B+
The rib just left of the crack of the route *The Grogan*.

12 Wollock Direct **V2** 5c
The extremely reach-dependent wall. Continue more easily solo to the top, or move right to the crack to descend.

13 Small is Beautiful **V6** 7A
The superb wall starting with your right hand on the side-pull.

Mutiny
Crack (HS)

Northern Peak

Sheffield Crags

Stanage Area

Burbage Valley

Derwent Edges

The Limestone

Central Grit

Staffordshire

South Peak

⑭ The Hanging Rib . . ⑬ ☒ ☒ [____] **V4** 6B
Climb the blunt arete using anything. It is slightly harder if you use the lip-pinch instead of the undercut.

⑮ Submergence . ☒ ☒ ☒ ☒ [____] **V9** 7C
A mega start to *The Hanging Rib* starting in the depths. Reach out to the lip, finger traverse left and dyno for break. A cunning heel-hook and a big mat saves a wet bum.

⑯ Zaff's Groove . . . . . . ☒ ☒ [____] **V7** 7A+
An eliminate up the vague groove. Avoid any holds on problems to either side and finish at the top of *Hanging Rib*.

⑰ Remergence . . . . . ⑭ ☒ ☒ [____] **V4** 6B
Through the middle of the roof. Essential for any aspiring gritstone climber. *Red Circuit continues on page 208.*

⑱ Blind Drunk . . ☒ ☒ ☒ ☒ [____] **V11** 8A
Rock up using a hold on the lip and a tiny dish up right to reach the start of *Remergence*.

⑲ Blind Date . . . . ☒ ☒ [____] **V8** 7B+
A classic product of the 80s which is now a standard test piece. Start on the crimp and flake under the roof and use everything else to get over the bulge. Continue over the next roof to the top break to get the full tick. A low start doesn't add much.

⑳ Blind Fig . . . . ☒ ☒ [____] **V9** 7C
Start as for *Blind Date* but match the sloper (not the edge to the left) then get the dreadful lip-holds and snatch for the finishing holds on *Remergence*.

Remergence
This superb wall has some of the best hard bouldering on Burbage North including the classics *Remergence* and *Blind Date*. In addition to the problems listed here, there are many combinations and eliminates. The landings are good if a little wet and muddy at times. It can stay dry in light rain if the wind direction is right.
Approach (see map on page 200) - Approach from the crag-top path or the main valley path.

㉑ Blind Fury . . . . ☒ ☒ [____] **V10** 7C+
The blank right-hand side of the roof is desperate.

There are four traverses at different levels.

㉒ Blind Ali . . . . . . ☒ ☒ ☒ [____] **V8** 7B+
A desperate traverse of the lower lip-edge holds and undercuts but not the back wall. Finishing up *Blind Date* is worth **V10** 7C+.

㉓ Break Traverse . . ☒ ☒ ☒ [____] **V10** 7C+
Traverse the fingery edges under the main roof from left to right.

㉔ Remergence Lip Traverse
. . . . ☒ ☒ ☒ [____] **V7** 7A+
Traverse the second roof lip either way.

㉕ Tiptoe . . . . ☒ [____] **V0+** 5a
A fun traverse of the higher break that can be used as an escape for most of the problems. Finish up *Mutiny Crack* for the full gritstone experience.

The Tiny Slab

About 50m right of Remergence area is a steep wall with a tiny, almost insignificant-looking slab on its right. This slab is home to four virtually independent problems.

Approach - See map on page 200.

❶ Tree Stump Traverse 🖫 **V3** *6A*
Traverse right from above the tree stump along the break until you pull up around the corner. Avoid the big flat foothold.

❷ Tiny Left Arete . . . . . . 🖫 **V0+** *5a*
The left-hand edge.

❸ Tiny Slab Left . . . . 🖫 **V1** *5b*
The slab to the crease, using chips.
Orange Circuit continues on page 212.

❹ Tiny Slab Right . . . 🖫 **V3** *6A*
The thin line on the tallest section of the slab, past some pebbles. Avoid holds on *Tiny Slab Left*.

❺ Tiny Right Arete . . . . . 🖫 **V5** *6C*
The right-hand arete. Awkward to keep your foot off the side block.

20m up and right of The Tiny Slab is a low roof.

❻ Tiny Roof . . . . . . 🖫 **V3** *6A+*
The roof, starting from the flake in the roof. Not as reachy as it may appear, just be gentle with the flake.
Red Circuit continues on page 212.

The next problem is about 30m further along. It is directly under a large tree, and can get a bit green.

❼ Solitude . . . . 🖫 **V5** *6C*
Start sitting at the break at the back. There is a direct version from the left at **V4** *6B*.

Northern Peak
Sheffield Crags
Stanage Area
Burbage Valley
Derwent Edges
The Limestone
Central Grit
Staffordshire
South Peak

Northern Peak | Sheffield Crags | Stanage Area | **Burbage Valley** | Derwent Edges | The Limestone | Central Grit | Staffordshire | South Peak

Nicholas Ecoffet on *The Terrace* (**V9**
7C) - *page 211* - on the blocks known as The
Terrace, near Ash Tree wall at Burbage North.
Photo: Adrian Berry

Striker

Ash Tree Wall

Ash Tree Wall is best known for its popular beginners' routes, but there is some good bouldering.
Approach (see map on page 200) - If you are at Remergence Area, rather than hacking across the bracken, it is better to drop down to the main path or head up to the cliff-top path.

❶ Ash Tree Little Slab . . . . [ ] **V1** 5b
The little slab leaning against the left-hand end of the edge, taken up its centre. No aretes allowed.

❷ Sunlight Caller . . . . 𝕏 [ ] **V1** 5b
The wall using some edges.

❸ Boggle Boothroyd . . . . 𝕏 ▯ [ ] **V0** 4c
A totally reach-dependent problem up the scoop to the right of the crack. Much harder for the short.

❹ Striker Left-hand . . . . 𝕏 🔒 [ ] **V7** 7A+
The wall and arete.

❺ Striker . . . . . . 𝕏 ▨ ◄ 🔒 [ ] **V10** 7C+
The wall just left of the arete requires a dyno from undercuts.

❻ Beach Tea One . . . . . 𝕏 ◔ [ ] **V3** 6A
The blunt arete is hard at the start. Finish up the cracks.

❼ Ivy Tree . . . . 𝕏 ◔ [ ] **V0+** 5a
The wall to the right of the arete. Move left to the arete and cracks to finish.

❽ All Stars' Goal . . . 𝕏 ▯ ◔ [ ] **V3** 6A
A high problem up the tall wall right of the gully. Move up to jams in a break and finish direct.

Above the approach path from the main valley path is a diamond-shaped slab.

❾ Ash Tree Big Slab . . . . . . 𝕏 [ ] **VB**
The big leaning slab can be climbed anywhere.

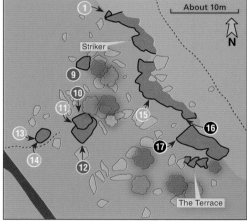

About 10m

Striker

The Terrace

Further down the hill is another big block with an undercut roof.

❿ Gruesome Mantel . . . 𝕏 ◄ [ ] **V3** 6A
Hang the break at the back then reach out via a block to the lip. A gruesome mantel to finish.

⓫ Jammed Block Mantel 𝕏 ◄ [ ] **V2** 5c
Pull past the jammed block steeply up left to another mantel.

⓬ Easy Arete . . . . 𝕏 [ ] **VB**
The far arete is pleasant. The face can be climbed anywhere at this grade.

Just above the main valley path is a small undercut boulder.

⓭ Undercut Block Left . . . . . ▨ [ ] **V0+** 5a
The left-hand side past a pocket.

⓮ Undercut Block Right . . . . ▨ [ ] **V0+** 5a
The right-hand side using edges on the lip.

Northern Peak

Sheffield Crags

Stanage Area

Burbage Valley

Derwent Edges

The Limestone

Central Grit

Staffordshire

South Peak

On the main wall behind the large block is a popular problem.

15 **Ash Tree Variation** . . . . . . ⬡ ☐ **V2** *5c*
The start of this route has frustrated many a keen beginner over the years. Climb direct between the cracks.

There are two hard problems near the block of Living in Oxford.

16 **Puck**. . . . . . . ⬡ ☐☐☐ ☐ **V8** *7B*
The highball arete via a pocket.

17 **Sitting in Oxford** . ⬡ ☐☐ ☐ **V6** *7A*
A sitting start to the left side of the arete, finishing at the break.

The Terrace
At a slightly lower level is a set of innocuous looking undercut blocks that are actually home to some really hard quality problems.
Approach - See map on page 200.

18 **The Terrace**. . . ⬡☐☐☐ ☐ **V9** *7C*
The steep arete from a sitting start. *Photo on page 209.*

19 **Jason's Roof**
. . . . ⬡☐☐☐☐ ☐ **V8** *7B+*
Starting from the low 'keel', make a long reach to face-holds and continue up the wall. From a standing start this is **V6** *7A*.

20 **Right Arete** . . . . . ⬡ ☐☐ ☐ **V6** *7A*
The hanging arete on its left. **V7** *7A+* from a sitting start.

21 **Hanging Wall** . . . ⬡ ☐☐ ☐ **V6** *7A*
Start from the low keel and climb the steep wall to pull round onto the pock-marked slab. **V5** *6C* from standing.

22 **La Terrace** . . . . . ☐☐☐ ☐ **V11** *8A*
Start up *The Terrace*, spin round onto the opposite wall, then drop down and finish up *Hanging Wall*.

Northern Peak | Sheffield Crags | Stanage Area | Burbage Valley | Derwent Edges | The Limestone | Central Grit | Staffordshire | South Peak

❶ Giza . . . . 〈3〉 ⚑ 〔 〕 **V8** *7B+*
Link up the thin breaks to a desperate rock-over.

❷ The Sphinx . . . . . 〈3〉 ⚑ 〔 〕 **V7** *7A+*
A bit high for a boulder problem really - but very good.

❸ Voyager . . 〈3〉 ✋ ⚑ 〔 〕 **V13** *8B*
Jump to grab the edge then make your way up the prow using tiny edges and heel-hooks. **V14** *8B+* from a sitting start.

❹ Sputnik . . . . ⚑ 〔 〕 **V8** *7B+*
The mirror line to *Voyager* up the other side.

❺ Cleo's Edge . . . . . . ⑲ ⑱ 〈3〉 〔 〕 **V2** 5c
The arete on its left-hand side is superb. *Photo on page 26.*

❻ Cleo's Right Hand . . . . ⑮ 〈3〉 〔 〕 **V0-** 4b
The right-hand side is easier.

❼ Cleo's Slab . . . . ⑯ 〔 〕 **VB**
The slab past a pocket. Nice done with no hands.

❽ Cleo's Other Edge . . . . . . ⑰ 〔 〕 **VB**
The arete is pretty straightforward.
Green Circuit continues on page 216.

Roof Goofe

From mid morning | 10 min | Windy

Afternoon | 10 min | Windy

The Sphinx Area
This small section of edge has little to offer the roped climber but there are some gems for the boulderer including one of the hardest in the Peak.
Approach (see map on page 200) - You can scramble across to it from Ash Tree Wall Area or reach it direct from below. *The Sphinx* itself is a little below the edge.

Northern Peak | Sheffield Crags | Stanage Area | Burbage Valley | Derwent Edges | The Limestone | Central Grit | Staffordshire | South Peak

Back up on the main edge, there are a number of good problems around the narrow tower of the **Jetty** and the walls to the right.

⑫ Jetty Aretty **V2** 5c
The little rib. Step off leftwards.
Orange Circuit continues on page 214.

⑬ Jetty Start . . . . **VB** 4a
The wall to the break.

⑭ Jetty Nose . . . . . . **V3** 6A+
The hanging arete taken on its left-hand side. A worrying finish.

⑮ Pocket Passer **V4** 6B
Jump to the pocket and pull up.

⑯ Jetty Bulge **V4** 6B
An interesting exercise up the rib to the left of the ledge. A two-finger pebble and a poor sloper are all you've got.

⑰ Safe Bet **V5** 6C
The left-hand side of the leaning arete has a scary finish.

⑱ Long Shot **V4** 6B
Climb the wall right of the arete.

⑲ Bedrock **V6** 7A
The thin centre of the wall.

⑳ Yabadabadoo **V5** 6C
Jump to the sloping ledge, without the block on the right. Finish direct. Morpho.

㉑ Answer the Phone **V1** 5b
The groove right of *Yabadabadoo*.

Through the gap formed by the Sphinx block is **Roof Goofe**.

⑨ Sphinx Slab **V0** 4c
The slab on the opposite side of the Sphinx block starting down by the supporting arete.

⑩ Roof Goofe **V4** 6B
An excellent mantel on the lip starting from the back.

⑪ Roof Goofe Right . . **V4** 6B
The right-hand side of the roof using some flakes and pockets.
Red Circuit continues on page 214.

Side tabs: Northern Peak | Sheffield Crags | Stanage Area | Burbage Valley | Derwent Edges | The Limestone | Central Grit | Staffordshire | South Peak

Boyager

Boyager

This hidden pair of blocks lies just down and slightly right (looking in) of the Knight's Move area.

Approach (see map on page 200) - Follow the diagonal path from the main valley path leading up to the edge, then head rightwards into the woods.

❶ Boyager . . . . **V7** 7A+
The upper of the two blocks is climbed in 'fridge-hugging' style.

❷ Monochrome **V8** 7B
Climb the left arete from a sit start on the low shelf.

Nicotine Stain

The main edge becomes higher and more continuous above the trees at this end. Most of the climbing is routes but there is some bouldering especially where the crag tapers away at the far right end. The main area of note is around the slab of *Nicotine Stain*.

Approach (see map on page 200) - From any of the other areas or the parking, go up onto the cliff-top path and walk along until you are just past the most continuous section of trees below the crag. Head down where you can.

The prow of The Fin is a prominent feature. This is about 15m right of the clean groove of Long Tall Sally.

❻ Right Fin. **V1** 5b
Another route that just about gains bouldering status. It follows the fine blunt flake in the side-wall of the fin.

❸ Mono Bulge. **V8** 7B
Start on the low shelf and pull past the mono up the steep left side of the prow's right arete to the nose. Pull up left to finish.

❹ Asylum Sika **V8** 7B
Sit-start on the creaky flakes up the side-wall to gain the good holds midway along the lip.

❺ Ripple Riser **V4** 6B
A rising right to left lip traverse of the right-hand wall from a sitting start.

❼ The Enthusiast. . . . . . . **V3** 6A+
The left-hand arete of the slab is sometimes very frustrating.

❽ Nicotine Stain **V4** 6B
A classic up the faint crack in the slab. Doing it more than once is hard.

❾ Nicarete **V1** 5b
The slab and arete just left of the wide, easy crack.

❿ Approach **V2** 5c
More frustrating climbing up the pockets and pebbles between the two cracks.

Nicotine Stain

The End
p.216

Beyond the End
p.217

Boyager

Velvet Roof

Nicotine Stain

Northern Peak
Sheffield Crags
Stanage Area
Burbage Valley
Derwent Edges
The Limestone
Central Grit
Staffordshire
South Peak

11 Spider Crack V1 5b
An easy *Nicotine Stain* up the next crack.
Orange Circuit continues on page 216.

12 Pest Control V4 6B
The desperate slab between two easy cracks.
Red Circuit continues on page 216.

Velvet Roof

Below the edge at this point is a cave which is partially hidden from above. This is the Velvet Roof.

13 Velvet Crab . . . . V7 7A+
The hanging left arete.

14 Velvet Roof V2 5c
The left-hand crack.

15 Right-Hand Roof . V4 6B
The right-hand crack.

Velvet Roof

Directly below the Nicotine Stain is a pair of blocks that converge into a triangular cave. This is home to some steep cracks and arete problems.
Approach (see map on page 200) - Approach from above by dropping down from the Nicotine Stain area.

16 Zaff Skoczylas V9 7C
The steep prow from a very low - lying down - start on the big pocket. The sitting version is unusually easier at **V8** 7B+. The right-hand finish is the same grade.

Northern Peak

Sheffield Crags

Stanage Area

Burbage Valley

Derwent Edges

The Limestone

Central Grit

Staffordshire

South Peak

The End

A worthwhile collection of short routes and problems located at the far end of the crag. Nearly always very quiet, and worth the extra walk.
Approach - See map on page 200.

1 Shelf Wall. . . . . . . 26 23 ☼ ▢ **V2** 5c
The middle of the wall.

2 End Slab. . . . . 18 ☼ ▢ **VB**
The gentle slab is nice and easy.

3 Two Pocket Sitter
. . . . 27 24 ☼ ▣ ▢ **V2** 5c
Start sitting at two pockets.

4 Front End Face . . . 25 19 ☼ ▢ **V0+** 5a
The arete is tricky on its right-hand side (but much easier on the slabby left-hand side).

5 Plank Sanction ☼ ▣ ▣ ▣ ▢ **V8** 7B
Starting from sitting, just right of the arete. Make powerful moves past an undercut pocket to gain the face.

6 Back End Slab . . . . ☼ ▢ **VB**
The slab up to the break. Continue for the full route.

7 Crack Habit 28 26 ☼ ▣ ▣ ▢ **V2** 5c
Starting from the back, jam through the roof. This is the sit-start to the route *Ender*.

8 Endest Arete . . . . 20 ☼ ▢ **VB** 4a
The left edge of the triangular slab.

9 Endste . . . . 21 ☼ ▢ **VB** 4a
The wall and flake above.

10 Grizzly Bear. . . . . . ☼ ▣ ▣ ▢ **V5** 6C+
From a sitting start, climb the way via poor breaks. The left-hand version takes the pocket with the right hand and moves out to the arete, the direct takes the pocket with the left hand.

11 Pocket Dyno . . . . ☼ ▣ ▢ **V6** 7A
From the lip of a low roof, dyno for a pocket.

12 Capped Rib . . . . 29 ☼ ▢ **V3** 6A
Climb the rib and continue directly through the overlap.
The last problem in the Red Circuit.

Beyond the End

The edge disappears for about 100m until a distinct square block. Another 50m beyond this is the final offering of the three square blocks making up the Three Bears.

Approach (see map on page 200) - Follow the crag top path the full length of the crag until these two isolated buttresses come into view ahead.

From mid morning | 22 min | Windy

13 Side-wall . . . . ㉗㉒⚡🏳 ☐ **VO+** 5a
The green side-wall requires a stiff pull to get going.

14 Little Cube Arete . . ㉘⚡▯▮ ☐ **V1** 5b
The sharp arete, avoiding the ledge. Easier for the tall.

15 Once Upon a Time . . . ⚡🏳 ☐ **V9** *7C*
The blank wall.

16 Beyond the End . . . ㉙㉓⚡ ☐ **VO** 4c
Delightful little arete that is worth the walk.

The Three Bears

Another 50m further on are **The Three Bears** *which give a set of similar reachy problems between breaks.*

17 Daddy Wall . . . . ㉔⚡ ☐ **VO** 4c
The front face of the left-hand boulder.

18 Daddy Bear Arete. . ㉚㉕⚡ ☐ **VO+** 5a
The right arete of the left-hand boulder.

19 Daddy Arete Right . ㉛㉖▯▮ ☐ **VO+** 5a
The right-hand side of the arete.

20 Daddy Right Arete . . . . . . ㉗ ☐ **VO-** 4b
The back arete of the Daddy block on its left.

21 Mommy Wall. . ㉜㉘⚡▯▮ ☐ **VO+** 5a
The front face of the middle boulder.

22 Mommy Bear Arete ㉝㉙⚡ ☐ **VO+** 5a
The right arete of the middle boulder.

23 Mommy Bear Right . . ㉞⚡ ☐ **V1** 5b
Climb the right-hand side-wall.

24 Don't Get Between . . . . . . ㉚ ☐ **VB**
The angular corner between *Mommy* and *Baby.*

25 Baby Bear Wall ㉟㉛⚡▯▮ ☐ **VO+** 5a
The front face of the right-hand boulder.
The last problem in the Orange Circuit.

26 Baby Bear Arete. . . . . ㉜⚡ ☐ **VO** 4c
The right arete of the right-hand boulder.
The last problem in the Green Circuit.

From mid morning | 23 min | Windy

Northern Peak
Sheffield Crags
Stanage Area
Burbage Valley
Derwent Edges
The Limestone
Central Grit
Staffordshire
South Peak

	No star			
VB to V0 Easy to 4c	1	6	2	-
V0+ to V2 5a to 5c	5	12	6	1
V3 to V5 6A to 6C+	1	17	16	1
V3 to V5 7A upwards	-	12	16	11

The main edge at Burbage South is a different kettle of fish to its popular and user-friendly neighbour down below in the valley (see page 234). Up on the edge the landings are often dreadful, the problems can be high and hard, it is often in the shade since it faces northwest, and many problems are gritty and green for much of the time. However, there are some superb challenges in amongst the jumbled blocks and higher sections of edge.

Circuits

Burbage South Edge isn't a great place for circuits. The landings are terrible and getting between the problems is awkward.

Approach   Also see map on page 179

The Burbage South Edge is best approached from roadside parking on the A6187 above the Fox House pub. From here locate a stile and follow a (sometimes muddy) path across the moor to arrive at the top of the South Quarry. Walk down a path between the two quarries for the bouldering at this end. Continue along the crag-top path for the other sections since the path below the crag is often awkward or non-existent.

Conditions

The edge faces northwest and only gets the sun late in the day. This means that it is often cooler, greener and damper than other nearby grit crags. It offers little shelter from the wind and is best considered a summer, autumn and spring crag after dry spells.

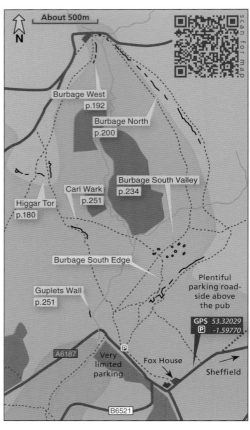

Northern Peak

Sheffield Crags

Stanage Area

Burbage Valley

Derwent Edges

The Limestone

Central Grit

Staffordshire

South Peak

Simon Wilson climbing *Gib's Rib* (**V6** *7A*) - *page 225* - on Burbage South Edge. Photo: Adam Long

Rascal Buttress

Evening | 20 min | Windy | Green

Pocket Wall 20m →

① 30m ←

Earl Area

This is the far, far northern end of Burbage South past where most people usually stop walking. It gets its name from its resemblance to Earl Crag in Yorkshire.

Approach (see map on page 218) - If you're starting here, the best approach is by walking along the top since the ground below the crag is hard going.

❶ What a Way to Spend Easter

. . . . **V5** 6C

The centre of the lone slab only 30m left of Rascal Buttress. The approach is hard - quickest to go via the crag top.

The next problems are on a small buttress about 30m right.

❷ Dizzie Rascal **V2** 5c

The left arete of the slab above a bad landing.

❸ Dirty Rascal **V6** 7A

The arete as far as the break. From here either traverse off or, if the landing is well-padded, jump.

❹ Rascal Groove **V6** 7A

The groove, moving right at the top (left is **Little Rascal, E4**). The very low sitting start is **V10** 7C+.

❺ Ronnie's Rib **V6** 7A

Climb the arete from a sitting start.

❻ Flake 'n' Blob **V0** 4c

Step of the block to the flake, then use the blob-pocket to finish.

❼ The Housebrick **V2** 6a

The set-back wall has fingery holds.

Rascal Buttress   Pocket Wall

Pocket Wall

Intense Wall 15m →

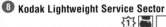

8 **Kodak Lightweight Service Sector**
. . . . **V5** *6C*
The arete on its left-hand side.

9 **Standup Arete** **V4** *6B*
The arete from, you guessed it, standing. The sit-start is **Fuji Heavy Industries, V7** *7A+*.

10 **Rail Thing** **V2** *5c*
Dyno to the top.

11 **Pocket Wall Left** **V6** *7A*
Sit-start the left-hand side of the wall.

12 **Pocket Wall** **V4** *6B*
The centre of the wall via a pocket. The sit-start from an undercut is **V8** *7B+*.

13 **Flat Wall Dyno** . . . **V5** *6C*
Leap between the breaks.

14 **Footy Rib** **V2** *5c*
The rib to the right.

Intense Wall

The following problems are on a short triangular wall.

15 **I'm Tense** **V8** *7B*
Starting from a low slot, head left then up.

16 **Intense** **V11** *8A*
Jump to the side-pull and continue. **V9** *7C* from standing.

Intense Wall

The Rib
p.222

Side tabs: Northern Peak · Sheffield Crags · Stanage Area · Burbage Valley · Derwent Edges · The Limestone · Central Grit · Staffordshire · South Peak

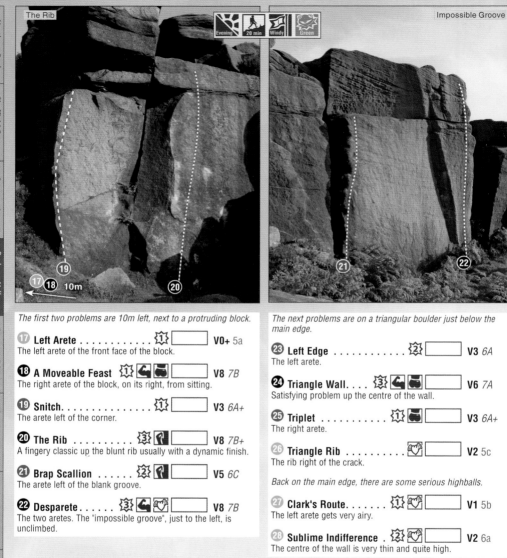

The Rib

Impossible Groove

Evening | 20 min | Windy | Green

The first two problems are 10m left, next to a protruding block.

17 Left Arete . . . . V0+ 5a
The left arete of the front face of the block.

18 A Moveable Feast V8 7B
The right arete of the block, on its right, from sitting.

19 Snitch . . . . V3 6A+
The arete left of the corner.

20 The Rib . . . . V8 7B+
A fingery classic up the blunt rib usually with a dynamic finish.

21 Brap Scallion V5 6C
The arete left of the blank groove.

22 Desparete V8 7B
The two aretes. The "impossible groove", just to the left, is unclimbed.

The next problems are on a triangular boulder just below the main edge.

23 Left Edge V3 6A
The left arete.

24 Triangle Wall V6 7A
Satisfying problem up the centre of the wall.

25 Triplet . . . . V3 6A+
The right arete.

26 Triangle Rib V2 5c
The rib right of the crack.

Back on the main edge, there are some serious highballs.

27 Clark's Route V1 5b
The left arete gets very airy.

28 Sublime Indifference . V2 6a
The centre of the wall is very thin and quite high.

Chockstone Layback   The Alliance

Intense Wall p.221

The Rib

Impossible Groove

Triangular Wall

Triangular Wall

Chockstone Layback

Chockstone Layback

Northern Peak
Sheffield Crags
Stanage Area
Burbage Valley
Derwent Edges
The Limestone
Central Grit
Staffordshire
South Peak

29 Home Cooking... **V6** *7A*
Clamp your way up the double aretes, finishing on the right.

30 Eating Out......... **V5** *6C*
The thin slab, avoiding the jammed block.

31 Chockstone Layback..... **V0-** 4b
Climb around the chockstone.

32 Green S-Groove....... **V2** 6a
As the name suggests, it can get a bit green.

33 Sweet Arete .... **V3** *6A+*
Starting on the right, climb over to the arete and finish up this.

34 The Wrestle **V4** *6B*
The wall left of the prominent corner crack is usually dirty.

35 The Alliance **V6** *7A*
Hug your way up the aretes to a high top-out. **V7** *7A+* from sitting.

36 Friar's Wall........... **V0** 4c
Follow the jugs up the green wall.

37 Guppy Arete **V2** 5c
The left-hand side of the arete aiming for the big hold.

38 Classic Arete........... **V5** *6C*
Climb the right-hand side of the arete from a low level to gain the good hold.

The Alliance

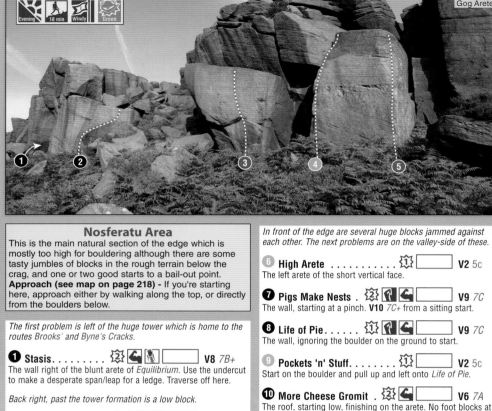

Gog Arete

Nosferatu Area

This is the main natural section of the edge which is mostly too high for bouldering although there are some tasty jumbles of blocks in the rough terrain below the crag, and one or two good starts to a bail-out point.
Approach (see map on page 218) - If you're starting here, approach either by walking along the top, or directly from the boulders below.

The first problem is left of the huge tower which is home to the routes Brooks' and Byne's Cracks.

1 **Stasis** . . . . **V8** *7B+*
The wall right of the blunt arete of *Equilibrium*. Use the undercut to make a desperate span/leap for a ledge. Traverse off here.

Back right, past the tower formation is a low block.

2 **Lip Barmy** . . . . . . **V8** *7B+*
Traverse right then move up more directly.

After another gap the edge presents some lower blocks.

3 **Fast Ledge** **V4** *6B*
The wall past the sloping ledge. Can be dirty.

4 **Gog Arete** . . . . **V0+** *5a*
The left arete on either side is superb.

5 **Ladder Rib** . . . . **V3** *6A+*
The right arete on its left-hand side. Harder on the right.

In front of the edge are several huge blocks jammed against each other. The next problems are on the valley-side of these.

6 **High Arete** **V2** *5c*
The left arete of the short vertical face.

7 **Pigs Make Nests** . . **V9** *7C*
The wall, starting at a pinch. **V10** *7C+* from a sitting start.

8 **Life of Pie** **V9** *7C*
The wall, ignoring the boulder on the ground to start.

9 **Pockets 'n' Stuff** **V2** *5c*
Start on the boulder and pull up and left onto *Life of Pie*.

10 **More Cheese Gromit** . **V6** *7A*
The roof, starting low, finishing on the arete. No foot blocks at this grade.

11 **Rock Bottom** **V4** *6B*
Rock up onto the slab.

12 **Definitive 5.11** . . . **V5** *6C+*
Go back into the cave and follow the crack out to daylight. Linking into *The Grazer* is **Definitive Burlesque V8,** *7B*.

13 **The Grazer** . . . . . **V5** *6C+*
Starting from the pedestal, span to the lip, then try and turn it onto the slab via a pocket.

14 **Sitting Duck** **V4** *6B*
Lunge right to the arete from *The Grazer* and finish up it.

Gog Arete   Definitive 5.11   Attitude Inspector

Definitive 5.11

Back up on the main edge is a classic dark wall.

15 Bad Attitude **V5** *6C*
Crimp up the wall left of the arete. The sitting start is **V8** *7B*.

16 Attitude Inspector **V6** *7A*
The dynamic arete is a classic of its type. **V7** *7A+* from a sitting start.

17 The Neck **V8** *7B*
The crimpy wall, finishing at the break.

18 The Knack Sit-start **V4** *6B*
Stop at the crack.

19 Old Macdonald **V6** *7A*
Climb the wall to gain the finish of the route *Nick Knack Paddywack*. Quite highball.

20 Nick Knack Paddywack Sit-start
.... **V6** *7A*
From the undercut, reach right for an edge then gain the break. Continuing direct from here is the highball **Bright Eyes V7** *7A+*.

21 Gib's Rib **V6** *7A*
The right arete to the break. *Photo on page 219.*

Attitude Inspector

Electrical Storm

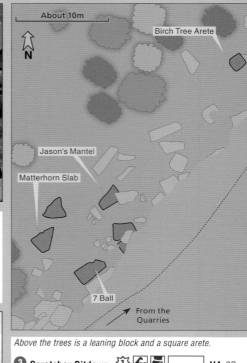

About 10m

N

Birch Tree Arete

Jason's Mantel

Matterhorn Slab

7 Ball

From the Quarries

Midway between the Nosferatu Area and the disjointed Oak Grove, is a short quarried wall with a classic hard problem.

❶ Electrical Storm . . 〔3〕 **V8** *7B*
From a sitting start, follow the line up and right.

❷ Grease Lightning . 〔2〕 **V8** *7B+*
Start as for *Electrical Storm*, but move left to finish.

Birch Tree Arete

Evening | 15 min | Windy | Green

Above the trees is a leaning block and a square arete.

❸ Scratcher Sitdown 〔1〕 **V4** *6B*
Pull onto the undercut slab and slap up the left arete.

❹ Little Artless . . . . 〔3〕 **V7** *7A+*
The short wall using edges to slap for a sloper.

❺ Birch Tree Arete . . . . 〔2〕 **V3** *6A+*
The right-hand arete.

15m further along are some more jumbled blocks.

❻ Big Block Wall . . . . 〔1〕 **V4** *6B*
The front of the next boulder on the right.

❼ Jason's Mantel . . . . . 〔2〕 **V6** *7A*
Mantel onto the slab left of its centre.

❽ Your Basic Mantel . . . 〔3〕 **V5** *6C*
The easier mantel just to the right.

Birch Tree Arete

Electrical Storm

Jason's Mantel

7 Ball

Matterhorn Slab

Oak Grove Boulders
A good little bouldering area situated in the trees between the classic hard routes *Nosferatu* and *Pebble Mill*.
Approach (see map on page 218) - Walk along the top, or approach directly along the path from the quarries.

Matterhorn Slab

7 Ball

Evening | 15 min | Windy | Green

Northern Peak
Sheffield Crags
Stanage Area
Burbage Valley
Derwent Edges
The Limestone
Central Grit
Staffordshire
South Peak

9 Curving Crimps **V4** *6B*
The wall, starting just left of the arete.

10 Oak Tree Arete **V4** *6B*
The arete.

11 7 Ball **V5** *6C*
Sit-start right of the groove, then follow the groove/rib.
V3 *6A+* from standing.

12 Middle Wall . . . . **V0+** *5a*
Climb the middle of the wall.

13 Corner Pocket **V4** *6B*
The arete. Slightly harder from a sitting start.

A little further below the edge is a delightful hidden slab.

14 Gentle Slab . . . . **VB** *4a*
The slab left of the arete on the block to the left (looking in).

15 Gentle Rib **V0** *4c*
The arete on the block to the left. A bit harder from sitting.

16 Matterhorn Left **V1** *5b*
The left edge of the slab using the arete. The slab just right,
without using the arete is **V2** *5c*.

17 Central Groove Thing **V2** *5c*
Use the sloper to gain the upper little groove. Superb!

18 Matterhorn Slab **V0-** *4b*
The groove can be reached much more easily from the right.

19 Matterhorn Right **V0-** *4b*
The right arete.

7 Ball

Jason's Mantel

Matterhorn Slab

Evening | 15 min | Windy | Green

Broddle's Baby

Pebble Mill

Pebble Mill (E5)

Pebble Mill Area

There are a few hard offerings on the edge and block around the tall prow of *Pebble Mill*.

Approach (see map on page 218) - Walk along the top, or approach directly along the path from the quarries.

The first few problems are to be found on a block just left of Pebble Mill.

1 Little Limmock **V4** *6B*
The slabby arete.

2 Broddle's Baby **V5** *6C*
The short, steep arete.

3 Trapped in Crows' Claws
. . . . **V7** *7A+*
Fridge-hug your way up the twin aretes, finishing on the left. The right-hand finish is **V6** *7A* but has a nasty landing.

The wall below Pebble Mill has some intense problems.

4 Pebble Mill Traverse
. . . . **V7** *7A+*
Starting at an undercut, traverse right across the scoop. Traversing in the reverse direction is the same difficulty. Traversing left and finishing up *Pepper Mill* is **V8** *7B+*.

5 Pepper Mill . . . . **V5** *6C+*
The arete on its right taken as far as the break.

6 Pebble Mill Stem **V6** *7A*
Traverse left with your feet on the handholds of *Pebble Mill Traverse* until you can finish up *Pepper Mill*.

7 We Aint Gonna Pay No Toll
. . . . **V4** *6B*
The wall just left of the right arete, moving left to the arete of the E5 *Pebble Mill* where you jump onto all those mats you brought.

8 Micro Mill . . . . **V0+** *5a*
The little arete.

7 Ball p.227

Matterhorn Slab p.227

Broddle's Baby

Pebble Mill

Dork Child

Above and Beyond

Rollerwall

Dork Child

The next problems are on the often-dirty aretes and walls between the two taller sections of the edge.

⑨ Dork Child Start .... 🎯 [ ] **V2** 5c
The first few metres are the most interesting, climb the arete on its left-hand side.

⑩ Dork Walk .... [ ] **V2** 5c
Rock onto the arete from the right.

⑪ Dork Slab .... [ ] **V1** 5b
The green side-wall requires a sharp pull.

⑫ The Dork .... [ ] **V2** 5c
Pull onto the shelf to the left of the blank groove.

Just up and to the right is a steep buttress with a prominent wide crack (Goliath) and a couple of striking aretes, the left of which has the following problems.

⑬ Above and Beyond the Kinaesthetic Barrier
.... 🎯🖐🫳 [ ] **V6** 7A
Micro-route or highball problem? Just about short enough to be done with plenty of mats, and too good to leave out. Start up the wall left of the arete to the big pocket then move right to the arete and finish at the top.

⑭ Above and Beyond... Direct
.... 🎯🖐🫳 [ ] **V7** 7A+
The direct start up the arete is better.

⑮ Samson ..... 🎯🖐🫳🫳 [ ] **V11** 8A
Originally climbed as a route, and a bit high for a boulder problem. It has been highballed, and is an obvious challenge for those at the highest level, so here it is.

⑯ Messiah Traverse .... 🎯🖊 [ ] **V6** 7A
Traverse the steep wall from the arete to a flake. The true devotee will start at the wide crack of David and descend the ramp but it doesn't add to the difficulty.

⑰ Rollerwall ...... 🎯🖐🖐 [ ] **V9** 7C
The ultra thin slab. Finish up Saul. Photo on next page.

⑱ Saul .... 🎯🫳 [ ] **V1** 5b
A much easier way up the slab but with a high top-out.

Above and Beyond

Rollerwall

Northern Peak

Sheffield Crags

Stanage Area

Burbage Valley

Derwent Edges

The Limestone

Central Grit

Staffordshire

South Peak

Dave Hesleden on *Rollerwall* (**V9** *7C*) - *previous page* - in the Above and Beyond Area on Burbage South Edge. Photo: Adam Long

Northern Quarry

The Quarries

The two big quarries at Burbage South have a few things of interest for the boulderer.

Approach (see map on page 218) - The approach from the road above the Fox House takes you straight to the top of the Southern Quarry. Break right if approaching from the southern end of the main valley path.

1 **Hanging Prow** **V5** *6C*
Pull onto the hanging prow and thrutch over onto its slab. The sitting start is **V7** *7A+*.

2 **Zorev** **V9** *7C*
The clean arete on the left side of the quarry above a flat landing. **V10** *7C+* from sitting.

3 **Violence** . . . .   **V7** *7A+*
Another arete, from a sitting start.

The slab opposite Violence offers some easy slab practice.

4 **Mini Millwheel** **V1** 5b
The third bouldery arete is much easier and a bit slippery.

Northern Quarry

Celtic Cross
p.232

Southern Quarry
p.232

Above and Beyond Area
p.229

Side-pull Arch
p.231

Northern Peak
Sheffield Crags
Stanage Area
Burbage Valley
Derwent Edges
The Limestone
Central Grit
Staffordshire
South Peak

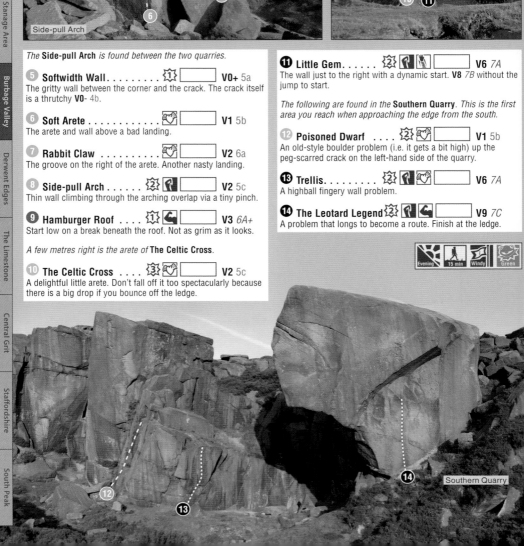

Celtic Cross

Side-pull Arch

The **Side-pull Arch** *is found between the two quarries.*

⑤ Softwidth Wall . . . . V0+ 5a
The gritty wall between the corner and the crack. The crack itself
is a thrutchy **V0-** 4b.

⑥ Soft Arete V1 5b
The arete and wall above a bad landing.

⑦ Rabbit Claw V2 6a
The groove on the right of the arete. Another nasty landing.

⑧ Side-pull Arch V2 5c
Thin wall climbing through the arching overlap via a tiny pinch.

⑨ Hamburger Roof . . . . V3 6A+
Start low on a break beneath the roof. Not as grim as it looks.

A few metres right is the arete of **The Celtic Cross***.*

⑩ The Celtic Cross V2 5c
A delightful little arete. Don't fall off it too spectacularly because
there is a big drop if you bounce off the ledge.

⑪ Little Gem V6 7A
The wall just to the right with a dynamic start. **V8** *7B* without the
jump to start.

The following are found in the **Southern Quarry***. This is the first
area you reach when approaching the edge from the south.*

⑫ Poisoned Dwarf V1 5b
An old-style boulder problem (i.e. it gets a bit high) up the
peg-scarred crack on the left-hand side of the quarry.

⑬ Trellis V6 7A
A highball fingery wall problem.

⑭ The Leotard Legend V9 7C
A problem that longs to become a route. Finish at the ledge.

Southern Quarry

Approach from above Fox House

Southern Quarry (and big drop)

Northern Peak

Sheffield Crags

Stanage Area

Burbage Valley

Derwent Edges

The Limestone

Central Grit

Staffordshire

South Peak

The Kindergarten

Inspite of its reputation for hard problems above nasty landings, Burbage South Edge is also home to one of the best baby boulderfields in the Peak. Above the Southern Quarry there is an assortment of beautiful small boulders scattered across the moor. This is a great spot to start them young with lots of low boulders above good landings. Just watch the boulders on the corner near the quarry edge where there is a big drop.

Approach (see map on page 218) - The approach from the road above the Fox House takes you straight to the Kindergarten.

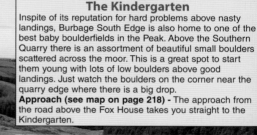

Only two problems are described. There are many more if you explore a bit.

15 Lilou . . . . 〔2〕 VB
The beautiful little groove is a great starter.

16 Kinderlibrium . . . . 〔1〕 VB
The arete is a little trickier.

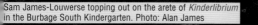

Sam James-Louwerse topping out on the arete of *Kinderlibrium* in the Burbage South Kindergarten. Photo: Alan James

	No star	⚅	⚅⚅	⚅⚅⚅
VB to V0 Easy to 4c	8	24	1	-
V0+ to V2 5a to 5c	14	37	14	1
V3 to V5 6A to 6C+	1	12	7	-
V3 to V5 7A upwards	1	8	6	2

The Valley Boulders at Burbage South offer some of the most friendly bouldering around. The landings are excellent and nothing gets too high. By following the chalk marks of the many visitors you can find almost 100 problems on these attractive blocks, but there will certainly be many more. The problems tend to be slabs and walls with some rounded aretes thrown in. It lacks steep power problems and really hard stuff but there are plenty of those elsewhere.

Circuits

This is a superb area for circuits and we have included three. They are easy to follow and make the most of the area.

Approach   Also see map on page 179

The Burbage South Valley Boulders are situated above and below the main Burbage Valley track. This is best approached from roadside parking on the A6187 above the Fox House pub. From here locate a stile and follow a (sometimes muddy) path across the moor to arrive at the top of the South Quarry. Walk down a path between the two quarries which leads down and across the moor to the boulders.

Conditions

The boulders face all directions and are exposed to strong winds but they may be okay when the edges are too windy. They are very quick drying and seldom green. The slabby, rounded holds require cool conditions.

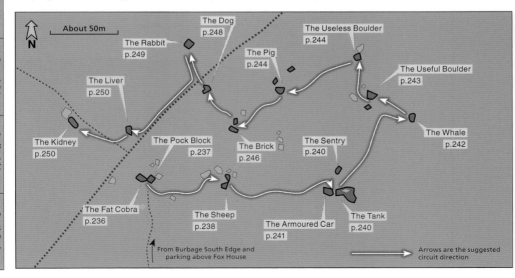

Northern Peak

Sheffield Crags

Stanage Area

Burbage Valley

Derwent Edges

The Limestone

Central Grit

Staffordshire

South Peak

Lev Jones doing the finger-tip mantel on *Wall Past Slot* (**V0+** 5a) - *page 237* - on the Pock Block at Burbage South Valley Boulders. Photo: Alan James

Northern Peak

Sheffield Crags

Stanage Area

Burbage Valley

Derwent Edges

The Limestone

Central Grit

Staffordshire

South Peak

The Fat Cobra

This boulder lurks above the path, just beneath the Pock Block. It has some nice easy problems on the slab facing the path. The actual cobra's head is at the other end. **Approach** - See map on page 234.

❶ Undercut Rib . . . . . ① ③ ❀ [ ] **V0** 4c
A high leg-up is needed for the hanging arete.

❷ Left of Crack . . . . ② ❀ [ ] **V0-** 4b
The undercut wall via some pock marks.

❸ Cobra Off-width . . . . [ ] **VB** 4a
Sadly this off-width requires no off-width technique at all.

❹ Cheesy Nose . . . . ① ❀ [ ] **V0-** 4b
The arete on pock marks.

[ ] The **Burbage South Green Circuit**
The best easy circuit in the book with 30 problems on the boulders above the path. Most have very good landings but a couple get quite high and many are more slabby making falls potentially nasty.

[ ] The **Burbage South Orange Circuit**
A long and taxing circuit that makes the most of the whole area. 30 problems in all, but good landings and no highballs makes it an attractive proposition.

[ ] The **Burbage South Red Circuit**
Just 20 problems in this one and only one at **V5** *6C*. Good landings mostly and not too many highballs.

The Pock Block

❺ Cobra Mantel . . . . . ❀ [ ] **V2** 5c
Tackle the cobra's head direct with a wicked mantel to finish. Watch yourself on the block behind.

❻ The Cobra . . . . ① ② ❀ [ ] **V2** 5c
An excellent low-level traverse. Start on the side-wall then swing around. Pull up onto the top, once past *Cobra Mantel*.

❼ The High Cobra . . . . . ❀ [ ] **V2** 5c
A high traverse. Pull up onto the top, once past *Cobra Mantel*.

⑧ Wall Past Slot . . . . ③ ④ 🌟 [ ] **V0+** 5a
The far left-hand side of the slab with your right hand in the good slot. Starting with your left hand in the slot is **V2** 5c.
Photo on page 235.

⑨ Highrishman . . . . 🌟 📷 [ ] **V7** 7A+
Jump off the boulder to catch a left-hand sloper on the bulge, and a right-hand crimp. A tough rock-over remains.

⑩ Scratch Scoop . . . . . . 🌟 📷 [ ] **V7** 7A+
The desperately thin centre of the slab.

⑪ Pock-man . . . . ② ④ 🌟 [ ] **V1** 5b
The right-hand side of the slab gives a superb and airy problem. Precarious first go but it gets much easier on subsequent attempts. **V3** 6A without the chipped footholds on the right.
Photo this page.

⑫ Pick . . . . ⑤ 🌟 [ ] **V0-** 4b
The pock-marked arete. *Green Circuit continues on page 238.*

⑬ Pack. . . . . ③ 🌟 📷 [ ] **V5** 6C
A worthy eliminate up the bulging wall to the left-hand crack. Keep away from holds on the right.

⑭ Pock. . . . . ④ ⑤ 🌟 [ ] **V2** 5c
A gem of a problem up the middle of the wall. Harder for the short. Sit start is **V5** 6C. *Orange Circuit continues on page 238.*

⑮ Puck. . . . . ⑤ 🌟 [ ] **V3** 6A
The arete is very hard to start. **V7** 7A+ from sitting.
Red Circuit continues on page 238.

The Brick
p.246

The Sheep
p.238

The Pock Block
The main centre of the Burbage South boulders is this big pock-marked block. It even has a pleasant gearing up spot. The problems mostly involve using the dish scars in the rock which are slowly eroding away making bigger footholds, but slopier handholds.
Approach - See map on page 234.

Jamie Vetch climbing *Pock-man* (**V1** 5b) - *this page*. Photo: Adrian Berry

The Fat Cobra

Northern Peak | Sheffield Crags | Stanage Area | Burbage Valley | Derwent Edges | The Limestone | Central Grit | Staffordshire | South Peak

Northern Peak

Sheffield Crags

Stanage Area

Burbage Valley

Derwent Edges

The Limestone

Central Grit

Staffordshire

South Peak

The Sheep's Backside

The Lamb

Left of the Sheep is the slabby wall of **The Lamb**.

❶ Lamb Slab Left . . . . VB
The slab can be climbed in several places getting higher as you move right. It is a good starter problem.

❷ Lamb Slab Right . . . . VB
Another good easy problem.

❸ Talk to Me Martin. V8 7B+
Mega-hard and thin pulls on the poor edges left of the arete.

❹ Sickle Crack V6 7A
The arete starting with your right hand in the curving crack. **V7** 7A+ from sitting.

❺ The Sheep V6 7A
A superb problem using the curving crack and pocket to gain a sloping ledge. **V8** 7B+ from sitting. Much harder for the short.

❻ The Shearing. V2 5c
The left-hand side of the arete has an awkward finish especially if you avoid rocking over right too early. *Photo opposite.*
Red and Orange Circuits continue on page 240.

There are more problems around on **The Sheep's Backside**.

❼ The Sheep Slab . . . . VB
Anywhere on the side slab. Try it with no hands.

❽ The Sheep's Backside V0- 4b
Move from the wide slot to a pocket.

❾ Sheep Easy V0- 4b
Rock onto the slab and smear up it.

❿ The Crook . . . . VB 4a
A fine little arete is best on its right-hand side.

⓫ The Crook Traverse . . V0- 4b
Follow the rising finger-traverse to the arete.
Green Circuit continues on page 240.

The Lamb

The Pock Block

The Sheep
It does ... honest, you just have to be standing in the right place. A fine boulder with a prominent curving crack in it which is the classic *The Sheep*. The nearby Lamb Boulder and the back of the Sheep also give some good easier problems. The routes are described anticlockwise round both boulders together.
Approach - See map on page 234.

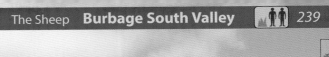

Jamie Vetch climbing *The Shearing* (**V2** 5c)
- *opposite*. Photo: Adrian Berry

Northern Peak

Sheffield Crags

Stanage Area

Burbage Valley

Derwent Edges

The Limestone

Central Grit

Staffordshire

South Peak

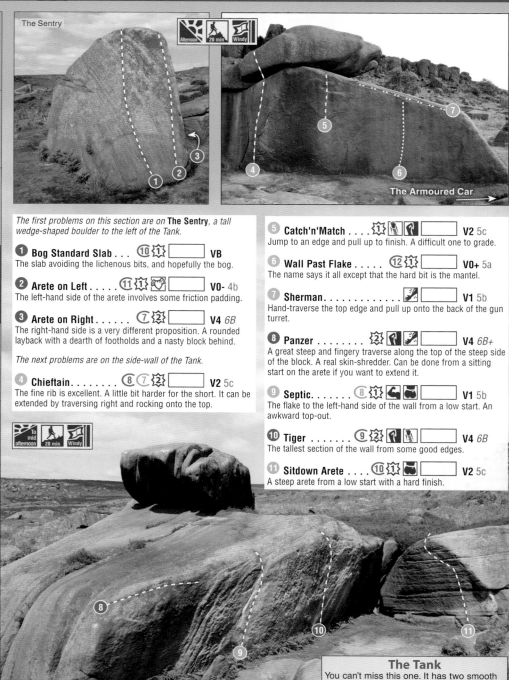

The Sentry

The Armoured Car

The first problems on this section are on **The Sentry**, *a tall wedge-shaped boulder to the left of the Tank.*

1 Bog Standard Slab . . . ⑩ 🌣 ⬜ **VB**
The slab avoiding the lichenous bits, and hopefully the bog.

2 Arete on Left . . . . . ⑪ 🌣 ⬜ **V0-** 4b
The left-hand side of the arete involves some friction padding.

3 Arete on Right . . . . . . ⑦ 🌣 ⬜ **V4** 6B
The right-hand side is a very different proposition. A rounded layback with a dearth of footholds and a nasty block behind.

The next problems are on the side-wall of the Tank.

4 Chieftain . . . . ⑧ ⑦ 🌣 ⬜ **V2** 5c
The fine rib is excellent. A little bit harder for the short. It can be extended by traversing right and rocking onto the top.

5 Catch'n'Match . . . . ⑪ 🌣 ⬜ **V2** 5c
Jump to an edge and pull up to finish. A difficult one to grade.

6 Wall Past Flake . . . . . ⑫ 🌣 ⬜ **V0+** 5a
The name says it all except that the hard bit is the mantel.

7 Sherman . . . . ⬜ **V1** 5b
Hand-traverse the top edge and pull up onto the back of the gun turret.

8 Panzer . . . . 🌣 ⬜ **V4** 6B+
A great steep and fingery traverse along the top of the steep side of the block. A real skin-shredder. Can be done from a sitting start on the arete if you want to extend it.

9 Septic . . . . ⑧ 🌣 ⬜ **V1** 5b
The flake to the left-hand side of the wall from a low start. An awkward top-out.

10 Tiger . . . . ⑨ 🌣 ⬜ **V4** 6B
The tallest section of the wall from some good edges.

11 Sitdown Arete . . . . ⑩ 🌣 ⬜ **V2** 5c
A steep arete from a low start with a hard finish.

The Tank
You can't miss this one. It has two smooth sides which give the bouldering interest but overall it promises more than it delivers.
Approach - See map on page 234.

⑫ Jigsaw Puzzle . . . . . . ⑬ ⟪ ⟫ **V0** 4c
Climb past an ear and a slot.

⑬ Mantel Past Slot . . . . ⑨ ⟪ ⟫ **V1** 5b
The wall past a distinct pebble.

⑭ Sloping Mantel . . . . . ⑩ ⟪ ⟫ **V1** 5b
Start at an eroded foothold. Easiest without a mantel.

⑮ Side pull Wall . . . . ⑪ ⟪ ⟫ **V2** 5c
An eliminate up the wall left of the arete avoiding the ledges and flakes on the right.

⑯ Big Flakes. . . . . ⑭ ⟪ ⟫ **VB**
Using the ledges and flakes is a nice easier problem.
Green Circuit continues on page 242.

⑰ Armoured Car Traverse ⟪ ⟫ **V2** 5c
A delightful traverse of the top of the wall left of the arete which tests your footwork. There is a lower traverse at **V4** 6B.

⑱ Armoured Cartwheel. . ⟪ ⟫ **V4** 6B
1m right of the arete to another awkward mantel finish.

⑲ Blind Crack . . . . ⑫ ⟪ ⟫ **V2** 5c
The wall above the intermittent pool via a flared crack.
Orange Circuit continues on page 242.

⑳ Rock and Mantel . . . . ⑪ ⟪ ⟫ **V3** 6A+
Rock up onto the break onto the right-hand side of the wall to reach a pocket. *Red Circuit continues on page 243.*

Nosferatu Area
p.224

The Armoured Car

In front of The Tank is a fine square block with a stepped arete. The wall to the right of this often has a puddle at its base. Both walls have some fine problems.
Approach - See map on page 234.

Northern Peak
Sheffield Crags
Stanage Area
Burbage Valley
Derwent Edges
The Limestone
Central Grit
Staffordshire
South Peak

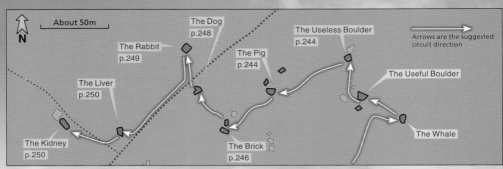

About 50m

N

The Dog
p.248

The Rabbit
p.249

The Useless Boulder
p.244

Arrows are the suggested
circuit direction

The Pig
p.244

The Liver
p.250

The Useful Boulder

The Kidney
p.250

The Brick
p.246

The Whale

The Whale

A big boulder, as you would expect, but it only has one face to offer really. Four problems above a good landing.
Approach - See map on page 234.

The Whale

① **Whale Rib** . . . . ⑮ ☆ [____] **V0+** 5a
The undercut left arete. Pull onto the slab on the left.

② **Centre Whale** . . . . . . ⑬ ☆ [____] **V1** 5b
A slight eliminate up the wall using the pocket. Swing up the arete to the top or pull around onto the slab.

③ **Right Whale** . . . . . ⑯ ☆ 🖼 [____] **V0** 4c
The centre of the wall is quite high for a problem of this grade.

④ **Whale of a Time** . . . . ⑭ ☆ [____] **V1** 5b
The far right problem using an undercut to reach up the rounded arete, then pull left to finish as for *Right Whale*.

The Useful Boulder

The Whale

The Useful Boulder

A fine boulder that doesn't look much until you get around the back where it has one excellent face plus a decent arete.
Approach - See map on page 234.

There are two isolated problems on and near The Useful Boulder.

5 Fun Slab **V0** 4c
The butt end of The Useful Boulder has this fun little slab.

6 Useful Crack . . . . ⑫ ☆ **V3** 6A+
Next to The Useful Boulder is a small boulder with this awkward little crack.

The main area of interest here is the uphill east-facing wall.

7 Left Flake **V1** 5b
Around the corner slightly is a hanging flake/crack thing.

8 Small Rib . . . . ⑮ ☆ **V1** 5b
The rib up the left-hand side of the wall.

9 Peasy Flake . . . . ⑰ ☆ **VB**
The grassy crack.

10 Flakeless **V0** 4c
A narrow eliminate between the two easy lines.

11 Easy Flake . . . . ⑱ ☆ **VB**
The pockets are easy and good. *Green continues on page 244.*

12 Scoop Eliminate . . ⑬ ☆ 🧗 **V3** 6A+
An excellent eliminate up the scoop onto the slab. No cracks are allowed. Usually very frustrating!

13 Open Flakeline . . . ⑭⑯ ☆ **V2** 5c
A super little problem up the flakes. *Photo this page.*

14 Careful Arete . . . . ☆ **V3** 6A
The arete climbed on its left-hand side.

Wayne Graham on *Open Flakeline* (**V2** 5c) - *this page*. Photo: Adrian Berry

15 Useful Arete . . . . ⑰ ☆ **V1** 5b
Climb the sharp arete on its right-hand side using unfamiliar square-cut edges. *Orange Circuit continues on page 246.*

16 It Hurts . . . . ⑮ ☆ 🧗 **V4** 6B
Crimpy wall to the right. *Red Circuit continues on page 244.*

The Useful Boulder

Northern Peak
Sheffield Crags
Stanage Area
Burbage Valley
Derwent Edges
The Limestone
Central Grit
Staffordshire
South Peak

Northern Peak

Sheffield Crags

Stanage Area

Burbage Valley

Derwent Edges

The Limestone

Central Grit

Staffordshire

South Peak

The Useless Boulder

From a distance the next boulder looks as though it may have something of interest but in the end it is a bit disappointing. The sheep seem to like it though.
Approach - See map on page 234.

1 The Useless Arete . . . . ☐ **V0-** 4b
The highest arete, on its far side. Previously graded at **V4** for some reason.

2 Pebble Wall . . . . ☐ **V0+** 5a
The pebbly wall.

3 Sloping Nose . . . . ☐ **V1** 5b
The left-hand side of the round arete.

4 Grapple with Flake . . . . . . ☐ **V2** 5c
A grovelling mantel onto the block using a flake.

The Pig

The Pig looks nothing like a pig but it is a big fat lump. It isn't very tall though so the only problems of interest are on the scooped south side with a couple of isolated offerings around the back.
Approach - See map on page 234.

5 The Basin . . . . (19) ☐ **V0+** 5a
Start on a low pocket and pull up into a pool/scoop.

6 The Trough . . . . (20) ☐ **V0+** 5a
Gaining the wide slot is surprisingly tricky.

7 Bacon Foot . . . . . (16) ☐ ☐ **V3** 6A+
Pull up slopers from a low start.

8 Little Pig . . . . . . (2) ☐ ☐ **V9** 7C
A desperate problem up the steep blunt arete from sitting.

9 Ice Cream Cone . . . . ☐ **V1** 5b
From two low pockets, heave onto the top.

10 Hidden Slab . . . . ☐ **V2** 5c
Scratch desperately up the smooth back slab.

This Little Piglet

That Little Piglet

The Useless Boulder

This Little Piglet

This small boulder behind the mass of the Pig has one attractive arete and a tiny fingerdish.
Approach - See map on page 234.

That Little Piglet

The second of the Piglets has a slabby face with four decent problems.
Approach - See map on page 234.

11 Caley Slab **V4** 6B
An eliminate up the slab which requires faith in your friction. No arete allowed.

12 Piglet Arete Left **V2** 5c
Caley Slab using the arete. Easy for the tall.

13 Piglet Arete **V2** 6a
The steep right-hand side of the arete.

14 Fingerdish Mantel . . . **V2** 6a
Locate the fingerdish, ... I'm sure you know what to do next!

15 That Little Arete Left . **V3** 6A+
The left-hand side of the arete. *Red continues on page 248.*

16 That Little Arete Right **V0-** 4b
The arete on the right is a nice slabby offering.

17 The Careful Trotter . . . **V0** 4c
More pleasant padding up the vague rib.
Green Circuit continues on page 246.

18 Oink Arete . . . . **V0+** 5a
A tricky pull on the flake is required on this one.

The Brick
p.246

The Briquette

① The Pig

The Dog

The Brick

An excellent boulder which is possibly even more popular than the Pock Block. The problems tend to be friendly and technical above good landings.
Approach - See map on page 234.

The Briquette *is next to The Brick and has one nice slabby face.*

❶ Slabby Rib . . . . ㉓ ⌗ ☐ **VO-** 4b
The arete requires a tricky pull to get started.

❷ The Windmill . . . . . . ㉔ ⌗ ☐ **VB** 4a
The left line on the slab. This is **V2** 6a without hands or knees.

❸ Gentle Slab . . . . ㉕ ⌗ ☐ **VB** 4a
The right line of the slab.

❹ Huggy . . . . ⑱ ⌗ ☐ **V1** 5b
A brilliant problem up the steep arete. The sit start is **V3** *6A*.

❺ Blunt Arete . . . . . . ㉖ ⌗ ☐ **VO+** 5a
The left arete requires a steep pull.

❻ Pocket Wall . . . . . ⑲ ⌗ ☐ **V1** 5b
The middle of the end wall. The pocket looks suspicious but the problem is the same grade with or without it.

❼ Short Arete . . . . ㉗ ⌗ ☐ **VO-** 4b
Past the eroding dish on the arete.

❽ Reachy Wall . . . . . ⑳ ⌗ ☐ **V1** 5b
A long reach proves helpful.

❾ Little Air . . . . ⌗ ☐ **V2** 5c
Jump from the neighbouring boulder to grab the edges, then mantel to finish. A much less serious undertaking than its big brother at Stanage (page 135).

The Pock Block

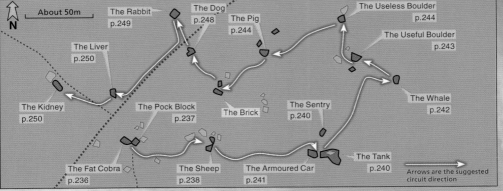

About 50m
N

The Rabbit p.249
The Dog p.248
The Pig p.244
The Useless Boulder p.244
The Useful Boulder p.243
The Liver p.250
The Kidney p.250
The Pock Block p.237
The Brick
The Sentry p.240
The Whale p.242
The Fat Cobra p.236
The Sheep p.238
The Armoured Car p.241
The Tank p.240

Arrows are the suggested circuit direction

10 Vague Rib . . . . 21 ☼ [ ] **V2** 5c
The vague rib. There are plenty of variations possible depending on which pocket you put your hands in to start.

11 Northern . . . . 22 ☼ [ ] **V1** 5b
Climb the wall past a pocket.

12 Exposure . . . . 28 ☼ [ ] **V0+** 5a
The left-hand side of the arete. *Green continues on page 248.*

13 KBHR . . . . 23 ☼ [ ] **V1** 5b
The arete on its right-hand side.

14 Cicely . . . . 24 ☼ ▨ [ ] **V0+** 5a
Straight up the end wall.

15 Alaska . . . . . . 25 ☼ ▨ ▨ [ ] **V2** 6a
The arete with a slot on its left-hand side, from a low start. *Orange Circuit continues on page 248.*

16 Alaska Right . . . . ☼ ▨ [ ] **V2** 5c
The right-hand side of the arete is frustrating to start. **V4** *6B* from sitting.

17 Crash 'n' Gurn . ☼ ▨ ▨ ▨ ▨ [ ] **V6** *7A*
Dyno from undercut and mono to the huge bucket.

18 Brick Back Wall . . . . [ ] **V0-** 4b
This and *Short Arete* are also the easiest ways off the top.

Sun and shade · 20 min · Windy

Northern Peak

Sheffield Crags

Stanage Area

Burbage Valley

Derwent Edges

The Limestone

Central Grit

Staffordshire

South Peak

The Dog

The dog's head boulder is right next to the main path. It has two sets of problems on opposite sides.
Approach - See map on page 234.

1 Dog Jump . . . . ⑲ ☆ 🖐 🧗 ☐ **V3** *6A*
Jump to the edge and heave over. **V2** 6a if you are tall enough to reach the edge.

2 Dog Sit . . . . . ☆ 🧗 ✋ 🍑 ☐ **V6** *7A*
Start on a low edge and snatch up poor holds. The footblock is allowed.

3 Dog Pound . . ☆ 🧗 ✋ 🍑 ☐ **V6** *7A*
From a sitting start, traverse left and up. The footblock is not allowed.

4 Walking the Dog . . . . ㉙ ☆ ☐ **V0** *4c*
Traverse the slabby face from right to left without using the top.

5 Doggy Bulge . . . . ㉚ ☆ ☐ **V0-** *4b*
The rounded arete above an eroding foothold.
The last problem on the Green Circuit.

6 Dog's Arse Left . . . . . ㉖ ☆ ☐ **V0+** *5a*
The left-hand side of the flared crack. Sit start is **V6** *7A*.

7 Dog's Arse Right . . . . . ㉗ ☆ ☐ **V1** *5b*
The right-hand side of the flared crack. Sit start is **V7** *7A+*.
Orange Circuit continues on page 250.

8 Doggy Style. . . . . . ⑳ ☆ 🍑 ☐ **V4** *6B*
Start low on the side of the dog's nose, follow the lip up leftwards as far as you can go.
The last problem in the Red Circuit.

The Rabbit

The Brick

The Rabbit

This boulder with rounded finishes is situated below the track. It isn't a great boulder. The problems are all very similar rounded pulls to mantels, with a dearth of footholds and plenty of shin-grinding potential. If you already have thin skin and bleeding shins keep away.

⑨ Reachy Arete **V2** 5c
At the lowest point is an arete. Much, much harder for the short.

⑩ Top of Ramp **V1** 5b
Climb through the left end of the diagonal overlap. Harder if you can't reach the pocket to start.

⑪ Jim's Slopes **V2** 5c
An eliminate but worthwhile. More awkward than it looks. *Photo this page.*

⑫ Deep Pocket **V2** 6a
The bulge has a helpful edge.

⑬ Bunny **V4** *6B*
The centre of the arete has some poor slopers.

⑭ Bugs **V2** 5c
The right-hand side of the arete.

⑮ Rabbit Wall **V2** 5c
The slopey wall.

⑯ Bunny Wall **V2** 5c
The wall just left of a rounded bulge.

Jamie Vetch climbing *Jim's Slopes* (**V2** 5c) - *this page*. Photo: Adrian Berry

Northern Peak

Sheffield Crags

Stanage Area

Burbage Valley

Derwent Edges

The Limestone

Central Grit

Staffordshire

South Peak

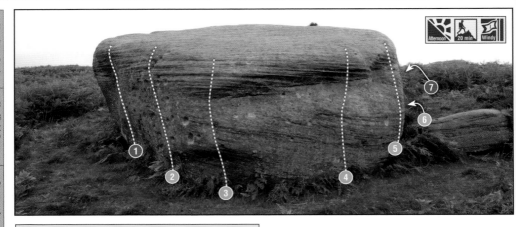

The Liver

This big slanting block is not a great boulder. Most problems involve identical swimming-mantels onto the sloping lower side and that is never very enjoyable. **Approach** - See map on page 234.

1 Green Scoop Mantel **V3** 6A
The left of two mantels appears to be desperate at first.

2 Left of Nose Mantel **V2** 5c
The mantel just left of the nose, using pock-marks.

3 Nose Mantel **V2** 6a
Flop over the nose.

4 Scoop Mantel **V2** 5c
Another mantel without enough footholds.

5 Over the Top **V1** 5b
Grovel over the wall above and left.

6 Bald Top **V1** 5b
The blunt arete past a short crack.

7 Flake and Scoop **V0** 4c
Short slab past a sloping ledge.

The Kidney Boulder has much more to offer.

8 Kidney Traverse 28 **V1** 5b
A delicate very low (for your feet) traverse, finishing up *4c Wall.* The extension move into the next foot pocket is **V3** 6A.

9 Mantel the Bulge 29 **V1** 5b
Pull up over a little roof.

10 Kidney Wall . . . . **V0+** 5a
The slab just right of the roof to a flared crack. If it feels harder then you are starting in the wrong place.

11 Slot Entry 30 **V1** 5b
Reach the flared crack. *The last problem in the Orange Circuit. Photo this page.*

12 4c Wall **V0** 4c
The short wall. Further right is similar but even shorter.

The Kidney

Below the track on the path which leads to Higgar Tor is a boulder on the left-hand side of the path which has a lovely south-facing slabby wall.

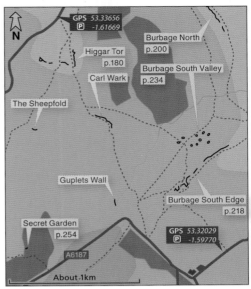

Guplets Wall

A decent pair of problems on the isolated Guplets Wall.
Approach - From the main valley track, head towards Carl Wark until you cross the stream, then break out left to the wall on a section which is often boggy.

13 Guplets on Toast . 🔲 **V8** *7B+*
The bulging wall from a sitting start. Standing is **V4** *6B+*.

14 Darkstar . . . . 🔲 **V10** *7C+*
The wall to the right of the crack is hard and quite high. The top may be in need of a brush. Worth E6.

Carl Wark

The flat-topped Carl Wark situated below Higgar Tor has one steep wall that has been developed by boulderers. The north-facing aspect means that it is green for much of the year and it sees little attention.
Approach - Follow any of the paths to Carl Wark and then scramble down to the tallest section of the crag.

15 Not Green Flag . . . . 🔲 **V6** *7A*
The left-hand side of the wall, on slopers, to the break.

16 Green Flag . . . . 🔲 **V8** *7B+*
The thin wall from using a good hold and side-pulls to the mid-height break. Scramble off left.

17 Rugosity Dinks . . . . 🔲 **V5** *6C*
Climb the wall just left of the thin crack to the break.

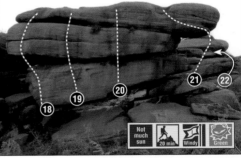

The Sheepfold

On the moor below the Leaning Block on Higgar Tor is a large rectangular sheepfold with a dark edge near it.
Approach - Drop down from Higgar Tor, or follow the path from Mother Cap.

18 Jean Marie . . . . 🔲 **V7** *7A+*
The left-hand side wall.

19 Just Walkin' . . . . 🔲 **V6** *7A*
Pull up the left side of the wall.

20 Sean . . . . 🔲 **V7** *7A+*
Straight up the centre, between the heather clumps.

21 Here Be Dragons . . . . 🔲 **V6** *7A*
Climb up then reach left to the scoop from the flake.

22 Roofless People . 🔲 **V5** *6C*
Around the back is a low roof. From a sitting start, follow edges to the lip.

Northern Peak · Sheffield Crags · Stanage Area · Burbage Valley · Derwent Edges · The Limestone · Central Grit · Staffordshire · South Peak

	No star	✶	✶✶	✶✶✶
VB to V0 Easy to 4c	2	6	1	-
V0+ to V2 5a to 5c	3	22	4	-
V3 to V5 6A to 6C+	3	16	8	9
V3 to V5 7A upwards	3	14	9	10

Northern Peak

Sheffield Crags

Stanage Area

Burbage Valley

Derwent Edges

The Limestone

Central Grit

Staffordshire

South Peak

Audrey Seguy on *Technical Master* (**V4** *6B*) - *page 266* - Millstone Edge. Photo: Adrian Berry

The Millstone area comprises several isolated areas of natural rock dotted across the moors above the large quarried crag of Millstone. For complete isolation there is the well-named Secret Garden hidden in the edge of the trees with its powerful roof problems. In complete contrast are the impressive monolith of Mother Cap and the smaller towers of Over Owler Tor; both are always busy, usually with walkers rather than boulderers. These areas offer pleasant vertical walls and aretes with a few steeper problems. Hidden a stone's throw from Mother Cap is another block with some desperate rounded roof problems known as Mother's Pet Rock. The final area is the quarry of Millstone itself which is an altogether different proposition. There are no rounded pulls here just delicate bridging on edges and technical laybacks up aretes.

Circuits

This area is quite spread out and getting between the various blocks isn't easy. The two circuits covered here are Orange and Red Circuits that take in Mother Cap, Over Owler Tor and Millstone but don't include the Secret Garden.

Approach

Also see map on page 179

Millstone is well known to most climbers, towering over the A625 as it drops down towards Hathersage. The other crags described are all situated on the moorland behind Millstone and all the areas are best reached from the Surprise View car park which is situated just east of the bend of Surprise View.

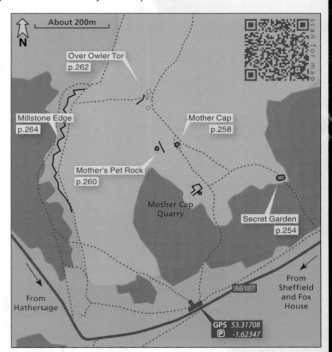

About 200m

N

Over Owler Tor
p.262

Millstone Edge
p.264

Mother Cap
p.258

Mother's Pet Rock
p.260

Mother Cap Quarry

Secret Garden
p.254

From Hathersage

From Sheffield and Fox House

A6187

GPS 53.31708
P -1.62347

Conditions

Both Over Owler Tor and Mother Cap are high and exposed, catching everything that is going. This also means that they dry quickly and are rarely green although some of Over Owler Tor faces north so can retain dampness in some conditions. There is a bit more shelter on the Pet Rock but nothing very significant. The Secret Garden gets more shelter from the trees and retains some dampness. Millstone gets lots of afternoon sun although the northernmost bays can offer shade in the summer months and are likely to be green in winter.

Northern Peak · Sheffield Crags · Stanage Area · Burbage Valley · Derwent Edges · The Limestone · Central Grit · Staffordshire · South Peak

The Secret Garden

This delightful little spot is not quite as secret as the name suggests, although it is still relatively quiet since the only people who come here are boulderers. The main problems are superb and steep above good landings. The traverse is a classic of its type and there is plenty to keep you busy for a few afternoons.

Approach (see map on page 253) - Park in the Surprise View parking on the A6187 Fox House to Hathersage Road. Walk back towards Fox House, to a stile on the left, just past an old milepost on the far side of the road. Cross the stile and walk straight up into the small woods. Keep on the main track until the boulders become visible up on your left.

1 First Bulge **V1** 5b
The left-hand side of the wall.

2 Sitdown Bulge **V4** 6B
Start low and move out left from the rightwards facing groove.

3 Sitdown Groove **V2** 5c
An awkward start up the groove. Easy if you start with your hands high.

4 The Harder Side . . **V6** 7A
A delightful little problem up the bulging arete. Start low and slap your way up it. **V8** 7B without the arete.

5 The Easier Side **V4** 6B
The pockets just right of the arete. **V2** 5c from standing.

6 Topless Crack **V2** 6a
The low crack is entertaining higher up.

7 Chockstone Crack **V1** 5b
A wide crack with an awkward finish.

8 Up From Recess . . . . **V3** 6A+
A weird little problem. Start with one hand on the lip and the other under the roof then pull up leftwards.

9 Beach Bum **V6** 7A
Starting at the back of the roof, follow the slopers.

10 Zaff's Problem . . . **V8** 7B
Awesome moves over the bulge.

11 Pistol Pinch . . . . . **V7** 7A+
Start at the back. Move left to gain the rounded pocket.

12 Beach Ball **V6** 7A
The direct line. *Photo on page 3.*

Lots of sun | 10 min

Side tabs: Northern Peak | Sheffield Crags | Stanage Area | Burbage Valley | Derwent Edges | The Limestone | Central Grit | Staffordshire | South Peak

13 Not Zaff's .... 🎯 [____] **V4** *6B*
The right-facing crack line has a hard rounded finish.

14 Beach Crack .... 🎯 🖐️ [____] **V1** 5b
The right-facing crack line has a hard rounded finish.

15 Secret Garden Traverse
.... 🎯 ✊ 🖐️ [____] **V4** *6B*
Superb! Traverse the 'orrible sloping break with your hands, finishing with *Up From the Recess*. Use your feet wisely.

16 Zippatricks ..... 🎯 ✊ 🖐️ [____] **V10** *7C+*
The *Secret Garden Traverse* but without your feet. Much harder for the tall.

17 The Runnel .... 🎯 ✊ [____] **V5** *6C*
Scratch desperately up the faint groove.

18 Nigel's Problem ..... 🎯 ✊ [____] **V7** *7A+*
Starting at a break, gain twin slopers then slap to the next break.

19 Left-hand Man ... 🎯 ✊ ✊ [____] **V8** *7B+*
Starting on the shelf, use slopers to reach the big pocket. Eliminating the arete and climbing the wall just to the right to reach the pocket is **V10** *7C+*.

20 Dick Williams 🎯 ✊ 🖐️ ✊ [____] **V8** *7B+*
The right arete is something of a classic.

21 Middle Man ..... 🎯 ✊ ✊ [____] **V9** *7C*
The diagonal line to gain the pocket on *Left-Hand Man*.

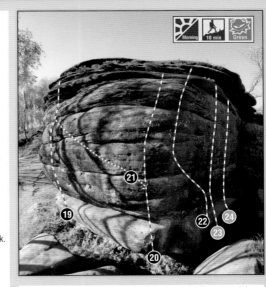

The wall around the corner has some delightful 'Buoux-style' pockets in it.

22 Right-hand Man ..... 🎯 ✊ [____] **V8** *7B+*
From a low start, use a mono to gain pockets then pull left to climb the right-hand side of the arete.

23 Buoux Left .... 🎯 [____] **V2** 5c
The left-hand side of the pockets.

24 Buoux Right .... 🎯 [____] **V1** 5b
The right-hand side of the pockets.

Northern Peak · Sheffield Crags · Stanage Area · Burbage Valley · Derwent Edges · The Limestone · Central Grit · Staffordshire · South Peak

The Garden Shed

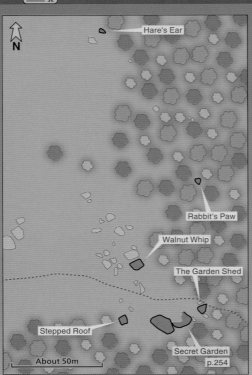

The Secret Garden - Outlying

The blocks around the main Secret Garden area have a few hidden problems for the enthusiast. These are marked on the map to the left. There are no real paths through the bracken and heather so finding them can be tricky. The Stepped Roof buttress is the best. The others can be green and dirty although they may give some shade in warmer weather.

Approach - See map on page 253.

The Garden Shed is opposite the Buoux pocket wall on the main area wall and looks, rather confusingly, like a walnut whip.

❶ Garden Shed Arete **V3** *6A*
Climb the steep back arete.

❷ Garden Shed **V5** *6C*
A stiff pull over the lower bulging arete.

Stepped Roof

Left (looking in) of the main Secret Garden area is a small stepped roof.

❸ Zaffatricks . . . . **V8** *7B+*
Traverse from left to right staying below the lip.

❹ The Duck **V5** *6C*
Starting at good jams, pass the sloper and finish via the break.

❺ Middle Duck . . . . **V4** *6B+*
Starting with your right hand on a side-pull and your left on the undercut/jam, span out to good holds in the roof and exit.

❻ Right-Hand Duck **V6** *7A*
Starting as for *Middle Duck*, move out right through the roof and finish with difficulty.

Map labels:
Hare's Ear
Rabbit's Paw
Walnut Whip
The Garden Shed
Stepped Roof
Secret Garden p.254
About 50m
N

Side tabs:
Northern Peak
Sheffield Crags
Stanage Area
Burbage Valley
Derwent Edges
The Limestone
Central Grit
Staffordshire
South Peak

Walnut Whip

Above the Secret Garden main wall and set slight back is a block with a shady northeast face.

7 Hulley Pulley . . . .  **V8** *7B+*
The short wall with a tiny pocket, from a sitting start and avoiding anything that makes it feel easy.

8 Fireball . . . . **V8** *7B+*
Another rounded arete, from a sitting start.

9 Walnut Whip **V5** *6C*
Another rounded arete.

Rabbit's Paw

Head about 50m through the woods from the Walnut Whip to a triangular slab in the trees.

10 Rabbit's Paw **V4** *6B*
The centre of the slab is thin.

11 The Fur Side **V0** *4c*
The right arete looks thin but has a useful flake.

Hare's Ear

The next block is about 100m further north along the edge of the tree line and faces northeast.

12 Hare's Ear Left **V5** *6C*
A big pull up left from the good hold on the lip using the intermediate sloper.

13 Hare's Ear **V6** *7A*
The more direct version straight up is a touch harder.

Northern Peak — Sheffield Crags — Stanage Area — Burbage Valley — Derwent Edges — The Limestone — Central Grit — Staffordshire — South Peak

Northern Peak

Sheffield Crags

Stanage Area

Burbage Valley

Derwent Edges

The Limestone

Central Grit

Staffordshire

South Peak

Mother Cap

The impressive square monolith of Mother Cap can be clearly seen from some distance and is usually very busy, although not with boulderers. The bouldering on its walls tends to be high and rounded but there are some decent problems and it combines well with a circuit at Owler Tor. *Conan the Librarian* is a classic and the landings are good so you can pad out the falls if required. It is very exposed to the weather but that does mean that it isn't green and will dry quickly.

Approach (see map on page 253) - Follow the main path from the Surprise View car park to Mother Cap, the distinct monolith that appears as you leave the woods.

① **Blue Cap Start** . . . . **①** 🎋 [ ] **V0+** 5a
The far left arete at the back of the block. The route pulls over the top at HVS.

② **Elf Cap Start** . . . . [ ] **V3** 6A
The centre of the wall feels quite bold. The route continues over the top at E2, but many will find the lower bit worth that as well.

③ **Oyster Cap Start** . . **①** 🎋 [ ] **V3** 6A+
The tallest arete on the block is quite high. Escape rightwards.

[ ] The **Millstone Area Red Circuit**
A 22-problem circuit on four different sections with some classic problems mostly below **V4** 6B+.

Descent

[ ] The **Mother Owler Orange Circuit**
This relatively easy orange circuit makes the most of Mother Cap and Over Owler Tor. It includes 17 problems with quite a few in the green zone.

Descent

4 David . . . . ⬚ ⬚ ⬚ [ ] **V8** 7B
Climb the left-hand side of the wall above a short crack.

5 **Conan the Librarian**
. . . . ② ⬚ ⬚ ⬚ [ ] **V4** 6B+
The best thing on Mother Cap. Thin moves above a good landing but most will need a mat. *Photo this page.*

6 Thin Wall . . . . ③ ⬚ ⬚ ⬚ [ ] **V3** 6A+
Climb the wall just left of the crack, eliminating the right arete.

7 Milk Cap . . . . ② ⬚ ⬚ [ ] **VB** 4a
The crack is a good old fashioned VDiff.

8 Ink Cap . . . . ③ ⬚ [ ] **V0** 4c
The wall left of the arete is tricky to get going on.

9 Flat Cap . . . . ④ ⬚ [ ] **V0+** 5a
Climb the arete mostly on its right-hand side, rocking over onto a ledge.

10 Dutch Cap . . . . . . ④ ⑤ ⬚ [ ] **V2** 5c
Thin moves up the centre of the side-wall. *The Red Circuit continues on page 260 and the Orange Circuit on page 262.*

11 Easy Cap . . . . [ ] **VB**
The right-hand side of the side-wall, avoiding the very easy way.

12 Mother's Cap Back Wall . . . . . [ ] **V1** 5b
The short wall on the back, between boulders.

13 Mama-Mia . . . . ⬚ [ ] **V0+** 5a
Traverse of the three biggest faces. Start at *Blue Cap* and keep fairly low on some disappointingly large foot-ledges. The last section on the *Dutch Cap* wall is known as **Baby's Traverse** and is **V0-** 4b.

Adrian Berry about to make the crux pull on *Conan the Librarian* (**V4** 6B+) - *this page* - at Mother Cap. Photo: Duncan Skelton

Northern Peak

Sheffield Crags

Stanage Area

Burbage Valley

Derwent Edges

The Limestone

Central Grit

Staffordshire

South Peak

Mother's Pet Rock

Hidden away to the west of Mother Cap is a small edge and a huge undercut boulder that promises little when viewed from above. The steep face of this boulder has a set of similar desperate problems most of which require ungracious beached-whale type struggles to finish.

Approach (see map on page 253) - Follow the main path from Surprise View car park to Mother Cap. Then head directly left (west) and scramble down to the block.

Over Owler Tor
p.262

Path to
Millstone

Mother Cap
p.258

Mother's Pet Rock

From Surprise View
car park

❶ Mother's Pet Arete . . . **V4** *6B*
The right-side of the left arete.

❷ The Blue Whale **V5** *6C*
Just climbing the face using the two pockets is harder.

❸ Orca . . . . **V8** *7B+*
Pull over past the wide section and a very rounded top out..

❹ Porker **V9** *7C*
Use a thin break to gain the rounded top out.

❺ Mother's Pride . . . **V8** *7B+*
Desperate sloper-pulling to a sloping top-out.

❻ Pet Cemetery . . . **V7** *7A+*
The slightly easier line just right. *Photo this page.*

❼ Ahab . . . . **V3** *6A+*
Rock onto the shelf, using anything in reach. Approach from *Pet Cemetery* at **V5** *6C*.

❽ Mother's Pet Traverse
. . . . **V7** *7A+*
The low traverse requires persistence. Finish up *Ahab*.

❾ Mother's Pet Long Traverse
. . . . **V8** *7B+*
... continue and finish up *Moby*.

Lee Pendleton on *Pet Cemetery* (**V7** *7A+*) - *this page*. Photo: Adrian Berry

Northern Peak
Sheffield Crags
Stanage Area
Burbage Valley
Derwent Edges
The Limestone
Central Grit
Staffordshire
South Peak

⑩ Top Shelf Mantel **V6** *7A*
Mantel the middle of the ledge.

⑪ Moby **V4** *6B*
Mantel the right-hand side of the ledge.

⑫ Proper Grit . . . . **V5** *6C+*
The wall to the right from a low start.

⑬ Pets Win Prizes **V8** *7B*
Wall to the right from sitting.

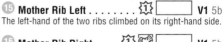

⑭ Mini Mother . . . . . **V3** *6A+*
The front face on the furthest block left. Start low and keep
going for further than you think.
Red Circuit continues on page 262.

⑮ Mother Rib Left **V1** *5b*
The left-hand of the two ribs climbed on its right-hand side.

⑯ Mother Rib Right **V1** *5b*
The next block right has a big rounded front. Awkward finish.

Mini Mother

Mother Ribs

Mother's Pet

Wafery Flake

Over Owler Tor

Further up the hill from Mother Cap is a collection of short walls and boulders below the jumbled mass of Over Owler Tor.

Approach (see map on page 253) - Continue up the main path from Mother Cap. Pass a 'walnut whip' like block, on the left, then bear left over the short edge just before you reach a 'mushroom' block.

❶ Cutaway **V5** *6C*
Wall above the cutaway.

❷ Scrunchy Slopes . . **V4** *6B*
The wall direct above a triangular ledge. Needs a spotter because of the 'pop-off' potential. **V2** 5c for the tall.

❸ Slopey Scrunch **V2** *5c*
The wall above a small broken flake.

❹ Lil' Arete **V0-** 4b
An arete and cracks.

❺ Wafery Flake . . . . . **V3** *6A+*
A smart little fingery wall from a tiny flake.

❻ Plop Start Left . . . . . . **V0+** 5a
The arete on its left-hand side is tricky to start.

❼ Plop Start Right **V0-** 4b
The arete is much easier on its right-hand side.

❽ Plip Start **V0** 4c
The wall right of the arete as far as the break.

❾ Flake Arete . . . . **VB**
A little arete with a flake.

Wafery Flake

Roof 1
Roof 2
Fingersplitter

⑩ ⑪ ⑫ ⑬ ⑭

⑩ Roof 1 . . . ⑪ V5 *6C*
From a very low start under the roof, move out right using a crimp and the right edge of the roof. Pull round to finish on the nose. Traversing left under the roof and up the left-hand side-wall is a poor **V3** *6A+*.

⑪ Roof 2 . . . . . . ⑫⑪ V2 *5c*
A very low roof. Start as far in as you can on two small crimps.

⑫ Left Tower. . . . . ⑫ V1 *5b*
The arete to the left of the crack.

⑬ Fingersplitter . . . . . . ⑬ V0+ *5a*
The crack. Much harder if you only use the crack.

⑭ Right Tower. . . . . ⑭ V0+ *5a*
The right arete.

⑮ Friend Slot Wall . . ⑮ V0+ *5a*
The wall left of the arete, using a 'Friend' slot. Much harder if you can't reach the slot.

⑯ Sisyphus. . . . . . V7 *7A+*
Sit start the arete on its left to gain the 'Friend' slot.

⑰ Golden Arete . . . . ⑬ V4 *6B+*
A brilliant problem up the steep arete with a crack.

⑱ Spider Crack . . . . V5 *6C+*
Golden Arete but just climbing the crack, with no arete allowed.
V7 *7A+* from sitting. *Photo on page 20.*

Golden Arete

㉑

⑳

⑮ ⑯ ⑰ ⑱ ⑲

⑲ Jawbone. . . ⑭⑯ V2 *5c*
Make a long move between the two ears. Dynamic for the short. A little harder from sitting but not much.

⑳ The Eye Socket . . . ⑮⑰ V2 *5c*
Start low as for *Jawbone* but move out right past some pockets. *The final problem in the Orange Circuit. The Red Circuit continues over at Millstone on page 264.*

㉑ Silver Arete. V0 *4c*
The arete in the back corridor.

Roof 1
Roof 2
Fingersplitter
Golden Arete

Northern Peak | Sheffield Crags | Stanage Area | Burbage Valley | Derwent Edges | The Limestone | Central Grit | Staffordshire | South Peak

North Bay

① ② ③ ④

North Bay to Green Death

The northern section of Millstone beyond the Embankment area has a few isolated problems including a couple of super-hard classics. The walls tend to be shadier, especially in the North Bay and hence can be green in the winter, but nice and cool at other times.
Approach (see map on page 253) - Take the path from Surprise View car park to the quarry. Then follow the path at the base of the crag passing the successive bays. You can approach easily from Over Owler Tor which brings you out above the North Bay.

① **Brigadoon** **V8** *7B*
The fingery wall hidden away on the far left of the bay.

② **Deceptive Rib** **V2** *5c*
A high problem up the steepening rib.

③ **Steady Arete** **V1** *5b*
Climb the arete on its left-hand side to a steeper finish.

④ **Bohemian Grove** **V11** *8A*
Ultra-thin wall climbing to good holds at around 4m. No arete.

Great Slab

⑤

⑤ **Sex Dwarves** . . . . . **V4** *6B+*
Frustrating friction climbing up the right-hand side of Great Slab. It is possible to step off right after the crux. Slippery.

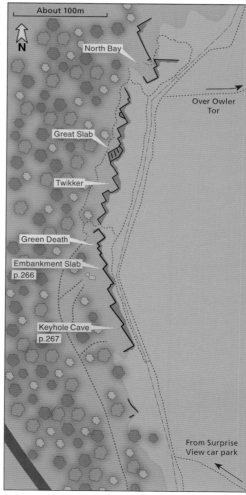

About 100m

N

North Bay

Over Owler Tor

Great Slab

Twikker

Green Death

Embankment Slab
p.266

Keyhole Cave
p.267

From Surprise View car park

Twikker

Green Death

6 The Bed of Procrustes

. . . . **V12** *8A+*
A stunning problem of utmost difficulty up tiny edges on the green streak below the route *Twikker*.

7 Cherry Bank Road . . . **V6** *7A*
Just left of the route *Great West Road*, climb the arete to finish at a good edge. Avoiding the shot-hole is **V10** *7C+*.

8 Green Death Start . **V5** *6C*
The thin edges on the left-hand side-wall lead to some sloping ledges. An excellent fingery problem.
Red Circuit continues on page 266.

9 Green Death Superdirect. . **V8** *7B*
Bridge the corner to a small edge and then larger ledges above. We have no symbols to describe the type of move needed for this problem but don't forget to squeak your rubber.
Photo this page.

Tom Haigh attempting the desperate friction bridging of *Green Death Superdirect* (**V8** *7B*) - *this page*. Photo: Adrian Berry

Northern Peak

Sheffield Crags

Stanage Area

Burbage Valley

Derwent Edges

The Limestone

Central Grit

Staffordshire

South Peak

Northern Peak

Sheffield Crags

Stanage Area

Burbage Valley

Derwent Edges

The Limestone

Central Grit

Staffordshire

South Peak

Embankment Slab

The popular central section of Millstone is home to many classic crack, corner and arete climbs. Hidden amongst all these towering walls are some surprisingly good boulder problems including one of the Peak's most famous. The walls here dry quickly and are seldom green. It can get hot in the afternoon sun.

Approach (see map on page 253) - Follow the path from the Surprise View car park. The Embankment area is the popular open area in the middle of the crag.

❶ Master Chef . . . . 🌀 🔗 [＿＿] **V8** *7B*
Manoeuvre up the blunt arete somehow. Reach at a good hold then stretch rightwards to *Technical Baiter*. **V9** *7C* from sitting.

❷ Technical Baiter. . . . . ⑱🌀 [＿＿] **V1** *5b*
The clean groove around the corner is often used as a descent, but make sure you have it wired first.

❸ Technical Master Left . 🌀 🔗 [＿＿] **V5** *6C*
If you layback up the left-hand side of the arete things get considerably harder and less delicate. **V7** *7A+* if you eliminate the crack.

❹ Technical Master . . . . . ⑲🌀 [＿＿] **V4** *6B*
One of the Peak's great problems follows the left arete of the Embankment slab. The trick is usually working out which foot to start with. *Photo on page 252.*

❺ Tip Top . . . . 🌀 🔗 [＿＿] **V9** *7C*
The thin crack left of the start of the route *Time for Tea*, to a good hold at 4m. Descent from here is tricky.

❻ Little Lotto Arete . . . . ⑳🌀 [＿＿] **V1** *5b*
The arete on its left-hand side via a handy pocket. It is an excellent **V3** *6A* without the pocket.

❼ Little Lotto Arete Right 🌀 🔗 [＿＿] **V5** *6C*
The sharp arete is desperate on its right-hand side.

❽ Seventies Style Wall . . ㉑🌀 [＿＿] **V4** *6B+*
The green slab. No arete allowed at this grade.

Keyhole Cave

The Keyhole Cave is in the second bay when approaching from the Surprise View parking via the lower path. The problems here are fingery traverses.

⑨ The Metal Rash Traverse

.... **V1** *5b*

The slabby wall left of the main Keyhole Cave wall can be traversed at a friendly height. Start by a block on the left and go all the way rightwards into the corner.

⑩ Keyhole Traverse

.... **V5** *6C*

The traverse below the cave is a unique exercise in sustained finger crimping on painful holds. Start at the furthest left crack or further left if you want to be pedantic. The grade depends on how far you go, this version is for reaching the 4th crack (*Jermyn Street*). *The final problem on the Red Circuit.*

⑪ Keyhole Traverse 2 **V6** *7A*

To the 7th crack (*Regent Street Direct*).

⑫ Keyhole Traverse 3 **V7** *7A+*

To the 8th crack (*Wall Street Crash*).

⑬ Keyhole Traverse 4 **V8** *7B+*

If you persist to the 10th crack (*Shaftesbury Avenue*) award yourself a pat on the back and go and nurse your fingertips.

⑭ Two Shot Holes **V2** *5c*

A little crack in the far back corner of the quarry to shot holes.

Regent Street (E2)

Northern Peak

Sheffield Crags

Stanage Area

Burbage Valley

Derwent Edges

The Limestone

Central Grit

Staffordshire

South Peak

	No star	🌟	🌟🌟	🌟🌟🌟
VB to V0 Easy to 4c	1	-	-	-
V0+ to V2 5a to 5c	8	8	-	-
V3 to V5 6A to 6C+	1	9	-	-
V3 to V5 7A upwards	1	1	-	-

Houndkirk Moor is situated to the east (Sheffield side) of Burbage and has two small bouldering locations. Neither is very significant but both are worth a look if you are in the area. Houndkirk Tor (False) has a small north-facing edge with a few decent blocks. The Ox Stones are a couple of large isolated blocks with one decent face. There isn't much scope for more problems beyond those detailed here.

Conditions

Houndkirk Tor (False) faces north and gets little sunshine. This leaves the place green for much of the winter. It is exposed to wind and so should dry quickly. A brush might be required to get rid of the lichen. The main Ox Stone is south-facing and much more exposed, although the rock is very gritty.

Duncan Campbell stretching through the roof on *Oxymoron* (**V1** 5b) - *opposite* - on the Ox Stones. Photo: Alan James

Northern Peak

Sheffield Crags

Stanage Area

Burbage Valley

Derwent Edges

The Limestone

Central Grit

Staffordshire

South Peak

Lots of sun | 5 min | Windy

The Ox Stones

The Ox Stones are a very minor venue but the largest one does have one good wall. It makes a good short evening venue or somewhere to stop off on a walk. The landings are good.

Approach - Park at the wide lay-by on the Ringinglow to Burbage road, just before the cattle grid on a bend. A rough path leads over a stile on the other side of the road across the moor. After only a very short distance the largest stone becomes visible on the left.

❶ First of a Thousand Oxs   **V3** *6A*
The hand traverse of the lip of the left-hand block is fun. Easier if you poke your toe onto a few ledges.

❷ Oxygen **V1** *5b*
The roof is easy at first, but there's a hard rock-over on the lip.

❸ Oxycute 'em **V2** *5c*
Start from the left-hand side of the flake/boss. The roof is easier than it looks.

❹ Oxymoron **V1** *5b*
Start from the other side of the flake/boss. Cross the roof on 'micro-jugs' and heave over on the 'bomber sloper'.
Photo opposite.

❺ Ox-Trail Soup **V1** *5b*
Traverse the lip from right to left. Footless is **V5** *6C*.

The wall around to the right of the steep section can be climbed anywhere and gives a few interesting easier problems.

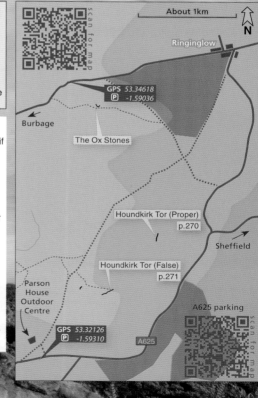

scan for map

About 1km

N

Ringinglow

GPS 53.34618
P -1.59036

Burbage

The Ox Stones

Houndkirk Tor (Proper)
p.270

Sheffield

Houndkirk Tor (False)
p.271

Parson House Outdoor Centre

A625 parking

GPS 53.32126
P -1.59310

A625

scan for map

Northern Peak · Sheffield Crags · Stanage Area · Burbage Valley · Derwent Edges · The Limestone · Central Grit · Staffordshire · South Peak

Buried Boomerang

⑤

Lots of sun | *15 min* | *Windy* | *Green*

Houndkirk Tor (False)

The short blocky edge has several decent boulders. The first are on a prominent spike-block.

Approach (see map on page 269) - The best approach is from a lay-by on the A625 by the turning to Parson House Outdoor Centre. Walk towards the centre but turn right along the wide track and follow this to the top of the hill until you drop down into a bowl. The bouldering is to the right beyond a short lollipop-shaped track.

❶ **Buried Boomerang** . . . . ☐ **V2** *5c*
The left-hand arete of the steep face. Avoid the ledge.

❷ **...and Tigger Too** . . . . ☼ ☐ **V3** *6A+*
Both aretes to finish direct.

❸ **Roo** . . . . ☐ **V2** *5c*
The left-hand side of the right arete of the leaning face.

❹ **Kanga** . . . . ☼ ☐ **V0+** *5a*
The right-hand side-wall of the block using both aretes.

❺ **Mantel** . . . . ☐ **V0** *4c*
Mantel the ledge on the back of the block. **V0+** *5a* from sitting.

The H.O.P.

Not much sun | *15 min* | *Windy* | *Green*

Uncoloured-in

The main areas are across rough terrain. The first walls are on the left section of blocks.

❻ **A Stoutness Exercise** . . . . 🔲 ☐ **V4** *6B+*
The leaning arete on the left.

❼ **Eeyore** . . . . ☼ ☐ **V3** *6A+*
Up the thin cracks.

❽ **Way of the Spaniel** . . . ☼ 🔲 ☐ **V5** *6C*
A thin eliminate on pebbles up the middle of the slab.

❾ **The H.O.P.** . . . . ☼ ☐ **V2** *5c*
The attractive blunt arete finishing on the shelf on the left.

❿ **Niche Crack** . . . . ☐ **V1** *5b*
The crack with a niche.

⓫ **Slotty Pockets** . . . . ☐ **V0+** *5a*
The wall right of the crack past a pocket.

⓬ **The Ramp** . . . . 🔲 ☐ **V2** *5c*
Sit-start the left-hand side of the wall.

⓭ **An Uncoloured-in Problem**
. . . . ☼ 🔲 📵 ☐ **V4** *6B*
A sit-down start left of the arete to holds on the lip. Stretch direct, or left to the ramp for an easy option **V3** *6A*.

⓮ **Undercut Arete** . . . . . ☼ 🔲 ☐ **V3** *6A*
Tackle the undercut arete directly from a sit-down start.

⓯ **We Stole Dave's Problem** . . . . ☐ **V0+** *5a*
The side-wall and right-hand side of the arete with pockets.

Friends and Relations

| Not much sun | 15 min | Windy | Green |

Across a gap are three more small walls.

16 Left Wall Mantel . . . . ☐ **V1** 5b
Steep wall to the left.

17 Friends and Relations 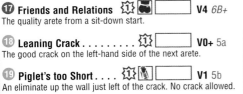 ☐ **V4** 6B+
The quality arete from a sit-down start.

18 Leaning Crack . . . . ☐ ☐ **V0+** 5a
The good crack on the left-hand side of the next arete.

19 Piglet's too Short . . . . ☐ ☐ ☐ **V1** 5b
An eliminate up the wall just left of the crack. No crack allowed.

20 The Crack Line . . . . ☐ **V1** 5b
The crack in the short wall.

21 An Expotition . . . . . . ☐ ☐ ☐ **V4** 6B+
Start from a side-pull.

22 Not the North Pole . . . ☐ ☐ ☐ **V4** 6B+
The blunt arete.

Houndkirk Tor (Proper)
The real Houndkirk Tor only has one decent problem.
Approach (see map on page 269) - Continue further on the main track then head across the moor towards the low west-facing edge.

23 Made in Sheffield  ☐ **V7** 7A+
A low roof about halfway along the Tor. From a sit start at the back, cross the roof to a hard move at the lip. Mantel to finish.

24 Made in Rotherham . . ☐ ☐ ☐ **V7** 7A+
Match holds on the right on the lip, then use a couple of crimps on the face above.

Uncoloured-in

The H.O.P.   Friends and Relations   Buried Boomerang

Northern Peak · Sheffield Crags · Stanage Area · Burbage Valley · Derwent Edges · The Limestone · Central Grit · Staffordshire · South Peak

Northern Peak

Sheffield Crags

Stanage Area

Burbage Valley

Derwent Edges

The Limestone

Central Grit

Staffordshire

South Peak

N

Grindleford

Froggatt
p.274

A621

Curbar
p.290

A623

Calver

Curbar

Baslow
p.310

Gardom's
p.322

Baslow

A619

Birchen
p.338

About 1km

Neil Kershaw on *Great White* (**V9** 7C) - *page 304* -
on the Curbar Field Boulders. Photo: Adam Long.

Northern Peak

Sheffield Crags

Stanage Area

Burbage Valley

Derwent Edges

The Limestone

Central Grit

Staffordshire

South Peak

	No star	✦	✦✦	✦✦✦
VB to V0 Easy to 4c	7	3	-	-
V0+ to V2 5a to 5c	1	14	6	1
V3 to V5 6A to 6C+	5	11	7	2
V3 to V5 7A upwards	4	16	13	3

Northern Peak

Sheffield Crags

Stanage Area

Burbage Valley

Derwent Edges

The Limestone

Central Grit

Staffordshire

South Peak

Froggatt has been bouldered on for years. Most of the problems are in amongst the routes on the crag itself and the list here is but a small fraction of what you could find. Due to the quarried nature of the rock, the stuff on the crag itself is technical and slabby, while the Pinnacle boulders contrast beautifully with their rippled and rounded gritstone. The harder problems require strong fingers as well as the usual grit prerequisites of balance, technique and an occasional dash of thuggery.

Circuits
There are two circuits described at Froggatt. The Pinnacle Orange Circuit is exclusively on the Pinnacle Boulders. There is also a much harder Red Circuit up to **V5** *6C/6C+* starting on the Hairpin Boulder.

Approach   Also see map on page 272
Approach 1 - The usual approach for Froggatt Edge is from the bend on the A625 Fox House to Froggatt village and Calver road, just below the Grouse Inn. Park either by the road on the bend, or in the car park in the trees. Note - if you park on the bend be sure to get your car off the road otherwise you will get a ticket. Follow the wide path through the gate which leads rapidly to the Hairpin Boulder and less rapidly (15 min) to the main crag.
Approach 2 - The more direct, but steeper approach, is from the Chequers Inn on the bends further down the A625. Park on the bend below the pub (or in the pub car park) and follow a path up through the trees directly to the Joe's Slab Area.

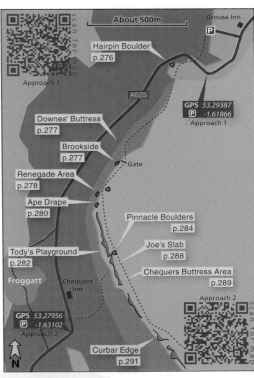

About 500m

Grouse Inn

Hairpin Boulder
p.276

Approach 1

A625

GPS 53.29387
P -1.61866
Approach 1

Downes' Buttress
p.277

Brookside
p.277

Gate

Renegade Area
p.278

Ape Drape
p.280

Pinnacle Boulders
p.284

Joe's Slab
p.288

Tody's Playground
p.282

Chequers Buttress Area
p.289

Froggatt

Chequers Inn

Approach 2

GPS 53.27956
P -1.63102
Approach 2

N

Curbar Edge
p.291

Conditions
The crag gets any weather going and can be as windy as any of the edges. The rock isn't green and will dry quickly, but there is little shelter if it rains except for the cave by *Rambeau*. It catches the afternoon sunshine and can be particularly pleasant on evenings with the added bonus of nice sunsets.

Duncan Campbell cutting loose on *Air Bear* (**V1** 5b) - *page 284* - the Froggatt Pinnacle Boulders. Photo: Alan James

Northern Peak

Sheffield Crags

Stanage Area

Burbage Valley

Derwent Edges

The Limestone

Central Grit

Staffordshire

South Peak

Hairpin Boulder

This is the first piece of rock you reach when approaching Froggatt from the north. It is close to the road so a popular spot with families wanting to get away from it all without having to go too far. The boulder is exposed and catches the wind and rain.

Approach - From the parking area on the bend of the A625, follow the broad cliff-top path for about 50m beyond the gate. The Hairpin Boulder is on the corner.

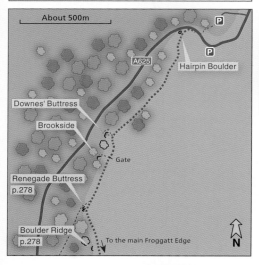

About 500m

A625

Hairpin Boulder

Downes' Buttress

Brookside

Gate

Renegade Buttress
p.278

Boulder Ridge
p.278

To the main Froggatt Edge

N

❶ Stray Bullit . . . . . . ③ ⚡ 🧗 [____] **V5** *6C*
Use a chipped hole at head height with your left hand to jump into the rounded groove up and right, then the top. **Bullit, V6** *7A,* goes straight to the top from the chip.
Red Circuit continues on page 280.

❷ Jelly Bomb . . . . ⚡ 🧗 [____] **V10** *7C+*
The sit-down start to *Stray Bullit* almost doubles the grade!

The **Froggatt Red Circuit**
This is a very hard circuit with 20 problems including several at **V5** *6C/6C+*. It starts on the Hairpin Boulder, then on to the main edge for the rest.

❸ Jump Before You Look . ② ⚡ [____] **V4** *6B+*
As for *Crash Test* but use flat holds to gain the crack up and left.

❹ Crash Test . . . . . . ① ⚡ 🧗 [____] **V2** *5c*
The arete from a low start is intricate and rewarding. Staying on the left of the arete is **V5** *6B*, staying on the right is **V4** *6A+*.

❺ Vanishing Point . . . . . ⚡ 🧗 [____] **V5** *6C+*
Traverse the ledges from the right at a low level. Drop down to go around the arete. Finish via the slanting crack and the rounded groove to its left.

❻ Hairpin Scoop . . . . . . ⚡ 🧗 [____] **V0+** *5a*
Mantel the ledge from a low start. Quite a grind.

❼ Hairpin Arete . . . . 🧗 [____] **V1** *5b*
The next arete is bisected by a large slot - surmount this.

❽ Flake Problem . . . . [____] **V0-** *4b*
To the left of the chips is a quick reach to the flake.

Descent

Hairpin Boulder

Downes' Buttress

There is one exceptional problem on Downes' Buttress which is situated right of a bend in the path, below a popular viewing point for walkers. Head rightwards to get down to the base to the small quarried bay.

❾ Glass Slipper ...... � ▣ ▭ **V7** *7A+*
Climb the blunt arete on its right-hand side to a rounded hold. It is **V6** *7A* from standing up. To the break is a hard highball.

Brookside

Hidden in the trees below the main Froggatt approach track are these small walls with a set of reasonable problems. Much of this area is green, really green, so green in fact that it may well be unclimbable for much of the year. Hit it after a dry spell though and you could be lucky. It is sheltered from the wind but is slow to dry.
Approach - From the upper bend parking area walk as far as the second gate. Go through the gate and then turn right to follow a small path through the trees down to the walls. *Old King Cascade* is on the other side of the brook and can be approached from a path before the gate.

There is one problem of interest on the north side of the brook. Reach this by taking the path before the gate.

❿ Old King Cascade 🔲 ◧ ◪ ▭ **V8** *7B*
The prow by the brook is excellent. Start from the very back. Straight up from the start holds is **Ol' Man River, V9** *7C*.

⓫ Ladies' Wall .... ◧ ◪ ▣ ▭ **V9** *7C*
The fingery wall from a sitting start.

⓬ Burnt Sienna ...... ◧ ◪ ▭ **V3** *6A+*
The wall and flake as far as the break, then go left.

⓭ Kimb's Limbs .... ▭ **V7** *7A+*
Climb the green rib on slopers.

⓮ Carry on Screaming ..... ◧ ▭ **V4** *6B+*
A mini *Screaming Dream* (page 278) up the crack.

⓯ Les Grands Doigts ...... 🔲 ▭ **V9** *7C*
The best problem on this section. **V10** *7C+* from sitting.

⓰ Bad Landing Crack .... ▭ **V3** *6A+*
The finger-crack is often dirty.

⓱ Flipworker .... ▣ ▭ **V3** *6A*
Hug your way up the short wall from a sitting start.

Northern Peak | Sheffield Crags | Stanage Area | Burbage Valley | Derwent Edges | The Limestone | Central Grit | Staffordshire | South Peak

Northern Peak

Sheffield Crags

Stanage Area

Burbage Valley

Derwent Edges

The Limestone

Central Grit

Staffordshire

South Peak

Renegade Buttress

A impressive buttress just below the main track. The routes *Screaming Dream* and *Renegade Master* rocketed the buttress to fame with the latter having become a much-desired highball target now. It shouldn't be long before its left-hand companion joins it on the boulderer's repertoire. The area is often green but it is open and hence cleans up relatively quickly in dry weather.

Approach (see map on page 275) - From the bend parking walk along the top path, through the gate. Continue for around 200m to a small path on the right. The buttress is just above the path.

③ The Screaming Dream

. . . . **V11** *8A*

A desperate highball of a famous trad route.

④ Renegade Master

. . . . **V10** *7C+*

The easy way up! The highball version of this route moves right at the top whereas the original route went straight up.
Photo opposite.

⑤ Dave's Dyno **V9** *7C*

Use the arete and an undercut to leap for the break.

⑥ Thuggy Bear **V6** *7A*

The right-hand side of the arete from sitting. Standing is **V2** *5c*.

❶ Renegade Bulge V5 *6C*
Mantel the bulge. The foot-ledge out left is out of bounds.

❷ Bulge Right-Hand. . . . V5 *6C+*
Mantel the bulge on the right arete.

Boulder Ridge

There are a number of isolated problems on the ridge running above Renegade Buttress, towards the bend in the path. This area is know as Boulder Ridge. The best wall here is about half way along from Renegade to the bend but is awkward to find from above however it is close to the top so don't start diving down into the undergrowth if you can't find it at first.

Approach - See map on page 275.

❼ Toasted V4 *6B*
Pull right up to the ramp.

❽ Hot Butter Knives. . . . V5 *6C*
From sitting, reach the ramp from the right.

❾ Stottie . . . . V8 *7B+*
The technical arete is well worth seeking out. It is a touch easier at **V8** *7B* from standing. *Photo this page.*

Jon Fullwood climbing *Stottie* (**V8** *7B+*) - *this page*. Photo: Alan James

Northern Peak

Sheffield Crags

Stanage Area

Burbage Valley

Derwent Edges

The Limestone

Central Grit

Staffordshire

South Peak

Jordan Buys on *Renegade Master* (**V10** *7C+*) - *opposite*
- on Renegade Buttress at Froggatt. Photo: Mike Hutton

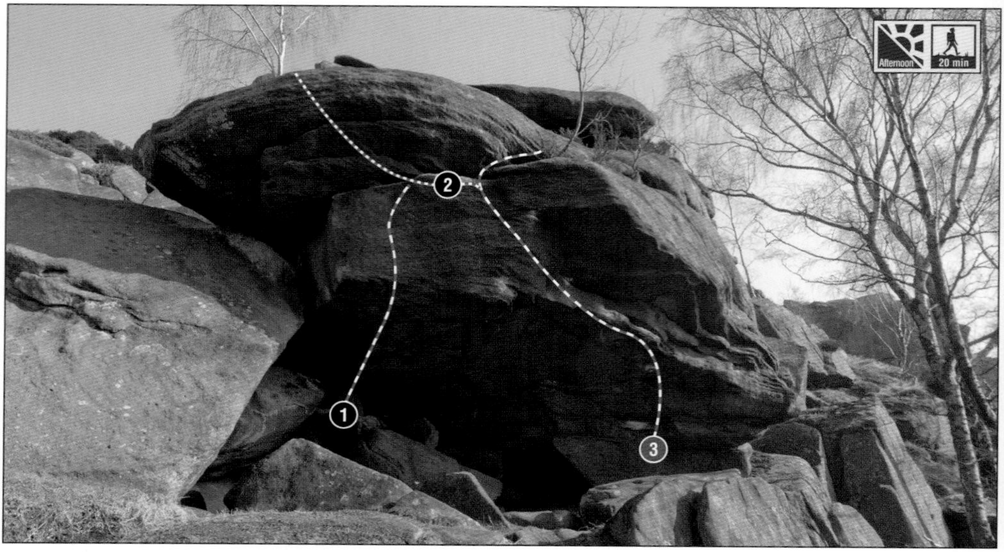

Ape Drape

This severely undercut boulder has a distinctive traverse with a couple of worthwhile variations. The traverse is steep and will stay dry in light rain. It is also below the line of the edge, which gives it a bit of shelter from the wind.
Approach (see map on page 275) - The boulder is below a small flat wall, below the track, 50m before the main climbing on the edge begins on the prominent north-facing side-wall of Strapadictomy Buttress. As another useful marker - it is about 70m after the boulder by the bend in the track.

1 Monkey Man . . . . 1 **V8** *7B+*
Starting from the block at the back of the overhang, follow the left lip, swinging left then right. Finish as for *Ape Drape Direct*. The slabby block on the left is out of bounds for your feet.

2 Ape Drape Direct . . . . 1 **V7** *7A+*
Follow *Ape Drape* to the break, then move left and mantel onto the top. Willing spotters with large baseball mits are essential.

3 Ape Drape. . . . 4 2 **V5** *6C+*
From a sitting start at the right side of the roof, follow the diminishing holds left. Exit to the right.

Leggit Wall and Rambeau

The main edge is mostly the domain of routes but there are a few worthwhile problems in amongst the taller stuff.
Approach (see map on page 275) - Follow the crag base path under the big roof of *Strapadictomy* and eventually you will arrive at the popular *Sunset Slab* which is next to the magnificent arete of *Beau Geste*. Just before *Sunset Slab* is a small hollow with a short wall and diagonal crack above it.

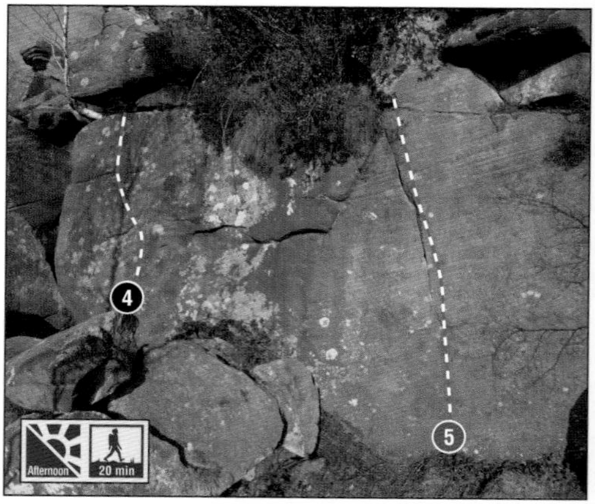

4 Pig Heart Boy 2 **V8** *7B*
The left-hand side of the wall has a couple of very sloping holds. Use these to gain the break.

5 Leggit. . . . . 5 2 **V3** *6A+*
The clean thin crack. Descent from the top can be awkward - right is scary and left is vegetated.
Red Circuit continues on page 282.

Cave Crack
(E2)

❻ **Rambeau** . . . . . . 🌀 ✊ 🧗 ▭ **V8** *7B*
Beyond *Beau Geste* is a large dirty brown cave. The route
through this is called *Cave Crack*. A desperate direct start to this
can be made up the arete and wall to the left of the cave. This is
still a bit easier than actually climbing *Cave Crack*.
Photo this page.

Adam Bailes on the steep start of *Rambeau* (**V8** *7B*) -
this page - on Froggatt Edge. Photo: Mike Hutton

Northern Peak · Sheffield Crags · Stanage Area · Burbage Valley · Derwent Edges · The Limestone · Central Grit · Staffordshire · South Peak

Northern Peak

Sheffield Crags

Stanage Area

Burbage Valley

Derwent Edges

The Limestone

Central Grit

Staffordshire

South Peak

Ape Drape
p.280

About 20m

N

Stradadictomy Buttress

Leggit
p.280

Sunset Slab

Beau Geste

Rambeau
p.280

Tody's Wall

Three Pebble Slab

Tody's Playground

Pinnacle Boulders
p.284

Turd Burglar

Valkyrie
Pinnacle

Joe's Slab
p.288

Chequers Buttress
p.289

Afternoon | 15 min

Tody's Playground

Under the main track beneath Tody's Wall is this divine little wall. The few problems here are fine and vertical although the bottom sloping section makes padding it out awkward. It is nice and sheltered and will be one of the last places on the crag to get wet.

Approach (see map on page 275) - Tody's Wall is easy to find since it is a large hanging slab in the centre of the main crag. At weekends there will be someone squatting down on a triangular-shaped block beneath the bulge.

❶ Hot Toddy . . . . 🔟 🎒   **V6** *7A*
From a sit start, pull up left then back right.

❷ Tree Wall . . . . ⑪ 🔟   **V1** *5b*
Well, there used to be a tree. From the flake follow small holds up the wall. *Red Circuit continues on page 286.*

❸ The Eyes . . . . ⑩ 🎋 🚩   **V3** *6A*
From the same start as *Tree Wall*, move right and climb through the small overlap.

❹ Tody's Pocket . . . . ⑨ 🎋 🚩   **V0+** *5a*
Climb the wall to the pocket and continue direct.

❺ Thin Wall . . . . ⑧ 🎋 🚩   **V2** *5c*
The wall to the right to some poor edges and stretch to reach edges above. Avoid the flakes on the right, and finish direct.

❻ Tody Boy . . . . ⑦ 🔟 🚩   **V2** *5c*
Use the small flakes to the right to gain the upper rails and exit any way you can.

❼ Tody Bear . . . . ⑥ 🎋   **V1** *5b*
A long reach gains the hollow flake below a juggier finish.

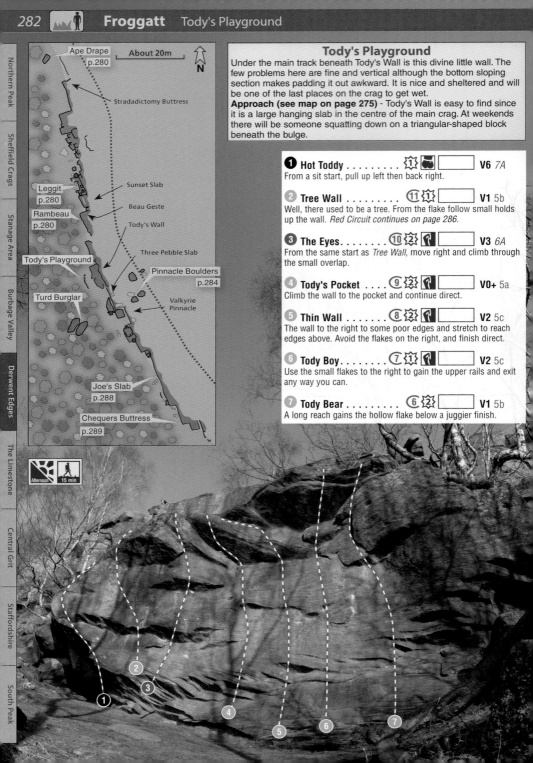

Turd Burglar Blocks

Below Three Pebble Slab are two huge boulders that have a few problems and some serious routes. Although many of the boulders in these trees are very green, the problems are mostly on fairly clean rock which will dry reasonably quickly.

Approach (see map on page 275) - From below Three Pebble Slab and the Valkyrie Pinnacle, find a vague path leading downhill to the right of the two huge boulders.

8 Jetpack **V6** 7A
Start on two low side-pulls and climb to the lip. Originally done as a dyno from the side-pulls at **V8**, 7B.

9 Pea Crab Shuffle . . **V9** 7C
From a sitting start, traverse the lip of the lower boulder all the way rightwards. Keeping your bum and legs off the ground is tricky in places.

10 The Sound of One Foot Slipping
. . . . **V7** 7A+
On the opposite wall, start at the break and pull up the arete and slightly left until you can rock back right onto the slab.

11 My Orange . . . . **V10** 7C+
Start as for the previous problem but continue leftwards along the lip to a scary top-out. Probably worth E6.

12 Scandalous **V8** 7B
In the middle of the wall on the downhill side of the lower boulder is a pumpy traverse line. Follow this and then the arete.

13 Gibsonitus **V8** 7B
Directly below Tody's Playground. Climb the rib from sitting.

14 The Green 45 . . . . **V6** 7A
Hidden about 30m below the main boulders. From the edge in the middle of the roof stretch to the lip and pull over onto the mossy slab.

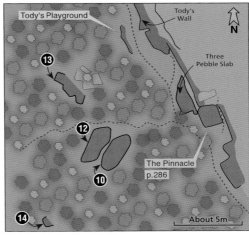

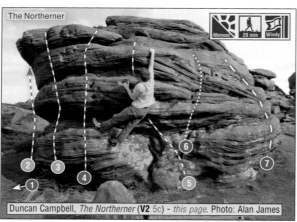

The Northerner

Duncan Campbell, *The Northerner* (**V2** 5c) - *this page*. Photo: Alan James

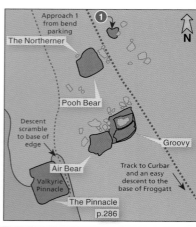

Approach 1 from bend parking

The Northerner

Pooh Bear

Descent scramble to base of edge

Groovy

Track to Curbar and an easy descent to the base of Froggatt

Air Bear

Valkyrie Pinnacle

The Pinnacle p.286

N

Pinnacle Boulders

This area makes a change from the more intense bouldering on the rest of the crag. Most of the problems are at an amenable grade and some are ideal as starting points for the beginner. The boulders are exposed to bad weather but they will dry quickly after rain.

Approach (see map on page 275) - Use either of the main approaches. The boulders are easy to find on the crag top behind the main Froggatt Pinnacle.

1 Baby Bear . . . . **VO** 4c
Surmount the small undercut boulder left of the path.

2 Areet . . . . ⑤ **VO+** 5a
Climb spaced holds on the blunt arete. Finish left at this grade or try pulling over the right-hand side at **V1** 5b.

3 Starter Motor . . . . ⑥ **V1** 5b
Just right of the arete. Start with your hands low.

4 Pick Pocket . . . . ⑦ **VO** 4c
The pocketed wall finishing direct over the bulge.

5 The Northerner . . . ⑧ **V2** 5c
Start low and pull out of the scoop leftwards to a sloping finish.
Photo on this page.

6 Teddy . . . . ④ **VO** 4c
The set of easy ledges lead up and right of the boulder. Starting as for *The Northerner* makes it a better **VO+** 5a.

7 Pooh Bear . . . . ③ **VO** 4c
The delightful slab can be climbed anywhere but is best taken direct past a low pocket.

8 Bear Poo . . . . ② **VO-** 4b
Up the chunky arete using all the ledges.

9 Rupert Bear . . . . **VB** 4a
The wall, trending left to the arete to finish.

10 Bare Rupert . . . . ① **VB** 4a
The edge of the wall.

Pooh Bear

The next problems are on the flat boulder on the wall facing the Valkyrie Pinnacle.

11 Where? . . . . **VO-** 4b
The easy-angled slab is a good Beginners' problem.

12 Flatulence . . . . ⑨ **VO+** 5a
Climb the wall to the left on flat holds.

13 Air Bear . . . . ⑩ **V1** 5b
The crack is easy, pulling over the top less so, especially if someone is watching! *Photo on page 275.*

14 Mini Mantel . . . . ⑪ **VO** 4c
Mantel over the left side of the low roof.

15 Care Bear . . . . ⑫ **V1** 5b
Swing along the lip of the roof to finish up *Air Bear*.

16 Mantelicious **V4** *6B*
Mantel over the right side of the low roof.

Northern Peak · Sheffield Crags · Stanage Area · Burbage Valley · Derwent Edges · The Limestone · Central Grit · Staffordshire · South Peak

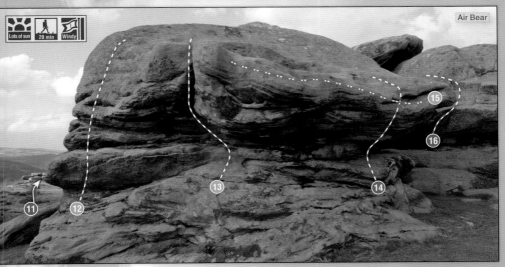

Air Bear

The next problems are on the taller of the two big flat boulders.

17 Naughty V1 5b
Climb past the short vertical seam using two chipped dinks above to mantel onto the slab. **V2** 5c without the chips.

18 The Broken Chair V4 6B
A desperate high rock-over using a sloping horror.

19 Groovy V2 5c
Use a high rock-over to pull past the short groove.

20 Rib Tickler V1 5b
From standing, tackle the flying flake on its left-hand side.

21 Come Together . . . . . . V0+ 5a
The crack climbed from standing is easier than it looks. Add the sitting start of the next problem and the grade goes up to **V2** 5c.

22 Nasal Passage V2 5c
From sitting in the middle of the low shelf, lurch up for a hold above then pull up and right, keeping off the crack. **V1** 5b from a standing start. *The last problem in the Orange Circuit.*

23 The Teddy Bear's Picnic
. . . . V4 6B
Start on a slot on the right-hand end of the lower wall and traverse left along the sloping shelf to *Nasal Passage*. Finish up any of the previous four problems although swinging left into *Groovy* is the best. The sit-down adds a bit but not to the grade.

Groovy

The **Pinnacle Orange Circuit** of 17 problems. Starting with some easy slabby problems on the Northerner block, and graduating to some harder stuff including *The Northerner* itself *Groovy*.

Northern Peak

Sheffield Crags

Stanage Area

Burbage Valley

Derwent Edges

The Limestone

Central Grit

Staffordshire

South Peak

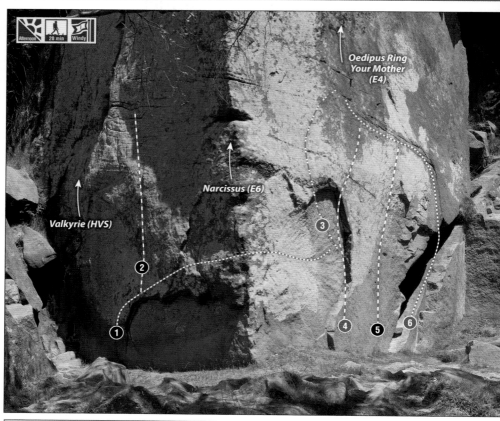

Valkyrie (HVS)

Narcissus (E6)

Oedipus Ring
Your Mother
(E4)

The Pinnacle

This is the fine pinnacle up which the classic route *Valkyrie* wends its way. The problems are fingery and technical and most end up in the middle of nowhere and involve either jumping off or reversing to get back down. A mat is strongly recommended as the floor is very stony and hard. You can continue up *Oedipus* to the cave on *Valkyrie* but this is also in the middle of nowhere and your options from there are definitely soloing and not highball. The bay can offer some shelter from the wind and can stay dry in the rain if it is coming from the right direction. After getting wet the wall dries very quickly. **Approach (see map on page 275 and 282)** - The Pinnacle is in the centre of Froggatt and can be approached from either of the main approaches. Once below the edge, you can't really miss it.

1 Pinnacle Traverse V8 *7B*
From the start of the curving flake on the left wall, reach the arete and swing around to gain *Oedipus Direct*. Climb this then reverse the *Oedipus* traverse!

2 Neon Dust Direct V10 *7C+*
Find a way to gain the poor slopers on the upper break above the curving low flake.

3 Glamourpuss. . . . . V5 *6C+*
Start below the arch on the right wall and gain the chipped holds above and left. A long move direct gains the loose flake above.

4 Oedipus Direct. . . . V4 *6B+*
From the arch swing out right and up to the edges low on the break of *Oedipus*. Possibly as hard as **V6** *7A* for those shorter than around 5'9". *Red Circuit continues on page 288.*

5 Mint400 Direct . . V8 *7B+*
Crimp up the thin breaks. Use the small shield on the right gain the better break above.

6 Oedipus Start V4 *6B*
Gain the in-cut slotted break out from the small cave and ape along to above the arch. Continuing upwards here is the route *Oedipus Ring Your Mother* but you have done the 6b bit, however the 5c reach for the chip on the hold below the break is quite exciting - as is the decent.

Northern Peak
Sheffield Crags
Stanage Area
Burbage Valley
Derwent Edges
The Limestone
Central Grit
Staffordshire
South Peak

Northern Peak

Sheffield Crags

Stanage Area

Burbage Valley

Derwent Edges

The Limestone

Central Grit

Staffordshire

South Peak

Adrian Berry on *Sole Power* (**V9** *7C*) - *page 289* -
Chequers Buttress, Froggatt. Photo: Adam Long

Joe's Slab

This tiny slab has been bouldered on for years by anyone and everyone and *Joe's Slab* must have had more ascents than any other problem in the Peak. Even by today's standards, it is not a path although it is the easiest way up the blank slabby wall. The problems are all slabby and feature small edges and pockets. Footwork is of the utmost importance. The rock is nice and clean. It has little shelter from the rain or wind but will dry quickly. **Approach (see map on page 275 and 282)** - Head for the popular south end of the edge using either of the main approaches. This is the area which is usually busy with climbers or groups below the clean slabs.

❶ Downhill Racer Direct

. . . . ☼ 🦶 ▢ **V7** *7A+*
The direct start to *Downhill Racer* is intense and fingery.

❷ Downhill Racer Start . ⑭☼ ▢ **V2** 5c
Just reaching the first slot is a decent little problem.

❸ Joe's Slab Arete . . . . . ⑮☼ ▢ **V4** *6B*
The impeccable arete can prove frustrating but also very engrossing.

❹ Thin Slab . . . . ☼ 🦶 ▢ **V7** *7A+*
Smear up the blank slab.

❺ Mono Seam . . . . . . ⑯☼🦶 ▢ **V5** *6C+*
From low edges gain the two tiny pockets above and direct to the semi-circular flake and ledge.

❻ Mono Seam Right-Hand ☼🦶 ▢ **V6** *7A*
Use the right-hand pocket to reach the flat hold on Joe's and finish up this.

❼ Joe's Slab . . . . . . ⑰☼🦶 ▢ **V2** 5c
Gain the flat pocket in the middle of the wall from bridging below. Use the rightwards undercut ramp as an aid to get there and then an optimistic move lands the half-moon finishing holds below the ledge. Masses of eliminates possible.

❽ Slab Pop . . . . ⑱☼ ▯ ▢ **V5** *6C*
The blank slab to the right above the undercuts requires some technique. You are not allowed to touch the edge of the crack.

❾ Joe's Slab Traverse . . ☼🦶 ▢ **V6** *7A*
Traverse the slab from right to left with your feet just above the crease in the slab and hands below ledge. Very delicate on the feet and remember to squeak your boots. Finish up the arete.

❿ Joe's Low Traverse . . ☼🦶 ▢ **V8** *7B+*
This time go from right to left with your hands on edges and slopes just above the crease. Again, finish up the arete.

Northern Peak

Sheffield Crags

Stanage Area

Burbage Valley

Derwent Edges

The Limestone

Central Grit

Staffordshire

South Peak

Chequers Buttress Area

There are a few good problems to be found on the far southern end of Froggatt Edge on or near the imposing Chequers Buttress. Most of the better ones are in the very high grades. The problems in this area dry quickly after rain, and get sun from late morning.

Approach (see map on page 275 and 282) - Head for the popular south end of the edge using either of the main approaches. If you are walking along the top, walk right to the end of the crag descend a grotty gully and you will find yourself at *The Whillans Direct*.

There are three reasonable problems further along the edge, past the Great Slab. A small cave split by a crack can be found in a block leaning against the edge.

⑪ Spinal Crack . . . . 🔄 ◀ 🍞 ⬜ V2 *5c*
Struggle up the crack. May feel harder than this - it depends on your mood.

⑫ Spinal Tap ⑲ 🔄 🔥 ◀ 🍞 ⬜ V5 *6C+*
From jugs in the back, pull out and up the slanting crack.

⑬ Lankaster Bomber . . . . . . 🔲 ⬜ V9 *7C*
The reachy problem to the right. The tall can knock off a couple of grades.

The next 'problems' both require a lot of very large, deep pads and to a lesser extent, spotters - and are quite high even then. It is sensible to top-rope them first - that will also make it possible to get back down.

⑭ Slingshot . . . 🔄 🔥 ◀ 🖐 ⬜ V10 *7C+*
A well-known problem, but rarely climbed on account of the difficulty in protecting it. The first half is easier for the tall, the second easier for the short.

⑮ Chequers Groove . 🔄 🔥 🌄 ⬜ V11 *8A*
Originally climbed un-roped above a very large gym mat.

The next problem on the edge is between the popular routes Chequers Crack and Chequers Buttress.

⑯ Business Lunch . . 🔄 🔥 🌄 ⬜ V9 *7C*
The wall left of *Sole Power.*

⑰ Sole Power . . . . . 🔄 🔥 🌄 ⬜ V9 *7C*
The superb arete - high, but doable with plenty of normal pads. Climbed on its right-hand side is **Our Soles** - also **V9** *7C*. *Photo on page 287.*

Around the corner is one final problem.

⑱ The Whillans Direct ⑳ 🔄 🖐 ⬜ V4 *6B+*
A steep direct start to *Jankers Groove* - the start offers a painful fist-jam - whether you use it is your call. Traverse off right. *The last problem in the Red Circuit.*

While here you may want to nip over to the far north end of Curbar since there are a few problems worth a look there - see next page.

The Big Crack (E2)

Chequers Crack (HVS)

Northern Peak · Sheffield Crags · Stanage Area · Burbage Valley · Derwent Edges · The Limestone · Central Grit · Staffordshire · South Peak

	No star	 ☆	☆☆	☆☆☆
VB to V0 Easy to 4c	12	11	-	-
V0+ to V2 5a to 5c	14	33	4	2
V3 to V5 6A to 6C+	5	30	6	4
V3 to V5 7A upwards	5	16	14	9

This area became popular after the first Peak Bouldering guides were published in the 1990s and it has remained one of the top destinations ever since. The area is split into two distinct sections; the Curbar Field Boulders are the best known and the Curbar Edge area offers bouldering in much more seclusion. Both areas are nicely balanced with plenty of warm-ups and slabs and also some number-crunching sensations which will require many visits for success. The Curbar Edge area tends to have a lot of highballs, especially in the higher grades. The Curbar Field Boulders are mainly walls and aretes with *Work Hard* being one of the hardest vertical problems in the Peak. There is also the brilliant and powerful *Gorilla Warfare* and its variants plus the Bad Landing Boulder and its plethora of hard eliminates. It is not all mega-desperates though and if you are operating at a slightly lower grade then there is still plenty of quality stuff to go at.

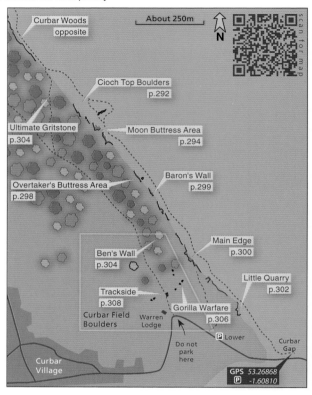

Circuits
Curbar Edge has an Orange and a Red Circuit both of which require a lot of walking, but take you on a good tour of the main areas. Both circuits start in the Little Quarry and work their way leftwards along to the Cioch Top Boulders eventually. Curbar Field has nice Orange and Green Circuits.

Approach   Also see map on page 272
Leave the car in the parking spots on the steep road below Curbar Gap or park up at the top car park (pay) or on the road opposite it especially if visiting the Edge Area. **Do not park anywhere near the bend by Warren Lodge**. For the Edge Boulders, walk up or along easily to the Main Edge which takes you past Little Quarry. The various sections are all described separately from here. For the Field Boulders walk down the road to a track on the sharp bend. This leads straight to the Trackside Boulder which is above the Warren Lodge. Please respect the privacy of the people in the house.

Conditions
The Field Boulders are slightly less exposed than the Edge area but they are still not places to be in bad weather although Trackside dries very quickly. The hillside faces southwest and catches plenty of sun and there is little to be found in hot weather although the Gorilla Warfare wall is shady and there are a few other spots tucked away. There is not much to be found here in wet weather although *Gorilla Warfare* can give some dry climbing.

Northern Peak — Sheffield Crags — Stanage Area — Burbage Valley — Derwent Edges — The Limestone — Central Grit — Staffordshire — South Peak

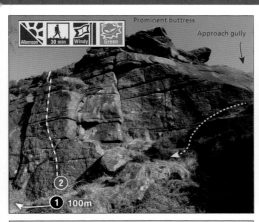

Prominent buttress

Approach gully

② ① 100m

Curbar Woods

The very far end of Curbar is closer to Froggatt and can easily be approached from there - see page 275. It offers a few isolated problems which are always quiet but often dirty and green.

Approach - Continue past Moon Buttress and 300m past a small wood on the crag top is a prominent buttress. Descend just before this and head right for the first two problems, or left for the others.

❶ Marx's Wall . . . . ⛶ 🪨 🍫 [____] **V6** 7A
Not on a topo. This is situated on a shady side wall, facing Froggatt. Make a sit start left of the crack - which is out of bounds. **V4**, 6B+ from standing.

❷ Curbar Your Enthusiasm . . ⛶ [____] **V3** 6A+
The wall to the right (looking out) of the approach gully.

❸ Happy Slapper. . . . . [____] **V1** 5b
Climb pockets up a rib down and left of the approach gully.

From approach gully

③ ④ ⑤ Greenacres (E1)

❹ Happy House . . . . . . ⛶ 🛡 [____] **V4** 6B
Another rib just right is a lot harder and undergraded at HVS!

❺ Blue Hawaii . . . . . . ⛶ 🛡 [____] **V5** 6C+
Tackle the desperate roof and continue up the slabby arete.

Things get a lot harder a little further to the right near the route Beech Layback.

❻ The Art of White Hat Wearing
. . . . ⛶ 🤚 [____] **V8** 7B
The distinctive groove up the middle of the wall.

❼ Jimmy Hat . . . . ⛶ 🪨 [____] **V9** 7C
Fingery wall climbing between the groove and the corner.

❽ Be Somebody or Be Somebody's Fool
. . . . ⛶ [____] **V7** 7A+
The pillar just right.

Beech Layback (VS)

⑥ ⑦ ⑧

30m from Greenacres Slab

Northern Peak
Sheffield Crags
Stanage Area
Burbage Valley
Derwent Edges
The Limestone
Central Grit
Staffordshire
South Peak

Cioch Top Boulders

Just beyond Moon Buttress are a couple of boulders on the crag-top with some good easier problems. Down below is a much harder one.

Approach (see map on page 290) - Walk along the top of Curbar Edge. Keep an eye out for Moon Buttress with its tall aretes and *Dog-leg Crack*. Walk around to the right of the Moon Buttress jumble to the cliff-top boulders near the Cioch Area.

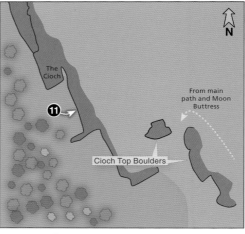

Cioch Top Boulders

① Left Arete . . . . ⑲ ⚄   **V0** 4c
The left arete of the block.

② Crispy Roof . . . ㉓ ⑳ ⚄ 🧗   **V1** 5b
Follow crimps up the leaning wall.

③ Crispy Noodling . . . . . . ㉕ ⚄   **V4** *6B+*
Make a hard move to a rounded hold on the arete.
The last problem on the Red Circuit.

④ Crispy Rib . . . . ㉔ ⚄   **V3** *6A+*
Up the right arete to the same hold as the previous problem.

⑤ Chekov . . . . ㉑   **VB** 4a
The short arete on its left or right.

⑥ Scotty . . . . ㉒ ⚄   **V0** 4c
Nice little rounded arete. Undercut away!

⑦ Bones . . . . ㉓   **V0** 4c
The crack just right. More interesting if you don't use the crack.

⑧ Mister Spock . . . . . ㉒ ⚄ 🎒   **V1** 5b
The high arete is excellent but has a worrying last move. The sit-down is **V3** *6A+.*

⑨ Uhuru . . . . ㉑ ㉕ ⚄ 🧗   **V2** 5c
Use a crimp on the edge to make upward progress. All over after the start. *The last problem in the Orange Circuit.*

⑩ Sulu . . . . ㉔   **V0-** 4b
The right side of the face is much easier than its left-hand neighbour. The upper slab is easy.

Tree Wall **(HVS)**

In complete contrast to the Cioch Top Boulders is this highball offering down on the main crag. Descend below the Top Boulders, then turn right (looking out) and head along for around 50m. The route is left of the classic Tree Wall.

⑪ Big Friday **V9** *7C*
The wall is intense and fingery. *Photo this page.*

James McHaffie climbing *Big Friday* (**V9** *7C*) - *this page* - near the Cioch Area of Curbar Edge. Photo: Adam Long

Northern Peak

Sheffield Crags

Stanage Area

Burbage Valley

Derwent Edges

The Limestone

Central Grit

Staffordshire

South Peak

Black Nix Wall

Moon Buttress Area

An area of Curbar well known for its classic routes also has some very fine bouldering with a range of grades that make a good mini-circuit.

Conditions - The area is exposed to the weather but dries quickly.

Approach (see map on page 290) - Walk along the top of Curbar Edge until you can see the distinctive wall featuring *Dog-leg Crack* and the tall arete of the route *The End of The Affair* down on the left.

These problems are on Black Nix Wall, which is found just left (looking in) of Moon Buttress and can be approached from the left (quickest) or right.

❶ Downhill Gardener... 〔〕 ▦ ☐ **V7** *7A+*
The short, curving arete on its left-hand side.

❷ Button Moon ..... ㉒ ⑱ 〔〕 ☐ **V2** 5c
The blunt flake on the wall to the right.
Both Red and Orange Circuits continue on page 292.

❸ Black Nix Wall...... 〔〕 ☐ **V2** 5c
Starting just right of the corner, climb up and right to the middle of the wall then finish up a short corner.

❹ Rat Scabies........ 〔〕 ☐ **V4** *6B*
An inviting feature with some tough moves. Follow the small roof right and gain the ledge with some difficulty. The best descent is to reverse a bit and jump - going upwards is soloing.

❺ Last Light....... ⑲ 〔〕 ☐ **V5** *6C*
The shady little wall.

❻ John's Arete.......... ☐ **V2** 5c
The arete as far as the ledge then scuttle left.

Eliminettes

The End of the Affair (E8)

The next problems are found on the short Eliminettes Wall directly below Moon Buttress.

❼ Wee-Wob .... ▦ ☐ **V1** 5b
The left-most line.

❽ The Start of the Affair. ⑱ 〔〕 ☐ **V4** *6B*
The steep line via thin cracks. Pitch 1 to bigger things above!

❾ Left Eliminette....... ⑯ 〔〕 ☐ **V2** 5c
The groove finishing through the left side of the small roof.

❿ Right Eliminette..... ⑰ 〔〕 ☐ **V2** 5c
The thin crack continuing through the right side of the small roof.

⓫ Middle T............. ☐ **V3** *6A*
The break from left to right.

The Trench

Above and behind Moon Buttress is a trench with a good supply of short problems mostly with good landings.

⑫ Left Arete . . . . ☐ **V0** *4c*
The left arete of the wall. A bit too short really.

⑬ Trench Wall . . . . . . ⑮☆▮▮☐ **V3** *6A+*
The wall to the right is easier for the tall.

⑭ Trench Flakes . . . . ⑯☆☐ **V4** *6B+*
Poor slopers up the middle of the wall.

⑮ Ringworm . . . . ⑰⑭☆☐ **V2** *5c*
Leg presses and slopers - excellent.

⑯ Trench Hole . . . . ⑮☆☐ **V0+** *5a*
Pull up the slab above the small pocket.

⑰ Pigeon Arete . . . . ☐ **V3** *6A+*
The left arete of the next block, starting on the rounded boss.

⑱ Cloud Cuckoo Land . . ☆▮☐ **V7** *7A+*
From a sit-down, reach the boss then make hard moves up right to the sloping ledge.

⑲ Clouded Judgement . . ☆▮☐ **V7** *7A+*
Just right of *Cuckoo*, via a mono, to the sloping ledge.

⑳ Never Spanned . . ☆▮☐☐ **V11** *8A*
From the mono on the previous problem, swing right to a side-pull then use the arete to gain the top. Poor landing.

The final four problems are the first you reach on the approach along the edge. They are on the wall with a dog-leg crack.

㉑ Ulysses or Bust . . . . . ☆☐☐ **V7** *7A+*
Very much a highball up the left arete.

㉒ The Unreachable Star
. . . . ⑭☆☐☐ **V4** *6B+*
The left-hand straight crack is also quite high.

㉓ Dog-leg Crack . . . . . . ☆▮☐ **V0-** *4b*
The crooked crack up the middle of the wall.

㉔ Trouser Jazz . . . . ☆☐ **V5** *6C+*
An eliminate up the thin seam just right of *Dog-leg Crack*.

㉕ The Dog's Hole . . . . . ⑬☆☐ **V4** *6B*
The short wall via a low pocket.

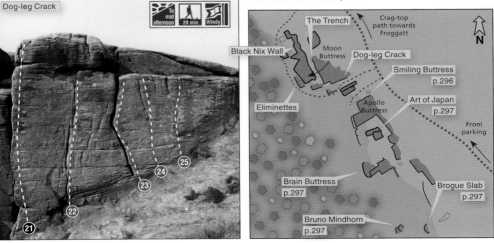

Dog-leg Crack

Northern Peak
Sheffield Crags
Stanage Area
Burbage Valley
Derwent Edges
The Limestone
Central Grit
Staffordshire
South Peak

The Trench
Crag-top path towards Froggatt
Black Nix Wall
Moon Buttress
Dog-leg Crack
Smiling Buttress p.296
Eliminettes
Apollo Buttress
Art of Japan p.297
From parking
N
Brain Buttress p.297
Brogue Slab p.297
Bruno Mindhorn p.297

Northern Peak

Sheffield Crags

Stanage Area

Burbage Valley

Derwent Edges

The Limestone

Central Grit

Staffordshire

South Peak

Smiling Buttress

Evening | 20 min | Windy

26

26 Smiling Buttress . V13 *8B*
The side-wall opposite *Dog-leg Crack* with the one smiling hold
has been climbed. The grade is a guess since Tyler Landman
didn't grade it.

Art of Japan (**V5** *6C*) - *opposite*. Photo: Mike Hutton

Art of Japan

Brogue Slab

The next problem is on a shady north-facing wall opposite Apollo Buttress - see map on page 295.

27 Art of Japan . . **V5** *6C*
The middle of the north-facing wall via side-pulls is superb. Gaining it from opposing undercuts on the left is **The Arse of Japan V7** *7a+. Photo opposite.*

Red Circuit continues on page 295.

*The following five problems are to be found on **Brogue Slab** at the far right-hand end of the lower tier of walls.*

29 Brogue Slab **V1** *5b*
The left side of the slab is easier for the tall.

30 Brogue Raider **V5** *6C*
The centre of the slab.

31 Gordon Brown Superhero
. . . . **V0+** *5a*
The arete on its left side.

32 Corner Mount . . . . **V0+** *5a*
The corner.

33 Crowbar **V1** *5b*
The middle of the wall just right.

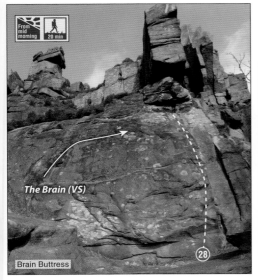

The Brain (VS)

Brain Buttress

*The next problem is down below **Brain Buttress**, a narrow pillar that projects from the edge - see map on page 295.*

28 Early Morning Day . . . **V4** *6B*
The right arete of the slab traversed by the start of the route *The Brain*. High but a good landing.

Brogue Slab

Bruno Mindhorn

Below and right (looking out) of Brogue Slab are a couple of blocks with these two problems.

34 Bruno Mindhorn . . **V7** *7A+*
From a big, low hold, pull through the roof and finish up the arete.

35 Break Out the Trumpets . . **V6** *7A*
The arete on the downhill side is climbed on its left side.

Overtaker's Buttress Area

The central section of Curbar has a number of problems, some more densely arranged than others but the best of them are hard and highball.

Approach (see map on page 290) - Walk along the crag top until the characteristic Mushroom Block appears. The beak above Overtaker's Buttress and the prow of *Fidget* are also conspicuous.

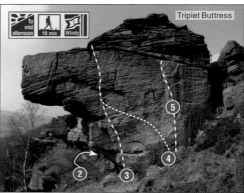

The next three problems are on the distinctive **Triplet Buttress** which is situated above and to the right of Overtaker's Buttress.

2 Lifeseeker **V5** *6C*
A similar line to *Fidget* up the other side of the fin.

3 Fidget **V5** *6C*
Follow the arete to the break then stretch for the top.

4 Six Syllables or Less **V5** *6C*
An alternative start to *Fidget* climbing up and left.

5 Rise of the Robots

. . . . **V3** *6A+*
The wall via the short crack. *Red Circuit continues on page 297.*

1 White Lines . . . . **V8** *7B+*
With plenty of mats this hard route becomes a highball boulder problem if ended at the big break.

At the top of the edge is a **Mushroom Block** with a number of short problems - three are listed here but you could tackle the block anywhere. Unfortunately the crux for all of them is the ungainly belly-flop finish in full view of everyone.

6 Paddestoel **V1** *5b*
The wall facing the edge. Grovel over the lip.

7 Champignon **V1** *5b*
The crack is much more graunchy than it looks.

8 Pilz . . . . **V0+** *5a*
Another awkward problem into the large scoop.

The next section of the edge is **The Sheep Pit**. It has a low roof with three problems.

9 Sheep Pit Crack Left **V1** *5b*
The roof taken directly to the crack.

10 The Sheep Pit . . . **V4** *6B*
From sitting, climb the groove then traverse left below the lip and finish up the crack.

11 Sheep Pit Crack Right . . . . **V0+** *5a*
The steep crack on the right above a nasty landing.

Baron's Wall

Northern Peak

Sheffield Crags

Stanage Area

Burbage Valley

Derwent Edges

The Limestone

Central Grit

Staffordshire

South Peak

Baron's Wall

The Baron's Wall has a good few problems that gain the mid-height break. From here you can either finish up the original or jump off from the ledge on *Talon Man*.
Approach (see map on page 290) - You can either approach from the Overtaker's area along the crag base, or drop down at the first point after passing the main climbing areas.

⑫ I Bet He Drinks Carling Black Label
. . . . **V6** *7A*
A hard highball linking cracks in the left side of the wall. The right-hand start up the groove is **Tube of Fosters, V5** *6C+* which is also highball.

⑬ Cartons and Curpets **V4** *6B*
The wall just right of the rib.

⑭ Smoke ont' Watter . . . **V3** *6A+*
The central line of the wall.

⑮ Talon Man **V4** *6B*
The wall past the side-pull. The dyno from the side-pull to the ledge is **V6** *7A*.

⑯ Baron's Direct **V3** *6A*
Climb direct to the finishing crack of *Baron's Wall*.

⑰ Baron's Wall **V1** *5b*
The easiest way up this wall but not as easy as you might think, especially if you continue up the top crack.

Mushroom Block

Triplet Buttress

Overtaker's Buttress

The Sheep Pit

Baron's Wall

Curbar Corner
p.300

Elder Buttress
p.301

Main Edge

This is the nearest part of Curbar Edge to the parking and is well known for its routes. There are a number of good problems to go at dotted along the edge.
Approach (see map on page 290) - From the upper or lower parking, follow the main path to the tall Eliminates Wall and beyond this to the various problems.

At the far left end of this area, beyond Kayak Slab, is **Inch Buttress** with these two good highballs.

1 Lepton . . . . **V5** 6C+
A great arete which is very highball, but has a good landing.

2 Lepton Wall **V3** 6A
The wall is easier towards the top, hence less scary.

On the main edge, down below Avalanche Wall is the fine clean-cut **Curbar Corner**.

3 Neat. **V2** 5c
The arete left of the corner.

4 Curbar Corner **V1** 5b
The perfect corner is superb.

5 Little Stiffer. **V2** 6a
The right arete is technical. Climbed on its right-hand side is **Jamie and his Magic Torch, V8** 7B.
Orange Circuit continues on page 295.

Elder Buttress

L'Horla Buttress

Elder Crack (E2)

Maupassant (HVS)

⑥ ⑦ ⑧ ⑨

The next two problems are on **Elder Buttress** *and are found left of the start of the route Elder Crack.*

⑥ Ramboid . . . . 🛏️ 🧗 [ ] **V8** *7B*
Make a chin-grinding mantel onto the triangular ledge.

⑦ Janus Start . . . . 🛏️ 🧗 [ ] **V3** *6A*
The start to this route makes a good highball.

⑧ Spray Mane . . . . 🛏️ 👋 [ ] **V8** *7B*
From twin pockets, dyno to the break.

⑨ Sean's Arete . . . . 🧗 🪨 🚪 [ ] **V8** *7B*
The arete climbed on its left. To the top break is **V9** *7B+.*

Cubism

⑩ ⑪ ⑫

Right of the imposing Eliminates Wall is a small section with a few problems - **Cubism**.

⑩ The Severed Garden . . 🚪 🧗 [ ] **V5** *6C*
The slab is quite taxing.

⑪ Cubism . . . . 🛏️ [ ] **V1** *5b*
The arete on its right-hand side.

⑫ The Boxer . . . . [ ] **V0+** *5a*
The slab is a bit easier.

Quad Quarry

⑬ ⑭

A little further along, above the lower approach walk is a quarried face. This is **Quad Quarry** *home to one of the oldest hard problems in the Peak.*

⑬ Walk on By . . . . 🧗 🪨 [ ] **V10** *7C+*
The stunningly blank wall. Amazingly first climbed in 1980 and graded E3 6c!

⑭ Buy Buy . . . . ⑤🛏️🧗 [ ] **V4** *6B+*
The small arete down below. *Page 299 if on Red Circuit.*

Northern Peak
Sheffield Crags
Stanage Area
Burbage Valley
Derwent Edges
The Limestone
Central Grit
Staffordshire
South Peak

Little Quarry

A small quarry at the top of the edge has some decent easier problems and is the start of the Circuits.
Approach (see map on page 290) - From the upper parking, walk along the edge and head left about 100m after going through the gate.

1 Curved Rib . . . . **VB** 4a
The rib is a nice starter.

2 One Inch Crack . . . . **VB** 4a
Climb the short crack.

3 One Inch Arete. . . . . **VB** 4a
The arete on its right-hand side.

4 The Letter L **V2** 5c
Reach the letter L hold. Quite polished.

5 Dressed Arete **V2** 6a
The arete on its left-hand side. A delight.

6 Dressed Right **V0** 4c
The same arete on its right-hand side.

7 Seams Simple Enough
. . . . **V2** 5c
The thin cracks have some crumbly holds.

First Buttress

8 Chimney Crack **V1** 5b
The crack at the right-hand side of the wall.

9 Ledge Wall **V0-** 4b
The left side of the wall with a big flake.

10 Thin Flake. **V0** 4c
Climb the thin right-facing flake.

11 The Sketch **V0** 4c
Thin cracks and the arete. No use of ledges on the left.

12 Front Crack . . . . **VB** 4a
Climb the crack.

13 Front On **V0-** 4b
The end of the blunt fin is a decent problem.

14 Fishy **V0** 4c
The arete used by *Front On* on its right-hand side.
Photo opposite.

15 Chippy **V2** 5c
The face on edges. *Orange Circuit continues on page 300.*

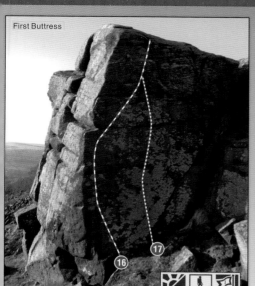

First Buttress

⑯
⑰

Morning | 3 min | Windy

50m to the right of the main quarry is a side wall to **First Buttress** *which has a couple of problems.*

⑯ Thomas the Tanked Up Engine

.... 🎖 📷 [ ] **V3** *6A+*
Climb the arete on its right-hand side. Quite scary.

⑰ The Phat Controller ④ 🎖 🧗 [ ] **V4** *6B+*

A direct version up the wall. *Red Circuit continues on page 301.*

[ ] The **Curbar Edge Orange Circuit**
This excellent circuit makes the most of the edge but is quite spaced out. The poorer problems and highballs have been omitted but you can add those to extend it a bit. The Little Quarry has plenty to get going on, then the next couple are by Avalanche Wall, before a final cluster by Moon Buttress and the Cioch Top Boulders. It is listed from right to left in the book.

[ ] The **Curbar Edge Red Circuit**
This is a much harder circuit with a couple of problems up to **V5** *6C*. Again, the highballs have mostly been left out and can be added if you are feeling confident. The problems are in clusters starting in the Little Quarries then on to Baron's Wall and finishing by Moon Buttress and the Cioch Top Boulders. It is listed from right to left in the book.

Red Circuit continues on page 301.

Northern Peak
Sheffield Crags
Stanage Area
Burbage Valley
Derwent Edges
The Limestone
Central Grit
Staffordshire
South Peak

⑭
⑮

Fishy (**V0** 4c) - *opposite*. Photo: Adrian Berry

The Ultimate Gritstone Experience

This isolated boulder is probably best combined with a visit to the problems in the Curbar Woods area on the far north end of the edge - see page 291.

Approach (see map on page 290) - From the Trackside Boulder continue for around 500m to a split in the path, Follow the right-hand branch uphill towards the edge. This boulder is on the right of the path just before you reach the edge.

Ben's Wall

A tall secluded boulder with its famous and impressive problem and a few extras to keep you busy. It is in the trees hence it can get green, but it tends to see enough traffic to keep clean for much of the time.

Approach (see map on page 290) - Walk along the main path from the Trackside Boulder for about 100m and Ben's Wall is hidden away to the right above the path.

Matt Kilner, *The Ultimate Gritstone Experience* (**V5** *6C*) - *this page.* Photo: Jamie Moss

❹ Pebble Wall **V3** *6A*
Climb the left arete. Balancy climbing and quite highball. It was originally done from the pockets on *Ben's Wall* at **V6** *7A*.

❺ Ben's Wall Traverse . . **V5** *6C*
Good footholds but sloping hands lead across to the crack. *Little White* makes a suitable finish.

❻ Ben's Wall **V9** *7C*
Gain the large sloping pocket dynamically and finish direct, or off left. It has been done static.

❼ Great White **V9** *7C*
Start just to the right of the previous problem (left hand in crack) and use a side-pull to gain a big pocket. Jump off; finishing from here is the scary **Greater White, V10** *7C+*. Photo on page 272.

❶ The Green Mile . . **V5** *6C+*
The left arete from sitting.

❷ The Ultimate Gritstone Experience
. . . . **V5** *6C*
The face, from a sitting start. Both aretes are 'in'. *Photo this page.*

❸ Touch Winky **V8** *7B*
The right arete from sitting.

❽ Little White **V5** *6C*
Follow *Great White* to the break, then traverse off right and follow the ramp to the top.

❾ Squat **V4** *6B*
Opposite *Ben's Wall*. A very low sit-down.

Bad Landing Boulder

The next boulder along has been intensely developed with some powerful eliminates and combinations. As you might expect from the name, the landings are bad so bring a few pads.
Approach - See map on page 290.

10 Bad Landing Arete . . . 19 ✪ ⬜ **V1** 5b
The arete at the left-hand end.

11 Drop Your Weapons . . ✪ 🔲 ⬜ **V9** 7C
Start on the side-pull in the groove, swing round the arete and drop down onto the lip. Traverse right and finish up *Bad Lip.*

12 Bad Landing Groove 20 ✪ 🔲 ⬜ **V2** 5c
The groove and holds right of the arete above the roof.
The last problem in the Orange Circuit.

13 Late Junction . . . ✪ 🔲 🔲 ⬜ **V8** 7B
From the low detached block, pull out to the lip then swing right and finish as for *Bad Lip.*

14 Le Musée Imaginaire . ✪ 🔲 ⬜ **V8** 7B+
From the start of *Bad Lip*, traverse the lip to finish up *Bad Landing Groove.*

15 Bad Lip. . . . . ✪ 🔲 🔲 ⬜ **V6** 7A
Hang the jug on the lip and pull up the small edges and slab without the block on the right. Finishing leftwards via a rockover and side-pulls is a slightly less scary **Detox Finish**, **V6** 7A.

16 Huffy's Roof . . . . ✪ 🔲 🔲 ⬜ **V10** 7C+
A sit-start to *Bad Lip*. Start with your right hand undercutting the pocket and left hand higher up the ramp.

17 Super Size Me. . . . . . ✪ 🔲 ⬜ **V12** 8A+
Starting matched on the undercut is Curbar's current hardest.

18 Left Turn. . . . . 🔲 🔲 ⬜ **V8** 7B+
From a matched hold, work left along the lip to *Bad Lip.*

19 Right Turn. . . . . 🔲 🔲 ⬜ **V8** 7B+
Head right from the matched hold to the arete.

Mini-Prow Boulder

This small boulder is situated 30m left of the Gorilla Warfare blocks. It has an attractive front prow.

20 Mini-Traverse . . . . . . ✪ 🔲 ⬜ **V3** 6A+
The traverse of the block has contrasting moves. Start on the fingery back side and finish up the prow.

21 Mini-Arete . . . . . . 9 16 ✪ ⬜ **V0** 4c
Small is beautiful, especially when it comes to aretes.

22 Mini-Crack . . . . . . 10 17 ✪ ⬜ **V0+** 5a
The small crack system.

23 Mini-Prow. . . . 11 18 ✪ 🔲 ⬜ **V1** 5b
The prow has endless variations. Any method is cute.
The last problem in the Green Circuit.

Northern Peak · Sheffield Crags · Stanage Area · Burbage Valley · Derwent Edges · The Limestone · Central Grit · Staffordshire · South Peak

Northern Peak

Sheffield Crags

Stanage Area

Burbage Valley

Derwent Edges

The Limestone

Central Grit

Staffordshire

South Peak

Gorilla Warfare

Uphill from the Trackside Boulder the grotty cleft of Gorilla Warfare oozes from the hillside. Behind the cleft is a dominating blank wall with two impressive aretes. Below this is a contrasting slabby block of Crescent Slab.
Approach - See map on page 290.

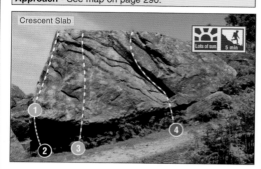

Crescent Slab

Lots of sun   5 min

1 Crescent Slab Arete ⑦ ⑨ 🏆 ☐ **V0+** 5a
Up the arete on either side, right is best. Both are hard to start.

2 Dan's Wall . . . . ☐ **V6** *7A*
The arete from a sitting start without the foot block.

3 Crescent Slab . . . . . . ⑩ ⑪ ☐ **V2** 5c
The slab is pleasant.

4 Diagonal . . . . ⑧ ⑪ ⑪ ☐ **V0-** 4b
The leftwards-leaning groove.
Green Circuit continues on page 305.

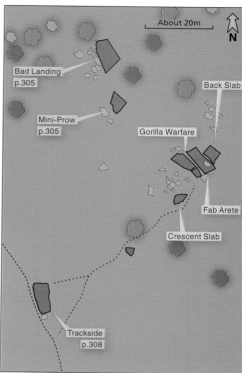

About 20m

N

Bad Landing
p.305

Mini-Prow
p.305

Back Slab

Gorilla Warfare

Fab Arete

Crescent Slab

Trackside
p.308

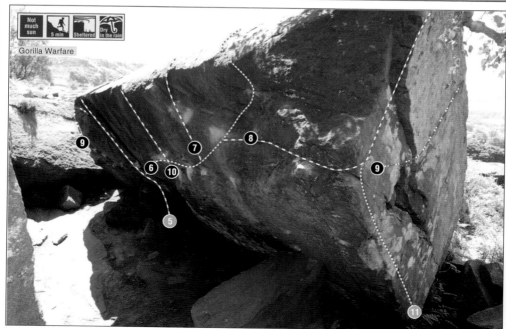

Not much sun   5 min   Sheltered   Dry in the rain

Gorilla Warfare

Fab Arete

Back Slab

The problems continue on the opposite boulder.

The most popular problems in this area are found in the deep slot between two huge boulders. The leaning face on the smaller boulder has a series of pumpy and powerful traverses on it.

5 Steve Clark **V2** 5c
Start low and thrash up the crack. Also called *The Offwidth*.

6 Gorilla Warfare . . **V6** 7A
From a sit-start and big flake right of the crack, traverse right on the vague line of features to reach some slopers. Make a blind reach around the top to some good edges.

7 Early Doors . . . . . **V7** 7A+
Follow *Gorilla Warfare* to the small spike edges then stretch for the upper ramp and edges on top.
Jihad, V8 7B reaches the same finish but eliminates the small spike edges by a powerful long move from the sloper.

8 Extended Warfare . . . **V6** 7A
Extend *Gorilla Warfare* by continuing the traverse across to the arete and then around to the right.

9 Original Warfare **V8** 7B
The original version of this problem. From the left-hand side of the boulder, traverse the lip, drop down *Steve Clark* then follow *Extended Warfare* around the arete. Finish by stretching right across the sidewall.

10 Hurricane **V9** 7C
From the first high slopers on the traverse, jump for the top. Holding the lip is the crux. It can be done statically and there is a sit-start at **V10** 7C+.

11 Humpin' **V2** 5c
From standing and using everything. The sit-start begins on pinches and is a poor eliminate **V7** 7A+.

12 Groovy Wall **V2** 5c
The usually green wall to the left of the big arete.

13 Veale Thing **V2** 5c
The tall arete above the cleft. Very high.

14 S-Crack Slap **V8** 7B
Pull on to the wall using S-shaped left hand hold and a poor crimp for your right. Slap the jug. Also called *Gutsy*.

15 The Scratcher **V8** 7B
Crimps to a larger crimp. Quite crimpy.

16 Baby Belle **V9** 7C
From the jug on *S-Crack Slap*, traverse right to finish up the left-hand side of *Fab Arete*.

17 Fab Arete **V1** 5b
The magnificent right-hand arete first on the left then on the right. Only a boulder problem if you don't fall off it.

18 Jordan's Wall **V5** 6C
The wall to the right is thin.

Further up the hill is a slabby block which can get a bit green.

19 Back Slab **V2** 5c
Climb up to the slight grooves.

20 Back Arete **V1** 5b
The right-hand side of the slab, via a vague ramp and some crimpy edges.

21 Dark Wall **V2** 5c
The shady wall facing the crag.
Orange Circuit continues on page 305.

Northern Peak · Sheffield Crags · Stanage Area · Burbage Valley · Derwent Edges · The Limestone · Central Grit · Staffordshire

1 **Bore-hole Wall** . . . . ⑥ [____] **V0-** 4b
The wall left of the bore-hole.
Green Circuit continues on page 306.

2 **Bore-hole Crack**. . . . . . . ⑤ [____] **V0-** 4b
The bore-hole.

3 **Bore-hole Traverse**. . . ⟳ ⬙ [____] **V1** 5b
Traverse the back of the block around to finish right of the arete.
Hands below the top.

4 **Side-wall Arete** . . . ④ ⑧ ⓫ [____] **V0** 4c
The small arete on its right-hand side.
Orange Circuit continues on page 306.

5 **Side-wall Crack** . . . ③ ⑦ ⟳ [____] **V0** 4c
The crack past the slot.

Trackside Boulder
This incredibly popular boulder is almost always busy with people when the conditions are good. Unfortunately this is showing in the wear to the ground under the main face.
Approach (see map on page 290) - From the lower parking on the road, walk down to the corner and follow the path.

6 **Side-wall Flake** . . . ⑥ ⟳ ▯ [____] **V1** 5b
Link the lower flake to the upper smaller flake.

7 **Side-wall Slot** . . . . . . ⑤ ⟳ [____] **V2** 6a
Mantel up past the slot. Easier if you use the arete on the right.

8 **Tracking High** . . . . . . ⟳ ⬙ [____] **V3** *6A+*
Traverse the lip of the recess rightwards then continue past the middle pocket, the flake and finish up the *Track Crack*.

9 Tracking . . . . **V8** 7B+
Traverse the very low break, from its start. Finish up
Strawberries, which is much harder from this side.
Continuing all the way to and up *Trackside* is **V10** 7C+.
Track Crack is out of bounds on all versions.

10 Crackside **V2** 6a
The short crack from the low break. Will feel harder if you do too
much crack climbing.

11 Three Pocket Wall . **V2** 5c
Use the three pockets and nothing else for your hands.

12 Trackside Scoop . . **V0+** 5a
The wall from a low start in the break. With the big pocket it is
a nice **VB**.

13 Strawberries **V4** 6B
Link the small vertical seams to attain a flat hold above. If it feels
harder than this then you're doing it wrong.

14 Track Crack . . . . . . **V0+** 5a
The deceptive crack is excellent.

15 Play Hard **V9** 7C
Slightly easier than *Work Hard* even though it looks harder.
Share the big sloper then reach up and left for a small hole. The
top is the next target. Needless to say, the crack is out.

16 Work Hard . . . . **V12** 8A+
The awesome wall via two slopers. Share the large middle
sloper, reach the next one and then lunge for the top.

17 Crack 'n' Pockets . . . . **V4** 6B+
Use the arete and crack above the roof and the thin vertical
seam out left to rock up for the pockets.
Crack 'n' Sloper, V5 6C, eliminate the seam out left.
Sloper 'n' Pockets, V6 7A, eliminate the crack and arete.

18 Trackside **V6** 7A
The deceptive arete can feel really easy, or completely
impossible, and can also prove addictive. Easy for the very tall.

19 Sidetrack **V6** 7A
The right-hand side of the arete requires a long reach to start
and finish. Without the foot-block is **V7** 7A+.

*There are a couple of boulders in the field below Trackside
Boulder. Access to these boulders is awkward and they have not
been described here.*

> The **Curbar Field Green Circuit**
> A mini-circuit of 11 problems takes you around
> the easier problems in The Curbar Field. It includes one
> Orange **V1** 5b problem to keep you on your toes.

> The **Curbar Field Orange Circuit**
> This testing circuit of 20 problems has mostly
> pleasant walls and the odd slab but just to spoil it we also
> included the offwidth in the pit of Gorilla Warfare. Quite a
> hard circuit with six problems at **V2** 5c/6a.

Northern Peak
Sheffield Crags
Stanage Area
Burbage Valley
Derwent Edges
The Limestone
Central Grit
Staffordshire
South Peak

	No star	⧼⧽	⧼⧽	⧼⧽
VB to V0 Easy to 4c	2	3	2	-
V0+ to V2 5a to 5c	8	14	4	-
V3 to V5 6A to 6C+	1	14	10	1
V3 to V5 7A upwards	-	20	1	4

Baslow has always lived in the shadow of its neighbours. The edge itself is never quite high enough for quality routes and never had the bouldering cachet of the near by Curbar. It is a beautiful location though and does offer plenty for the boulderer prepared to search around a bit. It may lack height for routing but it slightly overdoes it for many of the problems with highballs being in abundance. The problems are scattered along the edge on quarried and natural faces. There are also several free-standing boulders which actually give most of the best problems.

Circuits
Unfortunately this isn't a great edge for circuits. The quality Green and Orange problems tend to be either quite highball, or well spread out. We have included one Red Circuit up to **V5** *6C* which includes some good problems.

Conditions
Most of the edge is exposed to wind and rain, will dry quickly and is seldom green. The quarried sections tend to be more north-facing so might not dry as quickly. The boulders in the wooded sections have some shelter but will take longer to dry and can be green.

Approach   Also see map on page 272
Baslow Edge is the less imposing continuation of Curbar Edge and is usually approached from the Curbar Gap car park. From this car park walk down the hill towards Curbar village then follow a wide path off leftwards which curves around along the cliff top. This leads rapidly to the Square Stone and then along the top of the edge. The Eagle Stone is clearly visible ahead on the larger path set back from the edge.

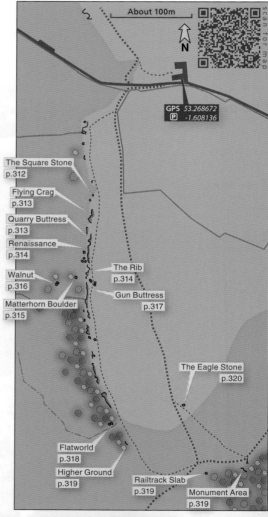

About 100m

N

GPS 53.268672
P -1.608136

The Square Stone p.312

Flying Crag p.313

Quarry Buttress p.313

Renaissance p.314

The Rib p.314

Walnut p.316

Gun Buttress p.317

Matterhorn Boulder p.315

The Eagle Stone p.320

Flatworld p.318

Higher Ground p.319

Railtrack Slab p.319

Monument Area p.319

Northern Peak

Sheffield Crags

Stanage Area

Burbage Valley

Derwent Valley

The Limestone

Central Grit

Staffordshire

South Peak

Duncan Campbell on the superb slab problem of *Renaissance* (**V1** 5b) - *page 314* - on Baslow Edge. Photo: Alan James

Northern Peak

Sheffield Crags

Stanage Area

Burbage Valley

Derwent Edges

The Limestone

Central Grit

Staffordshire

South Peak

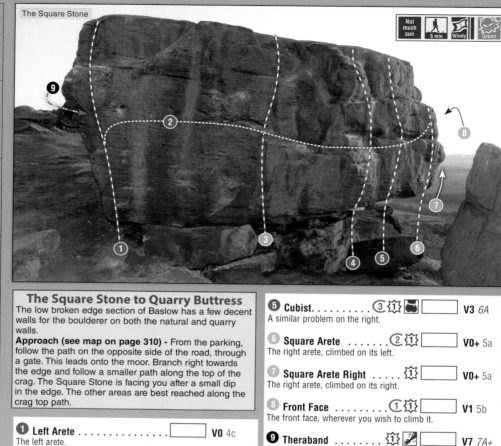

The Square Stone

Not much sun | 5 min | Windy | Green

The Square Stone to Quarry Buttress

The low broken edge section of Baslow has a few decent walls for the boulderer on both the natural and quarry walls.

Approach (see map on page 310) - From the parking, follow the path on the opposite side of the road, through a gate. This leads onto the moor. Branch right towards the edge and follow a smaller path along the top of the crag. The Square Stone is facing you after a small dip in the edge. The other areas are best reached along the crag top path.

1 Left Arete **V0** 4c
The left arete.

2 Square Dance . . . . **V4** 6B+
Traverse the face from the left arete to the right arete.

3 Short Wall . . . . **V0+** 5a
The easiest way up this face. **V3** 6A from sitting.

4 Square Wall **V3** 6A
Starting from a hold on the lip continue to the top.

5 Cubist. **V3** 6A
A similar problem on the right.

6 Square Arete . . . . . . **V0+** 5a
The right arete, climbed on its left.

7 Square Arete Right . . . . . **V0+** 5a
The right arete, climbed on its right.

8 Front Face **V1** 5b
The front face, wherever you wish to climb it.

9 Theraband . . . . **V7** 7A+
Starting on the arete right of problem 8, traverse the block, keeping below the top. Keep going as long as you want.

Directly below the Square Stone is a narrow buttress with a vague rib just left of an arete.

10 Has Shaun Got False Teeth? . . **V4** 6B
The faint rib avoiding the right arete.

The Square Stone

Flying Crag

Quarry Buttress

Flying Crag

Northern Peak
Sheffield Crags
Stanage Area
Burbage Valley
Derwent Edges
The Limestone
Central Grit
Staffordshire
South Peak

The Baslow Edge Red Circuit
A good 26-problem circuit with some classics.
There is one problem of **V5** *6C* but it is mostly **V4** *6B+* and
below, including some highball Orange Spots as well.

*The next problems are on Flying Crag, which is about 50m
further along the edge.*

⑪ **John Wilson** . . . . . ⑥ 🔲 **V3** *6A+*
The double prow above a dodgy landing.

⑫ **Flying Start** . . . . ⑤ 🔲 **V3** *6A*
Climb the groove which is more awkward than it looks.

⑬ **Flying Groove** . . . . . . 🔲 **V0+** *5a*
The slim groove on the right of the recess.

Quarry Buttress

*The next problems are on Quarry Buttress, about 50m further
along the edge.*

⑭ **Batu Motel** . . . . . 🔲 **V7** *7A+*
The steep slab requires a long reach.

⑮ **Cold Diggerty** . . . 🔲 **V5** *6C+*
Follow crimps diagonally across the wall.

⑯ **Hot Ziggerty** . . ⑦ 🔲 **V5** *6C*
Starting from the boulder, climb the wall. **V6** *7A* if started
without the boulder. *Red circuit continues on page 314.*

Red circuit continues on page 314.

⑰ **Arise Sir Freddy!** . . . . 🔲 **V4** *6B*
The arete, moving left then back right.

⑱ **Whatsit?** . . . . 🔲 **V1** *5b*
The face and arete just to the right.

Renaissance
p.314

The Rib
p.222

The Matterhorn Boulder
p.315

Gun Buttress
p.113

The Walnut
p.316

Renaissance

Renaissance to The Rib

As the edge becomes more continuous, there are more problems to be found.

Approach (see map on page 310) - Follow the crag-top path past the square stone and on for about 150m further to a popular section of natural edge. This is *Renaissance*.

The first three problems are really short solos on a popular beginners' slab. It can be climbed virtually anywhere.

1 Route 1 .... **VB**
High, but very easy. The arete to the left is a little easier still.

2 Route 1.5 .... **V0-** 4b
A decent eliminate. Just right is about the same grade.

3 Route 2 .... **VB** 4a
Trend right up the middle of the slab. A tricky start which can be avoided from the right.

The next slab is much steeper.

4 Resurgence **V1** 5b
A left-hand variation of *Renaissance*.

5 Renaissance **V1** 5b
The middle of the narrow wall is a gem. *Photo on page 311.*

6 Grounded Bees .... **V0+** 5a
The right arete feels artificial when you are on it.

Twin Roof

The following problems are found on a block just below Renaissance which is surprisingly hard to get to.

7 Twin Roof Left ...... **V3** 6A+
Rockover via a small pocket.

8 Twin Roof **V1** 5b
Climb the roof via some good holds.

The Square Stone
p.312

Flying Crag
p.312

Quarry Buttress
p.312

Northern Peak

Sheffield Crags

Stanage Area

Burbage Valley

Derwent Edges

The Limestone

Central Grit

Staffordshire

South Peak

The Rib

The Matterhorn Boulder

50m to the right, the bouldering continues at another north-facing quarried bay known as The Rib.

9 Pinch 'n' Push . . . . . . **V3** 6A+
The centre of the wall.

10 The Balls Test **V4** 6B
The arete that forms the left side of the crack.
Red circuit continues on page 316.

11 The Ripper . . . . **V7** 7A+
The wall right of the crack, avoiding the arete of the crack.

12 Truffle Pig **V6** 7A
Follow the rising line up the side-wall.

13 Ribless **V0** 4c
The wall, avoiding the arete is quite high.

The next problems are on the Matterhorn Boulder, well below the edge and on the way down to the Walnut.

14 Bone at it Direct . **V6** 7A
Starting low, reach out to the lip and pull over the the slab.

15 Smutt Ridge . . . . **V7** 7A+
Start as for the previous problem then traverse the lip right and finish up the arete.

16 Lion **V1** 5b
The right arete on its right-hand side.

The Rib

Gun Buttress
p.317

Renaissance

Twin Roof

The Matterhorn Boulder

The Walnut
p.316

Northern Peak

Sheffield Crags

Stanage Area

Burbage Valley

Derwent Edges

The Limestone

Central Grit

Staffordshire

South Peak

Northern Peak

Sheffield Crags

Stanage Area

Burbage Valley

Derwent Edges

The Limestone

Central Grit

Staffordshire

South Peak

The Walnut

The Walnut is a huge block situated in the fields below the main edge. It can be seen from the crag top just beyond the Square Stone. The main attractions are two powerful low-level traverses.

Approach (see map on page 310) - The Walnut Block is awkward to get to. It can be approached directly from above, past the Matterhorn Block although this can be tricky when the bracken is up. Alternatively, drop down a path in the gully before the square Stone and head across to it following vague sheep tracks.

❶ Hazelnut Whirl . . . . . . ⑫ ⚄ ☐ **V3** *6A+*
Climb into the scoop just right of the tree.

❷ Dry Roasted . . . . ☐ **V1** 5b
The wall. **V2** 5c from sitting.

❸ Praline . . . . ☐ **V2** 5c
The leftward trending line. Take care with the rock.

❹ Nut Job . . . . ⑬ ⚄ ☐ **V2** 5c
From sitting, climb through the lip and onto the slab.

❺ The Walnut . . ⑭ ⚄ ☐ **V4** *6B*
Traverse the steep wall. There are various eliminates but the basic rules are no holds on the top of the boulder, and finish by rocking onto the boulder at the end.

❻ Complete Nutter ⑮ ⚄ ☐ **V2** 5c
The fin from sitting.

❼ Whip Me Whip Me . . . ⚄ ☐ **V7** *7A+*
Start facing outwards, with hands undercutting slots. Climb feet first out of the cave, until you can spin round and top out.

The remaining problems are found on the north side of the smaller, adjacent boulder.

8 Nut Cracker . . . . ⑯ 🗘 ⬜ **V2** *5c*
Pull up to jugs from as low as you like.

9 Little Richard . . . 🗘 ⬛ ⬛ ⬜ **V6** *7A*
Start low on the left-hand side of the traverse and pull up through the bulge. Finish straight up.

10 Walnut Whip . 🗘 ⬛ ⬛ ⬛ ⬜ **V8** *7B*
Traverse the line of small edges and slopers across the middle of the boulder, below the good ledges. Top-out around the arete. It is **V4**, *6B+* with the big holds.

11 The Choker . . 🗘 ⬛ ⬛ ⬛ ⬜ **V10** *7C+*
A low, eliminate version of *Walnut Whip*. Start as for *Walnut Whip*, then drop down from the sloper and head left to easier ground.

12 Chunky Nut . . . . ⑰ 🗘 ⬜ **V4** *6B+*
Start as for *Walnut Whip*, then from the sloper move up to finish as for *Little Richard*.

Approach down here →

Gun Buttress

Back up on the edge, Gun Buttress is a small section of natural crag with a prominent 'gun barrel' on top of it.
Approach (see map on page 310) - Follow the crag-top path until the section of edge just before the wooded section begins below the edge. Continue past the 'gun' and descend and double back to the problems.

13 Rough Wall Climb . . . 🗘 🖐 ⬜ **V0** *4c*
The cracks up the centre of the wall.

14 Jolly Green Dwarf . . . 🗘 🖐 ⬜ **V0+** *5a*
The slabby arete.

15 Mad Bilberries . . . . ⑱ 🗘 🖐 ⬜ **V3** *6A+*
The friction slab.

16 Jolly Green Elephant ⑲ 🗘 ⬛ ⬜ **V4** *6B+*
Gain the hanging arete.

17 Pensioner's Bulge . . . . . . 🗘 ⬜ **V0+** *5a*
Climb through the roof on thin cracks.

18 Hair Conditioned Nightmare 🖐 ⬜ **V1** *5b*
The centre of the pillar is a HVS solo.

19 Hair Conditioned Rightmare
. . . . ⑳ 🗘 ⬜ **V2** *5c*
The arete above a ledge, climbed on its right-hand side.
Red circuit continues on page 318.

Northern Peak

Sheffield Crags

Stanage Area

Burbage Valley

Derwent Edges

The Limestone

Central Grit

Staffordshire

South Peak

Flatworld

A super little spot tucked away in the trees below the far southern end of the edge.

Approach (see map on page 310) - Walk along the crag top path, past the main edge until about level with the Eagle Stone. Head down right here to the block in the trees below, over a wire fence.

Up on the edge, behind the Flatworld boulders is a small projecting rib hidden in the trees and bracken.

❶ Heroes . . . . 🔆 ◪ ☐ **V7** *7A+*
The projecting nose direct without the block on the right. Finishing up and left to a jug-slot is **V6** *7A*.

The big leaning block of Flatworld has two impressive aretes.

❷ Spinal Fjord . . . . . . 🔆 ◪ ☐ **V4** *6B+*
Make a dynamic move to gain a short groove.

❸ Shakespeare's Theatre 🔆 ◪ ☐ **V4** *6B+*
The creaky flakes from sitting. A standing start is **V1** 5b.

❹ Leftworld . . . . . . 🔆 ◪ ◪ ☐ **V8** *7B+*
The arete of *Flatworld* on its left-hand side.

❺ Flatworld . . . . . . 🔆 ◪ ◪ ☐ **V8** *7B+*
The arete is a modern classic.

❻ Hurry on Sundown . . . ㉑🔆 ☐ **V4** *6B*
The arete to the right. **V6** *7A* from a sitting start.

❼ Lichen Slab . . . . 🔆 ☐ **V2** 5c
The centre of the green slab to the right.

❽ Milk Arete . . . . ☐ **V1** 5b
The left arete of the block.

❾ Milk of Amnesia . . . . 🔆 ☐ **V4** *6B*
Climb the slab just right of the arete.

❿ Elmer Fudd . . . . 🔆 ◪ ☐ **V6** *7A*
Start on the right then move into the middle on very small holds.

⓫ Fat World . . . . ㉒🔆 ☐ **V3** *6A+*
The arete on its left-hand side.
Red circuit continues on page 320.

In trees up on edge

Approach over fence

The next problem is on a wall about 50m further along the edge from the Flatworld approach point.

12 **Higher Ground . . .** 〔icons〕 **V9** *7C*
The centre of the wall to a hard and high finish.

Higher Ground

Monument Area

Beyond Flatworld is one further section of edge, and two more isolated blocks and walls down by the monument.
Approach (see map on page 310) - All three blocks can be reached from the crag-top path as it curves round towards the monument.

The Railtrack block is in the bracken down to the right, just before you reach the Wellington Monument.

13 **Snappy Flakes . . . .** 〔icon〕 **V1** 5b
The overhanging wall on big snappy flakes.

14 **Flaky Layback . . . .** 〔icons〕 **V0+** 5a
Layback up the flakes on the left side of the slab.

Railtrack Slab

15 **Railtrack . . . .** 〔icons〕 **V6** *7A*
Mantel onto the slab.

16 **Halfway Slab . . . .** 〔icons〕 **V2** 5c
Climb the slab.

The final area described is found hidden down below and west of the Wellington Memorial.

17 **Fact Hunt . . . .** 〔icons〕 **V7** *7A+*
The hanging arete from a sitting start.

18 **That Which Does Not Kill Me Makes Me Stronger**
. . . . 〔icons〕 **V9** *7C*
The crimps just to the right.

19 **Dirty Bitch . . . .** 〔icons〕 **V5** *6C*
From the start of *Fact Hunt*, shift right, then up onto the slab to finish.

There are a few more hidden walls in the woods passed as you walk from the Monument towards Gardom's. Check
PeakBouldering.info > Baslow *for details.*

Northern Peak
Sheffield Crags
Stanage Area
Burbage Valley
Derwent Edges
The Limestone
Central Grit
Staffordshire
South Peak

The Eagle Stone

This is one of the better free-standing boulders around with the extra bonus of good landings, unless it has been wet, when they become muddy pools. Historically, an ascent of the stone was a rite of passage for the young men of Baslow who were supposed to climb the stone before proposing marriage to a local maiden.

Approach (see map on page 310) - The stone is situated on the moor above Baslow Edge. You can't miss it if you follow the cliff top path towards the Wellington Monument.

1 A Fist Full of Beagles . **V7** 7A+
The roof and mantel.

2 Beagle's About **V2** 5c
Climb up to and through the scoop at the top.

3 Roundabout. . . . . . . **V3** 6A+
Traverse all the way around the block starting where you like but normally at *Beagle's About*.

4 For a Few Beagles More
. . . . **V8** 7B
The wall past some thin breaks.

5 The Good, the Bad and the Beagle
. . . . **V6** 7A
Aim for the pale streak.

6 A Beagle too Far **V4** 6B
The prominent groove climbed on its right edge. *Photo opposite.*

7 The Bright Concept. . . . **V8** 7B+
The nose on the left.

8 Dreaming the Beagle . **V7** 7A+
Just right of the nose.

9 The Beagle Has Landed
. . . . **V6** 7A
Thin crimps lead to a dyno.

10 Where Beagles Dare
. . . . **V7** 7A+
The wall via a small pocket for your right hand.

11 Like a Beagle Over Troubled Water
. . . . **V4** 6B+
The wall via rounded breaks. *The last problem in the Red circuit.*

12 Men Only **V0-** 4b
Tackle the sloping ledges and chipped holds to test your manhood. This is also the descent.

Northern Peak

Sheffield Crags

Stanage Area

Burbage Valley

Derwent Edges

The Limestone

Central Grit

Staffordshire

South Peak

A Beagle Too Far (**V4** *6B*) - *opposite* - The Eagle Stone, Baslow. Photo: Adrian Berry

	No star	☆	☆☆	☆☆☆
VB to V0 easy to 4	2	-	-	-
V0+ to V2 5a to 5c	3	16	1	-
V3 to V5 6A to 6C+	4	21	8	2
V3 to V5 7A upwards	2	14	5	10

The bouldering at Gardom's has two decent areas of concentrated problems with a whole range of smaller developed blocks in between. Most of the problems are hard though and, with the exception of a few problems on Gardom's North and South, there is little on offer for the Orange and Green Spot boulderer. For those operating in the mid and upper grades, there is plenty to go at including some super classics.

Circuits

This isn't a great crag for circuits but we have included a couple at Gardom's North.

Conditions

The crag faces west and northwest and has extensive tree cover for much of its length. This makes many of the blocks and walls green for much of the time and the crag is often slow to dry. The upside is that the shade from the trees can be useful in warmer weather. It doesn't catch the wind like other moorland crags

Approach   Also see map on page 272

Gardom's is situated above the A621 Sheffield to Baslow road. For most of the bouldering, it is best to approach from the north end by parking on a minor road at a diagonal junction on the A621. From the parking walk back to the junction and cross the gate onto the path. Bear right and make your way across the wet moorland. Alternatively, you can walk down the (dry) road and there is a small path leading directly up to Gardom's North from below. For the south approach, see page 336.

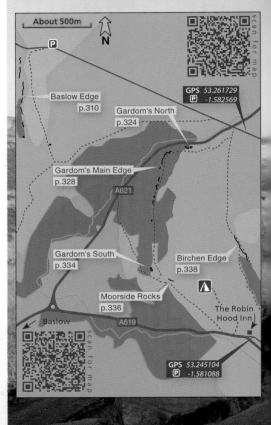

About 500m

N

Baslow Edge p.310

GPS 53.261729 P -1.582569

Gardom's North p.324

Gardom's Main Edge p.328

A621

Gardom's South p.334

Birchen Edge p.338

Moorside Rocks p.336

The Robin Hood Inn

Baslow

A619

GPS 53.245104 P -1.581088

Northern Peak

Sheffield Crags

Stanage Area

Burbage Valley

Derwent Edges

The Limestone

Central Grit

Staffordshire

South Peak

John Noakes on the lip of *Mark's Roof* (**V8** *7B*) - *page 325* - on the Gardom's North Boulders. Photo: Alan James

Northern Peak

Sheffield Crags

Stanage Area

Burbage Valley

Derwent Edges

The Limestone

Central Grit

Staffordshire

South Peak

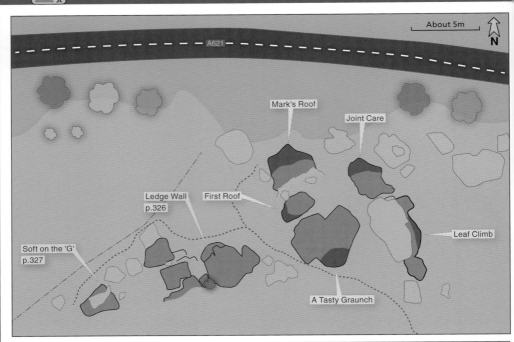

About 5m

N

Mark's Roof

Joint Care

Ledge Wall
p.326

First Roof

Leaf Climb

Soft on the 'G'
p.327

A Tasty Graunch

Leaf Climb

Morning   5 min   Windy

The first couple of problems are down to the right when you cross the fence on the normal approach across the moor.

1 Leaf Climb . . . . . ①❅🪧 [　　] **V4** *6B*
Traverse the lip from right to left without using the foot-block.

2 Percy's Roof . . . . . ②❅◀ [　　] **V5** *6C*
Start low and pull through the centre of the low roof. Keep your feet off the really useful footholds.

The **Gardom's North Red Circuit**
Only short but a hard 13-problem circuit with most of the problems being from **V4** *6B* to **V5** *6C+*. You can easily add the Orange problems to make it a more respectable length.

Gardom's North

This pleasant area is the first collection of rocks you reach on approaching Gardom's from the north and the A621. The boulders lie on a north-facing slope and are more shady than other areas, especially the roof problems. The rock remains green for much of the winter. It dries fairly quickly if there is a breeze.

Approach (see map on page 322) - The boulders can be seen on the usual approach to Gardom's Edge.

A Tasty Graunch

Lots of sun   5 min   Windy

Continue along the path for a short distance and you reach the low roof that is home to the next problem.

3 A Tasty Graunch. . . . . . . 🪧 [　　] **V7** *7A+*
A low right to left traverse, eliminating the top and heel-hooks. When you reach the crack pull up using the top. A bit silly.

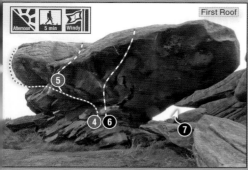

First Roof

Follow the rocks around to the right and you come to a steeply undercut block with some obvious roof problems.

4 First Roof Left . ③ 🔥 ⬅️ 📦 ☐ **V4** *6B+*
Follow big holds leftwards to a mantel finish on the left.

5 First Roof Middle
. . . . ④ 🔥 ⬅️ 📦 ☐ **V5** *6C*
From the same start, turn the roof in its centre.

6 Wishbone . . . 🔥 👊 ⬅️ 📦 ☐ **V8** *7B*
From the low start, use poor holds to stretch out right to turn the lip. Difficult to keep off the deck.

Behind First Roof is another jutting roof with a single problem over its lip.

7 Joint Care . . . . . . 🔥 ⬅️ ✏️ ☐ **V7** *7A+*
The flat nose above a poor landing.

Continue down in the direction of the road and turn right to Mark's Roof - home to some classic problems that combine thuggery and finesse.

8 Mark's Roof Left-hand
. . . . ⑤ 🔥 ✏️ ☐ **V5** *6C+*
Follow the line of holds on the left-hand side of the roof to the lip, then finish up the short flake. Brilliant and powerful.
Red Circuit continues on page 326.

9 Rock End Roll . . . 🔥 ✏️ 👊 ☐ **V7** *7A+*
Finish *Mark's Roof Left-hand* using the short, flared crack.

10 Nigel's Roof . . . . 🔥 ✏️ ⬅️ ☐ **V8** *7B+*
An eliminate between the two main lines. Start on the shelf of *Mark's Roof Left-hand* and use small crimps to gain the lip and finish as for *Mark's Roof*.

11 Mark's Roof . . . . 🔥 ✏️ ⬅️ ☐ **V8** *7B*
A classic roof. Cross the centre of the roof to a square hold. Swing left and pull desperately up the wall above. *Photo on page 323.* For **Mark's Roof Original, V6** *7A*, keep going left at the lip to join the finish of *Mark's Roof Left-hand*.

12 Mark's Roof Direct 🔥 ✏️ ⬅️ ☐ **V9** *7C*
As for the *Mark's Roof* to the square hold then scrabble up the ripples above.

13 Dylan's Variant . . 🔥 ✏️ ⬅️ ☐ **V7** *7A+*
As for the *Mark's Roof* to the square hold then use the arete to finish.

14 Full Circle . . . . 🔥 ✏️ ☐ **V8** *7B*
Start up *Mark's Roof*, then swing left and reverse *Mark's Roof Left-hand*, then traverse the back wall and go again.

Mark's Roof

Northern Peak · Sheffield Crags · Stanage Area · Burbage Valley · Derwent Edges · The Limestone · Central Grit · Staffordshire · South Peak

Ledge Wall

The left-hand side of the open central area starts with a small blunt rib.

15 Little Arete . . . V3 *6A*
Climb the blunt arete from a low start.

16 Seamstress V1 *5b*
Trend left up the blunt rib using a pocket.

17 Prowstress . . . . V3 *6A+*
The prow is frightening. A rounded pull gains safety.

18 Ledge Roof . . . V0+ *5a*
From a sit-start, climb the roof under *Ledge Wall*.

The next problems start from a high ledge - **Ledge Wall**.

19 Ledge Crack . . . . V0+ *5a*
The slab right of the crack.

20 Ledge Wall V2 *5c*
The slabby wall starting from the ledge. Take care not to bounce if you fall off.

21 Ledge Wall Right . . . . V0+ *5a*
The arete on its left-hand side.

22 West Wall Left V0 *4c*
The arete on its right-hand side.

23 West Wall V2 *5c*
The slabby side-wall requires some thought. No arete allowed.

Ledge Wall

The **Gardom's North Orange Circuit**
A short circuit only but a good one for a quick session especially in late afternoon sunshine. It includes mostly walls and aretes and there are no highballs.

24 Alcove Nose . . . . . . ⑩ V4 6B+
The blunt arete at the back of the recess. **V8** 7B+ from sitting.

25 Alcove Arete . . . . ⑧ V1 5b
The arete from a good hold.

26 Ben's Bulge . . . . V7 7A+
Use a horrible sloper and a leg jam to cross the bulge.

27 The Grasper . . ⑪ V5 6C
The jutting arete gets a little high but the landing is flat.

*The next problems are on the **Soft on the 'G'** block to the right.*

28 Soft on the 'G' V8 7B
A superb powerful arete. Easy if you know how.

29 Full Power V11 8A
A low start with your right hand in the pocket, and left on a ripple. Hard and dynamic moves above.

30 8 Ball . . . . . . V12 8A+
The even lower start on the right-hand front edge of the roof, using a low hold down for your left. Hang traverse the lip to join and finish up *Full Power*.

31 Rock Hard Bishop . . . ⑫ V4 6B+
Straight up the wall left of the little groove. Use holds on problems on either side.

32 Soft Groove . . . . ⑨ V1 5b
The central weakness of the wall.

33 Soft Groove Sit-down
. . . . ⑬ V5 6C
The sit-start is the real deal. No use of the block on the right. *The last problem in the Red Circuit.*

34 Soft Wall . . . . ⑩ V0+ 5a
Left of the arete is a useful hold high on the wall. Harder if you can't reach it.

35 Soft Arete . . . . ⑪ V0+ 5a
The arete on its right-hand side.

36 Soft Ribs . . . . ⑫ V0- 4b
Warm your fingers on this blunt rib off to the right. *The last problem in the Orange Circuit.*

Northern Peak · Sheffield Crags · Stanage Area · Burbage Valley · Derwent Edges · The Limestone · Central Grit · Staffordshire · South Peak

Soft on the 'G'

Northern Peak

Sheffield Crags

Stanage Area

Burbage Valley

Derwent Edges

The Limestone

Central Grit

Staffordshire

South Peak

Kidneystone

A621

Overhang Buttress

Traction Buttress

Gardom's North
p.324

From the
north parking

Pogle's Wood

Moyer's Buttress

About 50m

N

Gardom's Main Edge

There is a fair amount to go at along the edge, though it is mostly in the higher grades.

Approach (see map on page 322) - A path runs through the trees, passing above the Kidneystone after 50m, and along the top of the crag.

Kidneystone

Not much sun | 6 min | Green

Not much sun | 8 min | Green

Overhang Buttress

The Kidneystone is situated just inside the woods on the other side of the fence from Gardom's North. Follow the normal path then bear right for about 50m. It is visible in winter but hidden in summer.

❶ **Kidneystone** . . . . 🌓 🔲🔲🔲 **V8** 7B
From the low jug, head out left and up, avoiding the foot block.

❷ **Heartland** . . . . . . 🌓 🔲🔲🔲 **V9** 7C
Starting at the same jug, move right and up.

The next problems are at the base of the main edge. This is best reached by walking along the crag-top path and dropping down the gullies between the buttresses. Overhang Buttress is best approached down the first easy gully.

❸ **Afro** . . . . 🌓 🔲🔲 **V4** 6B
In the pit below a large overhang, climb the wall to the ledge.

Northern Peak

Sheffield Crags

Stanage Area

Burbage Valley

Derwent Edges

The Limestone

Central Grit

Staffordshire

South Peak

Traction Buttress

Pogle's Wood

The buttress on the left side of the first approach gully is Traction Buttress where there is one problem of note.

④ Bloc Steno **V5** *6C*
Eliminating the right arete, climb the short rib and groove as far as the overhang. It is **V3** *6A* with the arete.

Continue along the edge for about 100m and head down the third approach gully to reach the prominent Moyer's Buttress. On a small block in the woods below are two problems.

⑤ Pogle's Wood Left-Hand . . **V4** *6B*
The left arete is a bit of an eliminate. The sit-start is **V5** *6C*.

⑥ Pogle's Wood **V5** *6C*
The right arete. The sit-start is **V8** *7B*.

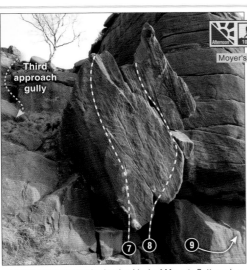

Third approach gully

Moyer's Buttress

Just left of the impressive leaning block of Moyer's Buttress is a diamond-shaped, undercut boulder with two problems on it.

⑦ The Gritstone Treaty
. . . . **V8** *7B*
The left arete.

⑧ Mo's Problem . . . **V7** *7A+*
The right arete needs some serious padding.

The right-hand side of Moyer's Buttress has a start to a route.

⑨ Perfect Day Direct Start
. . . . **V8** *7B*
The fingery wall - no French start allowed. Descend the crack on the left when you've reached the jugs. The French start version is worth **V7** *7A+*. (French start - one hand on the rock, one foot on the ground, then pop for the next hold).

Drum Roll

Lots of sun | 15 min | Green

⑩

After Moyer's Buttress is Elliott's Buttress. Beyond this the edge
becomes much more broken until Undertaker's Buttress with its
prominent beak overhang. About halfway along this section is a
short hidden wall just below the top of the edge.

⑩ **Drum Roll** . . . . 🌂 🖐 ▭ **V7** *7A+*
The centre of the quarried face. The sit-start is **V8** *7B*.

Bin Laden's Cave

⑪   ⑫

Not
much
sun | 15 min | Green

About 50m below Drum Roll is a hidden block facing away
from the edge. This can take some finding. It is also possible
to approach from Pogle's Wood by dropping down about 15m
to pick up a very vague path and following this carefully - it
bends round parallel to the main edge to eventually arrive at Bin
Laden's Cave after about 150m.

⑪ **Bin Lillemule** . . . . 🖳 ▭ **V7** *7A+*
The left arete of the block.

⑫ **Bin Laden's Cave** . . . 🌂 🗨 ▭ **V6** *7A*
The face and right arete is worth seeking out. *Photo opposite.*

A621

Pogle's Wood
p.329

Moyer's Buttress
p.329

Bin Laden's Cave

Drum Roll

Capillary Buttress
p.332

Apple Buttress
p.333

N

About 50m

Northern Peak

Sheffield Crags

Stanage Area

Burbage Valley

Derwent Edges

The Limestone

Central Grit

Staffordshire

South Peak

Northern Peak

Sheffield Crags

Stanage Area

Burbage Valley

Derwent Edges

The Limestone

Central Grit

Staffordshire

South Peak

Jim Hillard on *Bin Laden's Cave* (**V6** *7A*) - *opposite* - Gardom's Edge. Photo: Adam Long

Northern Peak

Sheffield Crags

Stanage Area

Burbage Valley

Derwent Edges

The Limestone

Central Grit

Staffordshire

South Peak

Capillary Buttress (left)

Afternoon   20 min

Capillary Buttress has some decent problems and is found just north of the popular Apple Buttress. To reach it, first locate the tall Apple Buttress, which is about 80m beyond where a wall crosses the path. Then double back and scramble down the approach gully. This leads steeply down to the front of the buttress where there is a big tree in front of an arete.

13 **Soloman** . . . . **V3** *6A+*
The left edge of the wall.

14 **A Fearful Orange** . . . . **V5** *6C+*
The short hanging crack starting matched on the big triangular hold. Leaning in higher is the start to the route *Squeeze Your Lemon* and is worth **V3** *6A+*.

15 **Neutral Milk Hotel** . . . **V3** *6A*
Tackle the arete on its left-hand side.

Afternoon   20 min   Green

Capillary Buttress (right)

16 **Two-Headed Boy** **V5** *6C*
The same arete on its right-hand side, continuing out right along the shelf. Mantel to finish.

17 **Ladder Coins** **V4** *6B*
Follow crimps up the wall.

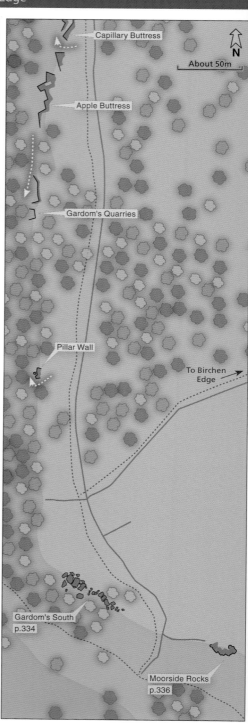

N

About 50m

Capillary Buttress

Apple Buttress

Gardom's Quarries

Pillar Wall

To Birchen Edge

Gardom's South
p.334

Moorside Rocks
p.336

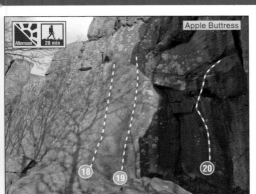

The tall Apple Buttress is a popular spot but doesn't have too much on offer for boulderers. The slabby wall to the right of the main buttress has some short routes most of which can be soloed. The two on the right-hand side are worthwhile and have no gear before the break anyway.

18 Cydrax **V1** 5b
The edges on the slab. At the break move left and descend the crack.

19 Cider . . . . **V0+** 5a
Climb the arete to the ledge.

20 Double Bum . . . . **V4** 6B+
The centre of the recessed wall right of the slab.

Just south of Apple Buttress is a wooded section of hidden quarries. A vague track leads from the Apple Buttress area underneath them. The smaller second quarry has a protruding block with some hard arete problems.

21 Dirty Business Left-Hand . **V4** 6B+
The arete on its left-hand side.

22 Dirty Business . . . . . . **V4** 6B+
The arete on the right. Eliminating the big holds on the face is **Plan D** and is **V9** 7C from sitting or standing.

23 Business as Usual **V5** 6C+
The centre of the wall with a dynamic start. Statically is **V8** 7B+.

24 The Forward Thinking Sound Engineer
. . . . **V7** 7A+
The left side of the right arete.

Charlotte Rampling (E6)

One final isolated buttress on the main edge has a decent arete problem. The buttress is situated about 100m before a stone wall crosses the path and you approach by descending down the far left (looking out) side.

25 English Voodoo . . . . . **V5** 6C+
Climb the arete mostly on its left-hand side. The crack and pocket to the right are not allowed. From sitting it is **V7** 7A+.

Gardom's South

Gardom's South is a relatively minor area that owes its popularity to a small set of decent problems that make the longish walk-in and green conditions worthwhile. *Suavito*, *Barry Sheen* and *G-Thang* are all Peak classics. The rest of the problems are less good but worth doing while you are here.

North Approach (see map on page 322) - From the north, continue until just after the second wall crosses the path then break out right to the rocks.

South Approach (see map on page 336) - Park in the car park by the Robin Hood Inn, just off the A619 Baslow to Chesterfield road as for Birchen Edge. Walk back down the road towards Baslow and pick up a marked path over the moor. Follow this for about 1km until you have just passed Moorside Rocks on your right. After a wall the main path drops down the hill. Break out right here along the wall then head leftwards to the boulders in the trees.

The left-hand side of the cluster has a short arete in front of the crag. There are more problems/routes here but they are all highball and a bit green most of the time.

Left Side

❶ Arete **V3** *6A*
Climb the arete on its left-hand side.

❷ Wall Past the Flatty **V2** *5c*
The wall to the right.

❸ Small Ones are More Juicy . . . **V4** *6B*
Follow the pockets up the slab.

In the through-cave a little further right are two problems on either side - see map opposite.

❹ The Sausage King of Meersbrook
. . . . **V10** *7C+*
The steep arete starting at the back.

❺ John Player Special **V6** *7A*
The other side of the through-cave. Ignore the supporting block on the right, follow the slopers and right arete.

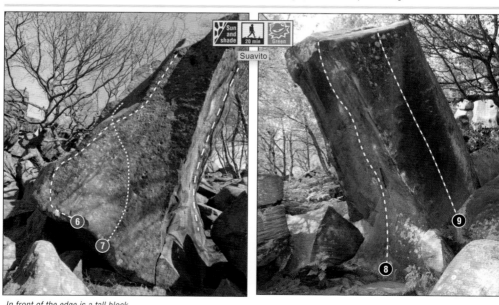

Suavito

In front of the edge is a tall block.

❻ Captain Cabinets . . . . **V4** *6B+*
From sitting, pull over the bulge then follow the right-hand side of the arete. The start and then manteling up left is **V4** *6B*.

❼ Wardrobe Ridge . . . . **V3** *6A+*
Use the pockets to pull up left and rock onto the ramp.

❽ Suavito **V8** *7B*
The superb leaning wall and arete to an airy finish.

❾ Escondido **V9** *7C*
Climb the side-wall using both aretes.

The most concentrated set of problems at Gardom's South is on three blocks split by cracks.

10 Left Triplet Arete V1 5b
The left arete of the first block.

11 Left Triplet Slab . . . . V0+ 5a
The slab left of the crack. The crack on its own is **VB** 4a.

12 Middle Triplet Arete V2 5c
The next arete.

13 Middle Wall . . . . V0+ 5a
Takes the front face of the middle block.

14 Middle Triplet Ridge V2 5c
The ridge.

15 China in Your Hands . . V8 7B+
The rightwards trending rail, started from the left by an inventive outward-facing bridging move (or a more conventional traverse).

16 Barry Sheene . . . V9 7C
Climb the wall direct, reaching the rail from undercuts.

17 G-Thang . . . . V4 6B+
The beautiful little groove. Using the arete out right drops the grade to **V4** 6B. The sit-down is **V5** 6C+.

The problems continue on the next block around to the right.

18 Stung V2 5c
Pop to the top from the obvious hold.

19 The Sting V2 5c
The right arete.

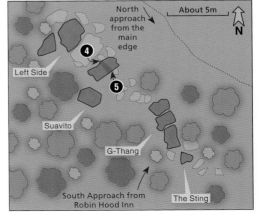

Northern Peak

Sheffield Crags

Stanage Area

Burbage Valley

Derwent Edges

The Limestone

Central Grit

Staffordshire

South Peak

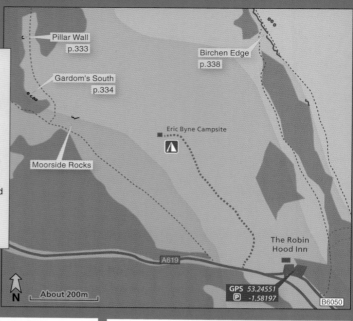

Moorside Rocks

A minor, but pleasant collection of blocks that has some great problems on offer, including one of the Peak's great hard classics. Unfortunately there is little here for those operating under **V4** *6B*. The rocks are well-exposed and south-west facing

Approach - Park in the car park by the Robin Hood Inn, just off the A619 Baslow to Chesterfield road as for Birchen Edge. Walk back down the road towards Baslow and pick up a marked path over the moor. Follow this for about 1km until Moorside Rocks is on your right. Gardom's South is a little further on in the trees.

Pillar Wall
p.333

Birchen Edge
p.338

Gardom's South
p.334

Eric Byne Campsite

Moorside Rocks

The Robin
Hood Inn

GPS 53.24551
-1.58197

A619

B6050

N   About 200m

---

1 Short Arete **V4** *6B*
The left arete.

2 Right Arete **V5** *6C*
The right arete of the small block.

3 Charlotte Dumpling . . **V4** *6B*
Move out right from the crack using a small edge to make a high rock-over. Eliminating the right side of the crack makes it **V8** *7B*.

4 Will's Dyno **V11** *8A*
Gain the finish of *Charlotte Dumpling* via an impressive dyno.

5 Superbloc . . . . . . **V12** *8A+*
The rounded right arete is an impressive ground-up target above a decent stack of pads. *Photo opposite.*

6 Batter Patter . . . . **V5** *6C+*
Climb the thin seam to an awkward leftwards exit onto the ledge.

7 Brazil Start **V5** *6C*
Climb the rounded arete to the break. The sit-start is **V5** *6C*. Continuing upwards are the routes *Homeless*, on the left, and *Brazil* on the right.

8 The Jackalope **V6** *7A*
A classic highball problem that tackles the flared crack, to an insecure top-out which is okay with a spotter.

From mid morning | 20 min | Windy

Ryan Pasquill *Superbloc* (**V12** *8A+*) - *opposite*. Photo: Adam Long

Northern Peak

Sheffield Crags

Stanage Area

Burbage Valley

Derwent Edges

The Limestone

Central Grit

Staffordshire

South Peak

	No star	 ☆	☆☆	☆☆☆
VB to V0 Easy to 4c	4	16	1	-
V0+ to V2 5a to 5c	3	22	3	-
V3 to V5 6A to 6C+	1	8	8	1
V3 to V5 7A upwards	-	4	7	2

Long regarded as a crag for novice climbers, Birchen Edge has a surprising amount of bouldering on offer to climbers of all abilities and is well worth a visit. The crag does get very popular at weekends, which can be awkward on sections shared with routes. The harder problems all tend to follow the same steep bulging undercut starts that the crag is littered with and they are surprisingly hard for a 'novice crag' with some reaching the lofty grades of **V10** *7C+*!

Circuits
The Three Ships provide an excellent Green Circuit that can be extended into an Orange very easily. The main crag has a short but very intense Red Circuit.

Conditions
Birchen is southwest facing and gets very little shade. It will dry very quickly after rain although it will catch any wind. The Three Ships are slightly more exposed which means a light breeze may keep the midges away in the summer.

Approach   Also see map on page 272
The usual approach is to park by the Robin Hood Inn in the (pay) car park, next to the pub car park (free for National Trust and RSPB members). From the car park, return to the road, turn left and walk for about 100m to a stile and a busy path. Follow the path for about 15 minutes to reach the main section of the crag. It is also possible to reach the north end of the crag from Gardom's South by following a path around the field - no short cuts.

Northern Peak | Sheffield Crags | Stanage Area | Burbage Valley | Derwent Edges | The Limestone | Central Grit | Staffordshire | South Peak

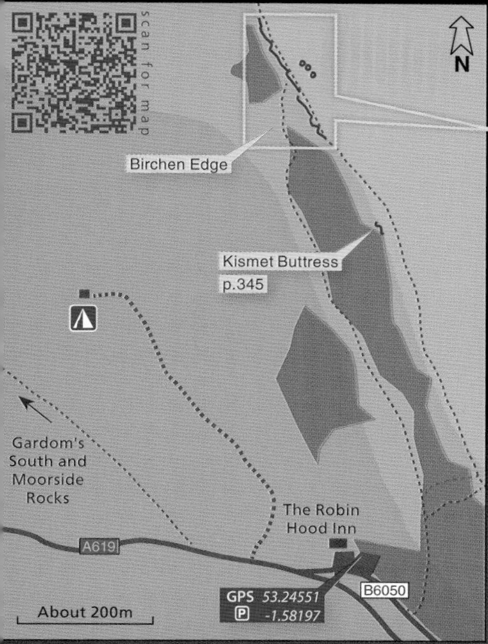
scan for map
N
Birchen Edge
Kismet Buttress
p.345
Gardom's
South and
Moorside
Rocks
The Robin
Hood Inn
A619
B6050
GPS 53.24551
P -1.58197
About 200m

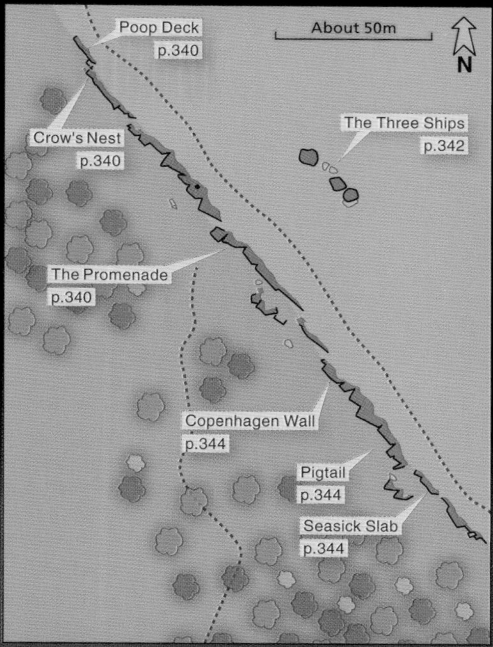
Poop Deck
p.340
About 50m
N
Crow's Nest
p.340
The Three Ships
p.342
The Promenade
p.340
Copenhagen Wall
p.344
Pigtail
p.344
Seasick Slab
p.344

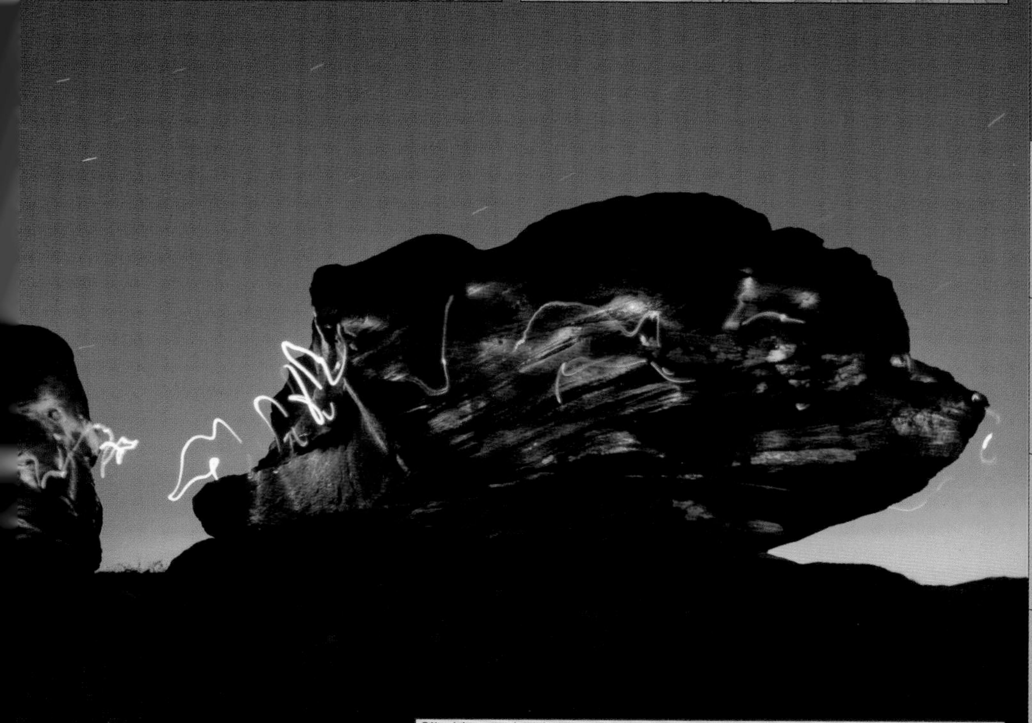

Climbing under the stars. Daniel Rushforth completes a head torch traverse of Victory, Defiance and Royal Soverin at Birchen Edge. Photo: Daniel Rushforth

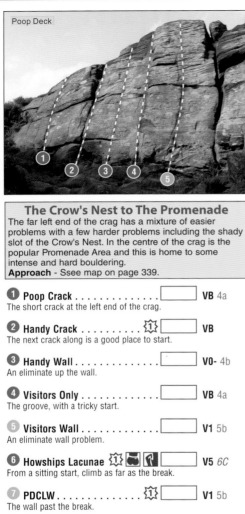

Poop Deck

Northern Peak

Sheffield Crags

Stanage Area

Burbage Valley

Derwent Edges

The Limestone

Central Grit

Staffordshire

South Peak

The Crow's Nest to The Promenade

The far left end of the crag has a mixture of easier problems with a few harder problems including the shady slot of the Crow's Nest. In the centre of the crag is the popular Promenade Area and this is home to some intense and hard bouldering.

Approach - Ssee map on page 339.

❶ Poop Crack . . . . VB 4a
The short crack at the left end of the crag.

❷ Handy Crack . . . . VB
The next crack along is a good place to start.

❸ Handy Wall V0- 4b
An eliminate up the wall.

❹ Visitors Only . . . . VB 4a
The groove, with a tricky start.

❺ Visitors Wall V1 5b
An eliminate wall problem.

❻ Howships Lacunae . . . V5 6C
From a sitting start, climb as far as the break.

❼ PDCLW V1 5b
The wall past the break.

❽ The Pirate V4 6B
The bulge is taken on slopers.

The next four problems are found on the north side of **The Crow's Nest** *tower, above Scrim Net.*

❾ Disabled Seaman . . . . . V3 6A+
The left arete on its right side.

❿ Cabin Boy V6 7A
Dyno from the low break.

⓫ The Cabin . . . . V3 6A+
The wall just left of the arete.

⓬ Log V2 5c
The arete on its left side.

⓭ Sling your Hammock . V1 5b
Full body bridge up the cleft. Harder for the short.

⓮ Dan's Arete V5 6C
The hanging left arete of the block.

⓯ Crow's Feet V2 5c
The hanging right arete of the block.

⓰ Scrim Net V3 6A
Up the crack.

⓱ Kiss Me Arse . . V5 6C
The arete from a sitting start. **V3** *6A* if you start standing.

⓲ Monocled Mono . . . V5 6C
The centre of the wall.

⓳ Kiss Me Softly V4 6B
The right arete from a sitting start.

⓴ Roger the Cabin Boy . V5 6C
The arete from a sitting start.

㉑ Technical Genius . V6 7A
The roof and flake from a standing start. **V7** *7A+* from sitting.

The Crow's Nest (left)

The Crow's Nest

In the centre of the crag, just left of the most popular section, are some savage undercut problems under **The Promenade**.

㉒ Promarete. . . . . ⑪ 🔲 **V3** *6A*
Rock onto the arete from its right-hand side.

㉓ Gritstone Megamix 🔲 **V6** *7A*
Tackle the roof direct - brilliant but quite high.

㉔ Megamix Left 🔲 **V7** *7A+*
Traverse the lip and finish up the arete.

㉕ HMS Daring . . 🔲 **V8** *7B+*
The arete on its left. On its right is *Splendide Audax,* **V8** *7B+*.

㉖ Thing on a Spring . ⑫ 🔲 **V6** *7A*
Launch for the break from the finger edge.

㉗ Oarsman Arete . . . ⑬ 🔲 **V4** *6B+*
The right side of the hanging arete. **V5** *6C* from sitting.

㉘ Oarsman. . . . . ⑭ 🔲 **V4** *6B+*
Layback off the thin crack. **V6** *7A* from sitting.

㉙ 'Oar 'Ouse. . . . . . . 🔲 **V6** *7A*
Layback the finger crack on its left.

㉚ Hornblower . . . . . . ⑮ 🔲 **V5** *6C*
The thin seams left of the arete.

㉛ Obstructive Pensioner 🔲 **V7** *7A+*
The nose on its left-hand side. On its right is **V7** *7A+*.

㉜ Jumpers for Trousers
. . . . 🔲 **V10** *7C+*
The scoop ignoring the left arete and the flake out right.

㉝ Eliminate Flake . . . . . 🔲 **V0+** *5a*
The steep flake, no bridging.

㉞ Bulbous Bow . . . . ⑯ 🔲 **V2** *5c*
The arete is hard for the short.
The last problem in the Red Circuit.

> The **Birchen Edge Red Circuit**
> This is a short and intense 16-problem
> circuit with several problems of **V5** *6C* and many of them
> involving powerful pulls over the undercut roofs.

The Promenade

Northern Peak | Sheffield Crags | Stanage Area | Burbage Valley | Derwent Edges | The Limestone | Central Grit | Staffordshire

Northern Peak

Sheffield Crags

Stanage Area

Burbage Valley

Derwent Edges

The Limestone

Central Grit

Staffordshire

South Peak

The Three Ships

Perched on top of the middle of Birchen Edge are three boulders, each named after one of the vessels that played a part in Nelson's victory at the Battle of Trafalgar. The names have been artfully carved into the rock. Plenty of good problems to go at, though you may have to share the top with agile walkers who have an eye for a challenge.

Approach (see map on page 339) - From the point where the main path arrives at the crag, scramble up the easy way to the top to the three boulders.

The first boulder is called **Victory**.

1 Orion **V1** 5b
A short wall to a rounded finish.

2 Neptune . . . . ① ⛭ **V0** 4c
The wall to the right.

3 The Victory Traverse . . . ② ⛭ **VB** 4a
Starting on *Neptune*, traverse up and right to the top.

4 Euryalus . . . . ③ ⛭ **V0** 4c
The wall.

5 V for Victory . . . . . . ④ ⛭ **V0-** 4b
Climb past the 'V'.

6 Prow Left . . . . ⑤ ⛭ **V0** 4c
The left side of the prow.

7 Prow Right . . . . ⑥ ⛭ **V0+** 5a
Just right of the prow. **V4** *6B* if done from sitting with a dyno.

8 Victor's Ledge . . . . . . ⑦ ⛭ **V0** 4c
A short problem - mostly a mantel.

Victory

Victory

Defiance

Royal Soverin

The **Birchen Three Ships Green Circuit**
A nice short circuit that makes the most of the delightful top boulders at Birchen. Nothing too hard and only 5 extra problems are required to make it into an Orange Circuit to tick the lot.

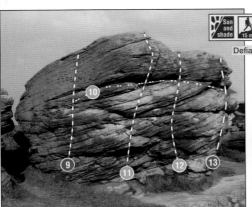

Defiance

The following problems are found on the middle ship, **Defiance**.

9 Finisterre . . . . ⑧ ⭐ [ ] **V0** 4c
The wall past the carved 'Defiance'.

10 The Defiance Traverse ⭐ [ ] **V2** 5c
Start from holds below the carved name, and continue to the east wall.

11 St. Vincent . . . . ⑨ ⭐ [ ] **V0+** 5a
From a sitting start, climb the crack.

12 Calvi . . . . ⑩ ⭐ [ ] **V0+** 5a
The scoop to the right.

13 Aboukir . . . . ⑪ ⭐ [ ] **V0** 4c
The wall past a hueco.

14 Tenerife . . . . ⑫ ⭐ [ ] **V0** 4c
From a sitting start, climb the prow.

15 Tenerife Right-hand ⑬ ⭐ [ ] **V0+** 5a
From a sitting start, climb up and right.

Royal Soverin

The final boulder is **Royal Soverin**.

16 Royal . . . . ⑭ ⭐ [ ] **V0-** 4b
A sitting start.

17 The Royal Soverin Traverse
. . . . ⭐ [ ] **V1** 5b
Start at the carved name and continue right.

18 Bilge . . . . ⑮ ⭐ [ ] **V0** 4c
The low arete.

19 Buccaneer . . . . . . ⑯ ⭐ [ ] **V0** 4c
The vague arete. *The last problem in the Green Circuit.*

20 Press Gang . . . . ⭐ [ ] **V1** 5b
The centre of the wall through the overhang.

21 Orlop . . . . ⭐ [ ] **V1** 5b
The wall to the right.

Northern Peak · Sheffield Crags · Stanage Area · Burbage Valley · Derwent Edges · The Limestone · Central Grit · Staffordshire · outh Peak

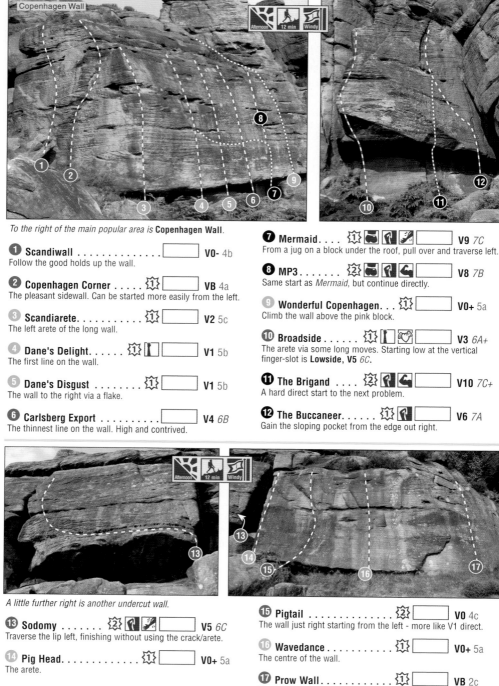

*To the right of the main popular area is **Copenhagen Wall**.*

1 Scandiwall . . . . [ ] **V0-** 4b
Follow the good holds up the wall.

2 Copenhagen Corner . . . . . [ ] **VB** 4a
The pleasant sidewall. Can be started more easily from the left.

3 Scandiarete. . . . . [ ] **V2** 5c
The left arete of the long wall.

4 Dane's Delight. . . . . . . [ ] **V1** 5b
The first line on the wall.

5 Dane's Disgust . . . . [ ] **V1** 5b
The wall to the right via a flake.

6 Carlsberg Export . . . . [ ] **V4** 6B
The thinnest line on the wall. High and contrived.

7 Mermaid. . . . . [ ] **V9** 7C
From a jug on a block under the roof, pull over and traverse left.

8 MP3 . . . . [ ] **V8** 7B
Same start as *Mermaid*, but continue directly.

9 Wonderful Copenhagen. . . [ ] **V0+** 5a
Climb the wall above the pink block.

10 Broadside . . . . . . [ ] **V3** 6A+
The arete via some long moves. Starting low at the vertical
finger-slot is **Lowside, V5** 6C.

11 The Brigand . . . . [ ] **V10** 7C+
A hard direct start to the next problem.

12 The Buccaneer. . . . . . . [ ] **V6** 7A
Gain the sloping pocket from the edge out right.

A little further right is another undercut wall.

13 Sodomy . . . . [ ] **V5** 6C
Traverse the lip left, finishing without using the crack/arete.

14 Pig Head. . . . . [ ] **V0+** 5a
The arete.

15 Pigtail . . . . [ ] **V0** 4c
The wall just right starting from the left - more like V1 direct.

16 Wavedance . . . . [ ] **V0+** 5a
The centre of the wall.

17 Prow Wall. . . . . [ ] **VB** 2c
The wall just to the right.

Northern Peak

Sheffield Crags

Stanage Area

Burbage Valley

Derwent Edges

The Limestone

Central Grit

Staffordshire

South Peak

Copenhagen Wall to Seasick Slab

The bouldering on the right-hand end of Birchen is dotted amongst the short routes here, indeed some of it is 'short routes' and circuits can be extended by those confident at soloing.

Approach (see map on page 339) - Follow the main path to the crag. This section is immediately to the right of where the path arrives at the crag.

Seasick Slab

About 50m further along the edge is **Seasick Slab**.

18 Seasick Arete . . . . ⚐ ☐ **V1** 5b
The perfect arete.

19 Seasick Slab . . . . ⚐ ☐ **V0-** 4b
The wall.

20 Seasick Steve . . . . ⚐ ☐ **V3** 6A+
Just to the right, start with a side-pull for your left hand and climb directly to a sloping top-out.

Just below is a pointed boulder with two problems.

21 Men United . . . . ⚐ ☐ **V1** 5b
The left arete and face.

22 Isle of Men . . . . ⚐ ☐ **V2** 5c
The right arete on its right-hand side after starting on the front face.

Kismet Buttress

The final three problems are found on Kismet Buttress, which is the right-most buttress on the edge and a little way from the main area

Approach (see map on page 339) - The buttress can be reached from the main path, by breaking right off the approach, however it is more common to reach it by walking right (looking in) from the main edge along the crag top path for about 200m to this isolated buttress.

23 Implosion . . . . ⚐ ☐ **V2** 5c
The wall right of the left arete.

24 Explosion . . . . ⚐ ☐ **V1** 5b
The middle of the wall.

25 Blast Hole Wall . . . . ☐ **V1** 5b
The wall left of the right arete.

The Limestone

Northern Peak

Sheffield Crags

Stanage Area

Burbage Valley

Derwent Edges

The Limestone

Central Grit

Staffordshire

South Peak

About 2km

N

Tideswell

A623

Litton

Eyam

Froggatt
p.274

A625

Froggatt

Stoney Middleton
p.348

Stoney
Middleton

Calver

Rubicon
p.356

Baslow

Raven Tor
p.360

Great Longstone

A619

Taddington

Blackwell Dale
p.365

A6

Ashford

Bakewell

Monyash

Alport
p.368

Stanton Moor
p.406

A515

Youlgrave

Rob Greenwood (left) working *Powerband* (**V9** *7C*) while James Thornton is on *Staminaband* (**V11** *8A*)- *page 364* - at Raven Tor. Photo: Alan James

	No star	⚝	⚝⚝	⚝⚝⚝
VB to V0 Easy to 4c	1	-	-	-
V0+ to V2 5a to 5c	3	4	-	-
V3 to V5 6A to 6C+	6	9	2	-
V3 to V5 7A upwards	4	10	12	3

Bouldering at Stoney is of the old-style micro-eliminate variety and only of any appeal to those operating in the upper grades. That said it has been a forcing ground for over forty years and many of the big names of Peak climbing have honed their technique on the slippery walls, leaving some classic problems.

The three areas covered here are vertical walls with a multitude of tiny holds that give endless eliminates and some very impressive dynos. The exception to this is Tom's Cave which is intense and obscure even by Stoney standards. All the holds at Stoney suffer from overuse and polish which has made many of the problems harder than they were when first climbed.

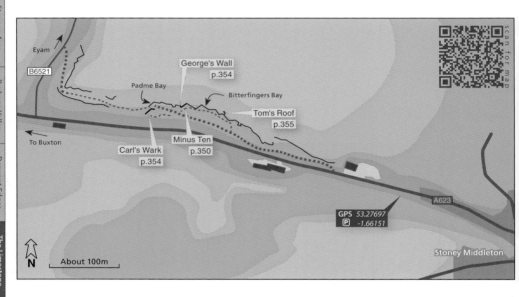

Approach   Also see map on page 347

All the areas can be accessed from the A623 Stoney Middleton to Buxton road, just west of Stoney. Park in the large lay-by which is on the left just as you leave the village towards Buxton. From the lay-by, walk up the road towards the crag. Follow the wide track up to the Bitterfingers Bay. The approaches from here are described in each section.

Conditions

Stoney is a popular mid-winter training ground. When dry it can be a great sun-trap and much of it stays dry in even quite heavy rain. Once wet it is slow to dry and it can get greasy in damp weather. It is very sheltered from the wind.

Northern Peak

Sheffield Crags

Stanage Area

Burbage Valley

Derwent Edges

The Limestone

Central Grit

Staffordshire

South Peak

Andy Healey in mid air on *One Armed Bandit* (**V8** *7B*) - *page 351* - on the Minus Ten Eliminate Wall at Stoney. Photo: David Bond

Minus Ten

Minus Ten was a major forcing ground for Peak bouldering in the 1980s when Sheffield's young guns used to hang out here throughout the winter months polishing up the holds whilst developing some cutting-edge vertical problems and dynos. It is less popular these days but still has its fans. Listed here are some of the basic problems and a few of the more significant eliminates. There are many more on offer - see peakbouldering.info for more details. Minus Ten is famously eccentric for its conditions. The wall can be at its stickiest during bad weather, when you least expect it, hence it is always worth a look. Generally the best periods are early spring and late autumn when the frost is biting.

Approach (see map on page 348) - Follow the crag-base path to the bay before the tall tower of the Pearly Gates Area is reached where the crag is next to the track.

4 Minus Wall Start . . . . 🛱 [ ] **V0+** 5a
Climb the crack to the break.

5 Minus Wall Right . . . . 🛱 📷 [ ] **V4** 6B+
Connect the breaks.

6 Minus Wall Traverse . 🛱 📷 [ ] **V4** 6B+
Traverse the lower break to the big crack.

1 Cracked Wall . . . . [ ] **V0-** 4b
Not a classic but okay for warming the cold fingers on. Climb the cracked wall to the grassy ledges.

2 Flat Wall . . . . 📷 [ ] **V0+** 5a
The wall has some small flat edges up to the break.

3 Triangle Link-up . . . . 🛱 📷 [ ] **V2** 5c
Link the two triangular pockets up to the break. Variations abound on this one.

7 Quent's Dyno . . . . 🛱 [ ] [ ] **V8** 7B
A famous dyno. Start on **1** and the edge of the crack, dyno elastically for jug **0**. The original is very picky on footholds.

8 Harris Problem . . 🛱 📷 📷 [ ] **V8** 7B+
Use **1** and the small edge **3** to reach edge **6b**. Right to break. Feet on smears only. Variation to top break is **V10** 7C+.

9 Not Ned's Problem . . . 🛱 📷 [ ] **V8** 7B+
Use small edge **3** and crimp **4** to reach the cluster of spiky edges **2**. Finish at top break.

10 White Ladder . . . . . . 🛱 📷 [ ] **V8** 7B+
Start on crimp **4** and **8** to reach edge **6a**. Left to good edge **6b** up and left, right to top break **6c**. Sit down is **V9** 7C.

11 The JABP . . . . . . ⬡ 🖐 📷 [ ] **V9** *7C*
A classic techno horror. Use the small shallow pocket **5**, the vague fin **6**, and any footholds, to reach the first break.

12 Sharp Pocket . . . . ⬡ 🖐 📷 [ ] **V8** *7B+*
Use **3** and **8** and stand up on poor smears below the low break. Cross over and reach the ramp **9** with your left, then match with your right. Pull up to the sharp pocket **13** and leap for the top break **33**.

13 Little Warm-up . . . . [ ] **V1** *5b*
A little warm-up. Use pocket **17**, pull up to **19** then the break. Up to top break **33**. Substitute hole **13** for break **20** for a **V3** *6A*.

The Rules - We numbered every featured hold on the central section in the 1998 guidebook and these numbers have stuck for most of the problems although a few new ones have been introduced. We have stuck with the old numbers and added the new ones as sub-divisions. Unless otherwise described, use your feet anywhere.

14 Egyptian Feet . . . ⬡ ✊ 🖐 [ ] **V7** *7A+*
Left in pocket **17**, right on poor **21**. Egyptian feet up onto small edges above the low break. Reach up to the edge **28** and crank through the edge in the groove **32**, using poor edges for your feet.

15 Egyptian Variation ⬡ 🖐 ✊ [ ] **V7** *7A+*
Variation on the previous problem. Left in pocket **17**, right on **21**, then get the edge **24**. Crank up to edge **28** and **30** for the right, to get **33**.

16 One Armed Bandit ⬡ ✊ 📷 [ ] **V8** *7B*
With your left in **17** and your right behind your back, dyno for the jug **31** with your left! *Photo on page 349.*

17 Easy Dyno . . . . ⬡ 📷 [ ] **V3** *6A*
As *One Armed Bandit*, but with your right hand as well, to **31**.

18 The Kirton Dyno . . ⬡ ✊ 📷 [ ] **V7** *7A+*
Start with your right on **19**, and your left hand in the break and toe in **17**, leap for **33**.

Photo on page 349.

Northern Peak

Sheffield Crags

Stanage Area

Burbage Valley

Derwent Edges

The Limestone

Central Grit

Staffordshire

South Peak

Northern Peak

Sheffield Crags

Stanage Area

Burbage Valley

Derwent Edges

The Limestone

Central Grit

Staffordshire

South Peak

19 Sean's Problem .. 🔲🔲🔲 **V8** *7B+*
Left on **34**, right on **36** and feet in the low break, reach the
shallow pocket **38** and crimp **24** (thumb around side edge) with
feet anywhere. Crimp edge **28** with right only, and incut **32** with
left, then top **33**. Replace side-pull **23** with edge **24** for **V9** *7C*.

22 Guidebook Eleven ..... 🔲 **V5** *6C+*
Left on **34** and right on **36** reach up to scoop **22** with right (or
left then swap). Reach up to **19** then **30** then **33**.

23 Slopey Side-pull .... 🔲🔲 **V7** *7A+*
Left on **34** and right on **36** left to slopey side-pull **21**, right **25**,
left **29**, feet anywhere. Variation, swap **25** for **26** at **V8** *7B*.

24 Gav's Problem...... 🔲🔲 **V8** *7B*
Left on **36**, right on **42** and feet in the low break. Left hand up
to **38**, right hand to **46**. Then undercut **40** to reach **51** and so to
the top **52**.

The next two problems have numerous variations. Check
peakbouldering.info for details.

20 Zippy's Sidepull .. 🔲🔲🔲 **V8** *7B+*
Left on **34**, right on **36** and feet in the low break. Get side-pull
23 with your right and put toe in shallow pocket **35**. Lurch for
jug **31**.

21 Lucian's Undercut ... 🔲🔲 **V6** *7A*
Left on **34**, right on **36** and feet in the low break. Get pocket **22**
and undercut up with toe in pocket **4**, to reach jug **31**.

25 Harris Problem 1 .... 🔲🔲 **V8** *7B*
Start with left on edge **36** and right on pinch **42**, feet anywhere.
Reach up left to the sloping edge **27** and cross over for edge **28**
with your right. Lock out for the in-cut **32** and the jug **33**.

26 Zippy's Problem.. 🔲🔲🔲 **V8** *7B+*
Start with left on edge **36** and right on pinch **42**. Get the sloper
44 with your left and reach the sloper **47** with your right. Slap up
for the left edge **48** and reach the top **52**. Small edges for feet.

30 The Double Double .. V5 *6C*
A classic double dyno from the good flakes **45** and edge **46** to get the opposing sides of the block **48** and the side below **53**. Then the jug **52**.

31 Prefab Brick Cake ... V1 *5b*
Start with your left on the polished edge **55**, and right on **56**. Reach up to the edge **58** and then **59**. Avoid the side-wall for your feet.

32 Face Off V4 *6B*
With your right on edge **55**, get the cluster of pockets **54**. Feel around for the best bit. Then up to **58** and **59** to finish.

33 Coffee High V4 *6B*
Start with both hands in cluster **54** then go for **59**.

34 Facade V5 *6C*
Start again with both hands in the cluster **54**, but crank direct to the edge **57** before reaching the jug **59**.

35 Megatron . . . . . . V7 *7A+*
Dyno from edge **55** to jug **59**.

Traverses - *There are three main traverses on the walls and all serve as good warm ups, warm downs and stamina workouts. The starts are marked on the previous page.*

36 High Break V1 *5b*
The highest break from the far left-hand end of the wall, finishing on hold **52** on the boot-shaped flake of *The Young American*.

37 Middle Break V4 *6B*
The middle break from the left-hand end is more technical and pumpy than the one above. The finish into the wide cracks on the right is awkward.

38 No Break . . . . V5 *6C+*
Traverse of the wall below the break, starting from the initial jug of *Quent's Dyno*. It is also technical in the other direction.

27 Pinch 2 . . . . V12 *8A+*
A famous product of the 1980s which is rarely repeated due to the polish on the crucial smear. Start with left on edge **36**, right on pinch **42** and outside edge of left foot on **41**. Up to sloper **44** with left, swap feet on **41**. Left toe onto smear **37** and dyno with right for pinch on lip **50**. Right foot up to **43** and dyno again for edge **51** which is hard to catch. Then the top **52**.

28 Jason's Variant . . V11 *8A*
An easier variation that eliminates the crucial smear **37** by jumping direct from **41** to the pinch on the lip **50**.

29 The Young American . V7 *7A+*
A classic dyno from the good flakes **45** and edge **46** to the jug **52**. Feet on **43** and edges to the left.

Northern Peak

Sheffield Crags

Stanage Area

Burbage Valley

Derwent Edges

The Limestone

Central Grit

Staffordshire

South Peak

George's Wall

This is a small wall situated around the corner from Minus Ten. It receives the afternoon sun but this is reduced by the tree cover in summer.
Approach- See map on page 348.

1 **George's Wall Eliminate 1** `V3` *6A*
Start on **A**, reach up left to edge **E** then make a long reach to edge **C**. Use this to get sloper **G** and then the break.

2 **George's Wall Eliminate 2** `V5` *6C*
Start on flat edge **B**, use edge **D** to reach break **F**.

3 **George's Wall Dyno** . . `V8` *7B*
A dyno from the big jug **J** to the break.

4 **Quent's Legendary Dyno**
. . . . `V9` *7C*
A super dyno from the big jug **J** to the sloper **G**.

5 **The Groove** . . . . `V3` *6A+*
The little groove using everything.

Minus Ten

Carl's Wark

Underneath the Padme Wall, the furthest bay on the main section of Stoney, is a lower bay with two bouldering sections either side of an open-book corner. The walls can stay dry in the winter, but because they are close to trees and the cave entrance, it can also be very damp. The bay is a sun trap from mid-morning onwards.
Approach (see map on page 348) - You can reach the walls from the upper tier by finding the descent path which drops through the trees just before the crag-bottom track reaches the end wall of Padme Bay.

6 **Carl's Wark Traverse**
. . . . `V8` *7B*
Start at the base of a little crack and follow a vague line of edges and head-height pockets to the bottom of a pillar. Continue across to meet the rightwards line of small flakes which form the start of *Bubbles Wall*. Battle up these to the break. Keeping low on this is a much harder **V9** *7C*.

7 **More Air Than Chocolate** . `V3` *6A*
The easiest way up the pockets to a little groove on the right.

8 **Au Revoir Mono Doigt**
. . . . `V8` *7B*
The flat wall above the traverse, to the right of the groove, yields to a tenacious effort.

9 **Bubbles Start** . . . `V3` *6A+*
A highball start to the break. The landing slopes a way to the right so take care.

The right side of the bay has a lower wall.

10 **Soapsuds Traverse** . . . `V4` *6B+*
Traverse the low break to the small crack. Ascend this and reverse the upper break back left.

11 **Soapsuds Left** . . . . `V1` *5b*
Reach up to the flakes above the break.

12 **Soapsuds Crack** . . . . `V0+` *5a*
The pleasant small crack to the upper breaks.

13 **Soapsuds Right** . . . . `V3` *6A*
Climb the flat wall via the small pocket.

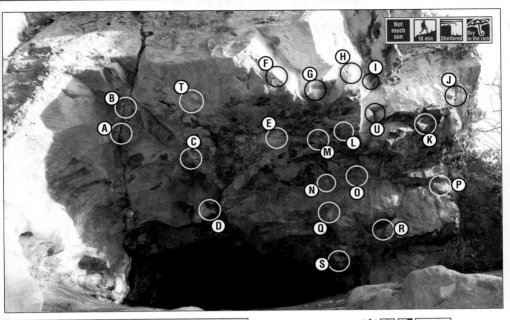

Tom's Roof

Tom's Roof can only be described as an acquired taste, it has attractions for the strong boulderer but will be found too intense, steep and powerful for most climbers. It is a complex roof so have patience or find a local if the topo proves too difficult to follow. The cave stays dry most of the time but can get greasy during damp spells.
Approach (see map on page 348) - Tom's Roof is situated halfway up the crag, formed by the left-hand of a pair of caves, just to the right of the Bitter Fingers Bay. The only way to access the roof is from a slippery gully beneath the cave

14 The Womb V5 *6C*
Jam out from the back of the hole to **D**, and then add a finish of your choice.

15 Tom's Original . . V6 *7A*
RH and LH - **C**, RH and LH - **E**, RH and LH - **H**, RH and LH - **J**, any feet.

16 Punker Bunker . . . V7 *7A+*
Tom's Original to hold **H**, but no side-wall for feet.

17 Power Allowance . V8 *7B*
RH and LH - **C**, RH and LH - **E**, RH - **G**, right foot toe jam **H**, RH - **E**, LH - **E**, LH and RH - **C**, any feet except side-wall.

18 Pete's Power Pull V9 *7C*
LH and RH - **C**, LH - **E**, LH and RH - **H**, feet on back-wall only.

19 Jerry's Problem . . . . . V10 *7C+*
RH and LH - **C**, RH and LH - **E**, footless, RH little crimp below LH slot **I**, and LH - slot **I**, RH - large jug **I**.

20 Armbandit . . . . . V7 *7A+*
LH - **B**, RH - **A**, RH - **E**, LH - **Q**, RH - **K**, LH and RH - **I**, feet anywhere.

21 Swing Thing V9 *7C*
LH - **B**, RH - **A**, RH and LH - **E**, RH and LH - **H**, feet on the back-wall only. There and back it is **V10** *7C+*.

22 Figure of 8 . . . . V8 *7B+*
LH and RH - **C**, RH - **E**, LH - **Q**, RH - **U**, LH - **E**, RH and LH back to **C**, feet on back-wall and **S**. In reverse it is **V9** *7C*.

23 One Summer Problem V9 *7C*
LH - **B**, RH - **A**, RH and LH - **E**, footless, RH - **U**, LH - **L**, LH and RH - **H**, feet on back-wall only.

24 Quintessence . . . V11 *8A*
LH - **B**, RH - **A**, LH - **T**, RH - **F**, footless, LH and RH - **H**, feet on back-wall only.

25 Rack and Ruin V9 *7C*
LH - small pocket left of **D**, RH - pinch lip right of **D**, RH - **E**, LH - **Q**, RH - **L**, RH and LH - **H**, feet back-wall for first move then side-wall.

26 Side Wall Traverse . . . V9 *7C*
D, **N**, **O**, **P**, feet anywhere.

27 Harris Problem 2 . V8 *7B+*
LH - **Q**, RH - **O**, LH and RH - **E**, LH - **B**, LH - **A**, feet on **S**, ramp below **S** and back-wall.

28 Jerryattricks . V10 *7C+*
Link the following problems without getting off: *The Womb, Swing Thing, Tom's Original* in reverse, and *Power Allowance*.

Northern Peak

Sheffield Crags

Stanage Area

Burbage Valley

Derwent Edges

The Limestone

Central Grit

Staffordshire

South Peak

	No star	⚝	⚝⚝	⚝⚝⚝
VB to V0 Easy to 4c	-	-	-	-
V0+ to V2 5a to 5c	3	3	-	-
V3 to V5 6A to 6C+	3	3	4	-
V3 to V5 7A upwards	-	5	4	2

Rubicon is a typical Peak limestone bouldering venue - tiny holds, powerful moves and countless eliminates. Some boulderers detest its polish and friable nature and others can't keep away from the intricate fingery problems. It is also famous for its traverses which provide stamina training exercises and are especially good when combined with each other. The problems listed here are mostly the basic non-eliminates. You could virtually fill this guidebook with a list of the variations that have been done. We shall leave them up to you and your imagination.

Conditions

The steep walls will stay dry during the heaviest of downpours. The crag is very sheltered from the wind but it is a big sun trap and can become impossibly hot. In winter there is a lot of seepage on the Rubicon Area and the lake often floods the base making access to the base of the crag impossible.

Northern Peak | Sheffield Crags | Stanage Area | Burbage Valley | Derwent Edges | The Limestone | Central Grit | Staffordshire | South Peak

Approach   Also see map on page 347

The crag is approached from the tiny village of Cressbrook which can be reached from the B6465 which connects the A623 to the west of Stoney Middleton with Ashford on the A6. At The Monsal Head Pub, follow the sign to Cressbrook down into the dale. Park by the large mill in Cressbrook and follow the footpath between the houses and past a small cafe. This leads to the dam. Cross a small wooden bridge to reach the crag.

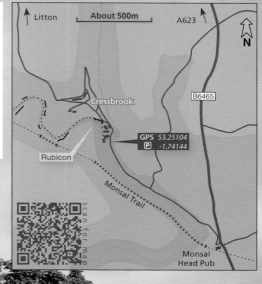

Litton   About 500m   A623

N

Cressbrook

B6465

GPS 53.25104
P   -1.74144

Rubicon

Monsal Trail

scan for map

Monsal
Head Pub

Access

The path below the crag is owned by a local fishing club and it is only with their permission that anyone is allowed access to the dale.

Northern Peak

Sheffield Crags

Stanage Area

Burbage Valley

Derwent Edges

The Limestone

Central Grit

Staffordshire

South Peak

Late afternoon bouldering at Rubicon. Photo: Adam Long

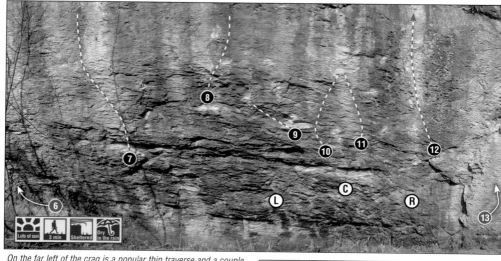

On the far left of the crag is a popular thin traverse and a couple of bouldering starts to routes.

1 **Dragonflight Traverse .** ⬚⬚⬚ **V3** *6A+*
Traverse the wall below the route *Dragonflight* in either direction.

2 **Barracuda Start . .** ⬚⬚⬚ **V10** *7C+*
Use sharp crimps and a pocket to reach the jug.

3 **Caviar Start . . . . .** ⬚⬚⬚ **V8** *7B*
Pull thinly up to a good hold.

4 **Piranha Start . . . .** ⬚⬚⬚ **V6** *7A*
Follow the drilled pockets as far as the flake.

The next area is just to the left of the big patch of ivy. We have only listed the main problems here. There are many eliminates possible - see PeakBouldering.info

5 **Piranha Traverse . . . .** ⬚⬚ **V7** *7A+*
Traverse from flakes on *A Miller's Tale* to the trees on the left.

6 **A Miller's Tale . . . . . .** ⬚⬚ **V4** *6B+*
Climb up to the spooky hole anyhow you can.

Kudos Area
This hard wall has many fine problems all of which need an iron will and iron fingers. It is a good idea to warm up well since tendons have audibly snapped here! To get back down, either reverse and jump, or traverse off along the break in either direction.
Approach - See map on page 357.

7 **Kudos . . . .** ⬚⬚ **V8** *7B*
From the glued flakes gain a shattered flake below a glued bolt. The easier method uses small layaways out to the right to reach into the flake. **The Hard Way** avoids the layaways out to the right and rocks straight for the flake - same grade but a bit harder. **The Original** is **V9** *7C* and involves rocking onto the polished sloper rather than the jug. The sit-start is **V8** *7B+*. **The Kudos Traverse** starts as for *Kudos* and finishes on the jugs of *The Press*, **V8** *7B*.

8 **A Bigger Tail . . . .** ⬚⬚ **V6** *7A*
Jump to gain small edges which lead up right, via a small pocket, to good holds. Starting a bit lower with your left hand in a poor dish and your right hand in the slot is **Johnny G 7C**, **V9** *7C*. Starting this from sitting is **A Bigger Belly, V13** *8B*.

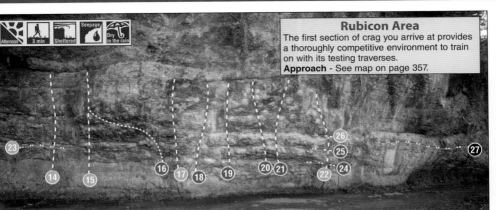

Rubicon Area
The first section of crag you arrive at provides a thoroughly competitive environment to train on with its testing traverses.
Approach - See map on page 357.

❾ The Pinch . . . . . . 🔥🖐️🫳 ☐ **V8** *7B+*
Start matching on the horizontal pinch under the hold of *Bigger Splash Direct*, and slap up left.

❿ Bigger Splash Direct . 🔥🫳 ☐ **V8** *7B*
Use the left-hand gaston of *The Press* as a side-pull and use a left hand undercut up and left. Slap into the jug on *A Bigger Splash*. Starting at the low rail **C** is **V8** *7B+*. Starting down right on **R** is **V9** *7C*. Starting at a slot **L** down and left is **Tsunamish, V10** *7C+*, or **Tsunami, V11** *8A*, without the two-finger pocket.

⓫ The Press . . . . . . 🔥🫳🫳 ☐ **V8** *7B+*
Gain the jug on *A Bigger Splash*, using tiny opposing gastons, and a crimp directly below. Starting at **C** is **V10** *7C+*. Starting at **R** is also **V10** *7C+*. Starting at **L** is **V11** *8A*.

⓬ A Bigger Splash . . . . . 🔥🫳 ☐ **V7** *7A+*
From low jugs gain a good jug via some leftwards-leaning flakes.

⓭ A Bigger Prize . . . 🔥🫳🫳 ☐ **V4** *6B+*
The wall, from sitting.

On the right of the crag is the huge roof of the route Rubicon.

⓮ Rubicon Start . . . . ☐ **V0+** *5a*
Up to the roof on pockets.

⓯ Left Flank . . . . ☐ **V1** *5b*
The left flank of the steep wall on shattered holds.

Rubicon Area

⓰ Toenail Left . . . . 🫳 ☐ **V3** *6A+*
Climb diagonally up and left to below the roof of *Rubicon*.

⓱ Toenail Pie Start . . . . 🔥 ☐ **V1** *5b*
The best bit of the route, past the strange small plaque.

⓲ Debris Groove . . . . . . 🔥🫳 ☐ **V3** *6A*
Struggle up the groove.

⓳ Crimps and Pockets . . . . . 🫳 ☐ **V4** *6B+*
Small holds just right of the groove.

⓴ Peg's Path . . . . 🫳 ☐ **V4** *6B*
From the low breaks, use small holds to gain the ledges.

㉑ Peg's Right . . . . 🔥 ☐ **V4** *6B*
From the low break move up and right.

㉒ Sharp Pockets . . . . 🔥 ☐ **V2** *5c*
From flakes climb the groove using sharp pockets.

There are a number of good traverses that can be combines to make up circuits of unlimited difficulty.

㉓ Warm-up Traverse . . . . . . 🫳 ☐ **V0+** *5a*
The standard warm-up. Traverse the breaks either way across the base of the wall. This can be linked to the other traverses to make for extra pump.

㉔ Low Break . . . . . . 🔥🫳🫳 ☐ **V4** *6B+*
Traverse the lower break either way.

㉕ Middle Break . . . . 🔥🫳 ☐ **V3** *6A*
The middle break.

㉖ Top Break . . . . 🔥🫳 ☐ **V2** *5c*
The top break is the easiest and the most polished.

㉗ Approach Traverse . . . 🔥🫳 ☐ **V6** *7A*
Traverse the line of edges below a ledge on the wall above the approach path. Start at a large hole and finish at some good flakes. Avoid only the large break/ledge.

Northern Peak | Sheffield Crags | Stanage Area | Burbage Valley | Derwent Edges | The Limestone | Central Grit | Staffordshire | South Peak

	No star	☆	☆☆	☆☆☆
VB to V0 Easy to 4K	-	-	-	-
V0+ to V2 5a to 5c	-	-	-	-
V3 to V5 6A to 6C+	-	4	3	-
V3 to V5 7A upwards	3	10	4	7

Raven Tor became synonymous with hard climbing in the UK in the 1980s. Most of the publicised development at the time was about the grade-busting routes that were being put up but this development was based on a strong foundation of hard bouldering much of which had taken place at the foot of the same crag. The traverse of *The Powerband* must rank as one of the most significant bouldering milestones in the Peak and many other cutting-edge problems have been added since.

For the average boulderer there isn't much on offer here except a sense of awe experienced by trying these famous problems. For the accomplished boulderer looking to improve their finger strength and stamina, this is one of the ultimate natural training locations.

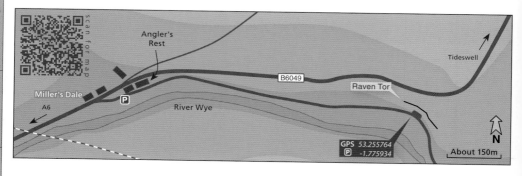

Access

Raven Tor is on land owned by the National Trust who are willing to allow access to the crag. Make sure that you park carefully and don't block the road - alternative parking is available 5 minutes walk away at the base of Tideswell Dale. Also, please avoid unnecessary disturbance of the vegetation and bird life, particularly at nesting time.

Approach   Also see map on page 347

Raven Tor is the perfect crag for the roadside generation. It should be approached from the B6049 at Miller's Dale, just south of Tideswell. A sharp turn off this road (signed to Litton Mill) leads past the Angler's Rest and on for about 1km to the crag, which is un-missable above the road on a bend. Parking is limited, if it is full DO NOT block the road as this has caused problems in the past. Alternative parking is available a 5 min walk further on at the bottom of Tideswell Dale.

Conditions

Raven Tor is a classic winter venue for bouldering. It stays dry during bad weather, and although it does seep, it is always worth a look since there are often dry sections. During the summer it can get impossibly hot but the trees sometimes give a little shade . If there is any moisture on the rock you will have to go somewhere else.

Northern Peak

Sheffield Crags

Stanage Area

Burbage Valley

Derwent Edges

The Limestone

Central Grit

Staffordshire

South Peak

Tim Banton on *Cave Problem* (**V8** *7B+*) - *page 362* - at Raven Tor. Photo: David Bond

Northern Peak

Sheffield Crags

Stanage Area

Burbage Valley

Derwent Edges

The Limestone

Central Grit

Staffordshire

South Peak

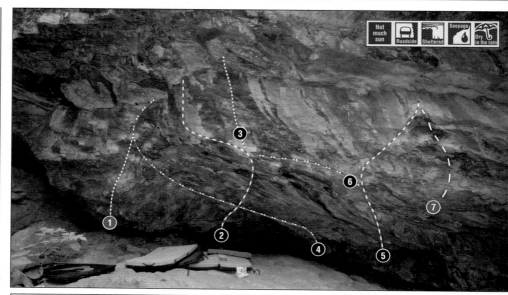

Weedkiller Area

This set of hard roof problems lurks beneath the massive overhang of the routes *Chimes of Freedom* and Weedkiller. The problems listed here are only a few of those that have been done, and those that remain to be done. There are plenty more combinations and eliminates listed at PeakBouldering.info

1 Too Hard for Mark Leach

. . . . **V5** *6C*

From the left-hand side of the cave, climb up to the finish of *Ben's Roof*. The footless version is **V8** *7B*.

2 Keen Roof **V13** *8B*

An impressive direct line out from the back left of the cave finishing at jugs under the higher roof. The extension from the very back of the cave is **Belly of the Beast, V14** *8B+*.

3 Hook . . . . **V10** *7C+*

From the good hold on the lip of *Keen Roof*, follow crimps right of better holds.

4 Ben's Roof **V10** *7C+*

Cross the cave from the back right-hand corner. Sit start on low side pulls and then move pout slightly leftwards.

5 Cave Problem . . . **V8** *7B+*

From a slot, pull past the lip moving right to finishing hold on *Weedkiller Traverse*. The sit-start is **V9** *7C. Photo on page 361.*

6 Fat Lip **V13** *8B*

Climb *Cave Problem* from the slot then traverse left to finish as for *Keen Roof*.

7 Chimes Start **V4** *6B*

The polished start to the route using everything to achieve the jug beneath the roof. **Converter** is the sitting start **V9** *7C*.

8 Basher's Problem . . . **V6** *7A*

Climb out on undercuts and up to a large flat hold. Finishing on the right on poor holds and a spike and pinch is **V7** *7A+*.

9 Weedkiller Traverse . . **V8** *7B*

This classic test-piece traverses the line of weakness across the first overlap. Start on the small pillar on in-cut jugs and swing across finishing up *Chimes Start*. **Perverse Reverse, V8** *7B* reverses the traverse starting from as high as you can reach.

10 High Green **V8** *7B*

Share a start with *WeedkillerTraverse* but reach up to the next overlap above and swing along the pockets to join *Basher's Problem*.

Pinches
Wall

The Toilet Area

This section has provided much entertainment for dedicated enthusiasts of steep eliminates with dreadful handholds and polished foot holds.

11 Toilet Traverse . . . . . . 🌓 🔧   **V4** *6B*
Traverse the low break from the recess on the left and finish at the last good pockets below the groove of *A Little Extra*. V8 7B+ If you traverse all the way to *Powerband*.

12 The Rib . . . . 🌓 🔧   **V4** *6B*
The rib finishing at the good holds.

The wall just right is Pinches Wall. We have left the million eliminates on this tiny section of wall, for you to find out. Most end at the upper flake.

13 Verbal Abuse Start . . . 🌓 💭   **V3** *6A+*
Climb the groove to prominent jugs.

14 A Little Extra Direct 🌓 🔧 💪   **V6** *7A*
Start in the break and reach a small hold with your left. A powerful pull rightwards gains a jug which is the finish.

15 Undercuts to Crimp 🌓 🔧 💪   **V8** *7B+*
From the break, use twin undercuts to span up for a crimp right of the finishing jug. For a **V9** *7C* eliminate start at the same place and move out right and past a poor pocket and side-pull to finish up at the same jug.

16 Pump up the Valium . . 🔧 💪   **V10** *7C+*
From a stack of mats, reach a pinch with your left hand and pull up to a poor side-pull and continue up the wall to finish at jugs.

17 Hooligan Start . . . . . . 🔧 💪   **V12** *8A+*
Start with a poor undercut with your left hand and poor pinch for your right. Slap up for a small edge and continue up and right to finish at flakes.

Powerband Area

This area lurks behind the roadside bushes underneath the bulging right wall of the Tor. It is a popular training area especially during winter.

① Boot Boys Start . . . **V5** 6C
From 2m left of the tree, climb through the initial bulge.

② Out of My Tree Start
. . . . **V8** 7B
A series of evil pocket jams deposits you out to the jugs.

③ Pump up the Power
. . . . **V10** 7C+
The pale groove has plenty of small holds. The finishing hold is 5m up so plenty of pads are needed, or use a rope and get 8a+.

④ The Steve Miller Band
. . . . **V9** 7C
Connect *Pump up the Power* to *Out of My Tree*.

⑤ Rattle and Hump Start
. . . . **V7** 7A+
From the pockets on the traverse, crimp your way up the steep wall to a jug at 3m. **Rattle and Hump Hard Way, V8** 7B, avoids the good holds on the left and the heel/toe lock.

⑥ Powerband **V9** 7C
A famous test-piece. Traverse the break from a small low set of good pockets below and right of the flake of *Rattle and Hump*. Finish on the pillar right of *Out of My Tree*. The crux is passing a glued pinch on the upper break and dropping under to reach the continuation line of pockets. *Photo on page 347.*

⑦ Power Humps . . . **V8** 7B
Follow *Powerband* into *Rattle and Hump Start*. **V8** 7B+ if you avoid the good starting holds on *Rattle and Hump*.

⑧ Influx **V11** 8A
From undercuts follow the rib to finish at an edge. Good holds out right are out of bounds.

⑨ Kristian's Problem **V8** 7B
Monkey up the twin edges to finish at a crimp on *Wild in Me*.

⑩ Wild in Me Start **V5** 6C
The flake, moving right to finish on the good side-pull.

⑪ Staminaband **V11** 8A
An extension start to the *Powerband*. Begin at the base of *Super High Intensity Body Building*, by a tree, and traverse left to reach the start holds from a series of pockets and undercuts.

⑫ Stamina Humps . . **V10** 7C+
Cut short *Staminaband* by finishing up *Rattle and Hump Hard Way*.

⑬ Staminaband Pump up the Power
. . . . **V14** 8B+
Staminaband into *Pump up the Power*.

To the right is a shorter wall with a few small problems based on the route *Saline Drip*. They have no topo.

⑭ Saline Drip **V6** 7A
From just right of a tree, head up leftwards on sharp holds to a jug. It can be gained direct as well at **V6** 7A and the sit-start is a slightly harder **V7** 7A+.

	No star	⚅	⚅⚅	⚅⚅⚅
VB to V0 Easy to 4c	-	-	-	-
V0+ to V2 5a to 5c	-	-	-	-
V3 to V5 6A to 6C+	2	4	-	-
V3 to V5 7A upwards	4	12	8	1

Blackwell Dale consists of three steep walls next to the B6049 road. The location isn't great and the road is busier than you might think, but the approach walks are very short and there are some good problems on offer. Much of the bouldering here continues the theme of the other limestone crags - powerful and fingery high-grade problems. There is little here for the average boulderer.

Approach

Also see map on page 347

The areas are found along the B6049 that runs between the A6, Miller's Dale and Tideswell and the A623. There is parking in a lay-by under Beginners' Wall and you can also park under the roof of Sean's Roof which is around 100m further up the road, directly opposite the Read or Dead Wall.

Conditions

Both Beginners' Wall and Sean's Roof suffer from seepage and are wet for much of the winter. The Red or Dead Wall actually dries more quickly although it can also get terminally wet. Once dry these walls offer the potential for sheltered and shady climbing during the summer months.

Chee Dale
not described

Millers Dale

Raven Tor
p.360

Blackwell Dale

GPS 53.252439
Ⓟ -1.802423

Priestcliffe

About 1km

Rob Greenwood, *Jerry's Traverse* (**V7** *7A+*)
- *page 367* - Blackwell Dale. Photo: Alan James

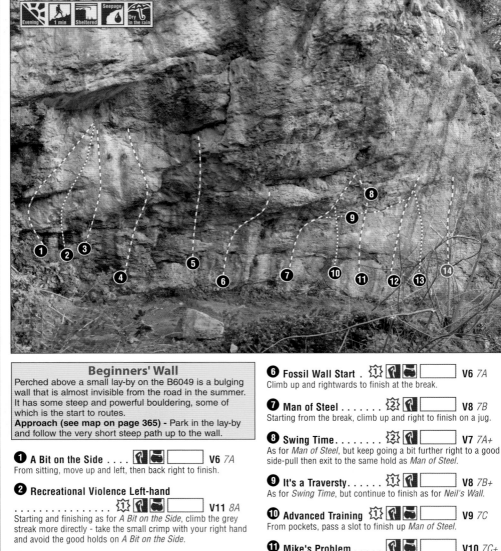

Beginners' Wall

Perched above a small lay-by on the B6049 is a bulging wall that is almost invisible from the road in the summer. It has some steep and powerful bouldering, some of which is the start to routes.

Approach (see map on page 365) - Park in the lay-by and follow the very short steep path up to the wall.

❶ A Bit on the Side . . . . ▢▢ **V6** *7A*
From sitting, move up and left, then back right to finish.

❷ Recreational Violence Left-hand
. . . . ▢▢▢ **V11** *8A*
Starting and finishing as for *A Bit on the Side*, climb the grey streak more directly - take the small crimp with your right hand and avoid the good holds on *A Bit on the Side*.

❸ Recreational Violence
. . . . ▢▢▢ **V12** *8A+*
The same as the above problem, only take the crimp with your left hand.

❹ The Love of Money Start . . ▢ **V8** *7B*
The initial moves of the route.

❺ Aurora . . . . ▢▢ **V9** *7C*
The wall following the dark streak on small holds.

❻ Fossil Wall Start . ▢▢▢ **V6** *7A*
Climb up and rightwards to finish at the break.

❼ Man of Steel . . . . ▢▢ **V8** *7B*
Starting from the break, climb up and right to finish on a jug.

❽ Swing Time . . . . ▢▢ **V7** *7A+*
As for *Man of Steel*, but keep going a bit further right to a good side-pull then exit to the same hold as *Man of Steel*.

❾ It's a Traversty . . . . . . ▢▢ **V8** *7B+*
As for *Swing Time*, but continue to finish as for *Neil's Wall*.

❿ Advanced Training ▢▢▢ **V9** *7C*
From pockets, pass a slot to finish up *Man of Steel*.

⓫ Mike's Problem . . . . . ▢▢ **V10** *7C+*
From sitting, climb the wall into the top of *Swing Time*.

⓬ Neil's Wall . . . . ▢▢ **V8** *7B+*
Starting at a couple of crimps, climb the wall to finish at the break. **V9** *7C* from sitting.

⓭ Neil's Wall Right . . . . ▢▢ **V11** *8A*
A low right-hand variation to *Neil's Wall* via a slot.

⓮ Groove . . . . ▢ **V4** *6B*
The groove.

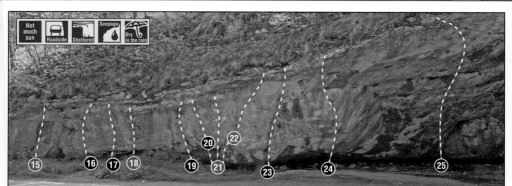

Sean's Roof Area

An often-dank roadside cave with some short problems on its left flank and one through the roof itself. On the opposite side of the road is the Read or Dead Wall.

15 Uno **V3** *6A*
The wall left of the crack.

16 Somebody's Head **V6** *7A*
From the very lowest holds, climb to the jug.

17 Orange Si **V8** *7B*
Another very low start, follow edges up the wall.

18 Twice a Slice **V5** *6C*
Start at the break.

19 My Friend Flicka . **V8** *7B+*
Follow small edges in and around a crack.

20 Fudge **V6** *7A*
From low jugs, climb the wall to a finishing jug.

21 Don't Jump **V5** *6C*
The central line from the same start as *Fudge*.

22 Push Me Pull You . . . . **V4** *6B+*
From the same start as *Fudge*, climb up rightwards following the feature.

23 Byker Groove . **V9** *7C*
The fingery groove to a finishing jug.

24 Paint it Black . **V9** *7C*
The vague prow marking the left side of the cave.

25 Sean's Roof . . **V12** *8A+*
The roof itself is an 8b+ sport route that can be highballed.

The Read or Dead Wall is on the other side of the road.

26 Left of Abattoir . . **V4** *6B*
The left-most line. Finish at the break.

27 Free Range Abattoir **V7** *7A+*
From the left side of the ledge, climb the wall.

28 Red or Dead . . **V7** *7A+*
From the right end of the sloping ledge move right to the pocket then continue up the pale streak.

29 Top Shop . . . . **V8** *7B+*
Gain the top of *Red or Dead* from the right. It is possible at various levels - the topo line is the lowest level.

5m right is another similar section of wall.

30 A Lack of Colour . **V8** *7B*
The slight groove to the top of the wall.

31 Jerry's Traverse . . **V7** *7A+*
The traverse which can be done either way. *Photo on page 365.*

Photo on page 365.

Northern Peak

Sheffield Crags

Stanage Area

Burbage Valley

Derwent Edges

The Limestone

Central Grit

Staffordshire

South Peak

	No star	⚐	⚐	⚐
VB to V0 easy to 4c	-	-	-	-
V0+ to V2 5a to 5c	3	1	1	-
V3 to V5 6A to 6C+	-	5	3	-
V3 to V5 7A upwards	4	5	2	-

Rheinstor has been climbed on way before the Plantation was trendy, though the style and height of the problems tends to put people off. To complete most of the problems you have to gain the break at about 5m, and a decent bouldering mat is essential, even then most will want to traverse off. The rock is superb solid limestone with lots of tiny pockets, however few of the pockets are sinkers with most only accepting two fingers to the first joint. Nuda's Tartan could not be more different, consisting of a couple of limestone roofs providing some very steep problems.

Access

Rheinstor is on land owned by Haddon Estates. There have never been many problems in the past but, since the area is popular with walkers, it is worth remembering that you are on show so keep the curse and celebration volume down.

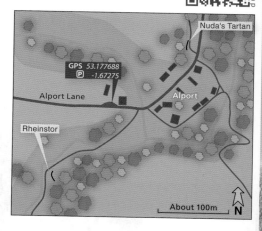

scan for map

Conditions

Rheinstor faces west and catches the afternoon sun. It is very sheltered and can be warm when other areas are cold. There is no seepage to speak of but also no shelter from the rain. Nuda's Tartan faces east, but is steep and sheltered by trees.

Approach   Also see map on page 347

Alport is situated off the B6046 which runs south from the A6 south of Bakewell. For both venues, park in the generous lay-by with a high kerb just west of the village of Alport (on nice days it fills quickly so either get there early or park somewhere else with consideration for residents). To reach Rheinstor, walk towards the village for 50m and turn off to the right down a lane.

Continue down the lane, over the river and you will find the wall on your left after 250m. For Nuda's Tartan, walk down the road for 250m to a lane leading off the left. Turn up here and walk for about 50m and you should see the rock through the trees on your left.

(Map labels: Nuda's Tartan, GPS 53.177688 / -1.67275, Alport Lane, Alport, Rheinstor, About 100m, N)

Northern Peak

Sheffield Crags

Stanage Area

Burbage Valley

Derwent Edges

The Limestone

Central Grit

Staffordshire

South Peak

Northern Peak

Sheffield Crags

Stanage Area

Burbage Valley

Derwent Edges

The Limestone

Central Grit

Staffordshire

South Peak

Rheinstor

Rheinstor offers vertical pocket-pulling, with many of the problems being the lower sections of trad routes. It is very sheltered and west-facing, so turn up later in the day for some sun. Most problems finish at the main break which is quite high. Traverse off from here and reverse one of the other easier problems to get back down.
Approach - See map on page 369.

1 Le Crepscule . . . . 🔲 V2 5c
The polished groove at the left-hand side of the crag. Good on the way up but the only way down is reversing it.

2 Little Flake Wall . . . . 🔲 V4 6B
Climb straight up to a little flake.

3 Wizard of Aus . . . 🔲 V4 6B+
Climb the wall with a tricky move to a flake. This includes most of the hard climbing on the route which is given E4!

4 Meridian . . . . . . 🔲 V5 6C
Climb the thin fingery wall to a thread then skedaddle off leftwards. Harder than *Wizard of Aus* but less bold ... just. *Photo page 368.*

5 Ron's Route . . . . 🔲 V4 6B+
The wall above and left of the eye. Fingery and painful.

6 Mjollnir . . . . 🔲 V3 6A+
Climb past a faint scoop to the break.

7 Valhalla . . . . 🔲 V1 5b
Two threads show the way. Probably better as an HVS.

8 Descent Route . . . . 🔲 V0+ 5a
The most common way back down.

9 Asgard . . . . 🔲 V1 5b
Up to a pocket then back down again.

The two low traverses are extremely testing on the tendons.

10 Lower Traverse . . 🔲 V6 7A
Traverse either way along the thin lower line at about head height.

11 Upper Traverse . . 🔲 V5 6C
The next break up is a touch easier and a touch higher!

12 Spirit Chaser . . . . 🔲 V2 5c
The main break is best used to get off the other problems.

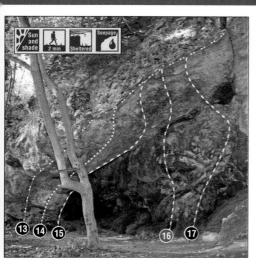

Northern Peak
Sheffield Crags
Stanage Area
Burbage Valley
Derwent Edges
The Limestone
Central Grit
Staffordshire
South Peak

Nuda's Tartan

A complete contrast to Rheinstor with some very steep hard problems. It is a sheltered, shady spot that seeps after prolonged rain.
Approach - See map on page 369.

⑰ Dave's Roof . . . . V7 *7A+*
Start right of the last problem and cross the roof in the direction of a good pocket, finish as for *The Meltdown*.

A few metres right is another steep piece of rock where the following problems are to be found.

⑱ Slap Happy . . . . . V4 *6B+*
From sitting, follow the holds straight through the steepness.

⑲ The Scenic Route. . . . V6 *7A*
Start as for *Slap Happy* then head out left all the way to finish on the slab. Foot-ledges are out of bounds.

⑳ Slot Machine. . . . . . . V7 *7A+*
Start up *Slap Happy* then head out right to finish up *Iron Flag*.

㉑ Calorie Count . . . V9 *7C*
From the back of the cave, pull through on a variety of holds to finish on jugs.

㉒ Enigma. . . . . V8 *7B+*
From sitting, make a low traverse to finish up *Slap Happy*.

㉓ Iron Flag. . . . . . . V8 *7B+*
Starting up the crack, climb through the roof.

㉔ Stumped. . . . . V10 *7C+*
The final line pulling through the roof at its right-hand end.

⑬ The Meltdown V8 *7B*
From sitting, traverse the lip.

⑭ Nuda's Tartan V8 *7B+*
A harder, right-hand start to *The Meltdown*. From the base of the pillar, climb the roof to meet *The Meltdown* at its mid-point.

⑮ Tarantula V9 *7C*
Harder still, climb the roof to join *The Meltdown* two thirds the way along.

⑯ Submission. . . . . V5 *6C+*
Start at the base of the back wall and cross the roof using an undercut and a pocket then follow *The Meltdown* to finish.

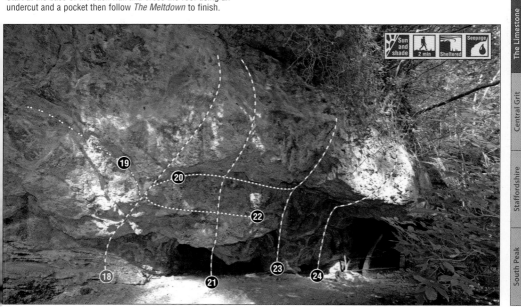

Northern Peak

Sheffield Crags

Stanage Area

Burbage Valley

Derwent Edges

The Limestone

Central Grit

Staffordshire

South Peak

Central Grit

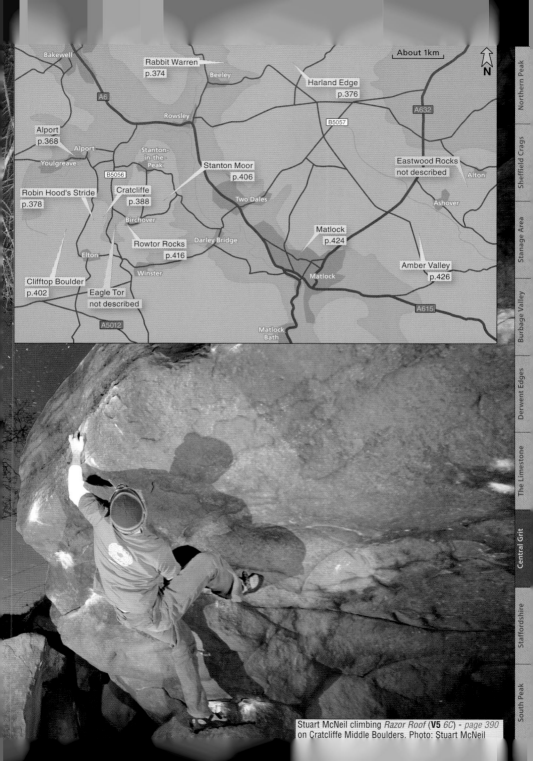

About 1km

N

Bakewell

Rabbit Warren
p.374

Beeley

Harland Edge
p.376

A6

Rowsley

A632

B5057

Alport
p.368

Alport

Stanton-
in-the-
Peak

Stanton Moor
p.406

Eastwood Rocks
not described

Alton

Youlgreave

B5056

Robin Hood's Stride
p.378

Cratcliffe
p.388

Two Dales

Ashover

Birchover

Matlock
p.424

Rowtor Rocks
p.416

Darley Bridge

Clifftop Boulder
p.402

Elton

Winster

Amber Valley
p.426

Eagle Tor
not described

Matlock

A5012

A615

Matlock
Bath

Stuart McNeil climbing *Razor Roof* (**V5** *6C*) - *page 390*
on Cratcliffe Middle Boulders. Photo: Stuart McNeil

Northern Peak

Sheffield Crags

Stanage Area

Burbage Valley

Derwent Edges

The Limestone

Central Grit

Staffordshire

South Peak

	No star	☆	☆☆	☆☆☆
VB to V0 Easy to 4c	2	2	-	-
V0+ to V2 5a to 5c	6	5	1	-
V3 to V5 6A to 6C+	1	1	-	-
V3 to V5 7A upwards	-	-	-	-

Rabbit Warren is a minor venue, but with some good rock and problems that are just about worth the hike. It is a good place to combine with a short walk on the moors above Chatsworth.

Approach

Also see map on page 373

The edge is approached from Beeley which is on the B6012 between Chatsworth and the A6 at Rowsley. In Beeley, turn east on Chesterfield Road and follow this for 2.7km to where the road turns right and an unpaved road leads off to the left. Park here

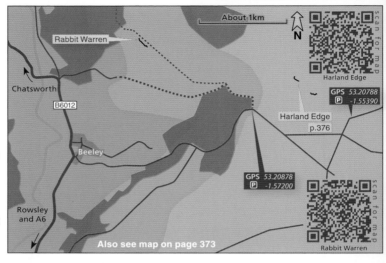

and continue on foot along the unpaved road for 0.5km to a stile on the right. Cross the stile and follow the track for 1.5km. The rocks are down to the left and you cannot see them from the track so they are easy to miss. At time of writing there are tree saplings planted between the rocks and the track - if you get to woodland you've gone a bit too far.

Conditions

Plenty of sun and exposure make this a quick-drying venue but it will catch any bad weather that is going.

Continue your approach to the left-end of the rocks to find the first problems.

① Bugs' Arete . . . . ☆   **V2** 5c
The arete on its right, eliminating the crack.

② Bunny Wall . . . . ☆   **V0+** 5a
The wall to the right, via the prominent flake.

The next bay has some good lines, but take care with the rock at the top as it tends to be a little loose.

3 Jessicarete . . . . ☐ **V0-** 4b
The arete just left of the crack.

4 Jessica Rabbit . . . . ☼ ☐ **V0** 4c
The crack.

5 Killer Bunnies . . . . ▯ ☐ **V4** 6B
From a thin crack, span up to a hold and continue up the wall.

6 Sinister Bunny . . . . ☼ ☐ **V2** 5c
The wall left of the corner.

7 Camateras Crack . . . . ☐ **V0+** 5a
The crack right of the corner.

8 Hannah Sporren Warren . . . . . ☐ **V1** 5b
The wall right of the crack.

9 Cwingen . . . . ☐ **V1** 5b
The wall just right of the arete.

10 Cwingod . . . . ☼ ☐ **V0+** 5a
The arete has good holds, but there are big moves between them.

The next mini-buttress has a prominent cut-away on its right.

11 Choux-Fleur . . . . ☐ **V1** 5b
From the higher break, climb the left arete.

12 The Seeker . . . . ☼ ☐ **V0+** 5a
The centre of the slab.

13 The Tomb . . . . . . ☼ ▤ ☐ **V4** 6B
From sitting, climb the underside of the arete.

14 The Bunny Run . . . . ☼ ☐ **V0-** 4b
The wall to the right.

15 Teal'c . . . . ▤ ☐ **V2** 5c
The off-width crack.

A few metres right are a couple more problems.

16 Bummer . . . . ▤ ☐ **V0** 4c
The undercut arete. Slightly harder on its right-hand side.

17 Spitsnswallows . . . . ▤ ☐ **V1** 5b
Climb the wall, eliminating the arete.

A couple of hundred metres further on is a slab next to a holly bush.

18 Ace in the Hole . . . . ☼ ☐ **V1** 5b
The right side of the slab.

Northern Peak · Sheffield Crags · Stanage Area · Burbage Valley · Derwent Edges · The Limestone · Central Grit · Staffordshire · South Peak

	No star	🌑	🌑🌑	🌑🌑🌑
VB to V0 Easy to 4c	-	1	-	-
V0+ to V2 5a to 5c	2	6	1	-
V3 to V5 6A to 6C+	-	3	2	-
V3 to V5 7A upwards	-	-	-	-

Harland Edge is a scenic and exposed spot with just enough value to justify the awkward approach. The range of bouldering isn't extensive but it will certainly be appreciated by those who like solitude in a beautiful and wild setting.

Access

Access is now permitted here under the CRoW act but the area is managed for nature conservation so care should be taken not to disturb nesting birds. Also, stick to the paths where you can find them and avoid damaging walls and fences. Where there are no real paths, take a direct line and don't wander all over the place.

Approach   See map on page 374

The edge is approached from Beeley which is on the B6012 between Chatsworth and the A6 at Rowsley. At Beeley, turn east on Chesterfield Road and follow this for 2.7km to where the road turns right and an unpaved road leads off to the left (parking for The Rabbit Warren). Continue along the road taking left turns at two junctions for a further 2km. Parking is possible on the right side of the road in a small lay-by just before the road turns to the right. Walk up the road in the direction of a mile-marker stone. Carefully hop over the wall and follow the vaguest path imaginable in a west-northwest direction, contouring the side of a low hill, heading for the rocks.

Conditions

Plenty of sun and exposure make this a quick-drying venue but it will catch any bad weather that is going.

The first five problems are on an isolated block a couple of hundred metres west of the first rocks you reach on the approach.

❶ Between the Bars. 🌑 **V3** *6A+*
The wall left of the arete, from sitting. V0+ 5a from standing.

❷ Swollen Tongue . . . . 🌑 **V2** *5c*
The arete on its left side.

❸ Miss Ohio . . . . 🌑🌑 **V1** *5b*
Follow the flakes just right of the arete.

❹ Me-Oh My-oh . . . . . . 🌑🌑 **V3** *6A+*
The centre of the wall.

❺ Harland Shuffle . . . . 🌑 **V2** *5c*
The right side of the wall.

Bread and Water   Come Harland High Water

Miss Ohio

Approach

Northern Peak
Sheffield Crags
Stanage Area
Burbage Valley
Derwent Edges
The Limestone
Central Grit
Staffordshire
South Peak

Bread and Water

Northern Peak

Sheffield Crags

Stanage Area

Burbage Valley

Derwent Edges

The Limestone

Central Grit

Staffordshire

South Peak

In the main section reached on the approach is a block with a distinctive break at half-height.

6 Overhung Mantel . . . . **V0+** 5a
Cross the overlap and mantel.

7 Bread and Water . . . . **V0+** 5a
The middle of the wall.

8 To Harland Back **V4** 6B
Traverse the break from right to left, then reverse to the start.

The next couple of problems are on the small block a few metres to the right.

9 Happy Feet **V2** 5c
The left side of the wall, starting in the low break.

10 Papa Hobo **V2** 5c
The groove.

A little further to the right is another isolated buttress with some good lines.

11 Spangle **V1** 5b
Follow the thin crack. Without the arete is **V3** 6A.

12 Meat Balls **V1** 5b
The short crack, from sitting.

13 Come Harland High Water . **V4** 6B+
Climb the arete. Everything left of the arete is out of bounds. The sit-start is **V6** 7A.

14 Harland Globetrotter **V3** 6A
The thin crack.

15 Fascism **V0-** 4b
The arete.

Come Harland High Water

	No star	☆	☆☆	☆☆☆
VB to V0 Easy to 4c	5	5	1	-
V0+ to V2 5a to 5c	7	8	7	2
V3 to V5 6A to 6C+	1	11	7	1
V3 to V5 7A upwards	2	8	8	5

Northern Peak

Sheffield Crags

Stanage Area

Burbage Valley

Derwent Edges

The Limestone

Central Grit

Staffordshire

South Peak

Robin Hood's Stride is a beautiful spot with a superb variety of quality problems, especially in the low-to-mid grades. The landings are mostly good, the rock quality solid and the setting is stunning - what more could you ask for? Like its close neighbour Cratcliffe, the Stride makes an excellent venue for a family picnic. There are problems on both the prominent Stride itself and the free-standing boulders that surround it. There is plenty to go at in the higher grades here as well, with a number of excellent hard classics like *Big Al Qaeda*, *Spine Left-hand*, *My Prune*, *Dry Wit in a Wet Country* and *Jerry's Arete*.

Circuits

The Green Circuit is excellent and straightforward, and great in combination with the Green at Cratcliffe. The Orange Circuit is also good although it finishes with a few highballs so take care. The Red Circuit takes in the whole of the Stride and includes some classic problems.

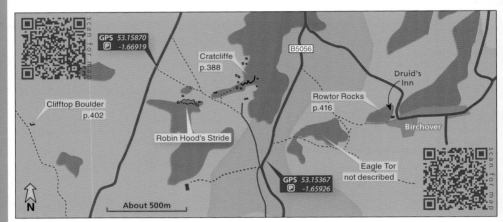

GPS 53.15870
P -1.66919

Cratcliffe
p.388

B5056

Druid's
Inn

Clifftop Boulder
p.402

Rowtor Rocks
p.416

Birchover

Robin Hood's Stride

Eagle Tor
not described

GPS 53.15367
P -1.65926

About 500m

N

Approach   Also see map on page 373

Robin Hood's Stride can be approached as for Cratcliffe, from a small lay-by on the B5056 that runs south from the A6 towards Winster. From the road, follow the track up towards the Stride. It can also be approached from the minor road that runs parallel to the B5056 connecting Alport and Elton. There is roadside parking here but take great care to keep your car tucked away and **do not block access to Harthill Moor Farm**. An easy walk across the field leads to the Stride.

Kaluza Klein Area
p.386

The Lower Boulders
p.380

Conditions

The Stride is exposed to the wind and has little to offer in the wet. It dries reasonably quickly after rain although some of the problems on the tree-covered south side can get very green.

Northern Peak

Sheffield Crags

Stanage Area

Burbage Valley

Derwent Edges

The Limestone

Central Grit

Staffordshire

South Peak

Nathan Lee on *Spinal Slab* (**V6** *7A*) - *page 384* - on the Square Block at Robin Hood's Stride. Photo: Rob Greenwood

Northern Peak

Sheffield Crags

Stanage Area

Burbage Valley

Derwent Edges

The Limestone

Central Grit

Staffordshire

South Peak

Map

Dorsal Fin
p.383

Main Edge
p.382

The Green Boulder

Square Block
p.384

The Innaccessible
Pinnacle

The Lower Boulders

Southwest Boulders
p.385

The Cave
p.386

Kaluza Klein Area
p.386

About 20m

N

The Lower Boulders

The first blocks you see when approaching from the south. Do not approach directly across the field, but continue past the boulders and approach from behind.
Approach - See map on page 378.

The Stride Green Circuit

An excellent short circuit on the boulders to the north and east of the Stride itself. Add a few **V1** 5b problems to make it a baby Orange Circuit.

The Stride Orange Circuit

19 good problems on the north and east of the Stride, then it goes a bit highball for the last four on the Southwest Boulders if you feel up to them.

Lots of sun   10 min

The right-hand of the two boulders has a T-crack in it.

1 Flake Slab Arete ② ③ ☼ ⬅ **V2** 5c
Make a powerful pull and rock up on your right foot.

2 Flake Slab ① ② ☼ **V1** 5b
Pull on the flake then climb the slab and arete.

3 Joy of Noledge ① ② ☼ **V0+** 5a
The centre of the slab, past a right hand finger slot - no ledge!

4 Joy of Ledge ① ☼ **VB**
The easy right-hand side has a friction slab start.

5 The Arch ③ ☼ **VB**
A nice easy one following the overlap.

6 Arch Direct ③ ☼ **V3** 6A+
A desperate static move with your right foot in the slot, or an easy pop off the deck at about **V1** 5b.

7 T Slab ④ ④ ☼ **V0+** 5a
The cracks, approached from the right. Direct is harder.

8 T Slab Arete ⑤ ⑤ ☼ **V0+** 5a
A steep pull up the right arete of the slab.
Green Circuit continues on page 383 and Orange Circuit continues on page 382.

The **Stride Red Circuit**
20 intense problems up to
V5 *6C+*, including a few highballs on
the Southwest Boulders.

The Green Boulder

In the shade of a tree behind the Lower Boulders is this solitary tall green boulder with an impressive east face.
Approach - See map on page 378.

9 Ben's Groove . . . . **V8** *7B+*
Mantel into the groove then pull out of the top.

10 Slap Bass Odyssey . . . **V8** *7B*
The arete via some poor seams. *Photo on page 7.*

11 Zaff's Mantel **V6** *7A*
Starting up as for *Slap Bass Odyssey,* move out right and mantel the prominent shelf.

12 Green Boulder Traverse **V5** *6C*
As for *Zaff's Mantel,* but keep hand-traversing right to finish up the arete on its left-hand side.

13 Short Arete **V4** *6B*
The short arete on its right-hand side.
Red Circuit continues on page 382.

14 Short Wall **V6** *7A*
The smeary wall. **V8** *7B+* without holds on the right.

15 Boysen's Crack . . **V5** *6C*
Gain and climb the short hanging crack.

16 King of Fools . . . . **V8** *7B+*
The rounded arete climbed on its left-hand side, using the edge of the crack to finish.

Northern Peak

Sheffield Crags

Stanage Area

Burbage Valley

Derwent Edges

The Limestone

Central Grit

Staffordshire

South Peak

The Green Boulder

The Main Edge

Although there isn't a Main Edge as such, the following problems are on the rocks that form the base of the jumble of boulders that make up Robin Hood's Stride. The first two problems are just above The Green Boulder. **Approach** - See map on page 378.

1 Boomerang Wall . . . . ⑥ **V2** 5c
The wall just left of the arete.

2 Boomerang-erang . ⑤⑦ **V2** 5c
The crooked arete starting from the block. **V3** *6A* from sitting.

20m further along the edge, the problems continue.

3 Grovel . . . . **V4** *6B+*
A shallow groove to a lichenous finish.

4 Burley's Bridge **V4** *6B*
The steep green arete.

5 Big Al Qaeda **V8** *7B*
The excellent hard arete requires some cunning footwork.

6 Nobody Knows **V4** *6B*
The wall just left of the arete. Enter the scoop and finish over the bulge on good holds.

7 Muscle Slab . . . . . ⑥⑧ **V1** 5b
The right side of the narrow pillar.

8 Left of Picalli's **V8** *7B*
From sitting, pull up to gain the rising diagonal line.

9 Picalli's Pickle **V7** *7A+*
From the far side of the tunnel, tackle the fearsome roof crack.

The Southwest Boulders (p.385) down and around to the right

The Dorsal Fin

This is one of the fine free-standing boulders to the north of the Stride. After wet weather, these are likely to dry first and tend not to be as green as some of the other boulders.

Approach - See map on page 378.

On a small slabby block before the main Dorsal block.

10 Shy Slab . . . . ⑨ ⑥ **V0+** 5a
Climb the friction slab up its centre. Easier on either side.

The next problems are on the distinctive Dorsal Fin boulder.

11 Dorsal Arete . . . . ⑦ **VB**
The left side of the south face of the block on big chips.

12 JT . . . . ⑩ ⑧ ⑪ **V0-** 4b
The wall past the letters 'JT'.

13 JT Crack . . . . ⑨ ⑫ **VB** 4a
Up past a crack.

14 Flipper Arete . . . . ⑦ ⑫ **V3** *6A*
Superb climbing up the arete using a crease on the right.

15 Flipper . . . . ⑧ ⑫ 🖐 **V5** *6C*
Excellent. Gain the crease from below and finish up it.

16 Vandals . . . . ⑨ ⑪ ⑫ **V1** 5b
Brilliant balancy climbing up the chips to a chip-less rock-over.
Red Circuit continues on page 384.

17 Jaws . . . . ⑪ 🖐 **V7** *7A+*
The ridge on the wall side, all the way to the top, without any chipped holds. **V3** *6A* with chips for feet.

18 Potty Time . . . . ⑫ ⑩ **V0+** 5a
The scoop requires a stiff pull to enter.
Orange and Green Circuits continue on page 384.

19 Black Arete **V2** 5c
Right of *The Dorsal Fin* (looking at the crag) is a block with a short arete that can be climbed on either side.

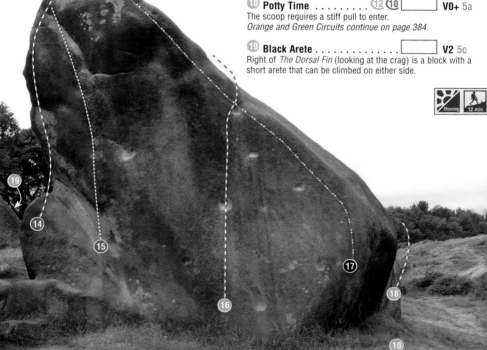

Northern Peak

Sheffield Crags

Stanage Area

Burbage Valley

Derwent Edges

The Limestone

Central Grit

Staffordshire

South Peak

The Square Block

Hidden at the far west end of Robins Hood's Stride is a large block with some good aretes and slabs.
Approach - See map on page 378.

❶ Ben's Wall . .   **V9** *7C*
Use a high side-pull then gain the top by going left. Exiting right is the same grade. The arete is out of bounds.

❷ Spine Left-Hand   **V4** *6B*
The left-hand side of the arete is hard to start and airy to finish.

❸ The Spine . . . . . .   **V0+** *5a*
A magnificent problem up the right-hand side of the arete. Getting your feet in the right order is the crux.
The last problem in the Green Circuit.

❹ Spinal Slab **V6** *7A*
The slab to the right has no holds. *Photo on page 379.*

❺ Angle Arete **V1** *5b*
The arete on its left-hand side.

❻ Angle Arete Right . . . .   **VB** *4a*
The right-hand side.

❼ Scoop Slab . . . .   **VB** *4a*
Make a friction move direct up the slab.

❽ Scoop Slab Traverse   **V0+** *5a*
Tiptoe across the slab all the way to the arete. Delightful. Going straight up the short slab is a fun easy problem.

❾ Shadow Slab . . . .   **VB**
Climb the slippery slab anywhere.

❿ Square Block Crack **V1** *5b*
The gnarly short wide crack. Starting from *The Nose*, then undercutting leftwards is **Milking the Cow**, **V1** *5b*.

⓫ The Nose . . . .   **V4** *6B+*
Reach right from the hole and then grovel onto the top. The nose direct hasn't been done yet.

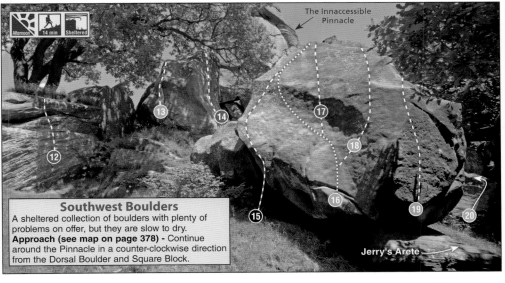

The Innaccessible Pinnacle

Southwest Boulders
A sheltered collection of boulders with plenty of problems on offer, but they are slow to dry.
Approach (see map on page 378) - Continue around the Pinnacle in a counter-clockwise direction from the Dorsal Boulder and Square Block.

Jerry's Arete

⑫ Jams O'Mantel V4 *6B*
From the break, reach the rounded nose and mantel this.

⑬ Back Bottom V2 *5c*
The rounded green arete.

⑭ Concave Crimper . . . . V3 *6A+*
Use crinkles to slide up the slab.

⑮ Ben and Jerry's Love Child V6 *7A*
The left arete from sitting.

⑯ Diamond Slab Left
. . . . V2 *5c*
Start in the scoop in the centre of the diamond-shaped slab and move to the arete. A good scary problem.

⑰ Diamond Slab . . . . V5 *6C+*
An even scarier direct version with thin holds.

⑱ Diamond Slab Right
. . . . V2 *5c*
From the scoop in the centre of the slab, reach right to the right-hand arete. Still scary but easier.

⑲ Front On V2 *5c*
The front face of the block.

⑳ Inside Groove V1 *5b*
Follow the groove to the arete, and finish up this.

㉑ Hoppin' Mud . . . . V8 *7B+*
The left-hand side of the side-wall. Jump to a sloper and top out.

㉒ Jerry's Arete V6 *7A*
The arete on its steep side starting at a finger-lock.

㉓ Boss Hogg . . . V1 *5b*
A steep start at the flake leads to a thought-provoking finish up the arete. Starting from the boss and swinging up left is **V3** *6A+*. *The last problem in the Orange Circuit.*

㉔ Bossa Nova V5 *6C*
Mantel the protruding nose with great difficulty and an awkward landing. Impossible for some body types.
Red Circuit continues on page 386.

㉕ Roscoe . . . . V3 *6A+*
Pull onto the right side of the slab using a high crimp.

㉖ Daisy V0 *4c*
Climb the blocky groove.

Jerry's Arete

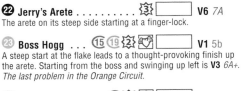

Northern Peak | Sheffield Crags | Stanage Area | Burbage Valley | Derwent Edges | The Limestone | Central Grit | Staffordshire | South Peak

Northern Peak

Sheffield Crags

Stanage Area

Burbage Valley

Derwent Edges

The Limestone

Central Grit

Staffordshire

South Peak

Kaluza Klein Area →

The Cave
Tucked away on the south side of The Stride is this small cave with a number of sheltered lines.
Approach (see map on page 378) - The Cave is reached by traversing the base of The Stride usually from the Kaluza Klein area.

Kaluza Klein Area
On the south side of The Stride is a prominent arete taken by the route *Kaluza Klein*. There are a number of problems (mostly hard) on the walls around this.
Approach (see map on page 378) - The area is best reached directly from the Lower Boulders.

1 Cave Left . . . . ⑰ **V3** *6A*
Reach from the pocket to the top. No arete at this grade.

2 The Foot Locker. . . . . ⑱ **V2** *5c*
From the chalky jug, move left to the pockets then finish via the arete.

3 The Haddon Haul **V1** *5b*
Haul up the crack.

4 The Blobs Eliminate
. . . . **V7** *7A+*
Out from the back, via blobs, to the sloper on the lip, then back left up the prow. Many variations are possible.

5 The Cave Problem
. . . . **V6** *7A*
Starting low, gain the sloper at the lip then traverse left to the edge of the roof.

6 Cave Problem Direct . ⑲ **V3** *6A+*
Start as for *The Cave Problem* then continue direct.

7 Hugo First. **V3** *6A*
From sitting, follow the flake left, then up.

8 The Kid. **V6** *7A*
Pull up to undercuts then right to a good hold and back left to finish. A more direct finish is **V7** *7A+*.

9 The Growler . . **V10** *7C+*
Follow crimps directly up the wall. A desperate start and a tricky upper wall on the E4 route *Mock Beggar's Wall*.

10 No Regrets **V9** *7C*
Traverse left after the start of *The Growler* into *The Kid*.

11 Grizzly Arete . . . . **V7** *7A+*
The superb arete.

12 Dry Wit in a Wet Country
. . . . **V6** *7A*
The thin slab leads to the hanging crack.

Down at a lower level.

13 Elderberry Layback **V0-** *4b*
Climb the layback crack. The slab to the right is **V0** *4c*.

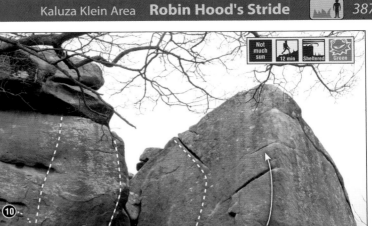

Kaluza Klein
(E7)

Northern Peak
Sheffield Crags
Stanage Area
Burbage Valley
Derwent Edges
The Limestone
Central Grit
Staffordshire

14 My Prune **V9** 7C
The arete on its right-hand side is high and hard.

A small block has a steep side with one very hard problem.

15 Sweet Thing . **V11** 8A
From low undercuts gain the sloping top via a chipped edge.

16 Sweet Arete . . . . . **V4** 6B+
The arete from a sitting start is climbed on its left and finished
rightwards. **V2** 5c from standing.

17 The Staircase . . . . **VB**
The low-angled, chipped slab is high but easy.

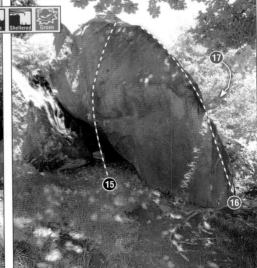

	No star	⊠	⊠	⊠
VB to V0 Easy to 4c	4	9	3	-
V0+ to V2 5a to 5c	7	15	6	-
V3 to V5 6A to 6C+	5	11	3	3
V3 to V5 7A upwards	2	11	8	5

Cratcliffe is a superb crag that combines some great bouldering with good routes in a beautiful location. It is also right next to Robin Hood's Stride which means there is masses here for plenty of visits for the keen boulderer. The Top Boulders are a good place to get going with short slabby problems above friendly landings. Moving into the trees things get a bit more serious for both grade level and the landings but the quality of the problems increases. For the harder stuff the area has a number of well-known destination problems such as *Jerry's Traverse* and *T Crack* plus more recent developments on the boulders and walls below Cratcliffe Tor have added several more good hard problems like *Brain Dead* and *Wish*.

For climbers with young families this is probably the most attractive bouldering venue in the Peak, and because of this it can get a bit busy on nice days.

Circuits

There are three great circuits here with the Orange and Green staying mostly on the delightful Top Boulders. A longer Red Circuit makes the most of all the areas covered.

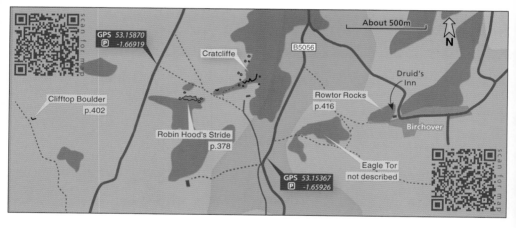

Approach   Also see map on page 373

Cratcliffe (and Robin Hood's Stride) are both approached from a small lay-by on the B5056 that runs south from the A6 towards Winster. From the road, follow the track up towards Robin Hood's Stride. Despite the fact that you can see Cratcliffe Tor crag off to your right, please continue up the track until you can head up rightwards into the trees. The rocks here are Cratcliffe Middle. **Do not follow the track to the house.** From Cratcliffe Middle, turn right towards the Tor. This brings you out at the stile in the trees by the Egg Boulder.

Conditions

The whole area is exposed to the wind and has little to offer in the wet although some of the steeper walls might stay dry in light rain. It dries reasonably quickly although some of the problems in the trees can get very green. The tree cover can give shade in the warmer months.

Ben Bransby and family on *T Crack* (**V8** *7B*) - *page 396* -
on the Cratcliffe Tree Boulders. Photo: Adam Long

Northern Peak

Sheffield Crags

Stanage Area

Burbage Valley

Derwent Edges

The Limestone

Central Grit

Staffordshire

South Peak

Northern Peak

Sheffield Crags

Stanage Area

Burbage Valley

Derwent Edges

The Limestone

Central Grit

Staffordshire

South Peak

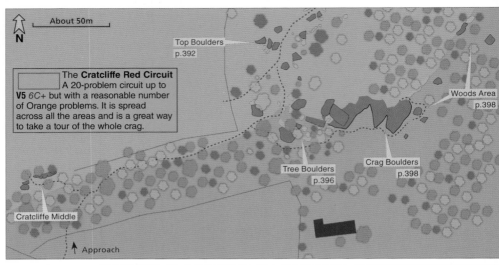

About 50m

N

Top Boulders p.392

The **Cratcliffe Red Circuit** A 20-problem circuit up to **V5** 6C+ but with a reasonable number of Orange problems. It is spread across all the areas and is a great way to take a tour of the whole crag.

Woods Area p.398

Tree Boulders p.396

Crag Boulders p.398

Cratcliffe Middle

↑ Approach

Razor Roof

Not much sun | 10 min | Sheltered | Green

① ② ③ ③ ④

Cratcliffe Middle

This small collection of boulders in the trees above the approach to Cratcliffe Tor has some great problems. The problems are almost always in the shade owing to the tree cover, hence they can get very green especially around The Blob.

Approach (see map on page 388) - The boulders are passed on the way to Cratcliffe Tor, just after you break up and back rightwards towards the crag.

❶ **Middle Slab** **V0** 4c
The centre of the slab from a sloping hold.

❷ **Middle Slab Right** **V2** 5c
The right-hand side of the slab via some dimples.

The next problems are just behind the previous ones.

❸ **Look at Me!** **V6** 7A
The roof crack starting at the far end, smoothly working your way out.

❹ **Look Right** **V1** 5b
The block is climbed using both aretes. The sit start is **V5** 6C. Climbing just the left arete on its right is **V6** 7A.

The best problems here are on the Razor Roof.

❺ **Razor Arete** . . . . **V5** 6C+
Start on the good hold and climb the little arete above.
The Red Circuit continues on page 395.

❻ **Razor Roof** **V5** 6C
Start low and reach up to gain some razor edges to finish from.
Photo on page 373.

❼ **RZA Roof** . . . . . . **V7** 7A+
Razor Roof's big brother gaining the right-hand side of the roof from the right and slapping to get the top.

❽ **Cave Wall** **V2** 5c
Start as for *RZA Roof* and continue directly.

❾ **Razor Traverse** . . **V7** 7A+
Starting up *RZA Roof*, continue along the lip until it is possible to finish as for *Razor Arete*.

10 Slab in the Middle V2 5c
The green slab between the two steeper sections.

Immediately right is a very green undercut block with a blob.

11 Crimps V1 5b
The left-hand side of the steep undercut block.

12 The Blob V6 7A
From the upside-down blob, heave up to the lip and pull over slightly rightwards.

13 Green Lipped Muscle
. . . . V9 7C
Starting low on the right, pull up and follow the lip leftwards to finish up *Crimps*.

14 Thrutch Over V5 6C
Mantel the lip with great difficulty.

15 Blob Over V4 6B
Another hard mantel on the far right.

Northern Peak

Sheffield Crags

Stanage Area

Burbage Valley

Derwent Edges

The Limestone

Central Grit

Staffordshire

South Peak

The Squirm

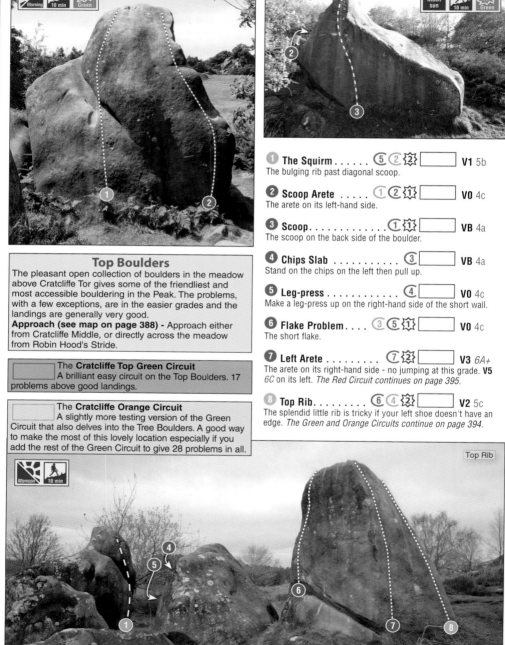

Top Boulders

The pleasant open collection of boulders in the meadow above Cratcliffe Tor gives some of the friendliest and most accessible bouldering in the Peak. The problems, with a few exceptions, are in the easier grades and the landings are generally very good.

Approach (see map on page 388) - Approach either from Cratcliffe Middle, or directly across the meadow from Robin Hood's Stride.

The **Cratcliffe Top Green Circuit**
A brilliant easy circuit on the Top Boulders. 17 problems above good landings.

The **Cratcliffe Orange Circuit**
A slightly more testing version of the Green Circuit that also delves into the Tree Boulders. A good way to make the most of this lovely location especially if you add the rest of the Green Circuit to give 28 problems in all.

① **The Squirm** **V1** 5b
The bulging rib past diagonal scoop.

② **Scoop Arete** **V0** 4c
The arete on its left-hand side.

③ **Scoop** . . . . **VB** 4a
The scoop on the back side of the boulder.

④ **Chips Slab** . . . . **VB** 4a
Stand on the chips on the left then pull up.

⑤ **Leg-press** **V0** 4c
Make a leg-press up on the right-hand side of the short wall.

⑥ **Flake Problem** **V0** 4c
The short flake.

⑦ **Left Arete** . . . . **V3** 6A+
The arete on its right-hand side - no jumping at this grade. **V5** 6C on its left. *The Red Circuit continues on page 395.*

⑧ **Top Rib** **V2** 5c
The splendid little rib is tricky if your left shoe doesn't have an edge. *The Green and Orange Circuits continue on page 394.*

Top Rib

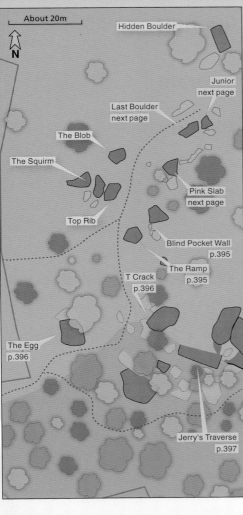

About 20m

N

Hidden Boulder

Junior
next page

Last Boulder
next page

The Blob

The Squirm

Pink Slab
next page

Top Rib

Blind Pocket Wall
p.395

The Ramp
p.395

T Crack
p.396

The Egg
p.396

Jerry's Traverse
p.397

The Blob

A low lump of a boulder with a couple of mantels.

9 Blob Mantel **V2** 5c
A little mantel, start at the distinctive 'blob'.

10 Bob Mantel . . . . **V0+** 5a
A tiny mantel on the back side of the boulder.

Hidden Boulder

The next boulder is hidden about 50m behind the main cluster, just beyond some larger trees. The wall of interest faces away from you (north) and is difficult to spot until you are under it.

11 Suicide Bummer . . . . **V3** *6A+*
The often-dirty wall left of the arete.

12 Hidden Arete **V1** 5b
From a sitting start, climb the left arete. Can be started from the left by a low traverse at **V2** 5c.

Last Boulder
p.394

Hidden Boulder

Pink Slab
p.394

The Blob

The Squirm

Top Rib

Blind Pocket Wall
p.395

Northern Peak

Sheffield Crags

Stanage Area

Burbage Valley

Derwent Edges

The Limestone

Central Grit

Staffordshire

South Peak

Northern Peak

Sheffield Crags

Stanage Area

Burbage Valley

Derwent Edges

The Limestone

Central Grit

Staffordshire

South Peak

The next problems are on the **Junior Boulder.**

13 Junior Flake . . . . 6 😊 ▢ **V0-** 4b
The flake and arete on the left side of the left boulder.

14 Junior Arete . . . . . 5 7 😊 ▢ **V0+** 5a
The little arete on its right-hand side. It is easier on its left.

15 Junior Slab . . . . . . 6 8 😊 ▢ **V0** 4c
The middle of the thin slab.

16 Junior Chips . . . . 9 ▢ **VB** 4a
The right-hand side of the thin slab on chips.

17 Hidden Wall . . . . 10 ▢ **V0** 4c
Anywhere up the back wall.

Blind Pocket Wall

The Ramp

The Ramp

*The steep face of the **Last Boulder** has some tough mantels.*

18 **Last Arete** . . . . ⑧ 🔆 🪨 🔲   **V4** *6B+*
The fine arete from a sitting start. **V1** *5b* from standing. A foothold was chipped here but it has now crumbled away.

19 **Through Mantel** . . . . 🔲   **V4** *6B*
Mantel the lip.

20 **Johnny's Groove** . . ⑨ 🔆 🔲   **V4** *6B*
Struggle up the vague groove. **V8** *7B* if you start low and squirm directly into the groove.

21 **Lip Slap** . . . . ⑩ 🔆 🔲   **V5** *6C+*
Traverse the lip from *Johnny's Groove* to the arete.

22 **Foot Tickler** . . . . . . ⑦ ⑫ 🔆 🔲   **V0+** *5a*
An excellent little rising traverse with your feet just above the lip.

23 **Right Slab** . . . . ⑪ 🔆 🔲   **V0-** *4b*
The right-hand side of the slab without touching the arete.

Pink Slab *is a triangular-shaped block with a number of prominent chipped holds.*

24 **Easy Slab** . . . . ⑬ 🔆 🔲   **V0-** *4b*
The left-hand side is smeary at the start.

25 **Pink Slab** . . . . ⑭ 🔆 🔲   **VB** *4a*
The chipped slab. **V3** *6A+* without chips.

26 **Pink Arete** . . . . ⑮ 🔆 🔲   **V0-** *4b*
The excellent arete. Eliminating the chips is **V1** *5b*.

27 **Pink Slab Right** . . . ⑪ ⑧ 🔆 🔲   **V2** *5c*
Climb the slab without the chips. **V0** *4c* with the chips. **V3** *6A+* just the slab without chips or the arete is excellent as well.

*The next boulder along is **Blind Pocket Wall**.*

28 **Blind Pocket Rib** . . . . ⑨ 🔆 🔲   **V1** *5b*
Left-hand side of the slab. Pull on up to the top or escape left at **V0+** *5a*.

29 **Blind Pocket Wall**

. . . . ⑫ ⑩ 🔆 ▮▮ 🔲   **V2** *5c*
Follow the pocketed wall top out for a flutter. **V1** *5b* for the tall.

30 **Blind Pocket Arete** . ⑬ ⑪ 🔆 🔲   **V2** *5c*
Arete and pocket with your feet left of the crack.
The Red Circuit continues on page 396.

31 **Blind Pocket Traverse** . . . . 🔲   **V2** *5c*
Traverse the slab from right to left.

The Ramp Boulder *to the right has two problems that cross.*

32 **The Romp** . . . . ⑫ ⑯ 🔲   **V0+** *5a*
Take a counter-diagonal to the ramp-line.
The Orange Circuit continues on page 396.

33 **The Ramp** . . . . ⑰ 🔆 🔲   **V0** *4c*
Climb the delightful rising ramp. **V3** *6A* with no hands.
The last problem in the Green Circuit.

Northern Peak
Sheffield Crags
Stanage Area
Burbage Valley
Derwent Edges
The Limestone
Central Grit
Staffordshire
South Peak

Northern Peak

Sheffield Crags

Stanage Area

Burbage Valley

Derwent Edges

The Limestone

Central Grit

Staffordshire

South Peak

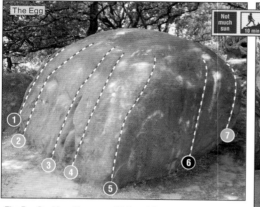

About 40m

N

Pink Slab
p.394

Top Rib
p.392

Blind Pocket Wall
p.395

T Crack

Jerry's Traverse

Serpico

The Egg

Hueco Wall
p.400   P Crack
p.400

Sparrow Block
p.399

Babu Yagu
p.399

Brain Dead
p.399

Hermit's Cave   Fern Hill
p.398   p.398

Slopey Green   Green Slopey

Brian's Private
p.398

The Egg Boulder offers some friction slabs on nothing holds.

1 **Left Egg Arete** **V0-** 4b
Climb the arete on its left-hand side.

2 **Left Egg** **V2** 5c
A similar line to *Left Egg Arete* but without the arete.

3 **Eggy Scoops** **V1** 5b
Centre of the wall, via scoops.

4 **Egg Arete Left** **V2** 5c
Wall just left of the arete, into a scoop.

5 **Egg Arete** **V4** 6B
The arete on its right-hand side rocking over leftwards.

6 **Eggs is Eggs** . . . . **V8** 7B+
The side-wall from poor slopers. **V6** 7A from the higher slopers.

7 **Egged On** **V2** 5c
The right-hand edge, via a flake. *The last problem on Orange.*

8 **T Crack** **V8** 7B
A magnificent problem out of the cave via a T-shaped crack and some slopers. The finishing pull off a rounded pocket is an exciting finale. The blocks down and right and the chipped dink out left are out of bounds. *Photo on page 389.*

9 **T Crack Lite** . . . . . **V7** 7A+
The same problem with the block down and right at the start.

10 **Mr T** **V8** 7B
Starting as for *T Crack*, avoid the break by moving out right to the arete from the base of the 'T' to a powerful finish.

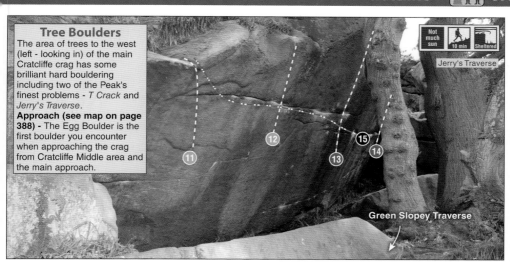

Tree Boulders

The area of trees to the west (left - looking in) of the main Cratcliffe crag has some brilliant hard bouldering including two of the Peak's finest problems - *T Crack* and *Jerry's Traverse*.

Approach (see map on page 388) - The Egg Boulder is the first boulder you encounter when approaching the crag from Cratcliffe Middle area and the main approach.

Jerry's Traverse

Green Slopey Traverse

The leaning wall of Jerry's Traverse is hidden in the trees but is obvious from its distinct line of horizontal cracks.

⑪ Robin Mantel **V1** 5b
Mantel the lip by the 'V' cleft.

⑫ Little Robin **V2** 5c
Lunge from good jugs to the top.

⑬ The Lark . . . . .   **V5** 6C+
Reach from some low slots to edges on the upper wall and so to the top. *The Red Circuit continues on page 398.*

⑭ Optimistic Meg **V4** 6B
The arete from the lowest break.

⑮ Jerry's Traverse   **V8** 7B
Traverse the break from right to left to finish at the V-shaped cleft. The tricky bit is where the break becomes inconveniently sloping in the middle. In reverse it is a bit harder, **V8** 7B+. There and back is worth **V9** 7C.

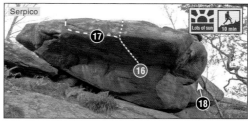
Serpico

On the level above Jerry's Traverse is a block forming a low roof.

⑯ Serpico **V5** 6C
Cross the roof using a small pocket and finish direct.

⑰ Shunting Biscuits . . . .   **V7** 7A+
Traverse left from the lip of *Serpico* to finish via a thin seam.

⑱ Converted . . . .   **V8** 7B+
Right of *Serpico*, past a corner crack. Reach through the roof to a ramp and mantel using the right arete of the crack on the left.

Slopey Green

Jerry's Traverse

Green Slopey

⑲ Slopey Green Traverse . . .   **V5** 6C+
This large leaning block, split by a wide crack, has a low traverse which is, not surprisingly, slopey and green!

⑳ Green Slopey Traverse   **V5** 6C
Just below *Jerry's Traverse* is a boulder with a long rounded edge. Swing along this from left to right. Footless is **V7** 7A+.

Northern Peak · Sheffield Crags · Stanage Area · Burbage Valley · Derwent Edges · The Limestone · Central Grit · Staffordshire · South Peak

The Hermit's Cave

Cratcliffe Crag and The Woods
The base of Cratcliffe Tor has a few good problems, and there are still more in the woodland below. The first problems are on the wall to the right of the Hermit's Cave. **Approach (see maps on pages 388 and 390)** - After crossing the field, follow the path along the bottom of Cratcliffe Tor to The Hermit's Cave.

1 Hermit's Cave Traverse. **V4** *6B*
Traverse from the fence rightwards to a crescent-shaped crack.

2 The Fence. **V0+** *5a*
Pull through the lip into the crack.

3 The Bishop **V3** *6A+*
Link the chipped holds.

4 Chip and Thin **V1** *5b*
Just left of the groove, follow the diagonal runnel.

5 Hermitage Rib **V3** *6A*
Climb the rib between the grooves.

6 Hermitage Hand Jam. **V0+** *5a*
Jam your way up to the rising crack of the route *Hermitage Crack* which continues to the top at VS.

Fern Hill

Fern Hill

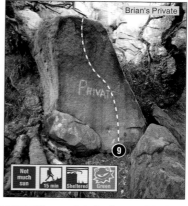

Brian's Private

Two hard problems are below the wall of the route **Fern Hill**.

7 Three Hundred Pounds of Musclin Man
V10 *7C+*
The stark arete. The sitting start is an extra impressive **V11** *8A*.

8 Percy's Cornflake. **V7** *7A+*
The wall starting from a jug on the low break in the cave.

Below the highest part of the crag, featuring the route Suicide Wall, is a block hidden in the woods, facing away from the crag.

9 Brian's Private Arete
V8 *7B*
From a sitting start with your right hand on the arete and left hand on the undercut, dyno up the right arete.

Brain Dead

Babu Yagu

*The **Brain Dead** block is in the jumble of trees below the tallest section of the crag featuring the route Suicide Wall.*

⑩ Near Death Experience V8 *7B*
The wall left of the arete using a rail. No tree allowed at the start.

⑪ Brain Dead ...... V4 *6B+*
The arete can be climbed on either side. **V7** *7A+* from sitting.
The Red Circuit continues on page 400.

Babu Yagu *has two more hard highballs which are directly above the Brain Dead block, just to the side of the descent path from the top of the crag.*

⑫ Babu Yagu V8 *7B*
Follow the break out to the arete to finish.

⑬ Chess Boxer .... V7 *7A+*
The arete on its left - highball and serious, although not as serious as the route **Grimoire** which tackles the right-hand side of the arete at E6 6c, or very highball **V7** *7A+*.

*As the edge drops in height there is the distinctive **Sparrow Block** overhanging arete thrusting out of the foliage.*

⑭ Sparrow/My Best Friend the Watermelon
.... V9 *7C*
A seriously highball arete, but it does get easier towards the top.

⑮ Sparrow Right-Wing V8 *7B*
Follow slopers leftwards to the finish of *Sparrow*.

Below the Sparrow block is a smaller block with a hanging prow.

⑯ Thigh Master .... V5 *6C+*
Climb the prow with some powerful hugging moves.

Sparrow Block

Northern Peak | Sheffield Crags | Stanage Area | Burbage Valley | Derwent Edges | The Limestone | Central Grit | Staffordshire | South Peak

Hueco Wall

The most hidden bouldering. Continue past the end of the crag, the descent gully and the Sparrow buttress for about 50m to the scoop-covered wall. It can also be reached from the top boulders by continuing past the Last Boulder and persevering.

17 Moss Ridge . . . . 🔄 ☐ **V2** 5c
The left arete.

18 House of the Holey 🔄 ☐ ☐ ☐ **V9** 7C
Follow the diagonal ramp as far as the break with feet out right in the crack.

19 Chapel of Rest . . . . . 🔄 ☐ ☐ **V6** 7A
Gain the left-hand of the two huecos and continue to the top.

20 Wish . . . . 🔄 ☐ ☐ **V7** 7A+
Gain the right-hand hueco and exit up and right.

21 No Hueco . . . . 20 🔄 ☐ ☐ **V5** 6C
The traverse is harder than it looks. *Photo opposite.*
The last problem in the Red Circuit.

P Crack

About 30m below Hueco Wall is a low green block.

22 Seventy-Two . . . . . 🔄 ☐ ☐ ☐ **V6** 7A
From under the roof gain the left arete via a big pocket and exit up leftwards.

23 Seventy-Two Direct 🔄 ☐ ☐ ☐ **V7** 7A+
Gain the lip of the roof then finish up the arete.

24 P Crack . . . . 🔄 ☐ ☐ ☐ **V8** 7B
Cross the roof from the back and finish up the short crack.

Northern Peak

Sheffield Crags

Stanage Area

Burbage Valley

Derwent Edges

The Limestone

Central Grit

Staffordshire

South Peak

Northern Peak

Sheffield Crags

Stanage Area

Burbage Valley

Derwent Edges

The Limestone

Central Grit

Staffordshire

South Peak

Tim Parkinson on the thin bit of *No Hueco* (**V5** *6C*) - *opposite* - in the Woods area of Cratcliffe. Photo: Adrian Berry

	No star	✪	✪✪	✪✪✪
VB to V0 Easy to 4c	-	-	-	-
V0+ to V2 5a to 5c	1	3	-	-
V3 to V5 6A to 6C+	-	6	2	-
V3 to V5 7A upwards	-	2	2	2

Close to Cratcliffe and Robin Hood's Stride, Clifftop Boulder offers more excellent bouldering in a pleasant setting. The boulder itself is actually the lower section of a medium-sized edge which overlooks some farmland. There is a small selection of quality problems which should give plenty of entertainment for the dedicated boulderer. The easy problems are little more than warm-ups.

Approach   See map on page 373

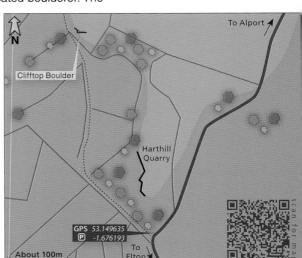

The best approach is from the back road which leads from Elton to Alport. From the west end of Elton turn north along a lane. Park at a bend, on a corner, by a gate and water trough. From here follow the path below a big quarry. Keep on the lower left-hand path and continue around into a field. From here the edge can clearly be seen beyond some trees. To get to the actual block you need to scramble over a drystone wall and an electric (ouch!) fence. Take care with both of these crossings, one for your sake and the other for the sake of the farmer's wall.

Conditions
The traverse should stay dry in heavy rain but it is exposed to the wind. It catches all the afternoon sun and is not particularly green.

Around 50m left of Clifftop Boulder is a low block with a prominent roof.

❶ The Golden Egg . . . . . ✪✪✪ 🔲 **V10** *7C+*
Start by clamping the left arete and side-pull, climb the prow.

❷ Furry Egg . . . . ✪✪ 🔲 **V10** *7C+*
Follow *The Golden Egg* until both hands are on the lip then move up to the boss, finishing out left.

❸ Sheep Dip . . . . ✪ 🔲 **V5** *6C*
The groove just left of the crack, moving out left to a slot before returning back right.

❹ Kong Wubba . . . . ✪ 🔲 **V5** *6C+*
Avoiding the move out left on *Sheep Dip*.

Left of the main buttress is a short block.

5 **Nose on Left** . . . . [ ] **V0+** 5a
The left-hand side of the arete.

6 **Nose Direct** . . . . ⛺ [ ] **V2** 5c
The arete direct.

7 **Right Nose** . . . . ⛺ [ ] **V1** 5b
Rock over from the flakes.

The business section is on the excellent central block with its undercut base.

8 **Emergency Room** . . . . ⛺ 📖 [ ] **V6** 7A
Dyno from the break to the top.

9 **Brad's Break** . . . . ⛺ [icons] [ ] **V5** 6C
Traverse the upper break from out of the cave to the furthest arete and slab. Then climb up to the top.

10 **Brad's Block Traverse**
. . . . ⛺ [icons] [ ] **V8** 7B
Drop down from the start of the previous problem and traverse the lower break. Finish up *Cracker Block*. There's a **V8** 7B+ extension that shuffles along from halfway up *Cracker Block* to finish *Steep Arete*.

11 **Clifftop Arete Left** . . . . ⛺ [icon] [ ] **V7** 7A+
The blunt arete from the low traverse is a little gem.

12 **Middle Wall** . . . . ⛺ [icons] [ ] **V4** 6B
Start as low as you like below the left-hand side of the scooped roof.

13 **Original** . . . . ⛺ [icons] [ ] **V3** 6A+
Start low on the right of the scoop and finish up the flake on the left-hand side of the main arete.

14 **Boing Boy** . . . . ⛺ [icon] [ ] **V6** 7A
The direct start to *Original*.

15 **Cracker Block** . . . . . . ⛺ [icon] [ ] **V4** 6B
From the low jugs on the traverse, pull up onto the slab using a curving sloper.

16 **Steep Arete** . . . . . ⛺ [icons] [ ] **V5** 6C
From sitting, climb the arete.

17 **Rib Arete** . . . . ⛺ [icon] [ ] **V3** 6A
The arete just right from a low start. Eliminating the hold on the left near the top is **Small Rib V5** 6C.

Up and right of the main face.

18 **Arete on Left** . . . . ⛺ [icon] [ ] **V2** 5c
The highball arete.

Northern Peak

Sheffield Crags

Stanage Area

Burbage Valley

Derwent Edges

The Limestone

Central Grit

Staffordshire

South Peak

On the hill on the other side of the road from Cratcliffe is a collection of shady boulders known as Eagle Tor. The land is privately owned and due to the actions of climbers, we no longer have permission to climb here:

"*The landowners of this small bouldering crag have unfortunately stated to the BMC they no longer allow access, and have installed fencing and signs near the rocks. The owners are decent people with a young family and appreciate the quality of the crag. However, large numbers of boulderers, damaged fencing, defecation near the house, toilet paper and noise have eroded their patience. The boulders are located on private land which is effectively the owner's back garden. The owners are within their rights to eject you. The BMC advises climbers to avoid Eagle Tor at present.*"
www.thebmc.co.uk

We have included reference to Eagle Tor only to state that you may not climb here.

Northern Peak

Sheffield Crags

Stanage Area

Burbage Valley

Derwent Edges

The Limestone

Central Grit

Staffordshire

South Peak

Pat King climbing at Eagle Tor. Photo: Adam Long

	No star	✿	✿✿	✿✿✿
VB to V0 Easy to 4c	-	-	-	-
V0+ to V2 5a to 5c	10	4	1	-
V3 to V5 6A to 6C+	12	12	3	1
V3 to V5 7A upwards	4	15	6	4

Stanton Moor is a beautiful place popular with walkers and those in search of stone circles. For boulderers there are a few small spots that have a limited amount on offer however the place is saved from ignominy by having a few hard and extremely high quality destination problems. *Brad's Wall, Brutal Arete, Stanton Deliver* and the *Andle Stone Wall* are all brilliant and are as good as any of their grade in the Peak - shame that they are all **V8** *7B* or above. For those looking for mid-grade problems, there is still a reasonable set to go at but you will need to dot about across the moor and it isn't great for circuits. There is nothing in the Green Zone here.

Conditions
The varied landscape should be able to offer something whatever the time of year. It isn't as exposed as the higher edges but can still catch the wind and some of the boulders will dry quickly. Others are more sheltered in the trees and are slow to dry and get very green.

Approach   Also see map on page 373
The various areas are usually approached from the minor road that connects Stanton-in-the-Peak with Birchover both of which can be reached from the B5056. The normal parking is in a lay-by on the road just north of Birchover although there are other parking spots to the south and by the big quarry. For approaches to the various boulders, see the boxes on the following pages.

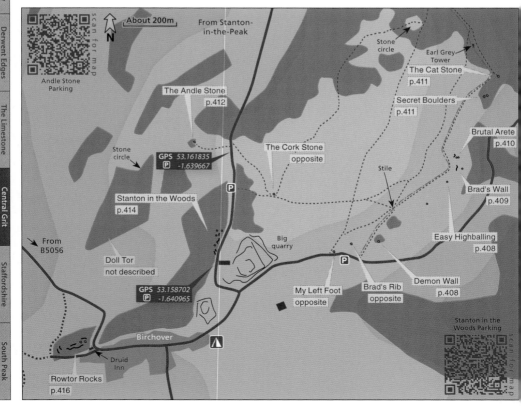

Side tabs: Northern Peak | Sheffield Crags | Stanage Area | Burbage Valley | Derwent Edges | The Limestone | Central Grit | Staffordshire | South Peak

Map labels: About 200m · N · From Stanton-in-the-Peak · Stone circle · Earl Grey Tower · The Cat Stone p.411 · Andle Stone Parking · The Andle Stone p.412 · Secret Boulders p.411 · Brutal Arete p.410 · Stone circle · GPS 53.161835 P -1.639667 · The Cork Stone opposite · Stile · Brad's Wall p.409 · Stanton in the Woods p.414 · Easy Highballing p.408 · From B5056 · Big quarry · Demon Wall p.408 · Doll Tor not described · GPS 53.158702 P -1.640965 · My Left Foot opposite · Brad's Rib opposite · Stanton in the Woods Parking · Birchover · Druid Inn · Rowtor Rocks p.416

The Cork Stone to Brad's Rib

Dotted across the southern end of Stanton Moor are some isolated blocks giving a few good problems. The Cork Stone is a striking free-standing block like a mini version of the Andle Stone. The other two give some steep wall problems.

Approach - You can't miss the Cork Stone 100m along the normal approach from the parking spot. My Left Foot is next to the southern entry to the moor and Brad's Rib is 100m right of here, above a bracken covered hillside.

Rock Quality - The Cork Stone is soft gritstone so please avoid brushing. It is so exposed that it isn't really necessary anyway.

① Tony's Problem **V9** 7C
The middle of the face using a left-facing flake and poor hold for your right. No chips at this grade.

② Dark Rites **V3** 6A
The arete on its left-hand side.

③ Bonsallitis **V6** 7A
The arete on its right-hand side.

④ The Mammoth Book of UFOs
. . . . **V8** 7B
The arete climbed on its left-hand side, from a low start.

⑤ Unidentified Flying People **V9** 7C
An eliminate up the arete on its right-hand. No chips or rungs obviously!

⑥ Corker **V1** 5b
The end of the block using both aretes.

Next to the south entry path to the moor is a block in the trees.

⑦ Overlook Arete . . . . . . **V7** 7A+
The left arete from sitting.

⑧ My Left Foot **V3** 6A
The wall and arete to the slot at the top. **V5** 6C from sitting.

Head along the main path past a rise on the right, then double back right once past it to find Brad's Rib.

⑨ Muhammad Ali **V4** 6B
The left side of the left wall, from sitting.

⑩ Mike Tyson . . . . . **V8** 7B+
From the break, use the thin seam at top to exit.

⑪ Brad's Rib . . . . . . **V7** 7A+
The arete is excellent and has a desperate finish.

⑫ Tom Thumb . . . . **V8** 7B+
The centre of the front face of the boulder.

⑬ Pulling Teeth **V4** 6B
Follow holds up the right-hand side of the front face.

Northern Peak | Sheffield Crags | Stanage Area | Burbage Valley | Derwent Edges | The Limestone | Central Grit | Staffordshire | South Peak

Northern Peak

Sheffield Crags

Stanage Area

Burbage Valley

Derwent Edges

The Limestone

Central Grit

Staffordshire

South Peak

Demon Wall to Easy Highballing

There is a series of miniature outcrops and blocks that skirt the southeast edge of Stanton Moor but are on the other side of the fence so technically are not actually on Stanton Moor.

Approach (see map on page 406) - From any of the parking spots, head towards a stile at the southeast corner of the moor. Cross the stile - the path here connects all the areas on this side of the moor. For *Demon Wall*, head south towards a small copse on a rise. The blocks are on the far side of this. For the other areas, head north along the path. *Rhododendron* is on the right after about 200m, and Easy Highballing about 80m further on. They are difficult to spot from the path but can be found more easily from *Brad's Wall*, if the bracken isn't too high.

In the jumble of green blocks is a massive oak tree sprouting from the rock. **Demon Wall** is just right of this.

① **A Rural Object** . . . . ☐   **V5** *6C*
From a break move out to the arete and a slopey mantel.

② **Demon Wall** . . . . 🔲🔲🔲 ☐   **V8** *7B*
From the break under the arete, use a tiny pocket and the left arete to gain the top. Not a great landing.

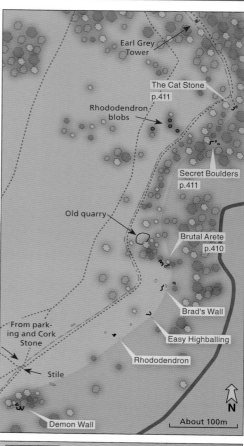

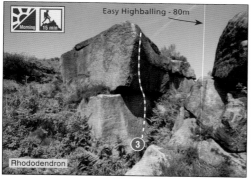

Rhododendron is in a trench which is difficult to spot from above and best approached from Easy Highballing Buttress.

③ **Rhododendron** . . . . . . 🔲🔲 ☐   **V4** *6B*
From the break, move up left to the arete and finish.

Around 50m south of Brad's Rib area is a square block buttress.

④ **Undone Rib** . . . . ☐   **V1** *5b*
The rib at the left-hand end of the buttress.

⑤ **Crack** . . . . ☐   **V0+** *5a*
The steep crack.

⑥ **Make it Stick** . . . . 🔲🔲🔲 ☐   **V5** *6C*
Tackle the block overhang, starting on the lip.

Brad's Wall

The biggest concentration of bouldering along the edge of Stanton Moor is around *Brad's Wall* and *Brutal Arete*. The problems here are certainly of better quality than elsewhere, they even include a few classics.

Approach (see map on page 406) - Follow the path next to the fence northwards. Where it bends around leftwards there is a rounded walnut-whip style block off to the right. Head across to here. *Brad's Rib* is pretty much straight ahead down the slope. You can also reach Easy Highballing and *Rhododendron* by crossing the moor in a southwesterly direction although this will be much harder when the bracken is up.

Chicken Ninja

7 Chick Factor . . . . **V3** *6A+*
The wall left of the arete.

8 Drizzle **V2** *5c*
The wall just right of the arete, starting in the break,

9 Brad's Wall **V9** *7C*
Follow edges up the wall left of the prow to a stopper finish.

10 Rex Regis of Rusticus Res
. . . . **V7** *7A+*
The prow via a mantel on the nose staying left of the arete.

*There are two problems on the **Chicken Ninja** Slab about 30m below Brad's Wall.*

11 Chicken Ninja . . . . **V3** *6A+*
The centre of the slab.

12 Chicken Ginger **V6** *7A*
The right arete on its right, from sitting.

Chicken Ninja - 30m

Northern Peak

Sheffield Crags

Stanage Area

Burbage Valley

Derwent Edges

The Limestone

Central Grit

Staffordshire

South Peak

Northern Peak

Sheffield Crags

Stanage Area

Burbage Valley

Derwent Edges

The Limestone

Central Grit

Staffordshire

South Peak

Brutal Arete

Brutal Arete is said to be one of the best of its grade in the Peak; it is certainly a beautiful line and is now accompanied by Dan Varian's incredible *Stanton Deliver*. **Approach (see maps on pages 406 and 408) -** Follow the path next to the fence northwards. Where it bends around leftwards there is a rounded walnut-whip style block off to the right. Head across to here and then break left down a rough path which leads steeply down to the wall.

❶ **Brutal Arete. . . . .** 　 V8 *7B*
A beautiful problem on side-pulls. Also known as 'Spare Rib' which is possibly a better name since it isn't really very brutal. Follow the narrow rib up to a hard and high finish.

❷ **Stanton Deliver** 　 V12 *8A+*
The stunning groove is sustained and high. Start standing below the rib with your right-hand out on the arete. Aim for the little crack.

Below Brutal Arete is a jumble of big green boulders with a few problems on the south-facing walls.

❻ **Wonder Bra. . . . .** 　 V5 *6C*
From sitting, climb the left arete of the upper block, rocking onto the wall.

❼ **Big Brother . . . . .** 　 V7 *7A+*
The big green arete of the upper boulder climbed on its left-hand side. There is a sit start but the arete is high enough anyway!

❽ **The Cresta Run . . . .** 　 V8 *7B*
Climb the left arete of the lower boulder on its right-hand side then move right with difficulty to join *Little Brother*.

❾ **Little Brother . . . .** 　 V4 *6B*
The right-hand arete of the lower boulder.

❸ **Stanton Warriors .** 　 V8 *7B+*
On the other side of the buttress is a big rounded arete. Climb it on its right without using the crack. At the top move right to the crack to finish. It needs a direct finish.

❹ **The Stanton Shuffle**
. . . . 　 V10 *7C+*
From the small grassy ledge past the start of *Stanton Warriors*, and keep heading left until you're on *Brutal Arete*.

❺ **Mini Prow . . . .** 　 V4 *6B*
The dirty rounded arete to the right of the main buttress.

Secret Boulders

Between Brutal Arete and The Cat Stone is a small collection of blocks with a couple of quality problems.
Approach (see maps on pages 406 and 408) - These boulders are hard to find. Follow the path north past the other areas. After a wooded section on the right is a small clearing. This is roughly opposite some rhododendron blobs on the moor to your left. Head into the woods here to approach the blocks from above. On your first visit, it's probably easiest to find The Cat Stone first, then hike 100m back, turning left when you come to the clearing.

The main block is a short wall with a huge tree sprouting out of the middle crack.

⑩ Secret Places . . . . 〔23〕☐ **V6** *7A*
The prow up the left side of the left-hand boulder.

⑪ Safe House . . . .☐ **V3** *6A*
Span your way up the wall left of the tree.

⑫ Brad's Arete 'The Presence of Absence'
. . . . 〔33〕☐ **V5** *6C+*
The arete just right of the tree on its right-hand side, obviously!

⑬ Sworn to Secrecy . . . . 〔〕☐ **V2** *5c*
The right arete, climbed on its left-hand side.

⑭ Secret Side-wall . . . . ☐ **V2** *5c*
The same arete on its right-hand side.

10m right is a pointed block.

⑮ Classified . . . . 〔〕☐ **V1** *5b*
Climb the steep side of the block.

Down the slope is a free-standing block.

⑯ To Have It All . . . . . . 〔1〕▨☐ **V5** *6C+*
A short problem up the lowest of the boulders. From the low sloper, pop to the lip and mantel.

⑰ The 1980s Were The Days!
. . . . 〔〕▧▨☐ **V6** *7A*
From sitting, traverse the lip left, finishing up the left side.

The Cat Stone

A solitary boulder with a rectangular carving that plays a part in the problems.
Approach (see maps on pages 406 and 408) - Follow the path to a junction and head right to the stone.

⑱ The Plaque . . . . 〔〕☐ **V4** *6B+*
From holds under the roof, climb the arete using the left side of the plaque, and the crack around left. Without the crack is a good **V6** *7A*.

⑲ The Green Man . . . . 〔〕☐ **V9** *7C*
The wall just right of the plaque, starting at the engraving, and jumping up right to a sloper.

⑳ Aces High . . . . 〔1〕▨☐ **V5** *6C+*
Directly to the right (facing the plaque) is a short wall with a prominent break at half-height problem. Start in the break and dyno to the top.

Northern Peak | Sheffield Crags | Stanage Area | Burbage Valley | Derwent Edges | The Limestone | Central Grit | Staffordshire | South Peak

The Andle Stone

This beautifully situated boulder stands alone in the middle of a field, surrounded by rhododendrons. The boulder is exposed to the sun, but sheltered from the wind by the dense surrounding undergrowth.

Approach (see map on page 406) - The stone is visible from the most northerly parking area and is reached by walking across the field.

❶ **Spook**. **V6** *7A*
Span from the break to gain the top.

❷ **No Bull** **V5** *6C*
The arete climbed on its left-hand side.

❸ **Witches' Sabbath** **V4** *6B*
The same arete on its right-hand side.

❹ **Andle Stone Wall** **V8** *7B*
The centre of the wall left of the metal rungs. *Photo opposite.*

❺ **Ron's Problem** **V9** *7C*
An eliminate between *Andle Stone Wall* and the metal rungs.

❻ **Nettle Tea** . . . . **V0+** *5a*
The arete right of the metal rungs.

❼ **Crack and Wall** **V1** *5b*
Follow the crack around the back side of the boulder.

❽ **Mug** **V4** *6B*
Traverse the boulder starting on the shelf right of Nettle Tea. Everything is 'in'.

Northern Peak • Sheffield Crags • Stanage Area • Burbage Valley • Derwent Edges • The Limestone • Central Grit • Staffordshire • South Peak

Northern Peak

Sheffield Crags

Stanage Area

Burbage Valley

Derwent Edges

The Limestone

Central Grit

Staffordshire

South Peak

Ben Meakin, spotted by Neil Amos and his huge shadow, on the fingery *Andle Stone Wall* (**V8** *7B*) - *opposite*. Photo: Paul Phillips

Stanton in the Woods

Though it has been climbed on for years, it is only since 2008 that access has been open to climbers. This is a very esoteric location that has a few good problems and a lot of very green and dirty ones. Most will need a brushing prior to an ascent but after a long spell of dry weather they should come into condition. There are almost twice as many problems here as described on this page but many of these have been reclaimed by the moss and lichen since their first ascent - it is perhaps best to leave them this way.

Approach (see map on page 406) - Park in the car park opposite the quarry site. Follow the large path that leads down towards Birchover, and immediately head right along a small path. Stick close to the wall and you will shortly come to the Leaning Block Boulder.

The furthest block described is **The Big Block**. *It is very green and dirty much of the time. Beyond this are some more developed blocks left for you to explore.*

❶ The Church . . . . 🔲🔲 ▭ **V5** *6C+*
The left-hand arete on its right-hand side.

❷ Green Chapel . . . . 🔲 ▭ **V6** *7A*
The right-hand arete, climbed on its left-hand side. Climbed on the right it is V4.

❸ Appliance Friction . . . . . . 🔲 ▭ **V4** *6B*
The green slab has cleaned spots for your feet.

One of the better problems here is on a diamond-shaped block perched on another block. This one tends to stay clean.

❹ Hangman . . . . . . 🔲🔲🔲 ▭ **V4** *6B+*
From the break where the boulders meet, climb the prow.

High up is a square block with a prominent arete.

❺ The Noose . . . . ▭ **V0+** *5a*
The flake up the left-hand side.

❻ Eliminate Slap . . . . 🔲 ▭ **V6** *7A*
The centre of the wall, without using holds out left or right.

❼ Clandestiny's Child . . . . . 🔲 ▭ **V6** *7A*
The right arete on its left-hand side.

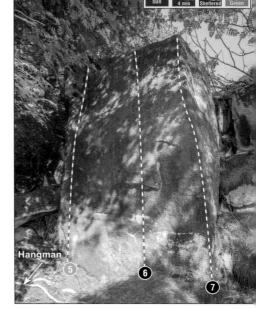

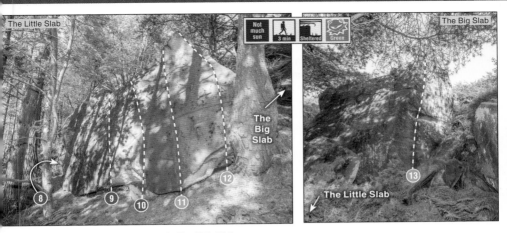

In the central area is a very green slabby block - **The Little Slab**.
This should clean up in drier weather.

8 Prow **V3** *6A*
The prow at the left-side of the slab.

9 Centre Left **V4** *6B*
The slab just left of centre.

10 The Seam **V3** *6A*
Climb the slab to the thin seam at the top.

11 Green Groove **V2** *5c*
The groove and slab above.

12 Right Arete **V1** *5b*
The right arete of the slab.

Above The Little Slab is **The Big Slab** *with one problem.*

13 Big Slab Arete **V1** *5b*
Follow holds up the wall just right of the arete.

The first block reached on the approach is also the most popular one here - **The Leaning Block**.

14 Left Arete **V1** *5b*
The back left arete of the block, from sitting.

15 Centre Wall **V2** *5c*
The wall just right of the back arete, without using the arete.

16 Arete and Mantel **V4** *6B*
The short, hanging arete, with a dirty mantel to finish.

17 Bumlog Millionaire . . . **V6** *7A*
The short wall from sitting.

18 Lean-to **V5** *6C*
The right arete, from sitting.

19 The Knife . . . . . . **V8** *7B+*
The square-cut arete.

Northern Peak · Sheffield Crags · Stanage Area · Burbage Valley · Derwent Edges · The Limestone · Central Grit · Staffordshire · South Peak

	No star	🗍	🗍	🗍
VB to V0 Easy to 4c	-	-	-	-
V0+ to V2 5a to 5c	5	-	1	-
V3 to V5 6A to 6C+	6	6	5	-
V3 to V5 7A upwards	4	7	5	8

This is a lovely little place on a small hill overlooking the village of Birchover. It consists of a series of blocks and caves in the trees with some interesting rock carvings and tunnels. Most of the climbing is in the higher grades requiring some big mantels and long pulls on the steep rounded breaks. There is little here for the Orange and Green Spot climber. The rock can be quite green but the best problems tend to stay clean, be prepared for some dirty experiences though if you are here after long periods of wet weather. It is sheltered from the wind and can be a cool retreat in summer when the trees give plenty of shade.

Access
Rowtor Rocks are a popular venue for all sorts of people wishing to view the caves and the carvings, or just sit on the summit. Please try and keep your impact to a minimum, with respect to the other visitors and the varied plant life. Avoid using too much chalk. Below *Pat's Roof* is a small chicken coup and the owner of this is very sensitive to climbers. Please make an extra effort to keep quiet if bouldering in this area and on no account use this area as a toilet.

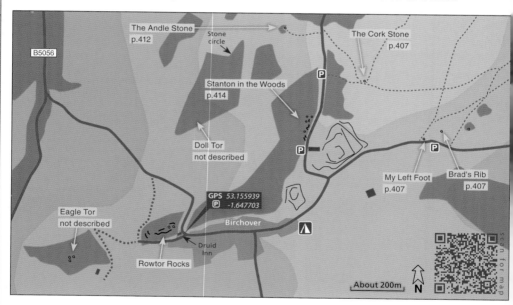

Approach   Also see map on page 373
Birchover is best approached from the B5056 road which runs south from the A6. As you arrive in the little village of Birchover the first thing you will see is the Druid Inn on the right-hand side of the road. Park on the main road in the village, not down the lane by the pub. The rocks are just behind the pub and are reached by a small path down the lane leading up behind it.

Conditions
As illustrated by the crag photos, Rowtor is a very green crag which can make some problems impossibly dirty after the winter. Most of the steeper rock remains clean though and the popular problems tend to clean up relatively quickly without excessive brushing. The area is very sheltered from the wind and will offer shady climbing in the summer due to the tree cover.

Northern Peak · Sheffield Crags · Stanage Area · Burbage Valley · Derwent Edges · The Limestone · Central Grit · Staffordshire · South Peak

Northern Peak

Sheffield Crags

Stanage Area

Burbage Valley

Derwent Edges

The Limestone

Central Grit

Staffordshire

South Peak

Stephen Horne on the lip of *Bus Stop Mantel* (**V8 7B**) - *page 419* - Rowtor Rocks. Photo: Alan James

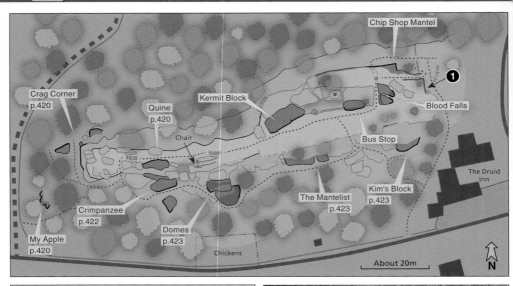

Rowtor Rocks

The bouldering is situated on the hill behind the pub. From the car park walk around the back, to the left of the pub. A path leads back right through the trees and past the first green looking rocks and one large cave. These rocks have not been climbed on and are best left alone since they are the most popular area with other visitors and there is little of quality. Continuing around takes you to a large curving roof carved out of the rock.

Approach - See map on page 416

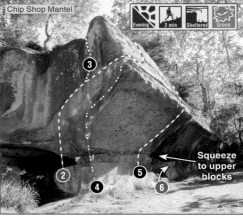

Chip Shop Mantel

Squeeze to upper blocks

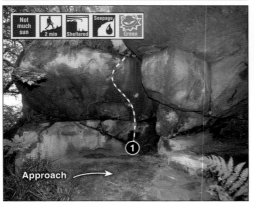

Approach →

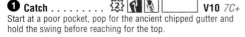

Approaching from behind the pub the first problem you reach is in the east-facing end wall.

❶ Catch . . . . **V10** *7C+*
Start at a poor pocket, pop for the ancient chipped gutter and hold the swing before reaching for the top.

❷ Chip Shop Mantel **V4** *6B+*
Hand traverse the gutter and keep going around the corner. Finish with a scary mantel. All the way to *Pink Lady* is **V4** *6B+*.

❸ The Brazillian . . . **V9** *7C*
From the gutter use a tiny crimp and rock over for the scoop.

❹ The Yoghurt Hypnotist **V8** *7B*
From sitting, and without using the gutter, follow the prow to the lip and finish either up the arete or as for *Chip Shop Mantel*.

❺ Pink Lady . . . **V11** *8A*
Climb the arete left of the cleft from sitting. The jump start is **V7** *7A+*. A static start from standing is **V10** *7C+*.

❻ The Abyss **V5** *6C*
The wide crack, upwards!

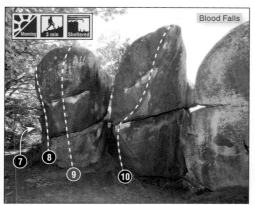

Squeezing through the cleft and following the steps brings you onto a terrace. Continue between the rocks and turn left to find the next problems.

7 Men in Small Cars 🔲🔲🔲 **V8** *7B*
From undercuts, dyno to the top.

8 The Cheek . . . . 🔲🔲 **V6** *7A*
The wall from sitting, eliminating the big holds on *Pig Trough*.

9 Pig Trough . . . . . 🔲🔲🔲 **V3** *6A+*
Climb the nose, starting in the break.

10 Blood Falls . . . . . 🔲🔲🔲🔲 **V7** *7A+*
Start in the low break, move up to a pockety seam and finally make a wild slap for the top. *Photo on page 421.*

Along the path a little further is a bus shelter on the right.

11 Bus Stop Traverse . . . . . . 🔲🔲 **V6** *7A*
Follow the sloping lip from left to right and mantel to finish.

12 Bus Stop Mantel . . . . 🔲🔲 **V8** *7B*
Mantel the roof of this and up the runnel in disbelief!
Photo on page 417.

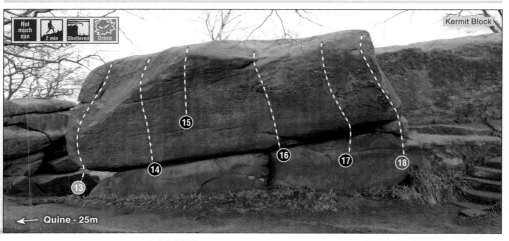

13 Kermit's Ears . . . . 🔲 **V1** *5b*
The left arete of the block. **V4** *6B+* from sitting.

14 Raw Deal . . . . . . 🔲🔲🔲 **V10** *7C+*
Pull onto the slab, using a small pocket.

15 Raw Power . . . . . 🔲🔲🔲 **V8** *7B*
Jump to start, then mantel the top of the block.

16 The Line . . . . . 🔲🔲🔲🔲 **V6** *7A*
From standing reach the small flake and mantel the top. The sit-down is a **V9** *7C*, that was **V8** *7B+* but holds snapped off.

17 Dissolution . . . . . 🔲🔲🔲 **V8** *7B+*
Follow edges up the wall left of the arete.

18 Kermit's Arete . . . 🔲🔲🔲 **V4** *6B+*
The right arete of the block using the arete out right. Without the arete from sitting is a good **V8** *7B+*.

Northern Peak · Sheffield Crags · Stanage Area · Burbage Valley · Derwent Edges · The Limestone · Central Grit · Staffordshire · South Peak

19 Quine V9 *7C*
From sitting, gain the lip and mantel.

20 Cute Bum V5 *6C*
Just right, start sitting at the short arete and pull to and through the lip.

21 Seal Traverse V2 *5c*
Traverse the lip and flop onto the top at the left-hand end.

Hidden away on the far corner are a few more problems for the keen. Follow a path down from the summit (past the Crimpanzee area - next page) and head rightwards under a tall section of crag covered with breaks. Past this and around the corner is a jumble of blocks with a flat block perched on top.

22 The Ornithologist V9 *7C*
This problem tackles this flat roof of the top perched block on its far side, above a very small ledge and a very big drop.

23 I am the God of Hell Fire . V7 *7A+*
The short end of the protruding block.

24 Unleash the Beast . . . . . . V5 *6C+*
Climb the arete on its right-hand side from sitting.

25 Hang 'em High V7 *7A+*
A few metres in front of the edge is a block with a sloping top edge. Start by a crack and traverse the lip up leftwards.

The left-hand branch of the path dropping down from the summit area leads down to the road and around to the left of a tall buttress with a tree in front of a cave.

26 My Buddy the Apple . . V9 *7C*
Manoeuvre over the stacked roofs to join the groove.

27 My Apple . . . . V7 *7A+*
Start up the short arete, use the chips to swing out then pull into the hanging groove.

28 Dass Crab V4 *6B*
The arete on the right of the buttress is highball.

Northern Peak

Sheffield Crags

Stanage Area

Burbage Valley

Derwent Edges

The Limestone

Central Grit

Staffordshire

South Peak

Northern Peak

Sheffield Crags

Stanage Area

Burbage Valley

Derwent Edges

The Limestone

Central Grit

Staffordshire

South Peak

Rob Greenwood on *Blood Falls* (**V7** *7A+*) -
page 419 - Rowtor Rocks. Photo: Alan James

Crimpanzee

Once you drop down from the terrace, there are some green blocks immediately on the left - **Crimpanzee**.

29 Jam and Blast It V5 *6C*
The steep crack.

30 Crimpy Flake V4 *6B*
The thin flake on the left side of the green boulder.

31 Crimpanzee .... V4 *6B+*
The crimpy wall. **V8** *7B+* from sitting.

32 Little Flatty V3 *6A*
Mantel the small flatty.

Just below is a green slab.

33 Slot Slab Arete .... V0+ *5a*
The arete of the slab.

34 Slot Slab V2 *5c*
The short slab with a slot at the top.

Domes

Access Warning - See introduction on page 414 for more information about access to this area.

Above the through cave is the impressive roof of **Domes**.

35 Domes . . . . 🔲🔲 V7 7A+
Climb the prow of the cave. Starting down to the right is **V9** 7C.

36 Pat's Arete . . . . 🔲🔲 V4 6B
The arete forming the left end of the roof on its left-hand side.

37 Pat's Roof . . . . . . 🔲🔲🔲 V6 7A
Gain the lip of the roof from undercuts, and move left to exit up the left arete.

38 Traverse . . . . 🔲🔲🔲 V4 6B+
Traverse the break from the left to finish up *Runnel Rummage*. Alternatively, finish up *Short Sean's Reachy Roof* at **V7** 7A+.

39 Runnel Rummage . . . 🔲🔲 V3 6A+
From the short arete, move out to holds on the lip and finish.

40 Short Sean's Reachy Roof
. . . . 🔲🔲🔲 V6 7A
From the break, gain the break in the nose and pop to the top. **V7** 7A+ without the foot block.

The Mantelist

Kim's Block

Continuing along brings you to the bulging walls of **The Mantelist** *which are usually green and grotty.*

41 Aloha . . . . 🔲 V3 6A+
The arete on its right.

42 Barbapapa . . . . 🔲 V5 6C
Mantel the belly.

43 Barbarete . . . . 🔲 V2 5c
Pull onto the rounded arete.

44 The Mantelist . . . . 🔲🔲 V6 7A
Mantel the blob using the right arete.

Kim's Block *is the last block is just above the approach path.*

45 Exit Stage Right . . . . 🔲 V2 5c
The left side of the wall without touching the capping roof.

46 Kim's Problem . . . . . . 🔲🔲 V8 7B+
Tiny crimps up the wall.

47 Final Thought . . . . 🔲 V3 6A+
The right arete on the left-hand side. Dynoing the top from the flake without using the arete is **V6** 7A.

Northern Peak | Sheffield Crags | Stanage Area | Burbage Valley | Derwent Edges | The Limestone | Central Grit | Staffordshire | South Peak

	No star			
VB to V0 *Easy to 4c*	-	-	-	-
V0+ to V2 *5a to 5c*	1	3	1	-
V3 to V5 *6A to 6C+*	2	4	3	-
V3 to V5 *7A upwards*	-	-	1	-

In the northern edge of Matlock town are two small bouldering spots with a few decent problems. Neither are major venues but they are worth a look if you are in the area. Bank Quarry has one tall block with some good highball aretes. Jackson Tor has a few more problems in the mid grades.

Conditions
Both are in a sheltered settings with plenty of shade from tree cover but they will be green in the winter and slow to dry after rain although they can be sun-traps in dry winters.

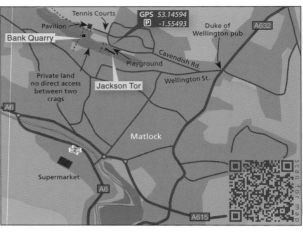

Approach
Also see map on page 373
From Matlock, head north on the A632 Chesterfield Road until you reach Wellington Street on the left (Duke of Wellington Pub on the corner). Turn off and follow Wellington Street for 100m and turn right up Cavendish Road. Continue for 650m and park next to a playground.

For Bank Quarry, walk up the road to two lanes leading off left. Take the second one past tennis courts and continue along a path that leads around the side of the pavilion. Just after the pavilion, a path next to a wire fence leads into the woods. Follow this to the cliff edge. The boulder is down and just to your left.

For Jackson Tor, the broken edge lies directly below the playground. Follow a path around the side of the playground, down some steps and make your way along the base of the edge when you spot it.

Not much sun | 4 min | Sheltered | Green

Bank Quarry
An isolated block with two good highball aretes.

❶ Jimmy . . . . **V4** *6B+*
The left arete has a tricky start (on its left side).

❷ The Chiseller. **V4** *6B*
Follow the chipped holds without using the aretes.

❸ Boulder Arete Left-hand **V1** *5b*
The right arete on its left-hand side.

❹ Boulder Arete . . . . **V0+** *5a*
The right arete on its right-hand side.

❺ Chisel On **V2** *5c*
More chipped holds on the right face of the boulder.

❻ Glory Days . . . . **V3** *6A+*
The left side of the back wall.

15m to the right is a sharp arete.

❼ Back Street Abortionist . . . **V7** *7A+*
Escape right at the break.

Jackson Tor

This hidden spot is prone to getting vegetated. The bouldering is found on two blocks and a quarried bay.

⑧ Moai . . . . 〔icons〕 **V3** *6A*
The arete can be climbed directly via some powerful moves, or by coming in from the right which is more technical.

⑨ Jackson Bollock . . . . 〔box〕 **V5** *6C*
Climb the rib. The arete to the left is **V0-** *4b*.

The next problems are on a pair of boulders below and to the right (looking in).

⑩ Spitting Cobra . . . . . . 〔icons〕 **V3** *6A*
The front of the left-hand block.

⑪ Cottonmouth . . . . 〔icon〕 **V3** *6A*
The wall right of the crack. The crack is **V0** *4c*.

⑫ Boomslang . . . . 〔icon〕 **V2** *5c*
The right arete on its left-hand side.

A little further along are the final problems in a square bay.

⑬ The Arete . . . . 〔icons〕 **V3** *6A*
The left arete finishing on the right. Moving left after half-height to reach the ledge on the left is **V4** *6B*.

⑭ The Sickle . . . . 〔icons〕 **V1** *5b*
Jam or layback up the corner crack.

⑮ Po . . . . 〔icons〕 **V5** *6C+*
The arete direct to a crack. This is the direct start to **The Stride, E1** *5b*.

〔side tab: Northern Peak | Sheffield Crags | Stanage Area | Burbage Valley | Derwent Edges | The Limestone | Central Grit | Staffordshire | South Peak〕

Northern Peak
Sheffield Crags
Stanage Area
Burbage Valley
Derwent Edges
The Limestone
Central Grit
Staffordshire
South Peak

	No star			
VB to V0 Easy to 4c	1	-	-	-
V0+ to V2 5a to 5c	6	4	-	-
V3 to V5 6A to 6C+	11	9	3	1
V3 to V5 7A upwards	3	8	3	3

The picturesque Amber Valley has a series of well-hidden outcrops buried in amongst varying levels of undergrowth. There is nothing of any great quality here but some good isolated problems especially in the harder grades.

Three crags are covered: Cocking Tor, Turning Stone Edge and Bradley Edge - the first two have some decent routes if you want to combine your visit with a bit of roped climbing. They can easily be visited in a single session although prepare to spend a bit of time bashing your way through the bushes on your first visit. The more open Cocking Tor and Bradley Edge suffer from bracken in the summer, whereas it is the dense rhododendrons that smother Turning Stone Edge. The area doesn't lend itself well to a circuit approach.

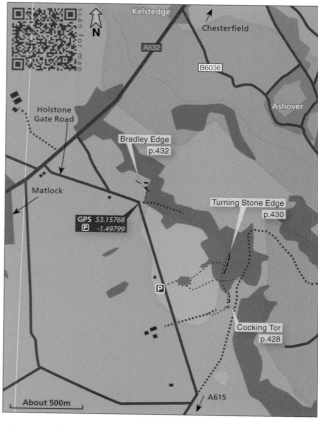

Conditions

The crags face east and northeast getting some morning sunshine. The vegetation will mean that they only dry slowly but also offer shade from the sun in hotter weather, and shelter from any wind. The rock is solid grit although there are some flaky sections on a few of the problems.

Approaches

Also see map on page 373

This area lies 6km east of Matlock. From Matlock, gain Holestone Gate Road from either the A632 (Chesterfield Road) or the A615 (Nottingham Road).

Bradley Edge - At a bend in the Holestone Gate Road a track leads off to towards a trio of mobile telecom masts. Park on a verge nearby taking care not to park on the track itself - as tempting as it might be. Walk down the track towards a green electricity substation until you reach the edge of the woods.

Turning Stone Edge and Cocking Tor - Park off the road directly opposite a distinctive round copse of trees. Follow the track to the copse, then around it to a wood. For Cocking Tor follow the edge of the field to the right and continue into the woods until you reach the path that runs parallel to the edge. For Turning Stone Edge head straight into the woods and continue in a similar direction to gain the cliff edge and a steep descent gully.

Northern Peak

Sheffield Crags

Stanage Area

Burbage Valley

Derwent Edges

The Limestone

Central Grit

Staffordshire

South Peak

Tim Burrows climbing *Swingers Party* (**V8** *7B+*) - *page 432* - at Bradley Edge. Photo: Christian Fox

Northern Peak

Sheffield Crags

Stanage Area

Burbage Valley

Derwent Edges

The Limestone

Central Grit

Cock End

Cocking Tor

A minor edge which has enough bouldering to justify a visit, especially to those operating in the higher grades. It is northeast-facing, so shady in the afternoon. There is a lot of vegetation, so expect it to stay a bit wet after rain. **Approach** - See maps on page 426 and 430.

The first problems are on **Cock End** *block which is reached down a path past Cocking Tor and heading off to the right.*

1 **Cock Jockey** . . . . [ ] **V1** 5b
The left arete of the block.

2 **Cock End.** . . . . [ ] **V5** 6C
The right arete of the block, moving left at the top. Eliminate both the pocket and arete to get a **V6** 7A tick.

3 **Split Tip** . . . . [ ] **V3** 6A
The wall just right of the corner from a sitting start.

The Tor

The Tor *is found at the base of Cocking Tor. The top is distinguished by a plethora of old carvings.*

4 **Jelly Tot Left** . . . . [ ] **V3** 6A+
The eliminate wall just left of the arete.

5 **Jelly Tot** . . . . [ ] **V3** 6A+
The arete.

6 **Jelly Start** . . . . [ ] **V1** 5b
Climb past the port-hole to the ledge.

Just below is a block with a single problem.

7 **Stridesque** . . . . [ ] **V4** 6B
From a sitting start move from flake to flake.

Follow the base of the crag to the right from the Tor (looking in) for 20m and you will reach **The Prow**. There is a pagan cross carved into a block below.

8 Crack 'n' Slope . . . . 🔟 ☐ **V1** 5b
Climb the crack on the left side of the buttress.

9 Sun Worship . . . . 🔟 ☐ **V2** 5c
Starting on the undercuts, follow the left side of the block.

10 Pagan Cross . . . . . . 🔟 ☐ **V4** 6B
Starting on the low flake, follow the right side of the block.

11 Wicker Man. . . . . 🔟 ☐ **V6** 7A
The groove just to the right.

20m to the right is **Monomantel**.

12 Rockabilly Rehab. . . . . . . 🔟 ☐ **V4** 6B+
The line just left of the ramp.

13 Monomantel . . . . 🔟 ☐ **V6** 7A
The clue is in the name.

14 Gravy Boatsmen . . . . . . 🔟 ☐ **V4** 6B
The ramp. Starting directly is worth **V5** 6C.

10m to the right is a fallen block with shot hole marks.

15 The Radjy Man . . . . ☐ **V5** 6C+
Make a sit start under the right arete, then pull left to finish up the left-hand side of the rib.

The next block over is **Salad Fingers**. The best approach is to come down from the top rather than along the base. The block is situated directly below where the main path meets the crag.

16 Salad Fingers . . . . 🔟 ☐ **V8** 7B
The wall left of the arete via slopers.

17 Hubert Cumberdale . . . . . 🔟 ☐ **V3** 6A+
The arete on its left-hand side.

18 Jeremy Fisher . . . . ☐ **V4** 6B+
The arete on its right-hand side.

Northern Peak
Sheffield Crags
Stanage Area
Burbage Valley
Derwent Edges
The Limestone
Central Grit
Staffordshire
South Peak

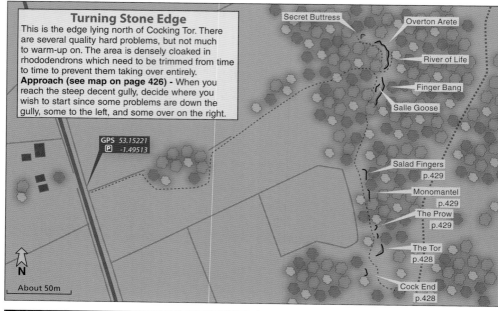

Turning Stone Edge

This is the edge lying north of Cocking Tor. There are several quality hard problems, but not much to warm-up on. The area is densely cloaked in rhododendrons which need to be trimmed from time to time to prevent them taking over entirely.
Approach (see map on page 426) - When you reach the steep decent gully, decide where you wish to start since some problems are down the gully, some to the left, and some over on the right.

GPS 53.15221
P -1.49513

N
About 50m

Secret Buttress
Overton Arete
River of Life
Finger Bang
Salle Goose
Salad Fingers p.429
Monomantel p.429
The Prow p.429
The Tor p.428
Cock End p.428

Salle Goose

Finger Bang

The first problem described is on the top of the crag. Head right from the top of the descent gully along the top of the crag for about 20m - the problem is above a ledge just below the top of the crag.

❶ Salle Goose . .  **V10** 7C+
From good holds in the break, turn the lip and follow the vague rib on poor holds. Easier for the tall.

To reach the next problem, head down the descent gully and turn right along the base of the edge.

❷ Finger Bang . . **V7** 7A+
The roof/prow is followed to a finish on the ledge. Descend either by traversing or jumping. Highball but a padded landing in the bushes.

River of Life

The next problem is found by heading left at the base of the descent gully, at a distinctive, chalky roof.

3 River of Life .... **V10** *7C+*
A highly-rated roof problem on a series of flat side-pulls.

About 30m further along the base of the crag is **Overton Arete**.

4 Gibbon Swing **V6** *7A*
The left arete is climbed dynamically from a sit start.

Overton Arete

5 Underton Arete .. **V5** *6C+*
From sitting, climb the dual aretes.

Secret Buttress

For **Secret Buttress**, *turn left along the crag-top path and tunnel through rhododendrons until you reach a large boulder - the Turning Stone, Secret Buttress lies below.*

6 Jumpin' on an Aphid .... **V3** *6A+*
The left arete of the slab.

7 The Cherub's Bit **V6** *7A*
The centre of the thin slab, starting from the left.

8 Velveteen Whisper......... **V4** *6B*
Continue right from *The Cherub's Bit*, to finish up the right arete.

9 Nice Pinch, Shame About the Ledge
.... **V6** *7A*
Gain the break from undercuts and continue past the eponymous pinch to finish up the arete. The ledge is out.

10 Riding the Stang .... **V7** *7A+*
Starting as for *Nice Pinch*, move right and climb the wall.

11 The Seeker **V9** *7C*
Start with the crescent-shaped ramp and climb the rib to a stretch for the top.

12 Secret Dyno .... **V8** *7B+*
From the ramp, gain the top via undercuts. It was named before the first ascent which turned out to be static.

13 Ha Hoo................ **V4** *6B*
Below Secret Buttress is another block with this problem taking the near arete.

Northern Peak · Sheffield Crags · Stanage Area · Burbage Valley · Derwent Edges · The Limestone · Central Grit · Staffordshire · South Peak

Bradley Edge

Though it isn't much of an edge, the jumble of blocks hold a fair few problems. There are quite a few more problems than described here, but many are poor or suffer from perilous landings.

Approach (see map on page 426) - From the parking, walk down the track towards a green electricity substation until you reach the edge of the woods. Now head left around a jumble of concrete debris and follow the path to the rocks.

The first problems are on the side wall of the first buttress you encounter on the approach.

❶ Vegetarian Cannibal . . 🔲🔲 **V4** *6B*
The off-width crack, starting back in the cave.

❷ Top Dog . . . . 🔲🔲 **V6** *7A*
The centre of the wall, via a dynamic start.

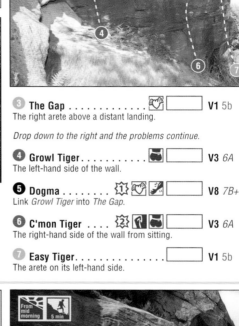

❸ The Gap . . . . 🔲🔲 **V1** *5b*
The right arete above a distant landing.

Drop down to the right and the problems continue.

❹ Growl Tiger . . . . 🔲🔲 **V3** *6A*
The left-hand side of the wall.

❺ Dogma . . . . 🔲🔲🔲 **V8** *7B+*
Link *Growl Tiger* into *The Gap*.

❻ C'mon Tiger . . . . 🔲🔲🔲 **V3** *6A*
The right-hand side of the wall from sitting.

❼ Easy Tiger . . . . 🔲 **V1** *5b*
The arete on its left-hand side.

Head down and continue along to reach the prominent roof.

❽ Morris Dancing . . 🔲🔲🔲 **V5** *6C+*
From the break in the side-wall, gain edges on the nose and use these to finish.

❾ Swingers Party . . 🔲🔲🔲 **V8** *7B+*
From the back of the roof, reach out to the lip and move leftwards to finish up the nose. Direct after the start is **V7** *7A+*. *Photo on page 427.*

Back up on the edge is this hanging arete - just right of a long low roof with distinctive brush marks.

❿ Wet Nettle . . . . . 🔲🔲🔲 **V8** *7B*
Climb the arete from a kneeling start.

Amongst the thick bracken below the edge are a few blocks, two of which have some worthwhile problems. The larger of the two is a few metres below the Swinger's Party overhang.

⑪ Spiderman 2 . . . . **V0-** *4b*
Step onto the left-hand side of the green slab.

⑫ Spiderman 1 . . . . **V0+** *5a*
Step onto a foothold on the right-hand side of the green slab.

⑬ Eat Less Bread . . . . **V4** *6B+*
Starting at the lip, climb the arete. **V7** *7A+* from sitting.

⑭ Three and Four Pence **V5** *6C*
Follow holds up a line left of the centre of the west face of the boulder.

⑮ Two n Six . . . . **V0+** *5a*
Climb the thin wall finishing on the arete of *Probably*.

⑯ Probably **V4** *6B*
The arete is sharp but good.

⑰ Western Front **V5** *6C*
The right-hand arete of the east face of the boulder.

The next boulder is found a little further down and next to the trees and has a '1915' inscription on it.

⑱ Crimp Master Nasty **V8** *7B*
From a low start, follow friable holds up and right.

⑲ The Big Push **V4** *6B*
The right arete on its left-hand side.

⑳ Uphill Arete Right-Hand **V1** *5b*
The left arete of the north side of the boulder. Much easier on the other side.

㉑ Slabby Wall **V2** *5c*
The wall just right.

Northern Peak

Sheffield Crags

Stanage Area

Burbage Valley

Derwent Edges

The Limestone

Central Grit

Staffordshire

South Peak

Northern Peak

Sheffield Crags

Stanage Area

Burbage Valley

Derwent Edges

The Limestone

Central Grit

Staffordshire

South Peak

Mark Katz on *Hats for Clowns* (**V8** *7B*), Eastwood Rocks. Photo: Adam Long

Northern Peak

Sheffield Crags

Stanage Area

Burbage Valley

Derwent Edges

The Limestone

Central Grit

Staffordshire

South Peak

Eastwood Rocks   See map on page 373

The best bouldering in the Amber Valley is at Eastwood Rocks. This hidden outcrop to the east of Ashover has some excellent problems and decent routes as well. Unfortunately the local farmer has not allowed climbing on his land for the last 30 years or so and this is unlikely to change in the near future. No further information is included in this guide. The problems are listed at PeakBouldering.info.

Staffordshire

Iain Hammond on the powerful *Teck Crack Direct* (**V5** *6C*) - *page 448* - on the Lower Tier of the Roaches. Photo: Simon Rogers

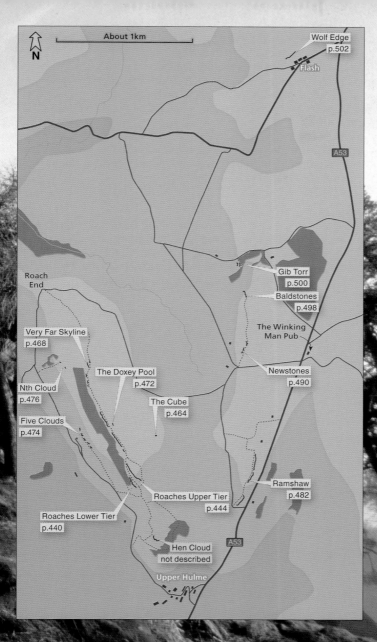

About 1km

N

Wolf Edge
p.502

Flash

A53

Roach
End

Gib Torr
p.500

Baldstones
p.498

The Winking
Man Pub

Very Far Skyline
p.468

The Doxey Pool
p.472

Newstones
p.490

Nth Cloud
p.476

The Cube
p.464

Five Clouds
p.474

Ramshaw
p.482

Roaches Upper Tier
p.444

Roaches Lower Tier
p.440

Hen Cloud
not described

A53

Upper Hulme

Northern Peak

Sheffield Crags

Stanage Area

Burbage Valley

Derwent Edges

The Limestone

Central Grit

Staffordshire

South Peak

	No star	☆	☆☆	☆☆☆
VB to V0 Easy to 4c	13	30	9	-
V0+ to V2 5a to 5c	22	53	18	-
V3 to V5 6A to 6C+	10	32	22	6
V3 to V5 7A upwards	5	10	17	5

The most extensive and best bouldering in Staffordshire is at the Roaches. Most of this is conveniently situated by the popular and accessible end of the crag in boulderfields, or at the base of the edge itself. There are some outlying areas along the Skyline which are covered in a separate chapter - see page 466.

The bouldering on offer here covers all styles but the area particularly excels in blank friction slabs and walls. The rock quality is excellent and exhibits some amazing features in the shape of scoops, grooves, pockets, flakes and aretes. For most climbers the Roaches is as good an area as any covered in this book.

Approach   Also see map on page 437

The Roaches is situated to the east of the A53 between Buxton and Leek. At busy times it is necessary to park at Upper Hulme, on the A53, from where the local council provides a bus link to the crag. At less busy times parking is available on the road below the crag but please park considerately. From here, a well-worn path leads to the two main tiers past the conspicuous Rockhall Cottage (the Whillans Memorial BMC hut).

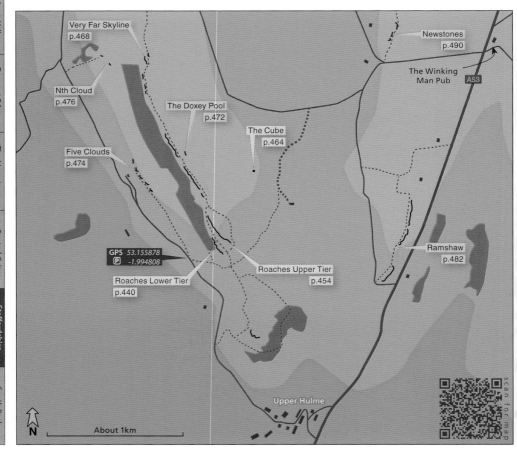

Northern Peak · Sheffield Crags · Stanage Area · Burbage Valley · Derwent Edges · The Limestone · Central Grit · Staffordshire · South Peak

Circuits

This is a great area for circuits although the wet nature of the Spring Boulders means that this area can be off limits during the winter months. We have included a Green, Orange and Red Circuit on both the Lower and Upper Tiers.

Conditions

The area faces southwest receiving the sun from mid morning. It is often beautiful in late-afternoon sunshine. It catches the wind and dries quickly after rain but offers little shelter from bad weather. Most of the rock is clean although some north-facing sections can be green. The area around the Spring Boulders is usually very boggy in the winter.

Access

The moorland in this area is environmentally sensitive. Please keep to the paths described.

Northern Peak

Sheffield Crags

Stanage Area

Burbage Valley

Derwent Edges

The Limestone

Central Grit

Staffordshire

South Peak

Meilee Rafe on *Joe's Arete* (**V3** *6A*) - *page 455* - Upper Tier Boulders. Photo: Adrian Berry

Northern Peak

Sheffield Crags

Stanage Area

Burbage Valley

Derwent Edges

The Limestone

Central Grit

Staffordshire

South Peak

The Spring Boulders

This delightful area has plenty to go at and much of it is of a different character to the problems found elsewhere. Some of the grit is smooth and featureless which makes for full body involvement on some excellent hold-less slabs. The major drawback is the often damp ground that becomes a fully-fledged bog during winter months. It is probably best visited in summer or a dry autumn, but keep away after sustained periods of rain. Concerns have been expressed over the condition of the moss and lichen on these boulders. Please clean the holds very gently and only when necessary, using a plastic brush.

Approach (see map on page 438) - A short stroll from the parking bays on the Upper Hulme Road up through the gated track towards Rockhall Cottage and the Lower Tier of the main crag. The Spring Boulders are to the left of the main track.

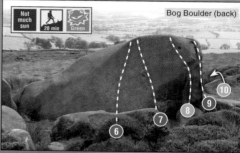

Lower Tier Boulders p.444

Fly Boulder p.443

Shothole Boulder p.443

Ramp Boulder p.442

Little Summit Boulder p.442

Rockhall Cottage

Bog Boulder

Spring Boulder

Little Boulder

Gentle Slab Boulder

About 50m

N

The left-hand boulder is the **Bog Boulder** *which, as expected, is usually above a bog.*

❶ Bog Arete Left . . . . . . ① 🏃 ⬜ **VB**
The arete on its left.

❷ Bog Arete Right . . . . . . ① 🏃 ⬜ **V4** *6B*
The right-hand side of the arete is much harder.

❸ Pebbles and Seam . . . . ② 🏃 ⬜ **V3** *6A*
Up the technical brushed wall, passing the vague slot, to a rounded finish.

❹ Bog Monster . . . . . ③ ① 🏃 ⬜ **V2** *5c*
The featured wall.

❺ Bog Standard . . . . ④ ② 🏃 ⬜ **V2** *5c*
The line of weakness is hard to start.

❻ Bog Slab . . . . ② 🏃 ⬜ **V0** *4c*
The slab up the back side of boulder - no chips.

❼ Poxy . . . . ③ 🏃 ⬜ **VB**
The chipped slab direct.

❽ The Swinger . . . . ⬜ **V0+** *5a*
Gain the hole in the slab either from below, or from the chips.

Not much sun | 20 min | Green

Bog Boulder (back)

❾ Runnel Arete . . . . ④ 🏃 ⬜ **VB**
The featured arete and runnel.

❿ Undercut Wall . . . . ⬜ **V0+** *5a*
The end wall using a side-pull for your right to a rounded top.

Lots of sun | 3 min

Bog Boulder

Spring Boulder

Little Boulder

The Gentle Slab Boulder

Spring Boulder (back)

The **Spring Boulder** *is the middle of the trio and has problems on both sides.*

⑪ Spring Slab . . . . 🔲 V6 *7A*
The brushed line right of the arete.

⑫ C3PO . . . . 🔲 V7 *7A+*
The slightly harder line just right.

⑬ Boba Fett . . . . 🔲 V8 *7B+*
The longest line on this slab is also the thinnest.

⑭ Bobarete . . . . 🔲 V6 *7A*
The big pink arete above the spring.

⑮ Sprung . . . . 🔲 V3 *6A*
From sitting, move left then up. Better than it looks.

⑯ Sprat . . . . 🔲 V0+ *5a*
Starting from the same hold as *Sprung*, climb up and right.

⑰ Sprite . . . . 🔲 V0+ *5a*
The arete on its left.

Little Boulder (back)

The smallest of the trio of is the appropriately-named **Little Boulder** *- see topo opposite.*

⑱ Spring Roll Left . . . 🔲 V2 *5c*
Climb the arete above the spring.
Red Circuit continues on page 442.

⑲ Spring Roll . . . . . . 🔲 V0+ *5a*
The rounded arete on the path side.

⑳ Slabby Seam . . . . 🔲 VB *4a*
The seam is steady.

㉑ Blunt Arete . . . . 🔲 V0 *4c*
The blunt rib right of the seam.

Gentle Slab Boulder

㉒ The Nose . . . . 🔲 V1 *5b*
Up to a small slot from the low slopers.

㉓ Wavy Slab . . . . . 🔲 V0+ *5a*
Smear up the right-hand side of the arete.

㉔ Centre Slab . . . . . . 🔲 V0+ *5a*
Excellent smearing up the centre of the slab.
Orange Circuit continues on page 442.

㉕ Gentle Slab . . . . 🔲 V0- *4b*
Smear up the right-hand side of the slab.
Green Circuit continues on page 442.

The Roaches Lower Circuits
We have included three circuits on the Roaches Lower area. All three include a significant number of problems in the Spring Boulders which tend to be too boggy after sustained periods of wet weather and in winter.

The **Roaches Lower Green Circuit**
A great test of your slab technique. 25 problems with no real highballs make this one of the best starter circuits around.

The **Roaches Lower Orange Circuit**
An excellent all-round circuit with plenty of slabs but also a good number of walls and aretes. 30 problems across the Spring Boulders, the Lower Tier Boulders and the Piece of Mind Boulders.

The **Roaches Lower Red Circuit**
This circuit just ups the difficult level a little from the Orange Circuit but has nothing harder than **V4** *6B+* making this a good target for those trying to push their level a bit. 30 problems across the Spring Boulders, the Lower Tier Boulders and the Piece of Mind Boulders.

Northern Peak | Sheffield Crags | Stanage Area | Burbage Valley | Derwent Edges | The Limestone | Central Grit | Staffordshire | South Peak

Ramp Boulder

Little Summit Boulder

*The lowest boulder is a brick-shaped block with a nice scoop in its east face - the **Ramp Boulder**. It is often very wet.*

26 The Ramp V2 5c
The blank groove is tricky.

27 Rampole of the Roaches
. . . . V2 5c
Gaining the hole and the top.

28 Flakes V1 5b
The flakes on the arete.

There are two problems on the back of the boulder.

29 Pod 'n' Up V2 5c
Go through the left end of the horizontal pod.

30 Mid Pod V1 5b
Up through the middle of the horizontal pod.

*The **Little Summit Boulder** is obvious from its name.*

31 Summit Arete V0- 4b
The slabby arete.

32 Slab to Summit . . . . V0+ 5a
The slab. *Green Circuit continues on page 445.*

The Fly Boulder

Shothole Boulder

Upper Tier Boulders
p.454

The Little Summit Boulder

The Ramp Boulder

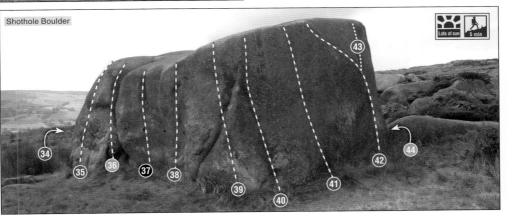

Shothole Boulder

The **Shothole Boulder** is named after the holes in its east face.

③③ Violence . . . . ⑨ 🔖 [ ] **V3** 6A
The scoop.

③④ Impotence . . . . ⑩ 🔖 [ ] **V3** 6A
The blunt nose to the right.

③⑤ Lout . . . . ⑪ 🔖 [ ] **V3** 6A
A balancy start leads to a rounded final pull.

③⑥ Seconds Out . . . . . ⑩ 🔖 🖐 [ ] **V1** 5b
Grope with the classic crack-line.
Orange Circuit continues on page 445.

Shothole Boulder

③⑦ The Grind . . . . 🔖 🪨 [ ] **V6** 7A
Gain the ear to the right and the top direct. Finishing is a
struggle.

③⑧ Skinned Rabbit . . . . . ⑫ 🔖 [ ] **V4** 6B
The shot-holes to a rounded top-out. **V6** 7A from sitting.

③⑨ Sin Left . . . . 🔖 [ ] **V5** 6C+
The blank flake in the square arete is baffling and leads to
another tricky top-out.

④⓪ Sin . . . . 🔖 [ ] **V5** 6C
The right-hand side of the same arete proves delicate.

④① Mr Nice . . . . ⑬ 🔖 [ ] **V4** 6B+
The face, using a chipped foot-hold.

④② Mr Left . . . . 🔖 [ ] **V5** 6C
From the arete step left into the scoop. Then move up to the top.
The direct start awaits an ascent.

④③ Arete on Left . . . . [ ] **V4** 6B
The left-hand side of the arete finishing directly.

④④ Shothole Flakes . . . . 🔖 [ ] **V0+** 5a
Juggy flakes and the other side of the arete to the top.

Fly Boulder

*The next two problems are on the **Fly Boulder**.*

④⑤ The Fly . . . . ⑭ 🔖 [ ] **V4** 6B
The prow. Starting from a low flake is **V7** 7A+.
Red Circuit continues on page 445.

④⑥ The Lurch . . . . 🪨 🤚 [ ] **V4** 6B
Jump to the scoop right of the prow, and top out.

Northern Peak | Sheffield Crags | Stanage Area | Burbage Valley | Derwent Edges | The Limestone | Central Grit | Staffordshire | South Peak

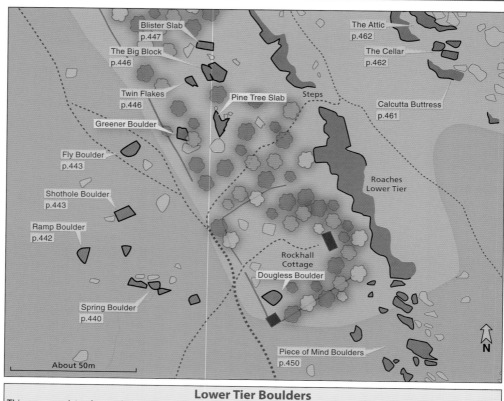

Lower Tier Boulders

This area consists of some independent boulders scattered amongst the pines below the crag, and some steep hard problems on the crag's base. Except the Douglas Boulder, the bouldering covered here takes place on, or below, the left-hand side of the steps which split the crag. The boulders will stay damp and green for long periods during the winter. The crag problems seem to dry more quickly, and not be quite as green. The lower tier is a big sun-trap which can make it a great spot in the winter, but desperately sweaty in the summer.

Approach (see map on page 438) - The best approach is from the parking down on the road. A pleasant stroll up the stony track brings you to the gate of Rockhall Cottage (a BMC hut). Go to the left of the garden to the boulderfield.

Dougless Boulder

Next to the distinctive Rockhall Cottage is a large boulder - **Dougless Boulder**. *There are a few good lines but they will usually need a good brush before you can realistically try them.*

❶ Particle Exchange . . . **V6** *7A*
Start up the crack then step to to the arete and finish up this.

❷ Dougless **V4** *6B*
From the crack, mantel the break and continue to the top.

❸ The Rumour . . . . **V7** *7A+*
The thin wall right of the crack and left of the arete.

❹ Sketchy Rib **V2** *5c*
The arete.

❺ Slabby Arete **V0-** *4b*
The next arete to the right.

Map labels: Blister Slab p.447; The Big Block p.446; Twin Flakes p.446; Greener Boulder; Fly Boulder p.443; Shothole Boulder p.443; Ramp Boulder p.442; Spring Boulder p.440; About 50m; Pine Tree Slab; Steps; The Attic p.462; The Cellar p.462; Calcutta Buttress p.461; Roaches Lower Tier; Rockhall Cottage; Dougless Boulder; Piece of Mind Boulders p.450; N

Not much sun | 8 min | Green

Pine Tree Slab

The first block you reach directly below the Lower Tier is the Easy Slab which can be climbed anywhere with no more than moderate trust in friction. Right of this is **Pine Tree Slab**.

⑥ Boss Slab . . . . ⑪⑬❄ ☐ **V0+** 5a
Climb the slab to the small flake at the top.

⑦ Pine Slab . . . . ⑮⑫❄ ☐ **V2** 5c
Climb the thin slab left of the crack eliminating all big holds.

⑧ Pine Crack . . . . ⑭❄ ☐ **VB** 4a
The crack up the centre of the slab yields willingly.

⑨ Squeezy Slab . . . . . . ⑬❄ ☐ **V1** 5b
Smear up the narrow blank slab. No chips or crack allowed.

⑩ Up Chips. . . . . ⑮❄ ☐ **VB** 4a
The pockets right of the crack and slab.

⑪ Arch. . . . . ⑭⑯❄ ☐ **V0+** 5a
The slab past the arch.

⑫ Pine Arete. . . . . . . ⑮⑰❄ ☐ **V0** 4c
The arete on the left-hand side is intricate.

⑬ Pine Arete Right . . . . ⑱❄ ☐ **V0** 4c
The arete and slab on its right-hand side is excellent. The slab without the arete is a poor eliminate, **Green Slab, V3** *6A+.*

⑭ Pine Martin. . . . . ⑯⑯⑲❄ ☐ **V0+** 5a
A super little problem up the flake.
Orange Circuit continues on page 446 and Green Circuit continues on page 447.

Towards the wall are two low boulders, one of which has a steep green face with a flake running across it - the **Greener Boulder**.

⑮ Greener Traverse . ⑰❄ ☐ **V4** *6B*
Traverse the rail from left to right and lurch to the top. Just the rail in reverse is **V2** 5c. Can be climbed from sitting at **V4** *6B+.*
Red Circuit continues on page 446.

⑯ Greener Mantel . . . . . ❄ ☐ **V3** *6A*
The final move of the traverse on its own.

⑰ Greenerete . . . . . ❄ ☐ **V4** *6B*
The arete from a sitting start.

Greener Boulder

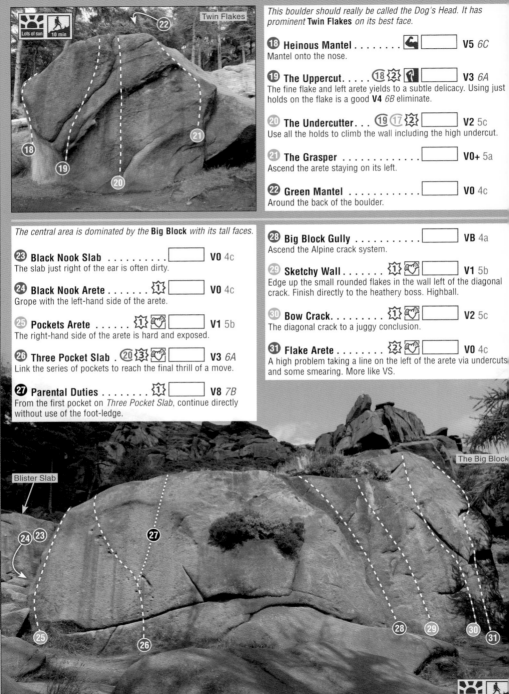

Twin Flakes

This boulder should really be called the Dog's Head. It has prominent **Twin Flakes** on its best face.

18 Heinous Mantel **V5** *6C*
Mantel onto the nose.

19 The Uppercut. . . . . 18 . . **V3** *6A*
The fine flake and left arete yields to a subtle delicacy. Using just holds on the flake is a good **V4** *6B* eliminate.

20 The Undercutter. . . 19 17 . . **V2** *5c*
Use all the holds to climb the wall including the high undercut.

21 The Grasper . . . . **V0+** *5a*
Ascend the arete staying on its left.

22 Green Mantel **V0** *4c*
Around the back of the boulder.

The central area is dominated by the **Big Block** with its tall faces.

23 Black Nook Slab **V0** *4c*
The slab just right of the ear is often dirty.

24 Black Nook Arete **V0** *4c*
Grope with the left-hand side of the arete.

25 Pockets Arete **V1** *5b*
The right-hand side of the arete is hard and exposed.

26 Three Pocket Slab . 20 . . **V3** *6A*
Link the series of pockets to reach the final thrill of a move.

27 Parental Duties **V8** *7B*
From the first pocket on *Three Pocket Slab*, continue directly without use of the foot-ledge.

28 Big Block Gully . . . . **VB** *4a*
Ascend the Alpine crack system.

29 Sketchy Wall **V1** *5b*
Edge up the small rounded flakes in the wall left of the diagonal crack. Finish directly to the heathery boss. Highball.

30 Bow Crack. **V2** *5c*
The diagonal crack to a juggy conclusion.

31 Flake Arete **V0** *4c*
A high problem taking a line on the left of the arete via undercuts and some smearing. More like VS.

Blister Slab

The Big Block

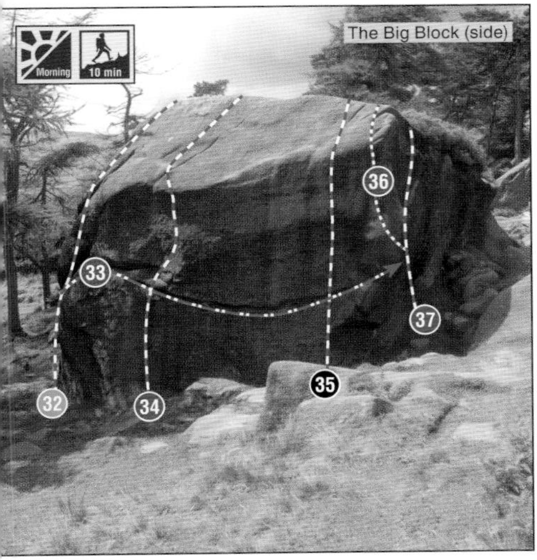
The Big Block (side)
Morning
10 min
32
33
34
35
36
37

㉜ **Big Block Arete** . . . . ☐ **V0+** 5a
The right-hand side of *Flake Arete*. A stiff start if you go direct.

㉝ **The Undercut Traverse**
. . . . ㉑ ☆1 💪 ☐ **V4** *6B*
Traverse along the break from left to right, or right to left.
Red Circuit continues on page 448.

㉞ **Stretch and Mantel** ☆3 ▮ ♡ ☐ **V5** *6C*
Yawn up to the ledge over the lip of the wall from the undercut break - dynamic for many. A naughty mantel remains.

㉟ **Undercut Dyno**. . . . ☆2 ✋ ♡ ☐ **V8** *7B*
Gain the boss on the lip from the break via a very big dyno.

㊱ **Stretch Left**. . . . . ☆1 ▮ ♡ ☐ **V4** *6B*
From the left-hand side of the arete gain a ledge on the upper slab, from the arete.

㊲ **Classic Arete**. . . . . ⑱ ⑳ ☆2 ☐ **V0** 4c
Climb the juggy flakes on the right side of the arete.

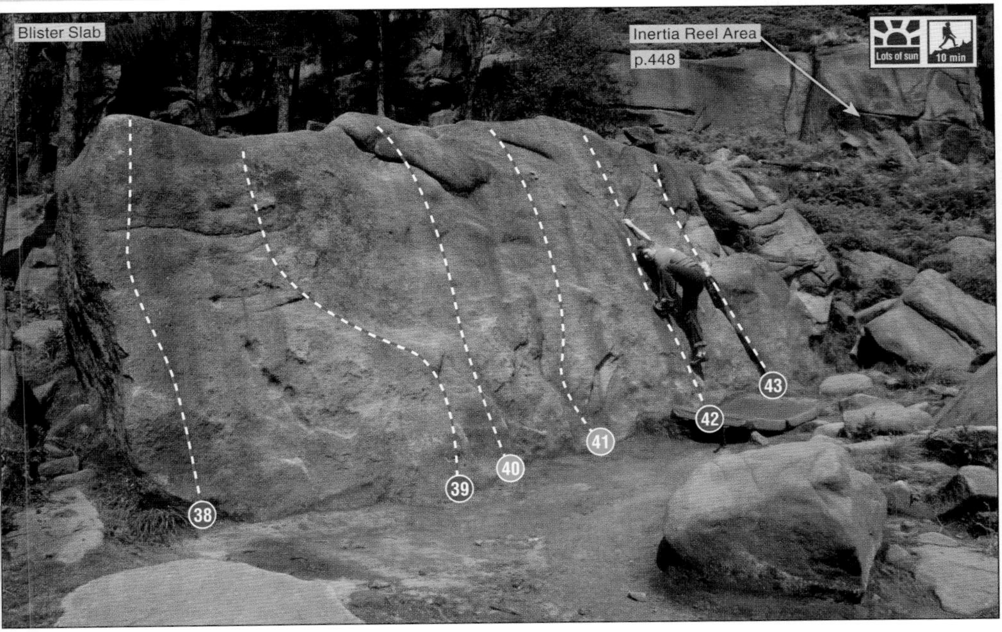
Blister Slab
Inertia Reel Area
p.448
Lots of sun
10 min
38
39
40
41
42
43

Blister Slab *is located just behind The Big Block.*

㊳ **Left Slab**. . . . . ⑲ ㉑ ☆1 ☐ **V0** 4c
Climb the minute arete.

㊴ **Slab 2** . . . . ㉒ ☆1 ☐ **VB** 4a
The slab to the right, trending left.

㊵ **Blister's Sister**. . . . ⑳ ㉓ ☆1 ☐ **V0+** 5a
Gain some small flakes below the top of the slab.

㊶ **Blister Slab**. . . ㉑ ㉔ ☆2 ▮ ☐ **V0+** 5a
Rock up on edges to gain the blisters. Harder for the short.
Orange Circuit continues on page 450.

㊷ **Back Slab Right**. . . . . . ㉕ ☆1 ☐ **V0-** 4b
A delicate wall left of the crack.
The last problem in the Green Circuit.

㊸ **Block and Crack**. . . . . ☐ **VB**
The crack is an easy way up or down.

Northern Peak

Sheffield Crags

Stanage Area

Burbage Valley

Derwent Edges

The Limestone

Central Grit

Staffordshire

South Peak

Inertia Reel Area

The left-hand end of the Lower Tier, directly above the Lower Tier Boulders, offers some hard problems at the base of the crag including one of the Peak's most famous traverses - shame it is so hard!
Approach - See map on page 438.

1 Apache Dawn ... **V7** 7A+
Scary pebble-pulling above the horizontal pod.

2 Catastrophe Internationale
.... **V6** 7A
The slab above the right-hand end of the pod is another highball frightener that sees few ascents.

3 Bareback Rider ..... **V4** 6B+
The arete on its right-hand side and the high slab above.

4 Traverse of Man **V3** 6A
Start in the cave and traverse left. Keep going around the corner and all the way across to the holly bush. Easy bits connected by hard moves.

5 Ascent of Man Start ㉒ **V3** 6A+
Start low in the back of the cave and climb up to good round jugs below the flake proper.

6 Ascent of Woman Start
.... ㉓ **V4** 6B+
Start low in the cave and reach the shallow pocket on the right. Link this to the flaky ramp and the break above.
Red Circuit continues on page 450.

The main buttress has a low line of sloping holds running all the way across it.

7 Inertia Reel Traverse
.... **V12** 8A+
Moffatt's stunning traverse. From the start of the low shelf travel desperately rightwards all the way to the end of the wall.

8 Ant Lives **V6** 7A
A celebration of obscure gritstone technique. From the shelf reach the next ledge above using a selection of body parts.

9 Inertia Reel ..... **V7** 7A+
Attain a small flake and the rounded ledges from a minute undercut in the low break. Escape off the upper ramp to the right, or jump. The sit-start is **Turbo, V10** 7C+.

10 Teck Crack Direct . **V5** 6C
Traverse the shelf rightwards and power up to the sloping top. The low start, with feet on the back wall is **Thud, V8** 7B.
Photo on page 436.

⓫ Teck Crack Superdirect ☼ 🔧 ☐ **V8** *7B+*
Reach the same seam as for *Teck Crack Direct* from the poor
crack and pebbles below. A hideous pull.

⓬ The Dignity of Labour . ☼ 🖐 ☐ **V6** *7A*
Although accepted as a route, this micro-gem is undoubtedly
an extended boulder problem. From the boulder, reach the
horizontal break and lurch to a grisly rounded finale.

*The next four problems are on the steep buttress right of The
Inertia Reel Traverse.*

⓭ A Modest Proposal . . . . ☐ **V6** *7A*
From the break, gain and finish up the steep prow. Alternatively
jump from the boulder to gain the nose - **Skydivin'**, **V5** *6C*.

⓮ Mushin . . . . ☼ 🔧 ✊ ☐ **V10** *7C+*
Use a glued undercut above the break to reach a cluster of
shallow pockets. Use these to gain the base of a hanging
groove. Finish up this.

⓯ The Boozy Traverse . . ✊ 🦶 ☐ **V5** *6C+*
Traverse the low break below the bulging wall and grooves of
Lightning Crack.

⓰ Pindles Numb . . . ☼ 🖌 🖐 ☐ **V5** *6C*
A highball hand traverse to gain the groove that *Mushin* gets to
from below.

*Matinee
(HVS)*

*Via Dolorosa
(VS)*

There is one worthwhile problem on the main routes section of
the edge. It is at the base of Raven Rock - the highest buttress
at The Roaches which is home to the classic route *Valkyrie*.

⓱ The Gutter . . . . ☼ 🔲 ☐ **V7** *7A+*
From the back of the cave follow the crack and arete to the
ledge. The side-wall to the right, including the heel-hook, is out.
Using the heel-hook drops the grade to **V5** *6C+*.

Northern Peak

Sheffield Crags

Stanage Area

Burbage Valley

Derwent Edges

The Limestone

Central Grit

Staffordshire

South Peak

Piece of Mind Boulders

The Piece of Mind area has a small set of described problems but there is plenty more to be found here for those who wish to explore amongst the jumble of blocks. It gets lots of sun and can be quieter than other areas. The rock will dry quickly but is exposed to any wind.
Approach (see maps on pages 438 and 444) - Walk under the Lower Tier to just past the trees and holly bushes and the boulderfield is ahead. Alternatively you can reach it directly from the main approach by taking a path to the right of Rockhall Cottage.

❶ Cottage Arete . . . . . . 22 ⛰   **V2** 5c
Next to the wall of Rockhall Cottage is this short arete. Climbed on its right at this grade. **V1** 5b on its left-hand side.

❷ Sketchy Arete **V2** 5c
The narrow arete on the block a little down the hill.

❸ Adventurous Arete **V3** 6A
A square arete above a nasty sloping landing.

❹ Open Bum Cleft . . . 24 ⛰   **V3** 6A
A little to the right (looking up at the crag) is an open scoop.

Back up on the main line of the crag is a steep crack-line.

❺ The Jams . . . . ⛰   **V2** 5c
The crack-line on the left.

❻ Hanging Arete **V1** 5b
The left side of the slab is exposed.

❼ The Teacup . . . . 23 ⛰   **V1** 5b
Follow the flakes up the slab.

The Square Room (page 452) is just behind this slab.

❽ Grewsome . . . . . . 25 ⛰   **V4** 6B
Hang the flat jug and mantel over the bulge. *Photo on page 31.*

❾ Twisted Crack . 26 ⛰   **V4** 6B
The crack climbed any way you can.

❿ Off Work . . . . . 27 24 ⛰   **V2** 5c
Struggle up the off-width crack. Sticking to the left arete is **Left Off, V3** 6A.

⓫ Flake and Arete . 28 25 ⛰   **V2** 5c
The arete with a flake. The sit-start from slopey holds is a soft **V6** 7A.

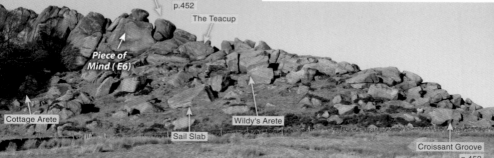

Square Room p.452

The Teacup

Piece of Mind (E6)

Cottage Arete

Sail Slab

Wildy's Arete

Croissant Groove p.452

Square Room
p.452

Wildy's Arete

12 Wildy's Arete..... V2 6a
The arete on its left-hand side. **V4** *6B* from sitting.

13 Wildy's Right....... V3 6A
The arete on its right-hand side is excellent. *Photo on page 453.*
The last problem in the Red Circuit.

14 Slab and Crack V0- 4b
The slab, finishing left of the crack. It is possible to finish on the
left with a rock-over at **V1** 5b.

15 Jobby............... V0- 4b
The right arete of the boulder.

16 Micky............... VB 4a
On the back of the *Slab and Crack* boulder is a thin crack.

*Over to the right is a trench formed by boulders, the following
problems are on the left side of the trench.*

17 Scab V2 5c
The crack, from a sitting start.

18 Buster V4 6B
From the start of *Scab*, move up and right, then follow slopers
along the top of the boulder until it is possible to top out.

Down below Slab and Crack is the easy-angled **Sail Slab**.

19 Sail Slab............. VB
The left-side of the slab.

20 Mantel and Pocket ...... VB 4a
The slab 2m left of the right arete.

21 Sail Arete .... VB 4a
The right, then left side of the arete.

22 Sail Rib .... V0+ 5a
The rib on the side of the slab.

23 Tittersworth Rib..... V2 5c
The arete of the next boulder up the hill. Same grade on its left
and right. The right side from sitting is **V4** *6B*.

24 Chips Ahoy V1 5b
The centre of the wave slab has a rounded and high finish.
The last problem in the Orange Circuit.

Sail Slab

Northern Peak | Sheffield Crags | Stanage Area | Burbage Valley | Derwent Edges | The Limestone | Central Grit | Staffordshire | South Peak

Square Room

There are some outlying problems. The **Square Room** is best approached by walking under The Teacup Slab (page 450).

25 Dropsy . . . . ☆ ▢ **V0+** 5a
The ramp above a big drop.

26 The Blob . . . . ▢ **V1** 5b
Climb the rounded arete to a blob feature.

27 Crinkles Wall . . . ☆ ▢ **V5** 6C+
A desperately thin wall.

28 Rock Room Slab . . . . ☆ ▢ **V1** 5b
The smearing slab opposite *Crinkles Wall*.

29 Annie's Egg . . . . . . ☆ ▢ **V5** 6C+
Jump onto the slab and follow the vague groove to the top.

The following problems are found at the lowest part of the Piece of Mind boulderfield.

30 Ramp . . . . ▢ **V0+** 5a
The short wall.

31 Potty . . . . ▢ **V0** 4c
The scoop.

32 Croissant Groove . . . . ▢ **V2** 5c
The groove on the lowest boulder.

Croissant Groove

Square Room

The Teacup
p.450

Cottage Arete
p.450

Sail Slab
p.451

Wildy's Arete
p.451

Croissant Groove

Northern Peak

Sheffield Crags

Stanage Area

Burbage Valley

Derwent Edges

The Limestone

Central Grit

Staffordshire

South Peak

Claire Carter on *Wildy's Right* (**V3** *6A*) - *page 451* - on the Piece of Mind Boulders. Photo: Alan James

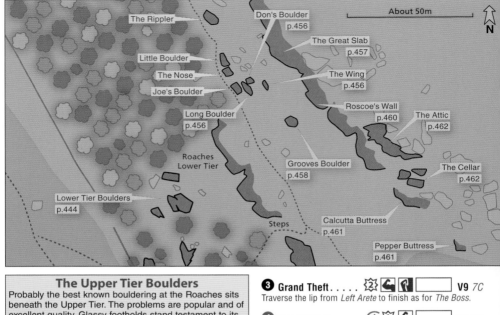

The Upper Tier Boulders

Probably the best known bouldering at the Roaches sits beneath the Upper Tier. The problems are popular and of excellent quality. Glassy footholds stand testament to its popularity and sometimes the usual gritstone friction is absent. The rock is solid and well-climbed on. There are few problems with dirty holds or green rock and due to its exposed nature the boulders dry very quickly.

Approach (see map on page 438) - From the parking area walk up past Rockhall Cottage and onto the steps which rise to the Upper Tier.

❶ Back Arete . . . . ☐ **VB**
The small arete on the back of the boulder.

❷ Left Arete . . . . ① ⑪ ☐ **V0** 4c
The left arete on its right-hand side.

❸ Grand Theft . . . . . ☆ ◣ ◪ ☐ **V9** 7C
Traverse the lip from *Left Arete* to finish as for *The Boss*.

❹ The Rippler . . . . . . ① ⑪ ◣ ☐ **V3** 6A
Climb up the slab, using a ripple to start. The sit-start is **V6** 7A.

❺ The Boss . . . . ☆ ◣ ☐ **V5** 6C
From a low round hold surmount the lip and the upper slab. The sit-start is **Lip Service**, **V7** 7B+.

The **Little Boulder** *has two easy offerings.*

❻ Nosy . . . . ② ☐ **VB** 4a
Climb through the nose.

❼ Upright . . . . ③ ☐ **VB** 4a
Climb up and right.

The Nose *is a slightly disappointing boulder opposite the famous Joe's Arete.*

8 Crimpy Wall . . . . . ① ④ ⚄ [　] **V0+** 5a
Climb the left wall on its right-hand side. Further left is **VB**.

9 Nose Arete . . . . . . ② ⑤ ⚄ [　] **V0+** 5a
The nose on its left side.

10 Nose Arete Right . . . . [　] **V2** 5c
The nose on its right side is harder but not as good as you tend to get pushed left onto the other side.

11 Nose Scoop . . . . [🔲] [　] **V3** *6A*
Mantel just right of the arete.

12 Nose Mantel . . . . [　] **VB**

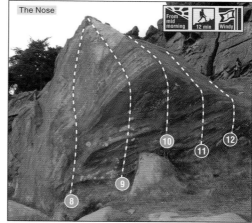

The Nose

much easier mantel on the right-hand side of the slab.

Joe's Boulder

3 The Bishop's Move . . . ⑥ ⚄ [　] **V0-** 4b
The big holes on the flat wall.

4 Joe's Arete . . . . ② ⚄ [　] **V3** *6A*
A classic rite of passage problem. The polished arete goes in many ways. It can look easy but it always feels sketchy at the top. *Photo on pages 12 and 439.*

5 Pink Wall Eliminate . . ⚄ [🏳] [　] **V6** *7A*
The blank wall to the right of the arete is excellent.

The **Roaches Upper Green Circuit**
A relatively short circuit considering how much bouldering there is on the Upper Tier. 18 problems including six at **V0+** 5a. and it finishes up in the Cellar.

The **Roaches Upper Orange Circuit**
a 24-problem circuit with problems on all areas including a few classic problems up to **V2** 5c.

16 Pink Wall . . . . ③ ③ ⚄ [🏳] [　] **V1** 5b
The wall just left of the holes, without using the holes.
Red Circuit continues on page 456.

17 Joe's Portholes . . . ④ ⑦ ⚄ [　] **V0+** 5a
Use both holes to gain the top. Direct from a sit start at the low hole, without the flakes on the left or the top hole, is **Mean Ol' Bastard, V8** *7B*. A dyno from the low hole to the top is **Apocalypse Now, V7** *7A+*.
Green and Orange Circuits continue on page 456.

18 Joe's Right . . . . [🏳] [　] **V1** 5b
A one-move-wonder up the sharp flake to the top.

The **Roaches Upper Red Circuit**
Another relatively easy Red Circuit with 25 problems but nothing more than **V4** 6B+. Add the extra problems from the Orange Circuit and you have a great work out.

Northern Peak · Sheffield Crags · Stanage Area · Burbage Valley · Derwent Edges · The Limestone · Central Grit · Staffordshire · South Peak

Northern Peak
Sheffield Crags
Stanage Area
Burbage Valley
Derwent Edges
The Limestone
Central Grit
Staffordshire
South Peak

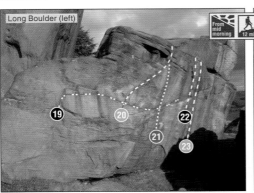

Long Boulder (left)

From mid morning | 12 min | Windy

Long Boulder (right)

*The **Long Boulder** is found just behind Joe's Boulder, in front of the Great Slab area of the Upper Tier.*

⑲ Nadin's Traverse . . . . | **V6** *7A*
Traverse right to finish up *Pixie*, or continue to finish as for *Reg* or *The Staircase* at **V7** *7A+*, or really go for it and link into *Cooper's Traverse* at **V8** *7B*.

⑳ Jug Up . . . . | **V0+** 5a
Pull up the short wall rightwards on big holds.

㉑ Glued Up . . . . | **V3** *6A*
The wall from the glued-on hold. Dynoing to the top from the glued-on hold is **Glued-Up Dyno, V8** *7B*.

㉒ Reg . . . . | **V6** *7A*
Another dyno, starting from the sloping edges.

㉓ Pixie . . . . | **V2** 5c
The same place as *Reg* but use the side-pull.

㉔ The Staircase . . . . | **V2** 5c
The stepped flakes. Start low to add a bit extra.

㉕ Cooper's Traverse . | **V3** *6A+*
Traverse the lip until the difficulties run out.

㉖ Long Boulder Mantel . . . . | **V0** 4c
The bulge from a sitting start.

Don's Boulder

To mid afternoon | 12 min | Windy

*The first three problems are on **Don's Boulder**, just between Long Boulder and Great Slab.*

㉗ Don's Crack. . . . . | **V1** 5b
The prominent crack.

㉘ Don's Eliminate . . . . | **V4** *6B*
The wall just right, without using the crack or the arete.

㉙ Don's Arete . . . . | **V0-** 4b
The right arete.

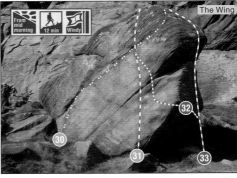

The Wing

From mid morning | 12 min | Windy

*Right of Don's Boulder is **The Wing**.*

㉚ Winger . . . . | **V2** 5c
Climb diagonally across the face to finish up the right arete.

㉛ Wing Wong . . . . . . | **V2** 5c
The face just left of the arete via breaks. *Photo on page 459.*

㉜ Broken Wing . . . . | **V5** *6C+*
From a position hanging from a slot, move out left to the arete, and climb to the break. Finish as for *Wing Wong*.

㉝ The Beak . . . . | **V4** *6B*
Pull steeply up the edge and continue up the nose.

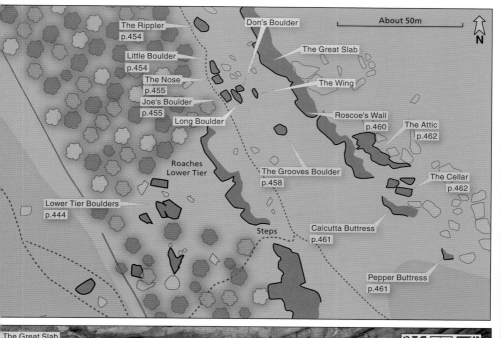

The Great Slab

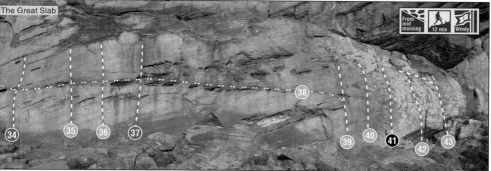

The following problems are **The Great Slab** at the base of the main edge, below the imposing roof of *The Sloth*.

④ Popper . . . . ⑨ 🌣 ☐ **V0-** 4b
Follow three pockets up the left side of the slab.

⑤ Slab Dancer . . . . . ⑨ ⑩ 🌣 ☐ **V0+** 5a
Climb the wall using the slot. Without the slot is **Flap Dancer,** ⑧ 7B.

⑥ The Lintel . . . . ⑨ ⑩ 🌣 ☐ **V2** 5c
Climb the wall above the ledge with a stretch to finish.

⑦ Cheesy Moon . . . . . . ⑪ 🌣 ☐ **V0-** 4b
The wall above the pod.

⑧ Long Traverse . . . . 🖉 ☐ **V1** 5b
Traverse from right to left. Continue to your heart's content.

㊴ Goat's Gruff . . . . . ⑪ ⑫ 🌣 ☐ **V0+** 5a
Follow the pockets up the wall.
Green Circuit continues on page 458.

㊵ Goat's Eye . . . . ⑩ ⑫ 🌣 ☐ **V2** 5c
Climb the slab above a low pocket. From a sit-start on the pocket it is **V4** 6B.
Red and Orange Circuits continue on page 458.

㊶ The Monodoigt . . . . . 🌣 🪝 ☐ **V8** 7B+
The wall via the monodoigt pocket.

㊷ The Flake Museum . . . 🌣 🖼 ☐ **V2** 5c
The wall above a small cutaway.

㊸ Scallop . . . . 🖼 ☐ **V0+** 5a
The flakes at the right end of the wall above a bad landing.
Escape is left.

Northern Peak · Sheffield Crags · Stanage Area · Burbage Valley · Derwent Edges · The Limestone · Central Grit · Staffordshire · South Peak

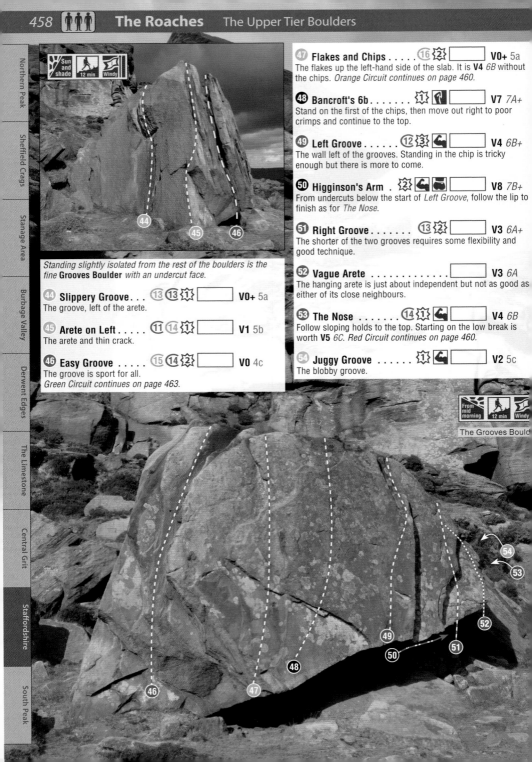

47 Flakes and Chips . . . . . ⑯ ✡ [____] **V0+** 5a
The flakes up the left-hand side of the slab. It is **V4** 6B without the chips. *Orange Circuit continues on page 460.*

48 Bancroft's 6b . . . . ✡ ▣ [____] **V7** 7A+
Stand on the first of the chips, then move out right to poor crimps and continue to the top.

49 Left Groove . . . . . . ⑫ ✡ ◀ [____] **V4** 6B+
The wall left of the grooves. Standing in the chip is tricky enough but there is more to come.

50 Higginson's Arm . ✡ ◀ ▣ [____] **V8** 7B+
From undercuts below the start of *Left Groove*, follow the lip to finish as for *The Nose*.

51 Right Groove . . . . ⑬ ✡ [____] **V3** 6A+
The shorter of the two grooves requires some flexibility and good technique.

52 Vague Arete . . . . [____] **V3** 6A
The hanging arete is just about independent but not as good as either of its close neighbours.

53 The Nose . . . . ⑭ ✡ ◀ [____] **V4** 6B
Follow sloping holds to the top. Starting on the low break is worth **V5** 6C. *Red Circuit continues on page 460.*

54 Juggy Groove . . . . . . ✡ ◀ [____] **V2** 5c
The blobby groove.

Standing slightly isolated from the rest of the boulders is the fine **Grooves Boulder** *with an undercut face.*

44 Slippery Groove . . . ⑬ ⑬ ✡ [____] **V0+** 5a
The groove, left of the arete.

45 Arete on Left . . . . . ⑪ ⑭ ✡ [____] **V1** 5b
The arete and thin crack.

46 Easy Groove . . . . . ⑮ ⑭ ✡ [____] **V0** 4c
The groove is sport for all.
Green Circuit continues on page 463.

The Grooves Bould...

Northern Peak

Sheffield Crags

Stanage Area

Burbage Valley

Derwent Edges

The Limestone

Central Grit

Staffordshire

South Peak

ne excellent *Wing Wong* (**V2** 5c) - *page 456* - on the
ing Boulder on the Upper Tier. Photo: Adrian Berry

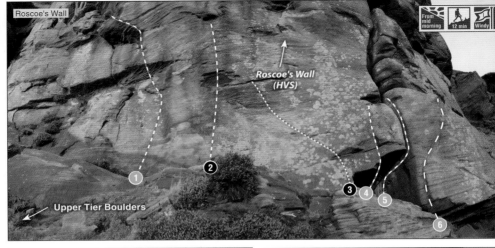

Roscoe's Wall

Roscoe's Wall
(HVS)

Upper Tier Boulders

Upper Tier - Right-hand

Right of Great Slab, the next buttress on the main edge of the upper tier is Roscoe's Wall where there are a number of good problems around the base. Continue another 50m to reach Calcutta Buttress. Pepper Buttress is another 30m along.

Approach - See maps on pages 438 and 457.

1 Magic Crossing . . . . ⟨⟩ ☐ **V1** 5b
From the flake, move up and left to a hole.

2 Toucan . . . . ⟨⟩ ☐ **V6** 7A
From a good edge, climb through the dark rock.

3 Lichenthrope . . . . ⟨⟩ ☐ **V7** 7A+
Just left of the cave is a low slot. Start here and climb up and left to latch the jug on *Roscoe's Wall*.

4 Crack Indirect . . . . ⑮ ⑰ ⟨⟩ ☐ **V2** 5c
From the back of the niche, follow the lip out to the slot, then follow the wall left of the crack - without using the crack.

5 Crack Start . . . . ⑱ ⟨⟩ ☐ **V1** 5b
Jam up the crack.

6 Babbacombe Start . . . ⑲ ⟨⟩ ☐ **V1** 5b
The arete and flakes. The sitting start is **Polish**, V7 7A+.

7 Sheep Shit . . . . ⟨⟩ ☐ **V7** 7A+
The wall starting from the thin rail.

8 Sheep Shit Crack . . . . ⟨⟩ ☐ **V5** 6C+
From the rail, move up to the short flake/crack.

9 Oik . . . . ⑯ ⟨⟩ ☐ **V3** 6A
From beneath the roof, continue up and right to the break.

The Grooves Boulder
p.458

The Attic
p.462

The Cellar
p.462

Roscoe's Wall

Calcutta Buttress

Pepper Buttress

Northern Peak · Sheffield Crags · Stanage Area · Burbage Valley · Derwent Edges · The Limestone · Central Grit · Staffordshire · South Peak

*The problems continue on **Calcutta Buttress**, about 30m further along the edge from Roscoe's Wall.*

⑩ Bombay Overhang . ⑰⑳🔲 ▢ **V2** 5c
Climb through the overhang and up the rounded nose.

⑪ Calcutta Crimp . . . . ⑱🔲🔲 ▢ **V4** 6B+
From a hold under the roof, pass the lip on crimps and continue to the break.

⑫ Dirtnap . . . . 🔲 ▢ **V8** 7B
Starting at the arete, follow the lip leftwards and finish at the top of *Bombay Overhang*.

⑬ Sleeping with the Flowers
. . . . 🔲🔲 ▢ **V5** 6C+
From sitting at the back, follow the arete to the break - no footblock at this grade. The standing start is **Sign Start, V2** 5c.

⑭ Mistral Start . . . . . ⑲🔲🔲 ▢ **V4** 6B
Through the double roofs of crimps. The low start is **V4** 6B+.

⑮ Limbless Limbo Dancer 🔲🔲 ▢ **V6** 7A
Start low under the roof and pull through to finish up the rib.

⑯ Dish Grab . . . . . . ⑳🔲🔲 ▢ **V4** 6B+
From a low start, gain the dish and continue to the break.

⑰ Calcutta Rib . . . . ㉑🔲 ▢ **V2** 5c
The rib. *Orange Circuit continues on page 462.*

⑱ Calcutta Traverse . . ㉑🔲🔲 ▢ **V3** 6A
Traverse from right to left, finishing up the crack. **The Black Hole Start, V5** 6C+, begins in the crack further right. Combining this into *Dirtnap* is **Delhi Belly, V9** 7C.
Red Circuit continues on page 462.

Pepper Buttress

*The final two problems are on **Pepper Buttress**, which is about 30m along the edge from Calcutta Buttress.*

⑲ Too Drunk . . . . 🔲🔲 ▢ **V6** 7A
The middle of the overhanging face, taking a rib.

⑳ Drunk Enough . . . . . . 🔲🔲 ▢ **V5** 6C+
The right arete of the face, from sitting.

The Cellar
p.462

Calcutta Buttress

Pepper
Buttress →

Northern Peak | Sheffield Crags | Stanage Area | Burbage Valley | Derwent Edges | The Limestone | Central Grit | Staffordshire | South Peak

The Attic

This area has never been very popular being overshadowed by its neighbours. There is a mix of problems from steep roofs to delicate slabs and heinous cracks. We have only described a few things but a bit of exploration will reap a reward. The area really catches the weather so keep away in high winds but this does mean that it dries quickly after rain.

Approach (see maps on pages 438 and 457) - The area sits on top of the right-hand Upper Tier. It is best approached walking up just left of Calcutta Buttress and either going through the Cellar crawl, or walking around. More direct scrambles exist but they are awkward with a pad.

1 The Squirm **V0** 4c
The short crack right of a corner leads to the roof where you creep off left through the cleft.

2 The Finger **V1** 5b
The fine arete below the large spiked roof and the finger above.

3 Handy Wall **V1** 5b
The wall to a ledge.

4 Mounty **V0-** 4b
The crack and slab, via a bulge.

5 Barley **V1** 5b
The rambling wall to a rounded rib finish.

6 Chasm Arete **V3** 6A
The arete on the left wall of the bay, avoiding the right wall.

7 Sexy Steve . . . . **V3** 6A+
Climb the slabby wall left of the crack.

From mid morning | 13 min | Windy

8 Scrack **V0** 4c
Jam up the perfect crack.

9 Reachy Wall **V2** 6a
The wall right of the crack has a long move to easier ground.

10 Runnel Rouser. . . . . . **V0+** 5a
The runnel and wall above. Highball with a terrible landing.

11 Arete **V0-** 4b
The arete.

12 Risky Runnel. **V1** 5b
The runnel to the right.

The Cellar

Next to The Attic is a ring of blocks with problems on both the inside and outside. The inside walls can be green.
Approach (see maps on pages 438 and 457) - Walk up left of Calcutta Buttress to arrive at the outside wall. Squeeze through a small gap to get into The Cellar itself.

13 The Gates **V6** 7A
The slab to the left of the scurry hole is technical and feels scary.

14 Crinkly Wall **V2** 5c
The wall opposite is delicate.

15 Ride my Pimp **V4** 6B
The large nobble on the arete proves to be both a hurdle and the key.

16 The Downpipe . . . . . . **V5** 6C+
On the wall to the right lurks a vague crack. Use this somehow to gain the upper slab then creep up this.

17 Pipe Entry **V6** 7A
Sit-start at a flake, pull to the lip and move left to finish as for *The Downpipe*.

18 Night Rider . . . . . **V8** 7B+
Traverse the lip from the right to finish up *The Downpipe*.

Northern Peak
Sheffield Crags
Stanage Area
Burbage Valley
Derwent Edges
The Limestone
Central Grit
Staffordshire
South Peak

The Attic

The Cellar (outside)

From mid morning | 13 min | Windy

Approach crawl

Inside The Cellar is a slabby wall.

19 Left Slab . . . . ⑮ 👤 [ ] **V0** 4c
The slab left of the groove.

20 Tiny Groove . . . . ⑯ 👤 [ ] **VB** 4a
Climb the central flake line easily.

21 Right Slab . . . . ⑰ 👤 [ ] **VB** 4a
Gain the slight flake on the slab.

22 Cellar Dwella . . . . . . 👤 👤 [ ] **V7** 7A+
The short arete is powerful and blank.

23 Cellar Slab 1 . . . . . ㉔ ㉓ 👤 [ ] **V1** 5b
The left side of the slab.

24 Cellar Slab 2 . . . . . ㉕ ㉔ 👤 [ ] **V2** 5c
The next line up the slab.
The last problem in the Orange and Red Circuits.

25 Easy Groove . . . . ⑱ 👤 [ ] **VB**
The large groovy flake. *The last problem in the Green Circuit.*

Sun and shade | 13 min | Windy | Green

The Cellar (inside)

Approach

To The Attic

Side tabs: Northern Peak · Sheffield Crags · Stanage Area · Burbage Valley · Derwent Edges · The Limestone · Central Grit · Staffordshire · South Peak

The Cube

This is an isolated collection of boulders on the moorland behind the Upper Tier of the main crag. The problems are quite high but the landings are okay. The moorland is exposed to most things but, as always, being exposed grit means it's quick to dry and seldom green. Most of the problems will catch the morning and early afternoon sun.

Approach (also see map on page 438) - Do not approach The Cube directly from the path that runs along the Upper Tier. Instead, approach as for the Spring Boulders/Lower Tier but follow a track off to the right that skirts the bottom of the Piece of Mind Boulders. Continue past a ruin and some old poles keeping an eye out for the faint remains of a very old track that leads directly across the moor to The Cube. This is very easy to miss, and if you reach a junction with a vehicle track, you've gone about 50m too far.

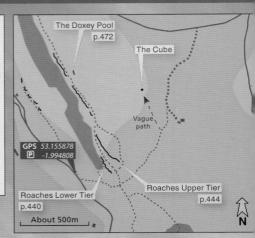

The Doxey Pool p.472
The Cube
Vague path
GPS 53.155878
-1.994808
Roaches Lower Tier p.440
Roaches Upper Tier p.444
About 500m
N

To mid afternoon | 30 min | Windy

① Flakes .... ⚅ ❤ ☐ **V1** 5b
The flake on the left wall, move left at the break to finish.

② Cube Crack .... ⚅ ❤ ☐ **V0-** 4b
The crack-line.

③ Period Drama ... ⚅ ✎ ❤ ☐ **V3** 6A
From *Cube Crack*, traverse right along the break and around the arete. Head to the top when you run out of break.

④ Jump ...... ⚅ ▮ ◨ ❤ ☐ **V5** 6C
The front side of the small undercut arete requires a long reach or a powerful move. **V7** 7A+ from sitting.

Northern Peak

Sheffield Crags

Stanage Area

Burbage Valley

Derwent Edges

The Limestone

Central Grit

Staffordshire

South Peak

5 The Cube Direct ⏣ 🧗 ❤️ [ ] **V8** 7B+
A direct start to *The Cube*.

6 The Cube ⏣ 🧗 ❤️ [ ] **V4** 6B
Although a qualified route, this brilliant flat wall could be deemed an extended boulder problem for the brave. You may need a cheat stone or an extra mat to reach the pebble to start.

7 The Pube ⏣ ❤️ [ ] **V3** 6A+
A right-hand finish to *The Cube*.

8 Right Pube ⏣ ❤️ [ ] **V3** 6A+
The right-hand side of the arete to the ledge and a hard finish.

9 Back Crack ⏣ 👤 [ ] **V1** 5b
The backside crack on The Cube requires jamming skills.

10 Cube Traverse ⏣ ↗️ [ ] **V3** 6A+
Traverse the main three faces from left to right with hands in the mid-height break.

Not much sun | 30 min | Windy

Triangular Slab

To mid afternoon | 30 min | Windy

The next five problems are found on **The Triangular Slab** *just below The Cube.*

11 K2 ⏣ [ ] **VB**
Struggle up the alpine ridge and plant your flag of choice.

12 K3 ⏣ [ ] **V0+** 5a
Climb the slab above the slot to the ridge.

13 Summit Slab ⏣ ❤️ [ ] **V2** 5c
Up the middle of the slab passing the porthole. A bit eliminate at the top where you need to keep your hands off the arete.

14 Notch Slab ⏣ [ ] **V2** 5c
Climb right of the porthole to the right arete.

15 2K ⏣ [ ] **VB**
The right-hand ridge.

Triangular Slab

The Cube

	No star	☼	☼☼	☼☼☼
VB to V0 *Easy to 4c*	5	9	3	-
V0+ to V2 *5a to 5c*	1	13	6	-
V3 to V5 *6A to 6C+*	5	13	3	2
V3 to V5 *7A upwards*	1	1	-	4

The Skyline Area of the Roaches is really just a continuation of the main edge running northwards up the ridge, presenting odd decent sections of rock in the shape of small buttresses and wind-worn boulders. The dramatic setting makes for a spectacular bouldering location which is added to by the excellent quality of many of the problems. There is a really good grade spread except perhaps in the very highest difficulty level.

Circuits

Circuits here involve quite a lot of walking, but it is well worth it with three of the best at Green, Orange and Red. It has been described assuming you are approaching from Roach End but all three circuits could easily be done in the other direction.

Conditions

Sitting at the highest point of the ridge, the Skyline catches all the weather going be it wind, rain or shine. This makes it a delightful place in good weather but best keep away when a cold westerly is blowing. It dries quickly and there isn't much green rock.

Approach   Also see map on page 437

The best approach is from the parking by the roadside at Roach End. This can be reached off the A53 by the road under the main Roaches crag, or the road around the back which leads past Ramshaw or the Newstones. From the parking head up the well-worn path to the summit trig point. Continue from here to drop down towards the main edge. Just after passing a line of soft undercut buttresses on the left, is a west-facing wall on the right - The Very Far Skyline. All the areas can also be easily reached from the top of the Roaches Upper Tier.

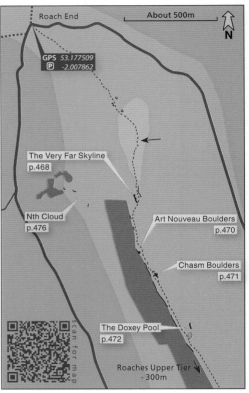

Roach End

About 500m

N

GPS 53.177509
P -2.007862

The Very Far Skyline
p.468

Nth Cloud
p.476

Art Nouveau Boulders
p.470

Chasm Boulders
p.471

The Doxey Pool
p.472

Roaches Upper Tier
- 300m

Lazy Trout (**V2** 5c) - *next page* - on the Very Far Skyline. Photo: David Hudson

The Very Far Skyline

This small outcrop provides some superb bouldering in a beautiful setting. It is quite exposed and has a relatively long approach walk, but the rewards are high when the conditions are good. It will catch any wind that is going, but is also south-facing and dries very quickly.

Erosion - Behind the two sections described here is an upper tier of undercuts slabs. Some of the footholds on these boulders have deteriorated due to the soft crumbly nature of the rock and will only get worse with more visitors. We have not included a topo for the upper tier and request that no one climbs there.

Approach (see map on page 466) - The boulders sit on top of the Roaches ridge at the northwestern end of The Skyline. You can approach from the main crag and the parking bays at the Upper Hulme End (page 438). This takes a while but clears the head and is a pleasant walk. A quicker route is from Roach End. Parking is available by the gates where the road bends and a short walk takes you past the impressive Bearstone Rock and up to the trig point on the ridge. The circuit lies on the small crag below the main path, behind the edge proper.

① **Rounded Arete** . . . . ① ⑪ ☐ **VB** 4a
The left arete of the slab is delicate and pleasant.

② **Open Groove** . . . . . ① ① ⚒ ☐ **V1** 5b
The faint groove in the left-hand side of the shield.

③ **Two Pocket Slab** ② ② ⚒ ▯ ☐ **V2** 5c
Direct up the middle of the slab using the shallow pockets. More like **V1** 5b for the tall.

④ **Lazy Trout** . . . . ③ ③ ⚒ ☐ **V2** 5c
The fine right side of the slab from a low shallow pocket direct. *Photo on previous page.*

⑤ **Eager Trout** . . . . . . ④ ④ ⚒ ☐ **V2** 5c
Trend up right to reach the arete.

⑥ **Clamp Arete** . . . . ⑤ ⚒ ☐ **V3** *6A*
The arete. **V7** *7A+* from sitting.

⑦ **Crack** . . . . ② ⑪ ☐ **VB** 4a
The wide traditional crack takes no prisoners.

The **Skyline Green Circuit**
One of the best easier circuits in the book although it involves quite a lot of walking. Only 15 problems but some real quality and only three at **V0+** 5a making it really manageable for beginners (watch out for *Harry Patch* though).

The **Skyline Orange Circuit**
A great mid-range circuit with plenty to test you but at quite a high level of difficulty for an Orange. Those who take some time to get going might prefer to do it in reverse starting at the Doxey Pool.

The **Skyline Red Circuit**
A long 29-problem circuit with problems up to **V5** *6C+*. This really makes the most of the Skyline area but is a hard circuit. Drop the harder **V5** *6C/6C+* problems for an easier, but still decent, circuit.

8 Harry Patch. . . . . . ③ ☼ 🖐 [ ] **V0** 4c
From the crack escape up the pockets. A highball finish but on good holds.

9 Bernie . . . . ⑥ ☼ [ ] **V3** *6A*
Layback the bay side of the next arete.

10 Off Fingers Crack . . ⑦ ⑤ ☼ [ ] **V2** 5c
In the left wall of the bay lurks another jamming school lesson.

11 Pinkies to Perkies . ⑥ ④ ☼ [ ] **V0** 4c
The crack splitting the bay wall provides a jamming test which requires a variety of widths.

12 Slab Crack . . . . [ ] **VB** 4a
Tackle the diagonal crack.

13 Slab Walk. . . . . . . ⑦ ⑤ ☼ [ ] **VB** 4a
Climb the hanging slab. Delightful.

14 Slab Arete. . . . . ⑧ ☼ [ ] **V1** 5b
Rock onto the arete from the right.

15 Inner Tube . . . . . ⑧ ☼ ▣ [ ] **V3** *6A+*
Start in a low hole and gain the top from slopers.

16 Wall and Rib . . . . ⑥ ☼ [ ] **V0-** 4b
The rib is a bit escapable.

17 Left Crack . . . . ⑦ ☼ [ ] **V0-** 4b
Climb the left-hand continuous crack.

18 Right Crack . . . . ⑧ ☼ [ ] **V0-** 4b
The disjointed cracks on the right of the wall.

19 Easy Ramp . . . . ⑨ ☼ [ ] **VB** 4a
Climb the easy groove above *Flight Exam*.
Green Circuit continues on page 471.

20 Flight Exam. . . . . . ⑨ ⑨ ☼ [ ] **V2** 5c
An eliminate but a good one. Use the pocket as your only hold to gain the top edge. With the rib it is a good **V0** 4c.

21 The Loner . . . . ⑩ ☼ 🖐 [ ] **V3** *6A*
As for *Flight Exam* but move out right from the pocket and pad up the slab avoiding the top of the boulder.

22 The Shepherd . ⑪ ☼ 🖐 ‖ [ ] **V5** *6C+*
Start directly below the flakes. Climb up to and past them with a long rock-over for the top.

23 Leek Hills . . . . ⑫ ☼ 🖐 [ ] **V4** *6B+*
Crimp the right-hand arete and a series of flakes.

24 Leek Flake . . . . . . ⑬ ⑩ ☼ [ ] **V1** 5b
Climb the firm flake avoiding any other holds.
Orange and Red Circuits continue on page 471.

There is a lot of potential for other problems here but, as mentioned before, please refrain from climbing on the upper tier due to soft rock.

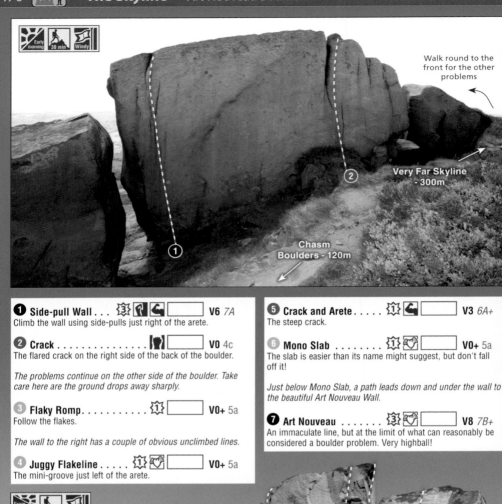

Early morning | 30 min | Windy

Walk round to the front for the other problems

Very Far Skyline ~ 300m

Chasm Boulders - 120m

From mid morning | 30 min | Windy

❶ Side-pull Wall . . . 　V6 *7A*
Climb the wall using side-pulls just right of the arete.

❷ Crack . . . . 　V0 *4c*
The flared crack on the right side of the back of the boulder.

The problems continue on the other side of the boulder. Take care here are the ground drops away sharply.

❸ Flaky Romp. . . . . 　V0+ *5a*
Follow the flakes.

The wall to the right has a couple of obvious unclimbed lines.

❹ Juggy Flakeline . . . . . 　V0+ *5a*
The mini-groove just left of the arete.

❺ Crack and Arete . . . . . 　V3 *6A+*
The steep crack.

❻ Mono Slab . . . . 　V0+ *5a*
The slab is easier than its name might suggest, but don't fall off it!

Just below Mono Slab, a path leads down and under the wall to the beautiful Art Nouveau Wall.

❼ Art Nouveau . . . . 　V8 *7B+*
An immaculate line, but at the limit of what can reasonably be considered a boulder problem. Very highball!

Art Nouveau Boulders
There are two large boulders on the crag next to the main path. They are just above the section of the edge with the classic route/highball *Art Nouveau*.
Approach (see map on page 466) - Continue along the Skyline path for about 300m from the Very Far Skyline. The back of the *Side-pull Wall* block is next to the path.

Northern Peak | Sheffield Craigs | Stanage Area | Burbage Valley | Derwent Edges | The Limestone | Central Grit | Staffordshire | South Peak

Chasm Boulders

This cluster of blocks is right on the Skyline path. The problems are not classic but one or two are worth seeking out.

Approach (see map on page 466) - These boulders are around 120m south along the Skyline path from the Art Nouveau Boulders.

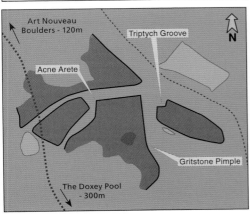

Acne Arete

The rest of the problems are in the narrow slot of **Acne Arete** between the boulders. Most require 'zit' starts!

⑫ Acne Arete **V6** *7A*
There's just enough room to climb the arete!

⑬ Squeezer's Spots **V5** *6C*
Climb the short wall, from sitting.

⑭ Spotter's Pop **V4** *6B*
A similar problem to the right.

⑮ Puss in Boots **V5** *6C*
The wall just left of the arete.

⑯ Spotter's Slop **V6** *7A*
Follow rounded holds up the opposite boulder.

⑧ Rounded Feature ⑭ ⑪ ⑩ ⚡ **V0+** *5a*
Climb past the distinctive, rounded hold.

⑨ Triptych Groove ⑮ ⚡ **V5** *6C+*
The groove and arete from sitting.

⑩ Gritstone Pimple . . ⑯ ⚡ **V4** *6B*
The short wall pulling to a mantel for the pimple.
Red Circuit continues on page 472.

⑪ Ramp . . . . ⑫ ⑪ ⚡ **V0+** *5a*
Climb the ramp to the break then flank the arete on its right-hand side. Direct is scarier.
Orange and Green Circuits continue on page 472.

The Doxey Pool
p.472

The Doxey Pool

Midway between the top of the Roaches, and the Skyline trig point is a strange pool that never empties, yet has no visible incoming water. The small outcrop above the pool is a mini crag that has a disproportionately good set of boulder problems considering its size and extent. A weird feature of the gritstone here is that it becomes softer and more prone to erosion after rain. It is probably best to keep away when there has been rain in the past day or so and not to climb here if the holds feel at all damp. The Doxey Pool catches any bad weather going but in the summer can be spot-on if there is a slight breeze. The ground is usually boggy in the winter and the few pools can swell making problems like *Staffordshire Flyer* and *The Drowning Pool* nonviable.

Approach (see map on page 466) - The boulders can be approached from either end and are easily spotted from the Skyline path.

❶ **Left Cheek** . . . . □ **V5** *6C*
Climb the left arete of the crack to a tricky top-out.

❷ **Soggy Bottom Crack** . . . . . □ **V2** *5c*
The really ugly and dirty crack can be climbed from the back if you really want to.

❸ **Ledge Jump** . . . . □ **V3** *6A+*
A jump lands you on the shelf which unfortunately means a mantelshelf.

❹ **Staffordshire Face** . ⑰ ⛾ □ **V5** *6C*
Starting on a sloper next to the crack, pull on and swing right onto the face which is climbed directly.

❺ **Staffordshire Flyer** . ⑱ ⛾ □ **V4** *6B*
Gain the lip break from the line of edges. A sketchy slap remains.

❻ **The Arete** . . . . ⑲ ⛾ □ **V5** *6C*
The next arete looks easy. Use all the cracks and features in vain. The sit-start is **V8** *7B*.

❼ **Another Nadin Traverse** . . ⛾ □ **V9** *7C*
From a sitting start on *The Arete*, follow the lip right until possible to continue as for *The Drowning Pool*.

❽ **The Drowning Pool.** . . ⛾ □ **V7** *7A+*
Gain the fine flake from a low start from the round jug down and right. A standing start (with a cheat stone if you really need to) reduces the grade to **V4** *6B*. *Photo opposite*.

❾ **Groovy Crack.** . . . . . ⑳ ⑬ ⛾ □ **V1** *5b*
The hanging, flared crack is reached from below. No chips at this grade and much better for it. **V0** *4c* with the chips.

❿ **Chipped Wall** . . . . ⑭ ⑫ ⛾ □ **V0-** *4b*
Use all the chips to climb the wall.

⓫ **Thin Flake.** . . . . . . ㉑ ⑮ ⛾ □ **V1** *5b*
The flake at the right-hand side of the block. No chips at this grade. The tall can bypass the move but what fun is that?

12 The Drowning Traverse

. . . . (16) (13) [ ] **V0+** 5a
A mid-height traverse from *The Flake* almost as far as *The Arete*.
It covers some good ground. Use the chips.

13 Side-wall . . . . (22) [ ] **V5** 6C
The side-wall on poor slopers.

14 Arete on Left . . . . (23) [ ] **V4** 6B
The left side of the arete has few useful holds but a subtle
approach gets you there.

15 Arete on Right . . . . . . (17) [ ] **V1** 5b
Ascend the right side of the arete using anything in reach. Just
using the arete is quite a test piece **V6** 7A.

16 Blind Flake . . . . . . (24) (18) [ ] **V2** 5c
Climb the blind flake without using the arete.

17 Little Pocket Slab Left . (25) [ ] **V5** 6C+
Gain a small pocket in the slab from down and left.

18 Little Pocket Slab . . . . (26) [ ] **V5** 6C
Gain the same pocket from down and right.

19 Archway . . . . (27) [ ] **V3** 6A+
Follow the rightwards arch to a finish up the slab above.

20 Little Flake . . . (28) (19) [ ] **V2** 5c
Make a big pull up onto the slab. After that it is easy.

21 Bulging Arete . . . . (29) [ ] **V5** 6C
Starting at poor low undercuts, power up the front of the block
using the arete. *The last problem in the Red Circuit.*

22 Hand Crack . . . . [ ] **V0** 4c
Right of the arete is a hand-jamming crack.

23 Easy Arete . . . . (14) [ ] **V0-** 4b
The left-hand arete can be absorbing and delicate on either side.

24 Pancake . . . . (20) (15) [ ] **V0** 4c
Climb up to, and through, the groovy flaked dish.
The last problem in the Orange and Green Circuits.

25 Li'l Crack . . . . [ ] **VB**
The crack in the left wall is a bit too trivial.

26 Li'l Arete . . . . [ ] **VB**
The arete on the right of the edge is very small.

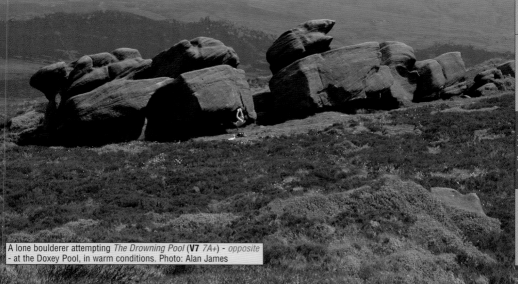

A lone boulderer attempting *The Drowning Pool* (**V7** 7A+) - *opposite*
- at the Doxey Pool, in warm conditions. Photo: Alan James

Northern Peak · Sheffield Crags · Stanage Area · Burbage Valley · Derwent Edges · The Limestone · Central Grit · Staffordshire · South Peak

	No star	☆	☆☆	☆☆☆
VB to V0 Easy to 4c	-	-	-	-
V0+ to V2 5a to 5c	2	-	3	1
V3 to V5 6A to 6C+	1	2	4	2
V3 to V5 7A upwards	-	2	4	7

The curious formation of the Five Clouds has left five distinct bumps of west-facing rock faces of varying size and extent. The first two have only limited bouldering on offer, and the third is the best for those looking for routes. The Fourth Cloud has the best bouldering including the brilliant Fourth Cloud Boulder with its set of hard classics. The Fifth Cloud has a few problems and finally there is the Nth Cloud just to confuse the numbering which is situated a little way further along the ridge. The difficulty level of problems is high here and this isn't an area for those looking for easy circuits.

Conditions
The Five Clouds are situated in front of the main Roaches edge at a slightly lower level. They receive plenty of afternoon sunshine, will dry quickly and are seldom green.

Approach   Also see map on page 437
Park as for the Roaches. Go through the gate then turn left along a sunken track. Follow this towards The Clouds, passing under the old quarries.

Very Far Skyline
p.468

Nth Cloud

The Doxey Pool
p.472

The Cube
p.464

Five Clouds

GPS 53.155878
Ⓟ -1.994808

Roaches Upper Tier
p.444

Roaches Lower Tier
p.440

Upper Hulme
A53

About 500m
N

Northern Peak

Sheffield Crags

Stanage Area

Burbage Valley

Derwent Edges

The Limestone

Central Grit

Staffordshire

Northern Peak

Sheffield Crags

Stanage Area

Burbage Valley

Derwent Edges

The Limestone

Central Grit

Staffordshire

South Peak

Simon Wren climbing *Finger of Fate* (**V4** *6B*) - *page 480* - on the Second Cloud. Photo: Dave Bond

Swivel Finger

The Nth Cloud

This collection of blocks and walls is some distance from the other Clouds. It has only a few problems but they of a very high quality. It dries quickly and catches the afternoon sun but despite these attractions, you can expect to have the place to yourself.

Approach (see map on page 474) - Continue along the approach road, past the usual parking area for The Roaches, for about 1.5km. Park by a small gate below some woods and the crag above right on the hillside. This gate is about 50m before a junction where a road joins steeply from the left. Park on the verge (not obstructing the gate). Pass through the gate and hike up the hill to the clearly visible rocks.

1 Swivel Flakes . . . . . . 🏵️ 🤍 ▭ **V4** *6B*
The flakes at the left side of the wall.

2 Swivel Finger . . . . 🏵️ ▭ **V4** *6B*
The big arete is brilliant and balancy. **V4** *6B+* from a sitting-start.

3 Nth Power . . . . . . 🏵️ 🖐️ ▭ **V12** *8A+*
From standing, tackle the wall direct starting from an undercut and a mono.

50m to the right is another set of short walls. The middle one of these has two good problems.

4 Crystal Voyager . . 🏵️ 🖐️ 🤍 ▭ **V8** *7B+*
The wall via a thin flake and some poor pockets.

5 Spankasaurus Does Chicago
. . . . 🏵️ 🖐️ ▭ **V4** *6B*
The arete to the right.

Crystal Voyager

Swivel Finger

Crystal Voyager

Northern Peak

Sheffield Crags

Stanage Area

Burbage Valley

Derwent Edges

The Limestone

Central Grit

Staffordshire

South Peak

Jordan Buys teetering up the upper slab of *Trust* (**V6** *7A*) - *page 479* - The Fourth Cloud, The Roaches. Photo: Mike Hutton

The Fifth Cloud

The Fifth Cloud is really a collection of blocks. The problems described are found on the blocks at either end of the area.

Approach (see map on page 474) - Follow the path along the base of The Clouds until you reach this, the final area.

Matchbox Slab

❶ The Imperfect Catch . . . . . ☆1   **V10** 7C+
The wall at the back of the pinnacle starting with your right on a sloper (on *Darkest Cloud*) and left on an undercut. Make a hard move up right then straight up using the left arete.

❷ The Darkest Cloud . . . ☆3   **V11** 8A
The arete starting from a pair of undercuts and continuing using crimps, slopers and pinches. **V8** 7B+ from standing.

❸ Ninestein **V3** 6A
A direct start to the route *Cloud Nine*. Traverse off left at the ledge.

❹ Dreamer **V2** 5c
The arete on the right of the buttress is climbed on its right.

The **Matchbox Slab** is at the far right-hand side of the Fifth Cloud, and faces the Fourth Cloud.

❺ Matchbox Arete . . . . ☆1   **V3** 6A
The slabby arete.

❻ Matchbox Slab. . . . . ☆2   **V2** 5c
This blank slab is a delight. Avoid escaping off right, or left, until the break is reached.

Cloud Nine (E2)

Matchbox Slab

The Fourth Cloud

A more substantial buttress which has some decent routes. The best bouldering is on the superb free-standing boulder below the crag. The grit is solid, blank and fine grained. It dries quickly and is never green.
Approach (see map on page 474) - Follow the path underneath the crags to the fourth outcrop.

Boysen's Delight (HVS)

7 Fourth Arete . . . . 🚶 [ ] **V2** 5c
The arete left of the flat wall is climbed making use of flakes on the front. **Forthright, V4** 6B, moves out right at the top.

8 Hard Arete . . . . . 🚶🧗‍♂️ [ ] **V7** 7A+
The right-hand arete on its left side.

9 Four Lions . . . . . 🚶🧗‍♂️ [ ] **V8** 7B
A left-hand finish to *Hard Arete*, following the lip out left. Sit-start as per *Tetris* at **V9** 7C.

10 Tetris . . . . 🚶🧗‍♂️ [ ] **V9** 7C
The sitting start to *The Hard Arete* starts low on the rib before moving left to finish.

11 Columns . . . . 🚶 [ ] **V10** 7C+
Follow *Tetris* to the lip, then hand traverse right to finish up the right arete.

12 Trust . . . . 🚶 [ ] **V6** 7A
A direct line over the lip and up the slab. *Photo on page 477.*

13 Thrust . . . . 🚶 [ ] **V6** 7A
From the start of *Trust*, traverse the lip right to the arete and finish up this.

Up on the crag is one solitary problem.

14 Milky Buttons . . . . . . 🚶 [ ] **V7** 7A+
The highball scoop.

Matchbox Slab

Main buttress

The Third Cloud
A sizeable buttress with many excellent routes, and a few decent problems at either end.
Approach (see map on page 474) - Follow the approach path past the first two Clouds.

❶ Persistence. . . . . 📋 **V4** *6B*
A vague flake up on the left-hand side, beyond the central section with the route **Appaloosa Sunset**.

❷ Who Needs Ready Brek?
. . . . 📋 **V9** *7C*
A hard right-hand finish to *Persistence* taking the thin break.

At the right end of the buttress are a couple more problems.

❸ Icarus Upstart . . . 📋 **V4** *6B+*
From a pocket in the lip, move out to the lip and continue up the arete. Exit out right if you don't wish to continue up the arete.

❹ The Pinnacle of Human Achievement
. . . . 📋 **V4** *6B*
The prow from sitting.

The Second Cloud
The Second Cloud is the first to offer anything for the climber. It has a number of good problems, though all are highballs.
Approach - See map on page 474.

❺ Nadin's Secret Finger. 📋 **V9** *7C*
Climb rightwards to finish as for *Finger of Fate*. Start a little up the slope. Desperate!

❻ Finger of Fate . . . . . . 📋 **V4** *6B*
The fine arete, climbed on its left. *Photo on page 475.*

❼ Communist Crack. 📋 **V1** *5b*
Climb the classy crack.

❽ Marxist Undertones . . 📋 **V2** *6a*
Snatch to a ledge from a pocket. There are variations on either side at **V4** *6B*. *Photo opposite.*

❾ Marxist Arete . . . . 📋 **V2** *5c*
The arete direct.

Steph Crowley on *Marxist Undertones* (**V2** 6a) - *opposite* - Second Cloud. Photo: David Hudson

Northern Peak

Sheffield Crags

Stanage Area

Burbage Valley

Derwent Edges

The Limestone

Central Grit

Staffordshire

South Peak

	No star	⟨1⟩	⟨2⟩	⟨3⟩
VB to V0 Easy to 4c	2	1	1	-
V0+ to V2 5a to 5c	6	6	5	1
V3 to V5 6A to 6C+	2	8	7	2
V3 to V5 7A upwards	2	3	6	3

A stone's throw from The Roaches, Ramshaw has plenty to offer the boulderer with excellent problems across the grade range. The edge is renowned for its savage steep cracks and routes that pack a real punch, but the bouldering is less formidable although it still commands respect. Many of the problems here are quite highball, particularly the harder ones, so plenty of pads and good spotters are advised.

Northern Peak

Sheffield Crags

Stanage Area

Burbage Valley

Derwent Edges

The Limestone

Central Grit

Staffordshire

South Peak

N↑

Baldstones
p.490

The Winking
Man Pub

Newstones
p.490

A53

Ramshaw

GPS 53.155323
Ⓟ -1.975276

scan for map

About 500m

Circuits
Ramshaw isn't a typical circuit crag being a bit spread out with quite a lot of isolated problems. There is enough for a short-but-good Orange Circuit and an excellent and hard Red Circuit.

Approach   Also see map on page 437
The distinctive edge is impossible to miss above the A53. It is reached by turning off onto a minor road between the junctions leading to Upper Hulme (and The Roaches) and The Winking Man pub. The minor road is followed up the hill and around to a parking area behind the edge.

Conditions

Ramshaw faces east, receiving morning sun on much of the crag, making it a good venue for cool conditions in the afternoon. A number of the problems in the Dangerous Crocodile Bouldering area face south and get a lot more sun. It is in an exposed position and catches any wind that is blowing. Despite the shady nature of many of the problems, it doesn't get too green.

Alan James climbing *Ossie's Bulge* (**V4** *6B+*) - *page 486* - on the Dangerous Crocodile Boulders at Ramshaw. Photo: Duncan Campbell

Northern Peak

Sheffield Crags

Stanage Area

Burbage Valley

Derwent Edges

The Limestone

Central Grit

Staffordshire

South Peak

Northern Peak

Sheffield Crags

Stanage Area

Burbage Valley

Derwent Edges

The Limestone

Central Grit

Staffordshire

South Peak

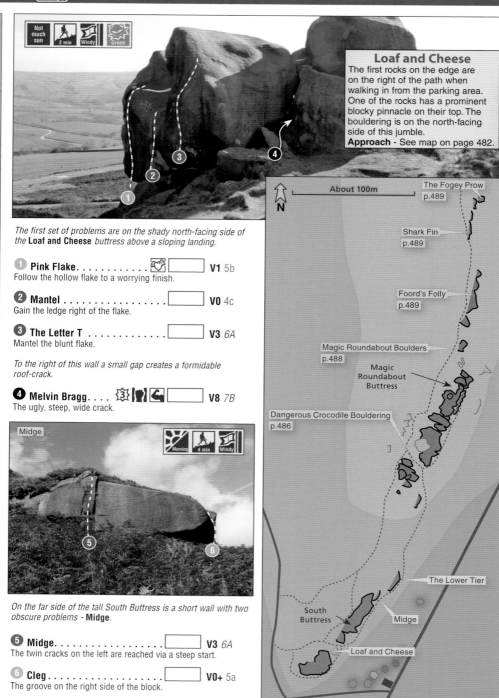

Not much sun | 2 min | Windy | Green

Loaf and Cheese
The first rocks on the edge are on the right of the path when walking in from the parking area. One of the rocks has a prominent blocky pinnacle on their top. The bouldering is on the north-facing side of this jumble.
Approach - See map on page 482.

*The first set of problems are on the shady north-facing side of the **Loaf and Cheese** buttress above a sloping landing.*

① Pink Flake **V1** 5b
Follow the hollow flake to a worrying finish.

② Mantel **V0** 4c
Gain the ledge right of the flake.

③ The Letter T **V3** 6A
Mantel the blunt flake.

To the right of this wall a small gap creates a formidable roof-crack.

④ Melvin Bragg **V8** 7B
The ugly, steep, wide crack.

About 100m

N

The Fogey Prow p.489

Shark Fin p.489

Foord's Folly p.489

Magic Roundabout Boulders p.488

Magic Roundabout Buttress

Dangerous Crocodile Bouldering p.486

The Lower Tier

South Buttress

Midge

Loaf and Cheese

Midge

Morning | 4 min | Windy

*On the far side of the tall South Buttress is a short wall with two obscure problems - **Midge**.*

⑤ Midge **V3** 6A
The twin cracks on the left are reached via a steep start.

⑥ Cleg . . . . **V0+** 5a
The groove on the right side of the block.

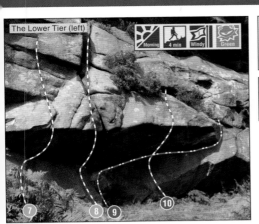

The Lower Tier (left)

The **Ramshaw Orange Circuit**
A short circuit with only 13 problems but including some of real quality. It starts with some steep stuff but has a few more delicate slabs in the middle and finishes with the classic *Shark's Fin* at the far end.

The **Ramshaw Red Circuit**
A decent length 24-problem circuit with a good spread of difficulty including five problems at **V5** *6C/6C+*. It builds to a big finish in the Foord's Folly area.

The Lower Tier

Below the main edge and to the right (looking in) of South Buttress is an undercut tier of rock offering some steep, sheltered bouldering.
Approach - See map on page 482.

7 Sensible Shoes ... **V1** *5b*
Crosses the roof just left of the crack.

8 Crab Walk Direct .. **V2** *5c*
Starting low, climb the crack through the roof.

9 Smoothment Traverse .. **V4** *6B*
From the crack, traverse right under the roof to finish up some flakes.

10 Roof Direct ... **V5** *6C*
Climb through the roof.

11 Rock Climbing in Britain
.... **V7** *7A+*
From sitting, traverse the ramp from left to right.

12 Roll Off **V2** *5c*
From the lip, move up and left to the ledge. The original desperate low start to this one has lost holds.

13 Cake **V3** *6A*
Starting on the lip, move up and right onto the ledge.

14 Collywood .... **V5** *6C+*
Starting from sitting at the crack, follow the lip leftwards until it is possible to finish in the groove.

15 Hem Line **V6** *7A*
The traverse of the crag from left to right - the meat of it can be consumed by starting easily just right of the crack (*Don's Crack*). Follow slopers into *Tierdrop*, then continue right to finish as for *Last Drop*.

16 Tierdrop ..... **V7** *7A+*
A classic highball, follow pinches and crimps through the steepness to a thought-provoking finish via a big chipped horizontal slot. The sitting start is **V8** *7B*. Going out left from the slot at the finish is worth **V8** *7B*.

17 Tier's End **V1** *5b*
Climbs into the groove. Linked from the sitting start to *Tierdrop* it is **V6** *7A*. *Orange and Red Circuits continue on page 486.*

18 Last Drop **V1** *5b*
Climb up from the prominent chipped slot.

The Lower Tier (right)

Northern Peak | Sheffield Crags | Stanage Area | Burbage Valley | Derwent Edges | The Limestone | Central Grit | Staffordshire | South Peak

Dangerous Crocodile Bouldering

Continuing along the main crag-top path is a jumble of blocks approximately 100m further on from South Buttress. It is a complex area that offers plenty for the explorer. Just key problems have been included here.
Approach - See maps on pages 482 and 484.

The first problems are on a short prow buttress with an open mouth, just right of the path.

1 Easy Prow . . . . ⑤ 🔯 ⬜ **V0+** 5a
The flake.

2 Little Prow . . . . 🔯 🔳 ⬜ **V5** 6C+
The rounded arete from the break.

Further along is another wedge buttress with a prominent flake on its side-wall.

3 The Scoop . . . . ⑨ ⑥ 🔯 ⬜ **V2** 5c
The prominent scoop. Harder for the short to get started.

4 The Lurch . . . . ⑩ 🔯 ⬜ **V4** 6B
Starting at the flake, traverse the slopers left then up.

5 Ossie's Bulge . . . . . . ⑪ 🔯 ⬜ **V4** 6B+
Pull up the flake then balance up left. A direct finish is possible, but harder - **V4** 6B. *Photo on page 483.*

6 Ram Air . . . . 🔯 🔳 🔳 ⬜ **V8** 7B+
High, hard and classic.

The next problem is on the far north-facing side of the large block that is home to the route Dangerous Crocodile Snogging.

7 Elastic Wall . . . . 🔯 🔳 🔳 ⬜ **V5** 6C
From a small side-pull, jump for the top.

The problems continue up and to the right.

8 The Arete . . . . . . ⑫ ⑦ 🔯 ⬜ **V2** 5c
The arete is the same grade on each side.

9 5c Wall . . . . ⑬ 🔯 🔳 ⬜ **V3** 6A
The crimpy wall.

10 Baby Groove . . . . 🔯 ⬜ **VB** 4a
The easy groove.

Further right and near the main path is a short, green block.

11 Mansize . . . . 🔳 🔳 ⬜ **V9** 7C
The steep arete via a pinch. Unfortunately it's located in a dank pit, and may need a gentle brushing.

12 Hanging Crack . . . . 🔳 ⬜ **V0+** 5a
The short hanging crack to the top of the block.

Follow the block around to the right to find a clean slab.

13 Classic Mantel . . . . ⑭ ⑧ 🔯 ⬜ **V2** 5c
Mantel the slab on dinks.
Orange and Red Circuits continue on page 488.

14 Saian . . . . 🔯 🔳 ⬜ **V5** 6C
The pillar in the chasm is a bit enclosed.

Lurking behind is the continuation of the edge which has a couple of nasty cracks waiting right of some easy-angled slabs.

15 Crocodile Slot . . . . . . 🔳 🔳 ⬜ **V1** 5b
The left-hand of two nasty cracks.

16 Right Slot . . . . 🔳 🔳 ⬜ **V1** 5b
The right-hand crack is harder.

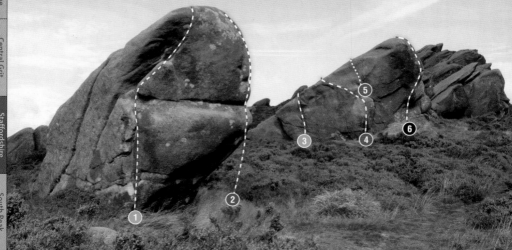

Lots of sun | 6 min | Windy | Green

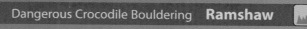

Not much sun | 6 min | Windy | Green

Little Prow and Ossie's Bulge Boulders hidden behind

From mid morning | 6 min | Windy

Northern Peak
Sheffield Crags
Stanage Area
Burbage Valley
Derwent Edges
The Limestone
Central Grit
Staffordshire
South Peak

Magic Roundabout Boulders

The first problems are actually on the back of the main edge section with the route Magic Roundabout.

❶ Magic Arete . . . . . 🔲🔲🔲 **V2** 5c
Climb the arete on its right-hand side.

❷ Be Calmed . . . . 🔲🔲🔲 **V4** 6B
Starting up the arete, move right and mantel. The direct start to the mantel is **V5** 6C.

❸ Be Calmed Right-hand 🔲🔲🔲 **V5** 6C+
Gains the top from the right.

❹ Force Nine . . . . 🔲🔲 **V7** 7A+
The thin slab, exit left when you reach the flake, or else it becomes a scary solo.

Beyond the main buttress is a short section of east-facing blocks with a set of steep problems - **Magic Roundabout Boulders**.

❺ Jamless . . . . . 🔲🔲🔲🔲 **V2** 5c
Curiously easier without getting into the crack.

❻ Arete on Left . . . . 🔲🔲 **V6** 7A
Climb the arete on its left-hand side.

❼ Epilogue . . . . 🔲🔲 **V6** 7A
The seam leads to a hard finish.

❽ The Rammer . . . . 🔲🔲🔲 **V0-** 4b
The chimney.

❾ Monologue . . . . 🔲🔲 **V8** 7B+
Clamp your way up the wall using both aretes.

❿ The Pinches . . . . 🔲🔲 **V4** 6B
The overhanging arete.

⓫ Practice Chimney . . . . **VB** 4a
The chimney for some practice.

⓬ Dialogue . . . . 🔲🔲 **V8** 7B+
Classic fridge-hugging.

⓭ Cracked Arete . . . . 🔲🔲🔲 **V2** 5c
Climb the short arete on the right-most block.

Magic Roundabout Boulders

North End
Some of the best bouldering at Ramshaw is at the north end of the edge, on the lower section of the main crag, and dotted across the various blocks.
Approach (see maps on pages 482 and 484) -
The first problems are on The Magic Roundabout Boulders, which are about 100m further on from Dangerous Crocodile Boulders.

Northern Peak

Sheffield Crags

Stanage Area

Burbage Valley

Derwent Edges

The Limestone

Central Grit

Staffordshire

South Peak

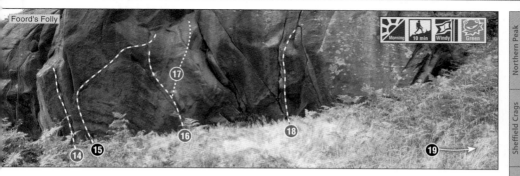

Foord's Folly

*Dropping down under the east-facing side of the next main edge buttress leads to **Foord's Folly** wall with some problem starts.*

14 Press Direct . . . . . 21 11 ▣ **V4** *6B*
Follow the twin seams as far as the crack. **V6** *7A* from sitting.

15 Lust Left-Hand. . . ▣ ▣ ▣ **V8** *7B*
Crimp along the crumbly rail to finish in the niche.

16 Night of Lust Start . 22 ▣ ▣ **V5** *6C+*
Follow poor holds up into the niche. Starting from the low jug is **V6** *7A*.

17 Runnel Entry . . . . . 23 11 ▣ **V5** *6C*
From the low start to *Night of Lust Start*, head up and right.

18 Foord's Folly Start . . . 24 ▣ **V3** *6A*
A fine crack. Either jump off at half-height or keep going and tick the E1 route. *The last problem in the Red Circuit.*

Another 50m further along, three isolated problems take you to the end of the edge - see map on page 484.

19 California Screaming . ▣ ▣ **V8** *7B*
The high hanging arete at the same level at Foord's Folly.

20 Shark's Fin . . . . . . 13 ▣ ▣ **V0+** 5a
The overhanging flake on the top of the edge.
The last problem in the Orange Circuit.

21 The Fogey Prow. . . . . ▣ **V9** *7C*
Back down at the same level as the pinnacle is this steep, hard arete which is climbed from a sitting start.

Shark Fin

The Fogey Prow

Northern Peak

Sheffield Crags

Stanage Area

Burbage Valley

Derwent Edges

The Limestone

Central Grit

Staffordshire

South Peak

	No star	✪	✪✪	✪✪✪
VB to V0 Easy to 4c	-	9	2	-
V0+ to V2 5a to 5c	4	18	4	1
V3 to V5 6A to 6C+	2	12	7	6
V3 to V5 7A upwards	2	2	5	2

Northern Peak

Sheffield Crags

Stanage Area

Burbage Valley

Derwent Edges

The Limestone

Central Grit

Staffordshire

South Peak

Neil Colquhoun on the fingery *Ripple* (**V4** *6B+*) and Duncan Campbell pulling through the bulge of *Crack and Arete* (**V3** *6A+*) - *page 494* - on the Newstones. Photo: Alan James

Two crags which are always treated as one, mainly because you have to walk past the Newstones to get to the Baldstones. They have a similar character being lumps of rock rather than edges - a little too tall for bouldering in parts, but also mostly too small for routes. The lovely location and easy access means that they are quite popular.

Circuits

These two make great crags for a circuit. There are a lot of problems in nice clusters and three circuits have been included - Green, Orange and Red. We have omitted some of the classic highballs.

Approach   Also see map on page 437

The two areas are approached from one parking spot on a side road off the A53, just south of The Winking Man pub. After you have turned off the A53, you will see the Newstones on your right. Continue to the first junction and park neatly by the road. Follow a track, to the right of the nearby house. Keep on the lower track and don't bnach left into the private burial ground. Remember this on your return as well since it is easy to stray down the burial ground path by accident. The Baldstones are 10 minutes further on.

Conditions

The crags are mostly east-facing getting morning sun. They are exposed to the wind but tend not to get too green. The rock can be gritty after rain.

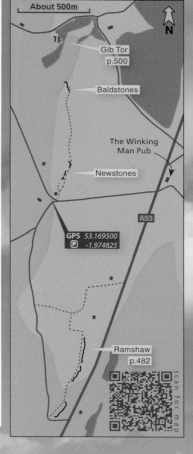

Charlie's Overhang

The first buttress you arrive at has an impressive flying overhang. It has some classic problems with very high finishes but the landing zone is almost perfect.

Approach - See map on page 490.

1 S and M .... 🏔 ▮▮ **V7** *7A+*
Gain a small crack in the left-hand side-wall, using the break and undercuts. Finishing out left is **V5** *6C*. Starting down and right gives a good low start, which gets **V8** *7B* if finished direct.

2 Leather Joy Boys 🏔 🍴🔲 **V8** *7B*
Pull over as for *S and M* then traverse out right on sickly jams to a very high finish.

3 Little Traverse ...... 🏔 📷🔲 **V3** *6A*
Traverse the low break beneath the roof, finishing on some jugs left of the crack.

4 Charlie's Overhang 🏔 📷🔲 **V4** *6B*
Climb up to the lip and contemplate the next move... then reverse it, or push on. Superb and very rewarding.

5 Moonshine .... 🏔🔲 **V1** *5b*
The bulging wall is easy until the last bit.

6 Praying Mantel Start
.... 🔲📷🔲 **V5** *6C*
Sit-down start the steep wedge-shaped arete.

7 Wraparound Arete ... 🏔🔲 **V5** *6C*
The rounded undercut arete.

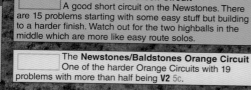

Charlie's Overhang — Top Block — Hazel Barn p.494 — Twin Aretes — Rhynose Buttress p.496 — Sly Buttress p.496

The Newstones Green Circuit
A good short circuit on the Newstones. There are 15 problems starting with some easy stuff but building to a harder finish. Watch out for the two highballs in the middle which are more like easy route solos.

The Newstones/Baldstones Orange Circuit
One of the harder Orange Circuits with 19 problems with more than half being **V2** *5c*.

The Newstones/Baldstones Red Circuit
A superb long 29-problem circuit that includes a lot of the best bouldering on these two crags. As described it is one of the easier Red Circuits at mostly **V3** *6A+* and below but you could easily add a few classic **V5** *6C/6C+* problems to bump up the difficulty level.

Twin Aretes

The next buttress on the lower level has inviting twin aretes.

8 Left Twin Arete . . . . . . ① ☆ ☐ **VB** 4a
The short and aesthetic arete.

9 Right Twin Arete . . . . . ② ☆☆ ☐ **V0** 4c
A big sister arete on the right.

10 Flake Slab . . . . ① ☆ ☐ **V1** 5b
The middle of the slab, via flakes. A sit-start gives a **V4** 6B alternative.

11 Flake Slab Eliminate
. . . . ① ② ☆ 🧗 ☐ **V2** 5c
An eliminate up the right-hand side of the slab avoiding all good holds.

Top Block
Set back from the main lower buttresses is a superb low block with a bulging face. It is home to a set of similar problems with low starts.
Approach - See map on page 490.

12 Square Cut Face . . ② ☆ 🪨 ☐ **V3** 6A
Pull up using some sloping edges.

13 Left Arete . . . . ③ ③ ☆ 🪨 ☐ **V2** 5c
The arete on its left-hand side.

14 Wall and Mono ④ ☆ 🧗 🪨 ☐ **V3** 6A+
Up to mono and upper breaks.

15 Varicose . . . . ⑤ ☆☆ 🪨 ☐ **V3** 6A+
Use the varicose vein. A bit of a physiological riddle.

16 The Grinding Sloper ⑥ ☆ 🪨 ☐ **V3** 6A
Some rounded breaks right of the *Varicose*.

17 Varicose Traverse . ⑦ ☆ 🪨 ☐ **V3** 6A
Traverse leftwards from *The Grinding Sloper* to finish up *Square Cut Face*.

18 Easy Slab . . . . ③ ☆ ☐ **VB** 4a
The slabby wall.

19 Easy Crack . . . . ④ ☆ ☐ **VB**
The crack.

20 Easy Slab Right-hand . ⑤ ☆ ☐ **VB**
The easy wall and breaks. *Green Circuit continues on page 494.*

21 Right Arete . . . . . . ⑧ ④ ☆ ☐ **V2** 5c
Nice little arete. *Orange and Red Circuits continue on page 494.*

Green Circuit continues on page 494.
Orange and Red Circuits continue on page 494.

Northern Peak | Sheffield Crags | Stanage Area | Burbage Valley | Derwent Edges | The Limestone | Central Grit | Staffordshire | South Peak

Hazel Barn

The jutting buttress of Hazel Barn has a number of classic problems including the beautiful *Ripple*.
Approach - See map on page 490.

❶ Ripple . . . . . . V4 6B+
Traverse the vein up rightwards to a high finish. Longer and harder than it looks. *Photo on page 490.*

❷ Martin's Traverse . . V1 5b
An awkward start gains access to the lower rising line. Excellent. *Photo opposite.*

❸ Martin's Direct . . V3 6A
From the base of the ramp of Martin's, climb straight up.

❹ Crack and Arete . . . V3 6A+
Beef up the crack in the arete, swing rightwards to finish. A sit-start adds a bit. You can also finish on the left. *Photo on page 490.*

❺ Short Wall V2 5c
Gain the right wall of the arete, using sharp flakes.

❻ Hazel Barrow Crack VB 4a
The delightful groove in the arete is really a route - **HS**.

❼ Hazel Barn . . . . . . VB
Another route up the right-hand side of the wall - **VDiff**.

❽ Hazel Traverse . . . . V3 6A+
Traverse right on good holds to finish as for *Hammy*.

❾ Hazel Groove V2 5c
The groove in the side-wall is brilliant after an awkward start.

❿ Nutmeg V0 4c
Pull up the flakes then move right.
Green Circuit continues on page 496.

⓫ Nutmeg Groove V2 5c
Up the wall just left of the overhanging arete.
Orange Circuit continues on page 496.

⓬ Hammy V3 6A
Up the nose and arete from a low start.
Red Circuit continues on page 496.

⓭ Mister Coconut . . . . V3 6A+
A grim mantel right around the back.

Northern Peak | Sheffield Crags | Stanage Area | Burbage Valley | Derwent Edges | The Limestone | Central Grit | Staffordshire | South Peak

Northern Peak

Sheffield Crags

Stanage Area

Burbage Valley

Derwent Edges

The Limestone

Central Grit

Staffordshire

South Peak

Dave Bishop on *Martin's Traverse* (**V1** 5b) - *opposite* -
Hazel Barn at The Newstones. Photo: Mike Hutton

Northern Peak
Sheffield Crags
Stanage Area
Burbage Valley
Derwent Edges
The Limestone
Central Grit
Staffordshire
South Peak

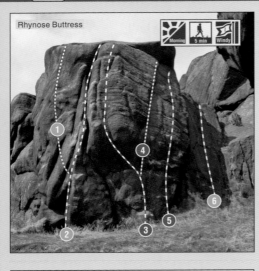

Rhynose Buttress

After a gap is a collection of larger blocks. The first of these is **Rhynose Buttress** and has a steep thrusting rounded arete.

① **Scratch Wall** . . . . ☐ **V2** 6a
The wall left of the crack is a bit artificial.

② **Scratch Crack** . . . . . . ⑨ ⟨⟩ ☐ **V1** 5b
The jamming crack.

③ **Scratch Arete** . . . . . . ⟨⟩ ☐ ☐ **V5** 6C
Gain the arete and cracks from powerful moves on the right wall.

④ **Itchy Groove** . . . . . ⑰ ⟨⟩ ☐ ☐ **V4** 6B+
Up the blank groove direct.

⑤ **Itchy Fingers** . . . . ⑱ ⟨⟩ ☐ **V3** 6A
The arete is gained from the right.

⑥ **Bridget** . . . . ⑩ ⑨ ⟨⟩ ☐ **V0+** 5a
The corner and slabs in the bay.

Sly Buttress
The largest buttress at Newstones is the tall block of Sly Buttress which is split by two cracks and has an attractive vein feature on its right-hand wall.
Approach - See map on page 490.

⑦ **Sly Traverse** ⑲ ⑪ ⟨⟩ ☐ ☐ ☐ **V2** 5c
Traverse the flakes along the steep wall with your feet on the ramp at this grade. Eliminating the ramp is **V6** 7A.

⑧ **Stallone Arete** . . . . ⟨⟩ ☐ **V5** 6C+
The bulging arete on rounded holds.

⑨ **Sly Stallone** . . . . ⟨⟩ ☐ ☐ **V5** 6C
Jump to the lip holds from small edges. Eliminating the foot ramp nudges the grade up a bit - **V6** 7A.

Past a pair of awesome cracks, which weigh in at HVS and VS, is a nice vein.

⑩ **Sly Mantelshelf** . . . ⑳ ⟨⟩ ☐ ☐ **V2** 5c
Traverse the vein rightwards and rock onto the upper slab.

⑪ **Sly Super Direct** . . . . ㉑ ⟨⟩ ☐ **V3** 6A
Gain the vein directly from below.

⑫ **Captain Quark** . . . . . . ⟨⟩ ☐ ☐ **V5** 6C+
A crimpy direct line to the vein.

⑬ **Sly Direct** . . . . ㉒ ⟨⟩ ☐ ☐ **V1** 5b
Up to the right-hand end of the vein then finish direct.
Red Circuit continues on page 498.

Rhynose Buttress

Stegosaurus

Northern Peak

Sheffield Crags

Stanage Area

Burbage Valley

Derwent Edges

The Limestone

Central Grit

Staffordshire

South Peak

Stegosaurus

At the back of Sly Buttress are some short problems and a block. The cracks here are completely the opposite of what you normally expect from 'rounded' gritstone.
Approach - See map on page 490.

⑭ Tiny Crack . . . . ⑩ 🛠 🖐 [____] **V0** 4c
The left-most crackline.

⑮ Left Crack . . . . ⑫ 🛠 🖐 [____] **V1** 5b
The thin crack is quite tricky.

⑯ Tyrannosaurus Hex. ⑬ ⑪ 🛠 [____] **V0+** 5a
Flakes up the middle are nice and juggy.

⑰ Prehistoric Offwidth
. . . . ⑫ 🛠 🖐 🥾 [____] **V0** 4c
Start low for the wider crack on the right.

There are two traverses.

⑱ The Clanger . . . . 🥾 🖐 [____] **V2** 5c
The low right to left traverse.

⑲ Soup Dragon . . . . 🥾 [____] **V1** 5b
Traverse the top from right to left.

Clammy Hands

The free-standing block has some more problems.

⑳ Clammy Wall . . . . . . ⑬ 🛠 [____] **V0** 4c
The wall and flakes to a rounded top.

㉑ Yo Clam . . . . . ⑭ ⑭ 🛠 🥾 [____] **V0+** 5a
Start at the horizontal vein and hand traverse right, pulling up at the end. Can be extended around the block at **V1** 5b.

㉒ Clammy Hands
. . . . ⑮ ⑮ 🛠 🖐 🥾 [____] **V0+** 5a
Gain the crack from the vein and climb it to the top.
The last problem on the Green Circuit. The Orange Circuit
continues on page 498.

Stegosaurus

Clammy Hands

Gold Rush Buttress

The Baldstones

The Baldstones is a continuation of the Newstones outcrop a little further north. It consists of several large buttresses with routes and two small concentrations of high quality bouldering. As with the Newstones, the buttresses face east getting morning sunshine only and are exposed to the wind.

Approach (see map on page 490) - From the Newstones, follow the path directly northwards to arrive at the Baldstones.

The first buttress gives some nice routes or solos.

❶ Original Route.... 23 16 ⚡ **V2** 5c
The start of the route is very awkward but not as hard as it looks. Traverse off left or jump off, or continue to the top - it's about HVS.

The next problems are on a steep, leaning wall below the tall **Gold Rush Buttress**.

❷ Baldy . . . . 24 ⚡ 🪨 💼 **V3** 6A+
From a low start (feet on the ramp) follow the flake and continue onto the ledge.

❸ Baldstones Dyno . . 25 ⚡ 🖐 **V4** 6B+
A classic dyno to the lip, from here continue onto the ledge.

❹ Throwball . . . . ⚡ 🖐 **V7** 7A+
Decent holds lead to flatties then a hard dyno.

❺ Baldstones Low . . ⚡ 📐 📐 **V8** 7B+
A low traverse following a line of small holds just below the original. Finish up *Baldy*.

Elephant's Ear Buttress

Ray's Roof (E7)

Gold Rush Buttress

6 **Baldstones Traverse** . V7 7A+
Traverse along the line of sloping holds, starting up the arete and finishing up *Baldy*. A hard alternative finish is up *Throwball* at **V8** 7B.

7 **Easy Exit** . . . . V3 6A+
An alternative easier finish to *Baldstones Traverse*.

8 **Crank Cuffin** V9 7C
From the arete use poor holds to reach the top.

9 **Last Banana Before Sunset**
. . . . V2 5c
Left of the big roof, start from the ledge and move up and right to finish just right of the small pinnacle.

Right of the route **Ray's Roof** *is a short square arete which can be climbed on either side.*

10 **Indirect Arete** . . . . V7 7A+
The square arete on the left.

11 **Indirect Arete Right** . . V2 5c
The other side of the arete proves to be much more pleasant.

Elephant's Ear Buttress

Past the terrifying Ray's Buttress with its man-eating crack, is the short **Elephant's Ear Buttress** *wall with some superb problems.*

12 **Ganderhole Crack** . . . . . . V0+ 5a
The crack.

13 **Fielder's Indirect** V1 5b
The wall and pockets left of the groove.

14 **Fielder's Corner** V3 6A+
The groove above a nasty landing.

15 **Fielder's Wall** . . . V8 7B
Climb the blank-looking wall using a sloping pocket - that's the only hold.

16 **Elephant's Eye** . . . . V4 6B+
Start on the ear and reach out to the top pocket on the wall.

17 **Elephant's Ear** . . . . V0+ 5a
Up the splendid flake. The sit-start is **V5** 6C.
The last problem in the Orange and Red Circuits.

18 **Clever Skin Left-Hand.** V8 7B+
The sloping arete on its left side.

19 **Clever Skin** . . . . V7 7A+
The sloping arete and wall with a skin-trashing hold.

On the right is a boulder shaped a bit like a bun.

20 **The Wart.** . . . . V7 7A+
From a poor pocket, mantel onto the left side of the boulder. The mantel on its own is **V3** 6A+.

Northern Peak | Sheffield Crags | Stanage Area | Burbage Valley | Derwent Edges | The Limestone | Central Grit | Staffordshire | South Peak

	No star	⭐	⭐⭐	⭐⭐⭐
VB to V0 Easy to 4c	-	-	-	-
V0+ to V2 5a to 5c	3	2	-	-
V3 to V5 6A to 6C+	3	3	-	-
V3 to V5 7A upwards	-	1	1	3

Gib Torr is the natural continuation of the Newstones - Baldstones ridge. It is best considered as a crag for the hard-core enthusiast. The problems are generally steeper than those on the Newstones - Baldstones edges and they tend to be hard and high.

Approach   Also see map on page 437

Gib Torr is situated very near a little road off the main A53 Leek to Buxton road. There is adequate parking for a few cars on the roadside from where the crag can be seen.

Conditions

The crag faces northeast and more significantly faces a deep forest - this means green! Despite this, a good winter's session can be had if the weather has been dry. Landings are good, although there are a few boggy areas.

Access

Do not try to get to the Baldstones from Gib Torr or the other way around. The area you would have to cross is an S.S.S.I. The area known as Flashbottom Rocks lies just to the north of Gib Torr. This area is owned by English Nature and has a number of rare species. Please do not climb there.

About 500m

GPS 53.180689
Ⓟ -1.974696

Gib Tor

Baldstones p.490

The Winking Man Pub

Newstones p.490

A53

Norman Gillman enduring *Extended Torrture* (**V4** *6B*) - opposite - on the upper section of Gib Torr. Photo: Mike Hutton

Northern Peak

Sheffield Crags

Stanage Area

Burbage Valley

Derwent Edges

The Limestone

Central Grit

Staffordshire

South Peak

The first two problems described are on the prominent block at the top of the crag which is approached on the left (looking in).

1 Gib Torrture **V2** 5c
Pull up to the short crack and top out. **Extended Torrture** continues right to finish up the next short crack **V4** 6B. *Photo opposite.*

2 Gibbering Wreck **V8** 7B
Following flakes through the roof to a hard move around the lip.

Set above the main lower tier is a smaller wall with an arete.

3 The Fin **V6** 7A
The wonderful arete from the low flake. **V8** 7B from sitting.

4 The Fink . . . . **V7** 7A+
Climb the wall just right of the arete. A series of sloping edges leads to the small cluster of pockets on the top ridge. The low start from a pocket is **V8** 7B+.

5 5c Wall **V2** 5c
The line up the right side of the wall.

The main lower tier has a triangular buttress on its left.

6 Gibbering Left . . . . . . **V4** 6B+
From edges reach up and left to the lip of the slab.

7 Gibbering Right . . . . . **V5** 6C+
From the same edges climb up to the scoops in the lip of the bulging wall. **The Gibbering Lip** continues along the lip to a good hold at **V7** 7A+.

8 Gibby Haines . . . . . . **V4** 6B+
Use two small pockets to reach a jug, left of the route *Gibber Crack*. The sit-start from a large side-pull pocket under the overhang is **Stayin' Alive, V8** 7B.

9 Maurice Gibb . . . . . . **V10** 7C+
Start up *Gibby Haines* then make a huge dyno to a hold up and left.

10 Porridge Wall **V2** 5c
The small flat wall right of the dirty cracks has a variety of problems on sloping holds.

11 Martin's Problem . . . . **V4** 6B+
From a low start follow small holds up the wall.

12 Stall **V6** 7A
Layback the perfect arete - the foot-ramp is off limits. The sit-start is **V9** 7C.

13 Little Traverse **V1** 5b
Traverse the lip.

14 Little Mantel **V4** 6B
Mantel through the middle of *Little Traverse*.

Set back and to the right is a small green wall.

15 Gary's 5c **V2** 5c
The arete to the right.

16 Seams Green . . . . **V3** 6A+
The green wall to the right.

	No star	✪	✪✪	✪✪✪
VB to V0 Easy to 4c	2	1	-	-
V0+ to V2 5a to 5c	11	5	-	-
V3 to V5 6A to 6C+	4	3	-	-
V3 to V5 7A upwards	1	-	-	-

Wolf Edge is an isolated spot that is of exclusive interest to boulderers. It's unlikely you will ever find crowds of people here, so it's particularly worth a visit if crowds are likely at the more well known nearby venues. The quality of the rock is improving with traffic, but could need a gentle brushing in places.

Approach   Also see map on page 437

The crag is best approached from the small village of Flash (highest village in England at 461m). This is situated just west of the A53 and north of the other Staffordshire crags in this book. Park in the village and walk a short distance west where a road leads steeply up to some houses. Follow this road, staying to the left, and pass through a gate to a track. Follow the track past fields, avoiding the right-hand fork, and you will soon see the edge. The areas right of the track are gained by following a vague path along the base. Areas left of the track (The Warren) need to be approached from above, so keep on the main track until level with the edge, then follow a path along the top of the edge until it is possible to descend.

Conditions

The edge faces southeast getting plenty of morning and early afternoon sun. It is exposed to the elements and will dry quickly but offers little shelter. It doesn't suffer from green rock.

Access

The area is mostly Open Access Land, but the field below The Warren isn't included, which means you do not have the right to climb on the rocks that form the edge of the field. If you choose to climb here, stay close to the rocks and avoid the field - don't use it as a shortcut or climb over the drystone walls.

The Warren
p.504

The Fin
p.505

Northern Peak

Sheffield Crags

Stanage Area

Burbage Valley

Derwent Edges

The Limestone

Churnet Grit

Staffordshire

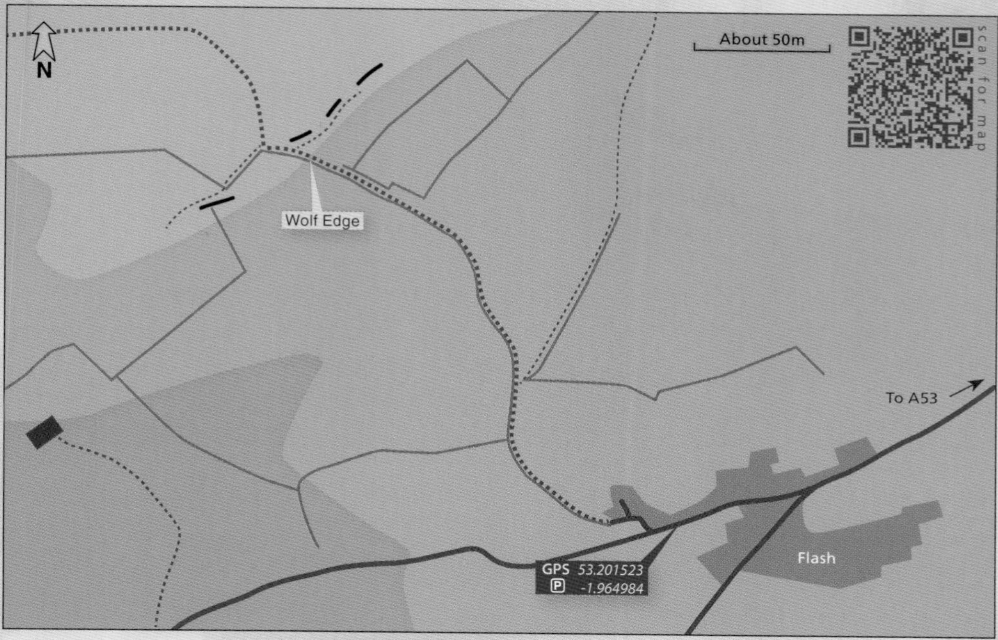

About 50m

N

Wolf Edge

To A53

Flash

GPS 53.201523
P -1.964984

Underground
p.505

Wolf Block
p.505

scan for map

Northern Peak

Sheffield Crags

Stanage Area

Burbage Valley

Derwent Edges

The Limestone

Central Grit

Staffordshire

South Peak

The Warren (left)

1 **Left Arete** . . . . ☐ **V0** 4c
The arete.

2 **Side-wall** . . . . ☐ **V2** 5c
Can be a bit dirty.

3 **Crack** . . . . ☐ **V1** 5b
The crack.

4 **Lair** . . . . ☆ ☐ **V3** 6A+
The face above the hole.

5 **Fine Slab** . . . . ☆ ☐ **V1** 5b
The slab.

6 **Fine Slab Arete** . . . . ☐ **V0** 4c
The right arete.

7 **Rock Fusion** . . . . ☆ ☐ **V3** 6A
The next arete.

8 **Claustrophobic Arete** . ☆ 🖼 ☐ **V2** 5c
The tower.

9 **Horseshoe Arete** . . . . ☆ 🖼 🔖 ☐ **V1** 5b
From sitting, climb the arete via the in situ horseshoe.

10 **Swiss Cheesed** . . . . 🖼 ☐ **V3** 6A+
Another high arete.

11 **Quantum Leap** . . . . ☐ **V8** 7B
The right arete on its left-hand side. The arete on its right-hand
side is **Project Quantum, V7** 7A+, and the sitting start on the
right is **V8** 7B.

The Warren (right)

The Fin

12 This is my Church . . . . [ ] **V5** *6C+*
The side-wall of the narrow fin.

13 The Fin. . . . . [ ] **V1** 5b
The edge of the narrow fin.

14 Ear Flake . . . . [ ] **V0+** 5a
The flake on the right side of the narrow fin.

15 Short Arete . . . . [ ] **V2** 5c
The short arete from sitting.

16 Crumble Left . . . . [ ] **V2** 5c
The left arete of the block.

17 Crumble . . . . [ ] **V4** *6B*
The middle of the block.

18 Crumble Right . . . . [ ] **V1** 5b
The right arete of the block.

19 Wolf Prow . . . . [ ] **V2** 5c
The prow from a sitting start.

Underground

Wolf Block

20 Underground Mantel . . . . [ ] **V0+** 5a
Mantel up the face.

21 The Underground . . . . [ ] **V4** *6B*
The arete.

22 Overground . . . . [ ] **V1** 5b
The next arete over is climbed on its right-hand side.

23 Overground Right . . . . [ ] **V1** 5b
The wall to the right.

24 Wolf Bite . . . . [ ] **V4** *6B*
From the sloper, climb the prow.

25 Wolf Bite Right . . . . [ ] **V2** 5c
The blunt arete just right.

26 Ramp Wall . . . . [ ] **V1** 5b
The wall.

27 The Ramp . . . . [ ] **V0** 4c
The prominent feature to the right.

Northern Peak

Sheffield Crags

Stanage Area

Burbage Valley

Derwent Edges

The Limestone

Central Grit

Staffordshire

South Peak

Simon Wren on *Jill the Traverse* (**V4** *6B+*) - *page 524* - on
Gentlemen's Rock in the Churnet Valley. Photo: David Bond

Northern Peak

Sheffield Crags

Stanage Area

Burbage Valley

Derwent Edges

The Limestone

Central Grit

Staffordshire

South Peak

Northern Peak

Sheffield Crags

Stanage Area

Burbage Valley

Derwent Edges

The Limestone

Central Grit

Staffordshire

South Peak

Hartington

Matlock
p.424

Matlock

Amber Valley
p.426

Matlock Bath

A515

Black Rocks
p.508

Cromford

A6

Harborough
p.512

Ambergate

A523

Shining Cliff
p.516

A52

Ashbourne

Belper

Churnet Valley
p.518

About 6km

South Peak

		No star	☆	☆☆	☆☆☆
VB to V0	Easy to 4c	2	1	-	-
V0+ to V2	5a to 5c	3	2	-	-
V3 to V5	6A to 6C+	3	5	1	-
V3 to V5	7A upwards	-	3	4	2

Black Rocks is a small venue, but well-known for its collection of high quality routes across the grades. There is limited bouldering to be found on the blocks below the main outcrop, and around the base of the outcrop itself, but this does include some major hard classics. Some of the problems are quite high and a good collection of mats is advantageous.

Approach   Also see map on page 507

Black Rocks is 1km south of Cromford, and just north of Wirksworth. From lights on the A6, turn south into Cromford and follow the B5036 uphill, forking left onto a minor road after 1.3km. Two left turns lead into the Black Rocks parking, the upper one is nearer the rocks. A path leads from here to the High Peak Trail and the crag just above.

Cromford

N

GPS 53.09783
P   -1.56748

B5036

Railway Slabs
p.510

Cemetery

South Gully Area
p.511

The Block
p.511

scan for map

Bolehill

About 100m

Conditions

Much of the rock here is more green than black, especially when conditions have been wet and during the winter months. Very little sun is to be found in the morning.

Northern Peak

Sheffield Crags

Stanage Area

Burbage Valley

Derwent Edges

The Limestone

Central Grit

Staffordshire

South Peak

South Gully Area
p.511

The Bloc
p.51

Gaia Area
p.510

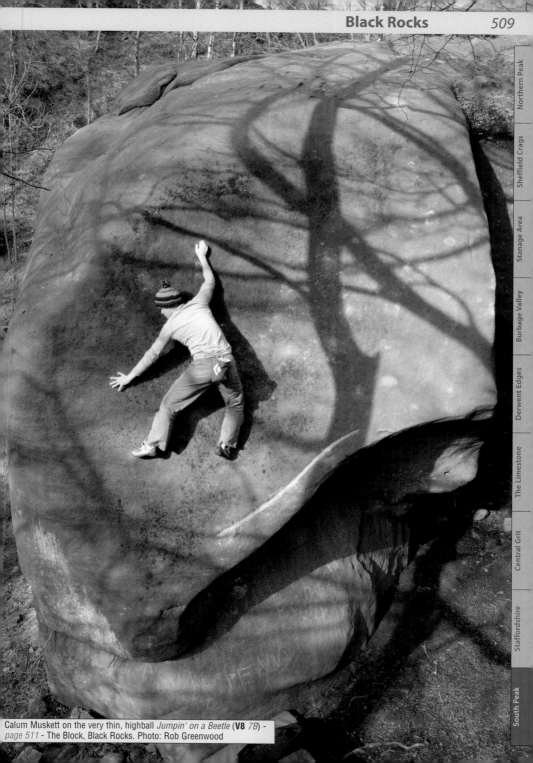

Northern Peak

Sheffield Crags

Stanage Area

Burbage Valley

Derwent Edges

The Limestone

Central Grit

Staffordshire

South Peak

Calum Muskett on the very thin, highball *Jumpin' on a Beetle* (**V8** *7B*) - page 511 - The Block, Black Rocks. Photo: Rob Greenwood

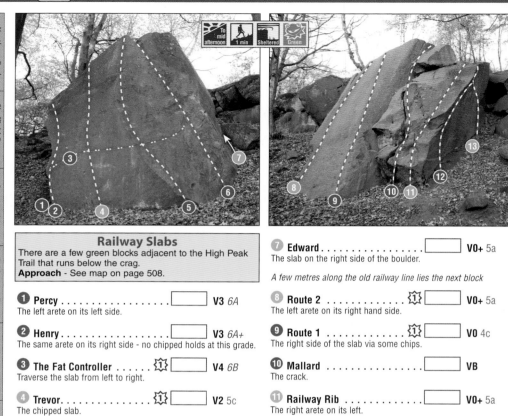

Railway Slabs

There are a few green blocks adjacent to the High Peak Trail that runs below the crag.
Approach - See map on page 508.

❶ Percy **V3** *6A*
The left arete on its left side.

❷ Henry . . . . **V3** *6A+*
The same arete on its right side - no chipped holds at this grade.

❸ The Fat Controller . . . . . . ☆ **V4** *6B*
Traverse the slab from left to right.

❹ Trevor . . . . ☆ **V2** *5c*
The chipped slab.

❺ Thomas **V4** *6B*
The poor arete via a chip.

❻ Gordon **V0-** *4b*
The slab just right.

❼ Edward . . . . **V0+** *5a*
The slab on the right side of the boulder.

A few metres along the old railway line lies the next block

❽ Route 2 . . . . ☆ **V0+** *5a*
The left arete on its right hand side.

❾ Route 1 . . . . ☆ **V0** *4c*
The right side of the slab via some chips.

❿ Mallard . . . . **VB**
The crack.

⓫ Railway Rib . . . . **V0+** *5a*
The right arete on its left.

⓬ Harold . . . . ☆  **V4** *6B*
The right arete on its right from a low start.

⓭ The Buffer **V2** *5c*
The short wall just right.

Gaia Area

Up on the main edge there are three problems around the base of the classic hard grit route *Gaia*.
Approach - See map on page 508.

⓮ Goya . . . . ☆ **V9** *7C*
The steep arete.

⓯ Curve Ball . . . . ☆☆ **V4** *6B*
Climb the crack but continue directly up the wall via a pocket.

⓰ Taxi to the Crag . . . . ☆☆ **V8** *7B*
The arete below *Gaia*.

⓱ Desert Island Disco . . . . . ☆ **V5** *6C*
The wall via some pockets and chips.

Gaia (E8)

Northern Peak | Sheffield Crags | Stanage Area | Burbage Valley | Derwent Edges | The Limestone | Central Grit | Staffordshire | South Peak

South Gully Area

To the right of the tallest section of the crag is another relatively tall wall which has some hard problems and starts to routes.
Approach - See map on page 508.

South Gully (VDiff)

The Block

Further right is tall wall with some thin starts that can be climbed as boulder problems.

18 Route 66 . . . . **V9** *7C*
From sitting at the slot, climb up rightwards to the lip, then traverse it left before pulling around onto the slab.

19 Hat Trick **V6** *7A*
The rib as far as the pocket.

20 Non Stick Vicar . . . . **V8** *7B+*
Follow the flake to gain the slab. No arete at this grade.

21 Runnel Rib . . . . **V4** *6B+*
The arete, exiting right at the ledge.

22 The Runnel **V5** *6C*
The technical groove.

The Block

Around to the right from Birch Tree Wall is a solitary green block with just one hold - a chiselled gutter - it is home to four hard highballs.
Approach - See map on page 508.

23 Jumpin' on a Beetle . . **V8** *7B*
Mantel onto the gutter and head up left to finish.
Photo on page 509.

24 The Angel's Share . . . **V9** *7C*
Direct up the middle of the slab.

25 Velvet Silence . . . . . . **V7** *7A+*
Traverse the gutter and finish up the right arete.

26 Make it Slappy . . . . . **V8** *7B+*
The right side of the arete, moving left onto *Velvet Silence*.

	No star	🌟	🌟🌟	🌟🌟🌟
VB to V0 Easy to 4c	7	7	1	-
V0+ to V2 5a to 5c	5	9	-	-
V3 to V5 6A to 6C+	-	-	-	-
V3 to V5 7A upwards	-	2	1	-

Harborough is a popular cliff made from heavily pocketed and solid dolomitic limestone. The bouldering here is mostly easier routes that are short enough to be considered boulder problems. Most are above good landings but they can be as tall as 6m high so care is needed if you are nervous or poushing your grade. The cave on the left-hand side of the crag provides some desperate enclosed hard bouldering which is a complete contrast to the easier open walls around it. The outlook over the High Peak Trail and the grassy base make it a good spot for a picnic although the nearby factory detracts a little.

Circuits
We have included a Green Circuit which is virtually all the Green problems on the crag. Add the Orange problems for a decent Orange Circuit.

Approach   Also see map on page 507
The crag is in the southern Peak, to the west of Wirksworth. There is parking on the side of the minor road that runs from Brassington to Wirksworth, just east of the prominent factory. A track leads past the edge of the works and up and over the High Peak Trail to the left-hand end of the cliff by the conspicuous cave and the tower of rock known as The Steeple.

Conditions
Harborough has a fine, sunny aspect and it is the limestone equivalent of the gritstone cliffs further north. There is no seepage and it dries quickly. Many of the problems are polished.

Lots of sun · 5 min

Problems are inside the cave

The Cave
On the far left-hand side of the crag is a cave which gives some desperate test-pieces which are very uncharacteristic of the rest of the crag. The roof itself is tackled by the route **Gobbler's Roof, E7 6c**.

❶ Blinding Lights . . ☆ 🔲 ◣ ▭ **V8** *7B+*
Tackle the prow in the back left of the cave. Finish on jugs just below the roof. An even lower lying start is **V9** *7C*. It can also be started from further back on underclings at **V11** *8A*.

❷ Banana Face . . . . ☆ 🔲 ▭ **V8** *7B+*
On the left wall, start low with right hand on a poor side-pull. Make dynamic moves up to jugs and finish rightwards.

❸ The Swarm . . . . . ☆☆ ◣ ▭ **V12** *8A+*
Climb the roof starting from the right-hand side-wall, finishing with hands matched in the crack.

The Steeple Area

The right-hand side of the crag has a prominent tower (The Steeple). Below this are a couple of short walls with good problems above a flat landing.

④ Pockets . . . . VO 4c
The arete on pockets has a sharp start.

⑤ Cracks V1 5b
Follow thin cracks up the wall to a tricky finish.

⑥ Jug . . . . VO+ 5a
Climb the wall via a prominent jug.

⑦ Jug Right-Hand V1 5b
The wall just left of the crack. No crack allowed.

⑧ Concave Wall . . . . VB 4a
The narrow wall right of the crack.

To the right of a brick ruin is a nice wall.

⑨ Little Arete . . . . VB
The arete right of the brick building.

⑩ Useful Gully Arete . . . . VO- 4b
The left arete (facing in) of the gully.

⑪ Bow Ridge . . . . VB
The arete on the left side of the wall.

⑫ Bow Corner . . . . VB 4a
The groove just right.

⑬ Bow Shaped Wall . . . . VO+ 5a
Follow thin cracks up the wall.

⑭ Bow Arete . . . . VB 4a
The wall just left of the arete.

⑮ Bow Arete Right . . . . VO- 4b
The arete taken on its right. *Green circuit continues on page 514.*

The **Harborough Green Circuit**

This circuit consists of most of the Green problems on the crag. Some are quite high, but most are above good landings.

Northern Peak

Sheffield Crags

Stanage Area

Burbage Valley

Derwent Edges

The Limestone

Central Grit

Staffordshire

South Peak

Left Bulge

The Arete

The Arete

The rest of the upper tier is a bit high for bouldering although worth a look if you are a confident soloist. At the right-hand end of the Upper Tier is a short wall with a prominent arete.

Approach - See map on page 512.

The problems continue after about 80m.

1 Shorty . . . . 9 ☐ **V0+** 5a
The arete.

2 Mantel Wall . . . . 10 ☐ **V0** 4c
The short wall.

3 Cracked Wall . . . . 11 ☐ **V1** 5b
Climb cracks up the left side of the wall.

4 Overhanging Crack . . . 11 ☐ **V0+** 5a
More cracks up the middle of the wall.

5 The Arete . . . . 12 ☐ **VB** 4a
The excellent arete.

6 Blinkers . . . . 13 ☐ **V0+** 5a
The thin crack.

7 Legs Over . . . . 14 ☐ **V0-** 4b
The wall.

Lower Tier

Below the right-hand side of the main Upper Tier is a long lower wall that never reaches any great height and offers some decent bouldering.

Approach - See map on page 512.

8 Left Bulge . . . . 11 ☐ **V1** 5b
The short bulge on the left.

9 Right Bulge . . . . 11 ☐ **V1** 5b
The short bulge on the right.

The Cave
p.512

The Steeple Area
p.513

Northern Peak · Sheffield Crags · Stanage Area · Burbage Valley · Derwent Edges · The Limestone · Central Grit

Cracked Arete

20m further on to the right are some clean vertical walls.

10 **Cracked Arete** . . . . ⑮ ☐ **VB** 4a
The arete on the left.

11 **Slab Wall** . . . . ☐ **V1** 5b
The wall.

12 **Flake Mantel** . . . . ⑯ ☼ ☐ **VB** 4a
The wall via a mantel and a flake.

13 **Cod Eye Wall** . . . . ☐ **V1** 5b
The wall via some pockets.

Flake Sitter

The final problems are on a short wall a little further to the right.

14 **Sharp Bulge** . . . . ☐ **V1** 5b
The bulge on the left.

15 **Flake Sitter Left** . . . ⑰ ☼ ☐ **V0-** 4b
The left-side of the wall, from sitting.

16 **Flake Sitter** . . . . . . ⑱ ☼ ☐ **V0+** 5a
The short wall, via a flake, from sitting.

17 **Final Wall** . . . . ⑲ ☐ **VB** 4a
The wall right of the crack.

The Arete

Cracked Arete

Flake Sitter

Left Bulge

Northern Peak

Sheffield Crags

Stanage Area

Burbage Valley

Derwent Edges

The Limestone

Central Grit

	No star	🗲	🗲🗲	🗲🗲🗲
VB to V0 easy to 4c	-	-	-	-
V0+ to V2 5a to 5c	-	2	2	-
V3 to V5 6A to 6C+	-	1	1	-
V3 to V5 7A upwards	-	1	2	1

Shining Cliff is a little known venue with a decent set of routes and some limited, but quality bouldering. It tends to get overlooked in favour of bigger crags further north. Although problems are few, and mostly in the mid-to-high grades, they are all high quality and worth seeking out. Sheltered and south-facing, this is a good place to head for in winter sun. In the summer the vegetation takes over.

Approach   Also see map on page 507

Approach by turning into Holly Lane off the A6 at Ambergate. Drive along this and the continuation called Jackass Lane, to possible parking at a lay-by outside a house and opposite a farm. Walk or drive down the track next to the house for around 250m to an open area in the woods. Follow the path on the right for 5 minutes to the first buttress.

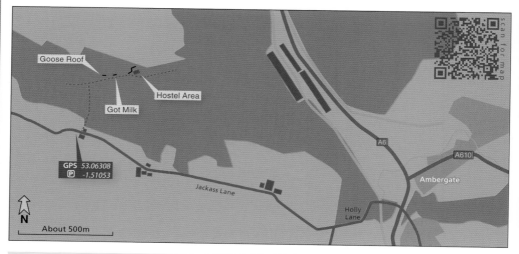

The first buttress is **Goose Roof**.

1 Foie Gras . . . . 🗲🗲🗲 ⬜ **V2** *5c*
The groove and juggy roof to finish.

2 Goose Cannon . . . 🗲🗲 ⬜ **V8** *7B+*
Start up *Foie Gras* and hand traverse the lip right to finish up *Goosecreature*.

3 Goosecreature . . . 🗲🗲🗲 ⬜ **V8** *7B+*
Cross the roof and gain the arete above, continuing up through the juggy roof. The *Goosegg Groove* ledge is out of bounds.

4 Goosegg Groove . . . . 🗲🗲 ⬜ **V3** *6A*
The groove on the right-hand side of the buttress.

Northern Peak
Sheffield Crags
Stanage Area
Burbage Valley
Derwent Edges
The Limestone
Central Grit
Staffordshire
South Peak

*The next problems are reached by descending back down to the path and heading along east for about 100m - **Got Milk**.*

⑤ Peaches and Crust . . . . 〰️ 🧗 ⬜ **V6** *7A*
Follow thin cracks and edges up the left side of the wall.

⑥ Got Milk . . . . 〰️ 🧗 ⬜ **V4** *6B*
The cracks up the right side of the wall, finishing direct.

*Continue along the track for a couple of hundred metres, past a wooden building on the right, and you reach a Youth Hostel. The following problems are next to the hostel - **Hostel Area**.*

⑦ Unidentified Flying Object
. . . . 〰️ 🐑 ⬜ **V2** *5c*
The centre of the face.

⑧ S.H.A.D.O. . . . . 〰️ 🐑 ⬜ **V2** *5c*
The wall just left of the arete.

Squeeze between the building and the rock to reach the next two problems.

⑨ Wet with Sweat . . . . . 〰️ 🐑 ⬜ **V2** *5c*
The right side of the right arete close to the building.

⑩ Moo Cow . . . . 〰️ ⬜ **V7** *7A+*
A direct start to the **E7** route **Gecko Blaster**. Jump off from the good ledge. The sitting start is **V8** *7B+*.

	No star	☆	☆☆	☆☆☆
VB to V0 Easy to 4c	-	1	-	-
V0+ to V2 5a to 5c	6	10	2	-
V3 to V5 6A to 6C+	7	28	15	1
V3 to V5 7A upwards	2	19	17	6

The Churnet is a beautiful little spot, tucked away to the south of the Peak District near Alton Towers, it's unlike anything else you will find in the Peak area. The steep-sided wooded valley has a series of small sandstone outcrops dotted along its length and on the hillsides above. The rock is of variable quality, but it is pretty solid on the buttresses described. Although it does have recorded routes, most people come here for the bouldering since the short steep buttresses have been developed with some superb problems. The valley is also famous for its long and sustained traverses.

Circuits

The Churnet hasn't much to offer the lower-grade boulderer - Wright's Rock and Gentlemen's Rock are mostly in the Black and Red zone. We have included one Red Circuit which takes a tour of the main walls and involves a fair amount of walking but will give a superb day out.

Approach   Also see map on page 507

The Churnet is to the east of Stoke, very close to Alton Towers. The presence of Alton Towers is useful since there are signs to it from everywhere. Once in the vicinity, look out for signs for the Red Road in Alton, or Oakamoor if you are at the other end. Halfway down the Red Road is a large cafe with parking. The crag approaches are described from here.

Conditions

The area is well-sheltered from the wind and will give shade on most buttresses in the summer making it a good warm weather retreat. In the winter months it can get dank and much of the rock will be green, although it is worth taking a look if the air is dry.

Naomi Buys pulling through the roof of *Wright's Unconquerable* (**V7** *7A+*) - *page 521* - at Wright's Rock in the Churnet. Photo: Mike Hutton

Northern Peak

Sheffield Crags

Stanage Area

Burbage Valley

Derwent Edges

The Limestone

Central Grit

Staffordshire

South Peak

Wright's Rock

This beautifully situated crag is perched above some fields high above the main valley. There is some excellent all-weather bouldering plus a few impressive routes that never get climbed. Although it is the most exposed crag, it faces north and can be damp. The crag is popular with livestock in bad weather so you may literally be 'in the shit' if you fall off.

Approach (see map on page 518) - Walk up the main path down the left-hand side of the mill. As you pass the dam above the mill, take a small path to the left up the hill. Follow this up and across a field. When you reach the track, turn left then immediately right through a gate and follow this path to the crag.

Left of the main crag are a few walls with plenty to go at. These are passed on the way to the main crag. The first problems are to be found on the **Out There Block** *which is close to the top of the approach path.*

❶ Out There and Back . . 🔄🔲 **V7** *7A+*
Start low and pull to the break then continue to the upper break to finish. **Instantly Out There, V8** *7A+,* uses the twin pockets on the left for the last move.

❷ Been Caught Stealing
. . . . 🔲🔲 **V6** *7A*
Just right, from sitting gain the break, and continue up and left to finish at the next break.

❸ Instant Funk . . . . 🔄🔲🔲 **V8** *7B*
From the right-hand end, traverse the break leftwards finishing left of *Out There and Back* via the distinctive pockets on the lip.

A few metres further on is a small red-streaked vertical wall - this is **Keith Sharp Holds Block.**

❹ Fatherhood . . . . 🔲🔲 **V7** *7A+*
The arete from sitting.

❺ Motherhood. . . . . 🔲🔲🔲 **V5** *6C+*
Sit at the pocket and climb the wall, moving left towards the top.

❻ Navuku . . . . 🔲🔲🔲 **V4** *6B+*
The pale streak up the middle.

❼ Wright's Giza. . . . . 🔲🔲 **V7** *7A+*
The brown streak, continuing past the break.

❽ Keith Sharp Holds . . . 🔲🔲 **V8** *7B*
The fingery wall.

Wright's Rock (left)

Not much sun | 10 min | Sheltered | Green

The Churnet Red Circuit
This is a long 31-problem circuit with problems up to **V5** *6C+*. There aren't too many highballs but it does require a lot of walking and all the various walls may not be in condition at the same time if it has been damp.

A little further along you reach the left wing of the main crag of **Wright's Rock** *at a cave.*

⑨ Wright's Unconquerable
. . . . ⚅ 🖐 [ ] **V7** *7A+*
A powerful line through the left side of the roof.
Photo on page 519.

⑩ Crumble Roof . ① ⚅ 🖌 🖐 [ ] **V3** *6A+*
From a low start, climb through the roof.

⑪ Dave's Traverse . . . . . ⚅ 🖐 [ ] **V4** *6B*
After the start of *Crumble Roof*, continue left to finish as for *Wright's Unconquerable*.

⑫ Jug Up Wall . . . . . ② ⚅ 🖐 [ ] **V4** *6B*
Follow positive holds up through the bulge.

⑬ Threapwood Bulge . ③ ⚅ 🖐 [ ] **V4** *6B*
The bulge a little to the right.

⑭ Threapwood Arete . ④ ⚅ 🖐 [ ] **V4** *6B*
The arete.

To the right is a recess known as The Niche.

⑮ Niche Traverse ⑤ ⚅ 🖌 🖐 [ ] **V4** *6B*
A left-to-right traverse of the recessed wall. Extending into *Saur Off* is worth **V5** *6C+*.

⑯ Rocket Ride . . . . . ⑥ ⚅ 🖐 [ ] **V5** *6C+*
The middle of the recessed wall to a flat hold.

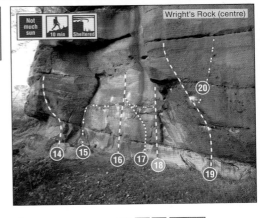

Wright's Rock (centre)

Not much sun | 10 min | Sheltered

⑰ Davros . . . . ⚅ 🖐 🖐 [ ] **V5** *6C*
From low on the right, pull up left to a side-pull then left again to the flat ledge. Pulling back right is **Albatross, V6** *7A*.

⑱ Saur On . . . . ⚅ [ ] **V1** *5b*
The corner, as far as the pocket.

⑲ Saur Off Sit Start . . ⑦ ⚅ 🖐 [ ] **V4** *6B*
The arete just right from sitting.
Red Circuit continues on page 522.

⑳ Iron Pebble . . . . ⚅ 🖐 [ ] **V4** *6B+*
Follow *Saur Off Sit Start* and exit rightwards.

Northern Peak

Sheffield Crags

Stanage Area

Burbage Valley

Derwent Edges

The Limestone

Central Grit

Staffordshire

South Peak

㉑ Thorns . . . . ⑧ 🔢 [ ] **V1** 5b
Into the overhung corner and exit left. Traversing right under the roof to the exit is worth **V2** 5c.

㉒ Blazes . . . . ⑨ 🔢 🔷 [ ] **V3** 6A+
Up the wall then leftwards through the roof. Finishing rightwards is a good **V4** 6B.

㉓ Quill. . . . . 🔢 🔷 🔷 [ ] **V10** 7C+
The desperate groove from a low start with your thumb on a gaston. The sit-down is **V11** 8A.

㉔ Simple Simon . . . 🔢 🔷 🔷 [ ] **V8** 7B
Gain the jug on the lip (jump or climb out) then crimp your way directly up the wall.

㉕ Sam Tan . . . . 🔢 🔷 🔷 [ ] **V8** 7B
A left-hand finish to *Simple Simon*.

㉖ Simple Simon Indirect
. . . . 🔢 🔷 🔷 🔷 [ ] **V6** 7A
The prequel to the previous problems. From sitting at some flakes, climb up and left to the jug on *Simple Simon*. Linked into *Simple Simon* is **V9** 7C.

㉗ Pie Hard . . . . 🔢 🔷 🔷 🔷 [ ] **V7** 7A+
The wall left of *Fingers*. Extending further is a scary **V8** 7B+.

㉘ Fingers . . . . 🔢 🔷 🔷 [ ] **V6** 7A
Starting at the pod under the roof, gain the lip and continue direct up the wall to the break.

㉙ Thumbs . . . . . 🔢 🔷 🔷 🔷 [ ] **V8** 7B+
From the lip on *Fingers*, follow edges left to finish as for *Simple Simon*. **V9** 7C from sitting.

㉚ Alternative Three . . ⑩ 🔢 🔷 [ ] **V4** 6B
Power through the bulges, and cross the roof to the break. **V5** 6C from sitting.

㉛ Johnny Utah . 🔢 🔷 🔷 🔷 [ ] **V7** 7A+
Start up *Alternative Three Sitting* and finish up *Fingers*.

㉜ Alternative Three Left-hand
. . . . 🔢 🔷 🔷 [ ] **V7** 7A+
A much harder alternative finish to *Alternative Three*.

㉝ Tyler . . . . . . 🔢 🔷 🔷 🔷 [ ] **V8** 7B
From sitting, follow a line parallel to *Alternative Three*, ignoring its holds until you're in the roof where you take the flake with your left hand.

The next mini-buttress is **Right's Rock**.

34 Point Break . . . . . ⬚⬚⬚⬚⬚ **V8** *7B+*
Gain the big pinch below the roof (**The Undercut, V5** *6C+*, to this point) now span through the roof to finish on the lip.

35 Warchild . . . . ⬚⬚⬚⬚⬚ **V10** *7C+*
Gain the break then move left and cross the roof.

36 Bhodi . . . . ⬚⬚⬚⬚⬚ **V7** *7A+*
The right-hand finish to *Warchild*.

37 Little Groove . . . . . . ⬚⬚⬚⬚ **V2** *5c*
The groove. Can be linked into the top of *Bhodi* at **V5** *6C*.

38 Last Wrights . . . . . ⬚⬚⬚⬚ **V2** *5c*
The front of the bulge to the first break.
Red Circuit continues on page 524.

39 Wright's Traverse . ⬚⬚⬚⬚⬚ **V8** *7B*
The reason most people come here. Start up *Thorns* and finish up *Last Wrights*.

40 Wrong's Traverse . ⬚⬚⬚⬚ **V8** *7B*
From a flake below *Simple Simon* traverse right below the good holds on *Wright's Traverse*.

41 The Crack . . . . . . ⬚⬚⬚⬚ **V6** *7A*
Climb the crack from sitting.

42 Calyx . . . . ⬚⬚⬚⬚ **V8** *7B*
The roof just right.

43 The Hob . . . . ⬚⬚ **V0+** *5a*
The easy line on the right.

44 The Hob Traverse . . . . ⬚ **V1** *5b*
Traverse the break in any direction.

Northern Peak · Sheffield Crags · Stanage Area · Burbage Valley · Derwent Edges · The Limestone · Central Grit

Not much sun | 15 min | Sheltered | Dry in the rain | Green

Gentleman's Rock

This is home to a bunch of up-problems and a tasty traverse. It faces north and can be great for shelter from wind and rain, but dreadful in damp and humid conditions.
Approach (see map on page 518) - Follow Dimmingsdale for roughly 1.5km and take a broad track up the south side for a short distance until you find a vague path leading left to the rock.

❶ Jill the Traverse. . . **V4** *6B+*
Traverse right on small edges as far as *Gentleman John*. Linked into *Low Traverse* and *The Nose* is **V7** *7A+*.
Photos on pages 506 and 526.

❷ Moon Jumper **V4** *6B*
The wall and roof above the start of *Jill* finishing on the sloping ledge on the lip of the overhang.

❸ Lunar Direct **V9** *7C*
Use pockets and slopey side-pull to the break, then pull up to the sloping hold on *Moon Jumper*.

❹ Electrofly **V6** *7A*
The green wall via a pocket to the break, then move left and finish as for *Lunar Direct*.

❺ Martin's Mono . . . **V7** *7A+*
Undercut the eponymous pocket and jump for the break.

❻ Fifty Pence Problem . . **V8** *7B*
The bulge via a hold that looks a little like a 50p coin (a heptagon if you don't know). Finish at the pocket.

❼ Humpty Dumpty . . . . . **V7** *7A+*
The groove.

❽ Gentleman John **V4** *6B*
The finger-crack to good holds.

❾ High Speed Imp Act **V6** *7A*
Pull up on edges to twin pockets then stretch across the steep ground, finishing at the good holds in the break.

❿ Crash Damage . . . **V8** *7B+*
A left-hand finish to *High Speed Imp Act* using a mono to reach a pocket at the lip.

⓫ Clover Field **V5** *6C*
Move right from *High Speed Imp Act* to the break and continuing up the dirty slab to the big break.

⓬ The Nose **V5** *6C*
From a sitting start, gain the flake in the roof then slap to the rounded nose. Dynoing from the start holds is **V8** *7B+*.

⓭ Low Traverse
. . . . **V4** *6B*
Start on the right on a very low break and traverse leftwards with a tricky move up between the two breaks. Finish on the jug on *Gentleman John*.

⓮ Slow Worm . . **V8** *7B*
From sitting, pull through the steepness to finish at the break.

⓯ Mindbender Jelly **V6** *7A*
Traverse from right of *Slow Worm* and continuing to *Gentleman John*.

Spooky Land

A small outcrop with a handful of problems. The rocks are under heavy tree cover, get little sun and stay wet after rain.
Approach (see map on page 518) - Follow Dimmingsdale for roughly 1.5km, then turn left up a broad track on the south side of the dale and continue for a couple of hundred metres to the two small buttresses.

Square Pusher 20m

The first couple of problems are on a short wall 20m beyond the first rock you come across on the approach.

⑯ Square Pusher... 🪨 V4 *6B+*
Pull onto a high edge, make a move and pop for the top.

⑰ Skint V4 *6B*
From sitting, climb the wall just right.

⑱ Spooky Wall .... V4 *6B+*
Slap between breaks up the left wall.

⑲ Spooky Arete .... V3 *6A+*
Starting at a distinct triangular hold in the niche, move up leftwards finishing up the arete.

⑳ Flowtation V5 *6C*
From the same starting hold as *Spooky Arete*, pull up and right.

The Chained Block

An isolated boulder on the north side of the river. Exposed and south-facing, this is a good option if the rest of the rocks here are wet and grotty.
Approach (see map on page 518) - Follow the path up Dimmingsdale for roughly 1.5km to a bridge (not to be confused with the small wooden bridges passed on the way). You can see the block up in the trees to the right - approach via a forestry track with a bit of bush whacking.

㉑ The Chained Block Traverse
.... V4 *6B+*
From just left of the short crack, follow the prominent break right, rising past a distinctive pocket to finish up the arete.

㉒ Superstring V4 *6B*
Starting low on the rounded arete, climb up and left, past the pocket, to finish on the sloping top.

㉓ The Revival .... V7 *7A+*
Starting as for *Superstring*, move right to the nose, then exit up left past a pocket.

㉔ The Awakening V8 *7B*
The right-hand finish to *The Revival* via a poor sloper.

㉕ Lean, Green, Bean Machine
.... V4 *6B+*
Starting right of the arete, follow slopers to finish up and right.
Red Circuit continues on page 527.

Northern Peak

Sheffield Crags

Stanage Area

Burbage Valley

Derwent Edges

The Limestone

Central Grit

Staffordshire

South Peak

Maggie Carroll on *Jill the Traverse* (**V4** *6B+*) - page 524 -
Gentleman's Rock, Churnet. Photo: Simon Rogers

Virgin Wall

This wall has the best traverse in the Churnet valley. The wall faces west but is very sheltered in the trees, hence it receives little sun. It can be damp and slimy but can also be crisp and dry when you least expect it.

Approach (see map on page 518) - Follow Dimmingsdale until you get to a bench with a dedication to Heidi Hunderhill - there is a bridge over the river at the same location. Continue for 50m and there is a rock on the left with 'LU' carved into it. Continue for another 50m to where an easy-to-miss trail leads off up into the woods to a wall.

❶ The Full Virgin Traverse

. . . . **V8** *7B*

Start on the far right-hand side and move left, dropping down slightly in the central section before moving up to the pebble-line. This leads left to ledges and a finish.

❷ Virgin Central . . . **V4** *6B*

The middle section starting at the tree and going as far as the pull-up. *Red Circuit continues on page 528.*

❸ Virgin Left **V6** *7A*

Start as for *Virgin Central* but continue all the way along the pebble-line to the flat ledges at the finish.

❹ Virgin Right **V5** *6C*

The start into *Virgin Central*.

Northern Peak
Sheffield Crags
Stanage Area
Burbage Valley
Derwent Edges
The Limestone
Central Grit
Staffordshire
South Peak

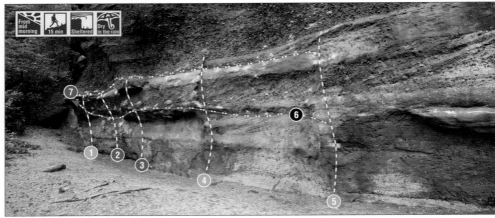

Northern Peak

Sheffield Crags

Stanage Area

Burbage Valley

Derwent Edges

The Limestone

Central Grit

Staffordshire

South Peak

Ousal Crag

Ousal Crag is similar to the crags in the Eifel in Germany - millions of pebbles, roughly arranged in bands, glued into sandstone. As with the Eifel, the pebbles have been known to detach themselves from the rock spontaneously. Ousal has a superb pumpy traverse and plenty of potential for hard up-eliminates. For most people the combination of Ousal Crag and Cottage Rocks will give them a good day out. The crag is south facing and is often relatively warm. It is very sheltered from wind and rain but can still be slippery in damp conditions.

Approach (see map on page 530) - Walk up the main path past the right-hand side of the mill. Fork right past a barrier, up the hill. Follow this path around the bend (Cottage Rocks) and back around another bend. Pass two small crags until you can see the pebble-dashed walls above you in the trees.

❶ Ooze . . . . 🔲🔲 **V1** 5b
Start low at the very left-hand end of the wall and pull up to the higher break.

❷ Sneezy . . . . ⑲🔲🔲 **V3** 6A+
Up from the flat sloper on the lower traverse.

❸ Booze . . . . ⑳🔲🔲 **V3** 6A
From low on crimps, pull up to good holds. **V0+** 5a from standing.

❹ Little Rib . . . . 🔲 **V1** 5b
Climb the little rib.

❺ Uzi Lover . . . . ㉑🔲🔲 **V1** 5b
From a low start right of the recess, move up on pockets.

❻ Ousal Low . . . . . . 🔲🔲🔲 **V7** 7A+
The low line is done from right to left. It starts easy, with an optional hands-off rest, but builds to a big fingery finish which is difficult to figure out.

❼ Ousal High . . . . . . ㉒🔲🔲 **V4** 6B+
A superb left-to-right upper line without any hard moves except for the ones at the end when you are pumped.

The next problem - **Bizarre** *- is next to the path to Ousal Crag.*

❽ Bizzare . . . . 🔲🔲🔲 **V8** 7B
From a sitting start on a flake, gain the top via the break.

The next problems are on Cottage Rocks and are passed on the approach to Ousal Crag.

❾ Adam's Arete . . . . 🔲🔲🔲 **V8** 7B
The arete.

❿ Billy Bunter . . . . 🔲 **V1** 5b
Climb direct up the wall past a large pebble.

⓫ Crusty . . . . 🔲 **V0** 4c
The thin cracks in the centre of the wall.

⓬ Sid the Sexist . . . . 🔲 **V1** 5b
The pocketed slab to the right of *Crusty*.

⓭ Cottage Slab . . . . 🔲 **V1** 5b
The wall to the hole.

⓮ Green Wall . . . . . . ㉓🔲🔲 **V4** 6B
Climb direct up the wall using a finger-ramp with your right hand to rounded ledges and a mantel finish.

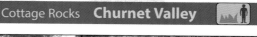

Pine Wall 20m

Cottage Rocks

The highest concentration of problems with some good stuff in the mid grades. Descend down and leftwards. It is the sunniest of the various Churnet crags and has two steep dry walls, however the slabby wall can turn fluorescent green in damp conditions.

Approach (see map on page 530) - Walk up the main path past the right-hand side of the mill. Fork right past a barrier, up the hill. Follow this to a bend where there is a very tall tree. The rocks are on the upper tier above the bend.

The next six problems share an awkward finish up the flake.

⑮ Sapling Bulge . . . . ㉔ ☆ 🔲 ⬜ **V4** *6B*
Use the finger-ramp with your left hand to get some pockets on the right. Move up to a small tree then the wide flake.

⑯ The Tufa . . . . ㉕ ☆ ⬜ **V3** *6A*
Pinch the tufa to jugs and the wide flake.

⑰ Orange Crush . . . . ⬜ **V2** *5c*
The left-hand side of the pocketed wall.

⑱ Pocket Wall. . . . . . ㉖ ☆ 👓 ⬜ **V4** *6B+*
The middle of the wall from a low start. The high start is **V1** *5b*. Traverse left at the top to finish up the flake.

⑲ The Wafer. . . . . ⬜ **V3** *6A*
From a little flake. It can be started low at **V3** *6A+*.

⑳ Strenuosity . . . . . . ㉗ ☆ 👓 ⬜ **V1** *5b*
Thrash up the wide crack on the right-hand side of the pocketed wall. At the top, traverse left to the wide flake to finish.

㉑ Cottaging . . . . . . ☆ 👓 🔲 ⬜ **V5** *6C*
Traverse the wall from right to left, starting on some poor holds.

㉒ Glory Hole . . . . . . ㉘ ☆ 👓 ⬜ **V4** *6B*
Traverse at mid-height from the crack to finish as for *The Tufa*.

The next block is further right and overlooks the track. It catches the direct morning sunlight.

㉓ Left Pine. . . . . . . ☆ 🖐 👓 ⬜ **V5** *6C*
Start on a low hold below the bulge and snatch your way up the wall above.

㉔ Pine Wall . . . . ㉙ ☆ 🔲 👓 ⬜ **V4** *6B*
Go up left from a good pocket. Tricky and excellent.

㉕ Right Pine. . . . ㉚ ☆ 🔲 👓 ⬜ **V4** *6B+*
Go up right from the good pocket past some edges.

㉖ Lonesome Pine . . . . . ☆ 🔲 ⬜ **V6** *7A*
From the right side of the wall, make a low traverse left to finish as for *Left Pine*.

Up and further right is the final wall on this section.

㉗ Push . . . . ㉛ ☆ ⬜ **V3** *6A+*
Climb the arete on the right. There are more problems on the walls to the left including some traverses.
The last problem on the Red Circuit.

Northern Peak
Sheffield Crags
Stanage Area
Burbage Valley
Derwent Edges
The Limestone
Central Grit
Staffordshire
South Peak

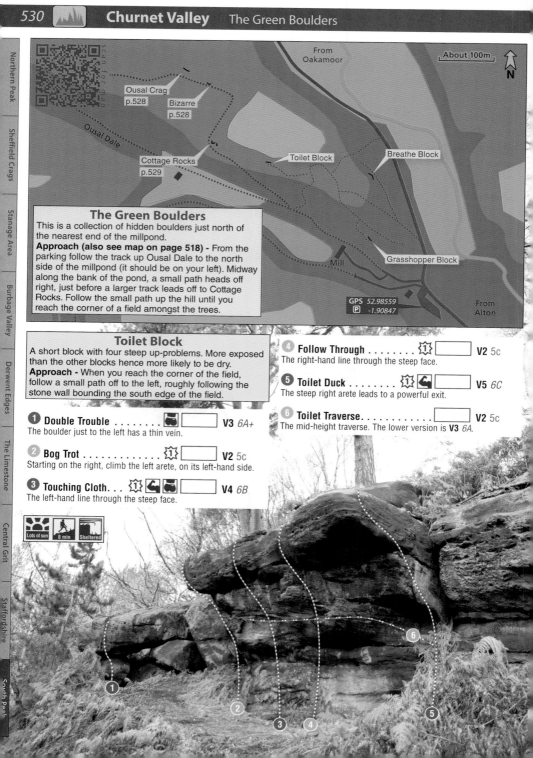

Ousal Crag
p.528

Bizarre
p.528

Cottage Rocks
p.529

From
Oakamoor

About 100m

N

Ousal Dale

Toilet Block

Breathe Block

Grasshopper Block

Mill

GPS 52.98559
P -1.90847

From
Alton

The Green Boulders

This is a collection of hidden boulders just north of the nearest end of the millpond.

Approach (also see map on page 518) - From the parking follow the track up Ousal Dale to the north side of the millpond (it should be on your left). Midway along the bank of the pond, a small path heads off right, just before a larger track leads off to Cottage Rocks. Follow the small path up the hill until you reach the corner of a field amongst the trees.

Toilet Block

A short block with four steep up-problems. More exposed than the other blocks hence more likely to be dry.

Approach - When you reach the corner of the field, follow a small path off to the left, roughly following the stone wall bounding the south edge of the field.

❶ Double Trouble . . . . ☐ **V3** *6A+*
The boulder just to the left has a thin vein.

❷ Bog Trot . . . . ☐ **V2** *5c*
Starting on the right, climb the left arete, on its left-hand side.

❸ Touching Cloth. . . ☐ **V4** *6B*
The left-hand line through the steep face.

❹ Follow Through . . . . ☐ **V2** *5c*
The right-hand line through the steep face.

❺ Toilet Duck . . . . ☐ **V5** *6C*
The steep right arete leads to a powerful exit.

❻ Toilet Traverse. . . . . ☐ **V2** *5c*
The mid-height traverse. The lower version is **V3** *6A*.

Lots of sun | 8 min | Sheltered

Breathe Block

This wall is found at the end of a north-facing edge that is mostly of little interest. The north-facing aspect and dense tree cover make this a dank place in winter, but a good place to hide from summer heat and sun.

Approach - From the corner of the field, follow the path around to the right and ignore the first path leading off to the left. Take the second path and follow it downhill towards the road. Keep an eye out for the rocks on the left. A path follows the base of the edge along its length. Follow this until you reach the block.

8 Breathe . . . . **V7** *7A+*
From thin edges, pass the sloper and finish. **V8** *7B* from sitting.

7 Footprints **V4** *6B*
From sitting, climb the left arete. **V2** *5c* from standing.

9 Suffocation . . . . **V3** *6A+*
Dyno for the break and go for the top. **V4** *6B* from sitting.

Grasshopper Block

This block is hidden away and wet for much of the time - it redeems itself with some inviting holds. Though south-facing, it is covered by trees and seeps badly after wet weather.

Approach - From the corner of the field follow the path around to the right, ignoring the two paths that lead off to the left. Keep an eye open for an easy-to-miss trail leading off to the right - there is a narrow log crossing it where it starts, which may help you find it. Continue along this narrow trail for about 20m and you will see the block on your left.

10 Down Under . . . . . . **V3** *6A+*
From sitting, follow holds up the left side of the block with a dynamic move to finish.

11 The Grasshopper . . . . **V3** *6A+*
The centre of the steep wall.

12 The Duck-billed Platypus
. . . . **V6** *7A*
Starting sitting just left of the right arete, pull up to the break and finish up the arete.

13 The Kookaburra **V2** *5c*
The right-hand start to the previous problem is much easier.

14 The Tomahawk Traverse
 . . . . **V7** *7A+*
A link-up traverse. Starting up *The Kookaburra*, follow the low break left passing *The Grasshopper* before moving up to the next level which is followed left. Traverse back right on the good break to finish.

There are more problems to the left of Down Under - see
PeakBouldering.info > *Churnet Sandstone*

Northern Peak | Sheffield Crags | Stanage Area | Burbage Valley | Derwent Edges | The Limestone | Central Grit | Staffordshire | South Peak

Northern Peak · Sheffield Crags · Stanage Area · Burbage Valley · Derwent Edges · The Limestone · Central Grit · Staffordshire · South Peak

Stars	Grade	Route	Photo	Page
*	V6	1980s Were The Days!, The		411
**	V0-	20 Foot Crack		203
*	V1	20 Foot Traverse		203
**	V3	21 Today Start		119
**	VB	2K		465
	V0	4c Wall		250
*	V2	5c Wall (Gib T)		501
*	V3	5c Wall (Ramshaw)		486
***	V5	7 Ball		227
***	V12	8 Ball		327
*	V3	...and Tigger Too		270
*	V4	A B Top		149
*	V4	A Beagle too Far	321	320
**	V4	A Bigger Prize		359
**	V7	A Bigger Splash		359
**	V6	A Bigger Tail		358
*	V6	A Bit on the Side		366
***	V8	A Case of Mistaken Identity		169
*	V5	A Day Without Pay		140
*	V5	A Fearful Orange		332
*	V7	A Fist Full of Beagles		320
*	V6	A Lack of Colour		367
*	V6	A Little Extra Direct		363
*	V4	A Miller's Tale		358
*	V3	A Minah Variation		113
	V6	A Modest Proposal		449
*	V4	A Moveable Feast		222
*	V5	A Rural Object		408
	V4	A Stoutness Exercise		270
	V7	A Tasty Graunch		324
	V0	Aboukir		343
***	V6	Above and Beyond the Kinaesthetic...		229
***	V7	Above and Beyond... Direct		229
*	V5	Abyss, The		418
*	V11	Acapella		55
	V1	Ace in the Hole		375
*	V13	Ace, The		154
*	V5	Aces High		411
*	V5	Acid Reign		100
*	V6	Acne Arete		471
*	V8	Adam's Arete		528
**	V4	Adults Only		138
*	V9	Advanced Training		366
	V3	Adventurous Arete		450
**	V4	Afro		328
*	V3	Ahab		260
	V1	Air Bear	275	284
*	V6	Al's Attic		166
	V2	Alaska		247
	V2	Alaska Right		247
	V1	Alcove Arete		327
	V4	Alcove Nose		327
	V2	Alcove Traverse		66
	V9	Alcove Wall		66
*	V4	All 14,000m Peaks		158
**	V7	All Quiet Direct		206
***	V3	All Quiet on the Eastern Front		206
	V2	All Sloping Arete		81
*	V3	All Stars' Goal		210
	V0+	Alleluia		104
	V0+	Alleluia Right		104
	V3	Altered		101
***	V6	Alliance, The		223
**	V5	Almost a Hold		174
	V3	Aloha		423
*	V4	Alternative Three		522
*	V7	Alternative Three Left-hand		522
*	V4	An Expotition		271
*	V4	An Uncoloured-in Problem		270
***	V8	Andle Stone Wall	413	412
**	V10	Andy Brown's Wall		152
**	V9	Angel's Share, The		511
*	V1	Angle Arete		384
*	VB	Angle Arete Right		384
*	V5	Angry Love		58
**	V4	Angus		42
*	V4	Angus Right		42
**	V5	Aniston Slap, The		138
*	V5	Annie's Egg		452
***	V9	Another Nadin Traverse		472
	V1	Answer the Phone		213
*	V6	Ant Lives		448
**	V7	Apache Dawn		448
*	V5	Ape Drape		280
*	V7	Ape Drape Direct		280
*	V4	Appliance Friction		414
	V2	Approach		214
**	V6	Approach Traverse		359
	V0+	Arch		445
	V3	Arch Direct		380
*	V6	Arch Enemy		49
	V0	Arch Right		84
	VB	Arch, The		380
	V0	Arched Roof		84
	V3	Archway		473
	V0+	Areet		284
*	V3	Arete (Gardom's)		334
	V0-	Arete (Plantation)		145
	V1	Arete (Plantation)		128
	V0-	Arete (Roaches)		462
	V4	Arete and Mantel		415
	V0+	Arete and Seam		81
	V0-	Arete of Cold Gloom, The		195
	V2	Arete on Left (Burbage S)		240
	V2	Arete on Left (Clifftop)		403
	V2	Arete on Left (Tintwistle)		52
*	V4	Arete on Left (Ramshaw)		488
	V1	Arete on Left (Roaches)		458
	V4	Arete on Left (Roaches)		443
*	V4	Arete on Left (Skyline)		473
**	V1	Arete on Right (Burbage S)		240
	V1	Arete on Right (Skyline)		473
*	V4	Arete on Right (Derwent)		82
	V2	Arete, The (Black Tor)		60
	V3	Arete, The (Derwent)		81
*	VB	Arete, The (Harborough)		514
**	V3	Arete, The (Matlock)		425
	V2	Arete, The (Ramshaw)		486
***	V4	Arete, The (Skyline)		472
*	V4	Arise Sir Freddy!		313
**	V7	Armbandit		355
	V2	Armoured Car Traverse		241
	V4	Armoured Cartwheel		241
	V1	Arrow Crack		117
***	V8	Art Nouveau		470
***	V5	Art of Japan	296	297
***	V8	Art of White Hat Wearing, The		291
	V0+	Artificial Route		42
*	V3	Ascent of Man Start		448
*	V4	Ascent of Woman Start		448
	V1	Asgard		370
*	VB	Ash Tree Big Slab		210
	V1	Ash Tree Little Slab		210
	V2	Ash Tree Variation		211
*	V8	Asylum Sika		214
**	V7	Atari		58
***	V6	Attitude Inspector		225
*	V8	Au Revoir Mono Doigt		354
*	V9	Aurora		366
*	V8	Awakening, The		525
	V1	Babbacombe Start		460
*	V8	Babu Yagu		399
	V0	Baby Bear		284
	V0	Baby Bear Arete		217
	V0+	Baby Bear Wall		217
	V9	Baby Belle		307
*	VB	Baby Bulge		81
*	VB	Baby Groove		486
	V2	Baby Wolverine		60
	V1	Back Arete (Curbar)		307
	VB	Back Arete (Roaches)		454
	V0	Back Bottom		385
**	VB	Back Cover		135
	V0	Back Crack		465
*	VB	Back End Slab		216
***	V8	Back in the YMCA		159
	V5	Back Side Arete		52
	V0	Back Slab		307
	V0-	Back Slab Right		447
***	V7	Back Street Abortionist		424
	V4	Back Wall Traverse		63
	V3	Bacon Foot		244
	V5	Bad Attitude		225
	V1	Bad Landing Arete		305
	V3	Bad Landing Crack		277
	V2	Bad Landing Groove		305
	V6	Bad Lip		305
*	V5	Badger		157
	V3	Bald Top		250
***	V4	Baldstones Dyno		498
*	V8	Baldstones Low		498
**	V7	Baldstones Traverse		499
	V3	Baldy		498
	V4	Balls Test, The		315
	V0+	Baltra Flake		78
	V5	Bamboozer		113
	V2	Banana Arete		205
**	V4	Banana Face		512
***	V3	Banana Finger		205
***	V5	Banana Finger Direct	201	205
***	V6	Banana Reverse		205
	V2	Banana Right-hand		205
*	V7	Bancroft's 6b		458
	V1	Banner's Ridge		106
	V5	Banner's Ridge Right		106
	V2	Barbapapa		423
	V2	Barbarete		423
	VB	Bare Rupert		284
	V4	Bareback Rider		448
	V1	Barley		462
	V3	Baron's Direct		299
	V3	Baron's Wall		299
	V10	Barracuda Start		358
**	V9	Barry Sheene		335
*	V6	Basher's Problem		362
*	V8	Basic Training Start		63
*	V3	Basic Traverse		63
	V0+	Basin, The		244
*	V5	Batter Patter		336
**	V5	Battered Sausage		177
*	V7	Batu Motel		313
*	V3	Baxter's Wall		42
	V2	Baxter's Wall Direct		42
*	V4	Be Calmed		488
*	V5	Be Calmed Right-hand		488
*	V7	Be Somebody or Be Somebody...		291
**	V6	Beach Ball	3	254
*	V6	Beach Bum		254
	V1	Beach Crack		255
**	V3	Beach Tea One		210
	V1	Beached Whale Crack		199
	V0+	Beady Eye		160
***	V6	Beagle Has Landed, The		320
	V2	Beagle's About		320
*	V7	Beak No Weevil		99
**	V4	Beak, The		456
	V3	Beaky Direct		122
	V0-	Bear Poo		284
*	V8	Beast, The		119
*	V5	Beauty		119
***	V12	Bed of Procrustes, The		265
**	V6	Bedrock		213
*	V6	Been Caught Stealing		520
*	VB	Beginners' Slab		44
	V1	Bell End		129
*	V5	Bell, The		129
	V6	Ben and Jerry's Love Child		385
*	V7	Ben's Bulge		327
***	V11	Ben's Extension		149
*	V9	Ben's Groove		381
**	V10	Ben's Roof		362
***	V9	Ben's Wall (Curbar)		304
**	V9	Ben's Wall (RHS)		384
*	V5	Ben's Wall Traverse		304
**	V8	Beneath the Breadline		134
	V8	Bentley's Going to Sort You Out		147
	V3	Bernie		469
	V3	Between the Bars		376
	V1	Between the Two		159
**	V0	Beyond the End		217
	V0-	BGM's Crack		128
	V0	BGM's Mantel		128
*	V7	Bhodi		523
*	V8	Big Air	109	135
***	V8	Big Al Qaeda		382
	V0+	Big Block Arete		447
	VB	Big Block Gully		446
*	V4	Big Block Wall		226
**	V7	Big Brother		410
	V1	Big Business		148
	V1	Big Flake		94
*	VB	Big Flakes		241
**	V9	Big Friday	293	293
*	V4	Big Push, The		433
	V0	Big Slab		54
*	V5	Big Slab Arete		415
	V0-	Big Slab Left		184
	V0+	Big Slab Right		184
	V0+	Big Slab, The	180	184
***	V8	Bigger Splash Direct		359
	V0	Bilge		343
	V1	Billy Bunter		528
***	V6	Bin Laden's Cave	331	330
	V7	Bin Lillemule		330
**	V7	Bionics Traverse		67
	V3	Bionics Wall		67
	V5	Bionics Wall Low Left		67
	V4	Bionics Wall Right		67
**	V3	Birch Tree Arete		226
	V0-	Bishop's Move, The		455
	V3	Bishop, The		398
*	V8	Bizzare		528
	V5	Black and Decker		130
	V2	Black Arete (RHS)		383
	V0+	Black Arete (Plantation)		148
	V0	Black Bulge		148
	V0	Black Nix Wall		294
	V0	Black Nook Arete		446
	V0	Black Nook Slab		446
	VB	Black Wall		148
	V1	Blast Hole Wall		345
	V3	Blazes		522
**	V11	Blazing 48s		197
*	V8	Blind Ali		207
	V1	Blind Crack		241
***	V8	Blind Date		207
***	V11	Blind Drunk		207
***	V9	Blind Fig.		207
	V2	Blind Flake		473
*	V10	Blind Fury		207
	V2	Blind Pocket Arete		395
	V1	Blind Pocket Rib		395

Problem Index 533

Stars	Grade	Route	Photo	Page
	V2	Blind Pocket Traverse		395
**	V2	Blind Pocket Wall		395
*	V8	Blinding Lights		512
	V0+	Blinkers (Harborough)		514
*	V1	Blinkers (High Neb)		117
**	V0+	Blister Slab		447
*	V0+	Blister's Sister		447
	V2	Blob Mantel		393
	V4	Blob Over		391
*	V6	Blob, The (Cratcliffe)		391
	V1	Blob, The (Roaches)		452
***	V7	Blobs Eliminate, The		386
**	V5	Bloc Steno		329
	VB	Block and Crack		447
**	V8	Block and Tackle Direct		182
*	V2	Block Arete		174
*	V1	Block Party		174
*	V2	Block Wall		174
*	V3	Blocky Rib		198
***	V7	Blood Falls	421	419
*	V2	Blow Out		121
*	V5	Blow Peter		121
*	V0+	Blue Cap Start		258
*	V0	Blue December Sky		161
*	V5	Blue Hawaii		291
*	V5	Blue Whale, The		260
*	V0+	Blunt Arete (Burbage S)		246
*	V0	Blunt Arete (Roaches)		441
*	V6	Blunted		95
	V0+	Bob Mantel		393
***	V8	Boba Fett		441
**	V6	Bobarete		441
	V4	Boffwidth		99
*	VB	Bog Arete Left		440
**	V4	Bog Arete Right		440
*	V2	Bog Monster		440
*	V0	Bog Slab		440
*	V2	Bog Standard		440
*	VB	Bog Standard Slab		240
*	V2	Bog Trot		530
*	V0	Boggle Boothroyd		210
*	V1	Bogside Arete		153
*	V1	Bogside Flakes		153
**	V11	Bohemian Grove		264
*	V6	Boing Boy		403
*	V1	Bolted Pillar		190
**	V2	Bombay Overhang		461
*	V6	Bone at it Direct		315
	V0	Bones		292
*	V6	Bonsallitis		407
**	V5	Bookend Right		112
**	V4	Bookend, The		112
*	V2	Boomerang Wall		382
**	V2	Boomerang-erang		382
*	V2	Boomslang		425
*	V5	Boot Boys Start		364
*	V3	Booze		528
	V5	Boozy Traverse, The		449
**	V5	Bop		75
	V0-	Bore-hole Crack		308
*	V1	Bore-hole Traverse		308
	V0-	Bore-hole Wall		308
	V6	Born Slappy		146
*	V9	Born Snappy		146
**	V1	Boss Hogg		385
*	V0+	Boss Slab		445
*	V5	Boss, The		454
**	V5	Bossa Nova		385
**	V10	Boston Mess		153
*	V1	Bottomless Crack Direct 1		119
*	V2	Bottomless Crack Direct 2		119
*	V0+	Boulder Arete		424
**	V1	Boulder Arete Left-hand		424
*	V5	Boulder Club		101
*	V0+	Bouldering Matt		161
**	VB	Bow Arete		513
	V0-	Bow Arete Right		513
*	VB	Bow Corner		513
*	V2	Bow Crack		446
*	VB	Bow Ridge		513
*	V0+	Bow Shaped Wall		513
	V0+	Boxer, The		301
**	V7	Boyager		214
*	V5	Boysen's Crack		381
*	V2	Bracken Traverse		206
***	V9	Brad Pit	139	138
***	V5	Brad's Arete		411
***	V8	Brad's Block Traverse		403
**	V5	Brad's Break		403
**	V7	Brad's Rib		407
***	V9	Brad's Wall		409
***	V4	Brain Dead		399
**	V5	Brap Scallion		222
***	V9	Brass Monkeys		159
*	V5	Brazil Start		336
*	V9	Brazillian, The		418
*	V0+	Bread and Water		377
***	V5	Breadline		134
	V6	Break Out the Trumpets		297
*	V10	Break Traverse		207
*	V2	Breakdance High Start		176
*	V3	Breakdance Start		176
***	V6	Breakfast		194
*	V0	Breaking		104
*	V1	Breakout		129
*	V7	Breathe		531
*	V5	Brian		194
**	V8	Brian's Private Arete		398
	V0-	Brick Back Wall		247
**	V2	Bridge Arete		198
*	V2	Bridge Traverse		198
*	V1	Bridge Wall		198
*	V0+	Bridget		496
*	V2	Brig, The		106
**	V8	Brigadoon		264
**	V10	Brigand, The		344
*	V8	Bright Concept, The		320
*	V6	Bristol Stool		145
*	V0+	Broad Rib		123
*	V0	Broad Slab		123
*	VB	Broad Slab Left		123
*	V0-	Broad Wall		123
*	V3	Broadside		344
**	V5	Broddle's Baby		228
*	V5	Brogue Raider		297
	V1	Brogue Slab		297
**	V4	Broken		136
*	V0-	Broken Arete		184
*	V4	Broken Chair, The		285
**	V6	Broken Moon		55
*	V0	Broken Wall		183
**	V5	Broken Wing		456
*	V0+	Brown's Unmentionable		106
*	V7	Bruno Mindhorn		297
***	V8	Brutal Arete		410
**	V3	Bubbles Start		354
*	V0	Buccaneer		343
*	V6	Buccaneer, The		344
*	V1	Buck Eliminate		125
*	V0	Buckaroo (High Neb)		125
*	V5	Buckaroo (High Neb)		125
*	V3	Buckette Arete		125
*	V1	Buckette Rib		125
*	V1	Buckrib		125
*	V3	Buckshelf, The		125
**	V4	Buckstone Bulge		124
***	V8	Buckstone Dyno, The		124
***	V1	Buckstone Groove	16	125
*	V4	Buckstone Traverse		124
	VB	Buckstone Wall	125	125
	V2	Buffer, The		510
*	V2	Bugs		249
*	V2	Bugs' Arete		374
*	V2	Bulbous Bow		341
*	V5	Bulge Right-Hand		278
*	V5	Bulging Arete		473
	V4	Bull Flakes		144
**	V4	Bullworker		144
*	VB	Bullworker Slab		144
*	V0+	Bullworker Slab Traverse		144
	V2	Bum Start Crack		186
*	V4	Bum-Slide		44
*	VB	Bumbler's Arete		160
*	V6	Bumlog Millionaire		415
	V0	Bummer		375
*	V4	Bunny		249
*	V0-	Bunny Run, The		375
**	V5	Bunny Wailer		133
	V2	Bunny Wall (Burbage S)		249
*	V0+	Bunny Wall (Rabbit Warren)		374
*	V2	Buoux Left		255
**	V1	Buoux Right		255
	V2	Buried Boomerang		270
*	V4	Burley's Bridge		382
*	V3	Burnt Sienna		277
***	V8	Bus Stop Mantel	417	419
	V6	Bus Stop Traverse		419
**	V5	Business as Usual		333
	V4	Business Launch		149
*	V9	Business Lunch		289
*	V0+	Busker, The		206
	V4	Buster		451
*	V2	Butter Knife		72
**	V0+	Butter Scoop		72
**	V2	Button Moon		294
*	VB	Buxless		125
*	VB	Buxom		125
*	V4	Buy Buy		301
*	V9	Byker Groove		367
**	V3	C'mon Tiger		432
**	V7	C3PO		441
**	V6	Cabin Boy		340
**	V3	Cabin, The		340
*	V3	Cake		485
**	V4	Calcutta Crimp		461
**	V2	Calcutta Rib		461
*	V3	Calcutta Traverse		461
*	V2	Caley Arete		154
*	V4	Caley Slab		245
**	V8	California Screaming		489
*	V9	Calorie Count		371
*	V0+	Calvi		343
*	V8	Calyx		523
	V0+	Camateras Crack		375
*	V1	Canary Traverse		170
*	V3	Cannon, The		45
**	V3	Capped Rib		216
*	V5	Captain Ahab		81
*	V4	Captain Cabinets		334
*	V8	Captain Hook		147
**	V5	Captain Quark		496
*	V8	Captain Underpants		206
*	V1	Care Bear		285
*	V3	Careful Arete		243
*	V0	Careful Trotter, The		245
***	V11	Careless Torque	137	136
**	V10	Careless Youth		136
***	V8	Carl's Wark Traverse		354
	V4	Carlsberg Export		344
*	V4	Carry on Screaming		277
*	V4	Cartons and Curpets		299
***	V6	Catastrophe Internationale		448
**	V10	Catch		418
*	V2	Catch'n'Match		240
	V2	Cave Dweller		49
***	V3	Cave Eliminate Start		162
*	V3	Cave Left		386
*	V8	Cave Problem	361	362
*	V3	Cave Problem Direct		386
**	V6	Cave Problem, The		386
*	V5	Cave Route		175
	V3	Cave Traverse		49
*	V2	Cave Wall		390
	V0+	Cavendish, The		85
*	V8	Caviar Start		358
	V7	Cellar Dwella		463
*	V1	Cellar Slab 1		463
*	V2	Cellar Slab 2		463
***	V2	Celtic Cross, The		232
**	V5	Central Buttress Direct		122
**	V2	Central Groove Thing		227
*	V0+	Central Pillar		189
*	V0+	Central Wall		184
*	V2	Centre		52
	V4	Centre Left		415
*	V0+	Centre Slab		441
	V2	Centre Wall		415
*	V1	Centre Whale		242
*	V4	Chained Block Traverse, The		525
	V1	Champignon		298
**	V0+	Chant, The		203
**	V6	Chapel of Rest		400
***	V4	Charlie's Overhang		492
*	V4	Charlotte Dumpling		336
**	V3	Chasm Arete		462
*	V6	Cheek, The		419
*	V8	Cheeks 'n' Beaks		98
*	V0-	Cheesy Moon		457
*	V0-	Cheesy Nose		236
	VB	Chekov		292
*	V11	Chequers Groove		289
*	V6	Cherry Bank Road		265
*	V6	Cherub's Bit, The		431
*	V7	Chess Boxer		399
*	V3	Chick Factor		409
*	V6	Chicken Ginger		409
**	V1	Chicken Head		84
**	V1	Chicken Head Rockover		85
**	V3	Chicken Ninja		409
**	V2	Chieftain		240
**	V4	Chimes Start		362
*	V1	Chimney Crack		302
	V7	Chimp A		101
***	V8	China in Your Hands		335
*	V5	Chinless Wonder		172
*	V1	Chip and Thin		398
***	V7	Chip Shop Brawl	9	116
**	V11	Chip Shop Buddy		116
**	V4	Chip Shop Mantel		418
**	V4	Chipless		194
*	V0+	Chipped Slab		197
*	V0	Chipped Slab Right		197
*	V0-	Chipped Wall		472
**	V0	Chipper (Wimberry)		44
*	VB	Chipper (Wimberry)		43
*	V2	Chippy		302
*	V2	Chips		177
*	V1	Chips Ahoy		451
	VB	Chips Slab		392
	V2	Chisel On		424
	V4	Chiseller, The		424
*	V1	Chockstone Crack		254

Northern Peak
Sheffield Crags
Stanage Area
Burbage Valley
Derwent Edges
The Limestone
Central Grit
Staffordshire
South Peak

Stars	Grade	Route	Photo	Page
*	V0-	Chockstone Layback		223
*	V10	Choker, The		317
	V1	Choux-Fleur		375
*	V4	Chunky Nut		317
	V5	Church, The		414
	V0+	Cicely		247
*	V0+	Cider		333
*	V8	Cinzano Roof		204
	V0+	Cixot.		130
*	V0+	Clammy Hands		497
*	V0	Clammy Wall		497
**	V3	Clamp Arete		468
*	V6	Clandestiny's Child		414
	V2	Clanger, The		497
*	V1	Clark's Route		222
**	V5	Classic Arete (Burbage S)		223
**	V0	Classic Arete (Roaches)		447
*	V2	Classic Mantel		486
*	V1	Classified		411
*	V2	Claustrophobic Arete		504
*	V0+	Cleg		484
***	V2	Cleo's Edge	26	212
	VB	Cleo's Other Edge		212
*	V0-	Cleo's Right Hand		212
*	V1	Cleo's Slab		212
**	V7	Clever Skin		499
**	V8	Clever Skin Left-Hand		499
**	V7	Clifftop Arete Left		403
***	V13	Close of Business		149
**	V7	Cloud Cuckoo Land		295
**	V2	Clouded Judgement		295
	V5	Clover Field		524
	V2	Cobra Mantel		236
	VB	Cobra Off-width		236
*	V7	Cobra, The		236
***	V6	Cock 'O The Rock		122
	V2	Cock Crack		122
*	V5	Cock End		428
	V3	Cock Groove		122
	V1	Cock Jockey		428
*	V9	Cock-a-doodle-doo		122
	V1	Cod Eye Wall		515
*	V4	Coffee High		353
*	V3	Cold Diggerty		313
*	V5	Collywood		485
**	V10	Columns		479
*	V5	Combine Harvester		182
*	V3	Come Harland High Water		377
*	V0+	Come Together		285
***	V11	Coming Up For Air		135
	V1	Communist Crack		480
*	V1	Complete Nutter		316
***	V4	Conan the Librarian	259	259
*	V3	Concave Crimper		385
	VB	Concave Wall		513
	V8	Converted		397
**	V4	Cool Running		99
**	V4	Cool Running Left-hand	96	99
*	V3	Cooper's Traverse		456
*	VB	Copenhagen Corner		344
*	V1	Corker		407
	V0+	Corner Mount		297
*	V4	Corner Pocket		227
**	V5	Cornflake, The		169
	V0+	Corporal Punishment		104
	V2	Cottage Arete		450
*	V1	Cottage Slab		528
**	V5	Cottaging		529
**	V3	Cottonmouth		425
**	V6	Course Traverse, The		48
*	V8	Courtesy of Jonboy		156
	V2	Crab Walk Direct		485
*	V4	Crack 'n' Pockets		309
*	V1	Crack 'n' Slope		429
	VB	Crack (Black Tor)		59
	V0+	Crack (Stanton M.)		408
	V0	Crack (Skyline)		470
*	VB	Crack (Skyline)		468
	V1	Crack (Wolf Edge)		504
**	V3	Crack and Arete (New/Baldstones)	490	494
	V3	Crack and Arete (Skyline)		470
	V1	Crack and Wall		412
*	V4	Crack Cave		175
	V2	Crack Habit		216
	V2	Crack Indirect		460
	V1	Crack Line, The		271
	V1	Crack Start		460
	V2	Crack, The (Black Tor)		60
*	V6	Crack, The (Churnet)		523
	VB	Cracked Arete (Harborough)		515
	V2	Cracked Arete (Ramshaw)		488
*	V0+	Cracked Rib		187
	V1	Cracked Wall (Harborough)		514
	V0-	Cracked Wall (Stoney)		350
*	V4	Cracker Block		403
*	V1	Cracks		513
	V2	Crackside		309
*	VB	Cranberry Crack		203
*	VB	Cranberry Wall		203
*	V9	Crank Cuffin		499
	V6	Crash 'n' Gurn		247
**	V8	Crash Damage		524
	V2	Crash Test		276
	V4	Crazy Legs Crane		95
	V2	Crepscule, Le		370
***	V2	Crescent Arete	4	134
***	V2	Crescent Arete Right-hand		134
	V2	Crescent Groovelet		134
**	V6	Crescent Slab Arete (Curbar)		306
	V0+	Crescent Slab Arete (Plantation)		134
	V0	Crescent Slab Arete		306
*	V0-	Crime		104
	V8	Crimp Master Nasty		433
	V8	Crimp Shrimp		121
	V4	Crimpanzee		422
	V1	Crimps		391
	V4	Crimps and Pockets		359
	V4	Crimpy Flake		422
*	V4	Crimpy Roof		175
	V0+	Crimpy Wall		455
*	V5	Crinkles Wall		452
	V2	Crinkly Wall		462
*	V4	Crispy Noodling		292
*	V3	Crispy Rib		292
*	V3	Crispy Roof		292
*	V0-	Crispy Wall		123
	V1	Crocodile Slot		486
	V2	Croissant Groove		452
*	V0-	Crook Traverse, The		238
**	VB	Crook, The		238
*	V7	Crouching Tiger		95
*	V0-	Crow Man Groove		195
	V2	Crow Man Meets the Psychotic		195
	V0+	Crow Man Wall		195
	V2	Crow's Feet		340
	V1	Crowbar		297
	V0	Crown, The		138
*	V4	Crozzle Arete		144
**	V3	Crozzle Arete Right-hand		144
*	V1	Crozzle Slab	145	145
	V3	Crozzle Wall		144
	V4	Crumble		505
	V2	Crumble Left		505
	V1	Crumble Right		505
**	V3	Crumble Roof		521
*	V0	Crusty		528
**	V8	Crystal Voyager		476
	V1	Cube Arete		169
	V0-	Cube Crack		464
**	V8	Cube Direct, The		465
	V1	Cube Left		169
	V3	Cube Root, The		169
	V3	Cube Traverse		465
***	V4	Cube, The		465
	V1	Cubism		301
	V3	Cubist		312
	V3	Curbar Corner		300
	V3	Curbar Your Enthusiasm		291
*	V1	Curly's Crack		71
*	V1	Curse, The		203
*	V7	Curvaceous		95
*	V4	Curve Ball		510
	VB	Curved Rib		302
*	V4	Curving Arete	87	87
*	V4	Curving Crimps		227
	V5	Cutaway		262
	V5	Cute Bum		420
	V1	Cutunder Crack		119
	V1	Cwingen		375
	V0+	Cwingod		375
	V3	Cydrax		333
***	V4	D.I.Y.		130
	V0+	Daddy Arete Right		217
	V0+	Daddy Bear Arete		217
	V0-	Daddy Right Arete		217
	V0	Daddy Wall		217
	V0	Daisy		385
	V5	Dan's Arete		340
	V6	Dan's Wall		306
	V1	Dane's Delight		344
	V1	Dane's Disgust		344
	V1	Dark Green Traverse		83
***	V9	Dark Matter		48
	V3	Dark Rites		407
*	V6	Dark Side, The		55
	V2	Dark Wall		307
**	V11	Darkest Cloud, The		478
**	V10	Darkstar		251
	V2	Darwin's Crack		78
	V4	Dass Crab		420
	V9	Dave's Dyno		278
*	V7	Dave's Roof		371
*	V4	Dave's Traverse		521
*	V8	David		259
*	V5	Davros		521
**	V3	Daydreamer	127	128
**	V7	Deadline		134
	V0+	Deb		113
*	V3	Debris Groove		359
*	V6	Debstar		54
	V0	Deception		67
	V2	Deceptive Rib		264
	V2	Deep Pocket		249
*	V2	Defiance Traverse, The		343
*	V5	Definitive 5.11		224
**	V5	Definitive 5.12		204
	V6	Deforestation		55
	V5	Defying Destiny Start		159
*	V11	Delayed Devotion		138
	V2	Delivarate		152
***	V8	Deliverance		152
***	V7	Deliverance Traverse		153
*	V9	Delusions of Grandeur		138
*	V8	Demon Wall		408
	V0-	Descent Route (Burbage W)		196
	V0+	Descent Route (Alport Area)		370
*	V5	Desert Island Disco		510
***	V8	Desperate		222
*	V3	Desperation Start		162
	V0-	Diagonal		306
	V0-	Diagonal Crack		44
*	V8	Dialogue		488
	V3	Diamond Slab		385
	V2	Diamond Slab Left		385
	V5	Diamond Slab Right		385
***	V8	Dick Williams		255
**	V6	Dignity of Labour, The		449
*	V5	Dijon Dip		133
	V1	Ding Dong		163
***	V8	Directissima		50
**	V8	Dirtnap		461
*	V5	Dirty Bitch		319
*	V4	Dirty Business		333
*	V4	Dirty Business Left-Hand		333
	V1	Dirty Higgar		191
	V0+	Dirty Protest, The		132
*	V6	Dirty Rascal		220
*	V4	Dirty Roof		93
*	V3	Disabled Seaman		340
*	V4	Dish Grab		461
*	V8	Dissolution		419
	V2	Dizzie Rascal		220
*	V3	Dog Jump		248
	V6	Dog Pound		248
*	V6	Dog Sit		248
	V0+	Dog's Arse Left		248
	V1	Dog's Arse Right		248
*	V4	Dog's Hole, The		295
	V0-	Dog-leg Crack		295
	V4	Doggy Bulge		248
	V4	Doggy Style		248
*	V8	Dogma		432
***	V7	Domes		423
*	V0-	Don's Arete		456
	V1	Don's Crack		456
	V4	Don's Eliminate		456
	VB	Don't Get Between		217
	V5	Don't Jump		367
**	V5	Doorstep, The		166
	V4	Dope Mantel, The		150
***	V7	Dope on a Slope		150
	V2	Dork Child Start		229
	V1	Dork Slab		229
	V2	Dork Walk		229
	V2	Dork, The		229
	VB	Dorsal Arete		383
	V4	Double Bum		333
*	V5	Double Double, The		353
	V0-	Double Flake		175
	V3	Double Trouble		530
*	V4	Dougless		444
**	V8	Dove from Above, The		87
	V5	Dowager's Hump		119
***	V3	Down to Earth		113
	V3	Down Under		531
*	V7	Downhill Gardener		294
*	V7	Downhill Racer Direct		288
	V2	Downhill Racer Start		288
**	V5	Downpipe, The		462
*	V7	Dragon Slayer		94
*	V3	Dragon's Den, The		94
	V1	Dragon's Slab		63
*	V3	Dragonflight Traverse		358
*	V4	Dream Boat		128
	V8	Dreamer		478
*	V7	Dreaming the Beagle		320
*	V3	Dressed Arete		302
	V0	Dressed Right		302
	V2	Drizzle		409
**	V9	Drop Your Weapons		305
*	V2	Dropsy		452

Northern Peak · Sheffield Crags · Stanage Area · Burbage Valley · Derwent Edges · The Limestone · Central Grit · Staffordshire · South Peak

Stars	Grade	Route	Photo	Page
***	V7	Drowning Pool, The	473	472
*	V0+	Drowning Traverse, The		473
*	V7	Drum Roll		330
*	V5	Drunk Enough		461
	V1	Dry Roasted		316
***	V6	Dry Wit in a Wet Country		386
*	V9	DT's, The		129
*	V5	Duck, The		256
*	V6	Duck-billed Platypus, The		531
	V2	Dutch Cap		259
*	V7	Dylan's Variant		325
	V2	Eager Trout		468
	V0+	Ear Flake		505
***	V7	Early Doors		307
*	V4	Early Morning Day		297
*	V4	Easier Side, The		254
	VB	Easy Arete (Burbage N)		210
	V0-	Easy Arete (Skyline)		473
	V2	Easy Breaks		196
	VB	Easy Cap		259
	VB	Easy Crack (Hobson M)		64
	VB	Easy Crack (New/Baldstones)		493
	V3	Easy Dyno		351
	V3	Easy Exit		499
	VB	Easy Flake		243
*	V0	Easy Groove (Roaches)		458
*	V0	Easy Groove (Roaches)		463
	VB	Easy Jamming		170
*	V4	Easy Picking		101
	V0-	Easy Problem 1		204
	V0-	Easy Problem 2		204
*	V0+	Easy Prow		486
	VB	Easy Ramp		469
*	V0-	Easy Slab (Cratcliffe)		395
*	V0+	Easy Slab (Higgar)		189
	VB	Easy Slab (New/Baldstones)		493
	VB	Easy Slab Right-hand		493
	V1	Easy Tiger		432
*	V2	Easy Walling		170
	V4	Eat Less Bread		433
*	V5	Eating Out		223
	VB	Eden Arete		128
	V0-	Edge of Love, The		77
	V1	Edge of Reason, The		77
	VB	Edgy Slab		64
	V0+	Edward		510
	VB	Eeny		173
	V3	Eeyore		270
	V4	Egg Arete		396
	V2	Egg Arete Left		396
	V2	Egged On		396
*	V8	Eggs is Eggs		396
	V1	Eggy Scoops		396
***	V7	Egyptian Feet		351
	V7	Egyptian Variation		351
*	V7	El Regallo del Mocho		195
**	V5	Elastic Wall		486
	V0-	Elderberry Layback		386
***	V8	Electrical Storm		226
*	V6	Electrofly		524
**	V4	Elephant's Arse		183
	V1	Elephant's Bum		44
*	V0+	Elephant's Ear		499
	V4	Elephant's Eye		499
	V3	Elf Cap Start		258
	V0+	Eliminate Flake		341
	V6	Eliminate Slap		414
	V2	Eliminator		46
	V0	Eliza		165
	V6	Elmer Fudd		318
	V6	Emergency Room		403
	VB	End Slab		216
*	VB	Endest Arete		216
	VB	Endste		216
**	V5	English Voodoo		333
*	V5	Enhancing Hero		44
	V8	Enigma		371
*	V11	Enigma, The		55
	V0	Entering		104
***	V3	Enthusiast, The		214
**	V6	Epilogue		488
	V3	Erganweasel		92
*	V6	Escape From Monday		59
*	V9	Escondido		334
*	V6	Europe After Rain		101
	V0	Euryalus		342
	V2	Exit Stage Right		423
	V1	Explosion		345
	V0+	Exposure		247
**	V6	Extended Warfare		307
**	V3	Eye Socket, The		263
**	V3	Eyes., The		282
*	V3	Fab Arete		307
	V5	Facade		353
*	V3	Face Off		353
*	V7	Fact Hunt		319
**	V5	Fallen Archangel		120
	V6	Fallen Slab Lip		206
**	V4	Falls, The		153
**	V8	Famous Grouse		194
	V0-	Fascism		377
*	V4	Fast Ledge		224
*	V4	Fat Controller, The		510
**	V13	Fat Lip		362
*	V4	Fat Slapper		43
*	V3	Fat World		318
	V7	Fatherhood		520
*	V8	Faze Action		99
*	V8	Femme Fatale, La		52
	V2	Femme Slab, La		52
	V2	Fence, The		398
	V0+	Fern Crack Start		133
***	V5	Fidget		298
	V3	Fielder's Corner		499
	V1	Fielder's Indirect		499
**	V8	Fielder's Wall		499
*	V4	Fierce Wall		128
*	V8	Fifty Pence Problem		524
*	V8	Fig Roll		175
*	V8	Figure of 8		355
*	V5	Fin, The (Black Tor)		59
***	V6	Fin, The (Gib T)		501
	V1	Fin, The (Wolf Edge)		505
*	V7	Final Thought		423
	VB	Final Wall		515
*	V3	Finale		163
	V1	Finale Direct		163
	V0	Fine Slab		504
	V0	Fine Slab Arete		504
**	V7	Finger Bang		430
***	V4	Finger of Fate	475	480
	V2	Finger, The		462
	V2	Fingerdish Mantel		245
***	V6	Fingers		522
	V0+	Fingersplitter		263
*	V4	Fingery Green Wall		186
*	V0	Finisterre		343
***	V7	Fink, The		501
	V5	Fire Fly		52
*	V8	Fireball		257
*	V0	First Bulge		254
	V3	First of a Thousand Oxs		269
*	V4	First Roof Left		325
*	V5	First Roof Middle		325
*	V1	First Wall Traverse		202
***	V6	Fish Arete		48
*	V4	Fish Dish		48
*	V0	Fish Eye		48
*	V4	Fish Groove		48
	V0+	Fish Slab Central		48
	V1	Fish Slab Right		48
	VB	Fish Slab, The		48
**	V0	Fish Traverse		48
	V0	Fishy	303	302
	V3	Flags of the World		117
	V0	Flagstone Roof Left		84
	V3	Flagstone Roof Right		84
	V0	Flake 'n' Blob		220
	V2	Flake and Arete		450
	V2	Flake and Scoop		250
*	VB	Flake Arete (Millstone)		262
**	V0	Flake Arete (Roaches)		446
	V0	Flake Bulge		81
*	VB	Flake Mantel		515
	V2	Flake Museum, The		457
*	V0	Flake Problem (Cratcliffe)		392
	V0-	Flake Problem (Froggatt)		276
*	V0	Flake Sitter		515
	V0-	Flake Sitter Left		515
*	V0	Flake Slab (New/Baldstones)		493
*	V1	Flake Slab (RHS)		380
*	V0	Flake Slab Arete		380
	V1	Flake Slab Eliminate		493
	V0	Flake, The		46
	V0	Flakeless		243
	V1	Flakes (Hobson M)		64
	V1	Flakes (Roaches)		442
	V1	Flakes (Roaches)		464
	V2	Flakes and Chips		458
	V1	Flaky Bake		60
*	V4	Flaky Fluster		112
	V0+	Flaky Layback		319
	V0+	Flaky Romp		470
	V2	Flat Cap		259
	V2	Flat Groove		174
	V2	Flat Wall		350
*	V5	Flat Wall Dyno		221
	V0+	Flat Wall Traverse		174
	V0+	Flatulence		284
***	V8	Flatworld		318
*	V5	Flight Exam		469
*	V3	Flipper		383
**	V3	Flipper Arete		383
	V3	Flipworker		277
*	V5	Flowtation		525
*	V5	Fly Frisching		177
*	V4	Fly, The		443
**	V4	Flying Arete Left		190
***	V7	Flying Arete, The		190
	V0+	Flying Groove		313
	V3	Flying Start		313
	V1	Flying Wall Left		190
	V0+	Flying Wall Right		190
	V2	Fo'.		173
	V9	Fogey Prow, The		489
	V5	Foie Gras		516
	V3	Follow Through		530
	V3	Foord's Folly Start		489
*	V6	Foot Locker, The		386
	V0+	Foot Tickler		395
	V4	Footprints		531
	V2	Footy Rib		221
***	V8	For a Few Beagles More		320
*	V7	Force Nine		488
*	V7	Force Tart		140
	V1	Forestation		55
	V1	Fork 'andles		157
*	V7	Forward Thinking Sound..., The		333
*	V6	Fossil Wall Start		366
	V2	Four Candles		157
	V2	Four Candles Arete		157
**	V8	Four Lions		479
*	V5	Four Star		140
	V2	Fourth Arete		479
	V0	Fragile Mantel		163
**	V7	Free Range Abattoir		367
	V0	Friar's Wall		223
	V0+	Friend Slot Wall		263
*	V4	Friends and Relations		271
	VB	Front Crack		302
	V0+	Front End Face		216
	V1	Front Face		312
	V0+	Front Flake		166
	V0-	Front On (Curbar)		302
*	V0	Front On (RHS)		385
*	V0	Front Wall		189
	V6	Fudge		367
*	V1	Fudgie Budgie, The		170
	V8	Full Circle		325
***	V8	Full Circuit, The		153
***	V11	Full Power		327
***	V8	Full Virgin Traverse, The		527
	V1	Fumf		101
*	V0	Fun Crack		189
	V0	Fun Slab		243
	V0	Fur Side, The		257
**	V10	Furry Egg		402
*	V4	G-Thang		335
	V4	G005.E		138
*	V6	Galaxy Dove		85
	V0+	Ganderhole Crack		499
*	V2	Gap, The		432
*	V5	Garden Shed		256
	V3	Garden Shed Arete		256
	V2	Gary's 5c		501
*	V6	Gates, The		462
*	V8	Gav's Problem		352
	V2	Genovesa		79
*	V0	Gentle Rib		227
	VB	Gentle Slab (Burbage S)		227
*	VB	Gentle Slab (Burbage S)		246
	V0-	Gentle Slab (Roaches)		441
*	V4	Gentleman John		524
	V8	George's Wall Dyno		354
	V3	George's Wall Eliminate 1		354
	V5	George's Wall Eliminate 2		354
***	V4	Germ		117
	V2	Get the Horn		174
	V2	Getaway	103	104
	V2	Gib Torrture	500	501
***	V6	Gib's Rib	219	225
*	V4	Gibbering Left		501
*	V4	Gibbering Right		501
**	V8	Gibbering Wreck		501
**	V6	Gibbon Swing		431
	V4	Gibby Haines		501
	V8	Gibsonitus		283
***	V6	Giza		212
*	V5	Glamourpuss		286
***	V6	Glass Hour		146
	V2	Glass Hour Left-hand		146
**	V7	Glass Slipper		277
*	V3	Glory Days		424
	V4	Glory Hole		529
	V3	Glued Up		456
	V2	Go West	192	196
	V2	Goat's Eye		457
	V2	Goat's Gruff		457
	V0+	Gog Arete		224
*	V4	Golden Arete		263
***	V10	Golden Egg, The		402
**	V9	Golden Path, The		161

Northern Peak · Sheffield Crags · Stanage Area · Burbage Valley · Derwent Edges · The Limestone · Central Grit · Staffordshire · South Peak

Side tabs (top to bottom): Northern Peak · Sheffield Crags · Stanage Area · Burbage Valley · Derwent Edges · The Limestone · Central Grit · Staffordshire · South Peak

Stars	Grade	Route	Photo	Page
*	V6	Good, the Bad and the Beagle, The		320
*	V8	Goose Cannon		516
***	V8	Goosecreature		516
*	V3	Goosegg Groove		516
	V0+	Gordon		510
*		Gordon Brown Superhero		297
***	V6	Gorilla Warfare		307
**	V4	Got Milk		517
*	V9	Goya		510
	V0+	Grand Larceny		104
**	V9	Grand Theft		454
	V2	Grand Theft Start		174
**	V9	Grands Doigts, Les		277
	V2	Grapple with Flake		244
*	V0	Grapsus		79
*	V5	Grasper, The (Gardom's)		327
	V0+	Grasper, The (Roaches)		446
*	V3	Grasshopper, The		531
*	V0	Grassy Mantel, The		186
*	V4	Gravy Boatsmen		429
**	V5	Grazer, The		224
**	V8	Grease Lightning		226
**	V9	Great White	272	304
*	V6	Green 45, The		283
**	V5	Green Boulder Traverse		381
	V6	Green Chapel		414
*	V5	Green Death Start		265
***	V8	Green Death Superdirect	265	265
	V8	Green Eliminate 1		150
	V8	Green Eliminate 2		150
**	V8	Green Flag		251
*	VB	Green Groove (Higgar)		187
	V2	Green Groove (Stanton M)		415
**	V9	Green Lipped Muscle		391
*	V9	Green Man, The		411
	V0	Green Mantel		446
*	V5	Green Mile, The		304
	V1	Green Parrot		113
	V0	Green Ramp		64
	V2	Green Roof		83
**	V7	Green Room Slap		118
	V3	Green Runnel		72
	V2	Green S-Groove		223
	V3	Green Scoop Mantel		250
*	V0	Green Slab		206
*	V7	Green Slap, The		150
	V5	Green Slopey Traverse		397
***	V6	Green Traverse, The	151	150
**	V4	Green Wall (Churnel)		528
*	VB	Green Wall (Hobson M)		64
**	V0	Green Wall (Wimberry)		42
	V3	Greener Mantel		445
***	V4	Greener Traverse		445
	V4	Greenerete		445
	V4	Grewsome	31	450
*	V7	Grim Reaper Direct		66
*	V7	Grim Reaper Traverse		66
**	V6	Grind, The		443
*	V3	Grinding Sloper, The		493
**	V3	Gripple Grapple		168
*	V4	Gripple Graunch		168
	V1	Gripple Nipple		168
	V0+	Gripple One		168
	V1	Gripple Three		168
	V1	Gripple Two		168
*	V4	Grit Style		46
***	V6	Gritstone Megamix		341
*	V8	Gritstone Pimple		471
**	V8	Gritstone Treaty, The		329
*	V7	Grizzly Arete		386
*	V5	Grizzly Bear		216
	V4	Groove (Blackwell D)		366
	VB	Groove (Wimberry)		49
**	V4	Groove (Wimberry)		45
	V7	Groove Traverse		45
*	V6	Groove, The (Black Tor)		60
	V3	Groove, The (Stoney)		354
	V1	Grooved Arete		135
	V0-	Grooves		49
**	V2	Groovy		285
	V2	Groovy Crack		472
	V2	Groovy Wall		307
	V0+	Grounded Bees		314
*	V4	Grouper		48
*	V4	Grovel		382
	V3	Growl Tiger		432
**	V10	Growler, The		386
*	V3	Gruesome Mantel		210
	V5	Guidebook Eleven		352
*	V2	Gully Crack		75
*	V2	Gully Flake		172
***	V8	Guplets on Toast		251
*	V5	Guppy Arete		223
**	V5	Gurgling Green Streak, The		81
*	V7	Gutter, The		449
**	V8	H - Top		148
*	VB	H Block		132
	V2	H.O.P., The		270
	V4	Ha Hoo		431
*	V0	Haahoo		73
	V1	Haddon Haul, The		386
*	V3	Hair Conditioned Nightmare		317
	V2	Hair Conditioned Rightmare		317
	V1	Hairpin Arete		276
	V0+	Hairpin Scoop		276
	V6	Half a World Huway		86
*	V3	Halfway Slab		319
	V0+	Hallelujah Start		67
**	V3	Hamburger Roof		232
**	V3	Hammy		494
**	V3	Hamper's Direct		172
***	V7	Hamper's Hang		172
	V0	Hand Crack		473
	V2	Handrail		45
*	VB	Handy Crack		340
	V0-	Handy Wall (Birchen)		340
	V1	Handy Wall (Roaches)		462
*	V7	Hang 'em High		420
	V1	Hanging Arete		450
	V0+	Hanging Crack		486
	V5	Hanging Prow		231
***	V4	Hanging Rib, The		207
**	V4	Hanging Wall		211
	V4	Hangman		414
	V0-	Hank Rack, The		129
	V1	Hannah Sporren Warren		375
*	V8	Happy Campus		98
	V2	Happy Feet		377
*	V4	Happy House		291
	V1	Happy Slapper		291
***	V7	Hard Arete		479
	V4	Hard Mantel		93
*	V9	Hard Moon		55
*	V6	Harder Side, The		254
*	V6	Hare's Ear		257
	V5	Hare's Ear Left		257
**	V3	Harevester Dyno		182
	V2	Harland Globetrotter		377
	V4	Harland Shuffle		376
*	V0	Harold		510
*	V4	Harris Problem		350
*	V8	Harris Problem 1		352
*	V8	Harris Problem 2		355
	V0	Harry Patch		469
	V5	Harry's Hole		190
	V2	Harvest Arete		182
	V0	Harvest Groove		182
**	V4	Harvester, The		182
*	V3	Has Shaun Got False Teeth?		312
**	V6	Hat Trick		511
**	V5	Hatchet, The		169
*	VB	Hazel Barn		494
*	VB	Hazel Barrow Crack		494
	V2	Hazel Groove		494
	V3	Hazel Traverse		494
	V3	Hazelnut Whirl		316
	V3	Headbanger		121
**	V4	Headspin		176
**	V9	Heartland		328
	V5	Heinous Mantel		446
*	V8	Help Right-hand		133
*	V7	Help the Aged		133
***	V7	Help the Young		159
**	V6	Hem Line		485
**	V7	Hemline		191
*	V1	Henge, The		166
	V1	Henge/ Hinge Connection, The		166
	V3	Henry		510
*	V6	Here Be Dragons		251
***	V4	Hermit Traverse		398
	V0+	Hermitage Hand Jam		398
**	V7	Hermitage Rib		398
*	V7	Heroes		318
*	V1	Hidden Arete		393
	V0+	Hidden Paradise		77
	V2	Hidden Slab		244
	V0	Hidden Wall		394
**	V5	Hideous Hidare		118
**	V8	Higginson's Arm		458
	V2	High		104
*	V4	High Arete (Burbage S)		224
	V2	High Arete (Hobson M)		64
*	V1	High Break		353
	V2	High Cobra, The		236
***	V6	High Green		362
*	V4	High Mantel		185
**	V0-	High Road, The		169
***	V0+	High School Musical	76	76
***	V6	High Speed Imp Act		524
	V0	High Wall		64
*	V9	Higher Ground		319
*	V7	Highrishman		237
**	V4	Hinge, The		166
	V5	Hip Hip Huway		86
*	V7	Hippo, The		130
*	V9	Hippocampus		158
	V4	Historical Arete		122
*	V8	Hit Man, The		138
***	V8	HMS Daring		341
*	VB	Ho'		173
	V1	Hob Traverse, The		523
	V0-	Hob, The		523
	V2	Holds Actually		76
**	V6	Home Cooking		223
**	V4	Honcho		67
**	V5	Honcho Left		67
	V5	Honcho Right-hand		67
**	V6	Honorary Caley		154
*	V10	Hook		362
*	VB	Hook, Line, and Sinker		166
	V12	Hooligan Start		363
	V8	Hoppin' Mud		385
	V2	Horn Arete		
***	V5	Hornblower		341
*	VB	Hörnli Ridge		46
	V5	Horse Roof		83
	V5	Horse Roof Direct		83
	V1	Horseshoe Arete		504
	V5	Hot Butter Knives		278
*	V6	Hot Toddy		282
***	V5	Hot Ziggerty		313
*	V4	Hourglass Left	24	146
	V2	Hourglass, The		146
*	V9	House of the Holey		400
	V2	Housebrick, The		220
*	V4	Howdy Rowdy		172
	V3	Howitzer		45
	V5	Howships Lacunae		340
	V3	Hubert Cumberdale		429
	VB	Huffer Puffer		129
**	V10	Huffy's Roof		305
	V0+	Huge Slab Mantel		169
	V3	Huggy		246
	V3	Hugo First		386
	V8	Hulley Pulley		257
	V2	Humpin'		307
*	V7	Humpty Dumpty		524
	V3	Hurkling Towards Earth		81
**	V9	Hurricane		307
*	V4	Hurry on Sundown		318
	V1	Hush		206
	V0+	Hush Arete		206
	V2	Huway-cold		86
	V1	Huway-day		86
	V7	I am the God of Hell Fire		420
*	V6	I Bet He Drinks Carling Black.....		299
*	V8	I'm Tense		221
*	V8	Iain's Arete		98
*	V5	Iain's Prow		122
**	V4	Icarus Upstart		480
	V1	Ice Cream Cone		244
	V4	Iggle		73
*	V7	Ill Defined, The		59
	V3	Imp Wall		92
*	V10	Imperfect Catch, The		478
	V5	Impish		92
	V2	Implosion		345
	V3	Impotence		443
*	V11	In the Flick of Time		206
**	V3	Incursion Direct		116
	V7	Indirect Arete		499
	V2	Indirect Arete Right		499
***	V7	Inertia Reel		448
	V12	Inertia Reel Traverse		448
	V11	Influx		364
	V0	Ink Cap		259
	V3	Inner Tube		469
	V1	Inside Groove		385
**	V8	Instant Funk		520
**	V11	Intense		221
**	V7	Interstellar Pigeon		85
**	V6	Iranu		123
	V3	Iraqu		123
*	V8	Iron Flag		371
	V4	Iron Pebble		521
	V0-	Isabela Slab		79
	V2	Isle of Men		345
	V2	Issue 53		135
**	V4	It Hurts		243
*	V4	It's a Traversty		366
	V3	Itchy Fingers		496
	V3	Itchy Groove		496
	V0+	Ivy Tree		210
**	V9	JABP, The		351
***	V6	Jackalope, The		336
	V5	Jackson Bollock		425
	V5	Jam and Blast It		488
*	V6	Jamie's Other Roof		120
	V5	Jamie's Other Roof Right		120
**	V8	Jamie's Roof		120
	V2	Jamless		488
	V2	Jammed Block Mantel		210

Stars	Grade	Route	Photo	Page
	V4	Jams O'Mantel		385
	V2	Jams, The		450
	V0-	Jan		104
	V3	Janus Start		301
**	V6	Jason's Mantel		226
	V6	Jason's Mono Problem		195
**	V8	Jason's Roof		211
***	V11	Jason's Traverse		149
**	V11	Jason's Variant		353
	V2	Jawbone		263
*	V7	Jaws (RHS)		383
*	V0-	Jaws (Woolpacks)		76
	V7	Jean Marie		251
**	V10	Jelly Bomb		276
	V1	Jelly Start		428
**	V3	Jelly Tot		428
	V3	Jelly Tot Left		428
	V4	Jeremy Fisher		429
***	V6	Jerry's Arete		385
*	V5	Jerry's Finish		148
	V10	Jerry's Problem		355
**	V7	Jerry's Traverse (Blackwell D.)	365	367
***	V10	Jerry's Traverse (Plantation)		148
*	V8	Jerry's Traverse (Cratcliffe)		397
*	V10	Jerrytricks		355
*	V0	Jessica Rabbit		375
	V0-	Jessicarete		375
*	V8	Jester, The		121
*	V6	Jetpack		283
	V2	Jetty Aretty		213
*	V4	Jetty Bulge		213
*	V3	Jetty Nose		213
*	VB	Jetty Start		213
*	V0	Jigsaw Puzzle		241
*	V4	Jill the Traverse	506, 526	524
	V2	Jim's Slopes	249	249
*	V4	Jimmy		424
*	V9	Jimmy Hat		291
*	V0-	Jobby		451
***	V3	Joe's Arete	12, 439	455
**	V4	Joe's Low Traverse		288
	V0+	Joe's Portholes		455
	V1	Joe's Right		455
***	V4	Joe's Slab		288
**	V4	Joe's Slab Arete		288
	V6	Joe's Slab Traverse		288
	V6	John Player Special		334
*	V3	John Wilson		313
	V2	John's Arete		294
*	V7	Johnny Utah		522
*	V4	Johnny's Groove		395
*	V7	Joint Care		325
***	V11	Joker, The	11, 155	154
*	V0+	Jolly Green Dwarf		317
*	V4	Jolly Green Elephant		317
	V5	Jordan's Wall		307
**	V8	Jorge		95
*	V4	Jorge Easy		95
*	V6	Jorge Jr		95
*	VB	Joy of Ledge		380
*	V0+	Joy of Noledge		380
*	V0-	JT		383
**	VB	JT Crack		383
*	V0+	Jug		513
	V1	Jug of Justice		85
*	V1	Jug Right-Hand		513
	V0+	Jug Up		456
*	V4	Jug Up Wall		521
*	V0+	Juggy Flakeline		470
	V2	Juggy Groove		458
**	V5	Jump		464
*	V4	Jump Before You Look		276
	V3	Jump to Slopers		191
	V10	Jumpers for Trousers		341
**	V8	Jumpin' on a Beetle	509	511
	V3	Jumpin' on an Aphid		431
**	V0+	Junior Arete		394
	VB	Junior Chips		394
**	V0-	Junior Flake		394
*	V0	Junior Slab		394
**	V7	Jupiter Collision		82
	V6	Just Walkin'		251
*	V4	K Kole Arete		112
**	VB	K2		465
	V0+	K3		465
	V0+	Kanga		270
	V1	KBHR		247
***	V13	Keen Roof		362
	V1	Keep Pedalling		161
**	V8	Keith Sharp Holds		520
**	V1	Kermit's Arete		419
	V1	Kermit's Ears		419
**	V1	Keyhole Traverse		267
***	V6	Keyhole Traverse 2		267
***	V7	Keyhole Traverse 3		267
**	V8	Keyhole Traverse 4		267
**	V6	Kid, The		386
	V1	Kidney Traverse		250
	V0+	Kidney Wall		250
***	V8	Kidneystone		328
	V4	Killer Bunnies		375
*	V6	Kim Span		93
**	V8	Kim's Problem		423
	V7	Kimb's Limbs		277
*	VB	Kinderlibrium		233
*	V8	King of Fools		381
	V7	Kirton Dyno, The		351
**	V5	Kiss Me Arse		340
**	V4	Kiss Me Softly		340
*	V4	Knack Sit-start, The		225
	V2	Knee-bar Crack		71
*	V8	Knife, The		415
*	V4	KO'd		112
	V5	Kodak Lightweight Service		221
*	V5	Kong Wubba		402
*	V4	Kookaburra, The		531
*	V8	Kristian's Problem		364
**	V7	Krush Regime		190
**	V8	Kudos		358
	V4	Ladder Coins		332
***	V3	Ladder Rib		224
	V9	Ladies' Wall		277
	V3	Lair		504
	VB	Lamb Slab Left		238
*	VB	Lamb Slab Right		238
	V9	Lankaster Bomber		289
**	V5	Lark, The		397
	V2	Larry's Launch		71
*	V4	Last Arete		395
	V2	Last Banana Before Sunset		499
	V1	Last Drop		485
	V2	Last Horse Roof		83
*	V5	Last Light		294
	V5	Last Wrights		523
**	V8	Late Junction		305
	V4	Layaway Wall (Tintwistle)		52
	V3	Layaway Wall (Black Tor)		59
	V0+	Layback Crack, The		186
**	V2	Lazy Trout	467	468
	V4	Leaf Climb		324
**	V4	Lean, Green, Bean Machine		525
*	V5	Lean-to		415
*	V8	Leaning Block Traverse		182
	V0+	Leaning Crack		271
	V0+	Leaning Wall Start		204
	V0+	Leap		49
***	V8	Leather Joy Boys		492
*	V0	Ledge Climb		138
	V0+	Ledge Crack		326
	V3	Ledge Jump		472
	V0+	Ledge Roof		326
	V0-	Ledge Wall (Curbar)		302
	V2	Ledge Wall (Gardom's)		326
	V0+	Ledge Wall (Higgar)		188
	V0+	Ledge Wall Right		326
	V0+	Ledgy Wall		197
	V1	Leek Flake		469
**	V4	Leek Hills		469
	V0	Left Arete (Baslow)		312
	V0+	Left Arete (Burbage S)		222
	V1	Left Arete (Burbage W)		196
**	V3	Left Arete (Cratcliffe)		392
	V0	Left Arete (Curbar)		292
	V0	Left Arete (Curbar)		295
	V4	Left Arete (Higgar)		185
*	V0	Left Arete (Higgar)		190
	V2	Left Arete (New/Baldstones)		493
	V1	Left Arete (Stanton M)		415
	V0	Left Arete (Roaches)		454
	V1	Left Arete (Wimberry)		43
	V2	Left Arete (Wimberry)		42
	V0	Left Arete (Wolf Edge)		504
	V1	Left Bulge		514
	V5	Left Cheek		472
	V1	Left Crack (New/Baldstones)		497
	V0-	Left Crack (Skyline)		469
**	V3	Left Edge		222
	V2	Left Egg		396
	V0-	Left Egg Arete		396
	V2	Left Eliminette		294
	V1	Left Flake		243
	V1	Left Flank		359
***	V4	Left Groove		458
	V4	Left Leg		172
*	V4	Left of Abattoir		367
	V0-	Left of Crack		236
	V2	Left of Nose Mantel		250
*	V8	Left of Picalli's		382
	V0+	Left Over Chips		194
**	V5	Left Pine		529
*	V2	Left Side		52
*	V0	Left Slab (Roaches)		463
*	V0	Left Slab (Roaches)		447
**	V3	Left Slab (Tintwistle)		52
	V0+	Left Slab (Wimberry)		44
	V2	Left Slab, The		58
	V6	Left Spur		263
	V1	Left Tower		335
*	V1	Left Triplet Arete		335
	V0+	Left Triplet Slab		335
	V8	Left Turn		305
*	VB	Left Twin Arete		493
	V8	Left Wall Mantel		255
***	V8	Left-hand Man		271
*	V8	Leftworld		318
	V0	Leg-press		392
	V3	Leggit		280
	V0-	Legs Over		514
	V5	Lembas		92
	V3	Lembas Arete		92
*	V3	Len's Areet	107	104
**	V3	Len's Edges		104
*	V8	Leon		52
**	V9	Leotard Legend, The		232
	V5	Lepton		300
	V3	Lepton Wall		300
**	V8	Leroy Slips Disc		176
	V2	Letter L, The		302
	V3	Letter T, The		484
	V2	Letterbox Slot		43
	VB	Li'l Arete		473
	VB	Li'l Crack		473
	V2	Lichen Slab		318
**	V7	Lichenthrope		460
**	V5	Life in a Radioactive Dustbin		205
*	V9	Life of Pie		224
	V5	Lifeseeker		298
*	V4	Like a Beagle Over Troubled Water		320
*	V4	Like Pommel		184
	V0-	Lil' Arete		262
*	VB	Lilou		233
*	V6	Limbless Limbo Dancer		461
*	V6	Line, The		419
	V3	Link Up		93
	V2	Lintel, The		457
	V1	Lion		315
**	V8	Lip Barmy		224
	V5	Lip Slap		395
	V2	Little Air		246
	VB	Little Arete (Harborough)		513
	V0+	Little Arete (Derwent)		81
*	V3	Little Arete (Gardom's)		326
*	V7	Little Artless		226
*	V4	Little Brother		410
***	V5	Little Brown Thug		205
	V1	Little Cube Arete		217
**	VB	Little Eden Arete		128
	V2	Little Flake		473
	V4	Little Flake Wall		370
	V3	Little Flatty		422
**	V6	Little Gem		232
	V2	Little Groove		523
	V3	Little Left Wall		174
	V4	Little Limmock		228
	V1	Little Lotto Arete		266
	V5	Little Lotto Arete Right		266
	V4	Little Mantel		501
	V7	Little Oedipus		117
**	V9	Little Pig		244
	V5	Little Pocket Slab		473
	V5	Little Pocket Slab Left		473
	V5	Little Prow		486
	V1	Little Rib		528
*	V1	Little Richard		317
	V2	Little Robin		397
***	V4	Little Roof		198
*	V0	Little Slab		183
	V2	Little Stiffer		300
	V3	Little Thug		176
	V3	Little Traverse (New/Baldstones)		492
	V1	Little Traverse (Gib T)		501
	V1	Little Warm-up		351
	V5	Little White		304
**	V0	Little White Jug Start		204
*	V4	Local Hero		42
	V2	Log		340
	V2	Lone Arete, The		141
*	V0	Lone Boulder		141
	V0+	Lone Boulder Arete		118
	V0+	Lone Boulder Arete Left		118
	V0+	Lone Boulder Slab		118
*	V3	Lone Ranger, The		141
*	V3	Lone Scoop		141
*	V3	Lone Slab, The		141
*	V3	Loner, The		469
	V6	Lonesome Pine		529
*	V0	Long Boulder Mantel		456
	V3	Long John		113
*	V4	Long John's Arete	91	92
*	V4	Long Reaches		160
*	V4	Long Shot		213
	V1	Long Traverse		457

Northern Peak · Sheffield Crags · Stanage Area · Burbage Valley · Derwent Edges · The Limestone · Central Grit · Staffordshire · South Peak

Stars	Grade	Route	Photo	Page
*	V7	Long's Lock		196
*	V6	Look at Me!		390
	V1	Look Right		390
*	V5	Looking Glass Arete, The		59
***	V7	Looking Glass, The		59
*	V3	Lose Hill.		112
*	V3	Lost in France		203
*	V3	Louis the Loon		140
*	V3	Lout		443
	V3	Love Handles		117
*	V8	Love of Money Start, The		366
	V0	Love You Rock		104
*	V3	Low		104
**	V4	Low Break		359
*	V3	Low Coach		82
	V2	Low Lip Traverse		145
***	V10	Low Rider		116
	V2	Low Roof Left		85
*	V3	Low Roof Middle		85
	V2	Low Roof Right		85
**	V4	Low Traverse (Churnet)		524
	V8	Low Traverse (Burbage W)		196
*	V4	Low Triangle Traverse		204
	V2	Lower Cube Traverse		169
*	V6	Lower Traverse		370
	V0+	Loyd Grossman		158
	V1	Loyd Left		158
**	V6	Lucian's Undercut.		352
*	V9	Lunar Direct.		524
*	V4	Lurch, The (Ramshaw)		486
**	V4	Lurch, The (Roaches)		443
**	V4	Lurcher Direct.		106
	V1	Lurcher's Nose		106
*	V3	Lurcher's Nose Front		106
	V0	Lurcher, The.		106
**	V8	Lust Left-Hand		489
*	V3	Mad as a Badger		54
**	V3	Mad Bilberries.		317
	V7	Made in Rotherham		271
*	V7	Made in Sheffield		271
	V2	Magic Arete		488
	V1	Magic Crossing		460
*	V3	Magnetic North Start		173
**	V8	Make it Slappy		511
*	V5	Make it Stick		408
	V3	Makka Pakka's Press		73
***	V13	Malc's Traverse		149
	VB	Mallard		510
	V0+	Mama-Mia.		259
**	V8	Mammoth Book of UFOs, The.		407
**	V4	Man Calls Horse.	80	82
**	V8	Man of Steel.		366
	V9	Mansize		486
	V0	Mantel (Houndkirk M).		270
	V0	Mantel (Ramshaw)		484
*	VB	Mantel and Pocket		451
	V1	Mantel Past Slot.		241
*	V1	Mantel the Bulge		250
	V0	Mantel Wall		514
*	V5	Mantel, The		59
	V4	Mantelicious.		285
	V6	Mantelist, The.		423
**	V1	Mantelpiece Buttress Direct.		163
***	V8	Mark's Roof	323, 6, 7	325
**	V9	Mark's Roof Direct		325
***	V5	Mark's Roof Left-hand		325
*	V3	Martin's Direct		494
*	V7	Martin's Mono		524
**	V1	Martin's Problem		501
**	V1	Martin's Traverse	495	494
*	V6	Marx's Wall		291
	V2	Marxist Arete		480
	V1	Marxist Undertones	481	480
	V2	Mary Whitehouse		161
**	V6	Massacre	171, 174	173
**	V8	Master Chef		266
***	V10	Master Kush.		99
	V3	Matchbox Arete		478
*	V2	Matchbox Slab		478
	V2	Mating Toads	171	173
	V1	Matterhorn Left		227
	V0-	Matterhorn Right		227
	V0-	Matterhorn Slab		227
*	V10	Maurice Gibb		501
	V0-	Maya		77
	V3	Me-Oh My-oh		376
	V6	Means to an End		60
	V1	Meat Balls		377
*	V3	Medicine Ball, The.		175
	V0-	Meeny.		173
*	V7	Megamix Left		341
	V7	Megatron		353
**	V8	Meltdown, The		371
***	V8	Melvin Bragg		484
	V8	Men in Small Cars.		419
**	V0-	Men Only		320
*	V1	Men United		345
	V2	Mental Peace		163
**	V5	Meridian.	368	370
**	V9	Mermaid (Birchen)		344
***	V6	Mermaid (Burbage W)		198
**	V6	Messiah Traverse		229
	V1	Metal Rash Traverse, The		267
*	V7	Mick's Problem		191
**	VB	Micky		451
	V0+	Micro Mill		228
*	V4	Microbe	114	117
**	V4	Microbe Left.		117
	V1	Mid Pod		442
*	V0	Middle Block Slab		58
*	V3	Middle Break (Rubicon)		359
*	V4	Middle Break (Stoney)		353
*	VB	Middle Duck.		256
*	V9	Middle Leg		172
*	V9	Middle Man		255
*	V0	Middle Slab		390
	V2	Middle Slab Right		390
	V3	Middle T.		294
**	V4	Middle Traverse		196
	V2	Middle Triplet Arete		335
	V2	Middle Triplet Ridge.		335
	V0+	Middle Wall (Burbage S)		227
*	V4	Middle Wall (Clifftop)		403
	V0+	Middle Wall (Gardom's).		335
	V3	Midge		484
	V2	Midmantel.		132
*	V6	Midnight Monster		55
*	V8	Mike Tyson		407
	V10	Mike's Problem		366
	V1	Milk Arete		318
**	VB	Milk Cap.		259
*	V4	Milk of Amnesia		318
***	V7	Milky Buttons		479
*	V5	Minah Variation		170
*	V6	Mindbender Jelly		524
**	V6	Mini Beak	88	99
*	V4	Mini Beak Rib		99
	V0	Mini Mantel		285
*	V1	Mini Millwheel.		231
*	V3	Mini Mother		261
	V4	Mini Prow		410
*	V0	Mini-Arete		305
	V0+	Mini-Crack		305
	V1	Mini-Prow		305
*	V3	Mini-Traverse		305
*	V8	Mint400 Direct		286
*	V4	Minus Wall Right		350
	V0+	Minus Wall Start		350
*	V4	Minus Wall Traverse.		350
	V0-	Miny.		173
	V2	Miss Ohio		376
	V2	Miss Sunshine		123
*	V7	Missile Toe		170
	V3	Mister Coconut		494
	V1	Mister Spock		292
*	V3	Mistral Start.		461
	V3	Mjollnir		370
	V0-	Mo Tucker.		133
	V0-	Mo'		173
*	V7	Mo's Problem		329
	V3	Moai.		425
*	V4	Moby		261
	V0-	Moe's Meander		71
	V2	Mollie Sugden.		60
	V0+	Mommy Bear Arete		217
	V0+	Mommy Bear Right		217
	V0+	Mommy Wall		217
**	V5	Monad		117
	V1	Monk On		205
	V0	Monk's Bulge		105
	V0	Monk's Other Bulge		105
	V2	Monkey Crack		204
*	V8	Monkey Man		280
**	V8	Mono Bulge		214
	V5	Mono Seam		288
*	V6	Mono Seam Right-Hand.		288
***	V7	Mono Slab (Plantation)		134
	V0+	Mono Slab (Skyline).		470
***	V8	Monochrome		214
	V5	Monocled Mono.		340
**	V8	Monodoigt, The		457
	V6	Monologue		488
**	V7	Monomantel.		429
	V6	Moo Cow		517
*	V4	Moon Jumper		524
	V5	Moonshine		492
**	V7	Moontan.		99
	V3	More Air Than Chocolate		354
*	V6	More Cheese Gromit		224
	V5	Morris Dancing		432
	V2	Moss Ridge		400
	V1	Mother Rib Left		261
	V1	Mother Rib Right		261
	V1	Mother's Cap Back Wall		259
*	V4	Mother's Pet Arete		260
**	V8	Mother's Pet Long Traverse		260
**	V7	Mother's Pet Traverse		260
***	V8	Mother's Pride		260
*	V5	Motherhood		520
**	V5	Mounting Frustration		160
*	V0-	Mounty		462
**	V8	MP3.		344
*	V5	Mr Left		443
	V0	Mr M'Quod and the Anti-rock Squad		117
*	V5	Mr Mole.		50
*	V4	Mr Nice		443
*	V8	Mr Sheen		206
*	V8	Mr T.		396
*	V6	Mr. Brightside		52
	V1	Mrs Mole		50
	V4	Mug		412
	V4	Muhammad Ali		407
	V1	Muscle Slab		382
**	V8	Musée Imaginaire, Le		305
***	V10	Mushin		449
*	V8	My Apple		420
***	V9	My Buddy the Apple.		420
*	V4	My Crazy Head		172
*	V8	My Friend Flicka.		367
*	V3	My Left Foot.		407
*	V10	My Orange		283
***	V9	My Prune		387
**	V9	Nadin's Secret Finger		480
	V6	Nadin's Traverse		456
	V0+	Nameless Block Mantel		135
	V2	Nasal Passage.		285
*	V8	National Breakdown		156
	V0+	Naughty		285
*	V4	Navuku		520
*	V8	Near Death Experience		399
	V2	Neat		300
*	V8	Neck, The		225
	V3	Neep.		75
*	VB	Negative, The		138
*	V8	Neil's Wall.		366
	V11	Neil's Wall Right.		366
*	V10	Neon Dust Direct		286
	V0	Neptune		342
	V0-	Nertsery Crack		71
	V0+	Nettle Tea		412
	V3	Neutral Milk Hotel		332
*	V11	Never Spanned		295
***	V4	New York, New York.		117
	V1	Nicarete		214
*	V6	Nice Pinch, Shame About the Ledge		431
	V1	Niche Crack		270
*	V4	Niche Traverse		521
*	V6	Nick Knack Paddywack Sit-start.		225
	V4	Nicotine Stain		214
*	V7	Nigel's Problem		255
*	V8	Nigel's Roof.		325
***	V5	Night of Lust Start.		489
*	V8	Night Rider		462
**	V3	Nightmare Slab		128
*	V4	Nightrider		128
**	V7	Nightsalt.		159
**	V11	Nik's Wall		98
*	V4	Nikita		52
	V3	Ninestein		478
	V2	Ninky Nonk		73
*	V3	Nipple, The		46
*	V5	No Break		353
*	V5	No Bull		412
*	V5	No Hueco		400
*	V9	No Regrets	401, 400	386
	V4	Nobody Knows		382
**	V0-	Nobody's Business		148
*	V7	Non Rib		98
*	V8	Non Stick Vicar		511
	V0+	Noose, The		414
	V1	North		172
*	V3	North Roof		202
**	V5	Northeast Face		153
	V1	Northern.		247
	V2	Northerner, The	284	284
	V6	Northwest Face		153
	V0+	Nose Arete		455
	V2	Nose Arete Right (Roaches).		455
	V2	Nose Arete Right (Bell Hagg)		106
	V2	Nose Direct		403
	V2	Nose Horn.		83
**	V2	Nose Mantel (Burbage S)		250
	VB	Nose Mantel (Roaches)		455
	V0+	Nose on Left.		403
	V3	Nose Scoop		455
***	V6	Nose, The (Burbage W)		196
***	V5	Nose, The (Churnet)		524
*	V4	Nose, The (RHS)		384
	V1	Nose, The (Roaches)		441
*	V4	Nose, The (Roaches)		458
**	V7	Nostril, The		196

Northern Peak · Sheffield Crags · Stanage Area · Burbage Valley · Derwent Edges · The Limestone · Central Grit · Staffordshire · South Peak

Stars	Grade	Route	Photo	Page
	VB	Nosy		454
*	V6	Not Green Flag		251
*	V2	Not Like Pommel		184
*	V8	Not Ned's Problem		350
*	V3	Not So Course		48
*	V4	Not the North Pole		271
***	V5	Not to be Taken Away	25, cover	136
*	V4	Not Westworld		197
*	V4	Not Zaff's		255
	V2	Notch Slab		465
*	V3	Novel Adaptation	38	77
***	V12	Nth Power		476
*	V8	Nuda's Tartan		371
**	V3	Nunn's Eliminate		105
*	V3	Nunn's Right		105
	V2	Nunn's Traverse		105
	V2	Nut Cracker		317
*	V2	Nut Job		316
*	V2	Nutmeg		494
	V2	Nutmeg Groove		494
**	V4	Oak Tree Arete		227
*	V6	'Oar 'Ouse		341
*	V4	Oarsman		341
*	V4	Oarsman Arete		341
*	V7	Obstructive Pensioner		341
*	V1	Odd Block		84
*	V4	Oedipus Direct		286
***	V4	Oedipus Start		286
*	V1	Of Old		160
	V2	Off Fingers Crack		469
*	V2	Off Work		450
*	V0-	Og-Pog		73
*	V4	Ogilvie's Direct		95
	V2	Ogilvie's Slab		95
*	V0	Oh Bubba		158
*	V3	Oik		460
*	V0+	Oink Arete		245
**	V8	Old King Cascade		277
*	V6	Old Macdonald		225
*	V0-	Older Still		160
**	V9	Once Upon a Time		217
	V1	One Arm		60
*	V8	One Armed Bandit	349	351
	VB	One Inch Arete		302
	VB	One Inch Crack		302
	V7	One More Inch		149
*	V1	One Move		58
*	V9	One Summer Problem		355
	V1	Ooze		528
	V3	Open Bum Cleft		450
*	V2	Open Flakeline	243	243
**	V1	Open Groove		468
*	V9	Opposition		116
*	V4	Optimistic Meg		397
	V2	Orange Crush		529
*	V8	Orange Si		367
*	V8	Orca		260
**	V3	Original		403
*	V4	Original Route		498
**	V8	Original Warfare		307
	V1	Orion		342
	V1	Orlop		343
	V9	Ornithologist, The		420
***	V4	Ossie's Bulge	483	486
*	V3	Other Arete		81
*	V4	Ousal High		528
**	V7	Ousal Low		528
*	V8	Out of My Tree Start		364
**	V7	Out There and Back		520
**	V3	Outlook Roof		93
	V1	Over the Top		250
	V1	Overground		505
*	V0	Overground Right		505
*	V0+	Overhanging Crack		514
*	V0+	Overhung Mantel		377
*	V7	Overlook Arete		407
	V2	Ox-Trail Soup		269
	V2	Oxycute 'em		269
*	V1	Oxygen		269
	V1	Oxymoron	268	269
**	V3	Oyster Cap Start		258
**	V8	P Crack		400
	V5	Pack		237
	V1	Paddestoel		298
***	V1	Pagan Cross		429
*	V9	Paint it Black		367
**	V0	Pancake		473
	V0-	Pancake Edge		72
	V0-	Pancake Wall		72
	V4	Panzer		240
	V2	Papa Hobo		377
	V3	Parallel Universe		77
	V8	Parental Duties		446
	V3	Parquet Wall		185
*	V8	Parson's Finch, The		95
*	V6	Particle Exchange		444
*	V0+	Pass the Buck		125
*	V4	Pat's Arete		423
***	V8	Pat's Roof		423
*	V1	PDCLW		340
*	V9	Pea Crab Shuffle		283
**	V6	Peaches and Crust		517
*	V5	Peas		177
*	V1	Peas of Mine		50
*	VB	Peasy Flake		243
*	V4	Pebble Arete		152
***	V0	Pebble Arete Left-hand	143	152
*	V5	Pebble Face		152
*	V4	Pebble Face Direct		152
*	V4	Pebble Flakes		152
**	V5	Pebble Ledges		152
**	V0	Pebble Ledges Left		152
***	V6	Pebble Mill Stem		228
**	V7	Pebble Mill Traverse		228
	V0+	Pebble Wall (Burbage S)		244
*	V3	Pebble Wall (Curbar)		304
**	V4	Pebbledash		153
*	V5	Pebbledash Arete		153
*	V3	Pebbles and Seam		440
*	V0+	Pedlar's Arete		161
*	V1	Pedlar's Rib		161
	V2	Pedlar's Slab		161
	V4	Peg's Path		359
*	V4	Peg's Right		359
**	V6	Pendulum, The		146
*	V1	Pennine Way Variation		61
	V0+	Pensioner's Bulge		317
*	V1	Pepper		72
**	V5	Pepper Mill		228
	V3	Percy		510
*	V3	Percy 97		64
	V2	Percy Left-hand		64
*	V2	Percy Right-hand		64
**	V7	Percy's Cornflake		398
*	V5	Percy's Roof		324
***	V3	Perfect Day Direct Start		329
	V0+	Perfect Porthole Problem		86
*	V3	Period Drama		464
***	V4	Persistence		480
	V0+	Pert Block Arete		168
	V0+	Pert Bloke		168
*	VB	Pert Wall		168
*	V4	Pest Control		215
***	V7	Pet Cemetery	260	260
**	V9	Pete's Power Pull		355
	V1	Pete's Route		93
*	V0	Petit Tank, Le		49
*	V8	Pets Win Prizes		261
	V2	Petty Larceny		174
	V2	Petty Theft		104
*	V4	Phat Controller, The		303
	V0+	Phi Phi		77
	V4	Piano, The		79
*	V7	Picalli's Pickie		382
*	V0-	Pick		237
*	V0	Pick Pocket		284
*	V7	Pie Hard		522
	V0+	Pig Head		344
**	V8	Pig Heart Boy		280
	V3	Pig Trough		419
	V3	Pigeon Arete		295
	V5	Piggle		73
	V0+	Piggy's Crack		66
*	V8	Piglet Arete		245
	V2	Piglet Arete Left		245
	V2	Piglet's too Short		271
**	V9	Pigs Make Nests		224
*	V0	Pigtail		344
	V0-	Pillar		189
	V1	Pillar Arete		63
	V3	Pillar Eliminate		183
*	V6	Pillar Face		63
	V0+	Pilz		298
	V3	Pinch 'n' Push		315
***	V12	Pinch 2		353
*	V8	Pinch, The		359
*	V4	Pinches, The		488
	V5	Pindles Numb		449
*	V0	Pine Arete		445
*	V0	Pine Arete Right		445
*	VB	Pine Crack		445
	V0+	Pine Martin		445
	V2	Pine Slab		445
	V4	Pine Wall		529
**	V7	Ping Pong Pocket Rib		112
*	V0-	Pink Arete		395
	V1	Pink Flake		484
**	V11	Pink Lady		418
*	VB	Pink Slab		395
*	V2	Pink Slab Right		395
*	V1	Pink Wall		455
**	V6	Pink Wall Eliminate		455
*	V0	Pinkies to Perkies		469
	V2	Pinky Ponk		73
**	V4	Pinnacle of Human Achievement, The		480
**	V8	Pinnacle Traverse		286
	V6	Pipe Entry		462
**	V6	Pippin Dyno		182
*	V6	Piranha Start		358
*	V7	Piranha Traverse		358
*	V8	Pirate, The		340
***	V8	Piss		191
**	V7	Pistol Pinch		254
*	V4	Pixie		456
*	V0+	Pixie's Arete		92
*	V1	PK's Hammer		60
**	V8	Plank Sanction		216
*	V4	Plaque, The		411
*	V9	Play Hard		309
*	V1	Play Huway		86
**	V11	Playing with Fire		58
*	V0	Plip Start		262
	V2	Plop Start Left		262
*	V0-	Plop Start Right		262
	V5	Plug		159
*	V4	Plumber has Landed, The		112
*	V5	Po		425
*	V0-	Poached		49
*	V2	Poc Poc	74	75
*	V2	Pock		237
***	V1	Pock-man	237	237
**	V6	Pocket Dyno		216
	V2	Pocket Money		76
*	V4	Pocket Passer		213
**	V4	Pocket Slab		55
*	V4	Pocket Wall (Burbage S)		221
	V1	Pocket Wall (Burbage S)		246
*	V4	Pocket Wall (Churnet)		529
	V0+	Pocket Wall (Higgar)		184
	V4	Pocket Wall (Plantation)		134
*	V6	Pocket Wall Left		221
	V2	Pockets 'n' Stuff		224
*	V0	Pockets (Harborough)		513
	V2	Pockets (Wimberry)		46
	V2	Pockets Arete		446
	V2	Pod 'n' Up		442
**	V5	Pogle's Wood		329
**	V8	Pogle's Wood Left-Hand		329
**	V8	Point Break		523
	V1	Poisoned Dwarf		232
*	V7	Polished Bump		133
*	V2	Pontipine Scoop		73
**	V8	Pooh		191
*	V0	Pooh Bear		284
**	V8	Pool Wall (Plantation)		159
	V0+	Pool Wall (Wimberry)		50
	VB	Poop Crack		340
*	V5	Popp's Pop		147
*	V0-	Popper		457
*	V9	Porker		260
*	V3	Porky's Wall		66
	V2	Porky's Wall Right-hand		66
	V2	Porridge Wall		501
**	V5	Porthole, The		55
	V0+	Positive, The		138
**	V4	Pothole Slab		81
*	V0	Potty		452
*	V0	Potty Time		383
***	V9	Poundland		130
**	V9	Power Allowance		355
***	V8	Power Humps		364
***	V9	Powerband	347	364
*	VB	Poxy		440
	VB	Practice Chimney		488
	V2	Praline		316
	V5	Praying Mantel Start		492
*	V0	Precarious Rib		186
*	V0	Prefab Brick Cake		353
*	V0	Prehistoric Offwidth		497
*	V4	Press Direct		489
*	V1	Press Gang		343
***	V8	Press, The		359
	V3	Pressed		77
***	V7	Pressure Drop		140
	V2	Pretty Petty		160
**	V6	Prince, The		133
*	V4	Probably		433
*	V0+	Problem Corner		117
**	V3	Promarete		341
	V5	Proper Grit		261
	V3	Prow		415
*	V0	Prow Left		342
	V0+	Prow Right		342
*	VB	Prow Wall		344
	V2	Prow, The		184
*	V3	Prowstress		326
**	V3	Puck (Burbage N)		211
*	V3	Puck (Burbage S)		237
	V5	Pudding		177
	V4	Pulling Teeth		407
*	V1	Pullover		140

Northern Peak

Sheffield Crags

Stanage Area

Burbage Valley

Derwent Edges

The Limestone

Central Grit

Staffordshire

South Peak

Northern Peak · Sheffield Crags · Stanage Area · Burbage Valley · Derwent Edges · The Limestone · Central Grit · Staffordshire · South Peak

Stars	Grade	Route	Photo	Page
*	V10	Pump up the Power		364
	V10	Pump up the Valium		363
*	V3	Punishment		104
**	V7	Punker Bunker		355
***	V7	Punklet		161
***	V7	Purple Haze		99
*	V3	Push		529
*	V4	Push Me Pull You		367
	V5	Puss in Boots		471
*	V8	Quantum Leap		504
**	V8	Quent's Dyno		350
*	V9	Quent's Legendary Dyno		354
*	V3	Quick Wall		166
**	V4	Quick Wall Traverse		166
*	V10	Quill		522
**	V9	Quine		420
**	V11	Quintessence		355
*	V6	Quintessential Higgarisms		191
	V2	Quiver		117
*	V9	R.I.P.O.D.B.		116
	V1	Rabbit Claw		232
	V2	Rabbit Wall		249
*	V4	Rabbit's Paw		257
	V9	Rack and Ruin		355
	V5	Radjy Man, The		429
	V3	Rail Thing		221
*	V6	Railtrack		319
	V0+	Railway Rib		510
***	V8	Ram Air		486
***	V8	Rambeau	281	281
**	V8	Ramboid		301
**	V0-	Rammer, The		488
	V0+	Ramp (Roaches)		452
	V0+	Ramp (Skyline)		471
	V2	Ramp Thing		134
	V1	Ramp Wall		505
*	V0	Ramp, The (Cratcliffe)		395
*	V3	Ramp, The (Houndkirk M)		270
*	V2	Ramp, The (Roaches)		442
*	V6	Ramp, The (Tintwistle)		55
*	V0	Ramp, The (Wolf Edge)		505
	V2	Rampole of the Roaches		442
*	V0-	Ramsgate		160
**	V6	Rascal Groove		220
*	V4	Rat Scabies		294
**	V7	Rattle and Hump Start		364
	V1	Raw		49
**	V10	Raw Deal		419
**	V8	Raw Power		419
*	V7	Rawhide		172
*	V7	Razor Arete		390
***	V5	Razor Roof	373	390
***	V7	Razor Traverse		390
	V2	Reachy Arete		249
	V1	Reachy Wall (Burbage S)		246
	V2	Reachy Wall (Roaches)		462
**	V0	Real 20 Foot Crack, The		170
*	V12	Recreational Violence		366
*	V11	Recreational Violence Left-hand		366
***	V7	Red or Dead		367
	V6	Reg		456
***	V4	Remergence		207
*	V7	Remergence Lip Traverse		207
	V1	Renaissance	311	314
	V5	Renegade Bulge		278
***	V10	Renegade Master	279	278
	V1	Resurgence		314
*	V7	Revival, The		525
*	V7	Rex Regis of Rusticus Res		409
*	V4	Rhododendron		408
	V1	Rib		64
*	V3	Rib Arete		403
	V1	Rib Left		42
	V1	Rib Right		42
	V1	Rib Tickler		285
***	V8	Rib, The (Burbage S)		222
*	V4	Rib, The (Raven Tor)		363
*	V4	Rib, The (Tintwistle)		55
	V0	Ribless		315
*	V4	Ride my Pimp		462
	V7	Riding the Stang		431
*	V0	Right Arete (Black Tor)		58
*	V4	Right Arete (Black Tor)		59
**	V6	Right Arete (Burbage N)		211
*	V5	Right Arete (Gardom's)		336
	V1	Right Arete (Higgar)		190
	V2	Right Arete (New/Baldstones)		493
	V1	Right Arete (Stanton M)		415
	V1	Right Arete (Tintwistle)		54
	V2	Right Arete (Wimberry)		42
	V1	Right Bulge		514
*	V0-	Right Crack		469
*	V2	Right Eliminette		294
	V1	Right Fin		214
*	V3	Right Groove		458
	V0-	Right Hook		166
*	VB	Right Leg		172
	V1	Right Nose		403
**	V4	Right Pine		529
*	V3	Right Pube		465
	V0-	Right Slab (Cratcliffe)		395
*	VB	Right Slab (Roaches)		463
	V0-	Right Slab, The		58
	V1	Right Slot		486
**	V5	Right Spur		140
	V0+	Right Tower		263
	V8	Right Turn		305
**	V0	Right Twin Arete		493
	V0	Right Whale		242
	V6	Right-Hand Duck		256
*	V8	Right-hand Man		255
*	V4	Right-Hand Roof		215
*	V4	Rim Extension, The		165
	V2	Rim Flake		165
	V1	Rim, The		165
	V4	Rimmer		165
*	V7	Ripper, The		315
***	V4	Ripple	490	494
*	V4	Ripple Riser		214
	V2	Rippled Slab		185
	V1	Rippled Slab Arete		185
*	V3	Rippler, The		454
*	V3	Rise of the Robots		298
	V1	Risky Runnel		462
***	V10	River of Life		431
	V1	Robin Mantel		397
	V1	Rock Ahoy		81
**	V3	Rock and Mantel		241
*	V4	Rock Bottom		224
*	V7	Rock Climbing in Britain		485
*	V7	Rock End Roll		325
*	V3	Rock Fusion		504
*	V4	Rock Hard Bishop		327
	V1	Rock Room Slab		452
*	V4	Rockabilly Rehab		429
**	V8	Rocket Man		198
*	V5	Rocket Ride		521
*	V3	Rocksucker		122
*	V5	Roger the Cabin Boy		340
	V2	Roll Off		485
**	V9	Rollerwall	230	229
	V0+	Romp, The		395
*	V9	Ron's Problem		412
	V6	Ron's Reach		150
*	V4	Ron's Route		370
	V8	Ron's Slab		134
*	V8	Ron's Slab II		152
*	V9	Ron's Wall		124
***	V4	Ron-Side Force-It		195
*	V6	Ronnie's Rib		220
	V2	Roo		270
*	V5	Roof 1		263
*	V4	Roof 2		263
*	V5	Roof Direct		485
*	V4	Roof Goofe		213
*	V4	Roof Goofe Right		213
*	V3	Roof Left		82
	V1	Roof Right		82
*	V4	Roof Route		84
*	V5	Roofless People		251
	V3	Roscoe		385
**	V7	Rose and the Self-employed		149
*	V0	Rough Wall Climb		317
*	V4	Round the Horn		172
*	V3	Roundabout		320
*	VB	Rounded Arete		468
	V0+	Rounded Feature		471
*	V4	Rounded Wall		189
*	VB	Route 1 (Baslow)		314
*	V0	Route 1 (Black Rocks)		510
*	V0-	Route 1 (Burbage N)		202
*	V0-	Route 1.5 (Baslow)		314
	V1	Route 1.5 (Burbage N)		202
*	VB	Route 2 (Baslow)		314
	V1	Route 2 (Black Rocks)		510
*	VB	Route 2 (Burbage N)		202
	V0+	Route 2.5		203
*	VB	Route 3		203
	V2	Route 4		203
*	V3	Route 5		203
*	V9	Route 66		511
	V0-	Royal		343
	V1	Royal Soverin Traverse, The		343
	V2	RT Wall		202
**	V3	Rubber 'ose		157
	V0+	Rubicon Start		359
	V2	Rugosity Dinks		251
*	V1	Rugosity Wall		163
	V1	Rumblefish		195
**	V7	Rumour, The		444
*	VB	Runnel Arete		440
*	V5	Runnel Entry		489
*	V4	Runnel Rib		511
	V0+	Runnel Rouser		462
**	V3	Runnel Rummage		423
*	V5	Runnel, The (Black Rocks)		511
	V0-	Runnel, The (Derwent)		83
*	V5	Runnel, The (Millstone)		255
	V0-	Runnel, The (Woolpacks)		76
	VB	Rupert Bear		284
	V2	Rusty		123
	V2	Rusty Crack		163
	V0+	Rusty Left		123
	V2	Rusty Wall		163
**	V7	RZA Roof		390
***	V7	S and M		492
*	V8	S-Crack Slap		307
	V2	S.H.A.D.O.		517
***	V5	Safe Bet		213
	V3	Safe House		411
	V5	Saian		486
*	VB	Sail Arete		451
	V0+	Sail Rib		451
*	VB	Sail Slab		451
*	V8	Salad Fingers		429
*	V6	Saline Drip		364
***	V10	Salle Goose		430
	V2	Salt		72
*	VB	Salt and Vinegar		177
***	V8	Sam Tan		522
***	V11	Samson		229
*	V3	Sandy Arete		66
*	V4	Sapling Bulge		529
	V2	Sarah		125
***	V6	Satin Start		140
	V1	Saul		229
*	V4	Saur Off Sit Start		521
	V2	Saur On		521
*	V10	Sausage King of Meersbrook, The		334
*	V3	Savage		157
*	V5	Savage Me Softly		177
	V2	Scab		451
	V0+	Scallop		457
**	V8	Scandalous		283
*	V4	Scandiarete		344
	V0-	Scandiwall		344
	V6	Scenic Route, The		371
*	VB	Scoop		392
*	V0	Scoop Arete (Cratcliffe)		392
	V1	Scoop Arete (Plantation)		141
	V2	Scoop Centre		46
*	V3	Scoop de Grass		129
*	V3	Scoop Eliminate		243
	V2	Scoop Left		46
	V2	Scoop Mantel (Burbage S)		250
	V2	Scoop Mantel (Wimberry)		49
	VB	Scoop Slab		384
	V0+	Scoop Slab Traverse		384
	V2	Scoop, The (Derwent)		82
	V2	Scoop, The (Ramshaw)		486
**	VB	Scoop, The (Wimberry)		46
*	V0	Scoops Arete		135
	V1	Scoops Groove		135
	V0+	Scoops Slab		135
	V4	Scooter		197
*	V0	Scotty		292
*	V0	Scrack		462
*	V5	Scratch Arete		496
	V1	Scratch Crack		496
**	V7	Scratch Scoop		237
	V2	Scratch Wall		496
	V4	Scratcher Sitdown		226
*	V8	Scratcher, The		307
*	V5	Scratchy Bun Left		188
	V2	Scratchy Bun Right		188
***	V11	Screaming Dream, The		278
*	V3	Scrim Net		340
*	V4	Scrunchy Slopes		262
	V2	Seal Traverse		420
**	V5	Seam Wall		54
	V1	Seam, The (Hobson M)		64
	V3	Seam, The (Stanton M)		415
	V5	Seamless		147
	V3	Seams Green		501
	V2	Seams Simple Enough		302
	V1	Seamstress		326
*	V7	Sean		251
*	V8	Sean's Arete		301
***	V8	Sean's Problem		352
**	V12	Sean's Roof		367
	V1	Seasick Arete		345
	V0-	Seasick Slab		345
	V3	Seasick Steve		345
	V3	Seconds Out		443
*	V8	Secret Dyno		431
***	V4	Secret Garden Traverse		255
**	V6	Secret Places		411
	V2	Secret Side-wall		411
*	V9	Seeker, The (Amber V)		431
	V0+	Seeker, The (Rabbit Warren)		375
***	V10	Seldom Seen Kid		61

Stars	Grade	Route	Photo	Page
*	V1	Sensible Shoes		485
*	V1	Septic		240
*	V4	Seranata Start		119
*	V5	Serpico		397
***	V4	Seventies Style Wall		266
*	V4	Seventy Degrees		186
*	V6	Seventy-Two		400
*	V7	Seventy-Two Direct		400
	V5	Severed Garden, The		301
**	V4	Sex Dwarfs		264
*	V3	Sexy Steve		462
	VB	Shadow Slab		384
*	V0-	Shady Slab		135
	VB	Shady Slab Right Arete		135
*	V5	Shaft, The		172
*	V4	Shakespeare's Theatre		318
	V3	Shallow Water		43
	V1	Shark Attack		77
***	V1	Shark's Fin		489
*	V0-	Sharp Arete		189
	V1	Sharp Bulge		515
***	V8	Sharp Pocket		351
	V2	Sharp Pockets		359
*	V6	Shatner's Bassoon		172
	V2	Shearing, The	239	238
*	V5	Sheep Dip		402
	V0-	Sheep Easy		238
	V1	Sheep Pit Crack Left		298
	V0+	Sheep Pit Crack Right		298
*	V4	Sheep Pit, The		298
	V7	Sheep Shit		460
**	V5	Sheep Shit Crack		460
*	VB	Sheep Slab, The		238
	V0-	Sheep's Backside, The		238
***	V6	Sheep, The		238
	V2	Shelf Route		138
	V2	Shelf Wall (Burbage N)		216
	V2	Shelf Wall (Derwent)		82
	V3	Shell Shock		45
	V0	Shell Shot		45
*	V5	Shepherd, The		469
	V1	Sherman		240
***	V9	Shirley's Shining Temple		129
***	V8	Shit		191
*	V6	Shiznit, The		170
*	V5	Shock Horror Slab		129
**	V2	Short 'n' Curly		71
*	V0-	Short Arete (Burbage S)		246
*	V0	Short Arete (Burbage W)		198
*	V4	Short Arete (Gardom's)		336
**	V4	Short Arete (RHS)		381
	V2	Short Arete (Wolf Edge)		505
	V1	Short Arete Traverse		198
***	V6	Short Sean's Reachy Roof		423
	V0+	Short Wall (Baslow)		312
	V2	Short Wall (New/Baldstones)		494
*	V6	Short Wall (RHS)		381
	V0+	Shorty		514
	V0+	Shothole Flakes		443
	V7	Shunting Biscuits		397
	V0+	Shy Slab		383
*	V3	Sick		191
**	V6	Sickle Crack		238
	V1	Sickle, The		425
	V1	Sid the Sexist		528
	V1	Side pull Wall		241
	V9	Side Wall Traverse		355
	V2	Side-pull Arch		232
*	V0-	Side-pull Slab		123
	V0+	Side-pull Stretch		82
***	V6	Side-pull Wall (Skyline)		470
	V1	Side-pull Wall (Derwent)		82
	V0+	Side-wall (Burbage N)		217
*	V5	Side-wall (Skyline)		473
	V0+	Side-wall (Wolf Edge)		504
*	V0	Side-wall Arete		308
	V0	Side-wall Crack		308
	V1	Side-wall Flake		308
	V1	Side-wall Slot		309
*	V6	Sidetrack (Curbar)		309
	V1	Sidetrack (Plantation)		132
**	V7	Silk Start	131	133
	V0	Silver Arete		263
***	V8	Simple Simon		522
*	V6	Simple Simon Indirect		522
**	V5	Sin		443
*	V5	Sin Left		443
	V2	Sinew Stretch		121
	V1	Sinister Bunny		375
**	V0	Sip in Side	50	50
*	V1	Sisyphus		263
*	V4	Sit Start Wall		59
	V2	Sitdown Arete (Burbage S)		240
	V1	Sitdown Arete (Burbage W)		199
	V4	Sitdown Bulge		254
	V4	Sitdown Groove (Millstone)		254
*	V4	Sitdown Groove (Bell Hagg)		106
	V1	Sithee		130
**	V5	Sithee Direct		130
**	V4	Sitting Duck		224
*	V6	Sitting in Oxford		211
*	V5	Six Syllables or Less		298
*	V0	Sketch, The		302
	V3	Sketchy Arete		450
**	V3	Sketchy Pillar		188
	V4	Sketchy Rib		444
	V1	Sketchy Wall		446
	V2	Skid, The		123
**	V4	Skimmington Ride		117
**	V7	Skinless Wonder		172
**	V4	Skinned Rabbit		443
	V4	Skint		525
*	V6	Sky Bouldering		140
	V1	Slab		128
*	VB	Slab 2		447
	V0-	Slab and Crack		451
	V3	Slab and the Beanstalk		92
*	V1	Slab Arete		469
*	V0-	Slab Arete Left		58
	VB	Slab Crack		469
*	V0+	Slab Dancer		457
	V2	Slab in the Middle		391
*	V5	Slab Pop		288
	V0+	Slab to Summit		442
**	VB	Slab Walk		469
	V1	Slab Wall		515
*	V0	Slab, The		43
*	V0	Slabby Arete (Burbage W)		198
*	V0-	Slabby Arete (Roaches)		444
	V0-	Slabby Rib		246
	VB	Slabby Seam		441
	V2	Slabby Wall		433
*	V6	Slabenger		121
	V2	Slanting Crack		183
**	V8	Slap Bass Odyssey	7	381
*	V4	Slap Happy (Alport Area)		371
**	V5	Slap Happy (Wimberry)		43
	V4	Slap Problem		60
*	V3	Slap Stick		71
	V5	Slapstick		43
*	V5	Sleeping with the Flowers		461
	V3	Sleepwalker		128
	V1	Sling your Hammock		340
**	V10	Slingshot		289
	V0-	Slippery Groove (Hobson M)		64
	V0+	Slippery Groove (Roaches)		458
	V5	Slope John A		174
	V4	Slope John B		174
	V5	Sloper Pull		205
*	V6	Sloper Traverse		174
	V2	Slopers Crimp Problem		174
	V5	Slopey Green Traverse		397
*	V4	Slopey Pokey		146
	V5	Slopey Scrunch		262
*	V7	Slopey Side-pull		352
	V1	Sloping Mantel		241
	V1	Sloping Nose		244
	V1	Slot Entry	250	250
	V7	Slot Machine		371
*	V4	Slot Sitdown		148
	V2	Slot Slab		422
	V0+	Slot Slab Arete		422
	V0+	Slots		169
*	V0	Slotted Arete		166
	V1	Slotted Wall		166
	V0+	Slotty Pockets		270
**	V8	Slow Worm		524
	V1	Sly Direct		496
	V2	Sly Mantelshelf		496
***	V5	Sly Stallone		496
*	V3	Sly Super Direct		496
	V2	Sly Traverse		496
	V5	Small Arete		52
*	V6	Small Blunt Rib		187
***	V6	Small is Beautiful		206
	V4	Small Ones are More Juicy		334
	V1	Small Rib		243
	V3	Small Roof Left		87
	V4	Small Roof Right		87
	V0+	Small Slab		185
	V0-	Small Slab Arete		185
	V0+	Small Wall		52
***	V3	Smear Test		152
***	V13	Smiling Buttress		296
*	V3	Smoke ont' Watter		299
	V0	Smoked		49
*	V4	Smoothment Traverse		485
	V7	Smutt Ridge		315
*	V0-	Snap	111	112
	V5	Snapper Arete		134
	V4	Snapper, The		134
	V1	Snappy Flakes		319
	V11	Snatch!		138
*	V6	Sneaky Little Fingers		92
*	V3	Sneezy		528
*	V3	Snitch		222
	VB	Snout Groove		165
	V0+	Snout Wall		165
*	V2	Snout, The		165
	V0+	Soapsuds Crack		354
	V1	Soapsuds Left		354
	V3	Soapsuds Right		354
*	V4	Soapsuds Traverse		354
**	V5	Sodomy		344
*	V4	Soft Arete (Burbage S)		232
*	V0+	Soft Arete (Gardom's)		327
	V3	Soft Groove		327
*	V5	Soft Groove Sit-down		327
***	V8	Soft on the 'G'		327
	V0-	Soft Ribs		327
*	V5	Soft Top Beetle		118
*	V6	Soft Top Traverse		118
	V0+	Soft Wall		327
	V0+	Softwidth Wall		232
	V2	Soggy Bottom Crack		472
***	V9	Sole Power	287	289
*	V5	Solitude		208
	V5	Solly's Arete		106
	V2	Solly's Island	78	78
	V3	Soloman		332
**	V10	Solomon's Seal		121
*	V6	Somebody's Head		367
*	V0	Something Else		112
*	V5	Something Silly		112
*	V4	Soul Deep		52
*	V7	Sound of One Foot Slipping, The		283
	V1	Soup Dragon		497
*	V0-	South Arete		46
*	V0-	South Face	47	46
*	V0-	South Face Direct		46
**	V7	Southwest Face		153
	V6	Spades		154
	V2	Spangle		377
**	V4	Spankasaurus Does Chicago		476
**	V8	Sparks		101
**	V4	Sparky		166
	VB	Sparky Slab		166
	V8	Sparrow Right-Wing		399
*	V9	Sparrow/My Best Friend the		399
*	V9	Spartacus		194
*	V0	Sphinx Slab		213
***	V7	Sphinx, The		212
	V1	Spider Crack (Burbage N)		215
*	V5	Spider Crack (Millstone)	20	263
	V0+	Spiderman 1		433
	V0-	Spiderman 2		433
***	V8	Spike		113
*	V8	Spike, The		105
*	V1	Spike Problem, The		105
	V2	Spinal Crack		289
*	V4	Spinal Fjord		318
**	V6	Spinal Slab	379	384
**	V5	Spinal Tap		289
	V4	Spine Left-Hand		384
	V0+	Spine, The		384
	V2	Spirit Chaser		370
	V1	Spitsnswallows		375
*	V3	Spitting Cobra		425
	V3	Split Tip		428
**	V6	Spook		412
*	V3	Spooky Arete		525
	V4	Spooky Wall		525
	V4	Spotter's Pop		471
	V6	Spotter's Slop		471
	V0+	Sprat		441
*	V8	Spray Mane		301
	V0+	Spring Roll		441
	V2	Spring Roll Left		441
**	V6	Spring Slab		441
**	V9	Spring Voyage		124
	V0+	Sprite		441
*	V3	Sprung		441
*	V5	Spur Traverse		140
	V8	Sputnik		212
*	V0+	Square Arete (Baslow)		312
	V2	Square Arete (Burbage W)		194
*	V0+	Square Arete (Wimberry)		49
	V0+	Square Arete Right		312
	V1	Square Block Crack		384
	V1	Square Buttress Direct		163
*	V3	Square Cut Face		493
*	V4	Square Dance		312
*	V4	Square Pusher		525
*	V3	Square Wall		312
	V4	Squat		304
*	V4	Squawk		85
**	V5	Squawk Traverse		85
*	V7	Squawk Traverse Direct		85
	V5	Squeezer's Spots		471
*	V3	Squeezy Slab		445
	V1	Squirm, The (Cratcliffe)		392
	V0	Squirm, The (Roaches)		462
	V0+	St. Vincent		343

Northern Peak · Sheffield Crags · Stanage Area · Burbage Valley · Derwent Edges · The Limestone · Central Grit · Staffordshire · South Peak

Northern Peak | Sheffield Crags | Stanage Area | Burbage Valley | Derwent Edges | The Limestone | Central Grit | Staffordshire | South Peak

Stars	Grade	Route	Photo	Page
*	V5	Staffordshire Face		472
***	V4	Staffordshire Flyer		472
*	V2	Staircase Flake		166
*	VB	Staircase, The (RHS)		387
*	V2	Staircase, The (Roaches)		456
***	V6	Stall		501
*	V5	Stallone Arete		496
***	V10	Stamina Humps		364
***	V11	Staminaband		364
***	V14	Staminaband Pump up the Power		364
**	V7	Stanage Without Oxygen		172
*	V4	Standup Arete		221
**	V12	Stanton Deliver		410
*	V10	Stanton Shuffle, The		410
**	V8	Stanton Warriors		410
*	V4	Start of the Affair, The		294
*	V3	Starter Motor		284
**	V8	Stasis		224
*	V8	Stateside		44
*	V1	Steady Arete		264
*	V5	Steep Arete		403
*	V1	Steep Nose		82
*	V0+	Steep Side		141
***	V5	Steep Traverse		147
*	V2	Steep Traverse Arete		147
*	V1	Steeple, The		66
*	VB	Steps		166
*	V2	Steve Clark		307
**	V9	Steve Miller Band, The		364
*	V4	Steve Ring Home Start		63
**	V7	Steve's Wall		46
*	V2	Sting, The		335
*	V2	Stingray Arete		85
*	V0+	Stone Dove Crack		85
*	V1	Stone Dove Left		85
*	V1	Stone Dove Right		85
*	V0	Stone Dove Sidewall		85
***	V8	Storm, The		134
**	V8	Stottie	278	278
*	V1	Straight Crack		183
*	V4	Strawberries		309
*	V5	Stray Bullit		276
*	V0	Stream Arete		43
*	VB	Stream Slab		43
*	V3	Strenuosity		529
***	V5	Stretch and Mantel		447
*	V4	Stretch Left		447
*	V3	Stretching Wall		190
*	V4	Stridesque		428
**	V10	Striker		210
*	V7	Striker Left-hand		210
*	V10	Stumped		371
*	V2	Stung		335
***	V8	Suavito		334
*	V2	Sublime Indifference		222
**	V9	Submergence		207
*	V5	Submission		371
*	V3	Suffocation		531
*	V5	Sugar Loaf Girdle		42
*	V3	Suicide Bummer		393
*	V0-	Sulu		292
*	V0-	Summit Arete		442
*	V0+	Summit Bid		82
*	V2	Summit Slab		465
*	V1	Sun Worship		429
*	V1	Sunlight Caller		210
*	V0+	Sunny Barger		123
*	V3	Sunshine Traverse		63
*	V0+	Super Duper Direct Start		133
*	V12	Super Size Me		305
***	V12	Superbloc	337	336
*	V4	Superstring		525
*	V2	Surprise		130
*	V4	Surprise Direct		130
*	V0	Suspended Sentence		104
*	V2	Suzanne		163
**	V12	Swarm, The		512
*	V0+	Sweep		129
*	V3	Sweet Arete (Burbage S)		223
*	V4	Sweet Arete (RHS)		387
*	V8	Sweet Move		94
*	V10	Sweet Release		95
*	V11	Sweet Thing		387
*	V9	Swing Thing		355
**	V7	Swing Time		366
*	V0+	Swinger, The		440
***	V8	Swingers Party	427	432
*	V2	Swings		161
*	V3	Swiss Cheesed		504
**	V4	Swivel Finger		476
**	V4	Swivel Flakes		476
*	V2	Swollen Tongue		376
*	V2	Sworn to Secrecy		411
***	V8	T Crack	389	396
**	V7	T Crack Lite		396
*	V0+	T Slab		380
*	V0+	T Slab Arete		380
**	V7	Take Cover		45
**	V8	Talk to Me Martin		238
*	V1	Tall Arete		188
**	V4	Talon Man		299
*	V0-	Tanked Up		44
*	V9	Tarantula		371
**	V8	Taxi to the Crag		510
*	V4	Tea Break, The		175
*	V4	Tea Leaf		174
*	V1	Teacup, The		450
*	V2	Teal'c		375
*	V1	Technical Baiter		266
**	V6	Technical Genius		340
*	V1	Technical Love		58
***	V4	Technical Master	252	266
***	V5	Technical Master Left		266
*	V8	Technician's Day Out		60
*	V5	Teck Crack Direct	436	448
*	V8	Teck Crack Superdirect		449
	V0	Teddy		284
*	V4	Teddy Bear's Picnic, The		285
*	V8	Ten Shadows to Midnight		157
*	V0	Tenerife		343
*	V0+	Tenerife Right-hand		343
	V11	Terrace, La		211
***	V9	Terrace, The	209	211
*	V9	Tetris		479
*	V3	That Little Arete Left		245
*	V0-	That Little Arete Right		245
*	V9	That Which Does Not Kill Me		319
*	V7	Theraband		312
*	V5	These Vagabond Shoes		117
*	V5	Thief, The		54
*	V9	Thigh Master		399
*	V0	Thin Flake (Curbar)		302
*	V1	Thin Flake (Skyline)		472
*	V1	Thin Problem Crack		117
*	V7	Thin Slab (Froggatt)		288
*	V4	Thin Slab (Plantation)		152
	V2	Thin Wall (Froggatt)		282
**	V6	Thin Wall (Millstone)		259
**	V6	Thing on a Spring		341
*	V4	Think Tank		44
*	V5	This is my Church		505
*	V3	Thomas		510
*	V3	Thomas the Tanked Up Engine		303
	V1	Thorns		522
*	V4	Threapwood Arete		521
*	V4	Threapwood Bulge		521
*	V5	Three and Four Pence		433
*	V4	Three Breaks		161
***	V10	Three Hundred Pounds of Music		398
***	V3	Three Pocket Slab		446
	V2	Three Pocket Wall		309
**	V4	Three Real Men Dancing		113
*	V1	Three Tiered Cake		175
*	V4	Through Mantel		395
*	V1	Through the Keyhole		158
**	V7	Throwball		498
*	V6	Thrust		479
*	V5	Thrutch Over		391
	V8	Thug's Day Out		60
*	V8	Thuggy Bear		278
**	V8	Thumbs		522
	V1	Tier's End		485
***	V7	Tierdrop		485
*	V4	Tiger		240
*	V0	Tiny Crack		497
*	VB	Tiny Groove		463
*	V0+	Tiny Left Arete		208
*	V5	Tiny Right Arete		208
*	V3	Tiny Roof		208
*	V3	Tiny Slab Left		208
***	V3	Tiny Slab Right		208
*	V9	Tip Top		266
*	V0+	Tiptoe		207
**	V7	Tittersworth Rib		451
**	V7	To Be or Not to Be		136
*	V4	To Harland Back		377
*	V5	To Have It All		411
*	V8	Toasted		278
*	V1	Tody Bear		282
*	V2	Tody Boy		282
*	V0+	Tody's Pocket		282
*	V3	Toenail Left		359
*	V1	Toenail Pie Start		359
*	V8	Toilet Duck		530
*	V2	Toilet Traverse (Churnet)		530
*	V2	Toilet Traverse (Raven Tor)		363
**	V8	Tom Thumb		407
*	V6	Tom's Original		355
*	V7	Tomahawk Traverse, The		531
*	V3	Tomb, The		375
*	V0	Tombliboo Trouble		73
*	V0+	Tonto		141
*	V9	Tony's Problem		407
*	V6	Too Drunk		461
**	V5	Too Hard for Mark Leach		362
**	V3	Too Much		101
*	V2	Top Break		359
	V6	Top Dog		432
*	V1	Top of Ramp		249
*	V2	Top Rib		392
*	V8	Top Shelf Mantel		261
*	V8	Top Shop		367
*	V2	Topless Crack		254
*	V0+	Toppled Block Arete		189
*	V6	Tortoise, The	69	78
**	V6	Torture Garden		130
*	V6	Toucan		460
*	V8	Touch Winky		304
*	V4	Touching Cloth		530
*	VB	Toxic		130
*	V8	Track Crack		309
*	V8	Tracking		309
*	V3	Tracking High		308
***	V6	Trackside		309
*	V0+	Trackside Scoop		309
*	V0+	Trainer Failure		170
*	V7	Trapped in Crows' Claws		228
*	V4	Traverse		423
*	V3	Traverse of Man		448
*	V4	Traverse, The		59
*	V3	Tree Stump Traverse		208
*	V1	Tree Wall		282
*	V6	Trellis		232
*	V4	Trench Flakes		295
*	V0+	Trench Hole		295
*	V3	Trench Wall		295
*	V2	Trevor		510
**	V4	Triangle		64
*	V2	Triangle Arete		64
*	V1	Triangle Buttress Direct		204
**	V3	Triangle Left		64
*	V2	Triangle Link-up		350
*	V2	Triangle Rib		222
*	V3	Triangle Traverse		204
***	V6	Triangle Wall		222
*	V3	Triple Cracks Arete		189
*	V0	Triple Cracks Left		189
*	V0+	Triple Cracks Right		189
*	V3	Triplet		222
*	V5	Triptych Groove		471
*	V3	Trivial Pursuits 1		100
*	V3	Trivial Pursuits 2		100
*	V0+	Trough, The (Burbage S)		244
*	V1	Trough, The (Plantation)		132
*	V5	Trouser Jazz		295
**	V8	True Git		194
*	V6	Truffle Pig		315
*	V6	Trunk, The		186
***	V6	Trust	477	479
*	V3	Tufa, The		529
*	VB	Tweedle Dee		166
*	VB	Tweedle Dum		166
*	V5	Twice a Slice		367
**	V6	Twin Cam		170
*	V5	Twin Crack Arete		198
*	V1	Twin Roof		314
*	V3	Twin Roof Left		314
*	V4	Twins		59
*	V4	Twisted Crack		450
*	V8	Twister		153
*	V2	Two n Six		433
*	V2	Two Pocket Sitter		216
*	V2	Two Pocket Slab		468
*	V4	Two Pocket Wall		54
*	V2	Two Shot Holes		267
*	V5	Two-Headed Boy		332
**	V8	Tyler		522
*	V0+	Tyrannosaurus Hex		497
*	V2	Uhuru		292
***	V5	Ultimate Gritstone Ex..., The	304	304
**	V7	Ulysses or Bust		295
	?	Unclimbed Dyno		44
*	V3	Unconquerable Direct Start		159
*	V3	Undercut Arete		270
*	V0+	Undercut Block Left		210
*	V0+	Undercut Block Right		210
**	V8	Undercut Dyno		447
*	V0	Undercut Rib		236
*	V4	Undercut Traverse, The		447
*	V0+	Undercut Wall		440
*	V8	Undercuts to Crimp		363
*	V2	Undercutter, The		446
*	V0+	Underground Mantel		505
*	V4	Underground, The		505
*	V5	Underpass		52
**	V5	Underton Arete		431
*	V1	Undone Rib		408
*	V9	Unidentified Flying Object		517
*	V9	Unidentified Flying People		407
*	V5	Unleash the Beast		420
*	V3	Uno		367
*	V2	Unpredictable		157

Stars Grade	Route	Photo Page
*** V4	Unreachable Star, The	295
** VB	Up Chips	445
* V3	Up From Recess	254
* V0	Up Up and Huway	86
V1	Uphill Arete Right-Hand	433
V0+	Upper Cube Traverse	169
* V5	Upper Traverse	370
** V3	Uppercut, The	446
VB	Upright	454
* V1	Upsy Daisy	73
** V1	Useful Arete	243
* V3	Useful Crack	243
V0-	Useful Gully Arete	513
V0-	Useless Arete, The	244
* V8	Uvanu	123
V1	Uvavu	123
* V1	Uzi Lover	528
V0-	V for Victory	342
V3	Vague Arete	458
* V4	Vague Nose	194
* V2	Vague Rib	247
* V1	Valhalla	370
* V1	Vandals	383
** V5	Vanishing Point	276
** V3	Varicose	493
* V3	Varicose Traverse	493
V2	Vaudeville Crack	71
V2	Veale Thing	307
* V8	Vegetarian Cannibal	432
** V7	Velvet Crab	215
V2	Velvet Roof	215
*** V7	Velvet Silence	511
V4	Velveteen Whisper	431
* V1	Verandah Buttress	161
* V7	Verandah Buttress Direct	161
** V3	Verbal Abuse Start	363
V2	Via Dexter	163
* V1	Via Media	163
V0+	Viaduct Crack	67
* V5	Viaduct Eliminate	67
** V3	Viaduct Wall	67
V1	Viaduct Wall Traverse	67
V0	Victor's Ledge	342
* V10	Victorian Over Mantel	149
VB	Victory Traverse, The	342
* V7	Violence (Burbage S)	231
** V3	Violence (Roaches)	443
V4	Virgin Central	527
* V6	Virgin Left	527
* V5	Virgin Right	527
V2	Virginia Arete	133
VB	Visitors Only	340
V1	Visitors Wall	340
V0	Volcan Wolf	79
*** V13	Voyager	212
V3	Wafer, The	529
** V3	Wafery Flake	262
*** V10	Walk on By	301
V0	Walking the Dog	248
V3	Wall Above Flake	81
* V3	Wall and Mono	493
V0-	Wall and Rib	469
* V3	Wall End Grab	133
V0	Wall End Slab Direct Start	133
V0+	Wall End Start	133
V0+	Wall Past Flake (Burbage S)	240
* V3	Wall Past Flake (Derwent)	81
V2	Wall Past the Flatty	334
V0+	Wall Past Slot (Burbage S)	235 237
* V0	Wall, The	59
** V8	Walnut Whip (Baslow)	317
** V5	Walnut Whip (Millstone)	257
** V4	Walnut, The	316
** V10	Warchild	523
* V3	Wardrobe Ridge	334
V0+	Warm-up Traverse	359
V7	Wart, The	499
* V4	Wavedance	344
V2	Wavelength	132
* V0-	Wavelength Arete	132
V0+	Wavy Slab	441
* V0-	Way Down	42
V5	Way of the Spaniel	270
** V4	We Aint Gonna Pay No Toll	228
* V4	We Stole Dave's Problem	270
V1	Wednesday Climb	205
V1	Wee-Wob	294
*** V8	Weedkiller Traverse	362
** V4	West Arete	197
* V3	West Arete Right	197
* V4	West End Girls	194
*** V9	West Side Story	178 195
* V4	West Side Traverse	195
V2	West Wall	326
V0	West Wall Left	326
V2	West's Route	46

*** V10	Western Eyes	17 196
V5	Western Front	433
*** V11	Westworld	197
* V8	Wet Nettle	432
V2	Wet with Sweat	517
V1	Whale of a Time	242
V0+	Whale Rib	242
* V8	Whale Traverse	46
V0	Whalebone	46
V5	What a Way to Spend Easter	220
V1	Whatsit?	313
*** V7	Where Beagles Dare	320
* V4	Where Bulldykes Daren't	100
V0-	Where?	284
** V4	Whillans Direct, The	289
* V7	Whip Me Whip Me	316
* V12	Whippet, The	106
** V6	Whispa Loudly	55
** V8	White Ladder	350
V8	White Lines	298
*** V9	Who Needs Ready Brek?	480
* V6	Wicker Man	429
V0-	Wide Crack	187
V4	Wide Eyes Shut	77
V1	Wilbur's Corner	117
V1	Wilbur's Rib	117
V2	Wilbur's Wall	117
V5	Wild in Me Start	364
V2	Wildy's Arete	451
** V3	Wildy's Right	453 451
** V11	Will's Dyno	336
V0+	Win Hill	112
* VB	Windmill, The	246
V2	Wing Wong	459 456
V2	Winger	456
** V8	Winner Stays On	159
V2	Winnie the...	191
*** V7	Winsome	46
*** V7	Wish	400
* V8	Wishbone	325
* V4	Witches' Sabbath	412
** V6	Witness the Gritness	182
* V4	Wizard of Aus	370
V4	Wobbleblock	199
V5	Wobbleblock Direct	199
V1	Wobbly Wall	101
* V4	Wolf Bite	505
V2	Wolf Bite Right	505
V2	Wolf Prow	505
V2	Wollock Direct	206
* V5	Womb, The	355
V5	Wonder Bra	410
V0+	Wonderful Copenhagen	344
** V3	Woolly Pully	140
*** V12	Work Hard	309
V2	Wottinger Scoop	73
V5	Wraparound Arete	492
V4	Wrestle, The	223
V0	Wriggly Crack	112
* V7	Wright's Giza	520
*** V8	Wright's Traverse	523
** V7	Wright's Unconquerable	519 521
V8	Wrong's Traverse	523
V6	Wu Tang Span	121
V5	Yabadabadoo	213
V0+	Yo Clam	497
*** V8	Yoghurt Hypnotist, The	418
V8	You're Joking	48
** V7	Young American, The	353
* V6	Youngster's Wall	121
V5	Your Basic Mantel	226
** V9	Zaff Skoczylas	215
* V7	Zaff's Groove	207
** V6	Zaff's Mantel	381
** V8	Zaff's Problem	254
* V8	Zaffatricks	256
V0+	Zero Point	157
*** V10	Zippatricks	255
** V7	Zippattrocity	176
** V8	Zippy's Problem	352
** V8	Zippy's Sidepull	352
** V8	Zippy's Traverse	148
V8	Zmutt Ridge	46
** V9	Zorev	231
* V1	Zorro	174

Crag Index

Amber Valley	426
Baldstones	490
Bamford	110
Bank Quarry	424
Baslow	310
Bell Hagg	102
Birchen Edge	338
Black Rocks	508
Black Tor	56
Blackwell Dale	365
Bradley Edge	432
Burbage North	200
Burbage South Edge	218
Burbage South Valley	234
Burbage West	192
Carl Wark	251
Churnet Valley	518
Clifftop Boulder	402
Cocking Tor	428
Cratcliffe	388
Curbar	290
Derwent	80
Eagle Tor	404
Eastwood Rocks	434
Five Clouds, The	474
Froggatt	274
Gardom's	322
Gib Torr	500
Harborough Rocks	512
Harland Edge	376
Higgar Tor	180
Hobson Moor Quarry	62
Houndkirk Moor	268
Jackson Tor	425
Millstone	252
Mother Cap	258
New Mills Tor	65
Newstones	490
Nuda's Tartan	371
Over Owler Tor	262
Ox Stones	269
Rabbit Warren	374
Ramshaw	482
Raven Tor	360
Rheinstor	370
Rivelin	96
Roaches, The	438
Robin Hood's Stride	378
Rowtor Rocks	416
Rubicon	356
Secret Garden, The	254
Shining Cliff	516
Skyline, The	466
Stanage Far Right	164
Stanage High Neb	114
Stanage Plantation	126
Stanage Popular End	160
Stanton Moor	406
Stanon in the Woods	414
Stoney	348
Tintwistle Knarr	51
Turning Stone Edge	430
Wharncliffe	90
Wimberry	40
Wolf Edge	502
Woolpacks, The	68

Northern Peak

Sheffield Crags

Stanage Area

Burbage Valley

Derwent Edges

The Limestone

Central Grit

Staffordshire

South Peak

Northern Peak.... 38
Wimberry 40
Tintwistle Knarr.... 51
Black Tor....... 56
Hobson Moor Quarry 62
New Mills Tor 65
Woolpacks, The ... 68
Derwent 80

Sheffield Crags 88
Wharncliffe 90
Rivelin..........96
Bell Hagg 102

Stanage Area...... 108
Bamford 110
Stanage High Neb .. 114
Stanage Plantation . 126
Stanage Popular End 160
Stanage Far Right .. 164

Burbage Valley 178
Higgar Tor...... 180
Burbage West....192
Burbage North ... 200
Burbage South Edge .218
Burbage South Valley 234
Carl Wark 251
Millstone 252
Secret Garden ... 254
Mother Cap..... 258
Over Owler Tor ... 262
Houndkirk Moor .. 268
Ox Stones........269

Derwent Edges 272
Froggatt........ 274
Curbar......... 291
Baslow 310
Gardom's 322
Birchen Edge ... 338

Central Grit 372
Rabbit Warren ... 374
Harland Edge ... 376
Robin Hood's Stride . 378
Cratcliffe 388
Clifftop Boulder .. 402
Eagle Tor....... 404
Stanton Moor ... 406
Stanon in the Woods . 414
Rowtor Rocks ... 416
Bank Quarry 424
Jackson Tor..... 425
Amber Valley.... 426
Cocking Tor..... 428
Turning Stone Edge . 430
Bradley Edge 432
Eastwood Rocks...434

The Limestone .346
Stoney....... 350
Rubicon 356
Raven Tor 360
Blackwell Dale . 365
Rheinstor 370
Nuda's Tartan ... 371

Staffordshire ... 436
The Roaches ... 438
The Skyline..... 466
The Five Clouds . 474
Ramshaw 482
Newstones 490
Baldstones 498
Gib Torr....... 500
Wolf Edge..... 502

South Peak 506
Black Rocks 508
Harborough Rocks .512
Shining Cliff 516
Churnet Valley 518

N

Barnsley

M1

Manchester

A628

Chapeltown

Peak District
National Park

M67

Rotherham

M18

Stockport

Sheffield

M1

A623

Macclesfield

M1

Buxton

Chesterfield

Bakewell

A515

Central Grit

Matlock

Mansfield

A52

Leek

Alfreton

M1

Stoke on Trent

Ashbourne

Nottingham

About 10km

Access......................... 22
Accommodation..................16
Acknowledgements 10
Advertiser Directory..............10
Bouldering Mats.................. 24
Camping 16
Circuits........................ 32
Climbing Shops 16
Climbing Walls...................18
Colour-codes 30
Contents 3
Destination Planner 34, 36
Erosion 22
Feedback (Rockfax Database)...... 8
First Ascents 6
Font Grades....................30
Getting Around..................14
Grades........................30
Guidebooks..................... 6
Introduction 4
Landing 24
Map Key.............. 28, Front Flap

Mobile Phone Coverage 14
Other Guidebooks................... 6
Parking 22
Problem Names.................... 6
Pubs 16
QR Codes 8
Rockfax Publications ....Back Flap
Route Database................... 8
Satellite Navigation 8
Shops 16
Smartphones..................... 8
Spotting 26
Symbol Key .... 28, Front Flap
Topo Key .... 28, Front Flap
Tourist Information Offices...........14
UK Tech Grades 30
UKC Logbooks 8
V Grades 30
Weather.......................14
Website 8
When to Go 14
Where to Stay 16

Mountain Rescue
Dial 112 - Ensure you have details of your location and what the incident involves.
This number works on any mobile.

Northern Peak | Sheffield Crags | Stanage Area | Burbage Valley | Derwent Edges | The Limestone | Central Grit | Staffordshire | South Peak